Nobel Laureates in Literature

Garland Reference Library
of the Humanities
(Vol. 849)

Other biographical
dictionaries in this series

NOBEL LAUREATES IN ECONOMIC SCIENCES

NOBEL LAUREATES IN PHYSIOLOGY OR MEDICINE

NOBEL LAUREATES IN PHYSICS

NOBEL LAUREATES IN CHEMISTRY

NOBEL LAUREATES IN PEACE

GENERAL EDITOR, Bernard S. Katz

NOBEL LAUREATES IN LITERATURE
A Biographical Dictionary

EDITED BY Rado Pribic

Garland Publishing, Inc.
NEW YORK & LONDON 1990

Library of Congress Cataloging-in-Publication Data

Pribic, Rado.
   Nobel laureates in literature : a biographical dictionary / edited
by Rado Pribic.
      p.   cm. — (Garland reference library of the humanities : vol.
849)
   Includes index.
   ISBN 0-8240-5741-4
   1. Authors—Biography. 2. Nobel prizes. I. Title. II. Series.
PN452.P7   1990
809′.04—dc20   89-11803

Design by Alison Lew

Printed on acid-free, 250-year-life paper

Manufactured in the United States of America

TO MY PARENTS
NIKOLA AND ELISABETH

CONTENTS

ALFRED NOBEL AND THE NOBEL PRIZE IN LITERATURE

Alfred Nobel, the Swedish chemist and industrialist, was born in Stockholm on October 21, 1833, and died in San Remo, Italy, on December 10, 1896. By the time of his death he had established, on the basis of his inventions covered by more than three hundred fifty patents, a multinational conglomerate with more than ninety companies and plants in over twenty countries and on five continents. In his will he left a fortune of more than thirty-three million Swedish crowns (in 1989 one U.S. dollar was worth about six Swedish crowns), most of which (thirty-two million) was to be used to create the Nobel Foundation.

The Nobel Foundation is commissioned to use most of the interest drawn from the Nobel fortune for five prizes in the fields of literature, chemistry, physics, physiology or medicine, and peace efforts and awards them annually to those, who in the previous year "benefitted humanity most" regardless of nationality. A sixth prize, that in economic sciences, was added in memory of Alfred Nobel in 1968 and is being funded by the Swedish Imperial Bank (Sveriges Riksbank).

The Nobel family originally came from a small village in the south of Sweden, Nöbbellöv. Alfred's great-great-grandfather adopted the latinized form of Nobelius as his family name, which eventually became Nobel, still in reference to the village of Nöbbellöv. Alfred's father, an architect by training, experimented early in his life with explosive devices to be used for construction and military purposes. His firm in Sweden, however, went bankrupt, and in 1842 he moved to St. Petersburg, Russia (today's Leningrad), where through hard work and inventiveness he established a successful industrial enterprise. The firm's new generation of land and sea mines were successfully used by the Russians in the Crimean War.

Alfred, a very shy, introverted, but optimistic young man, received an excellent education in St. Petersburg, mostly from private tutors, especially in sciences and languages. Beside his native Swedish, Alfred learned to speak Russian, French, German, and English. From 1850 till 1852 he traveled throughout Europe and even to the United States. After his return to Russia, he became very interested in his father's research and became a professional chemist. In 1853 he moved to his father's explosives plant at Heleneborg, near Stockholm, as research chemist. Already by 1864 Alfred succeeded in developing a revolutionary new blasting method based on nitroglycerine, which was invented a few years earlier by the Italian scientist Ascanio Sobrero. Unfortunately, however, in the same year Alfred's younger brother was killed during an explosion in a nitroglycerine plant.

In addition to this tragedy, Alfred Nobel faced other difficulties, but in 1865 he was able to establish his first factory in Sweden to produce explosive devices. The most important of Nobel's many inventions was that of dynamite, patented in 1867 and developed at his German plant in Krümmel, near Hamburg. Dynamite changed military strategies, but, more importantly, it revolutionized construction methods in the construction of roads, canals, tunnels, and mines.

The profits earned from the dynamite patent were, of course, the prime basis for Nobel's substantial wealth and his growing worldwide industrial empire. After founding factories in Sweden and Germany in 1865, he expanded his multinational company with factories in Austria (1868), the United States (1868), France (1871), and Scotland (1871). The Nobel enterprise before Alfred's death had subsidiaries in more than twenty countries on five continents. They were the forerunners for such world-famous companies as Kema Nobel AB in Sweden, Dynamit Nobel AG in Germany, Société Centrale de Dynamite in France, and Imperial Chemical Industries in Great Britain.

Besides his patent for dynamite, Nobel held many other patents—his most important being those for blasting gelatine (1875) and ballistite (1887), a smokeless nitroglycerine powder that became the prime

source for cordite, a key element in the development in firearm ammunition. Other patents were granted for inventions in the field of synthetic materials, such as artificial leather and rubber, and in the area of telecommunications. The success of Alfred Nobel, however, cannot be attributed solely to his genius as a chemist and scientist. One also has to admire Nobel's shrewdness as an international entrepreneur and his idealistic weltanschauung.

From 1869 to 1891 Nobel lived primarily in Paris, moving in 1891 to San Remo on the Mediteranean, where he died in 1896. He also spent much time in his home in Bofors, Sweden. Even in his later years he was shy and as a rule would not grant public interviews. He refused to write his autobiography and repeatedly asked that no pictures or drawings be made of him. Nobel never married, though he maintained a long friendship with the Austrian peace activist Baroness Bertha von Suttner. Later in his life, he had a love affair with a simple Austrian girl twenty-three years younger than he. This relationship became an exercise in frustration since the two came from completely different social, cultural, and intellectual milieus.

Although Nobel never found a life companion and never established his own family, "the wealthiest vagabond in Europe," as he was repeatedly described, was very close to his older brothers Robert (1829–1896) and Ludwig (1831–1888). The two also contributed significantly to the industrial and scientific progress of their time. They were both instrumental in exploration and development of one of the major oil fields of the time, the Caspian Sea near the city of Baku. Their concern for their employees was exemplary, and the social security they provided was certainly the reason there was never a strike in their factories, a rarity for the times.

Why Alfred Nobel donated most of his estate to the Nobel Foundation is not completely clear. The theory that he wanted to clear his conscience after he saw the devastating power of his invention is not very convincing. After all, he was hoping that his inventions would be used to benefit mankind in building and improving a modern world rather than for military purposes. It is clear, however, that Alfred Nobel greatly respected the pioneering spirit of inventors and explorers in general. He believed in progress, and with progress in scientific, social, and political areas he saw possibilities for great improvements, happiness, and comfort for mankind. Nobel's prizes were intended to support the innovative spirit and the young struggling scholars and artists with new ideas. Of course, the history of awards, especially in literature, shows that older more established thinkers were generally given preference over the younger ones, contrary to Nobel's original intent.

As mentioned before, Nobel left thirty-two million Swedish crowns of his total estate of more than thirty-three million to the Nobel Foundation. This resulted in controversy. Since Alfred's relatives and friends received "only" about a mil-

lion-and-a-half crowns, they contested the will, which had been drawn up by Nobel without legal advice. In addition, several European countries claimed that they were also entitled to award the Nobel Prizes since Nobel's empire was multinational and his estate was located in eight different countries (Austria, France, Germany, Great Britain, Italy, Norway, Russia, and Sweden). Finally, Swedes themselves entered the controversy. They asked the inevitable questions: Why should these large sums be given to foreigners? Should not the prizes be awarded only to Scandinavians? Both the conservative and liberal Swedish parties criticized the will. But Nobel's instructions were clear, and all controversies eventually calmed down. After lengthy debate, the institutions that were asked by Nobel to carry out the provisions of his will agreed to accept the great responsibility, although they knew it would be difficult to judge by international standards and most decisions would be difficult and controversial. Much of the credit for the happy outcome has to be given to Ragnar Sohlman, the youngest of Alfred Nobel's assistants and one of the two executors of the will, for his persistent and skillful work on behalf of his deceased superior.

Alfred Nobel made provisions for five different Nobel Prizes to be awarded annually to those who in the previous year "benefited humanity most," regardless of their nationality. The interest drawn from the principal of the Nobel Foundation was to be used for the five prizes. After deducting administrative costs and a percentage added annually to the principal sum, the remainder of the interest income is divided into five equal parts for the prizes. The Nobel Prize for Literature is awarded by the Swedish Academy, the Chemistry and Physics Prizes are decided by the Swedish Royal Academy of Sciences, and the Prize for Physiology or Medicine is given by the Karolinske (Medical-Surgical) Institute in Stockholm.

Only the Nobel Peace Prize is awarded outside of Sweden. A five-person committee selected by the Norwegian parliament decides on the recipients of this prize. One should remember that during Nobel's lifetime the king of Sweden was also the king of Norway. At the turn of the century, the relations between Sweden and Norway became strained, and in 1905 Norway succeeded in peacefully gaining its independence from Sweden.

After Nobel's death, time was needed to organize the Nobel Foundation. Finally, on June 29, 1900, the statutes of the Foundation were announced. The Foundation was set up as an independent, nongovernmental agency. It officially came into existence on January 1, 1901, and the names of the first laureates were announced on December 10, 1901, the fifth anniversary of Alfred Nobel's death. Since then it has been customary for the awards to be announced annually before November 15 and for the Swedish king himself to present each laureate in Stockholm (except the Peace Prize, which is awarded simultaneously in Oslo) on December 10 with a check, a certificate, and a specially made gold coin with the portrait of Alfred Nobel on one side and the name of the laureate with the year of the award on the other. All laureates are requested to give a formal lecture in Stockholm (Oslo for the Peace Prize) within six months of the announcement of their awards, the topics for the lectures to be based on the work for which the awards were given. The lectures are published in the *Les Prix Nobel*, the official annual of the Nobel Foundation.

It is obvious why Nobel designated the awards for chemistry, physics, and physiology or medicine. He was, after all, a well-known natural scientist himself. But why did Nobel establish the prizes for peace and literature? The Peace Prize, according to his will to be awarded for "the best work for fraternity between nations," was probably influenced by the already mentioned Austrian peace activist Bertha von Suttner. She not only corresponded with Alfred Nobel regularly (increasingly so in Nobel's later years), but also for a short period of time served as Alfred Nobel's private secretary and undoubtedly prompted the successful industrialist to familiarize himself with pacifist thought. According to his correspondence, Nobel hoped for international disarmament, and the Peace Prize was supposed to award those who helped in bringing about friendship among peoples and nations who worked for a removal of armies and for arms reduction and who organized international peace meetings and congresses. Bertha von Suttner received the Nobel Peace Prize herself in 1905.

An earlier version of Alfred Nobel's will did not mention the Literature Prize but looking closer at Nobel's education and activities, it is not surprising that the prize was included in his final testament. The Nobel brothers had a well-rounded education in which the study of humanities played at least as important a role as that of natural sciences. Alfred traveled often and learned to speak several languages. He enjoyed reading many writers in their original languages. He often quoted, in addition to the Scandinavian writers, William Shakespeare, Immanuel Kant, and Victor Hugo in their native tongue. Alfred Nobel was acquainted with many literary personages. He knew Hugo personally, and he especially liked the English poet Percy B. Shelley, also a pacifist, who definitely contributed to Nobel's own weltanschauung. By imitating Shelley, Nobel tried to write poems, of which only one, "A Riddle," survives. In 1895 Nobel even wrote a tragedy, *Nemesis*. The poorly written play was published after Nobel's death. All but three copies were destroyed by relatives in order not to cause embarrassment to the famous man. Although Nobel did not succeed in creating any quality literature himself, he demonstrated an intense interest and appreciation for this field.

The Nobel Committee for Literature of the Swedish Academy annually sends a request for nominations for the Nobel Prize to the members of the Swedish and other Academies, to national and international literary organizations, and to selected professors of literatures around the world. The nominations have to be received by February 1 of each year, and the five-member committee secretly submits its recommendations by the end of September to the Swedish Academy as a whole. The Academy can overrule the recommendation of its committee, but all deliberations and votes are kept secret. The decision on each year's recipient is final, without appeal, does not need to be justified in more than one sentence, and has to be announced before November 15.

The Nobel Prize for Literature was not awarded in seven years (1914, 1918, 1935, 1940, 1941, 1942, and 1943). In 1964 Jean-Paul Sartre refused to accept it; in 1925 George Bernard Shaw wanted to reject the prize, but he did accept it reluctantly and used the prize money to establish a foundation promoting English-Swedish cultural relations; in 1958 Boris Pasternak under political pressure had to refuse the award. In 1904, 1917, 1966, and 1974 the prize was shared by two recipients.

Since the Nobel Prize for Literature is the highest honor that a writer can achieve, the selections have been viewed very critically. The list of writers who historically are considered as great but did not receive the award is long. The reasons for their absence are debatable: Was Paul Claudel too religious (Roman Catholic)? Were Maxim Gorki and Bertolt Brecht too ideological (Communist)? Were Franz Kafka, James Joyce, and Virginia Woolf too experimental? Did Henrik Ibsen, August Strindberg, and Anton Chekhov not receive the prize because they were primarily known as playwrights? To these names one could add those of many more influential writers, such as Gabriele D'Annunzio, Günter Grass, Stéphane Mallarmé, Rainer Maria Rilke, Dylan Thomas, and Émile Verhaeren.

One has to recognize that an unusually high number of recipients have been from Scandinavian countries and that the selections also definitely favored European and U.S. writers. Even the Indian laureate Rabindranath Tagore (1913), the only recipient before 1945 who was not European or American, was awarded the prize for his popularity in Europe rather than for his contributions to Indian literature. After 1945 writers from South America, Australia, Israel, and Japan were awarded the prestigious prize. But the first writer from Africa, Wole Soyinka, received the prize only in 1986, and the first laureate writing in Arabic, the Egyptian author Najīb Maḥfūẓ, had to wait until 1988 to be granted the Nobel Prize.

The Selection Committee for Literature did and does not have an easy task in meeting Alfred Nobel's demand for a representative of "idealistic" literature. However, it seems to have deviated from Nobel's other demand that the award be given for a "performance from the preceding year." In general, whereas Nobel Prize laureates in natural sciences often have not reached the age of thirty or forty at the time of their awards, Nobel Prize winners in literature are typically in the twilight of their lives and creativity when they receive the honor. Even the first laureate in literature, Sully Prud-

homme, did not meet the "preceding year" qualifications, since he had hardly published anything recent at the time of his award when he was seventy-two years old. The prize was given to him for his lifelong contribution to literature rather than for a "performance from the preceding year." Similarly, other laureates have been honored for work done several years before the awarding of the Nobel Prize. For example, Władisław Reymont received his prize in 1924 for his epic *Chlopi* (1904–09), Thomas Mann in 1929 for the novel *Buddenbrooks* (1901), and John Galsworthy in 1932 for the *Forsyte Saga*, published between 1906 and 1921. The major exception is Boris Pasternak, who was honored in 1958 for his novel *Doctor Zhivago*, published the previous year.

Finally, one can also look at the list of the past recipients of the Nobel Prize in literature and judge the quality of the selections by today's standards. Whereas one misses some of the great names in world literature, as discussed before, one can also question the selection of several historically insignificant writers. If we take German-language literature as an example, only four of the ten recipients, Gerhart Hauptmann (1912), Thomas Mann (1929), Hermann Hesse (1946), and Heinrich Böll (1972), can be considered as truly great writers.

Moreover, the first two German Nobel Prize Laureates for literature were not in the mainstream of belles lettres (the Nobel Foundation guidelines specify that the recipient does not have to be a belletristic writer); Theodor Mommsen (1902) was a historian and Rudolf Eucken (1908), today completely unknown to students of German literature, was a philosopher. The other German-language laureates, Paul Heyse (1910), Carl Spitteler (1919), Nelly Sachs (1966), and Elias Canetti (1981), are good and distinguished writers but they are hardly better and certainly not as influential as, for example, Franz Kafka, Bertolt Brecht, Robert Musil, and Günter Grass, who were not honored by the Swedish Academy.

Judging by selections in recent years, the future laureates in literature should show more international and cultural diversity. They will represent more literatures outside European traditions. However, controversies will continue, and one will often hear the question: How politically motivated is the presentation of the awards? The convention that the prize be given to older, established writers for their total contribution to literature, although against Alfred Nobel's original will, will also be continued. In any case, the Nobel Prize in literature, the best known and the most prestigious of all literary prizes, will continue to carry with it for all recipients a high moral responsibility in addition to worldwide prestige.

Rado Pribic

Nobel Laureates in Literature by Year

1901   René-François-Armand Sully Prudhomme

1902   Theodor Mommsen

1903   Bjørnstjerne Bjørnson

1904   José Echegaray y Eizaguirre and Frédéric Mistral

1905   Henryk Sienkiewicz

1906   Giosue Carducci

1907   Rudyard Kipling

1908   Rudolf Eucken

1909   Selma Lagerlöf

1910   Paul Heyse

1911   Maurice Maeterlinck

1912   Gerhart Hauptmann

1913   Rabindranath Tagore

1914   Not awarded

1915   Romain Rolland

1916   Verner von Heidenstam

1917   Karl Adolph Gjellerup and Henrik Pontoppidan

1918   Not awarded

1919   Carl Spitteler

1920   Knut Hamsun

1921   Anatole France

1922   Jacinto Benavente y Martinez

1923   William Butler Yeats

1924   Władysław Reymont

1925   George Bernard Shaw

1926 Grazia Deledda

1927 Henri-Louis Bergson

1928 Sigrid Undset

1929 Thomas Mann

1930 Sinclair Lewis

1931 Erik Axel Karlfeldt

1932 John Galsworthy

1933 Ivan Bunin

1934 Luigi Pirandello

1935 Not awarded

1936 Eugene O'Neill

1937 Roger Martin du Gard

1938 Pearl S. Buck

1939 Frans Eemil Sillanpää

1940 Not awarded

1941 Not awarded

1942 Not awarded

1943 Not awarded

1944 Johannes V. Jensen

1945 Gabriela Mistral

1946 Hermann Hesse

1947 André Gide

1948 T. S. Eliot

1949 William Faulkner

1950 Bertrand Russell

1951 Pär Fabian Lagerkvist

1952 François Mauriac

1953 Winston Churchill

1954 Ernest Hemingway

1955 Halldór Laxness
1956 Juan Ramón Jiménez
1957 Albert Camus
1958 Boris Pasternak
1959 Salvatore Quasimodo
1960 Saint-John Perse
1961 Ivo Andrić
1962 John Steinbeck
1963 George Seferis
1964 Jean-Paul Sartre
1965 Mikhail Sholokhov
1966 S. Y. Agnon and Nelly Sachs
1967 Miguel Angel Asturias
1968 Yasunari Kawabata
1969 Samuel Beckett
1970 Alexandr Solzhenitsyn
1971 Pablo Neruda
1972 Heinrich Böll
1973 Patrick White
1974 Eyvind Johnson and Harry Martinson
1975 Eugenio Montale
1976 Saul Bellow
1977 Vicente Aleixandre
1978 Isaac Bashevis Singer
1979 Odysseus Elytis
1980 Czeslaw Milosz
1981 Elias Canetti
1982 Gabriel García Márquez
1983 William Golding

THE CONTRIBUTORS

JOSEPH K. ADJAYE
Assistant professor of African Studies at the University of Pittsburgh. He has extensive experience in African studies curriculum development and teachers' workshops on the use of literary art forms as a tool for teaching about African society.

ROGER ALLEN
Professor of Arabic and Comparative Literature at the University of Pennsylvania. He is the author of several books and internationally recognized authority on modern Arabic literature.

JOSEPH R. ARBOLEDA
Associate professor of Spanish at Lafayette College. He is an expert on the Spanish theater, Romanticism, and civilization.

ANN BIDLINGMAIER
Chair of the English department at Lincoln High School in Tallahassee, Florida, where her areas of teaching include classical and British literature.

DOREEN L. BUCHMAN
A free lance writer and former teacher of college-level English. Currently she is working for the Department of University Publications at Rutgers University.

BIRUTA CAP
Associate professor of French at Kutztown State University. Her publications deal with seventeenth- and twentieth-century French studies, Franco-German literary relations, Baltic studies, and women studies.

JEAN-PIERRE CAP
Professor of French at Lafayette College. He is the author of several books on eighteenth- and twentieth-century French literary and historical studies.

RICHARD L. CHAPPLE
Professor of Russian at Florida State University. He has published two books and several articles on nineteenth- and twentieth-century Russian and Soviet literature.

AXEL CLAESGES
Associate professor of German at West Virginia University. He has published works on nineteenth- and twentieth-century German literature.

ERASMO G. GERATO
Professor of Italian at Florida State University. He has published extensively on twentieth-century Italian literature.

RICHARD B. HILARY
Associate professor of Italian at Florida State University. His publications are primarily in the area of the Italian Renaissance.

DAVID R. JOHNSON
Associate professor and chair of the English department at Lafayette

College. He is interested in nine-teenth- and twentieth-century popular American literature and thought and has authored articles on Ernest Hemingway.

ALBERT A. KIPA
Professor of German and Russian and chair of the department of foreign languages at Muhlenberg College. He is primarily interested in Germano-Slavic literary relations and has written and edited several books and articles.

FRITZ H. KÖNIG
Professor of Germanic literatures and languages and head of the department of foreign languages at the University of Northern Iowa. He has published several articles on Scandinavian literature.

KONSTANTIN KUSTANOVICH
Assistant professor of Slavic Languages and Literatures at Vanderbilt University, specializing in contemporary Russian literature. He is currently completing a book on V. Aksenov.

JEAN-PIERRE LALANDE
Associate professor of French at Moravian College. Most of his research focuses on the theater of the absurd and French surrealism.

ROXANNE DECKER LALANDE
Associate professor of French at Lafayette College. Her special research interests are in the area of seventeenth-century French drama and comic theory.

HOWARD MARBLESTONE
Associate professor of languages at Lafayette College where he combines teaching and research interests in classical literature and semitic philology.

MARIA G. MARIN
Instructor of Spanish at Lafayette College. Her scholarly interest is in the area of colonial literature of Latin America.

JOSEPH J. MARTIN
Associate professor of English at Lafayette College. His main scholarly interests are in nineteenth- and twentieth-century British fiction, and he has published several articles on Joseph Conrad.

EDWARD R. McDONALD
Associate Professor of Languages at Lafayette College. His main scholarly interests are in nineteenth- and twentieth-century German and Austrian literature.

JACQUELINE MUELLER
Independent scholar of Japanese literature. She has formerly taught Japanese language, culture, and literature on a college level.

JEAN PEARSON
Poet, teacher, editor, and translator. She is the author of one book of poems, the coauthor of a history of women in literature, and her translations of Swedish and German nature poetry have appeared in many journals and anthologies.

ELISABETH PRIBIĆ
Professor of Slavic Philology at Florida State University. She is the author and coauthor of several books and articles on Slavic linguistics and Czech and Slovak literature.

NIKOLA R. PRIBIĆ
Professor emeritus of Slavic literature at Florida State University. He has published numerous articles and several books, primarily on South Slavic literature.

RADO PRIBIC
Professor of Languages at Lafayette College and head of the international affairs program. His main research interests are in the area of Germano-Slavic literary, cultural, and linguistic relations.

ROBERT P. PULA
An independent scholar who writes on Polish literature.

STEVEN D. PUTZEL
Assistant professor of English at the Pennsylvania State University, Wilkes-Barre. He is the author of a book on William Butler Yeats and a contributor to various journals.

JAMES REIBMAN
Assistant professor of English at the Pennsylvania State University, Mont Alto. He is the author of articles on Samuel Johnson, on law and literature, and on historiography in the Scottish Enlightenment.

GEORGE M. ROSA
Assistant professor of Languages at Lafayette College. His research and publications focus primarily on the nineteenth-century French novelist Stendhal.

KATHRYNE ROSS
Research assistant for German literature at Lafayette College.

LORI SCARPA
Research assistant for Russian literature at Lafayette College.

STACEY SCHLAU
Director of the Women Studies Center and Assistant professor of Spanish at West Chester State University. Her publications focus on the Latin American women writers.

JUNE SCHLUETER
Associate professor of English at Lafayette College. She is the author and coeditor of several books on American, English, and German literature.

PAUL SCHLUETER
Independent scholar specializing in American literature. He has taught college-level courses in American literature, has published numerous articles and reviews, and has edited several books.

SCOTT C. SCHWARTZ
Graduate fellow of Spanish at New York University.

JAMES W. SCOTT
Professor of German at Lebanon Valley College. He has published on medieval and modern German literature.

LARRY E. SCOTT
Associate professor and chair of the department of Scandinavian Studies at Augustana College. He has published numerous articles and translations dealing with Swedish America.

ANTOINE SPACAGNA
Associate professor of French at Florida State University. He is the author of a book and several articles on twentieth-century French literature.

SUSAN SWANSON
Holds degrees in Scandinavian Studies and Linguistics from the University of California, Berkeley. She is currently an adjunct lecturer in English at Lehigh University.

ALFRED R. WEDEL
Associate professor of Romance Philology at the University of Delaware. His publications are mostly in the area of German-Spanish literary relations.

ERIC WILLIAMS
Assistant professor of German at the University of Hawaii. He specializes in lyrical poetry and has written on twentieth-century German literature.

HANA WIRTH-NESHER
Senior lecturer in English and department head at Tel Aviv University. She has written extensively on Jewish literature, the British and American novel, narrative techniques, and urban poetics.

REINHOLD WOLF
Free-lance writer, journalist, and currently a graduate fellow for comparative literature at the University of Oregon.

JOSEPHINE WTULICH
Author, tutor, and translator in several major languages including Polish. Her book and most of her other publications are in the field of historical sociology.

HANS WUERTH
Professor of German and chair of the foreign language department at Moravian College. He specializes in German literature of the twentieth-century, particularly the literature of the German Democratic Republic.

ARVIDS ZIEDONIS
The John and Fannie Saeger Professor of Comparative Literature and director of Russian studies at Muhlenberg College. He is the author of several books and numerous articles on Baltic and Russian literature.

THE LAUREATES

S. Y. Agnon   *1966*

Samuel Joseph Agnon (1888–1970), Israeli writer of novels and short fiction, was born Shmuel Yosef Czaczkes, on July 17, 1888, in Buczacz, Eastern Galicia, then in the Austro-Hungarian Empire. The area, part of the new Polish state after World War I, was occupied by the Germans in World War II, after which it became part of the western Ukraine in the USSR. Czaczkes's upbringing was comfortable, bourgeois, and Orthodox in the manner of East European Jews; that is, both reverential and erudite. He studied the classics of Jewish spirituality and literature, first with his father, a fur merchant and an ordained rabbi, and later at the *Bet Hammidrash* ("House of Study").

From the age of nine Czaczkes wrote poetry and prose both in Yiddish, the everyday language of the Jewish people, and in Hebrew, traditionally the language of Jewish prayer and scholarship. His works were first published in 1903, and in 1906 he became the assistant editor of a Yiddish weekly. Czaczkes continued to write in both languages until 1907, when he immigrated to Jaffa, Palestine, about the time of the Second Aliyah (wave of immigration), c. 1908–1913, which brought to Palestine approximately forty thousand Jews, mostly Russian and Ukrainian, imbued with Labor Zionism, the secular, socialist movement for the restoration of "the Land." Although Czaczkes did not belong, either by upbringing or by temperament, to the Labor Zionists, he was soon at the hub of Palestine Jewish society. He became secretary, first of the Jewish court in Jaffa, then of the Lovers of Zion Society and of the Land of Israel Council, a "parliament-in-the-making" (in his words) for the settlers. He encountered in Palestine "a human landscape as colored and varied as any novelist could wish for . . . " (Fisch 1975).

In 1908, "Agunot" ("Deserted Wives": in Jewish law an *'agunah* is a wife who, her husband having disappeared [or been presumed, but not proved, dead] without divorcing her, may not remarry), his first story published in Palestine, in Hebrew, brought Czaczkes literary fame. He then adopted the pen name "Agnon," derived from the root of "Agunot" (see below), and thereafter, Hebrew was his "native" tongue. He traveled widely in Palestine, writing as he did, and met regularly with distinguished writers, critics, intellectuals, and Zionist dignitaries. He enlarged his study of literature, particularly German and Russian. As his intellectual vista expanded, Agnon abandoned the outward appearance and the inner bearing of his Orthodox youth in Galicia and Palestine. For an extended time after 1911 he lived in Jerusalem, wherein both the Hasidic culture of some Jewish settlers and the secular, modern learning of others impressed him profoundly. His story "Vehaya He'akov Lemishor" (1912; "And the Crooked Shall be Made Straight") brought him further adulation in Palestine.

Apparently to expand his intellectual vista yet further, Agnon left for Berlin in 1913. He had planned to remain in Germany only a few years. But the outbreak of World War I and unstable political conditions caused him to prolong his stay, ultimately until 1924. In Germany, then the center of Jewish culture, and in Berlin particularly, he encountered other leading Hebrew writers, such as Hayyim Nahman Bialik, Ya'akov Fichman, and Ahad Ha'am. He came to know Martin Buber, Gershom Scholem (who would become the world authority on *Kabbalah*, Jewish mysticism), and Franz Rosenzweig, among others. Esther Marx, the cultivated daughter of a prominent Jewish family from Königsberg, became Agnon's wife in 1920; the Agnons' two children, a daughter and a son, were born in the next two years. In Germany Agnon acquired a Maecenas in Salman Schocken, philanthropist and publisher, who provided him with a life annuity to support his writing. Schocken's firm, later moved to Tel Aviv, became the chief publisher of Agnon's work as the New York branch thereof is for the English translations. In 1924, near the end of Agnon's sojourn in Germany, a fire in his house at Bad Homburg destroyed his library of some four thousand classic Jewish works plus all of the manuscripts he had written since his arrival in Germany, including a large novel, *Bitsror Hahayyim*

("Eternal Life"), and a book he had written with Martin Buber.

In early 1924 Agnon returned to Jerusalem, where he resided the rest of his life except for brief visits in Europe and America. The color and variety of the city, its vibrant intellectual life, especially with the founding of the Hebrew University in 1925, and its traditional Jewish culture made Jerusalem "the city of his heart" (Band, 1968). He resumed his Orthodoxy, this time without the traditional somber garb. He adopted his pen name as his family's surname. From his tranquil home in the southern suburb of Talpiot he could gaze upon the Old City with the Dome of the Rock to the north, the hills of the Judean desert to the south, and the Dead Sea to the east. But during Arab attacks on the Jewish settlement in 1929, the Agnon home, together with its library, was ransacked. Invaluable books, papers, and manuscripts were thus lost. Soon after this disaster, Agnon left for Germany, as Schocken planned to issue a four-volume edition of his writings. The edition, published at Berlin in 1931, contained works published or completed before the summer of 1929. In 1930 Agnon also made a "sentimental journey" through Galicia and to Buczacz, the city of his birth. As he would later recall, the events and experiences of 1929–30 marked a turning point in his life and in his oeuvre.

The thirties were to prove broadly and deeply productive for Agnon. Among his major works, the first full-length novel, *Hakhnasat Kalla* (*The Bridal Canopy*), upon which he had worked several years in Jerusalem, appeared in 1931 as did *Me'az Ume'attah* ("From Then and from Now") and *Sippure Ahavim* ("Love Stories"). The tale *Bilvav Yamim* (*In the Heart of the Seas*), the collection of stories *Beshuvah Vanahat* ("Easy and Quiet"), and the novel *Sippur Pashut* ("A Simple Tale") were published in 1935 to be followed in 1938 by *Yamim Nora'im* (*Days of Awe*), a collection of lore and homilies on the Jewish High Holy Days, Rosh Hashanah and Yom Kippur. *Oreah Natah Lalun* (*A Guest for the Night*), Agnon's second full-scale novel, his acknowledged masterpiece, appeared in 1939. *Elu Ve'elu* ("These and Those"), a collection of stories, was published in 1941, while the novel *Tmol Shilshom* ("The Day before Yesterday") appeared in 1945.

In 1951 an enlarged edition of *Sepher Hamma'asîm* ("Book of Fables," original edition, 1931) and the collection of stories *Samuch Venir'eh* ("Near and Visible") were printed, followed by *Ad Hena* ("To This Point") in 1952. In 1953 Schocken published a seven-volume edition of Agnon's collected works, 1931–52; its second edition in eight volumes, which included works from 1953 to 1962, has become the standard collection of Agnon's fiction published in his lifetime. To be sure, the bibliography of these works is not only enormous (approximately 250 works of fiction), but complex, as Agnon throughout his life revised his works for each new edition. An exhaustive primary (and secondary) bibliography compiled according to "historically oriented scholarship" is found in Band (1968), a work indispensable for the study of Agnon. Further, in 1953 appeared the collection of stories *'Al Kappot Hamman'ul* ("At the Handles of the Lock"), in 1959 *Attem Re'item* ("You Have Seen"), a collection of Rabbinic *dicta*, and in 1962 *Ha'esh Veha'etsim* ("The Fire and the Wood"), a collection of stories.

Agnon had manifestly become the most distinguished Hebrew writer of the twentieth century. In recognition of his vast and individual contribution to Hebrew letters he was awarded the Israel Prize for Literature in 1954 and in 1958. Owing to the extensive translation of his work into English and into European languages, international recognition came in 1966 with the Nobel Prize in literature, which the Swedish Academy awarded "for his profoundly distinctive narrative art with motifs from the life of the Jewish people"; this was the first Nobel Prize to a Hebrew writer. He shared the award with Nelly Sachs. Further honors included a Ph.D. from the Hebrew University in 1959 and membership in the Hebrew Language Academy.

At his death on February 17, 1970, Agnon left a large corpus of unpublished material. Published in nine volumes so far, this work includes *Shira* (1971); *'Ir Umelo'ah* (1973; "A Teeming City"), a collection of stories; *Bahanuto Shel Mar Lublin* (1974; "In Mr. Lublin's Shop"), and much else (see Aberbach: 1984, Bibliography).

Agnon's work inhabits two worlds: one of Orthodox Jewish life embraced and sustained by a warm tradition of sanctification, celebration, and study; the other of the modern era beset by change, uncertainty, and breakdown. His first nineteen years, until he left Galicia for Palestine (1907), became for Agnon the era of books and stable tradition; the period in Jaffa (1907–13) introduced him to the "varied human landscape," as the sojourn in Germany broadened his intellectual vista. Agnon's synthesis of this diverse experience is symbolized in the uneasy geographical and metaphysical oscillation between Buczacz and Jerusalem. As Fisch observes: "The ultimate question to which Agnon's writing addresses itself is this: How is one to mediate between Shebush [Agnon's Hebrew tag, meaning "breakdown," "disorder," "confusion," for Buczacz] and Jerusalem, between the past and the present, between nation-building and the pieties of Old World Hasidism, between God and socialism, between vision and reality?" and on a metaphysical level, between permanence and change? The past with its comfortable tradition is also the bitterness of exile from the Land of Israel; the present, with its prospect of redemption in the Land is, with its manifold challenges, alienated from the spiritual tranquillity of the past. The name, Agnon, adopted by the writer in 1908, betokens in Hebrew both "anchoring" and "forsaken [as a wife]," hence, "continuity and cutoff" (Brandwein). The double loss of his library of classic Jewish texts may have been for Agnon emblematic of the disastrous loss of tradition joined with the need to persevere (at his death Agnon left a library grander and richer than those lost).

Agnon is neither the apologist for the traditional ways nor the pioneer into the future. His work is fraught with religious, social, and metaphysical tension. The world of learning and of fantasy and that of reality painfully intersect in Agnon. His vision of the Jewish cultural heritage has been compared with those of two major twentieth-century writers of Jewish background: that of Proust in its "nostalgia" and that of Kafka in its "nightmare" (Band). But Agnon's vision in its complexity and tensions is utterly individual, even protean (Band).

Although Agnon's background and style are bookish, his subjects are at all times people in their astonishing diversity and complexity. He spoke in his Nobel address of the "influence, which I have received from every man, every woman, every child I have encountered along my way, both Jews and non-Jews. People's talk and the stories they tell have been engraved on my heart and have flown into my pen." His Hebrew style is "a modern distillation of traditional pietistic expression [derived chiefly from the Bible, Talmud, Midrash (Rabbinic Homily), and Classical Commentaries], together with strata from all [historical] levels of the language" (G. Kressel). Hebrew, though not spoken for nearly two thousand years, had nonetheless undergone a literary evolution in distinct phases; in Agnon's early years it was being revived as a spoken language in Palestine. For the cultivated reader or speaker of Hebrew its historical strata were all comprehensible as an organic whole; Agnon's style is thus an extraordinary amalgam inseparable from the content of his tales. His tone is consistent and steady as his manner is playful and even mysterious.

The following are some of Agnon's most significant and popular works: *Hakhnasat Kallah* (1931; *The Bridal Canopy*) a picaresque tale of Reb Yudel in the early nineteenth century, oscillates between his "inner world of joy and holiness" (Fisch) and the harsh realities of his life. *Sippur Pashuṭ* (1935; "Simple Tale"), a psychological novel, mediates between the simple desires of the individual and the demands of his society for conformity grounded in sloganism. In *Oreaḥ Naṭah Lalun* (1939; *A Guest for the Night*), inspired by Agnon's return to Galicia and Buczacz, Agnon offers his "epic vision of the shtetl [the traditional Eastern European Jewish village] in decline and of modern Jewish history at the crossroads" (Fisch, 1975). Realism and symbolism interact powerfully, especially in the symbol of the brass key to the House of Study, an image that brings together past, present, and future. *Temol Shilshom* (1945; "The Day Before Yesterday"), a tale of travel from the *shtetl* to Palestine, describes a search by the descendant of Reb Yudel for "the union of old and new" (Brandwein) and "the

frustrations and difficulties of the incipient Jewish nation" (Fisch). The second edition of *Sepher Hamma'asim* (1951; "Book of Fables") is a collection of Kafkaesque tales quite unlike those of the earlier oeuvre. These are "marked by a surrealistic abandonment of normal continuity and a technique akin to stream of consciousness. As in a dream, time and place are confused; the symbolic and everyday worlds are yoked together. . . . " (Fisch). Finally, the posthumous novel *Shira*, set in Palestine during the British mandate, portrays through the affair of an intellectual with the nurse Shira "the bond not with the past, but with the enchantments of a new world in which past beauty has faded . . . the fierce attractions of alienation itself, the shadow cast not by the past upon the present, but by the present upon the past" (Fisch).

HOWARD MARBLESTONE

Selected Bibliography

PRIMARY SOURCES

Agnon, Samuel Joseph. *Days of Awe.* Translated by M. T. Galpert. New York: Schocken Books, 1948.

———. *A Guest for the Night.* Translated by Misha Louvish. New York: Schocken Books, 1968.

———. *In the Heart of the Seas.* Translated by I. M. Lask. New York: Schocken Books, 1948.

———. *Twenty-One Stories.* Edited by Nahum N. Glatzer. New York: Schocken Books, 1970. [About one-

half of the stories herein are translated from *Sepher Hamma'asim*.]

SECONDARY SOURCES

Aberbach, David. *At the Handles of the
Lock. Themes in the Fiction of
S. Y. Agnon*. The Littman Library.
Oxford: Oxford University Press,
1984.

Band, Arnold J. *Nostalgia and Nightmare. A Study in the Fiction of
S. Y. Agnon*. Berkeley and Los Angeles: University of California
Press, 1968.

Fisch, Harold. *S. Y. Agnon*. Modern
Literature Monographs. New York:
Ungar, 1975.

Goell, Yohai. *Bibliography of Modern
Hebrew Literature in English
Translation*. Jerusalem: Israel Uni-
versities Press, 1968. Pp. 58–60.

Goldberg, Isaac, and Amnon Zipper.
*Bibliography of Modern Hebrew
Literature in Translation*. Tel Aviv:
Institute for the Translation of He-
brew Literature: 1979–82.

Hochman, Baruch. *The Fiction of S. Y.
Agnon*. Ithaca, N.Y.: Cornell University Press, 1970.

*Prooftexts. A Journal of Jewish Literary
History.* "Special Issue on S. Y.
Agnon." Vol. 7, No. 1, January
1987.

VICENTE ALEIXANDRE   *1977*

Vicente Aleixandre (1898–1984) is a
representative of what is called in
Spanish literature the Generation of
1927, or the Generation of the Dictatorship (of Franco). The Spanish
critic Dámaso Alonso characterizes
Aleixandre as a mystic pantheist; in
the rest of Europe he is known as a
poet of surrealism. His poetry is difficult to read due to his use of complicated associations of ideas and
bold metaphors that are often out of
context. Although the poet never
considered himself a surrealist in the
strict sense of the word, he shares,
nonetheless, with other representatives of this literary movement a distrust of the logical mind and an interest in the subconscious and
hallucinatory states of the mind.

Vicente Aleixandre was born in
Seville on April 26, 1898. His father,
an engineer, in 1900 was transferred
to Málaga, where young Vicente
and his sister spent their early childhood. From 1909 to 1913 Vicente
lived with his family in Madrid,
where he received his secondary
education at the Colegio Teresiano.
From 1914 to 1920 he studied law
and mercantile management. He
also took courses in Spanish literature. After graduation he taught
mercantile law. In 1924 he became
ill with tubercular nephritis and had
to retire to a sanatorium. During the

long days of convalescence, Aleixandre spent his time writing verses. His first poems appeared in the journal *Revista de Occidente* in August 1926.

Similar to the Spanish modernist poet Jimenez, who searched for the essence of poetry, the members of the Generation of 1927 also engaged in the search for this concept. The French writer and literary critic Henri Brémond had declared that emotion lay at the base of all poetry. Another French author, Paul Valéry, however, was of the opinion that intelligence and reason were the moving forces in poetry. The young Spanish poets who followed this debate were divided in their opinion. Jorge Guillen, for instance, another member of the Generation of 1927, followed Valéry's thesis. He rejected realism and sentimentalism. For him, as for most members of this group, pure poetry was neither description nor effusion. This poetry devoid of all emotionalism could only give way to a poetry in search of aesthetic principles or to a poetry of human and social concern. Carlos Bousoño, a critic and Aleixandre's biographer, declares that the main driving forces behind Aleixandre's work were his irrationalism and his individualism.

In 1927 Aleixandre returned to Madrid and settled in the outskirts of the capital. In 1928 he published his book of poetry entitled *Ambito* ("Ambit"). In addition to reading Spanish authors Quevedo, Lope, and Unamuno, he began to read such foreign authors as Freud, Joyce, and Rimbaud. In 1932 he published another book, *Espadas como labios* ("Swords like Lips"). He again took ill and had a kidney removed, but by 1933 he was back home again. The same year a jury of fellow writers gave him the National Prize in Literature for his unpublished work *La destrucción o el amor* (*Destruction or Love*). In 1934 Aleixandre traveled in England, France, and Switzerland. In 1935 he wrote *Mundo a solas* (*World Alone*), which was not published until 1936. In 1935 his book *La destrucción o el amor* (*Destruction of Love*) finally came out along with another one entitled *Pasión de la tierra* ("Passion of Earth").

During the Spanish Civil War, which raged from 1936 to 1939, the poet lay bedridden in his apartment. After the war the young poets of Madrid began to visit him there. In 1941, during World War II, the poet published his book of poetry entitled *Nacimiento último* ("Final Birth"), and toward the end of the war, in 1944, another book that bears the title *Sombra del paraiso* (*Shadow of Paradise*) came out.

Bousoño considers all these works as belonging to Aleixandre's first period. The main themes deal with the elemental nature of all things. That is, individual beings are viewed as part of the same cosmic matter. A tiger or a rose are unequal representatives of what the poet considers to be the same thing. Love in the poems written from 1928 to 1936 is nothing but passion and madness, reflecting Aleixandre's erotic pantheism. His style can also be characterized as oscillating between grandiose descriptions and minute details. The poem "Ven siempre ven" ("Come Always, Come") in *La destrucción o el amor* and the poem "El poeta" ("The Poet") in *Sombra del Paraiso* illustrate this oscillation:

> No te acerques, porque tu beso se
> prolonga como el choque imposi-
> ble de las estrellas,
> como el espacio que subitamente se
> incendia,

Translated edition of Lewis Hyde:
> Don't come closer, because your kiss
> goes on and on like the impossible
> collision of the stars,
> like space that suddenly catches fire.

> oye este libro que a tus manos envio
> con ademán de selva,
> pero donde de repente una gota
> fresquísima de rocío brilla
> sobre/ una rosa,

Translated edition of Lewis Hyde:
> listen to this book I put in your hands
> with my forest gestures,
> but where an incredibly fresh dew-
> drop suddenly shines on a rose.

During Aleixandre's second period, he speaks, as Bousoño has pointed out, of the spiritual unity of all human beings. Man is no longer seen as the creature torn between tellurian forces, but man shares, between his good and bad sides, the same destiny as his neighbor and, consequently, no longer has to fight a lonely battle. Life is, indeed, a constant struggle, but the poet considers that not to be alive is worse. Life must be understood as a continual growth that proceeds through stages. The representative work of this period is his book of verse en-

titled *Historia de corazón* ("History of the Heart") published in 1953. In one of these poems, "Entre dos oscuridades un relámpago" ("Between Two Nighttimes, Lightning"), Aleixandre deals with the paradox that life, which seems on the one hand so long because of its unbearable constant struggle, is really, on the other hand, of an incredibly short duration:

> Sabemos adónde vamos y de dónde
> venimos. Entre dos oscuridades./
> un relámpago.

Translated edition of Lewis Hyde:
> We know where we're going and
> where we came from. Between two
> nighttimes, lightning.

There is a third period in the poet's work that Bousoño considers to be a synthesis of the previous two. Whereas in the beginning Aleixandre dealt with the ultimate connection of all things in nature, and later he speaks of humanity and of life as a constant struggle, in his third period the poet presents the material world as something that possesses will. The matter becomes spirit through successive stages of evolution. A typical example of this weltanschauung appears in his poem "La oreja–la palabra." ("The Ear—The Word") in the collection *En un vasto dominio* ("In a Vast Dominion"), published in 1961:

> Y el cartilago avanza casi animal y
> casi mineral y se asoma.

Translated edition of Lewis Hyde:
> And the cartilage—part animal and
> part mineral—comes forward and
> looks out.

Aleixandre believed that man must develop his sensory and intellectual capacities. Society, however, can suffocate the impulse to grow. In the opening lines of his book *En un vasto dominio* (1962; "In a Vast Dominion"), the poet declares that he is not composing verses for the well-dressed gentleman, nor for the lady in a carriage, but for those who do not read him. The implication is that he is going to write for the plain folk, who are really the ones who care for him, even if they are not aware that he exists. The poem "Felix" expresses the poet's human and social concern. This composition deals with a country boy named Felix who is condemned to remain a primitive peasant for the rest of his life because society does not permit him to grow.

Aleixandre published another book of poetry when he was about to turn seventy. It is a collection entitled *Poemas de consumación* (1968; "Poems of Consummation") in which we find the theme of youth as the giver of love. The vision of death is now different from his earlier visions. It is no longer identified with the consummation of love, nor with the consuming fire of passion, but with the natural process of decay. Yet this view has the redeeming feature that death is like a dream that brings the long-awaited peace. Vicente Aleixandre was elected to the Spanish Academy in 1949,

and in 1968 the publishing house Insula issued a volume honoring him. Among the prominent people who remained in Spain after the victory of the Nationalists, not all were loyal to General Franco. Some went into an inner exile. Aleixandre was one of those who imposed upon themselves this inner exile. In 1977 he was awarded the Nobel Prize in literature. On December 13, 1984, the Spanish-speaking world lost one of its greatest poets of the twentieth century.

ALFRED R. WEDEL

Selected Bibliography

PRIMARY SOURCES

Aleixandre, Vicente. *A Bird of Paper*. Translated by Willis Barnstone and David Garrison. Athens: Ohio University Press, 1982.

———. *A Longing for Light: Selected Poems of Vicente Aleixandre*. Edited by Lewis Hyde. New York: Harper & Row, 1979.

———. *Shadow of Paradise*. Translated by Hugh A. Harter. Berkeley: University of California Press, 1987.

———. *Twenty Poems*. Translated by Lewis Hyde and Robert Bly. Madison, Minn.: The Seventies Press, 1977.

SECONDARY SOURCE

Schwartz, Kessel. *Vicente Aleixandre*. New York: Twayne, 1970.

IVO ANDRIĆ *1961*

Ivo Andrić (1892–1975) was awarded the Nobel Prize in literature in 1961 and was the first Yugoslav writer to be so honored. Although his parents lived in Sarajevo, where his father worked as a craftsman, Andrić was born in Travnik while his mother was there on a visit. Andrić attended elementary school in Višegrad, *gymnasium* in Sarajevo (1903–12), and studied Slavic languages and literature in Zagreb (1912–13), Vienna (1913–14), and Kraków (1914). He received his doctorate in philosophy in 1923 at the University of Graz, Austria, with a dissertation on the cultural development of Bosnia under the Turks. As a member of the Yugoslav National Movement, he spent three years in prison during World War I. After the war he went to Zagreb, and, together with N. Bartulović and B. Mašić, he helped edit the literary journal *Književni Jug* ("The Literary South") in 1918–19.

In 1919 Andrić moved to Belgrade and worked in the Ministry of Religion and later in the Ministry of Foreign Affairs. Thus he began a twenty-two-year diplomatic career that took him to various European centers: Vatican City, Bucharest, Trieste, Graz, Paris, Brussels, and Geneva. His career ended in 1941 with the outbreak of World War II while he was serving in Berlin as the last Yugoslav ambassador to Germany. During and after the war he was a free-lance writer in Belgrade, where for many years he presided over the Federation of Yugoslav Writers. He died there in 1975 at the age of 83.

Andrić's main source of inspiration was his native Bosnia—a diverse country with its mixed population of Orthodox Serbs, Catholic Croats, and large numbers of Moslems. Most of the Moslems are descendants of the Bogumils, heretics of the Middle Ages who, until the Turkish conquest of Bosnia in 1463, were very often the decisive factor in political struggles in that region.

Although born in Travnik and a lifelong devotee of that city, Andrić considered Višegrad his home. Višegrad was a remote Turkish *kasaba* (old Turkish-style town) with fewer than two thousand inhabitants, most of them illiterate. Although the Turkish occupation lasted almost four centuries, the Turks did little to improve the lives of the Višegrad population. Nevertheless, the town did have something to distinguish it—its bridge. The bridge had been built by the local bey Mehmed Pasha Sokolović (a.k.a. Sokollu) who as a young boy had gone to Istanbul and attained the highest rank of great vizier at the sultan's court. Andrić himself maintained that this bridge was the sole inspiration for his greatest work, *Na Drini Ćuprija* (1945; *The Bridge on the Drina*).

Early in 1911 Andrić began to publish poems in various Yugoslav literary journals: *Bosanska Vila* ("The Bosnian Fairy"), *Vihor* ("The Gale'"), and *Savremenik* ("The Contemporary"). The most significant outcome of his literary efforts of this period were the collections of poems in free verse, *Ex Ponto* (1918; "From the Bridge"), *Nemiri* (1920; "Unrest"), and *Put* (1920; "The Journey"), and the short story "Put Alija Derzeleza" (1920; "The Journey of Alija Derzeleza"), as well as three books of short stories (1924, 1931, and 1936). In addition, he published literary essays pertaining to Francisco Goya, St. Francis of Assisi, Petrarch, Walt Whitman, the great Serbian poet Njegoš, and other national and international writers.

Three of his most important novels appeared in 1945: *Na Drini Ćuprija* (The Bridge on the Drina,) *Travnička Kronika* (*The Bosnian Chronicle*), and *Gospodjica* (*The Woman from Sarajevo*). The first two are historical novels that elaborate on both actual and fictional characters. *The Bridge on the Drina* spans four centuries, from 1516 to 1914; the bridge's construction and destruction, and its function as a link between the east and west, are central to the book. Andrić's tracing of the history of the bridge is an ethnographic chronicle that provides the reader with a thorough, credible portrait of the rise and fall of the Ottoman civilization in Bosnia. The Nobel committee cited the epic force of this novel as justification for its decision to award the 1961 prize in literature to Andrić. *The Bosnian Chronicle* focuses on the Napoleonic Wars from 1806 to

1814 and their effect on Bosnia. Due to the brief time span the novel covers, Andrić was able to present more psychological nuances embedded in the characters and to stress intellectual, moral, and philosophical conflicts.

To the familiar theme of parsimony, Andrić added new flavor in *The Woman from Sarajevo*. Whereas his Višegrad novel left no room for detailed characterization, this work is primarily a psychological study. In this relatively short novel of some two hundred pages, the entire life of a peculiar, rather exceptional individual passes before the reader—a type that has since inspired many other writers. The protagonist, a young girl named Rajka Radaković, becomes a slave to one passion: the wish to accumulate money. Her entire life is directed toward this goal. Yet Rajka's pathological egotism dissolves when she meets the Belgrade spendthrift Ratko; she is attracted to him and surrenders large amounts of money to his control. Thus Rajka mirrors the same unpredictable conflict of values that many of Andrić's other characters embody.

The unfinished novel *Omar Paša Latas* (1976), which was posthumously published, is a historical work permeated with intense drama. The hero, Christian Michael, is a historical figure who left an unsuccessful career in the Austrian army, went to Turkey, and became a well-known Turkish conqueror. In this novel Andrić develops not so much the historical aspect of the protagonist, but the personal struggle of the individual.

Many of Andrić's stories and writings during the three postwar decades are continuations of the Bosnian themes of the previous chronicles. One of the more popular is a longer story, "Priča o vezirovom slonu" ("The Vizier's Elephant"), first published in 1948. The setting is Travnik in 1820, in the *čaršija*, the predominantly Moslem business district. In contrast to the depressed atmosphere of the town and the oppression of its population by a tyrannical vizier, the appearance of a young African elephant brought to town on the whim of the vizier provides some comic relief, but at the same time it is an ironic symbol of tyranny. Eventually, the vizier falls into disgrace, takes his own life, and the troublesome pet dies soon afterward.

Andrić's volume of short stories entitled *Nove Pripovetke* (1948; *New Stories*) is concerned mostly with the post-World War II years. The most significant story is "Zeko" (Bunny). An average Belgrade citizen, Zeko is a short man, very modest and timid, a calligrapher in the office of Royal Orders—and thus akin to Nikolai Gogol's Akaki Akakievich in the novella *The Overcoat*. Another well-known story of the postwar period is "Prokleta Avlija" (1954; *The Devil's Yard*). The main character, a Franciscan monk Petar, is captured by the Turks and spends time in a Turkish prison near Istanbul. After his release he returns to his native Bosnia, where he dies. Petar's encounter with tyranny, lawlessness, and cruelty at the hands of the Turks, and the tragic fates of some of the

inmates, are described after Petar's death by two friars as they take stock of the deceased's belongings.

During his years in diplomatic service, Andrić traveled extensively; his journeys to Italy, Spain, Portugal, Poland, Austria, the Soviet Union, and China are vividly described in travel books that harmoniously supplement his narrative works.

Andrić used colorful language like Thomas Mann, whom he considered his mentor, rich in figures of speech. He combined lyrical subjectivity and epic objectivity with the lucidity of modern essayistic art. His heroes are characterized by detailed references to their own personal pasts and by a thorough sociohistorical picture of their environment which has a profound effect on their private and public lives.

NIKOLA R. PRIBIĆ

Selected Bibliography

PRIMARY SOURCES

Andrić, Ivo. *Bosnian Chronicle*. Translated by Joseph Hitrec. New York: Knopf, 1963.

———. *The Bridge on the Drina*. Translated by Lovett F. Edwards. Chicago: University of Chicago Press, 1977.

———. *Correspondence*. Translated and edited by Ž. Juričić. Toronto: Serbian Heritage Academy, 1984.

———. *The Devil's Yard*. Translated by Kenneth Johnstone. Westport, Conn.: Greenwood Press, 1975.

———. *The Pasha's Concubine and Other Tales*. Translated by Joseph Hitrec. New York: Knopf, 1968.

———. *The Vizier's Elephant.* Translated by Drenka Willen. Chicago: Regnery, 1970.

———. *The Woman from Sarajevo.* Translated by Joseph Hitrec. New York: Knopf, 1965.

———, ed. *Sabrana dela.* Vol. 10. Belgrade: Prosveta, 1965.

SECONDARY SOURCES

Eekman, Thomas. *Thirty Years of Yugoslave Literature (1945–1975).* Ann Arbor: Michigan Slavic Publications, 1978.

Goy, E. D. "The Work of Ivo Andrić." *The Slavonic and East European Review* XLI, 97 (1963): 301–326.

Ivo Andrić. Bibliografija dela, prevoda i literature. Belgrade: Serbian Academy of Sciences, 1974.

Juričić, Želimir B. *The Man and the Artist. Essays on Ivo Andrić.* Lanham, Md.: University Press of America, 1986.

MIGUEL ANGEL ASTURIAS *1967*

When the Swedish Academy in 1967 awarded the Nobel Prize in literature to the Guatemalan writer and diplomat Miguel Angel Asturias (1899–1974), it acknowledged both the significance of his writing and his commitment to resolving the Latin American political situation. Writing in a variety of genres— poetry, fiction, drama, journalism, essays—Asturias was especially effective in describing life in his own country from its indigenous past to its problematic present.

Born in Guatemala City on October 19, 1899, Asturias grew up under a dictatorship that he and others helped topple in 1920, and in his writings he forcefully criticized social injustice in Guatemala and by implication as well in all of Latin America. He was born during the dictatorship of Manuel Estrada Cabrera, who governed from 1898 to 1920. Asturias's father, an attorney, joined the opposition to Estrada Cabrera, necessitating the family's move from Guatemala City to the town of Salamá.

Asturias continued his studies in Guatemala City in 1907; in 1916 he enrolled in the medical school at the Universidad de Guatemala but switched to the law school the following year. During his university years there was increasing active opposition to Estrada Cabrera, and Asturias received his degree in the midst of political activity and violence in 1922 with a thesis on "Sociología guatemalteca: el problema social del indio" ("Guatemalen Sociology") in which he denounced the social injustice directed against his country's indigenous peoples.

To escape Guatemala's continuing despotic government, after graduation Asturias went to London, moving to Paris in 1923, where he continued his studies at the Sorbonne. He stayed in Paris for the next ten years and became familiar with important artistic movements, such as surrealism. During the period he wrote poems, for example, "El caso de hablar" ("Let's Talk"), shorts novels *La señorita de la vecindad* ("The Girl from the Neighborhood") and *Dos de invierno* ("Two of Winter"), as well as his first major prose work, *Leyendas de Guatemala* (1930; "Legends of Guatemala"). The latter, describing Mayan life before Spanish settlement in Guatemala, was praised by the famous French poet Paul Valéry. From the beginning of his literary career, Asturias was noted for combining Mayan mysticism with a strong social conscience, qualities found in much of his later work as well. While in Paris he submitted a piece to a literary competition in the Guatemalan newspaper *El Imparcial*, but his entry was refused. It was a short work, "Los mendigos políticos" ("Political Beggars"), written in 1926, which Asturias called the genesis of what would be his most widely known novel, *El señor presidente* (1946; *Mr. President* completed in 1932).

Asturias returned to Guatemala in 1933, where he wrote for different newspapers and published several volumes of poetry, including *Sonetos* (1936; "Sonnets"). His friendship with Juan Arévalo Martínez, democratic president of Guatemala from 1945 to 1951, led to a diplomatic career, first as a cultural attaché in Mexico and subsequently in diplomatic positions in several Central and South American countries.

In 1946 *El señor presidente* was published to wide acclaim, though at first its quality of social protest and depiction of gruesome political repression was emphasized to the exclusion of its symbolic, hallucinatory style. Though in this work he continues in the tradition of protest literature going back to *Facundo* (1845) by the Argentine writer Domingo Faustino Sarmiento, Asturias also experiments with the structure of the novel and a new kind of language. In one sense a vivid critique of life under Estrada Cabrera, the novel is also a picture of an archetypal character who incarnates all Latin American dictators, indeed the very essence of dictatorship. The character of the dictator, between the myth and the reality, permeates the entire novel and is a constant presence whom no one sees or knows but whom everyone knows does exist. The world controlled by Mr. President is a hell peopled by repugnant men, such as one of the novel's characters who is ironically called Cara de Angel ("Angel Face"). At the same time this hell is inhabited by a series of beings who suffer without giving in. The novel denounces the reality of the past and the reality of the future in which another Mr. President might appear. *El señor presidente* is therefore an emblematic text both in Asturias's writing and in Latin

American literature in general. It is a hallucinatory, magical, cruel tale.

A very important factor in the writing of *El señor presidente* was the *tertulias* or "get togethers" Asturias enjoyed with other Latin American intellectuals, writers, and friends during his years in Paris. Their intellectual talks and chats in Parisian cafés focused on different aspects of Latin American dictatorships from the past to the present. Every participant in these discussions shared ideas, anecdotes, and knowledge of the dictators and the political situations in their native countries.

While in the diplomatic service in Argentina, Asturias published *Sien de Alondra* (1948; "Temple of Alondra")—a collection of his poetry from 1918 to 1948, with an introduction by Alfonso Reyes—and a play, *La audiencia de los confines* (1956; "The Last Trial"). His novel *Hombres de maíz* (1949; *Men of Corn*), explores the magical conceptions of culture found among Guatemalan Indians. In it he emphasizes the Indian ancestral myths as these are intertwined with the hopeless conditions under which the Indian peasants must live.

Indian oppression is also prominent in his epic trilogy *Viento fuerte* (1949; *The Cyclone*, or, *Strong Wind*), *El papa verde* (1954; *The Green Pope*), and *Los ojos de los enterrados* (1960; *The Eyes of the Interred*). This trilogy describes the malevolent effect of the United Fruit Company's incursions in Guatemalan affairs, the gradual control over the country's government by the huge corporation, and the strike that topples the country's dictator.

Asturias also published *Weekend en Guatemala* (1956; "Weekend in Guatemala"), a collection of eight stories focusing on the 1954 coup by right-wing dictator Carlos Castillo Armas, which again brought oppression to Guatemala after its brief experience with democracy. *Mulata de tal* (1963; *Mulata*), is a work utilizing magic and focusing on cultural clashes between Indian deities and Roman Catholic priests. *Malandrón* (1969; "Bad Thief"), subtitled "Epic of the Green Andes," describes the Spanish conquest of Latin America and the subsequent mixture of Spanish and Indian cultures. In 1969 he also collaborated with Pablo Neruda on *Comiendo en Hungría* ("Eating in Hungary").

Asturias's versatility enabled him to excel in several genres. His fiction, for which he is best known outside Spanish-speaking countries, has been widely translated and has been the subject of monographs and theses in several universities. Although his poetry is clearly indebted to modernist influences, it centers on Indian culture and conditions as well as on nationalism and family. Together with such other Guatemalan poets as Luis Cardona y Aragón, César Braños, and Rafael Arévalo Martínez, Asturias established a type of poetry that reflected the poetic techniques of Latin American modernism while at the same-time attempted to rediscover Guatemala's authentic values and traditions. His five plays—notably *Soluna* (1955; "Sun Moon")—also contrast modern Guatemala with the country's Indian past. They are not widely known outside Latin America.

Asturias left Guatemala in 1954. He lived in different countries including Argentina, Italy, and Switzerland. Finally, he returned to Paris as a permanent resident. He served there as Guatemalan ambassador from 1966 to 1970. He traveled extensively throughout Latin America, Europe, and the Soviet Union in his last years, giving numerous speeches and participating in conferences. He died in Madrid on June 9, 1974. Before his death he published an anthology, *Lo mejor de mi vida* (1974; "The Best of My Life").

In 1966 Asturias received the Soviet Union's highest literary prize, the Lenin Prize. He received the Nobel Prize in literature in 1967, with the Swedish Academy citing his "colorful poetry rooted in the particularity of his people and the Indian traditions." UNESCO has sponsored a continuing twenty-four volume edition of his complete works that is currently being published simultaneously in Paris and México.

MARIA G. MARIN

Selected Bibliography

PRIMARY SOURCES

Asturias, Miguel Angel. *Miguel Angel Asturias: tres obras* (*Leyendas de Guatemala, El Alhajadito, El señor presidente*). Caracas: Biblioteca Ayacucho, 1977.

———. *Obras completas*. 3 vols. Biblioteca de Premios Nobel. Madrid: Aguilar, 1968.

SECONDARY SOURCES

Bruswood, John S. *The Spanish American Novel*. Austin and London: University of Texas Press, 1975.

Callan, Richard J. *Miguel Angel Asturias*. Boston: Twayne, 1970.

Davis, William. "Maya-Quiché Myth in Asturias *El señor presidente*." *Philologica Pragencis* XIII, 2 (1970):95–104.

Dorman, Ariel. "Myth as Time and Word." *Review* 15 (1975):12–22.

Giacoman, Helmy F. Ed. *Homenaje a Miguel Angel Asturias*. Madrid: Anaya, 1971.

Harss, L., and B. Dohmann, eds. *In to the Mainstream*. New York and London: Harper & Row, 1977. Pp. 68–101.

Martin, G. "Evolution of Critical Theories Concerning *Hombres de maíz*." In *Publications du Centre Miguel Angel Asturias*. Paris: Université de Paris X-Nanterre, 1976.

———. "*El señor presidente* and How to Read it." *Bulletin of Hispanic Studies* 47 (1970):223–43.

Meneses, C. *Miguel Angel Asturias*. Madrid: Juncar, 1975.

SAMUEL BECKETT 1969

Samuel Beckett (1906—) was born in Foxrock, near Dublin, on April 13, 1906. The second son of a prosperous Irish Protestant family, he was educated at exclusive public schools in Ireland before attending Trinity College, where he took his B.A. in French and Italian language and literature in 1927 and then his M.A. in 1931. His first publications came while he held a prestigious two-year teaching appointment in Paris, where, during these years, 1927–29, he also became a close associate of the great expatriate Irish writer James Joyce. After a brief stint as a lecturer at Trinity, Beckett resigned in 1932 to devote himself fully to writing and to a six-year period of wandering, marked by stays in Paris, Berlin, London, and Dublin. He left Ireland for good in 1938 to settle permanently in France. A member of the French Resistance hunted by the Gestapo, he spent several years of World War II hiding in Vichy France. During this period he worked as a farm laborer by day and wrote at night. At war's end he returned to Paris, and he and his wife, Suzanne Dechevaux-Dumesnil, whom he married in 1948, have lived there since.

As poet, critic, playwright, and fiction writer, Beckett toiled in relative obscurity during the first quarter-century of his writing career. His early published work, which included a book on Proust, essays on Joyce, some poetry, a collection of short stories, and two novels, was written in English and received scant attention from critics or the public. In 1945 Beckett began writing in French and in doing so found his voice. The ten-year period following the war was the most fertile in his career and culminated in the sudden worldwide fame the play *En Atendant Godot* (1952; *Waiting for Godot*) brought him in the mid-fifties. Although most of Beckett's best novels and plays were originally written in French, he himself painstakingly translates them into English; consequently, he can be regarded as a major writer in both languages. Beckett, however, is a writer of truly international appeal and stature, as the translation of his work into dozens of languages and his being awarded the Nobel Prize in literature for 1969 attest.

The Swedish Academy cited Beckett for "a body of work that, in new forms of fiction and the theatre, has transmuted the destitution of modern man into his exaltation." No one really familiar with Beckett's fiction and plays, peopled with cripples and derelicts, would dispute the Academy's description of his subject as the destitution, spiritual and physical, of modern man, or its praise for his artistic originality. Only the claim that Beckett exalts modern man might puzzle or disturb those who know his work. But the nature of his subject and the originality of his treatment must be examined before we can directly approach this problem.

Although Beckett himself and most of his best critics consider his fiction more important than his plays, it is the latter upon which his fame largely rests and in which his originality in technique is most obvious. *Waiting for Godot*, his first play to be published and produced on stage, is the major case in point. What initially made this play, which has revolutionized modern theater, such a *succès de scandale* is that nothing seems to happen in it, no progress seems to be made. From a formal standpoint, its two acts represent essentially the same repeated waiting by its two tramp heroes for the title character, who will presumably give meaning to their lives but who, of course, never comes. Despite the relatively small, but significant, variations in the way Vladimir and Estragon kill time in the two acts, the larger pattern of repetition is more important and represents a striking assault on traditional expectations of development and resolution in drama. No less surprising than the puzzlement and frequent anger of early audiences over these formal properties was the plethora of divergent interpretations. Whether the play implies, for example, that human life has no meaning, as some critics maintain, or, to take one other common view, that its protagonists find no meaning because they merely passively wait for it, one thing is certain: *Waiting for Godot* is profoundly suggestive of many possible meanings without clearly committing itself to any—or at least to any yet captured in an abstract formulation that has been widely accepted. The concreteness and resonance of the play's indeterminacy owes a great deal to its formal innovativeness.

If Beckett's first major play concerns waiting for a new beginning, his second concerns waiting for an end. While the two only subtly differentiated acts of *Godot* suggest an infinite series, the single long act of *Fin de Partie* (1957; *Endgame*) suggests a final state after all important moves in life have been tried. The nearly bare, skull-like room in which the circular and unresolved actions of the two chief characters, Hamm and Clov, take place, as well as their names, their symbiotic relationship, and their complementary disabilities (Hamm cannot stand, Clov cannot sit) indicate the drama of the single consciousness half desirous of an end, yet half wanting to continue. That the room also appears to be a shelter for the only survivors of a nuclear catastrophe suggests that the characters represent all humanity. As in *Godot*, the two protagonists spend most of their time trying to distract themselves from their situation through actions reminiscent of vaudeville routines, through memories of the past, through quarreling in the present. In *Endgame*, however, both the pathos and the comedy is darker, for here the game is closer to its end and both characters more aware of the futility of their moves. The most conventionally dramatic of these is Clov's decision to leave the tyrannical Hamm (who may well be his father as well as his employer), but at play's end he has not left the shelter. Once again Beckett defies the traditional notion of resolution in drama, but in *Endgame* more than *Godot* he uses a variety of metafictional devices to remind the audience that they are witnessing a play, a fiction disjoined from life, one that is not an imitation of reality but a complex refraction of it. We are made to feel the theatricality of human life even at its most extreme stage at least as intensely as we can sense the mysterious referentiality of theater.

After *Endgame* Beckett's plays become shorter and increasingly economical in matter and form. The playwright begins to cut down his use of, and in some instances to abandon, many of the traditional resources of theater, such as dialogue and complex character interaction, and to adopt simpler, more primal theatrical methods for presenting the psychological and philosophical problems his characters face. For his next plays Beckett abandoned French and wrote directly in English. In *Krapp's Last Tape* (1958), about an old writer who has renounced all discourse except with the voices of his earlier selves recorded on tapes, and in *Happy Days* (1961), about a woman who inanely, but heroically, amuses herself with paltry possessions and memories while being literally as well as metaphorically buried by the sands of time, Beckett moves decisively toward monologue. In subsequent plays his minimalism becomes even more radical as he creates works built largely on carefully patterned gestures and stage movements, in *Come and Go* (1965), or as he creates a drama of disembodied voices, in *Not I* (1972). The same general process of essentializing—a

kind of voluntary poverty on Beckett's part—continues in the dramatic pieces of the eighties. While these pieces lack the tragicomic richness of the earlier masterpieces, they have an austere and suggestive beauty of their own.

Like his drama, Beckett's fiction is concerned with humanity facing the ubiquity of suffering and the twin abysses of death and apparent meaninglessness. The gallery of maimed and destitute characters of the novels and short stories is, however, more intensely aware than the stage characters of the implications of their dilemmas and more intent on solving their problems. In general, the fiction is more overtly philosophical in its grim playing, as its solitary characters ruminate obsessively on such questions as the nature of the self and the capacity of language to define ultimate reality. Withdrawal from the world toward discovery of the essential self is the project of the heroes of Beckett's first two published fictions, the short story collection *More Pricks Than Kicks* (1934) and the novel *Murphy* (1938), but in each case entanglements with women lead to a series of misadventures that prevent the heroes from attaining their aims. Beckett's second novel, *Watt* (finished in 1944 but not published until 1953), probes the problem of knowledge with a deeper and darker humor than the clever earlier works. While a servant in the employ of an inscrutable Mr. Knott, the title character, an incurable rationalist, witnesses a series of solid, yet strangely undefinable phenomena and finds his confidence in the simple referentiality of language shattered and with it, his sanity. Watt is the first of a line of Beckett heroes victimized by the obsessive need to find a fixed meaning in the flux of inner and outer experience.

Beckett's most brilliant and sustained exploration of these problems comes in the trilogy of novels he wrote between 1947 and 1949. Although the narrator heroes of *Molloy* (1951) and *Malone Meurt* (1951; *Malone Dies*) are eventually revealed to be earlier authorial selves of the speaker of *L'Innomable* (1953; *The Unnamable*), they are not aware in their original incarnations that they are masks to be stripped away in a progressive excoriation of the self. Beckett's new move here is to make his narrators writers who, by trying to limit their subject to the self in the act of writing, think they can capture experience in words. But the desperate attempts of the two narrators of the first novel, the tramp Molloy and his bourgeois double, Moran, to define the self in autobiographical narratives and in commentary on these stories of their disintegration fail hilariously. Both Molloy, who tells of the quest for his mother's room, and Moran, who recounts his quest for Molloy, are forced to admit defeat, and Molloy tells us, "There is a convention about writing: you either lie or hold your peace." Malone, the moribund narrator of the second novel, has apparently learned this lesson, for he decides to spend his last hours distracting himself by telling pure fictions. When these stories, however, begin to show an alarming resemblance to his past life

and present situation, he attempts to achieve a final convergence between life and writing by ending his main story exactly at the point of his death. This project, too, is futile, of course, and once again language and life fail to coincide. The narrator of *The Unnamable*, though, returns with a vengeance to the direct pursuit of the self with language. He decides to abandon storytelling, names (which he sees as signs of former false selves), and even human shape (by mid-novel he describes himself as a round shape speaking from an urn) to concentrate on speaking the pure words, untaught by human culture, that will finally define his primal self as both subject and object simultaneously. Since language is, of course, a cultural artifact and self-consciousness is inescapably dualistic, the project, though pursued with ingenuity and obsessive intensity, is doomed to failure.

Although Beckett's subsequent fiction lacks the scale and weight of the trilogy, it is brilliantly experimental in its own way. Like the later plays, it represents a minimalist approach to the problems it addresses, but it also marks a more striking departure from the work of Beckett's middle period than do his late plays. While the narrators of the trilogy fail with tragicomic ingenuity to find the patterns of meaning they seek in experience, and unintentionally create a kind of fictional formlessness the reader perceives as meaningful, the narrators of such later fiction as *Comment C'Est* (1961; *How It Is*), *Morte Imaginez* (1958; *Imagination Dead Imagine*),

Le Dépeupleur (1971; *The Lost One*), *Mal vu mal dit* (1981: *Ill Seen, Ill Said*) tyrannically impose coldly allegorical and geometrically precise forms on human life. By a variety of subtle techniques, however, Beckett leads the reader to see that the brilliant worlds and systems created by his speakers are overdetermined and, as such, ultimately reductive. There is pathos and grim comedy in these narrators' mania for meaning, but the rich complexity of life escapes them. Beckett, however, makes us aware of its implicit presence by the desperate exclusions of his reductive narrators.

All of Beckett's alienated and decrepit characters fail, and most seem to lack even dignity in their destitution. Impotent, ignorant, and sometimes even cowardly and dishonest, they only manage to survive in the failing light. Their endurance through wit, however sardonic, and determination, however perverse, is their only victory, but hardly a heroic one. Except, perhaps, in their indefatigable pursuit of meaning, they are not symbols of the exaltation of modern man. What does exalt us is the art of Beckett, an art that confronts the darkest possibilities with a grim gaiety and an integrity that does not offer easy consolations.

JOSEPH J. MARTIN

Selected Bibliography

PRIMARY SOURCES
Plays

Beckett, Samuel. *Come and Go: Dramaticule* (produced Paris, 1966; Dublin, 1968; London, 1970). London: Calder and Boyars, 1967. In *Cascando and Other Short Dramatic Pieces*, New York: Grove, 1968.

————. *En Attendant Godot* (produced Paris, 1953). Paris: Editions de Minuit, 1952. Translated by the author as *Waiting for Godot: Tragicomedy* (produced London, 1955; Miami and New York, 1956). New York: Grove Press, 1954; London: Faber & Faber, 1956.

————. *Fin de Partie; Suivi de Acte sans Paroles* (produced London, 1957). Paris: Editions de Minuit, 1957. Translated by the author as *Endgame: A Play in One Act; Followed by Act Without Words: A Mime for One Player* (*Endgame*, produced New York, 1958; *Act Without Words*, produced New York, 1960). New York: Grove Press; London: Faber & Faber, 1958.

————. *Krapp's Last Tape* (produced London, 1958; New York, 1960). Included in *Krapp's Last Tape and Embers*, London: Faber and Faber, 1959; and in *Krapp's Last Tape and Other Dramatic Pieces*, New York: Grove, 1960.

————. *Not I* (produced New York, 1972; London, 1973). London: Faber & Faber, 1973.

Novels

Beckett, Samuel. *Comment C'Est*. Paris: Editions de Minuit, 1961. Translated by the author as *How It Is*. New York: Grove Press, 1964; London: John Calder, 1964.

————. *L'Innommable*. Paris: Editions de Minuit, 1953. Translated by the author as *The Unnamable*. New York: Grove Press, 1958; London: John Calder, 1959.

———. *Malone meurt.* Paris: Editions de Minuit, 1951. Translated by the author as *Malone Dies.* New York: Grove Press, 1956; London: John Calder, 1958.

———. *Molloy.* Paris: Editions de Minuit, 1951. Translated by the author and Patrick Bowles. Paris: Olympia Press, 1955; New York: Grove Press, 1955; London: John Calder, 1959.

———. *Murphy.* London: Routledge, 1938; New York: Grove Press, 1957.

SECONDARY SOURCES

Abbott, H. P. *The Fiction of Samuel Beckett: Form and Effect.* Berkeley: Univeristy of California Press, 1973.

Bair, Deirdre. *Samuel Beckett: A Biography.* New York: Harcourt Brace, 1978.

Cohn, Ruby. *Back to Beckett.* Princeton, N.J.: Princeton University Press, 1962.

Esslin, Martin, ed. *Samuel Beckett: A Collection of Critical Essays.* Englewood Cliffs, N.J.: Prentice-Hall, 1965.

Kenner, Hugh. *A Reader's Guide to Samuel Beckett.* London: Thames & Hudson, 1973.

Knowlson, James, and John Pilling. *Frescoes of the Skull: The Later Prose and Drama of Samuel Beckett.* New York: Grove Press, 1980.

Worth, Katherine, ed. *Beckett the Shape-Changer.* London: Routledge & Kegan Paul, 1976.

SAUL BELLOW *1976*

Saul Bellow (1915—) was born in Lachine, Quebec, on June 10, 1915 to parents who had emigrated two years earlier from St. Petersburg, Russia. In 1924 the family moved to Chicago. Bellow grew up in a Yiddish-speaking environment. He studied at both the University of Chicago and Northwestern University, where he received degrees in sociology and anthropology. A three-time winner of the National Book Award—in 1953 for *The Adventures of Augie March*, in 1964 for *Herzog*, and in 1971 for *Mr. Sammler's Planet* (1970)—and winner of the Pulitzer Prize in 1976 for *Humboldt's Gift* (1975), he received the Nobel Prize in literature in 1976, the first American to win the prize since John Steinbeck's award in 1962. Among his numerous novels, short stories, and essays, are *The Victim* (1947), *Henderson the Rain King* (1959), *Mosby's Memoirs and Other Stories* (1968), *The Dean's December* (1981), and *More Die of Heartbreak* (1987).

Bellow's fiction places him within two literary tradotions: American and Jewish. His comic novel *The Adventures of Augie March* is clearly the direct descendant of Twain's *Adventures of Huckleberry Finn*, with its vast midwestern spaces, picaresque hero, and spirited episodes. His blunt realism and urban settings bear the stamp of Dreiser and of Howells, and the self-reliance and freedom of Augie March testify to the transcendental strains of Emerson and Whitman—"I am an American, Chicago born—Chicago, that somber city—and go at things as I have taught myself, free style, and will make the record in my own way."

In Bellow's introduction to a collection of Jewish short stories, he characterized Yiddish fiction as literature where "laughter and trembling are so curiously mingled that it is not easy to determine the relations of the two." This accurately describes Bellow's own work—it not only achieves this balance, but also draws on his second tradition by the infiltration of Yiddish words and phrases, which carry with them entire concepts from Jewish culture, by the dominance of Jewish characters and their milieu, and by a spirit of compromise, skepticism, and "approximate understanding," which he himself characterizes as Jewish. This alternate tradition is also reflected in his frequent allusions to a Central European intellectual legacy, rather than an Anglo-American one, and to his deliberate playing with Jewish and Gentile stereotypes, as in *The Victim* and *Mr. Sammler's Planet*.

This major presence of Jewish culture in Bellow's works has had an important influence in redefining American literature from an Anglo-Saxon mainstream canon to recognition of ethnic elements and pluralism in American culture itself. While the early reception of Bellow's works at times treated him as an immigrant intruder whose argot, in the words of a fellow novelist, revealed "an appalling bankruptcy in language" that was out to destroy English, Bellow's eventual recognition as a truly American writer marked a turning point in American literary history. Moreover, in the aftermath of World War II with its unparalleled human suffering and manifestations of evil, the character of the Jew in American fiction as portrayed by Bellow and other Jewish-American authors was perceived as an appropriate representation of the modern Everyman. Thus, Bellow has played a major role in bringing about the recognition of Jewish-American fiction as a significant part of the national literature.

The dominant form in Bellow's works is the novel of ideas. The major action is the struggle of the main character to understand his identity, status, and responsibility as a human being. These characters tend to be male, middle-aged and older, antiheroic, and intellectual who reach a stage in their development, sometimes as the result of some failure in their personal lives, when they seek answers to questions about the nature of a moral and meaningful existence. As Bellow formulated this in 1964 concurrent with his publication of *Herzog*, "In what form shall life be justified? That is the essence of the moral question." Or much earlier, in 1944 in *Dangling Man* (his first novel), the question plaguing his central character, "How should a good man live; what ought he to do?" Bellow's characters launch into long meditations on these subjects that take varied forms, such as letters to great thinkers of the past (Herzog addresses Heidegger, Nietzsche, and Spinoza, for example), dialogues among characters that draw upon the whole tradition of Western civilization, or extended interior monologues. These intellectual explorations tend to be argumentative, taking issue with accepted ideas, particularly those movements fashionable in the twentieth century. Bellow's central protagonists roam widely in their ruminations about man, requiring that the reader be equally well versed in the history of ideas.

These philosophical excursions, however, take place in a realistic universe, usually an urban setting, where everyday life is recorded down to its smallest naturalistic detail. Metaphysical flights are regularly interrupted by the sound of a coffee grinder, the deluge caused by deteriorating plumbing, the smell of city garbage bins, or the threat of a mugger in a New York City doorway. Bellow treats his intellectual characters with an ironic distance, and his world is also peopled with an energetic assortment of gangsters, speculators, pimps, bag ladies, and thieves, as well as with scholars and academics. In their pursuit of a few truths about human life, his characters also are constantly tempted by the flesh and find themselves in comical, even farcical, situations.

Distracted by women, who are almost invariably sensual traps in Bellow's universe, his male protagonists attempt to overcome their sexual desires in their quest for self-definition and a meaningful existence.

In his talkative novels, where action is a series of suppositions never carried to their conclusions, Bellow challenges many of the accepted notions of modern life, both social and philosophical. An intensely social writer, whose characters are entangled in human relationships and whose minds are repositories of the overstimulated age in which they live, Bellow persistently challenges prevailing stereotypes of that social world. This challenging treatment of stereotypes is already evident in his second novel, *The Victim* (1947), where he draws on myths of Jews and Gentiles as victims and victimizers, only to reveal the psychological complexity of each of these characters' need for an "other." In *Mr. Sammler's Planet* over twenty years later, Bellow portrays a Holocaust survivor without the sentimentality that is the trademark of much popular literature on the subject. Artur Sammler is a cosmopolitan, Old-World, refined, and rational septuagenarian who has not been ennobled by his sufferings in the war. Instead, he is depicted as the European uncle revered by his American relatives as a survivor sage, while the reader recognizes his emotional handicaps and human flaws. In the same work, a wealthy gynecologist with Mafia connections betrays more generosity and humanity than any of the other characters. And in a technique of role reversal of stereotypes, an Indian scientist sees salvation in technology, while rational Sammler embraces a mystical philosophy. Thus, Bellow is not content to deliver up the stock types of his own time.

In the same vein, throughout his career Bellow has challenged what he perceives to be the dominant ideas of his age. In a post-Holocaust world he has condemned the two responses of nihilism and celebration of madness. The latter he attributes to an excessive emphasis on the self, on a narcissistic pursuit of originality. The former he associates with philosophical and artistic movements that devalue individuality, that spotlight the absurdity of existence, "the theme of annihilation of Self," which he claims characterizes the writings of many of his contemporaries. While Bellow's fiction is remarkable for its interweaving of realistic contexts with philosophical debate, it is not innovative in its narrative techniques. In his Nobel lecture he attacked self-consciously avant-garde texts, what he termed "the message of Robbe-Grillet," fiction that demonstrates fragmented perception over moral discoveries. "Can it be that human beings are at a dead end?" In an essay published one year earlier, he posed a question central to his vision, "Why, since the unconscious is by definition what we do not know, should we not find in it traces of the soul as well as of aggression?" It is the word *soul* that is most revealing about Bellow's perspective on art and society. For he is one of the few major writers of the second half of this century who is unabashedly in search of that essence that preoccupied earlier artists, "something we all hesitate to mention though we all know it intimately—the soul." Bellow repeatedly asserts that existence has inherent value, and it is imperative for every person to attempt to define what it means to be human. The garrulousness of his characters and their rich inner lives are testimony to their engagement with the social and cultural world. Bellow, then, is basically a humanistic writer. "Undeniably, the human being is not what he commonly thought a century ago," he writes. "The question nevertheless remains. He is something. What is he?"

HANA WIRTH-NESHER

Selected Bibliography

PRIMARY SOURCES

Bellow, Saul. *The Adventures of Augie March*. New York: Viking Press, 1953.

———. *Dangling Man*. New York: Vanguard, 1944; New York: Penguin, 1988.

———. *The Dean's December*. New York: Harper & Row, 1981, 1982.

———. *Henderson the Rain King*. New York: Viking Press, 1959.

———. *Herzog*. New York: Viking Press, 1964.

———. *Him With His Foot in His Mouth and Other Stories*. New York: Harper & Row, 1984; London: Secker & Warburg, 1984.

———. *More Die of Heartbreak*. New York: Morrow, 1987.

———. *Mosby's Memoirs and Other Stories*. New York: Viking Press,

1968; London: Weidenfield & Nicolson, 1969.

——. *Mr. Sammler's Planet.* New York: Viking Press, 1970.

——. *Seize the Day.* New York: Viking Press, 1956.

——. *To Jerusalem and Back: A Personal Account.* New York: Viking Press, 1976.

——. *The Victim.* New York: Vanguard, 1947.

SECONDARY SOURCES

Clayton, John J. *Saul Bellow: In Defense of Man.* Bloomington: Indiana University Press 1968; 2nd ed., 1979.

Cronin, Gloria L., and Blair H. Hall. *Saul Bellow: An Annotated Bibliography.* 2nd ed. New York: Garland, 1987.

Fuchs, Daniel. *Saul Bellow: Vision and Revision.* Durham, N.C.: Duke University Press, 1984.

Harris, Mark. *Saul Bellow: Drumlin Woodchuck.* Athens, Ga.: University of Georgia Press, 1980.

Newman, Judie. *Saul Bellow and History.* New York: St. Martin's Press, 1984.

Rovit, Earl, ed. *Saul Bellow: A Collection of Critical Essays.* Twentieth Century Views. Englewood Cliffs, N.J.: Prentice-Hall, 1975.

JACINTO BENAVENTE Y MARTINEZ   *1922*

Jacinto Benavente y Martinez (1866 – 1954) was born in Madrid on August 12, 1866. He is known as a playwright, but he also wrote poems (*Versos*, 1893; *Verses*), short stories (*Vilanos*, 1905; *The Down of the Thistle*), articles on the theater (*Teatro del pueblo*, 1909; *People's Theater*), newspaper articles (*De sobremesa*, 1910–16; *Table Talk*), lectures (*Conferencias*, 1924; *Lectures*), and memoirs (*Recuerdos y olvidos:* Memorias, 1962; *Memoirs*). In addition, he did a translation of Shakespeare's *King Lear*, which was never performed, and in 1897 Molière's *Dom Juan*. All of his works are included in the eleven-volume *Obras completas* (1952–64; *Complete Plays*).

Few modern playwrights have been as prolific as Benavente. The vast majority of his plays, in which he often appeared, have been produced in Spain and abroad. His recognition in the form of tributes is difficult to surpass. The first official tribute came when he was elected to the Spanish Royal Academy in 1912; Benavente never filled the post because he neglected to write, and therefore deliver, an acceptance speech. In 1946, however, the academy made him an honorary member. He was awarded the Nobel Prize in 1922, elected Favorite Son of Madrid in 1924, made president of the Montepio pension fund for widows and orphans in 1929, and received the Mariano de Cavia Prize for the best newspaper article published in Spain during 1947. His greatest artistic achievement was the successful transformation of the Spanish theater from the outdated drama that had carried José Echegaray y Eizaguirre (1832–1916) to fame, fortune, and even the Nobel Prize (1904), to social drama in which Benavente exposed and censured the middle class. With satire, wit, and imagination he brought to the twentieth century a new type of drama that opened the way for other innovations. His sympathy for the oppressed made him their champion and an early feminist.

Jacinto Benavente y Martinez was the youngest of three sons born to Venancia Martinez, a native of Villarejo de Salvanés, and Dr. Mariano Benavente, a native of Murcia who had struggled to achieve success as a pediatrician. Among his patients were the children of prominent literary and political figures and some of their parents as well; he was director of the Hospital of the Child Jesus, a member of the Royal Academy of Medicine, and a recognized author of professional articles; he was even honored with a statue erected in his memory in Madrid's Retiro Park. Hence, the Benavente family was firmly ensconced in the upper middle class of the time. Dr. Benavente supervised the education of his children, who had in their home library a wide range of books. He was clearly the stronger figure of the two parents; biographers of his son agree that the mother remained in the background, attending to the children's religious and social education, and that she often took her youngest son with her on afternoon social visits. It was during these visits, no doubt, that Benavente was first exposed to the dialogue of middle-class ladies and the bourgeois problems that he later portrayed in his plays.

As a child, Benavente was quiet and studious. He was an avid reader, fascinated by the theater, and took pleasure in creating skits in which he would appear with his friends. He often dressed as a clergyman, delivering his sermons to playmates and his mother's guests. He attended the nearby Colegio San José and the Instituto San Isidro without distinction; he read Shakespeare, Alfred de Musset, and Molière in addition to the Spanish classics. He was said to have learned English, French, and Italian during his adolescent years, and eventually he was able to translate works from those languages into Spanish. After his father's death in 1885, he gave up his law studies at the University of Madrid, traveled extensively in Europe, and for a brief period acted in the company of the prominent actress Maria Tubau.

Benavente became active in literary *tertulias* (gatherings) in the cafés of Madrid. In these cafés he became friendly with the young writers who would later be dubbed by Azorin (José Martinez Ruiz)

the Generation of 1898. One prominent habitué of the *tertulia* in the
Café Madrid was Ramón Maria
del Valle-Inclán; when Benavente's
conservatism clashed with Valle-
Inclán's radicalism, they went their
separate ways to establish *tertulias*
with their own followers.

Benavente is traditionally considered part of the Generation of
1898, but this association can be
made only because of his interest in
social and artistic reform. He lacked
the philosophical convictions and
creative genius that characterized
the Generation of 1898. He initiated
his literary career by publishing a
volume of plays in 1892, *Teatro
fantástico* ("Theater of the Fantastic"), and in 1893 one of poems,
Versos, and another of essays,
Cartas de mujeres ("Women's Letters"). His first performed play, *El
nido ajeno* (1894; "Another's Nest"),
was produced with little notice, but
Gente conocida (1896; "Well-
Known People") was widely acclaimed. At about this time he succeeded Clarin (Leopoldo Alas) as
editor of *La vida literaria* (*Literary
Life*), and from time to time contributed to *Madrid cómico* (*The Madrid
Stage*) and other magazines.

Benavente soon became such a
controversial dramatist that he was
driven by adverse criticism to renounce writing more plays; he left
Spain on a tour of America as director of the company of the actress
Lola Membrives, the most widely
acclaimed interpreter of his plays.
While on tour, he occasionally acted
and often lectured to audiences. He
spent the Spanish Civil War years
(1936–39) in Valencia (where the

Republican government had established its headquarters) and in those
years wrote no plays. In 1949, he
resumed residence in Madrid, where
he continued to write and lead an
active public life until his death in
1954.

Benavente's first produced
work, *El nido ajeno*, is a psychological drama that explores the results
of a married couple sharing their
home with the husband's bachelor
brother, Manuel, referred to as "the
intruder"; this play involves numerous rivalries, jealousies, resent-
ments, and gossip, as well as Manuel's lust for Maria, his sister-in-law.
At the end of the play, the intruder
announces that he will go away for
the sake of restoring peace and harmony in his brother's home, where
"three is a crowd"; he suggests that
he may return after the fire of youth
is spent, when he no longer desires
Maria, at which time he may share
his brother's life without temptations, perhaps no longer as an intruder.

His next play, *Gente conocida*,
a social satire, was widely acclaimed
by critics and the theatergoing bourgeoisie, whose drawing rooms Benavente mirrored in the play. From
that time on, Benavente's plays were
sound commercial successes, although critics differed in their opinions. These first two plays, moreover, established two of the four
major categories into which scholars
and critics have divided Benavente's
work. The other two major classifi-
cations are rural plays and fantastic
plays. In his comprehensive study
Jacinto Benavente, Marcelino C.
Peñuelas distributes the plays as fol-

lows: twenty-seven satiric plays, twenty-three psychological plays, three rural plays, and seven fantasy plays; in addition to these major groupings, there are, in Peñuelas's reckoning, eleven comic plays, six sentimental plays, thirty-five miscellaneous works, forty-nine short plays, and eleven translations and adaptations, all written during Benavente's active years as playwright. Peñuelas cites critics who, on the other hand, limit Benavente's plays to three categories: psychological plays (including rural dramas and character studies), social satires, and plays based on imaginary tales. Still other critics group Benavente's plays by chronological periods; in this case, the year normally cited as the turning point in Benavente's creativity is 1930.

Whichever approach one takes, thematic or chronological, by 1931 Benavente had already written his most important dramas; his work was becoming increasingly repetitious and uninteresting, losing originality in subject matter and form, yet still pleasing his followers. While his new plays were staged almost exclusively in Spain, outside his native country producers relied increasingly on two early plays that have retained their dramatic interest to this day: *Los intereses creados* (1907; *The Bonds of Interest*) and *La malquerida* (1913; *The Passion Flower*). The advent of the cinema, however, gave his plays added life and allowed his works to reach wider audiences than he ever dreamed.

Henrik Ibsen influenced almost everyone at this time, including Benavente and Echegaray. Indeed, both Spaniards had to defend their works from accusations of imitation and even plagiarism, both claiming that their works were authentically Spanish, although neither of them denied familiarity with the theater of Ibsen. The controversial themes of Ibsen were applied to traditional themes from the Spanish repertory. Hence, Echegaray adapted the theme of Ibsen's *Ghosts* to *El hijo de Don Juan* (1892; "*The Son of Don Juan*"), and Benavente admitted that in writing *Gente conocida* he had merged a typical Spanish situation with some ideas that he tapped from Ibsen.

Benavente's social satires were revolutionary because their cast was held to minimal number and there were recognizable personalities from Madrid's elite among the characters portrayed. The fact that the playwright was known by so many of his devotees, however, limited the severity of his rebukes. His characters were drawn from real life, and he did criticize their shortcomings. But he was intimidated, and the plays were little more than a mild rebuff that ended satisfactorily for all the characters. It cannot be said that Benavente was disillusioned with Spanish society: He was at most annoyed.

The majority of the social satires are set in a salon or reception room in which dialogue replaces action. The characters reveal their problems to one another, or a maid narrates to a visitor what has taken place, thus exposing the theme of the play, or the characters speak about their friends, weaving into their tales the conflicts that will be discussed in the play. Although Benavente thus eliminates histrionic superfluity and rhetoric, he does not altogether break away from traditional Spanish themes; as in the works of Lope de Vega Carpio and Pedro Calderón de la Barca, honor is often an underlying theme. Benavente, however, does not penetrate the obviousness of the conflict; he does not analyze the reasons for a man's adulterous behavior, for example, nor does he attempt to define life itself, either in its existential or sociological sense. José Monleón superbly summarizes the morality of Benavente's characters in his observation that the mundane frivolities and preoccupations of the aristocracy are as detestable to the playwright as are the insecurities and seediness of the middle class. Nevertheless, Benavente never truly juxtaposes those hollow values with other, superior values: The characters can be better than they are or they can be worse than they are, but they cannot adopt a totally new set of values.

Benavente's masterpiece is generally considered to be *The Bonds of Interest*, a social satire that combines fantasy, psychology, brilliant dialogue, and even aesthetics within the framework of the old Italian *commedia dell'arte*. In this play, set in an imaginary city of dual character (one for the rich, one for the poor), Benavente touches problems similar to those that plague the middle class of his other satires: honor, financial ruin, hypocrisy, ostentatiousness, even a criminal past. The characters range from the destitute

Crispin, a type of picaro, and his master, Leandro, who arrive in that imaginary land with only the clothes on their backs and hope in their hearts, to a wide array of character types drawn from the *commedia dell'arte*: Harlequin, a wreck of an old soldier; Polichinela, a starving poet; a scribe; a go-between obviously reminiscent of the Spanish bawd Celestina, all motivated by materialism, all willing to compromise in order to realize their ambitions. The love story that Crispin spins around Silvia and Leandro is the only element untainted by selfishness, but the girl's parents allow the marriage only because of the interests at stake. The play moves swiftly from beginning to end with the aid of witty dialogue, exaggerated action onstage, spectacle, and intrigue. No element of society escapes criticism, and love triumphs in the end. A sequel or continuation of *The Bonds of Interest*—*La ciudad alegre y confiada* (1916; "The Happy and Confident City")—is pitifully inferior and is virtually forgotten.

The psychological play that is traditionally associated with Benavente's theater is *The Passion Flower*, which is also a rural play. Together with *The Bonds of Interest*, it overshadows almost every other play that brought success and acclaim to Benavente. It is the only one that he wrote between 1911 and 1915, and although it suffers from certain weaknesses, it may indeed vie for first place in public esteem. In 1923, for example, it enjoyed 750 performances in the United States and it was made into a film starring Norma Talmadge. The theme of *The*

Passion Flower is an inverted Phaedra story. In Benavente's version, Raimunda's second husband, Esteban, is in love with her daughter, Acacia. He has caused her first betrothal to Norberto to be broken, and now, on the eve of her marriage to Faustino, he has the groom killed by his peon, Rubio. Confronted with the facts, after long interrogations that constitute enough subject matter for another play, Raimunda attempts to smooth things over. She wants to send Acacia to the home of relatives until everything is forgotten, and she tries to effect a reconciliation between Acacia and Esteban, but instead of embracing Esteban and calling him father, as Raimunda commands, the girl embraces her stepfather passionately, and their kiss confirms the semi-incestuous attraction that had, until that moment, manifested itself in Acacia as hostility and in Esteban as devoted rejection of his paternal role. Raimunda's effort to stop her husband and Acacia from running away together ends with Esteban's shooting his wife, whose dramatic death will forever stand in the way of the lovers and, at the same time, save her daughter's honor.

The rural setting has been identified as Aldeaencabo, in Castile, where Benavente maintained a country home, and the plot is apparently based on a true story. One of the remarkable features of the play is the dialect; Benavente's interpretation of Castilian country dialogue dazzled and even distracted the audiences of the time. The intensity of a family situation in which honor is at stake, as well as the semi-incestu-

ous relationship between Acacia and Esteban, give the play a compelling psychological tension. Benavente may have been acquainted with the recent psychoanalytic theories of Sigmund Freud when he conceived *The Passion Flower*; whether he fully understood these theories or not, the principal characters all conform to Freudian patterns, as demonstrated by Professor Harold K. Moon (1971), who interprets the main characters as Freudian subjects.

The play poses two problems: It introduces what is, for all practical purposes, a detective story, and it flirts with the traditional honor theme without fully developing it. When the curtain falls on the first act, the question that has been raised is not "Whom does Acacia love?" but, "Who killed Faustino?" The honor theme, which could inspire a different type of play, is dropped almost as soon as it is mentioned. The work nevertheless projects great theatrical effects; it restores to twentieth-century drama the rural settings of Golden Age national drama, and it strongly suggests the consequences of repressed passion.

The plays discussed up to this point hardly reveal the range of Benavente's repertory, but they represent the best of his work; indeed, they may be the most enduring of his dramas, along with *Una senora* (1920; "A Lady") *La noche del Sábado* (1923; *Saturday Night*). The common denominator in Benavente's work is good taste and elegant restraint. His dialogues are carefully written so that although his characters speak the truth, they are never vulgar or commonplace; there is seldom violence or unpleasant action onstage. When there is action in addition to dialogue, it is swift, as in *The Bonds of Interest*, and highly effective. There are no wasted words or deeds on Benavente's stage. These plays share another common denominator. The strong characters are almost always women. It is a woman who is normally sacrificed, deceived, scorned, abused, slandered, and generally mistreated. It is also a woman who sacrifices, is truthful, respectful, submissive, virtuous, and forgiving. Women's rights are normally violated by selfish husbands, brothers, suitors, or even lovers, but the women respond with kindness, strength, compassion, understanding, and generosity. They replace their husbands as breadwinners, and their blood is shed as the sacrificial lamb's, to save others (as in *The Passion Flower*). Benavente's theater portrays familiar characters drawn from his own experience: the drawing rooms or living rooms in which he was reared, the country estate where he vacationed. Even in a play such as *The Bonds of Interest* the moral, philosophical thesis of the play differs little from the convictions that he expresses in drawing-room satires, his rural dramas, or his psychological plays.

Benavente wrote until his death, and his last plays were produced posthumously. Nevertheless, by the end of the 1920s he had spent his talent, and although he wrote copiously, his later plays reflect a stagnated talent without direction. His plays, which had initially achieved celebrity and recognition via his brilliant dialogues, had become more like long episodes with monotonous overtones. Dialogues run away from his characters so that they often lose connection with either character or plot, and they tend to be repetitious without subtley, sting, or sharpness. With few exceptions, the epigrammatic observations that had caused some critics to compare him with Oscar Wilde or George Bernard Shaw gave way to sentimentality and sermonizing. One such exception, *La melodia del jazz band* (1931; "The Jazz Band's Tune"), concerning the kindness of a "bad" woman, depends for its action neither on inner passion nor on moral conflict, but on the strains of a jazz song that is played throughout.

Although Benavente's late plays may not be up to the standards that he established earlier in the century, they are nevertheless an accurate chronicle of Republican, post–Civil War, and even contemporary Spain, particularly faithful in their portrayal of modern Spanish women faced with new privileges (divorce, suffrage) and confronted with problems of making a livelihood.

During the monarchy and before the war, Spanish women had lived under the protection of their men; with the exception of a tiny intellectual minority, they normally did not go out into society to earn a living. In some of the plays from the 1930s, Benavente, obviously unsettled by the new wave of women, portrays some who are somewhat bewildered by their new roles. Adelina in *El pan comido en la mano* (1934; "Bread Eaten from the

Hand"), for example, is so carried away by her talents as a novelist that she almost loses her marriage; the new institution of divorce ushered in briefly by the Republic comes to the stage in 1932 in *La moral del divorcio* ("The Moral of Divorce"), a rather clever exposition of Benavente's prodivorce ideas. His awareness of new lifestyles kept him active, except for the sojourn in Valencia, and occasionally he even attempted, not entirely without success, to rekindle the spark of his genius. *La infanzona* (1945; "The Noble Lady") is a late effort to create a rural drama (similar in setting to *The Passion Flower*); once more, the theme of incest is presented carefully, and the tragic outcome of the play, like that of *The Passion Flower*, is not lacking in dynamism, horror, or surprise. *Mater imperatrix* (1950) is the only other play from this late period that can be considered a worthy effort.

Benavente's theater, then, is a combination of new forms and themes combined with a chronicler's account of the society in which he lived. His followers and imitators include Manuel Linares Rivas, Gregorio Martínez Sierra, and the Alvarez Quintero brothers, Serafín and Joaquín.

JOSEPH R. ARBOLEDA

Selected Bibliography

PRIMARY SOURCES

Benavente, Jacinto. *Obras completas*. 11 vols. Madrid: Aguilar, 1952–64.

——. *Plays, by Jacinto Benavente.* First series. Translated by John Garrett Underhill. New York: Scribner, 1917.

——. *Plays, by Jacinto Benavente.* Second series. Translated by John Garrett Underhill. New York: Scribner, 1919.

——. *Plays, by Jacinto Benavente.* Third series. Translated by John Garrett Underhill. New York: Scribner, 1923.

——. *Plays, by Jacinto Benavente.* Fourth series. Translated by John Garrett Underhill. New York: Scribner, 1924.

SECONDARY SOURCES

Lázaro, Angel. *Vida y obra de Benavente*. Madrid: Alfrodisio Aguado, 1964.

Moon, Harold K. "Freud and Benavente's *La malquerida.*" In *Proceedings: Pacific Northwest Conference on Foreign Languages* XXII, 1971.

Peñuelas, Marcelino C. *Jacinto Benavente*. Translated by Kay Elnger. New York: Twayne, 1968.

Pérez de Ayala, Ramón. *Las máscaras*. Buenos Aires: Espasa-Calpe, 1944.

Sánchez Estevan, Ismael. *Jacinto Benavente y su teatro*. Barcelona: Ariel, 1954.

Underhill, John Garrett. *Plays by Jacinto Benavente*. New York: Scribner, 1921–24.

Vila Selma, José. *Benavente, fin de siglo*. Madrid: Rialp, 1952.

Viqueria, José Maria. *Asi piensan los personajes de Benavente*. Madrid: Aguilar, 1958.

HENRI-LOUIS BERGSON   *1927*

Henri-Louis Bergson (1859–1941) was born in Paris, the second son of Michel Bergson, an immigrant from Poland, and Catherine Levison of Doncaster, England. His father was a talented pianist and composer. The family moved from Paris to Geneva (Boulevard des Philosophes!), back to Paris, and later settled in England. The year 1868 marked the beginning of Henri-Louis's formal schooling at the Lycée Impérial Bonaparte in Paris. Serious, studious, polite, somewhat solitary, and endowed with a keen intellect, Bergson was the ideal student—as the proliferation of honors and awards conferred upon him during the next ten years confirm. In 1878 it seemed only natural that the doors of the prestigious Ecole Normale Supérieure be open to him.

The earliest influences on the thinking of young Henri-Louis were Lachelier, Ravaisson, and Rousseau. With Lachelier came the revelation to this student of the sciences and mathematics that philosophy was not a trivial pursuit but a serious endeavor. He admired Rousseau for never having abandoned the intuitive notion of the absolute in an age of rationalist thought and materialist philosophy, as well as for the literary value of his philosophical writings.

At the Ecole Normale Supérieure an intellectual rivalry soon sprang up between Bergson (ranked third) and Jean Jaurès (ranked first), who was later to become a socialist revolutionary and a political martyr. Debates pitted the tight logic of the politically conservative and anti-Kantian Bergson against the inspiring eloquence of his classmate and rival.

In 1881 Bergson embarked upon a distinguished teaching career. In those days, however, it was necessary to work one's way up through the ranks. During the next fifteen years he taught philosophy at *lycées* in Angers, Clermont-Ferrand, and Paris.

In 1889 he defended two theses: *Les Données immédiates de la conscience* (1910; rpt. 1971; translated as *Time and Free Will*) and *Quid Aristoteles de loco senserit*. These works reveal Bergson's discovery of time as duration, a discovery that was to be the foundation of his entire philosophy. In them, Bergson affirms that "experienced time," or the time of our consciousness, is radically opposed to chronological time. The latter can be measured by scientific instruments and is basically a quantitative perception that assumes spatial attributes. Chronological time is perceived as a series of juxtaposed dots on a linear continuum. The basic opposition between durative and punctual time lies in the qualitative nature of the former impression, which is indivisible and integrative. Duration is a function of memory: a fusion of individual moments in which the past becomes assimilated into the present in an ever-changing dynamic structure whose total is always more than the sum of the parts. The dynamics of this multitude of interconnected moments is what gives significance to experience; it is the principle that allows us to comprehend the sense or essence of things.

After distinguishing between experienced and chronological time, Bergson defines intelligence as our analytical and conceptual faculty, which separates, juxtaposes, and measures but which cannot *comprehend*, in the deeper, intuitive sense of that word. Intelligence is indeed a vital and necessary faculty that concerns itself with processing the quantitative and repetitive elements of human experience. For the intelligence, the principle of causality is the logical mode of explication. However, overemphasis on our analytical faculty can lead to rationalism and determinism, which do not allow penetration into the true meaning of things. It is intuition that permits the mind to pivot back upon itself and observe its own process. Intuition is essentially durative thinking that allows the subject to penetrate and coincide with the object. This is a conscious, reflective process, not a passive absorption. It allows the subject to apprehend that which is distinctive and consequently unduplicable in the object; that is, its essence.

In 1892, three years after the publication of *Time and Free Will*, Henri Bergson married Louise Neuburger. Marcel Proust, second cousin to the Neuburger family, served as best man at their wedding. A year later, the couple's only child was born. Jeanne Bergson, who was deaf from birth, later became a talented sculptress and painter in her own right.

One of Bergson's lifelong ambitions was to teach at the Sorbonne, but this was never to be. However, following the 1896 publication of *Matière et Mémoire* (translated in 1988 as *Matter and Memory*), perhaps his most important work, he became *maître de conférence* at the Ecole Normale and in 1900, professor of philosophy at the Collège de France. Bergson's lectures were social and intellectual events attended by the Parisian intelligentsia, including such celebrities as Gabriel Marcel, Charles Péguy, and Charles Blondel and a large feminine contingent (Bergson was a popular figure in the literary salons). Bergson's oratorical style was known for its imagery, clarity, and the mathematical precision of its enunciations: qualities on which the French have always prided themselves.

Bergson's popularity has also been attributed to his being the philosopher of the middle classes. His humanistic philosophy corresponded to the needs of the French bourgeoisie at that particular moment in history. He saw the intelligentsia, whose generosity benefitted the lower classes, as the primary forgers of history, not the violent movements of the masses. Antirevolutionary, antideterministic, and antimaterialistic, Bergson reintroduced a sense of the sacred to philosophy.

In *Matter and Memory* Bergson reveals himself to be a forerunner of the phenomenologists. There are no things, only events, which lie at the intersection of mind and matter, for they are the projection of abstract mental phenomena into the material world of matter and space. The self and the world are inextricably fused, and intuition is the qualitative understanding of this integration; it is thought seizing itself in action together with the phenomena it perceives. Bergson differentiates between conceptual space, which measures space quantitatively, and perceived space, which is the qualitative distance between the subject (the perceiver) and the object perceived. Reality itself is a dynamic process, a counterbalancing of qualitative and quantitative responses.

The publication of *Le Rire* (translated in 1956 as *Laughter*) in 1900 proved Bergson's interest in aesthetics. In it, Bergson, unlike Freud, concentrates primarily on the artistic manifestations of the comic, which allow him to apply his philosophical theories to the literary text. For Bergson, the comic is the perception of a gesture or word divorced from its content or meaning. Action and language separated from intention are habit, automatic gesture, and empty form. The comic character in literature is perceived as an automaton, a monomaniac, a general type devoid of individuality, flexibility, and adaptability to changing situations. Bergson defines the comic as "the mechanical encrusted upon the living." As stated above, Bergson believes that reality's true meaning lies in its dynamic diversity, which can be sensed through intuition. The comic perception is based upon the absence of the meaningful dynamics of life and is a prod-

uct of conceptual apprehension that is relative to the intent of the perceiver. It calls into play our intelligence, but it requires "anaesthesia of the heart." In short, Bergson sees the comic perception resulting from the predominance of the intellectual over the intuitive function. *Le Rire* also deals with the social implications of laughter. Laughter is viewed as a social corrective: Bergson apparently considers society to be a dynamic organism that chastises those unable to adapt appropriately to unpredictable changes. If Bergson seems to isolate the comic perception from the full range of human emotions, it must be remembered that his literary model was Molière, whose comic vision is more satirical and less broad than that of Shakespeare.

Bergson reached the height of his glory during the first decade of the twentieth century. In 1901 he was awarded membership in the prestigious Académie des Sciences Morales et Politiques; in 1902 he received the Légion d'Honneur; and in 1909 came recognition from abroad with an honorary doctor of science degree from Oxford. During these years Bergson finished his work on *L'Evolution créatrice* (1907; 1911; rpt 1984; translated as *Creative Evolution*), in which he applies his ideas in *Matière et Mémoire* to the theory of evolution. Here he argues that beyond material forms, words, and physical existence lies the intention that gives them sense. This is what Bergson calls the *élan vital* or the vital impulse. Matter is simply habitual and repetitive movement. One single vital impulse is giving sense to the whole range of created acts, events, and forms and to the evolutionary process itself. Each new creation owes its novelty to the dynamic scheme of life itself, yet admits of a partial resemblance to the past in that it relies for its articulation on acquired and established signs. Creation is therefore heterogeneous, alogical, and dynamic, yet tends toward a unified goal: the expression of the vital impulse that gives meaning to its diversity.

In 1917 Bergson was sent on an unusual mission for a philosopher. He became a diplomatic envoy to Washington, D.C., during World War I. It is said that his attempts to sway Woodrow Wilson into military involvement were in some measure responsible for American participation in the war. He later became a member of the International Commission for Intellectual Cooperation, a forerunner of the United Nations.

These political activities did not, however, divert him from his philosophical writings. The publication of L'Enérgie spirituelle (1920; Mind-Energy) was closely followed by Durée et simultanéité ("Duration and Simultaneity") in 1921.

In 1925, four years after his retirement, Bergson became prey to debilitating attacks of rheumatism, which gradually led him to a life of complete immobility. He would sit behind his desk for hours: even writing had become a painful effort.

His successful career was crowned by award of the Nobel Prize in literature in 1928. The literary value of Bergson's philosophical writings is undisputed. This is due not merely to the clarity of his style, but to his striking use of imagery as well. His use of imagery is not fortuitous, nor simply ornamental, for images play a vital role in his philosophical system. Unlike formal concepts and analytical symbols, which are primarily logical instruments devoid of evocative content, the image has the capacity to conjure up other images, thereby generating intuitive responses in the reader. Bergson's definition of intuition cannot be comprehended by our rational faculty alone. The image, of course, is not an intuition per se, but can produce a dynamic dialectic of images.

Neither the Nobel Prize nor his painful condition diminished Bergson's productivity. In 1932 Les Deux sources de la morale et de la religion (translated, 1954, as The Two Sources of Morality and Religion) appeared. This was the work of his maturity, the one toward which all previous works had aimed. Bergson had always alleged that mind can attain knowledge of the absolute through intuition, for it can become cognizant of the transcendant nature of its own processes. Unlike Kant, he did not uphold the view that all awareness is relative, rather that spiritual, religious experience is an authentic mode of knowledge. In light of Bergson's previous definition of the universal creative process, it is clear that for him all human endeavors have ultimately a sacred and transcendant significance. In Les Deux sources, Bergson makes a distinction between "open" and "closed" morality. The latter is a product of societal elements that apply pressure on one another for self-preservation. Enforced from without, this form of moral onus is felt as a constraint, an imposition. Open, dynamic morality is felt from within, as a longing to share in the principle of universal and divine creativity. It is a boundless, intuitive yearning in which the individual feels a form of emancipation. The mystical experience is not a passive evasion; rather it depends upon an inward resolve to give it shape and endurance. Bergson was to publish once more, in 1934, *La Pensée et le mouvant* (translated, 1946, as *The Creative Mind*).

Though a Jew, Bergson felt increasingly drawn toward Catholicism, in which he saw the culmination of Judaism. However, as a witness to the rise of anti-Semitic feelings of the late thirties, Bergson preferred to maintain solidarity with those brothers and sisters who were about to become the victims of persecution. His wife later confirmed, contrary to popular opinion, that Henri Bergson had never been baptized. He died in 1941, at the age of eighty-one, of pulmonary congestion. A Catholic priest said prayers at his deathbed.

ROXANNE DECKER LALANDE

Selected Bibliography

PRIMARY SOURCES
Bergson, Henri-Louis. *Creative Evolution*. Translated by Arthur Mitchell. 1911. Reprint, Lanham, Md.: University Press of America, 1984.

———. "Laughter." In *Comedy*. Edited and with an introduction by Wylie Sypher. 1956. Reprint, Baltimore: Johns Hopkins University Press, 1980.

———. *Matter and Memory*. Translated by Nancy Paul and W. Scott Palmer. New York: Zone Books, 1988.

———. *Oeuvres*. Edited by A. Robinet. Paris: Presses Universitaires de France, 1959.

———. *Time and Free Will; An Essay on the Immediate Data of Consciousness*. Translated by F. L. Pogson. 1910. Reprint, New York: Humanities Press, 1971.

———. *The Two Sources of Morality and Religion*. Translated by R. Ashley Audra and Cloudesley Brereton. 1954. Reprint, Notre Dame, Ind.: University of Notre Dame Press, 1977.

SECONDARY SOURCES
Alexander, Ian. *Bergson, Philosopher of Reflection*. New York: Hillary House, 1957.

Deleuze, Gilles. *Bergsonism*. Translated by Hugh Tomlinson. New York: Zone Books, 1988.

Gallagher, Idella. *Morality in Evolution. The Moral Philosophy of Henri Bergson*. The Hague: Nijhoff, 1970.

Kennedy, Ellen. *Freedom and the Open Society: Henri Bergson's Contribution to Political Philosophy*. New York: Garland, 1987.

Pilkington, Anthony. *Bergson and His Influence: A Reassessment*. Cambridge, U.K.: Cambridge University Press, 1976.

Russell, Bertrand. *The Philosophy of Bergson*. 1914. Reprint. Norwood, Pa.: Norwood Editions, 1978.

BJØRNSTJERNE BJØRNSON   *1903*

Bjørnstjerne Bjørnson (1832–1910) was born on December 8, 1832 in Kvikne/Østerdalen, Norway, the eldest son of Peder Bjørnson, a Lutheran minister. In 1837 the family moved to Nesset/Romsdal, where Bjørnstjerne came in close contact with nature and farm life. From 1844 on he lived in Molde, where he went to school, and in 1850 he entered Heltberg's preparatory school in Christiania (Oslo since 1925). At Heltberg's, Bjørnson met Ibsen, Vinje, and Lie. He established a life-long friendship with Ibsen and Lie. He had already decided to become a writer and poet and read extensively in order to prepare himself. In 1852 he entered the university at Christiania as a theology student. However, he soon discovered that theology was not for him and he left the university. He turned to journalism and ultimately became editor of *Illustreret Folkeblad*, the journal where he anonymously published his first peasant stories. These stories are didactic works in which Bjørnson tries to show the positive traits of farm life as well as some of the problems. His recognition came with the peasant story *Synnøve Solbakken* (1857), which became very popular throughout Scandinavia and soon after on the Continent. Between 1857 and 1860 Bjørnson published several other stories, all of them instant successes.

In 1856 he made his first trips abroad to Uppsala and Stockholm, where Sweden's history, as manifested in many buildings and museums, made a big impression on him and to Copenhagen, where he came into contact with young writers and read extensively, especially the German classics, in particular Goethe and Schiller. These experiences prepared him for writing historical plays. His first attempts were *Mellem Slagene* (1857; "Between the Battles") and *Halte-Hulda* (1858; "Limping Hulda"). In *Kong Sverre* 1861; "King Sverre") and the trilogy *Sigurd Slembe* (1862; "Sigurd the Bad"), with Schiller's *Wallenstein* as a model, he reached Shakespearean heights. Bjørnson brought much practical experience to his plays. From 1857 to 1859 he directed the theater in Bergen. While working at the theater, he fell in love with one of the actresses, Karoline Reimers, whom he married in 1858. In the same year he became very interested in politics and agitated in favor of liberal and nationalistic politicians. Through these activities he made many enemies and did not have the tranquility he needed to write. Therefore, in 1860 he went to Italy—the first of many journeys south.

When he returned to Norway, he again worked in a theater, as the artistic director of the Christiania Theater (1865). In 1866 he also took over as the editor of *Norsk Folkeblad*, which soon became his vehicle for expressing his religious and political convictions. As far as religion is concerned, he accepted the liberal ideas of the Danish reformer Bishop Grundtvig, whose undogmatic message was that brotherly and divine love and the continuous operations of the Word were the focal points of Christianity. This came at a time when religious gloom reigned in Norway, caused largely by Kierkegaard's philosophy, as expressed, for instance, in Ibsen's play *Brand*. In 1878 Bjørnson announced his severance from the church; he had now become a freethinker. But he remained a theist and a religious man and sympathized with Grundtvigianism to the end of his life. Politically he tried to support Sverdrup's work to unify the opposition to the conservative bureaucratic establishment and to found a new party: Venstre, i.e., a liberal party of the left (1869). For the disciples of Grundtvig, politics was the expression of the will of the people. Bjørnson ardently promoted this idea, which led to the introduction of parliamentary government in Norway fifteen years later.

Thus in the sixties Bjørnson became more and more involved with contemporary issues; at the same time his writings, until then idyllic peasant stories and historical dramas conceived in an aura of national romanticism, turned more realistic. He became interested in bourgeois plays and the realistic novel. Results of this development are the two-act play *De Nygifte* (1865; "The Newlywed") and the short novel *Fiskerjenten* (1868; *The Fisher Maiden*). The first, which is set in a drawing room, is a problem play about matrimonial frictions caused by the wife's devotion to her par-

ents, and it reflects the influence of French plays that Bjørnson had seen in Paris in 1863. A Danish critic pointed out that *De Nygifte* was "the first play which put questions and doubts into the bourgeoisie of the generation"—a function also performed eloquently by Georg Brandes, the Dane instrumental in advancing realistic and naturalistic writing in Scandinavia. *Fiskerjenten* is a problem novel. A young girl, Petra, after several scandalous affairs, wants to become an actress but is refused. After much dedication and study she is accepted. The gist of the novel is that Petra's acting is a manifestation of God's will and thus socially acceptable—or, to be an artist is to be respectable. It seems that Bjørnson tried to legitimize his own profession here.

Not unlike Goethe, Bjørnson mastered most literary genres. He did not limit himself to prose and drama, but was also a prolific author of poetry. He liberally sprinkled his peasant stories with lyrical folkloristic and nature poetry and liked to compose poems on special occasions, such as births, weddings, and deaths. Most of his poems have a strong rhythmic, musical quality and can easily be sung. His most famous poem—"Ja, vi elsker dette landet" ("Yes, We Love this Country")—is the Norwegian national anthem. Many of Bjørnson's poems were published in 1870 in a collection entitled *Digte og sange* (*Poems and Songs*). The same year also saw the publication of the epic-lyrical *Arnljot Gelline*, a cycle of poetry with topics taken from early Norse literature. Models were Oehlenschläger's *Helge*, Tegnér's *Frithiof's Saga*, and Runeberg's *King Fjalar*. In the seventies Bjørnson again became strongly involved in politics, fighting for the sovereignty of each Scandinavian country, the common vote, and the introduction of the republic and against the idea of a state church. As before, he made many enemies, this time even from the ranks of the Grundtvigians. Finding the atmosphere in the capital oppressive, he moved in 1874 to the farm Aulestad that he had purchased in Østre Gausdal. With longer trips abroad, Bjørnson was to live here the rest of his life.

After settling in Aulestad he turned out social problem plays in quick succession: *En fallit* (1875; *Bankruptcy*), *Redaktøren* (1875; *The Editors*), *Kongen* (1877; "The King"), *Det Nye Systemet* (1879; *The New System*), *Paul Lange og Tora Parsberg* (1898; "Paul Lange and Tora Parsberg"). All expose political corruption and abuse. In *Kongen* he attacked the monarchy, the union with Sweden (dissolved in 1905). Other plays—*Leonarda* (1879) and *En hanske* (1883; *The Gauntlet*) and *Når den ny vin blomstrer* (1909; *When the New Wine Blooms*)—home in on the role of woman, marriage, and divorce. *Over ovne I* (*Beyond Our Powers I*), in the same year, represents Bjørnson's long and agonizing religious struggles. While the plays perhaps represented Bjørnson's best work in the seventies and eighties (the later plays *Laboremus* [1901], *På Storhove* [1902], and *Daglannet* [1904] were rather weak), he also continued to write prose. His friend Georg

Brandes had advised him to learn from French naturalism. Bjørnson's attempts resulted in several novels—*Magnhild* (1877), *Kaptejn Mansana* (1879; "Captain Mansana"), *Det flager i byen og på havnen* (1884; *The Flags are Out in Town and Harbor*), *På guds vejne* (1889; "On God's Path"), *Mary* (1906)—and a collection of short prose, *Nye fortællinger* (1894; "New Stories"). The latter contrast strongly with the earlier peasant stories; there is a complete change of milieu, perception, and style. Turgenev's influence is tangible, but Bjørnson's didacticism is still present: the doctrine of work versus the dangers of sexuality. In 1903 he was awarded the Nobel Prize "as a tribute acknowledging his noble, splendid, and varied works of art, which have always been distinguished by freshness of inspiration, and, at the same time, by unusual purity of soul."

In the last years of his life his health failed. He died in 1910, at the age of seventy-eight. To the very end he was involved in public debate and surrounded by controversy. Bjørnson's collected works were first published in nine volumes in 1919.

Bjørnson's creative life clearly evidences a caesura around 1870. Before this year he wrote largely peasant stories, historical drama, and lyrical poetry in the national-romantic vein. During the last two thirds of his literary career he wrote problem plays and problem novels, political songs, and poems, very much influenced by French realism and naturalism.

One of his first peasant stories, still published anonymously, was

"Aanun." The story is somewhat tedious because Bjørnson addresses schoolmasters and Lutheran ministers directly and demands changes in education and in the church. He was to keep this didactic trait in most of his stories. The first one in which he really mastered the genre was *Synnøve Solbakken* (1857). It is about two farm children, Synnøve and Thorbjørn, growing up on neighboring farms—one in the sun (Synnøve), one in the shade (Thorbjørn). The two are intended for each other but kept apart because of Thorbjørn's violent temper and his taciturnity. The happy ending can only come when Thorbjørn overcomes his flaws of character. This is another basic trait of Bjørnson's early stories: the protagonist has to conquer himself in order to prosper. *Arne* (1858) has a different problem. Arne has to decide whether he will stay and work hard on his farm or follow his dreams and immigrate to America. Øyvind in *En glad gutt* (1859; *A Happy Boy*) has to show that he can handle his own life before he wins Marit, whom he loves. In the stories we do not meet the farmers in their daily toil but rather at turning points in their personal lives. Usually the women are ideal, ethereal figures; the men are often flawed but have the potential to overcome their flaws. The nature and landscape described, as in most of Bjørnson's work, is generically Norwegian, but not narrowed to a certain area (there are exceptions in the later plays). Descriptions are realistic, the figures are sentimental, and there is a general atmosphere of the idyll. Criticism of his time called Bjørnson's peasants "Sunday Farmers." Fifty years after publishing his peasant stories Bjørnson explained his reasons for writing them: "I wrote something in favor of the peasants. . . . We had learned that the saga's language was alive in the countryside and that the peasants' lives came close to the saga. Our nation's life was to be built on our history, and the peasants should be its foundation."

For much the same reason, namely, to provide the Norwegians with a picture gallery of their ancestors and to demonstrate the richness and vigor of their lives, he undertook the composition of historical dramas. Originally he envisaged a collection that was to cover the period of civil strife in Norway from about 1100 to 1300, much as Shakespeare had written about the Wars of the Roses in England. The most important of these plays is *Sigurd Slembe* (1862; "Sigurd the Bad"), which is divided into three parts. *Sigurds første flugt* (*Sigurd's First Flight*) is a one-act play. Sigurd exudes power and self-confidence and wants peace and good laws. But the lust for power is also present, and when he learns that he is the king's son, he wants to share the throne immediately with his brother, who, in the meantime, had become king. Upon learning that his ambition has placed him in danger, Sigurd decides to go on a crusade without heeding his mother's advice to stay. However, the crusade does not materialize. In *Sigurds anden flugt* (*Sigurd's Second Flight*) we find Sigurd in the Orkneys in the service of the local duke. Soon again the lust for power emerges, and he contrives a scheme by which he can seize power in the Orkneys, rejoin them with Norway, and thereby become king of Norway. The duke, by sacrificing himself, wrecks the plan, and this time Sigurd really does go on a crusade. In *Sigurds hjemkomst* (*Sigurd's Return*) he is in Norway again, ready to serve his country. His brother is now ready to share the throne with him, but the counselors are opposed. They kidnap Sigurd, but he escapes and murders his brother, who was not worthy to be king. The murder unites all his opponents and even the people who have, until this point, supported him. Again he takes flight, this time to northern Norway, still thinking that he has a call to save and serve the country. But his enemies grow stronger, and there is no doubt who will win the final battle. Sigurd's tragedy is that although he has many ideas, enormous potential, and enough resourcefulness to serve his country, he is thwarted by his hunger for power and his failure to conquer his selfishness. His opponents start out with revenge in mind and a scant moral basis, but in the end their mission becomes necessary for the survival of the state.

The three plays are different in nature. The first part is short and lyrical, dominated by Sigurd and his monologue; the second part is long and complex, full of action, with Sigurd as one of many important figures; the third and longest part has an action that stretches over three years, with the emphasis on personal psychological struggles, reflected in long monologues; Sigurd is again the main character. Yet the three parts definitely hang together, and all the dramatis personae shed light on Sigurd's character. When Sigurd becomes more and more enveloped in feelings of hate and revenge, the skald Ivar Ingemundson talks to Sigurd's better ego.

Bjørnson conducted detailed historical studies before writing this trilogy. Literary models were Schiller's *Wallenstein* and Shakespeare's dramas. In Schiller, Bjørnson admired the ability to bring an entire era to life and express a society through a play's characters. Shakespeare's influence is found in the blank verse of the first part and in the power of the prose dialogue. Sigurd evidences traits of Macbeth, whereas Harald Jarl, duke of the Orkneys, is a second Hamlet. Last but not least, Bjørnson had encountered classical antiquity on his stay in Italy from 1860 to 1862. Sigurd, like a hero out of Greek drama, upsets the balance, is guilty of hubris and consequently struck by nemesis. In contrast to his peasant stories, which had ended with reconciliation and restoration of balance, all of Bjørnson's historical plays end in tragedy.

Sigurd Slembe is, without doubt, Bjørnson's best historical play, yet better known abroad is his *Maria Stuart i Skotland* (1863; *Mary Stuart in Scotland*), mostly because of a theme that was not limited to Norwegian history. It is an attempt to round off Schiller's *Maria Stuart*. Bjørnson's historical plays have often been compared with those of Ibsen. It has been said that Ibsen's characters have more depth, better psychological conceptions and development, whereas Bjørnson offers more historical perspective and better mass scenes. Yet *Sigurd Slembe* is on a par with Ibsen's best historical drama, *Kongsemnerne* (*The Pretenders*).

Bjørnson's personal and artistic development in the late sixties and early seventies, his change from a national-romantic to a naturalist, has already been briefly outlined. In 1875 two of Bjørnson's great problem plays appeared: *En fallit* (*A Bankruptcy*) and *Redaktøren* (*The Editor*). Bjørnson had read many of the French bourgeois plays then in vogue, especially those of Angier. But Bjørnson's plays are not epigonic; he uses living models from his own sphere of experience. In Bergen he had seen many bankruptcies, and he himself was often plagued by money troubles. Tjælde, the protagonist in *En fallit*, has many involved business connections and speculates with borrowed money. He lives in a small city, and many people depend on him for their livelihood. He is convinced that he is a commercial genius. But he is overextended. His "passiva" surmount his "activa," and bankruptcy cannot be avoided. The city administrator, Berent, who personifies honesty and serves as speaker for the ethical standards of the community, helps Tjælde to face his failure, become honest, and start over again. In doing so, Tjælde finds success on a smaller scale, which brings happiness, because he becomes closer to his family. There are two subplots. Valborg, one of his daughters, in love with Sannæs, his assistant, finally proposes marriage

herself—a very unconventional move in the late nineteenth century—because Sannæs is too humble and bashful. The second daughter, Signe, is being pursued by Lieutenant Hamar, a knight of fortune, but is deserted in the middle of disaster. In the background the industrial revolution is visible, as disgruntled and misled workers threaten employers. Another theme, women's position in society, contrasts the attitudes of Mrs. Tjælde—the passive, submissive wife—with those of Valborg, who breaks with tradition, not only by proposing marriage to Sannæs, but also by becoming active in the firm and having a solid interest in her own career.

The topic in *Redaktøren* is the danger of misguided journalism: Venomous attacks and personal persecution can lead to personal disaster, even death, and to political conflict. Or in other words, when the press no longer discusses principles, but resorts to personalities, it can initiate a reign of terror. It was obvious to Norwegian readers of the time that Bjørnson here portrayed one of his bitterest enemies, Christian Friele, editor of the archconservative paper *Morgenbladet*. The conservative editor is the villain who even causes murder; the liberal politicians appear in a positive light. Bjørnson leaves it open whether the protagonist reforms; as in Tjælde's case, there is no happy ending.

Toward the close of the seventies, Bjørnson underwent a severe religious crisis. Much of this struggle found expression in the play *Over ævne I* (1883; *Beyond Our Powers I*). The protagonist is the

Reverend Sang, a minister who is an absolutely perfect and positive Christian, strong in his faith and willing to sacrifice everything. It is said that he can perform miracles through prayer. He tries to cure his paralyzed wife, but both die while he attempts the healing with extended prayer and praise of God. Whereas Christianity in the peasant stories always yielded support, it is different here; religion and reality part ways. Like the businessman Tjælde, Sang, too, overestimated his powers and his spirituality. Again the basic Bjørnson theme: Hubris is punished. Bjørnson cleverly attacks Christianity by using as protagonist a flawless minister. But the figure of Sang is exaggerated; so much faith and goodness in one person seems unrealistic. The surroundings, a somber and threatening north Norwegian landscape where day is night and night is day, raise the level of expectancy, set the stage for a miracle. Other ministers and their flock who arrive on a mission ship serve as comic relief and voice, choruslike, conventional and opportunistic beliefs. Sang's children provide a contrast of realism; they lose their faith. Sang's own first inklings of doubt kill him after the miracle does not happen. The play casts doubt on Christianity as the favored among all religions. It is probably one of Bjørnson's best dramatic efforts, in structure, characterization, psychological analysis, and style. In 1899 Georg Brandes accorded it the highest praise.

Over ævne II (1894; "Beyond Our Powers II"), on the other hand, was not successful. Bjørnson, trying to be more positive, emphasized a rather naive type of sociology more than religion. One might call the play melodrama about an industrial dispute. Another play published in the same year, *En hanske* ("The Gauntlet"), caused just as much discussion as *Over ævne I*. Svava, the main figure, demands that men should subject themselves to the same rigid sexual behavior codes as women. When she finds out that her fiancé does not conform to these demands, she strikes him in the face with a glove. When she discovers, however, that her father is also promiscuous, she becomes confused and depressed and promises reconciliation. The well-known Norwegian writer Arne Garborg made fun of the "gauntlet-morality," the Protestant ministers attacked the play, women's rights advocates supported it. In *Geografi og kærlighed* (1885; "Love and Geography") Bjørnson proved that he also could produce high-spirited comedy.

If Bjørnson's bourgeois problem plays were by and large very successful, his realistic problem novels were much less so. *Magnhild* (1877) and *Captain Mansana* (1879) make for tedious reading. Slightly better is *Det flager i byen og på havnen* (1884; *The Flags are Out over Town and Harbor*). But here too it is difficult to keep track of the large number of figures and the rambling structure. The point of departure is a girl's school; Bjørnson follows the girls' individual fates. One promptly gets "into trouble," but the father of her child decides to marry someone else. The unwed mother flings herself with her baby melodramatically at the altar during the fashionable wedding ceremony, for which all the flags are out. Further examples of Bjørnson's Victorian prose are the novels *På guds veje* (1889; "On God's Paths") and *Mary* (1906).

Bjørnson's long authorship yielded a very varied oeuvre, of which perhaps his historical and contemporary plays and his short prose are most successful. It also spans several literary schools of thought and artistic development during a turbulent time of literary history. It ranges from the romantic-sentimental to strict logical-psychological analysis. Bjørnson, therefore, has been called a Scandinavian Goethe. That claim may be slightly exaggerated. But together with Ibsen and Strindberg, he is one of the giants in Scandinavian and European literature in the second half of the nineteenth century.

FRITZ H. KÖNIG

Selected Bibliography

PRIMARY SOURCES

Bjørnson, Bjørnstjerne. *Arnljot Gelline.* Translated by William Morton Payne. New York: American-Scandinavian Foundation, 1917.

———. *The Fisher Maiden.* New York: Collier, n.d.

———. *Mary Queen of Scots.* Translated by Aug. Sahlberg. Chicago: Specialty Syndicate Press, 1912.

———. *Plays by Bjørnstjerne Bjørnson.* Translated by Edwin Björkman. 2 vols. New York: Scribner, 1913. (Contains: *The Gauntlet, Beyond Our Powers I, The New System, Love and Geography, Beyond Human Might II, Laboremus.*)

———. *Poems and Songs.* Translated by Arthur Hubbell Palmer. New York: American-Scandanivan Foundation, 1915.

———. *Sigurd Slembe.* Translated by William Morton Payne. Boston: Houghton Mifflin, 1888.

———. *Synnøve Solbakken.* Translated by Julie Sutter. New York: Macmillan, 1895.

———. *When the New Wine Blooms.* Translated by Lee M. Hollander. Boston: Badger, 1911.

SECONDARY SOURCES

Anker, Øyvind. *Bjørnstjerne Bjørnson: The Man and His Work.* Follebu: Aulestad, 1955.

Beyer, Harald. *A History of Norwegian Literature.* Translated by Einar Haugen. New York: New York University Press, 1970.

Larson, Harold. *Bjørnstjerne Bjørnson: A Study in Norwegian Nationalism.* New York: King's Crown Press, 1944.

HEINRICH BÖLL *1972*

Heinrich Theodor Böll (1917–1985) was awarded the Nobel Prize in literature in 1972 when he was fifty-four years old. He was born on December 21, 1917, in Bornheim-Merten in the vicinity of Cologne. He died on July 16, 1985 and was buried in a local cemetery. He maintained a cottage at Dugort on Ireland's Achill Island, the setting for some of the sketches in his *Irisches Tagebuch* (1957; *Irish Journal*), yet for all his travels throughout Europe, the United States, the Soviet Union, and the Middle East, Böll remained a steadfast son of the Rhineland. He spent most of his life in the vicinity of Cologne. Böll maintained that the poisonous seeds of National Socialism never could have taken root in Cologne, since it was a city with a strong tradition of antimilitarism and liberal Catholicism. This belief was reinforced by his homelife that was influenced by parents who were pious, tolerant, open-minded, and unpretentious humanists. His father was a sculptor and cabinetmaker who worked chiefly for the church.

Early on, Böll was apprenticed by a bookseller in Bonn from whom he received a good training. He was automatically enrolled in the *Arbeitsfront*, the Reich's Labor Service. He studied language and literature at the University of Cologne, specifically Germanistics along with classical philology. But after three months he was drafted into the German army for several weeks of training. War broke out, and the few weeks turned out to be a total of six years. He served as an infantryman on both the Eastern and Western fronts, including an extended period on the Russian line. He was wounded in combat four times. Of those males born in 1917 along with him, Böll had estimated their chances of surviving the war to be one in three. He expressly wanted to see his country lose the war and at times considered deserting, yet fear of reprisals against his family made him banish such thoughts. No doubt his contempt for the military is reflected in the fact that despite his combat experience, he never rose above the rank of corporal.

On April 9, 1945, he was captured by English and American troops near Cologne, and he quickly came to regard his prisoner-of-war status as a liberation. After his release in the same year, Böll returned to Cologne, a city with a mere twentieth of its prewar population. He enrolled once again at the University of Cologne in order to obtain the official designation of student, since he desperately needed to obtain a ration card. Unofficially, he worked in the carpenter shop of his brother, Alois, who had inherited it from their father. Böll also took a job in the city's Bureau of Statistics and was able once again to resume a family life. In 1942 he had married a schoolteacher and former childhood friend, Annemarie Cech, who subsequently bore him three sons. She was a tremendous support, helping Böll not only to overcome a paralyzing sense of shame induced by the war, but also to struggle to realize his long and heartfelt ambition—to become a writer.

In 1951 Böll decided to become a free-lance writer. Throughout his writing career he remained unswerving in his convictions, never shying away from the burning social issues and political controversies that arose in his postwar homeland. Within a few years Heinrich Böll had managed to gain a reputation as a disquieting social critic, a thorn in the side of the German political and Catholic ecclesiastical authorities, but also the herald of an unflappable national conscience that could neither be badgered nor bribed.

His works received many citations within and outside of Germany, including the first prize in 1951 of Group 47, a loose organization of postwar German writers that sought to revive literature in their country. He received the German Critics' Prize in 1953; in 1955 he was awarded the prize of the *Paris Tribune*; the state of North Rhine and the city of Wuppertal honored him with their respective state and city prizes in 1958; in 1959 the state of North Rhine-Westphalia conferred upon him its grand prize for art; in 1961 the city of Cologne honored him with its prize for literature; in 1965 he received a cultural and then in 1966 a literary award from the Italians; in 1967 the Bulgarians awarded him first prize for humorous short stories; in 1967 he received

the Georg Büchner Prize from the German Academy. In 1971 Böll was elected president of PEN, the international writers guild.

Böll's work depicts the ravages of war and the difficult rebirth of the German people during its aftermath. Thematically, his acceptance by the Communist authorities in Eastern Europe is understandable, yet it also is most interesting in light of Böll's criticism of the Eastern Bloc. While president of the Pen Club, he used his position to assist oppressed and suppressed writers in Eastern Europe. In 1971, for example, because of the deliberate intervention of Böll on behalf of Peter Huchel, a great East German lyricist who had been forced into silence by the government, the poet was allowed to emigrate from the German Democratic Republic to the Federal Republic of Germany.

Although Böll was brought up within a strongly Catholic environment, he nevertheless was no friend of the Roman Catholic hierarchy. Just prior to the announcement in October 1971 that he was to be awarded the Nobel Prize in literature, Böll had been served notice from the Cologne revenue office that he faced confiscations for refusing to pay his 10 percent church tax. A most generous philanthropist when it came to helping distressed people, Böll refused to yield to what he termed a "fiscalization of faith." As a Christian humanist par excellence, he inveighed against the church, for he contended that it had lost touch with the fundamental message of its founder, Jesus Christ. Thus, Böll's *Brief an einen jungen*

Katholiken (1958; *Letter to a Young Catholic*) expressed his deep discontent with the papal encyclical *Humanae Vitae* and presented his strong views on the need to change what he contended was a warped sense of morality within the institution of the Catholic Church. Here Böll addressed a fictitious draftee of the new German army and warned him of the moral dangers inherent in military life. Simultaneously, he criticized the church for equating sexual immorality with immorality in general. Implicit in his letter is the author's contention that just as the church once made a grave error by refusing to speak out against Hitler, again it was in error when it went along with the rearmament of West Germany.

In the political arena of 1965, when Böll's preferred political party, the Social Democrats (SPD), opted to team up with the Christian Democrats (CDU/CSU) to form a "Grand Coalition," he stood in vigorous opposition. Böll's voice was heard time and again decrying the shift in his country's leadership from an unpalatable fanatical devotion to National Socialism to an equally unpalatable fanatical devotion to ruthless materialism. He maintained that *Wirtschaftswunder*, or the "economic miracle," and the attitudes brought about by West Germany's rapid financial recovery from the devastation of the war, had also brought to the nation an ungodly social callousness. Böll railed out against nuclear armament and preached strongly for human rights. In 1962 he went to Russia, where he visited fellow pacifist and later (1970) fellow Nobel Prize winner, Alexander Solzhenitsyn. When Solzhenitsyn was stripped of his citizenship in 1974 and forcibly expelled from his homeland by the Soviet authorities, the Russian novelist's first stop in the West was at the home of Heinrich Böll.

Perhaps more than any other writer of contemporary literature, Heinrich Böll can be called a national writer, for his works have been read in both East and West Germany with equal fervor. Böll remains one of the few West German writers whose works have received the official sanction first needed in order to be published in the East.

A member of Germany's "war generation," Böll, in his earliest work, dealt with the question of guilt and redemption in the light of the horror and absurdity of World War II, with the Nazis who waged and glorified the war, with the young men who died as a result of it, and with the parents, wives, and children who were left homeless and psychologically crippled because of it. Böll initially focused realistically on the soldier in the war time setting, but his later books describe the aftermath of the war with a similar unsentimental realism. Even after his discharge the former soldier feels strange and alienated. As a civilian, he first encounters confusion, corruption, and anguish but gradually finds a semblance of normalcy. However, this period ends abruptly and is followed by a social malaise that is in no small part rooted in the sudden material prosperity of the nation.

Shortly after the war, when short stories such as *Die Botschaft*

(1947: *The Message*) and *Kumpel mit dem langen Haar* (1947; *My Pal with the Long Hair*) were published in a literary monthly, Böll's work caught the eye of a publishing house that wanted to expand beyond its usual fare of technical publications. It was at this time that Böll started his career as chronicler and interpreter of a society that in defeat and recovery reflected moral issues that concern us all. Throughout the four decades of his professional career as a writer, his work never seems dated. His short novel *Der Zug war pünktlich* (1949; *The Train was on Time*) deals with the frustrating moments in the last five days of the life of a furloughed German soldier from the time he boards the train at home to his return to the horror of the Eastern front. In unemotional language, Böll portrays the spiritual desolation and hopelessness that engulf the young soldier and his comrades at arms. Many of Böll's subsequent stories take place in railroad stations or field hospitals, and they convey the somber mood that man is powerless in this universe. His fate seems to be to await the unknown.

His second novel, *Wo warst du Adam* (1950; *Adam, Where Art Thou?*), is constructed in episodes that are linked by a central figure. Through the use of an episodic structure, Böll is able to achieve a wide diversity of perspectives, i.e., to portray social forces, which in their various guises, can undermine human existence. The nine loosely connected chapters mirror the experiences and fates of soldiers during their retreat from Rumania through

Hungary toward the end of the war. War is equated with a disease that is debilitating and utterly unromantic. Böll also directs literary barbs against the German postwar mentality. Without outright moralizing, he successfully debunks the "noble war" myth. False heroism, mendacity, and hypocrisy are relieved only in moments when true courage, decency, and hope prevail.

A collection of twenty-five short stories appeared under the title *Wanderer, kommst Du nach Spa* (1950; *Traveller, If You Come to Spa*). *Stranger, Bear word to the Spartans We . . .* , the title story, is one of the small masterpieces in this collection. It is set in 1945. A hallucinating, young soldier on the brink of death attempts to discern whether the emergency hospital to which he was transported is the "humanistic" high school from which he had graduated three months ago. By effective contrast, Böll suggests that a connection exists between the horrors of the war, the educational system, and the ideology of the Nazis. Only during the last seconds of his life is the answer of his whereabouts revealed to the mutilated soldier when he espies a quotation on the blackboard written in his own handwriting. The inscription by the poet Simonides of Ceo, "Stranger, if you should come to Sparta, then announce there that you have seen us lying here as the law commanded," commemorated the valor and martial discipline of the three hundred Spartans who fell in 480 B.C. at the pass of Thermopylae. It points ironically to Böll's disgust with senseless sacrifice in war, especially in this one that already had been lost. Here Böll shows all the signs of becoming a master of the short story. He reveals an ability for understatement and is able to sustain the mood and create a gripping atmosphere by concentrating on details. In juxtaposing war and school Böll suggests that the sacrifices in the name of ideology can be attributed to the German academician's hero worship and to the Prussian-Spartan militaristic tradition that the Nazis embraced as their ideal.

In these early short stories, Böll began his unmitigating attacks on all forms of tyranny, protesting against forces within a social structure that tended to mechanize and dehumanize a human being. This concern is already apparent in the Russian sentry's behavior toward the German POW in the story *Auch Kinder sind Zivilisten* (1950; *Children are Civilians Too*). For his short story *Die schwarzen Schafe* (1951; *Black Sheep*) Böll was awarded first prize by Gruppe 47 (Group 47). The story depicts totally passive characters whom the war psychologically debilitated. These people are incapable of the purposeful action that the new society asks of them, yet their apathy stems less from sheer laziness and more from their inability to get caught up in the sudden profit-oriented enthusiasm of postwar Germany. Another story about the consequences of the war that highlights Böll's growing compassion for the weak and the suffering is *Nicht nur zur Weihnachtszeit* (1952; *Not Only at Christmas Time*), which was adapted for television in 1970. It is a

study of an obsession that is rooted in a common frustration, a longing for the good old days, for a Germany that no longer exists. A disillusioned grandmother living in the destruction of 1945 suddenly decides that she should celebrate Christmas as it had been celebrated prior to the war, when things were to be found in abundance. She then continues to celebrate the holiday beyond the Yuletide and throughout the year by repeatedly singing carols. During the early fifties Böll resorted more and more to humor, irony, and satire in his prose works to render his message of compassion.

Cologne's bombed buildings and the rubble and the kiosks of the early postwar years are the setting for Böll's first widely acclaimed novel *Und sagte kein einziges Wort* (1953; *And Never Said a Word*). It became an immediate success. The title of the novel was taken from the words of a Black spiritual: "And they nailed Him to the cross and He never said a mumbling word." The allusion is to the suffering of Käte Bogner, whose husband, a disturbed veteran of the war, is unable to cope with postwar life in Germany. Fred, Käte's husband, cannot adjust to life with his family in a miserable one-room flat. Through the tribulations of a single family, the novel reflects the postwar chaos and the growing materialism of the Adenauer years that Böll increasingly despised. This novel marks the initial attempt by a German author to depict the effects of the war on German family life, and here Böll's technical virtuosity as a writer begins to manifest itself.

Through a skillful use of flashback and leitmotif, Böll's next novel, *Haus ohne Hüter* (1954; *Tomorrow and Yesterday, The Unguarded House*), confronts the issue of children who were turned into orphans as a result of the war. Much of the action is seen through the eyes of an eleven-year-old boy whose father was killed on the Russian front. A novella on adolescence, *Das Brot der frühen Jahre* (1955; *The Bread of Our Early Years; The Bread of Those Early Years*), contains a note of optimism, as two young lovers reject materialistic values. A young washing machine repairman suddenly has the chance to marry the boss's daughter, but he thereby must pay the price of a probable empty life. He does not succumb and spurns the offer. At this time Böll also wrote *Die Stimme Wolfgang Borcherts* (1955; *The Voice of Wolfgang Borchert*), an essay about a great lyrical talent that had little time to mature, for Borchert died as a result of war-sustained illness at the age of twenty-seven. The collection of stories *So Ward Abend und Morgen* (1955; *And There Was the Evening and the Morning . . .*), which contained Böll's short story *Der Tod der Elsa Baskoleit* (1951; *The Death of Elsa Baskoleit*), was followed shortly after by a collection of light, mostly satirical prose entitled *Unberechenbare Gäste* (1955; *Unexpected Guests*). The stories contained in the two collections had been written between 1951 and 1956 and reveal a new optimisim that favors a potentially positive social development. We note, for example, that although the young Elsa Baskoleit is dead, those moments of

beauty she had produced in the lives of sensitive people by means of her graceful dancing will not be forgotten, and the plight of her demented father helps to increase the moral awareness of a major figure, the truck driver, who is also the narrator of the story. The novella *Im Tal der donnernden Hufe* (1957; *In the Valley of the Thundering Hooves*) focuses again on adolescence and the problems of puberty. The ending is open, yet again we are left with the positive impression that a potential suicide crisis has been checked.

In the same year Böll's first nonfiction work, *Irisches Tagebuch* (1957; *Irish Journal*), was published. It is not only an informational travel guide based on the author's impressions of Ireland, but also a reflection of his desire to flee the hectic materialism of his homeland and to escape into a realm of unsullied nature. The simple piety of the country Irish is contrasted to the urgent need among Böll's compatriots to acquire wealth. In his collection of short stories entitled *Die Waage der Baleks* (1958; *The Baleks' Scale and other Tales*), Böll's position as an intensive seeker of truth and justice is displayed in his criticism of society. For Böll literature's purpose was not merely to transform the material of everyday life into a higher poetic reality, but also to unmask social injustice. For him literature that did not do this simply was not literature. He confronts the reader with disturbing realities that prompt a reaction, require a moral stance.

His collection of short stories *Der Bahnhof von Zimpern* (1959; *The Train Station of Zimpern*) is reminiscent of the preceding collection. It unites older tales with new ones. In the title story Böll draws a comical picture of the havoc that is caused by the use of high-pressure publicity and promotion techniques in modern industry.

Böll was also a successful writer of short stories that were written as plays for the radio, and his collection of satires published under the title *Doktor Murkes gesammeltes Schweigen* (1958, *Doctor Murke's Collected Silences*) is a satire on sterile broadcasting techniques. The title story helped Böll earn the reputation of being one of the leading satirists of his day. Social phenomena such as the frenetic desire of his countrymen to return as quickly as possible to a normal state of affairs, while simultaneously proceeding to forget the past, and the fact that there ever was a Hitler, are caustically parodied.

Böll capped off the late fifties with the novel *Billard um halbzehn* (1959; *Billiards at Half-Past Nine*). Although he again returns to the theme of the material and spiritual problems created by World War II, his experiments with the time and form in literature become increasingly ambitious. Language at times is more obtuse and more symbolic. In alluding to the Nazi past, a character in the novel refers to that period in history when "a motion of the hand and a misconstrued word could cost one one's life." Past and present are skillfully interlocked, as the conflict of the new generation with the fathers who fought the heinous war comes to a head. Böll traces the history of three genera-

tions of the Fehmel family, a respectable family of architects. The plot revolves around each one's connection with the Abbey of St. Anthony, which was built by the grandfather in 1908 as his first important commission; in 1945, it was blown up by his son, as a protest against the church's policy that officially tolerated Hitler; in the narrative present, the grandson is commissioned to help rebuild the abbey. The novel indicts a society that views the destruction of monuments as being anathema, yet not so the wanton death of innocent human beings. The symbolic core of the novel is the controversy between the recipients of "The Sacrament of the Lamb" and those of the "Sacrament of the Buffalo." For Böll the novel was intended to reflect the conflict of true Christian humanism, as expressed by the spirit of the biblical Sermon on the Mount, with the despotism and totalitarianism of the ruthless group of worshipers of a beastly power that has emerged in the West German constellation of economic success.

Following the publication of this novel, criticism against Böll became more vocal and decidedly harsh. Because of this antipodal view of good and evil, Böll was accused of being too simplistic in his approach to reality and of offering resolutions that were sentimental and emotional. For Böll the world had always been shaped by the antinomies of fear and love. Thus, he had no problem with the portrait he painted of a world consisting in varying degrees of ruthless, insensitive, and cunning manipulators, on the one hand, and individuals motivated by basic human decency, on the other, such as the people who helped to save both his mother's and his own life when she was denounced for anti-Hitler remarks or those who helped them to survive the immediate postwar famine. In effect, the latter are kind souls who have an abundance of love to share with their families and friends and who have compassion for the downtrodden and rejects of society. It is no coincidence that the family stands as a major source of strength for the alienated in Böll's representations, a condition that no doubt is a reflection of the strong human bond that family life had given him personally.

When his one play, *Ein Schluck Erde* (1962; *A Mouthful of Earth*) appeared, the critics rebuked it for lacking dramatic construction. It depicts a group of people who reside on rocks and artificial islands after a deluge caused by an atomic holocaust has radically altered their mode of existence. They aspire to nothing more than bread, love, and a bit of land.

While Böll's novels and stories speak of the little man and his plight, or thematically deal with the terrible experiences he himself had to go through simply to survive, Böll's irony holds his sense of shame and outrage in check. For example, in the two stories *Als der Krieg ausbrach* and *Als der Krieg zu Ende war* (1962; *As the War Broke Out; As The War Ended*) he relentlessly exposed sham values and fraudulent assurances, yet in a most jocular way. In Böll's work conflicts frequently cause a crisis that hardly seems tragic; often it is pathetic and grotesquely comical. This is certainly true of Böll's treatment of the dilemma experienced by Hans Schnier, the main character in *Ansichten eines Clowns* (1963; *The Clown*). Here Böll pillories the social policies of the land of the economic miracle, while at the same time indicting the hierarchy of the Catholic Church as being thoroughly hypocritical and heartless cohorts. They are more interested in dry clerical ritualism and abstract principles of order than in poor people who are in dire need of their help. The clown is the "natural" human being in a world of sterile pseudointellectualism, hypocrisy, and ruthless ambition. Here sharp-witted opportunists traffic in anything from antiwar slogans to religion. Although the scion of a wealthy industrialist family, Schnier has become a social pariah because of his views. He protests on the threshold of a society in which he is condemned to try to exist, but his attacks on the apathy of the privileged few are in vain. Böll's portrait of a consumer society that seems to have dulled the moral sense of communal responsibility reflects his growing pessimism.

The element of irony that pervades *The Clown* recurs in his next two novels—*Entfernung von der Truppe* (1965; *Absent Without Leave*) and *Ende einer Dienstfahrt* (1966; *End of a Mission*)— but here the butt of his satire is primarily the federal army. In *Absent Without Leave* the narrator, a social dropout like Hans Schnier, maintains that he needed to become a deserter in order to become a human being. *End of a Mission* satirizes the so-called efficiency of the military and is written in a style that parodies the language of German military and judicial officialdom. Indeed, Böll's writing is not always easy, especially when he resorts to linguistic satire through elevated journalese or military jargon. Some sentences are so convoluted that they defy translation; yet, by and large, his humorous writing is crisp and clean. The action in *End of a Mission* takes place in the foothills of the Eifel range, where Böll spent most of his time at a farmhouse in a tiny hamlet. The plot focuses on the trial of a young draftee who with his father is accused of trying to stage a happening by setting fire to a jeep. Böll gives an account of the tenuous relationship of the individual to social institutions that produce conflict and moral dilemma; yet again the account of the protagonist's uncertainties, though often moving, is fraught with humor.

Böll was awarded the Nobel Prize in Literature for his intricate and accomplished novel *Gruppenbild mit Dame* (1971; *Group Portrait with Lady*). He focuses as usual on a present that nettles him, and on a wartime past that he abhors, since its ill effects can never again be made right. Leni Pfeiffer, the heroine of this novel, has suffered the loss of her Russian lover-prisoner. Leni's life is colored through the multiplicity of perspectives of the characters who have known her. In his own inimitable style, Böll again depicts destructiveness, political madness, and general absurdity, yet

with a certain sardonic humor. Through the kaleidoscope of minibiographies, each laden with biting satire, there emerges the portrait of Leni as the romantic idealist in an inhumane society. In the world of "cash and carry" she is another of Böll's representatives of a positive existential possibility.

Böll sought repeatedly to define the oppressive effects of every sort of institutionalized power. He vehemently protested against anything he considered wrong. In *Die Verlorene Ehre der Katharina Blum oder Wie Gewalt entstehen und wohin sie führen kann* (1974; *The Lost Honor of Katharina Blum or How Violence Develops and Where It Can Lead*), Böll indicts yellow journalism and judicial malpractice. He castigates the monopolization of the press and the harmful consequences of distorted news coverage on West German society. Starting with an act of violence and proceeding in search of truth through a series of flashbacks, Böll unfolds the events leading up to the murder of a journalist. The thinly disguised background for the novel was the terrorism of West Germany's Baader-Meinhof group and the paranoia evoked by Axel Springer's newspaper, the *Bildzeitung*. As a result of an encounter with a young radical whom she likes, a sensitive young woman, Katharina Blum, becomes the exploited subject of cheap newspaper sensationalism. Rather than receiving assistance from the law, she becomes the subject of intensive police surveillance, and as a result of further attacks on her integrity, she is driven to shoot the journalist, whereupon she turns herself in to the chief criminal investigator. The work, a brilliant statement on the complexities of social truth, is linked thematically to Böll's following novel, *Fürsorgliche Belagerung* (1979; *Safety Net*). Once again the reaction of West German society to terrorism informs the work. In *Safety Net* Böll portrays the ill effects of constant police surveillance on the capitalist-industrialist Fritz Tolm and his family.

As the 1970s came to a close, Böll also published a selection of short stories under the name of his title story *Du fährst so oft nach Heidelberg* (1979; *You've Been Going so Often to Heidelberg*). This title story is a scathing attack on "Berufsverbot," the governmental practice that was aimed at keeping supposedly unsavory characters, Communists, and radicals from pursuing their job occupations. Suspected of being a political radical because of his frequent excursions to Heidelberg, a young biking enthusiast suddenly finds himself impeded from earning his livelihood.

Das Vermächtnis (1982; *The Legacy*) concerns a soldier named Schnecker, who has been missing in action since 1943. It comes to light that Schnecker is dead, killed however not by the Russians, but rather by a German officer named Schelling, who was once the dead soldier's schoolmate. Like the ruthless "buffalo" in *Billiards at Half-Past Nine*, Schelling has been able to forget the past, to exploit life, and to continue effectively with his oppression of the "lambs." Here, as in much of his prose, Böll's position as a moralist

can be attributed in part to his ability as a writer to create a sense of identification and intimacy between the reader and the oppressed individuals in the narrative. To this end he usually employs the first-person narrative and the interior monologue. It is his built-in narrator who tells the family the news of Schnecker's death. Clearly, like Leni Pfeiffer, the narrator comes across as a representative of a superior countersociety. His dictum, like Hans Schnier's, is that the past may not be forgotten; and, akin to Böll, he is a moral conscience of his generation.

Böll's final novel, *Frauen vor Flußlandschaft. Roman in Dialogen und Selbstgesprächen* (1985; "Women at the Front of a River Landscape. Novel in Dialogues and Monologues"), appeared shortly after his death. The plot unfolds in contemporary Bonn. This quaint town of the early eighties is no longer the temporary capital of a divided country, as the Adenauer administration had envisioned it would be. The politicians in the novel are now concerned with perpetuating their positions, but they believe that in order to do this effectively, it is necessary to bring the foibles of any and all of their potential successors to light. Böll's interest, therefore, lies less in daily politics and more in the invidious scale that determines the positions of these "leaders." Böll shows how his characters are all connected by a web of social interaction. The wives of the politicians who weave the social web are moved to the forefront, but, of course, they too are enmeshed in it by the intrigues of their husbands. The women are consummate actresses, and through their social interplay we learn of the power struggles, schemes, and coverups in which their men are involved and of the scandals that pervade their world. The characters remain indistinguishable from actual politicians, for in Böll's landscape the latter have been painted over. Since they are unidentifiable characters within a world of fiction, Böll gives them full rein to speak their minds without equivocating. In an admixture of dialogues and monologues, the unspeakable in politics is gradually aired and harshly exposed by Böll within this final open forum of ideas.

A controversial writer because of his interpretation of the spiritual, cultural, and political realities of his country, Böll continues to be revered by his followers. Criticism of him, however, still runs the gamut. He is accused of being a maudlin sentimentalist by some literary critics and a besmircher of the good name of the Fatherland by mindless jingoists. Böll, nevertheless, has earned the reputation of being a great humanist of the post-World War II era. He was committed to a moral rejuvenation of his countrymen that he had hoped would be based on love of one's neighbor. His concern with the everyday life of his fellowman, who is overpowered by injustices within the social system, has elevated Böll's position beyond that of a mere chronicler of the war generation. Stylistic excellence, the skillful use of such literary devices as metaphor, allegory, and symbol, and an irrepressible sense of humor

have transformed the language and world of the man of the street into first-rate literature. Empathy, coupled with integrity as an artist and a poetic ability to reveal his deep-felt concerns with the plight of the underdog, all join together in raising Böll's work above the criticism of those who have dubbed him a mere exponent of *Kriegs-, Trümmer-, and Heimkehrerliteratur* ("war, debris, and homecoming literature"). The final word on Heinrich Böll has yet to be written, but he will continue to be held in esteem by posterity as a writer, who, through his talent and ethical views, has helped his generation to gain deeper insight into the meaning of human dignity. He will no doubt be remembered as one of the incorruptible moral consciences in Germany's troubled history.

Böll's polemical writings appeared in a number of collections, including *Erzählungen, Hörspiele, Aufsätze* (1961; "Tales, Radio Plays, Essays"); *Hierzulande* (1963; "In This Country"); *Aufsätze, Kritiken, Reden* (1967; "Essays, Criticism, Speeches"); *Neue politische und literarische Schriften* (1973; "New political and literary Writings"); *Einmischung erwünscht. Schriften zur Zeit* (1977; "Butting In Is Desired. Contemporary Writings"); *Gefahren von falschen Brüdern. Politische Schriften* (1980; "Dangers from Fraudulent Brothers. Political Writings"); *Spuren der Zeitgenossenschaft. Literarische Schriften* (1980; "Traces of the Union of Contemporaries. Literary Writings"); *Vermintes Gelände. Essayistische Schriften*, 1977–81 (1982; "Mined

Landscape. The 1977–81 Essayistic Writings"); *Antikommunismus in Ost und West. Zwei Gespräche* (1982; "Anticommunism in East and West. Two Conversations").

The short biographical sketch *Über mich selbst* (1958; "About myself") focuses on the local environs and Böll's forebears. The period dating back to his formative years in school are mirrored in *Was soll aus dem Jungen bloß werden? Oder: Irgendwas mit Büchern* (1981; "And What's To Become Of The Boy? Or Something to do with Books").

Collections of his radio plays, *Zum Tee bei Dr. Borsig. Acht Hörspiele* ("Teatime at the Home of Dr. Borsig. Eight Radio Plays") and *Hörspiele* ("Radio Plays") appeared in 1964 and 1980 respectively; *Gedichte* ("Poems"), two volumes of his poems, were published in 1972 and 1975, respectively.

Gesammelte Erzählungen ("Collected Tales") appeared in two volumes in 1981. His opus, *Werke* ("Works"), was published between 1977 and 1980. It was edited by Bernd Balzer, and it comes in ten volumes: *Romane und Erzählungen* ("Novels and Tales," in 5 volumes); *Essayistische Schriften und Reden* ("Essayistic Writings and Speeches," in 3 volumes); *Interviews* ("Interviews," in 1 volume); and *Hörspiele, Theaterstücke und Drehbücher, Gedichte* ("Radio Plays, Theater Plays and Film Scripts, Poems," in 1 volume); the collection *Ein-und Zusprüche. Schriften, Reden und Prosa 1981-1984* ("Objections and Consoling Bits of Advice") appeared in 1984.

All of Heinrich Böll's major work has appeared in English translation, and several film adaptations of Böll's work have met with success.

EDWARD R. McDONALD

Selected Bibliography

PRIMARY SOURCES

Böll, Heinrich. *Absent without Leave, and Other Stories.* Translated by Leila Vennewitz. New York: McGraw-Hill, 1965.

———. *Adam, Where Art Thou?* Translated by Mervyn Savill. New York: Criteron, 1955.

———. *Adam and The Train: Two Novels.* Translated by Leila Vennewitz. New York: McGraw-Hill, 1970.

———. *And Never Said a Word.* Translated by Leila Vennewitz. New York: McGraw-Hill, 1976.

———. *Billiards at Half-past Nine.* Translated by Leila Vennewitz. New York: Avon, 1975.

———. *The Bread of Those Early Years.* Translated by Leila Vennewitz. New York: McGraw-Hill, 1976.

———. *Children Are Civilians Too.* Translated by Leila Vennewitz. New York: McGraw-Hill, 1970.

———. *The Clown.* Translated by Leila Vennewitz. New York: McGraw-Hill, 1965.

———. *End of a Mission.* Translated by Leila Vennewitz. New York: McGraw-Hill, 1967.

———. *Group Portrait with Lady.* Translated by Leila Vennewitz. New York: McGraw-Hill, 1973.

———. *The Lost Honor of Katharina Blum.* Translated by Leila Vennewitz. New York: McGraw-Hill, 1975.

———. *Missing Persons and Other Essays.* Translated by Leila Vennewitz. New York: McGraw-Hill, 1977.

———. *The Train Was On Time.* Translated by Leila Vennewitz. London: Secker & Warburg, 1973.

———. *The Train Was on Time.* Translated by Richard Graves. New York: Criterion, 1967.

———. *Traveller, if you come to Spa.* Translated by Mervyn Savill. London: Arco, 1956.

———. *The Unguarded House.* Translated by Mervyn Savill. London: Arco, 1957.

———. *Werke.* Edited by Bernd Balzer. 10 vols. Cologne: Gertraud Middelhauve Verlag and Kiepenheuer & Witsch, 1977–80.

SECONDARY SOURCES

Conrad, Robert C. *Heinrich Böll.* Twayne World Authors Series, Vol. 622. Boston: Twayne, 1981.

Lengning, Werner. *Der Schriftsteller Heinrich Böll: Ein biographisch-bibliographischer Abriss.* 5th ed. Munich: Deutscher Taschenbuch Verlag, 1977.

O'Neill, Patrick. *German Literature in English Translation: A Select Bibliography.* Toronto: University of Toronto Press, 1981.

Smith, Murray F. *A Selected Bibliography of German Literature in English Translation.* Metuchen, N.J.: Scarecrow Press, 1972.

JOSEPH BRODSKY *1987*

Joseph Brodsky (1940—) was born Iosif Aleksandrovich Brodskii in Leningrad on May 24, 1940, to a Russian Jewish family. During World War II his father was employed by the navy as a photojournalist; his mother worked as a translator. At age four Brodsky had learned to read; at five he was reading Pushkin's poetry to his mother. Mostly in the care of his grandparents, Brodsky lived through the German blockade of Leningrad, attended public schools through eighth grade, and then deliberately left school at age fifteen when he felt persecuted because of his Jewish background. He supported himself with a variety of jobs—in Leningrad factories and laboratories and on geological expeditions to the regions of the White Sea (1957), the Far East (1958), and the Caspian Sea (1959 and 1960).

Recalling the Hungarian invasion of 1956, Brodsky said that "pain, shock, sadness, and embarrassment at our helplessness" were the overwhelming feelings of his generation. At that time, Brodsky decided to learn the Polish language in order to read and translate the best modern Polish poets, especially Zbigniew Herbert and Czeslaw Milosz, as well as Kafka, Faulkner, Proust, and other Western authors unavailable in Russian translation. He belonged to the Leningrad Union of Writers as a translator, having been guided by the outstanding theoretician and practitioner of poetic translation, Professor Efim Etkind. Brodsky also began writing his own poetry, which was nonpolitical, pessimistic, and highly individualistic, and thus contradictory to the aims of official Soviet literature. He read extensively Russian literature, religous thought, and philosophy, as well as Greek mythology and, since 1963, the Old and New Testaments. He presented his works at private poetry readings and kept in touch with other Leningrad poets, to whom he dedicated some of his early verse. When Brodsky met the poet Anna Akhmatova (1889–1966) in 1960, they immediately became friends. She inspired him with a link to the great Russian lyric tradition of the past. Akhmatova believed him to be an outstanding poet of the younger generation, the first great poet since Osip Mandelstam, who died in Stalin's death camps. Brodsky also admired Mandelstam as well as Marina Tsvetayeva. He tried to work with official poets Natalia Grudinina and Gleb Semenov, but they denied him this opportunity.

In February–March 1964 he was arrested and labeled a "social parasite" (*tuneyadetz*), even though he stated his profession to be "poet-translator." His trial in Leningrad was actually an attack on all those outside the "official ranks" of poetry. The transcript of the trial, taken by literary critic Frida Vigdorova, was smuggled out of the Soviet Union and caused a scandal in the West. In Russia, Anna Akhmatova and three Lenin Prize winners—scientist Kornei Chukovsky, poet Samuil Marshak, and composer Dmitry Shostakovich—as well as several other official poets, including Natalia Grudinina, defended Brodsky vigorously, having recognized his talent as a poet; Efim Etkind of the Herzen Institute praised him as a gifted translator. Nevertheless, the bureaucratic judge sentenced Brodsky to five years of forced labor on a state farm in the Arkhangelsk region of Siberia. During this exile the first collection of Brodsky's poetry, entitled *Stikhotvoreniya i poemy* ("Shorter and Longer Poems"), was smuggled to the United States and published in 1965. This volume is important for the study of his earliest verse. While Brodsky was in Siberia, he seriously continued his studies of the English language. Through Akhmatova's vigorous campaign on his behalf, declaring Brodsky the most gifted lyric poet of his generation, public opinion was aroused in the Soviet Union, and in November 1965, eighteen months after his banishment, Brodsky was pardoned.

Brodsky translated from English the works of Donne, Marvell, Behan, and Stoppard. Two volumes of Brodsky's translations were published in the USSR. The modern Western poets W. H. Auden and

Robert Lowell also profoundly influenced him. His most outstanding long poem of this period was "Bol'-shaya elegiya Dzhonu Donnu" ("The Great Elegy of John Donne"), which gave him worldwide reputation when Etkind, presently living in Paris, smuggled it to the West in 1964. Brodsky continued writing poetry in his own now fully developed "metaphysical" style. The official campaign to discredit him took on certain undertones of anti-Semitism; his work was doomed to annihilation by suppression. Only four poems of this time up to 1972, considered to be his mature Leningrad period, were published in the Soviet Union in *Molodoi Leningrad* (1966; "Young Leningrad") and *Den' poezii* (1967; "Day of Poetry"). In the meantime, Brodsky's poetry continued to circulate actively in *samizdat* because he was understood by the people: He was spiritual, religious, even "formal"; he used the language of an aristocrat as well as the jargon of a soldier or a villager; he combined tradition and modernism in his poetry, which he recognized as a gift of God.

In June 1972, without apparent cause, the Soviet authorities told Brodsky to emigrate. He was the first literary figure to be expelled; Solzhenitsyn and others followed. Brodsky was enthusiastically received in Vienna by W. H. Auden, in London by Robert Lowell, and a month later in the United States by George L. Kline, eminent translator of Brodsky's technically very difficult verse into English, who in 1964 and 1967 had smuggled out many of his friend's poems from Warsaw and Leningrad. Brodsky became a U.S. citizen and in October 1977 officially changed his name from Iosif Aleksandrovich Brodskii to Joseph Brodsky. Since September 1972 he has been poet-in-residence and special lecturer at the University of Michigan. He has been a visiting lecturer at Queens College (New York City), the Five Colleges (Amherst, Smith, Mt. Holyoke, Hampshire, and the University of Massachusetts), and the Russian Institute of Columbia University. He has recited his poetry, usually by heart, in the United States, as well as in Canada, Mexico, and Western Europe. His poetry has been translated into many languages. Brodsky is a member of the Bavarian Academy of Fine Arts and of the American Academy of Arts and Sciences, has been a Guggenheim Fellow in poetry (1977–78), and is serving on the editorial board of the Russian-language journal *Kontinent*. He holds an honorary degree of Doctor of Letters from Yale University (1978).

In 1987 he received the Nobel Prize in literature for his poetry collection in English, *A Part of Speech* (1980), and his essay collection *Less Than One* (1986).

Brodsky's verse consists of the short lyric poem and the long poem, called *poema*, which usually is dramatic. His poetry recitations convey with a certain urgency his concern for the human predicament. His voice expresses a great measure of sadness and pessimism, irony about personal loss, or general anxieties over current situations and events, misfortunes, and death. These feelings are alleviated at times with humor, puns, comic-grotesque statements, and startling lighthearted wit. Brodsky is equally at ease with a wide variety of rhythms and meters, free verse, iambics, anapestics, short and long lines, masculine and feminine rhymes, and especially "slant" rhymes, which are characteristic of twentieth-century Russian modernist poetry, such as "shadows/meadows" in Brodsky's "Babochka" ("The Butterfly"), masterfully translated by George Kline. Brodsky's symbolism bridges classicism, mythology, and the Russian tradition of the past with his unique interpretation of the present and the future. Thus he, in turn, becomes the link between the old Russian tradition and a younger generation of Russian modernist poets who are learning from him to express the truth of the meaning of existence—word by word, line by line—as they continue reviving modern Russian verse, which had been endangered through the Stalin years.

From the beginning, starting with his first collection of poetry of 1965, *Stikhotvoreniya i poemy*, Brodsky felt compelled to seek his roots in Russian literature, classical antiquity, history, metaphysics, religious thinkers such as Berdyaev, Dostoyevsky, and Shestov, and the Bible. From the beginning, his verse has been intensely personal and melancholy, and philosophical over the helplessness of man in the face of evil and suffering, although in it man tries to change and to overcome his loneliness and the alienation caused by other human beings or a system of government. Brodsky's verse was not political at the outset, but it has become increasingly so. He is also a champion of human rights, urging others to see the truth, and is saddened if they, like he himself, are involved in a never-ending struggle until death to achieve these rights. Brodsky feels that man's ultimate purpose in life is to learn to accept the reality of death, which restores wholeness to the soul.

The second major collection of Brodsky's poetry, *Ostanovka v pustyne* (1970; "A Halt in the Wilderness"), expresses his deep understanding of the reality and finality of human separation and loneliness. It deals with the themes of lost love and suffering from within and as inflicted by others. Noteworthy also are the dialogue of two mental patients, "Gorbunov and Gorchakov," the dreamer and the informer; "Letter in a Bottle," an exploration of Brodsky's thoughts of death in the snowy wastes; "Verses on the Death of T. S. Eliot," an eloquent tribute to the great poet. In this volume the iambic pentameter is prevalent; however, Brodsky achieves new iambic fullness by employing predominantly one- and two-syllable words for maximum density.

Brodsky's substantial third volume of poetry, *Konets prekrasnoi epokhi* 1964–1971 (1977; *The End of a Beautiful Era*), includes such poems as "Two Hours in an Empty Tank," one of Akhmatova's favorites. Brodsky explores man's spiritual existence, his alienation from wholeness due to life's circumstances, and sadly realizes what time does to human beings as they are separated from fulfilling love and the miracle of life. As the title indicates, Brodsky tried to accept the fact that his works would never be published—that it was the end of his career as a poet.

The fourth volume, *Chast'recki: stikhotvorenija 1972-1976* (1977; *A Part of Speech*) contains eight poems written before exile; the remainder were composed between 1972 and 1976 and deal more with political and moral concerns, as well as with his own solitary situation. He reflects on his new comfortable environment and Western civilization's spiritual values with little joy. In a sense, the solitude of his first exile continues into the final solitude of his second. Brodsky welcomes solitude because "solitude teaches the essence of things, for their essence too is solitude." At the same time, in the poem "1972" he realizes what he is gradually losing: "My hair and teeth, my verbs and endings" (*"volosy, zuby, glagoly, suffiksy"*). Permanent exile can mean a poet's eventual silence in his native tongue. As Kline explains, the poem "1972" and some subsequent poems were written in triple dactylic rhymes where each position has a rigidly associated symbolic level: That associated with the first position is moral-spiritual-intellectual; with the second, emotional-psychological; with the third, biological-physical. *A Part of Speech* in English contains translations of Brodsky's poems by several of his friends, some assisted by the author, with this explanation: "I have taken the liberty of reworking some of the translations to bring them closer to the original, though perhaps at the expense of their smoothness. I am doubly grateful to the translators for their indulgence." Brodsky's literary English by then was so keen and subtle, his use of English idioms so remarkable, that his criticisms and suggestions were both penetrating and helpful to his translators. Two poems, "A Part of Speech" (1975-76) and "December in Florence" (1976), were translated from the Russian by the author himself.

An earlier volume, *Joseph Brodsky: Selected Poems*, which was translated and introduced by George L. Kline, with a foreword by W. H. Auden, in 1973, contains many of Brodsky's best poems up to that time, including "New Stanzas to Augusta," which was published, along with fifty-eight others, in the original Russian, as *Novye stansy k Avguste: stikhi k M.B., 1962-1982*, in 1983. *Verses on the Winter Campaign 1980* (1981) deals with the shameful invasion of Afghanistan, which upset Brodsky even more than the 1956 invasion of Hungary. Another volume is entitled *Mramor* (1984; *Marble*). His latest collection of poetry is *Uraniia* (1987; *To Urania*). It contains mostly short poems but does include also the long poem "V Anglii" ("In England"), which had been published separately in 1977 (translated in 1987). Like Thomas Mann, who in his exile in the United States stated, "Where I am, there is German poetry," Brodsky likewise insists on writing poetry in Russian, so that wherever he is, there is Russian poetry. He is not a nationalist: "I am a bad Jew, a bad Russian, a bad American, a bad . . . whatever, but I believe that I am a good writer" (*Die Zeit*, October 30, 1987). When Brodsky received the Nobel Prize in 1987, *Novi Mir* expressed interest in publishing his poetry.

Brodsky has written a number of remarkable critical essays on poets and poetry, many of them directly in English. Eighteen of these are compiled into his first collection of essays, *Less Than One: Selected Essays* (1986), and express his full range of poetic, literary, political, and historical interests. The volume may be considered an intellectual autobiography. "Less Than One," the first essay, is a eulogy to his native Leningrad, actually Petersburg; the last essay in the collection, "In a Room and a Half," is written in loving memory of his parents, who passed away in 1983 and 1984, while he tried in vain to visit them. His essays "On Tyranny" and "Flight from Byzantium" profoundly analyze history and politics of the modern age. "Catastrophes in the Air" deals with the history and future of Russian prose. Like Brodsky's mentors W. H. Auden, T. S. Eliot, Marina Tsvetaeva, Osip Mandelstam, and Czeslaw Milosz did before him, Brodsky successfully employs this genre for penetrating critical studies of Akhmatova, Tsvetaeva, and Mandelstam, as well as of Western poets Auden, Montale, Cavafy, and Derek Walcott.

Brodsky's Nobel lecture of 1987 is another penetrating, soul-searching essay on the question of individuality in art, especialy literature, which "is not exactly favored by the champions of the common good, masters of the masses, heralds of historical necessity," but which "transforms each zero" in the masses into a human being with an individual face by direct interaction between the poet and the reader. Brodsky believes that in this awareness of a person's uniqueness lies the meaning of human existence. Brodsky insists that creative literature is at once "dynamic, logic, and of the future." Creative literature is more durable than any form of social organization—which is temporary, a thing of the past, a "cliché." For this reason, literature is often "ahead of progress" because in literature "every new aesthetic reality makes man's ethical reality more precise"; therefore, "literature is much more dependable than a system of beliefs or a philosophical doctrine." Brodsky stresses here again the necessity for a continuity of language and literature: from ancient times to the present, to the future. Out of the ruins of tyranny, his generation has accepted the challenge to become the means for language to express new, contemporary literary content. Brodsky contends that "the language prompts, or simply dictates, the next line" through the poet's analysis, but even more so through his intuition and revelation, leading him into fields beyond his own imagination; all he can do is willingly respond and fill old forms with new words.

ARVIDS ZIEDONIS

Selected Bibliography

PRIMARY SOURCES

Brodsky, Joseph. *Chast'rechi: Stikhotvoreniya 1972-1976.* Ann Arbor, Mich.: Ardis, 1977.

———. *Joseph Brodsky: Selected Poems.* Introduction and translation by George L. Kline. Foreword by W. H. Auden. Baltimore: Penguin, 1973.

———. *Konets prekrasnoi epokhi: Stikhotvoreniya 1964-1971.* Ann Arbor, Mich.: Ardis, 1977.

———. *Less Than One: Selected Essays.* New York: Farrar, Straus & Giroux, 1986; Viking Press, 1986.

———. *Mramor.* Ann Arbor: Ardis, 1984.

———. *Novye stansy k Avguste: Stikhi k M.B., 1962-1982.* Ann Arbor, Mich.: Ardis, 1983.

———. *Ostanovka v pustyne: Stikhotvoreniya i poemy.* New York: 1970.

———. *Stikhotvoreniya i poemy.* Washington and New York: 1965.

———. *Urani-i-a.* Ann Arbor, Mich.: Ardis, 1987.

SECONDARY SOURCES

Emmanuel, Pierre. "A Soviet Metaphysical Poet." *Quest* 52 (1967):65-72.

Kline, George L. "Revising Brodsky." In *Modern Poetry in Translation: 1983: An Annual Survey.* Edited by Daniel Weissbort. London and Manchester: Carcanet, 1983. Pp. 159-68.

———. "Working with Brodsky," *Paintbrush* 4, Nos. 7-8 (1977):25-27.

———. and Richard D. Sylvester. "Iosif Aleksandrovich Brodskii." In *Modern Encyclopedia of Russian and Soviet Literature* 3 (1979):129-37.

Knox, Jane E. "Iosif Brodskij's Affinity with Osip Mandel'štam: Cultural Links with the Past," Ph.D. dissertation, University of Texas at Austin, 1978.

Kreps, Michael. *O poezii Iosifa Brodskogo.* Ann Arbor, Mich.: Ardis, 1984.

Proffer, Carl R. "A Stop in the Madhouse: Brodsky's *Gorbunov and Gorchakov.*" *Russian Literature TriQuarterly* No. 1 (1971):342-51.

Sylvester, Richard D. "The Poem as Scapegoat: An Introduction to Joseph Brodsky's *Halt in the Wilderness.*" *Texas Studies in Literature and Language* 17 (1975):303-25.

PEARL S. BUCK   *1938*

Born in the United States and raised amid the political unrest of revolutionary China in the early twentieth century, Pearl Sydenstricker Buck (1892–1973), exhibits a divided East-West sensibility in both her life and her writing. Cited by the Swedish Academy "for her rich and truly epic descriptions of peasant life in China," she was awarded the Nobel Prize in literature for 1938, the first American woman selected for Nobel recognition in any field. The award confounded early critical predictions of would-be publishers and literary agents, who warned that Western readers would take no interest in her fictional accounts of the ancient lands and peoples of Asia. Today her work is internationally acclaimed, and she remains one of America's most widely translated authors.

Pearl Buck was born to Absalom and Caroline Sydenstricker on June 26, 1892, at her mother's childhood home in Hillsboro, West Virginia. Her father was a Presbyterian missionary who lived and worked in China, where her mother had lost three of four children to tropical diseases. When "Carie" herself contracted and barely survived a bout of cholera, the family returned temporarily to the United States. Here, following an extended convalescence, Carie gave birth to Pearl, her fifth child and third daughter, to whom she gave the middle name Comfort.

American by heritage and birth, Pearl Comfort Sydenstricker did not remain long in her native country. With their three-month-old daughter and twelve-year-old son, Edwin, the Sydenstrickers soon left for Chinkiang, a distant inland river port located in the Chinese province of Kiangsu. Except for a brief visit to the United States at the age of nine, Pearl did not see her own country again until she returned for college. She did not live in the States permanently until she was forty years old, after the Communists had forced white foreigners out of China. By then the name Pearl S. Buck was well established as one of America's best-selling authors.

Despite her foreign isolation, Buck grew up with a strong sense of her own American identity, a blue-eyed, blond-haired minority in an oriental land. By the turn of the century, China's Manchu dynasty was coming to an end and civil wars posed an increasing threat. When the Boxer Rebellion broke out and the Empress Dowager issued an imperial edict decreeing death to all whites, eight-year-old Pearl and her family sought temporary refuge in Shanghai. Out of her childhood experiences during this turbulent political era, Buck developed a dual cultural alliance that combined fierce American loyalty with a deep sympathy for China and its people.

Apart from a brief stint at a Shanghai boarding school in her early teens, she was educated at home, studying American lessons under the instruction of her mother in the morning and learning Chinese language and literature under a hired Confucian tutor each afternoon. Her father also provided a strong moral and intellectual presence during her childhood. An independent-minded theologian who often found himself at odds with the Presbyterian Board of Missions, Absalom Sydenstricker was a noted scholar in his own right, in later years completing the first translation of the New Testament from Greek into Chinese vernacular.

Buck's early academic instruction provided sound preparation for her undergraduate studies at Randolph-Macon Women's College in Lynchburg, Virginia. Majoring in psychology, she graduated in 1914 with prizes in fiction and poetry. Meanwhile across the Pacific, China's ancient empire had been overthrown by rebel forces under Sun Yat-sen, and World War I was beginning. Despite this threatening political environment, Buck decided to return to China when she learned that her mother was seriously ill, obtaining a teaching appointment at a missionary school for boys in Chinkiang through the Presbyterian Missions Board.

In 1917, she met and married John Lossing Buck, a young American agriculturalist working and teaching in China. Their first child was born in 1921, a daughter whom they named Carol. That same year her mother died, and in expression of her love and sorrow, she set to work on her first extended manuscript, a biographical portrait of Caroline Sydenstricker entitled *The*

Exile. Although she considered the finished memoir too personal for immediate publication, *The Exile* marked the beginning of Buck's career as an author, and she now began to write in earnest, placing a number of articles in American newspapers and magazines.

In addition to her responsibilities as a mother and her commitment to writing, Buck began teaching courses in English and American literature at the University of Nanking, where her husband had been appointed to teach agriculture. During this period civil turmoil escalated throughout China. Unable to establish a secure political footing after overthrowing the imperial throne, Sun Yat-sen's revolutionaries accepted aid from the Soviet Union, and Chiang Kai-sek's military regime was initiated.

Personal tensions compounded Buck's political and professional concerns during this time. An increasing dissatisfaction with her marriage was matched by a growing awareness that Carol, now almost four years old, was not developing at a normal rate. In 1925 the Bucks returned to the United States to seek medical consultation for their daughter and to enroll in graduate programs in their separate fields at Cornell University. On the voyage back to her native land, still vividly aware of the growing conflict in China and the impact of Westernization, Buck began writing "A Chinese Woman Speaks," the story of a young heroine who finds herself caught between the traditions of the past and the opportunities of the modern world. The tale appeared in

the April 1926 issue of *Asia* magazine and was later published with a
companion piece, "West Wind,"
under the title *East Wind, West
Wind* (1930) as her first novel.

A specialist at the Mayo Clinic
in Rochester, Minnesota, diagnosed
that Carol suffered from a metabolic
deficiency known as phenylketonu-
ria, a curable condition today but
not so in 1925. Buck learned that her
daughter was, as a result, severely
retarded and would never mature
mentally beyond the age of four.
She would later write about Carol in
The Child Who Never Grew Up
(published in 1950) in an attempt to
provide guidance and support for
parents of similarly handicapped
children. In her grief, knowing that
she was unable to give birth to
another child, Pearl adopted a
three-month-old baby girl named
Janice. (In time, her adopted children would total nine.) Their studies
complete, the Bucks decided to return to China with their two daughters.

In 1927 violence swept across
China during the second revolution,
and the city of Nanking was invaded
by the Kuomintang and Communist
armies. The rebel forces robbed and
killed white residents, and the Bucks
were forced into hiding, eventually
escaping to Shanghai. From there
they sought refuge in Japan to wait
out the battle between the Communists and Conservative Nationalists,
returning to the Chinese mainland
later that year after Chiang Kai-
shek's National Party had reestab-
lished control.

In 1929 Buck traveled to the
United States to enroll her daughter

Carol in a school for mentally
handicapped children. Upon her return to Nanking, working in an attic
study, she began writing what was to
become her most famous novel, *The
Good Earth*, completing the manuscript in just three months. Published by John Day Company in
1931, the book was an immediate
success.

Written in a spare and simple
prose style, *The Good Earth* tells the
poignant tale of a Chinese peasant
named Wang Lung and his long-suf-
fering wife, O-lan. Together they
struggle to farm the land they love,
fighting flood and drought and starvation. In time Wang Lung becomes
an affluent landowner and the father
of a prosperous household. The family takes up residence in a great
house in the city, and as Wang Lung
approaches death, his sons plot privately to divide and sell their inheritance, the land to which their father
has devoted his life.

The book was praised by critics
for its realistic portrayal of characters and for its probing sympathy
and understanding of Chinese life
and customs. For American readers,
The Good Earth brought the mysterious East to life in simple human
terms. The book was a tremendous
popular success, selling 1,811,500
copies in the first year of publication. In 1932 *The Good Earth* was
awarded the Pulitzer Prize and in
1935 the Howells Medal of the
American Academy of Arts and Letters. It earned international celebrity
for Pearl Buck as an author and,
eventually, more than $1 million in
royalties.

In the next few years, Buck

completed *The Mother*, an intensely personal story of a Chinese peasant woman (published in 1934), and a sequel to *The Good Earth* entitled *Sons*, which continued the family epic of the house of Wang through the next generation (published in 1932). Next she undertook an English translation of the great classic novel of ancient China, *Shui Hu Chuan*, published in 1933 under the title *All Men Are Brothers*. When her father died in 1931, she memorialized him in the figure of Andrew in *Fighting Angel*, which appeared together with her earlier biographical account of her mother, *The Exile*, as *The Spirit and the Flesh* in 1936. In addition to her fictional accounts of Chinese life, the Swedish Academy would later cite these "biographical masterpieces" in her selection for the Nobel Prize.

As Pearl Buck's literary reputation grew, her estrangement from her husband increased. During a one-year visit to the United States in 1932 to meet her American public while her husband completed his doctoral studies at Cornell, her publisher, John Walsh, admitted that he had fallen in love with his best-selling author. Unhappily married himself, Walsh asked her to consider divorce and remarriage. Buck refused, and for the next three years Walsh pursued the relationship, following his top writer halfway around the world and back.

Feeling a strong sense of separation from her oldest daughter, Buck made the decision to leave her husband and return permanently to the United States in 1934. A year later, she purchased an old farmhouse in Bucks County, Pennsylvania, and finally consented to marry Walsh. They were both divorced and remarried in Reno, Nevada, on the same day, arousing—not unexpectedly—strong public criticism.

That same year Buck published a second sequel in the Wang family epic. Together with *The Good Earth* and *Sons, A House Divided* completed a literary trilogy called *The House of Earth*. However, the succeeding novels failed to match the widespread popularity of Wang Lung's original tale, and the early success of *The Good Earth* began to overshadow Buck's career. Indeed, *The Good Earth* became the measure by which readers judged all subsequent works. Critics began to condemn her as a literary anomaly in twentieth-century fiction, lacking the intellectual vision, psychological depth, or stylistic innovation of such great modern writers as T. S. Eliot, James Joyce, Virginia Woolfe, or D. H. Lawrence.

No one was more surprised than Buck herself when she was selected for the Nobel Prize in 1938. Unaware that she was even being considered for the award, she responded incredulously to the announcement, insisting upon firsthand confirmation from Stockholm. Her selection prompted vocal disapproval from a number of sources—not an unusual occurrence in the history of the awards. Nevertheless, Buck was hurt deeply by the sharply negative response of American literary critics, many of whom considered Theodore Dreiser, Carl Sandburg, or Willa Cather—to name a few— more likely national candidates.

Despite persistent criticism, Buck's post-Nobel output continued unchecked. Most of her later work was accused of being stridently moralistic and overtly didactic. Many readers typed her simply as "a writer of Chinese stories," the author of *The Good Earth*. Between 1945 and 1953, in an effort to sidestep the critical stereotypes in which she was trapped, she published five novels under the pen name "John Sedges," of which *The Townsman* (1945)—the tale of a Kansas farmer named Jonathan, who offers a model for the American Western hero—enjoyed the greatest public acclaim. Altogether she produced almost seventy books, including an autobiographical account entitled *My Several Worlds* (1954), as well as numerous articles, short stories, lectures, and screenplays—a most prolific writer by any standards.

In later years Buck became actively involved in humanitarian reform, founding an adoption agency for children of mixed parentage called Welcome House and establishing the Pearl S. Buck Foundation for the advancement of Amerasian children. Her compassion for children was deeply felt, and many of her books, both early and late, were written for young readers: *The Chinese Children Next Door* (1942), *Yu Lan: Flying Boy of Japan* (1945), *The Big Wave* (1947), and *Little Fox in the Middle* (1966), to name a few.

After her husband's death in 1960, Buck lived alone in Danby, Vermont, where she had acquired and developed considerable real estate holdings. She became a close companion of W. Ernest Hocking, retired chairman of Harvard's philosophy department, refusing, however, to marry again. After a yearlong illness, Buck died in Danby on March 6, 1973.

DOREEN L. BUCHMAN

Selected Bibliography

PRIMARY SOURCE
Buck, Pearl S. *My Several Worlds*. New York: Day, 1954.

SECONDARY SOURCES
Doyle, Paul A. *Pearl S. Buck*. Twayne's United States Authors Series, No. 85. Boston: Twayne, 1980.
Harris, Theodore F. *Pearl S. Buck: A Biography*. New York: Day, 1969.

IVAN BUNIN *1933*

Ivan Alekseevich Bunin (1870–1953), the first Russian writer to be awarded the Nobel Prize in literature, was born into an impoverished family of the nobility in Voronezh in 1870. He had little formal education past the gymnasium, but he read widely and traveled extensively, visiting Ceylon, Palestine, Egypt, Turkey, Italy, Sicily, Greece, Syria, Tunisia, and Algeria in addition to the exotic southern part of his native Russia, all prior to World War I. Such broadening experiences prompted him to abandon a position in the rural administration in Central Asia and to dedicate his life to self-expression in the arts.

An interest in painting as a teenager was transformed into active production as a poet and as a translator of such writers as Longfellow, Byron, and Tennyson. His first volume of verse appeared in 1891, and he was thereafter awarded the prestigious Pushkin Prize three times for his poetic endeavors. Bunin's verse continues the Russian classical tradition. His poetic world is filled with pictures of nature and twilight moods, which are presented with accomplished aesthetic expression and control. His form and themes are traditional. Bunin's verse attracted little public acclaim, largely because it was written initially at a time when modernist poetic modes, particularly symbolism, were in vogue. In the main, the author was little reflective of his age.

Bunin wrote verse throughout his life, and even after prose became his primary voice, it was decidedly the lyrical and evocative prose of the poet, characterized by a masterful control of language, detail, and rhythm. He was thus not a poet who became a prose writer, and his first short stories appeared in 1892 shortly after his debut as a poet. These initial attempts generally portrayed the peasantry and the rural landowners of the end of the nineteenth century, a milieu with which he was most familiar and which he depicted with precision and detachment. The primary focus of these stories is the disintegration of traditional rural Russian life. The disintegration is portrayed graphically and with detachment, yet one commonly feels a sense of loss. The stories blend classical realism with careful symbolism and link Bunin with the nineteenth-century tradition of Ivan Turgenev, Sergey Aksakov, Leo Tolstoy, and Anton Chekhov. This legacy placed Bunin outside the prevailing modernist trends.

Following almost twenty years of creative endeavor, Bunin was honored in 1909 by the Russian Academy of Sciences, which selected him as one of its twelve honorary members. Buoyed up by this singular recognition, Bunin then embarked on his most creative period.

Popular acclaim came with the publication of the long story *Derevnya* (1910; *The Village*). The tale depicts village life in its complexity and depth without adornment, and the impact is stark and tragic. *The Village* is a picture of life painted more by an artist and a poet than by a chronicler of events. In fact, there is little plot—the lack of a well-constructed story is common for Bunin's work. The tale portrays the lives and feelings of two brothers of the landed gentry who are depressed by everything that they see about them. Tikhon and Kuzma come from a family and a social class with a history of abuse, barbarism, and lack of love, and they see the same factors in the lives of all of the peasants around them. Life is bestial and without hope. Solace is sought in writing and in having a family, but nothing lightens the murky tedium. A traditional peasant wedding of two people who do not care for each other or for life concludes the story and serves as a representation of the despair of existence. All of Russia is compared with this single, miserable village.

The Village was followed in 1912 by the even more stark *Sukhodol*, meaning "dry valley." The setting is again a village and a manor house within which generations, individuals, and the entire social and economic system decay. This time the perspective is provided by an old servant who reflects upon her master's heyday. Buildings and lives crumble through misuse and disuse. Insanity, murder, rape, and unrequited love are rampant, and there is the sense that barbarism has always characterized events. Bunin's family chronicles convey a strong sense of history and the passing of time, and there is the feeling that nothing changes for the better.

Both *The Village* and *Sukhodol* were viewed by some as indictments of the prevailing system even though Bunin's literary concerns were never political. In his work the rural gentry lead a tragic life and throughout emit an odor of moral decay and wistful doom. The power of these works is in the telling—language, description, and mood—as elemental characters grapple with the elemental forces of life.

International acclaim came to Bunin with the publication of *Gospodin iz San-Frantsisko* (1916; *The Gentleman from San Francisco*). Bunin exchanges the Russian village for an ocean liner on which the wealthy, unnamed gentleman and his family are traveling to Europe. They are treated with a servile condescension that serves to underscore the essential emptiness of their lives. When the august gentleman unexpectedly dies, his family is no longer catered to and is treated with a cynical disdain by those who had previously groveled in their presence. His body is returned to San Francisco in the hold of the ship, bereft of any honor or solicitude, while the facade of life moves steadily onward in the more sociable areas of the liner. In his detached manner Bunin shows that life is largely inconceivable and that man is poorly equipped to fathom its depths.

The Bolshevik Revolution of 1917 posed a crisis for Bunin, who had never abandoned a certain aristocratic aloofness. He had previously affiliated himself literarily with Maxim Gorky's Znanie group, but he could never share the group's progressive social and political aspirations. This feeling of dissonance was aggravated by the Revolution, and Bunin abandoned his homeland in 1920, living the remainder of his life in Western Europe, primarily in Paris. Bunin was every whit a political and philosophical exile and became a focal point of the émigré community, although these feelings were not manifested in his writing.

Abroad, he continued his literary output. The stories written in emigration are characterized by an increased feeling of pessimism and by a more in-depth examination of two of his popular themes—love and death. Exemplary are *Mitina lyubov* (1925; *Mitya's Love*) and *Solnechny udar* (1925; *Sunstroke*). In *Mitya's Love* the young central character becomes a psychological case study of love. He suffers through an attachment to a young actress, never progressing beyond a physical attraction and always testing her devotion. He ultimately betrays her with a peasant girl, whom he pays for her favors, while the actress tearfully leaves him for a director. Mitya comes to feel that all of his relationships have been dirty and unnatural and that love cannot be retrieved. The pain is so intense that he shoots himself with enthusiastic pleasure in order to escape. In *Sunstroke* two travelers meet on a liner and share the night. The initial response of the traveling lieutenant to the woman's insistence that they can never see one another again is extreme distress and thoughts of suicide. The following morning he is able to continue his journey calmly, although he is conscious that he has aged ten years.

Mitya's Love and *Sunstroke* depict love as a blinding moment that cannot endure with the same intensity. Love thus becomes mostly memory, and while it is the supreme enchantment of life, it is also doomed to a tragic ending. By contrast, death is man's constant shadow and produces continual anxiety. Nothing in life can merit deep attachment because all will turn to ashes and dust as all go to their prescribed end. Bunin, like Tolstoy, lived in fear and awe of death, and he found himself beset by it, particularly in his later years. The characters that evince these feelings are typically sketchy. Their feelings, ideas, and moods are more important than their physical appearance, and the details that Bunin provides lead to psychological understanding rather than visual perception.

Bunin envisioned his major work in exile to be a fictionalized autobiography entitled *Zhizn' Arsenieva* (1932–33; "The Life of Arsenev"), published in English under the title of its first part *The Well of Days* (*Istoki dney*). Here he returned to the theme of the disintegration of the gentry. The work is not a novel per se, even though it is Bunin's only one of novelistic length. Rather, it is a combination chronicle, autobiography, and confession that is based in introspection and responses to nature. The strength of the work is its vigorous, poetic style. Although the characters feel stalked by death and find love and happiness only as blazing memories, Bunin emerges not as a poet of doom, but as one whose love and affirmation of life, frequently expressed in very sensuous terms, is stronger than the aura of death. One finds oneself sharing in Arsenev's perceptions of life, perceptions that are very much those of a poet and an artist who concludes that art is immortal. To illustrate this, there are many quotations from scripture and other sources and many references to Russian writers that give substantive meaning to life. Throughout, however, life is for the moment, and the remainder is memory. The tale is full of a sense of time and history and is concerned with the evolution of personality and consciousness.

Bunin was awarded the Nobel Prize for literature in 1933 "for the firm artistic skill with which he has represented the Russian classical line in the art of poetic prose." The citation referred to this rapport with the past, which he realized through his art, and praised his lyric-poet nature, which was able to render pictures of life with exact fidelity. *The Village, Sukhodol, The Gentleman from San Francisco, Mitya's Love,* and *The Life of Arsenev* were specifically commented upon in the citation. In accepting the prize, Bunin acknowledged his youthful passion for painting and its impact upon his writing. He also noted the pain of the previous years and the sadness surrounding his exile from his homeland.

The work of Bunin's later years was characterized by sketchlike stories in which he confined himself to specific scenes and moods. The collection *Tyomnye allei* (1943; *Dark Alleys*) is illustrative of his post–Nobel Prize work. The stories generally examine the theme of love and feature subdued moods and pictures. He also wrote memoires and essays that were characterized by spite, faultfinding, and an inability to appreciate anything Soviet. He died in 1953, impoverished, in ill health, and comparatively ignored following his worldwide recognition twenty years prior.

Bunin left a legacy of well-crafted fiction but no inheritors of his craft. In great measure he is more of a nineteenth-century writer than a twentieth-century one, and because he was somewhat of a transition from one era and style to another, those who followed were caught up in modernism. His love of lyricism in an age of modernism, his propensity for understatement, his lack of great ideas, and his aloof personality kept him rather isolated. He left, however, several volumes of finely crafted work, full of clear pictures, evocative turns of phrase, and an almost clinical approach to people and events.

RICHARD L. CHAPPLE

Selected Bibliography

PRIMARY SOURCE

Bunin, Ivan. *Sobranie sochinenii.* 9 vols. Moscow: Khudozhestvennaya literatura, 1965–67.

SECONDARY SOURCES

Baborenko, Aleksandr. *I. A. Bunin. Materialy dlya biografii.* Moscow: Khudozhestvennaya literatura, 1967.

Connolly, Julian W. *Ivan Bunin*. Boston: Twayne, 1982.

Kryzytski, Serge. *The Works of Ivan Bunin*. The Hague: Mouton, 1971.

Poggioli, Renato. "The Art of Ivan Bunin." *Harvard Slavic Studies*. Vol. I. Cambridge: Harvard University Press, 1953.

Struve, Gleb. "The Art of Ivan Bunin." *Slavonic and East European Review* 11, 32 (1933): 423–436.

Woodward, James B. *Ivan Bunin: A Study of His Fiction*. Chapel Hill: University of North Carolina Press, 1980.

ALBERT CAMUS *1957*

Albert Camus (1913–60) is not only a giant among French moralists—an important and characteristic strain in French literature—but he stands as one of the most profound thinkers of the twentieth century as well. His literary works, comprising approximately one-half of his non-journalistic writing, are illustrations of his philosophical concepts. His thought centered on man's existence: its purpose, justification, and fulfillment. And he elaborated it in three essentially successive but somewhat overlapping phases: confrontation with the absurd, revolt leading to commitment, and the need for moderation.

Camus' anthropocentric world developed early from his personal experiences. Born in 1913 in Mondovi, Algeria, of a French father and a Spanish mother, he lost his father to World War I the next year, before he had a chance to know him. His mother was reduced to earning a living for herself and her two sons by menial work in Algiers, and Albert in his early years experienced poverty. Nevertheless, his teachers, having discovered his exceptional intellectual aptitudes, recommended him for scholarships and encouraged his development—first, Louis Germain in middle school and later, at the university of Algiers, Jean Grenier, his professor of philosophy and himself a philosopher. However, his schooling was interrupted by the onset of tuberculosis when he was seventeen, and by his need to hold part-time jobs. Between 1928 and 1936, while preparing his degree in philosophy, he explored a number of paths that soon proved to be deadends: playing soccer for a sports club; getting married, only to be separated two years later; joining the Communist party, which nevertheless procured him the direction of a *Maison de la Culture* (cultural center); working for the university's meteorological service and for administrative and commercial establishments as a clerk—changing lodging as often as he changed jobs. After writing his thesis on the relationship between Hellenism and Christianity, Camus tried his hand at editing a newspaper and directing a theatrical troupe. The frequent changes in occupation and residence, which characterized the rest of his life, were necessitated by the events of World War II, the relapse of his illness, and frequent trips, not only within France and to Algeria, but also to central Europe, Italy, Greece, North and South America. Although he had remarried in 1940 and was the father of twins, Camus did not buy a house until late 1959—in southern France near Lourmarin—a few months before his absurd death in an automobile accident.

Death, as the absurd and arbitrary end of man's joy and striving, preoccupied Camus from his early youth—as a personal threat in the guise of tuberculosis. On the positive side, he experienced the throbbing, precarious life under the implacable Mediterranean sun as something beautiful, no matter how limited by personal circumstances. The quest for a personal code of conduct in a seemingly incoherent world led Camus to the study of philosophy, culminating in the comparison of two of the major systems of Western thought, Hellenism and Christianity. Camus was attracted to Hellenism not only because it was a culture that had evolved in the Mediterranean setting he knew and loved, but also because he recognized contemporary reality in some of its myths, particularly those of Sisyphus and Prometheus. He could see the persistence of Sisyphus—performing a seemingly useless task, constantly undone—in the humble occupations of his family as well as in the rise and fall of civilizations. Yet it was also evident that there are those who, like Prometheus, have a personal inner mission to help humanity through their discoveries and convictions, but at the expense of great personal suffering. Inspired also by his reading of Epictetus, Descartes, Pascal, Kierkegaard, Nietzsche, Spengler, and his French contemporaries Gide and Malraux, Camus elaborated a coherent philosophy with an inherent, positive morality.

Rejecting God and reason, like Descartes, Camus begins by doubting all certainties except the only evident one: death. Faced with the certainty of dying, he asks, how is man to spend the time he has to live? First, Camus insists that man must face this reality rather than obfuscate it with hopes and promises of another life, or even of tomorrow; second, he argues that given the reality of life now, a man must live it to the fullest. The fact that anyone may lose one's life at any time is absurd, and a lucid man is inevitably led to revolt at this evidence. Yet he is not alone; all men share this ineluctable destiny. It is through the realization of this bond, the solidarity with others, that man can find joy and meaning in a common fight against all that threatens sacred life.

Camus gives a negative example of man in his first novel—which has also been the most widely read worldwide,—*L'Etranger* (1942; *The Stranger*), written in early 1940.

Meursault, a young worker living alone in Oran, is summoned to his mother's funeral at the home where she had been interned. The officials of the institution are shocked at the fact that he shows no emotion and commits the improprieties of smoking and drinking coffee during the wake. Right after the funeral, Meursault resumes his normal life, continuing his relations with Marie, going to the movies and to the beach. He goes through all these actions without any conviction or desire, merely out of habit or forced by circumstances. He goes through life like a sleepwalker, automatically, without any feeling or reason. He observes, without any empathy, the euphoric crowds after a soccer victory, and watches, without any reaction, his neighbor's sadistic beating of his dog. And it is also without any reason or emotion that he pumps four bullets into an Arab on the beach. Sentenced to death for this crime, Meursault refuses the last ministrations of a priest; and while he awaits execution, his inner being cries out against the indifference of men and the black starry sky. . . . But Meursault (*meurt seul* = "dies alone") had been indifferent to other men himself. In the end, however, he does assume his fate and thus partakes of humanity.

In his next novel, *La Peste* (1947; *The Plague*), finished in 1946, Camus gives a positive image of man's existence. During an outbreak of the plague in Oran, a doctor, Rieux, who at first simply performs his professional responsibilities in a normal manner, is overcome by compassion for the victims and soon leads the fight against the scourge with selfless sacrifice and devotion. He is joined by Jean Tarrou, the chronicler of the extraordinary as well as the ordinary events, who carries on the administrative and political aspect of the fight. Rambert, a journalist from Paris, caught in Oran by the quarantine, also becomes a member of the team. The men find their task lightened by the understanding of Joseph Grand, a civil servant who helps to expedite bureaucratic matters. In contrast to their valiant effort stands Cottard, a selfish black-market profiteer who refuses to participate in their solidarity. The prayers of the priest Paneloux also prove to be of no avail against the pitiless ravages of the scourge.

While *L'Etranger* and *La Peste* are the two major novels that exemplify the first two phases of Camus' triptych philosophy—the recognition of the absurdity of death followed by revolt against it and commitment to perserve life—the third phase, the need for moderation, is illustrated by another negative example, *La Chute* (1956; *The Fall*), Camus' third major novel. Jean-Baptiste Clamence, a Parisian lawyer, has enjoyed playing God during his successful career. One evening, on a walk along the Seine, he hears a sinister laugh and remembers that once he let a woman drown without summoning help. Haunted by this memory, he abandons his career and all his values, leaves Paris, and moves to the underworld in Amsterdam, where he tries to subvert to nihilism all those who have unwittingly wandered into it. Like Meursault, Clamence is a failure because he has rejected life by refusing to save it. This is the fault that causes his downfall, his fall into Hell. But Clamence has another dimension. By exercising life and death decisions over his clients, he judged them—he played God. Thus, Clamence has renounced human solidarity twice. Camus has Clamence, the advocate of darkness, tell his story as a confession. Furthermore, the setting—the dark mists of Amsterdam, as opposed to the sunny Mediterranean shores—sustains the image of the confused, fallen hero who did not see man's limitations in the clear, sharp light of the noonday sun, but aspired to sit in judgment over others.

Abhorrence of all inhibiting isms or ideologies—in the form of nazism, communism, Christianity, or simple bureaucracy—was one of Camus' constants, for he perceived all of these systems as inhibitors of personal freedom and a threat to life. Institutions in general, but the Church and courts of law specifically, were regarded by Camus as insensitive, unwieldy, and ineffective in dealing with human problems. Camus also took issue with Sartre and the French Left in general for siding with the Soviet Union while knowing all along that it was governed by a tyrannical regime that had been mercilessly and hypocritically brutalizing its people.

Camus' personal philosophy with its social implications opposes existentialism, to which it has been often but incorrectly linked. In 1944 Camus issued a public statement denying any link to existentialism and

to Sartre, whose philosophy he regarded as negative, founded on the ugliness of life. Camus, on the other hand, celebrated its beauty.

While Camus achieved his greatest success with his novels, he also used other forms to convey his vision of the world: short stories, plays, and an important body of essays. Among his short stories, two, published in the volume *L'Exil et le Royaume* (1957; *Exile and the Kingdom*), are particularly striking, written in the same terse, precise, and concrete style as his longer works. "Le Renégat ou l'esprit confus," ("The Renegade or a Confused Mind") set in North Africa, shows the horrible fate of a missionary who had volunteered to bring Christianity to a fiercely savage desert tribe against the advice of his superiors. Mutilated and enslaved, the priest revolts by adopting the beliefs of his cruel masters and shoots the next missionary who comes to liberate him. "L'Hôte" ("The Host [Guest]"—in French the word may mean either) takes place on the eve of the Algerian war of independence. It is the story of a French teacher, Daru, in charge of a one-room school in a remote area of Algeria. One day a mounted policeman brings an Arab, on foot, whom Daru is to deliver to the next village to be tried for having killed his cousin in a dispute over grain. However, appealing to the Arab's conscience, Daru offers him the choice of returning to his village or to the French prison. The Arab chooses the latter and sets out alone and free on the road to town. Ironically, however, the Arab's friends believe Daru has been instrumental in his conviction and swear revenge.

Although *L'Exil et le royaume* was published in 1957, Camus had been planning the volume since 1952, and most of the stories were already in varying stages of completion in the early fifties. The title suggests the positive and negative sides of man's most essential aspects of existence: alienation/integration, which is the main theme of all the stories. They illustrate the anguish of those who find themselves in an alien group and are faced with decisions of allegiance. Camus believed that society reflected divine order and whoever transgressed it had to suffer grave consequences.

The tragic effects of alienation from one's group, precipitated by circumstances, but also consecrated by choice, are illustrated in Camus' theater as well. *Caligula*, written in 1938 but performed for the first time only in 1945, is the story of the incestuous young Roman emperor who does not accept the most evident fact of the human condition, death. In his revolt, which appears as sheer madness, he flouts every value of organized society before he is assassinated by a conspiracy that restores order. *Caligula*, as well as the next play, *Le Malentendu* (*The Misunderstanding*), begun in 1942 and performed in 1944, were inspired by Nietzsche's *The Origins of Tragedy*. *The Misunderstanding* is set in Budejovice, Czechoslovakia, but the legend of the plot is shared by a number of cultures, including the French, the German, and the Chilean. In Camus' version, a woman who keeps an inn, pressured

by her daughter, murders her son, who, having done well after leaving home, had returned incognito to visit his family. Both *Caligula* and *The Misunderstanding* belong to the first cycle of Camus' thought: the preoccupation with the absurd. These works invite meditation on the theme of death. They are the most frequently performed of Camus' plays.

Camus' involvement with the theater began early, in Algiers. As director of the *Maison de la Culture*, he founded a troupe, The Theater of Work, which was later called The Team (*L'Equipe*). It was with his collaborators in this troupe, in 1935–36, that Camus wrote his first play, *Révolte dans les Asturies* ("Revolt in the Asturias") about an incident in pre–civil war Spain. With its frequent changes of scene and sound effects, this Brechtian tragedy already shows Camus' preoccupation with staging. The play was banned by the Algerian government because of its political content.

Camus was to make an attempt at "total theater" with the production of *L'Etat de siège* ("State of Siege") in 1948, in collaboration with the mime actor and director Jean-Louis Barrault and incorporating Honegger's music. However, the public found the alternation of lyricism and irony disconcerting, and the original production failed. Camus had hopes of reworking this drama about the plague, based on Antonin Artaud's theories, and specified it should be performed outdoors, as the setting is the medieval walled town of Cadiz.

Les Justes (1950; *The Just Assassins*), originally entitled *La Corde* ("The Rope"), is the drama of self-sacrifice for a higher human ideal by Russian terrorists in the revolution of 1905. This play belongs to the second phase of Camus' creativity, which emphasized positive action in solidarity with others. It was elaborated between 1947 and 1949, concurrently with its fictional and philosophical counterparts, *The Plague* and *The Rebel*. The hero of *The Just Assassins* is an historic figure. Camus had incorporated extensive research in writing this play, even quoting the revolutionary Kaliayev. Moreover, it is the only one of Camus' works where love is an important theme.

After Camus became known as a dramatist, he was asked on occasion to adapt classics for contemporary productions and thus came to revamp Calderón's *Devotion to the Cross* (1952), Larivey's *Spirits* (1953), Dino Buzatti's *An Interesting Case* (1955), Lope de Vega's *The Knight of Olmedo* (1957), Faulkner's *Requiem for a Nun* (1957), and Dostoyevsky's *The Possessed* (1959). Camus believed that theater was a means of educating the masses and the highest form of literary expression.

Camus' philosophic essays are equally important. They parallel his creative works. The first cycle, that of the absurd, contains *The Myth of Sisyphus* (1942), which delves into a fundamental aspect of man's condition; the second, that of revolt, *L'Homme révolté* (1951: *The Rebel*) expresses in lyrical prose man's claim to his dignity, which can exist

only in freedom. During his phase of moderation and before his accidental death on January 4, 1960, Camus had begun work on a play, *Dom Juan*, a novel, *Le Premier homme* ("The First Man"), which was to have been his most important one, and essays, including a "Myth of Nemesis." Besides his work as journalist and editor of the Resistance newspaper *Combat*, Albert Camus also produced eight volumes of literary and political essays. His *Carnets* (*Notebooks*) were published in 1962.

Shortly after accepting the Nobel Prize in literature in 1957 and two years before his death, Camus wrote in the preface to a new edition of one of his earlier works, *L'Envers et l'endroit* (1937; "The Wrong Side and the Right Side" in *Lyrical and Critical Essays*, 1968), that his work was not even begun.

BIRUTA CAP

Selected Bibliography

PRIMARY SOURCES

Camus, Albert. *Essais*. Edited by R. Quillot and L. Faucon. Paris: Gallimard, 1965.

———. *Théâtre, Récits, Nouvelles*. Edited by Roger Quillot. Paris: Gallimard, 1962.

SECONDARY SOURCES

Brée, Germaine. *Camus*. New Brunswick, N.J.: Rutgers University Press, 1959.

Cruikshank, J. *Albert Camus and the Literature of Revolt*. London: Oxford University Press, 1959.

Fitch, B., and P. Hoy. *Albert Camus. Essai de bibliographie des études en langue française consacrées à Albert Camus, 1937–1967.* Paris: Lettres modernes, 1969.

Lottman, Herbert R. *Albert Camus.* Paris: Edition du Seuil, 1978.

Quillot, Roger. *La Mer et les prisons.* Paris: Gallimard, 1956. Rev. ed. 1970.

Roeming, R. *Camus, a Bibliography.* Madison: University of Wisconsin Press, 1968.

ELIAS CANETTI *1981*

Elias Canetti (1905—), winner of the 1981 Nobel Prize in literature, was born in Ruschuk, Bulgaria, on July 25, 1905. His parents, Jacques Canetti and Mathilda Arditti, were Sephardic Jewish merchants who spoke a Ladino dialect of Spanish, Elias Canetti's first language. Canetti's parents also spoke German, a language that Elias mastered and in which all his later literary works are written.

At the age of six, Canetti and his parents moved to Manchester, England. Canetti began school and learned English, as his second language. One year later, his father died of a sudden heart attack, and he moved with his mother to Vienna, Austria, in 1913. His mother taught him enough German to allow him to enter school at the normal level for his age group, and shortly afterward he was sent to school in Zurich, Switzerland.

At the age of sixteen Canetti attended a *Realgymnasium*, and in 1924 he entered the University of Vienna, where he received a doctorate in chemistry in 1929. It was during this time that Austrian society, as a result of the lost war, the terms of the Versailles Treaty, and eventually the economic depression, experienced widespread political and social upheaval and change. Political protests and public demonstrations made a memorable impression on Canetti's thinking, and eventually Canetti, influenced by his firsthand experiences, became preoccupied with the phenomenon of mass psyche. The writers Karl Kraus and Franz Kafka also influenced Canetti, and he began researching the behavior of the masses, which culminated in his later work *Masse und Macht* (1960; *Crowds and Power*).

Canetti's first published work, *Die Blendung*, was released in Vienna in 1935. It was later translated in England as *Auto-da-Fé* in 1946 and in the United States as the *Tower of Babel* in 1947. Canetti intended *Die Blendung* to be the first novel in a series of eight, illustrating madness in society. The other works, however, were never completed. Canetti also began writing plays in the 1930s, two of which became well known, *Die Hochzeit* (1932; *The Wedding*) and *Komödie der Eitelkeit* (1934; *Comedy of Vanity*). Both plays were published separately, but most of his later plays were published together in the volume *Dramen* (1964; *Plays*). Other writings include three autobiographical volumes entitled *Die gerettete Zunge* (1977; *The Tongue Set Free*), *Die Fackel im Ohr* (1980; *The Torch in My Ear*), and *Das Augenspiel* (1985; *The Play of the Eyes*); numerous essays; and excerpts from his personal notebooks.

In recognition of his work, Canetti is the recipient of several literary awards. He received the Prix International in Paris for *Die Blendung* in 1949, and in 1966 he won the Author's Award of the City (Dichterpreis der Stadt) in Vienna. A year later he was awarded the German Critics' Prize (Deutscher Kritikerpreis) in Berlin and in 1968 the Austrian State Prize for Literature. In 1972 Canetti received the prestigious Georg Büchner Prize and in 1980 the Kafka Prize. Although Canetti is often referred to as the first native Bulgarian to win the Nobel Prize in literature, Canetti is generally recognized as an Austrian writer because he writes exclusively in German and many of his experiences are based in Vienna.

On February 26, 1934, Canetti married Venetia Toubner-Calderon. The couple had no children, and Venetia died in May 1963. Canetti was married again in 1971 to Hera Buschor, and in 1972 their daughter Johanna Canetti was born. Canetti now lives in both London and Zurich and is a full-time writer and lecturer.

The main themes found in Canetti's works include the psychology of the masses, the rejection of death, transformation and isolation, and the conditions of power. In these he incorporates concepts of the religions, languages, and cultures of the contemporary world. Like many writers, poets, and philosophers, Canetti attempts to present the problems of society and continues to believe in the potential of mankind.

Canetti's analyses of society are often presented in satirical form, as they are in *Der Ohrenzeuge* (1974; *Earwitness*). *Earwitness* is a collection of fifty character sketches in which each personality has a number of real human traits that have been combined to create narrow-minded monstrosities. Among such characters are the "Never-must," the "Narrow-smeller," "Name-licker," and the "Woe Administrator." *Earwitness* is a satiric protest against the isolation of contemporary man and his one-sided view of society.

To create such isolated, specialized characters, Canetti uses a combination of dialects and other linguistic differentiations for which he coined the term *acoustic mask*. An acoustic mask is defined as the dialect, word choice, specific idiomatic expressions, and speech habits of a certain character. Canetti also uses a Viennese dialect, which appears in many of his plays and also in *Die Blendung*. Through the use of acoustic masks, one may discover a character's background, social class, and often his social aspiration.

The most important and recurring theme in Canetti's writing is the struggle against death. The death of Canetti's father, which occurred on the same day as the outbreak of war in the Balkans in 1912, deeply impressed him as a youth, subsequently creating a connection between war and death. As a result, Canetti's works often discuss the nature of life and death. According to Canetti, the only way in which life may be fully explored is if it is not defined by death. He considers death unnatural and refutes its inevitability.

Die Hochzeit, Canetti's first published drama, reflects this attitude toward death, and the author approaches death with satire and irony typical of his later works. The play revolves around a group of corrupt, monstrous people who are vying for ownership of the apartment building in which they live. This group is gathered at a wedding celebration where perversions of commitments, greed, and brutality are indicative of a rotten society beyond help. The society must therefore be destroyed, which occurs when an earthquake causes the building to collapse, thus signifying the fall of a helpless community.

A second drama, *Komödie der Eitelkeit*, is based on the psychology of the masses. The first part describes a society in which a law against vanity is decreed, which causes the destruction of all mirrors, films, and photographs. In this case, the mirrors symbolize truth and their destruction is the mass separation from reality. The law is largely accepted by the masses because people who were formerly regarded as outcasts of society are now given a chance to advance.

Loss of one's identity is the price paid throughout the society as the inhabitants adopt their new roles. The world without mirrors becomes one of suspicion and denunciation. Finally, a violent resistance destroys all societal order. As the masses fight over the repossession of mirrors, one sees how easily mass movements can destroy the identity and self-awareness of an individual.

This aspect of the mass psyche is among the many ideas collected in Canetti's *Masse und Macht*, a work resulting from twenty-five years of original research and preparation. *Masse und Macht* can be seen as a protest against tyrannical power and power retainment. Canetti presents his societal analyses by primarily using examples from mythology and primitive folklore.

Die Blendung, Canetti's only novel, may actually be described as an introduction to *Masse und Macht*, for it touches on many themes that are later expanded and more fully developed.

Die Blendung is an allegorical novel depicting an array of individuals driven by their own self-centered motives in contemporary Viennese society. The main characters, the sinologist Peter Kien, his wife Therese, Pfaff, and Fischerle all are examples of the one-sided characters typically used by Canetti. Peter Kien is a recluse intellectual who lives in an apartment with twenty-five thousand books on all subjects. This is

Kien's world, and he is blind to reality and the world apart from his library. Kien's power lies in his books as he regards reading and knowledge as the ultimate truth. Until he is separated from his library and forced into the dark underworld of society, Kien avoids contact with the "masses" as much as possible.

Kien's fear of losing his books to fire motivates him to marry his housekeeper, Therese. He thinks of her as a protector of his books, blind to the fact that she cares only about herself. As Therese takes advantage of her legal rights as Kien's wife, she infringes on his paradise and he realizes his mistake too late. In an act of desperation he calls on his books to form a "united front" against the enemy. Therese remains stolid and forces Kien into the city, where he faces reality and a trial of degradation.

Amidst the underworld, Kien acquires a partner, the dwarf Fischerle. Fischerle represents society's filth and dishonesty, and he succeeds in cheating Kien out of his money.

Kien, by now mentally deranged, returns to his library only to set fire to the books and to himself. This inferno is both his punishment and expiation in which his isolation from the world and his blindness to reality is condemned. However, he is once again united with his books, and he dies with the power of truth and knowledge. Kien had sworn that he would choose death over separation from his books, and this was the option he chose to escape the loneliness, cruelty, and filth of reality.

Fundamental to Kien's actions throughout the novel, which ultimately leads to his demise, is the role of the masses and the mass psyche. Kien's hatred of the masses and his struggle to suppress this within himself is the factor that keeps him secluded in his own "world in the head." As his wife encroaches upon this world, she becomes representative of the threatening masses against which Kien finds himself defenseless. He is thus expelled into an underworld in which he is forced to confront his enemy. Upon the final return to his library, Kien cannot return to his former state of isolation. The inferno that concludes the novel is an act of release in which Kien has, in essence, returned to face the masses. He realizes that he cannot substantiate his scholarly writings with merely individual, isolated experiences. The triumph of Kien's death is presented to shock the reader and illustrates the only way left for him to rescue himself from the reality of society.

Elias Canetti has made a great contribution to literature through his satirical criticism of society and his clear, exact use of language. His sincere desire to improve society is visible in all of his works, and his spirited view of life fills the reader with a hope for the future of mankind. Canetti presents the reader with classic social questions that he examines time and again in his analyses of society. The original theories and solutions that these studies produce illustrate Canetti's gifted abilities and his success as one of the most important thinkers in contemporary literature.

RADO PRIBIC AND
KATHRYNE ROSS

Selected Bibliography

PRIMARY SOURCES

Canetti, Elias. *Auto-da-Fé*. Translated by C. V. Wedgewood. New York: Stein and Day. 1946.

——. *Earwitness*. Translated by Joachim Neugroschel. New York: Seabury Press. 1979.

——. *The Tongue Set Free*. Translated by Joachim Neugroschel. New York: Seabury Press. 1979.

——. *The Wedding*. Translated by Gita Honegger. New York: PAJ Publications. 1986.

SECONDARY SOURCES

Barnouw, Dagmar. *Elias Canetti*. Stuttgart: Metzler, 1979.

"Elias Canetti." *Text+Kritik, Zeitschrift für Literatur*. No. 28. Munich: Heinz Ludwig Arnold, September 1982.

GIOSUE CARDUCCI   *1906*

Giosue Carducci (1835–1907), the first Italian recipient of the Nobel Prize in literature, was born on July 27, 1835, in Valdicastello, a village near Lucca, into an old, impoverished Tuscan family that could trace its ancestry back to the penultimate gonfalonier of the Florentine Republic. The poet's father, Michele, a physician, was an ardent liberal who believed in Italian independence and unity and who had spent time in prison and in exile before his son's birth for having participated in the Romagnol revolt of 1831; his mother, Ildegonda Celli, was an intelligent, loving woman who actively fostered her son's precocity. When Giosue was three years old, his father accepted an appointment as a public health officer in the Tuscan Maremma, a desolate yet beautiful area south of Pisa. During the eleven years that Carducci spent in the Maremma, he was educated at home, where he learned Latin and avidly read the classical Greek, Roman, and Italian authors in his father's library—Homer, Virgil, Horace, Ovid, Phaedrus, Dante, Tasso, and Alfieri—as well as some nineteenth-century Italian literature and significant historical works. Michele Carducci successfully communicated his patriotism and love of literature to his son, but his insistence that Giosue study Alessandro Manzoni's *Osservazioni sulla morale cattolica* (1819; "Observations on Catholic Morals") and Silvio Pellico's *Doveri degli uomini* (1834; "The Duties of Man") led the boy to despise both Catholicism and romanticism and to consider the two inextricably linked.

In 1848, the year in which Italy and much of Europe were convulsed

by a series of popular and nationalist insurrections and revolutions,
Michele Carducci fell victim to political persecution and was forced to
leave home. He took his family to
Florence. There he enrolled his son
in a clerical school, the Scuole degli
Scolopi, where Giosue distinguished
himself in the study of the classics
and of Italian literature and where a
friend introduced him to the works
of Schiller, Scott, and Byron. At the
age of eighteen, Carducci was
awarded a scholarship to the Scuola
Normale at Pisa, from which he
graduated in 1856 after completing a
thesis entitled "Della poesia caval-
leresca del Medio Evo al Mezzogi-
orno d'Europa" ("On Medieval Chi-
valric Poetry in the South of
Europe"). Soon after, Carducci obtained a position teaching rhetoric
at the Gymnasium of San Miniato al
Tedesco and published his first book
of verse, Rime (1857; "Rhymes"), a
collection of imitatively classical
poems exhibiting antiromantic,
anti-Catholic, and fiercely patriotic
sentiments. The Rime are laden with
unwieldy archaisms borrowed from
Dante, Petrarch, Tasso, and others,
yet are enlivened by Carducci's use
of the vigorous Tuscan dialect,
which he continued to turn to account in much of his subsequent
verse.

As a result of his attacks on the
literary, religious, and political Establishment, Carducci incurred the
hostility of the Tuscan governmental authorities, and he felt obliged to
resign his post at San Miniato al
Tedesco in 1857. In the same year,
Carducci lost his brother, Dante,
who committed suicide. His father

died the year after, and Carducci assumed the burden of responsibility
for his mother and younger brother,
Valfredo, who were left virtually
without resources. Since the government had denied Carducci's election
to a teaching post at Arezzo in 1858,
he earned a small income in Florence by tutoring and by collaborating with the publisher Barbera, a
friend for whom he edited various
reprints of Italian classics, work that
added to the range of his learning
and that he continued to do for
many years after his financial wor-
ries were over. He devoted much of
his free time in Florence to a literary
society that he had helped to found,
Gli amici pedanti (The Pedantic
Friends), which pugnaciously strove
to promote classical literary and
civic values. The society's official
organ was Il Poliziano ("Politian"),
a short-lived periodical named in
honor of a fifteenth-century Florentine poet and humanist renowned
for his prodigious classical scholarship. In the six issues that appeared,
Carducci published poetry, fulmi-
nated against romanticism, and
argued the need for a patriotic, classical revival. Toward the end of his
stay in Florence, Carducci married
Elvira Menicucci, fathered a child
(the first of four), and obtained an
appointment from the newly in-
stalled liberal government as a
teacher of Greek at Pistoia.

The year 1860 marked a turning
point in Carducci's life. Shortly after
Garibaldi landed with his thousand
red-shirts in Sicily—an event that
Carducci joyfully celebrated in
Manzonian decasyllables in "Sicilia
e la rivoluzione" ("Sicily and the

Revolution")—Carducci, who was dissatisfied with his job at Pistoia and had been searching for new employment, was appointed to the chair of Italian literature at the prestigious University of Bologna. He continued to reside in Bologna until his death in 1907, a span of forty-six years that saw him become the most widely acclaimed Italian writer of his day.

During his first few years at Bologna, Carducci, who was passionately interested in the unfolding drama of the Risorgimento, endorsed the moderates' plan to seek Italy's unification as a constitutional monarchy under Victor Emmanuel II of the House of Savoy. The poet, however, was so disgusted by the monarchist party's political maneuverings, particularly by its accommodations of Pope Pius IX and of Napoleon III, that he soon defected from that camp and reaffirmed his republican principles. "A Satana" ("To Satan"), written in 1863 and published in 1865 under the patriotic pseudonym Enotrio Romano (which Carducci also used in some of his later works), articulates an impatient radicalism. In that poem, Satan, whom Carducci depicts not as an embodiment of evil but as a joyful pagan god of reason, freedom, science, and art, crushes the forces of oppression and superstition, including all monarchies and the Church. The poem is a somewhat extravagantly enthusiastic hymn to the spirit of progress; it ends with Satan riding triumphantly in a locomotive after he has vanquished Jehovah. "A Satana" enjoyed a predictable *succès de scan-* *dale*, was acclaimed by extreme republicans, and made its author famous. Encouraged by his growing influence, Carducci agitated more and more vigorously against the monarchists and the Church and actively participated in the leadership of the republican *Unione democratica di Bologna* (Democratic Union of Bologna). The authorities responded in 1867 by attempting to transfer the poet away from Bologna, where he had many devoted followers among the students. The charges against Carducci were dropped after he promised to avoid political activity and resigned from the *Consiglio direttivo* (board of managers) of the *Unione democratica di Bologna*, though he insisted on maintaining his membership in the rank and file of the organization.

In 1868 Carducci published *Levia gravia* ("Light and Serious Things"), a collection of poems that, like those in the *Rime*, are elaborately and for the most part pedantically derivative in style. The volume, which was not well received, includes poems expressing Carducci's love of freedom and hatred of tyranny and some lyrical verse that is sorrowfully meditative in tone, including several sonnets concerning the death of Carducci's brother. Three years later, Barbera published a collected edition of Carducci's *Poesie* (1871; "Poems") divided into three sections. The first section, *Decennali* ("Decennia"), which contains the republican and anti-Catholic poems Carducci had written after 1860, is the most interesting and inventive part of the volume: In it, Carducci, inspired by the example of Victor Hugo's *Les Châtiments* (1853; "Chastisements"), produced forcible invective relatively unencumbered by classical ornamentation. The other two sections were reprints of earlier publications: a shortened, restructured version of *Levia gravia* and a collection of *Juvenilia*, which is the title Carducci used to designate all the verse that he had written before his arrival at Bologna. The volume came out at a time when Carducci was shaken by a double misfortune; in 1870 he had lost both his mother and his only son, Dante, named after the poet's brother. The death of Dante, Carducci's favorite child, inspired him to write two moving elegies: "Funere mersit acerbo" ("Plunged into Untimely, Bitter Death"—the words of the title, a quotation from Virgil's *Aeneid*, once commonly were used as a funerary inscription), and "Pianto antico" ("Ancient Lament"). Carducci's personal life was further transformed when he fell in love with an admirer, Carolina Cristofori-Piva, who is evoked throughout the "Aeolian," "Doric," and "Alexandrian" odes (as Carducci called them) that comprise *Primavere elleniche* ("Hellenic Springtimes"), published in 1872. Carolina Cristofori-Piva was Carducci's mistress from 1872 until her death in 1881, inspiring some of his best-known poems and a passionate correspondence that expresses with remarkable vividness and directness many of Carducci's most deeply personal desires, feelings, and thoughts.

The changes in Carducci's life in the early 1870s tinged his poetry with a new intensity of feeling to which the reading public responded very favorably upon the publication in 1873 of *Nuove poesie* ("New Poems"), which betray the influence of Victor Hugo and of certain German romantics, notably Heinrich Heine. Ironically, at the time Carducci wrote *Nuove poesie* he still was an avowed enemy of romanticism, which he attacked in that book in such poems as "Classicismo e romanticismo" ("Classicism and Romanticism") and the parodic "Anacreontica romantica" ("Romantic Anacreontic"). Carducci considered romanticism antithetical to his pagan, classical, and republican ideal of culture: He condemned it not only for its being foreign and Nordic, but also for its glorification of medievalism, feudalism, mysticism, and Christianity. While Carducci was not unaware of the links between romanticism and liberalism in Italy and elsewhere, he persisted in dismissing the romantic movement as a whole as an instrument of political and cultural repression. Yet his own turbulent, sentimental nature was in many ways attuned to romanticism, as the *Nuove poesie* attest. While writing that work, Carducci discovered that the romantic ballad, a genre he previously had despised, offered him a rich source of artistic inspiration, as did romantic lyricism, the romantic epic, and romantic irony. As Carducci grew older, he began to take a more favorable view of the romantic poets and increasingly perceived his literary vocation in romantic terms, partly modeling himself on that fellow enemy of Napoleon III, Victor Hugo, whom he hailed in a necrological article of May 1885 as "vate dell'umanità nel secolo decimonono" ("bard of humanity in the nineteenth century")—an epithet that recalls the one Carducci sought and earned for himself: "vate d'Italia" ("bard of Italy"). Like Hugo, Carducci eventually came to regard the mission of the poet as that of a seer and prophet serving as a guide to mankind. Toward the end of his career, Carducci learned to admire even Manzoni, whom he once had denounced as a wholly pernicious influence on Italian literature.

As Carducci's views of romanticism evolved, so did his political perspective. In 1878 he met the queen of Italy, Margherita of Savoy, and was so delighted by her company and by the compliments she addressed him that he published an encomiastic ode "Alla Regina d'Italia" ("To the Queen of Italy") shortly thereafter, thus incurring the contempt of many republicans. Though he argued in an essay entitled "Eterno femminino regale" (1882; "Eternally Regally Feminine") that the ode was a purely personal tribute to the queen rather than a political statement, the very arguments put forward in that essay reveal that Carducci had begun to hold the ideas of the constitutional monarchists in higher regard. In 1890 the poet broke completely with republicanism: His ode "Piemonte" ("Piedmont"), published in September of that year, effectively proclaimed his allegiance to the House of Savoy. The government rewarded Carducci in December 1890 by making him a senator.

Throughout the late 1870s and the 1880s Carducci wrote prolifically. In 1877 he produced his first collection of *Odi barbare* ("Barbarian Odes"), poems written in classical rather than Italian meters that were followed by *Nuove odi barbare* ("New Barbarian Odes") in 1882 and by *Terze odi barbare* ("Third Barbarian Odes") in 1889. Carducci's other projects of the period included numerous literary studies, contributions to several periodicals including the fashionable *Cronaca bizantina* ("Byzantine Chronicle"), and various books of verse: *Intermezzo* (1878; "Interlude"), Carducci's last attack on the romantic school and his last satirical poem apart from a piece entitled "A proposito del processo Fadda" ("On the Fadda Trial," written in 1879); *Giambi ed epodi* (1882; "Iambics and Epodes"), an edition of the political and satirical poetry Carducci had written from 1867 through 1879; *Ça ira* (1883; "It Will Be All Right"), an interesting historical poem whose title echoes that of a famous French revolutionary song and whose subject is the period of turmoil in France that culminated in the Battle of Valmy (September 1792); and *Rime nuove* (1887; "New Rhymes"), which combined extracts from *Nuove poesie* with a substantial amount of new poetry.

Odi barbare, which Carducci reorganized and republished in a definitive, two-book edition in 1903, is widely believed to constitute his most significant contribution to Italian literature. Carducci, who had developed a deeper understanding of classical and especially of Greek poetry as a result of his study of

Shelley and Goethe, conceived the idea of roughly duplicating the quantitative meters of Greek and Latin verse in Italian, as Gabriello Chiabrera had tried to do in the seventeenth century, by using a system of versification based on unrhymed lines of different lengths whose grammatical rhythms determine the pattern of stress. Carducci wanted to produce the kind of verse that might have been written in antiquity by a "barbarian" who had adapted classical prosody to his own idiom. A number of the *Odi barbare* are classical in theme as well as in meter, offering lyrical-epic evocations of Italy's former glory, as do "Dinanzi alle terme di Caracalla" ("In Front of the Baths of Caracalla") and "Alle fonti del Clitumno" ("By the Sources of Clitumnus"). Throughout *Odi barbare*, Carducci laments the passing of the ancient Roman world but also expresses fervent hopes for its renewal in verse whose classical dress often exhibits a romantic coloration. Many of the poems in the collection conjure up imposingly wide historical vistas linking remote periods and places, but the one that is perhaps most famous of all, "Alla stazione in una mattina d'autunno" ("At the Station on an Autumn Morning"), focuses on a distinctly up-to-date scene, describing the poet's separation from his mistress in a railway station. Whatever the setting of the *Odi barbare*, the effect they produce is curiously modern, owing to their lack of rhyme, their unusual meters, and the variable number of syllables in the lines.

Though Carducci occasionally evinced contempt for traditional Italian verse forms during the years he was writing *Odi barbare*, he did not hesitate to utilize them, notably in *Rime nuove*. Some of Carducci's most memorable poetry appears in this volume, including several pieces that nostalgically evoke his youthful wanderings in the Maremma: "Idillio maremmano" ("Idyll of the Maremma," previously published in the *Nuove poesie* of 1873), "Davanti San Guido" ("Before San Guido"), and "Traversando la Maremma pisana" ("Crossing the Pisan Maremma"), better known under the title "Traversando la Maremma toscana" ("Crossing the Tuscan Maremma"). After the publication of *Rime nuove* and of the three original collections of *Odi barbare*, the aging Carducci devoted himself largely to works of erudition, composing treatises on Tasso, Parini, and Leopardi, editing major collections of literary and historical texts, and preparing a collected edition of his own works that was completed after his death. His last volume of verse, *Rime e ritmi* ("Rhymes and Rhythms," published in December 1898 though dated 1899), contains poems in both "barbarian" and traditional meters and bears witness to a growing conservatism: In it, the former radical republican defends the Italian monarchy and its aggressively nationalistic and colonialist policies under autocratic prime minister Francesco Crispi. One of the most famous poems in *Rime e ritmi*, "La chiesa di Polenta" ("The Church at Polenta"), reveals that Carducci had begun to take an indulgent view of the religious as well as the political Establishment. This mystical ode, which caused a furor when first published in 1897 in the periodical *L'Italia*, led many people to think that its author had converted to Christianity, a supposition that Carducci emphatically denied. In reality, his new attitude toward the Christian religion, which had been evolving since the late 1880s, was based on a reassessment of its role in history and on a growing Mazzinian conviction that only faith in God could provide the spiritual bulwark of the Italian state. Whereas Carducci once had opposed Christianity because he had considered it an enemy of progressive, enlightened government, he now perceived it as a needed source of national solidarity. In both cases, he was motivated primarily by patriotism, which is the keynote of so much of Carducci's poetry and which informs even the final, valedictory poem in *Rime e ritmi*, "Congedo" ("Envoy"), where Carducci made it clear to the public that his career as a poet was effectively over.

Carducci died at Bologna on February 16, 1907, just over two months after he was awarded the Nobel Prize in literature. He is remembered today principally as the author of *Odi barbare*, as a spokesman of the Risorgimento, and as the chief instigator and oracle of Italy's nineteenth-century classical revival. His reputation has declined greatly since World War II, partly because the bellicose patriotic rhetoric of his later political verse in some ways anticipates that which prevailed in Fascist Italy and partly because his poetry in general is marred by an excessively thick veneer of bookish learning and verbal ornament. He is at his best in those of his poems that achieve the classical purity and simplicity he always espoused. Though the prestige Carducci once enjoyed has faded, he remains an important figure in the history of European letters, for he significantly influenced the development of Italian poetry in the late nineteenth and early twentieth centuries.

GEORGE M. ROSA

Selected Bibliography

PRIMARY SOURCES

Carducci, Giosue. *Edizione nazionale delle opere di Giosue Carducci*. 30 vols. Bologna: N. Zanichelli, 1935–40.

———. *Edizione nazionale delle opere di Giosue Carducci: Lettere*. 22 vols. Bologna: N. Zanichelli, 1938–68.

Translations

Carducci, Giosue. *The Barbarian Odes of Giosue Carducci*. Translated by William Fletcher Smith. Menasha, Wis.: G. Banta, 1939.

———. *The Lyrics and Rhythms of Giosue Carducci*. Translated by William Fletcher Smith. Colorado Springs, Colo.: Privately printed, 1942.

———. *The New Lyrics of Giosue Carducci*. Translated by William Fletcher Smith. Colorado Springs, Colo.: Privately printed, 1942.

———. *Political and Satiric Verse of Giosue Carducci*. Translated by William Fletcher Smith. Colorado

Springs, Colo.: Privately printed, 1942.

SECONDARY SOURCES

Biagini, Mario. *Il poeta della terza Italia: Vita di Giosue Carducci*. Milan: U. Mursia, 1961.

Bickersteth, Geoffrey L. *Carducci. A Selection of his Poems, with Verse Translations, Notes, and Three Introductory Essays*. New York: Longmans, Green, 1913.

Jeanroy, Alfred. *Giosue Carducci: l'homme et le poète*. Paris: Champion, 1911.

Klopp, Charles. "Giosue Carducci." In *European Writers*. Edited by George Stade et al. Vol. 7. New York: Scribner, 1985. Pp. 1495–1516.

Robecchi, Franco. *Carducci poeta barbaro*. Milan: Cooperativa Libraria, 1981.

Williams, Orlo. *Giosue Carducci*. New York: Houghton Mifflin, 1914.

WINSTON CHURCHILL *1953*

Sir Winston Leonard Spencer Churchill (1874–1965), statesman, soldier, journalist, historian, and parliamentarian, was born at Blenheim Palace, the elder son of Lord Randolph Spencer Churchill, politician, and his socialite wife, the former Jennie Jerome of New York City. Born prematurely, he endured an unhappy childhood in which he received constant and sincere affection only from his nanny. Churchill entered the prestigious public school, Harrow, where he survived as an undistinguished student, achieved a better record later at the Royal Military College at Sandhurst, and finally earned a commission on February 20, 1895, into the Fourth Queen's Own Hussars. An aristocratic background and social position enabled Churchill to chart an independent military career and, at the same time, begin the journalistic activities that sustained him financially throughout his public career.

Although a newly commissioned junior officer, Churchill, granted a special leave of absence, journeyed to Cuba to cover the Spanish-American War for the *Daily Graphic*. Called from Cuba, Churchill joined his British regiment in India, where he saw action on the northwest frontier (1896–97). Through the intercession of his London connections, Churchill joined Lord Kitchener's army in the Sudan (1898), resigning the following year to seek election to Parliament as the Conservative party candidate for Oldham. From this unsuccessful venture Churchill returned to South Africa, first as a war correspondent, later as a military officer. He was finally captured by the Boers and held as a prisoner of war but escaped and returned to Britain. All of these exploits added to his political capital and in 1900 Churchill was returned as a Conservative member of Parliament for Oldham.

During this period Churchill wrote press dispatches from Cuba (1895) and from India, the Sudan, and South Africa (1897–99). In 1898 he published *The Story of the Malakind Field Force*, a romantic and imperialistic impression of his Indian military experience. *The River War* (2 vols., 1898) was "an historical account of the reconquest of the Sudan." This was followed in 1900 by the publication of *London to Ladysmith via Pretoria, Ian Hamilton's March*, and his only novel, *Savrola*, revealing Churchill's habit of mind and the shape of his early ideals. *Savrola* is an imaginative fulfillment of his self-portrait—one revealed through his journalistic-historical memoirs—and one which refocuses the writer's position as both participant and observer. This initial phase of Churchill's writing reflects an intellectual pattern worked out in his later historical works—the man of action shaped by imperial notions of patriotism and individuality. In a true case of nature imitating art, Churchill became the embodiment of how his own aristocratic principles were able to flourish in a parliamentary democracy.

Entering Parliament as a Tory in 1901, Churchill crossed benches in 1904 to membership in the Liberal party over the issue of free trade. After a succession of government positions he became home secretary (1910–11). Inheriting a family tradition as a parliamentary radical, Churchill became a filiopietistic biographer with the 1906 publication of *Lord Randolph Churchill* (2 vols.). In this effort to resurrect the reputation of his father, Churchill aggressively embraced Lord Randolph's political principles and advanced the idea that the individual shapes the course of history. In addition he published his early speeches and travel books: *Mr. Broderick's Army* (1903), *For Free Trade* (1906), *My African Journey* (1908), *Liberalism and Social Problems* (1909), and *The People's Right* (1910). These volumes chart Churchill's odyssey from soldier to politician.

In 1908 Churchill received his first cabinet appointment as the Liberal party's president of the Board of Trade, and on September 12 married Clementine Ogilvy, eldest daughter of the Seventh Earl of Airlie and recent widow of Col. Sir Henry Hozier. She and Churchill had five children: Diana (1909–63), Sarah (b. 1914), Marigold (1918–21), Mary (b. 1922), and Randolph (1911–68), who in keeping with family tradition wrote the first two volumes of the standard biography of Sir Winston, now being completed by Martin Gilbert. Churchill's family life, especially the relationship he shared with Clementine, who died in 1977, are recounted in daughter Lady Soames's *Clementine Churchill* (1979), which details Clementine's role in this dynamic political family.

Churchill's early political career reveals a pattern of controversial actions and positions. As home secretary, Churchill used troops in an effort to save the lives of rioting Welsh miners at Tonypandy and then led troops in a fire fight to defeat a group of anarchists in Sidney Street, London. Churchill's prominence in both incidents brought charges of irresponsibility. Nevertheless, at this time Churchill did learn from Lloyd George a "language of Radicalism," which acted as a counterpoint to his Whig notions of aristocratic responsibility. Although he certainly accepted the legitimacy of class distinctions, Churchill did show a concern for the poor and underprivileged. His efforts at reform under the guidance of Lloyd George—the Mines Act of 1911, prison reform, early shop closing laws, and issues of law and public order—were in accord with the Liberal party's political agenda. In an effort to improve conditions for working people Churchill took an active leadership role as home secretary.

Although a home secretary is concerned mostly with domestic issues, the additional responsibility of that office for some areas of national security fitted in with Churchill's military interests and experience. Moreover, as became his custom, Churchill extended his cabinet mandate to include an interest on the Committee of Imperial Defence. During this period he was an invited observer to the Kaiser's army maneuvers. His observations plus his appreciation of German aggressiveness during the Agadir crisis, 1911 (where Germany dispatched a gunboat to frustrate French designs on Morocco) led Churchill to speculate on the necessity for British military preparedness, a theme that dominates the course of his political career and shapes much of his writings.

Churchill's appointment by Prime Minister Asquith as first lord of the Admiralty (October 25, 1911), recognized his interest, ability, energy, and tenaciousness to develop a strong British military presence. As first sea lord Churchill immediately embarked on a program to strengthen and modernize the navy. In this process he encountered resistance from entrenched members of the naval establishment. Personnel changes as well as strategic modifications, such as the introduction of the *Queen Elizabeth*-class of oil-fired battleships and a reconstituted Royal Navy Air Service, highlighted Churchill's efforts to ready the navy for the inevitable war with Germany. Churchill's four-year tenure as first lord of the Admiralty ended during World War I in 1915 as a result of what is known as the Gallipoli debacle. The Gallipoli campaign was a major military operation designed to seize control of the Gallipoli Peninsula, thus giving the British control of the Dardanelles. The Gallipoli plan was an effort to reshape the direction of World War I and its failure, with its immense loss of life and material, damaged for a considerable time Churchill's political career. However, Churchill's strategic vision of opening a Balkan front to cut through the war of attrition on the French front was later vindicated by military historians Lord Ismay and Captain Roskill, who rightly place the failure for the Dardanelles campaign to the vascillations of Lord Kitchener, who neglected to carry out Churchill's plan for joint army and navy action.

After Churchill resigned as sea lord, he joined, as a lieutenant colonel, the 6th Royal Scots Fusiliers in France, while retaining his seat in Parliament. When Lloyd George became prime minister in 1916, he recalled Churchill to serve as minister of munitions (1917). Later Churchill became secretary for war and air (1918–21). In the November 1922 general elections he lost his parliamentary seat.

Now out of parliament, Churchill focused his attention on journalism, writing a series of articles on the "Great War." These articles, begun February 1923, were later gathered together and published in book form as the first four volumes of the *World Crisis* (1923–29). *The World Crisis* and *The Unknown War: The Eastern Front* (1931) together form an autobiographical and self-justifying historical narrative, concentrating on the significance of Churchill's actions in the shaping of wartime policy. His announced intent in the writing of these works was to "make a contribution to history" and "to expose [his viewpoint] to historical judgment." The third volume of this series reveals the changing nature of his historical writing reflecting his recent reading of Daniel Defoe's *Memoirs of a Cavalier*. Churchill writes:

In this delightful work the author hangs the chronicle and discussion of great military events upon the thread of the personal experiences of an individual. I was immensely encouraged to find that I had been unconsciously following with halting steps the example of so great a master of narrative (Introduction to vol. 3).

The recognition of this literary influence is indicative of Churchill's intellectual development and his understanding of historiography. "His gift for exposition, for disentangling the essential from the ephemera of politics and war as he looked back upon the panorama in which he had featured only in a few scenes, makes the purely historical part of his narrative glow as vividly as that of a Gibbon or a Macaulay and outshine the full lights shed by lesser writers" (Ashley 1968, 73). Churchill's grand narrative sweep in these volumes comes from his method of composition and his immersion in the British historical writing tradition of Robertson, Gibbon, and Macaulay.

Over the course of his career, Churchill developed a method of historical writing that enabled him to produce a narrative that clearly resonated with his own voice. In addition to setting his subject within a broad theme, Churchill stressed the element of grandeur as he highlighted the strengths and weaknesses of his principal characters. Surprisingly, he dictated much of his writing, cognizant of its narrative qualities, made clever use of documentation, and presented arguments on many sides of issues to create a work that for him would let the history speak for itself. Later Churchill would employ research assistants to provide material, to appreciate his performance, and to check out his facts. If possible, Churchill demanded to see a draft in type of each section when written, considerably raising the cost of production. Churchill's expansive imagination and oratorical style in his well-arranged books combine with his own experience of events and men, especially in war and politics, to shape his understanding of what had occurred and how the participants felt when they contemplated the actions taken.

After returning to Parliament in 1924, Churchill rejoined the Conservative party, rising to the senior cabinet post of chancellor of the Exchequer. This post allowed Churchill to don Lord Randolph's robe of office and thus, to his mind, restore his father's reputation. An effort to return to the gold standard marked Churchill's ingenious budgets. Nevertheless, his management of the economy did not fundamentally change Britain's position in the postwar international economy. During the general strike of 1926 he assumed a vigorous antistrike posture as editor of the *British Gazette*. With his inflammatory rhetoric he alienated the labor voters and Social Democrats in much the same manner as his actions did when home secretary during the Tonypandy affair. Nevertheless, Churchill did try to solve coal industry dislocation and did seek to lower tax rates, arguing these actions would help the laboring classes. Churchill was out of government in 1929.

The 1930s were a turbulent period for Churchill. Seen as a prophet

in the wilderness, especially after his 1931 resignation from Baldwin's "shadow cabinet," Churchill maintained a nineteenth-century imperialist posture. He was at odds with Conservative plans for dominion status for India and was almost alone in supporting Edward VIII in his desire to marry divorcée Wallis Simpson and to avoid abdication. Churchill again warned of German rearming and ambitions and from 1933 until 1939 consistently argued for British military preparedness. Over the issues of India and Germany, Churchill endured political isolation.

During this period he published several works: *A Roving Commission* (1930), *My Early Life* (1930), *India* (1931), *Thoughts and Adventures* (*Amid These Storms*) (1932), *Great Contemporaries* (1937), *While England Slept* (*Arms and the Covenant*) (1938) and *Step by Step* (1939), as well as numerous newspaper and magazine articles. His primary intellectual achievement of this period was the biography of his ancestor John Churchill, the first Duke of Marlborough.

Marlborough: His Life and Times (1933–38) is a four-volume study of exceptional skill and historical understanding. Churchill, who had unrestricted access to the muniment room at Blenheim Palace, conceived this study as the biography of a hero who influenced the course of British history. Yet this work proved problematic because Marlborough was a man whose actions did not coincide with Churchill's own notions of loyalty and political principle. The strength of Churchill's writing comes, however, from his profound understanding of political motivation and the waging of war. On the one hand, Churchill shrewdly scrutinizes the actions of men and, on the other hand, offers some simplistic interpretations on the Age of Anne, the last Stuart monarch (1702–14). *Marlborough* resonates Whig interpretations as Churchill sets up a "harmony of interests" to evaluate Marlborough's actions either as pragmatist or principled hero. In addition, this biography functions "not only as (looking back to the 1920s) a critique of the World War I generals and (looking ahead to the 1940s) a portrait of a heroic ideal Churchill would try to emulate, but also as another expression of Churchill's pervasive theme of the 1930s: the hideousness of modern life" (Weidhorn 1974, 112). In his effort to do the utmost justice to his ancestor's reputation, Churchill wrote a political and military history that in many ways explained his own political thought and military strategy.

Churchill's days in the political wilderness ended when the reality of German ambitions became clear with the invasion of Poland in 1939. He returned to government as first lord of the Admiralty. Prime Minister Chamberlain, weakened by the failure of the Munich agreement of 1938, nevertheless held on until May 10, 1940, when debate in the House of Commons demanded a coalition government. Churchill, whose dire prophecies had come true, now became prime minister. Of this he writes, "At last I had authority to give directions over the whole scene.

I felt as if I were walking with destiny. . . ." (*The Second World War*, Vol. 1 1948, 526–27). Thus Churchill took center stage on the world scene, fulfilling the grandeur of his own historical imagination.

Churchill embodied British determination and valor. He led his nation on to victory, was accorded the hero's garland, yet suffered defeat in the postwar election of 1945. He became leader of the opposition and was received as a world statesman. He finally returned to power in 1951.

Wartime and the immediate postwar period saw some of Churchill's most important and inspiring speeches, which he published: *Blood, Sweat, and Tears* (*Into Battle*) (1941); *The Unrelenting Struggle* (1942); *The End of the Beginning* (1943); *Onwards to Victory* (1944); *The Dawn of Liberation* (1945); *Victory* (1946); *Secret Session Speeches* (1946). From 1948 to 1953 he published his six-volume *The Second World War*. More personal than his earlier volumes on World War I, Churchill clearly set out his desire in this work to make a contribution to history from the standpoint of the British prime minister and minister of defence. These volumes reflected his concern for European unity facing a powerful, postwar Communist Russia and his hope that the United States would handle with maturity its obligations as the leading world power. Churchill tried not to accept the reality of Britain having survived the war only to lose her empire.

Knighted and awarded the Nobel Prize in literature in 1953,

Churchill pursued a moderate Conservative policy for Britain. Becoming increasingly deaf and suffering from poor health, Churchill was persuaded to release the reigns of power, and he resigned the prime ministership in 1955. Nevertheless, he remained a member of Parliament until retiring in 1964. He died January 25, 1965, at the age of ninety.

During this final period of his career, Churchill published several volumes of speeches: *The Sinews of Peace* (1949); *Europe Unite* (1950); *In the Balance* (1952); *Stemming the Tide* (1954); and *The Unwritten Alliance* (1961). These speeches reflect Churchill's embrace of Edmund Burke's "slow and noiseless" organic growth of the British political process as the appropriate model for the world to adopt. "The story of postwar diplomacy—of British alertness, American participation, western firmness, Korea instead of Munich—is therefore for Churchill a parable illustrating how men and nations should have acted in the 1930s, and the history of Europe in his lifetime is a narrative of redemption" (Weidhorn, 182). But only with the death of Joseph Stalin does Churchill with his belief in the "great man of history" theory accept the validity of "peaceful coexistence" as a way of achieving accommodation and reconciliation.

His last major work, *A History of the English-Speaking Peoples* (1956–58), was designed to stress the common heritage of Great Britain and the United States of America. In this work Churchill presents "a personal view of the processes whereby the English-speaking peoples throughout the world have achieved their distinctive position and character." To argue for an historical special relationship between Great Britain and the United States, Churchill focuses on war and politics in setting out a narrative of events rather than an evolution of ideas. The history that Churchill fashions perpetuates myths of British imperial greatness. The Constitution of the United States, for example, is presented as "a reaffirmation of faith in the principles painfully evolved over centuries by the English-speaking peoples." The British navy is credited for "the best part of a century . . . [as] the stoutest guarantee of freedom for the Americas." This effort, however, does not relieve American suspicion of British imperial aims, rather it raises them. *A History of the English-Speaking Peoples* neglects those people whose ancestors did not come from the British Isles, nor does it fully consider the importance of egalitarianism to the American mind.

JAMES REIBMAN

Selected Bibliography

PRIMARY SOURCES

Churchill, Winston. *The Collected Works of Sir Winston Churchill.* London: Library of Imperial History, 1973–75.

James, Robert R., ed. *Winston Churchill: His Complete Speeches: 1897–1963.* London: Bowker, 1974.

Wolff, Michael, ed. *The Collected Essays of Sir Winston Churchill.* London: Library of Imperial History, 1976.

SECONDARY SOURCES

Ashley, Maurice. *Churchill as Historian.* London: Martin Secker & Warburg, 1968.

Churchill, Randolph, S. *Companion Volumes.* Vol. 1, Part 1; Vol. II, Part 3. Boston: Houghton Mifflin, 1967–69.

———. *The Official Biography of Sir Winston Churchill.* Vols. 1–2, Boston: Houghton Mifflin, 1966–67.

Gilbert, Martin. *Companion Volumes.* Vol. III, Part 1; Vol. V, Part 3. Boston: Houghton Mifflin, 1973+.

———. *The Official Biography of Sir Winston Churchill.* Vols. 3–8. Boston: Houghton Mifflin, 1971–88.

Manchester, William. *The Last Lion: Winston Spencer Churchill: Visions of Glory 1874–1932.* Boston: Little Brown, 1983.

———. *The Last Lion: Winston Spencer Churchill: Alone 1932–1940.* Boston: Little Brown, 1988.

Weidhorn, Manfred. *Churchill's Rhetoric and Political Discourse.* Lanham, Md.: University Press of America, 1987.

Weidhorn, Manfred. *Sword and Pen: A Survey of the Writings of Sir Winston Churchill.* Albuquerque: University of New Mexico, 1974.

Woods, F. B. *A Bibliography of the Works of Sir Winston Churchill.* London: Kaye & Ward, 1969.

GRAZIA DELEDDA *1926*

Grazia Deledda (1871–1936), the second Italian citizen to be awarded the Nobel Prize in literature, was born in Nuoro, Sardinia, September 27, 1871, and died in Cervia, Emilia-Romagna, on August 15, 1936.

The fourth of six children of a well-to-do, middle-class family, Deledda received the standard elementary education permitted girls of that era. She was self-educated and in effect read everything available from the Bible and Homer through the Russian writers Tolstoy, Gorky, and Dostoyevski, to the Englishman Thomas Hardy, the French authors Sue and Hugo, and the Italians Negri, Guerrini, Manzoni, Verga, Carducci, and D'Annunzio. This rather eclectic literary exposure and lack of formal training resulted in an inability of the critics to categorize her in a convenient literary package. Deledda's contributions were unique in many respects.

Deledda had an innate sensitivity to characterizations, a keen psychological insight, and a fundamental gift as a good storyteller.

At age seventeen she began a literary career with the publication of short stories and poetry in a Sardinian magazine. Deledda's collaboration with magazines and newspapers throughout Italy lasted her entire career. She maintained a lengthy, lively correspondence with publishers, editors, and a few contemporary authors, including Federigo Tozzi and Marino Moretti. On January 11, 1900, she married Palmiro Madesani, a civil servant in the Ministry of Finance. They moved to Rome in April 1900, and she lived there the rest of her life, raising two children, writing constantly, and maintaining strong contacts with her native Sardinia.

Even though Roman literary circles were now available to her, Deledda remained essentially shy and secluded in a domestic atmosphere.

Deledda's literary life was dedicated to narrative, and the years 1900 to 1920 emerged as both productive and successful. From this period came her greatest novels: *Elias Portolu* (1900), *Cenere* (1903; "Ashes"), *Colombi e sparvieri* (1912; "Pigeons and Hawks"), *Canne al vento* (1913; "Reeds in the Wind"), *Marianna Sirca* (1915), *L'incendio nell'uliveto* (1917; "Fire in the Olive Orchard"), *La madre* (1920; "The Mother") and the collected short stories *Chiaroscuro* (1912; "Light and Shade"). Her autobiographical work *Cosima* was published posthumously in 1937. Deledda's lengthy career saw the production of fifty-nine novels and short story collec-

tions, three books of essays, two dramas, one edition of poetry, and one translation.

It has been somewhat rare that a writer's early environment should be such a determining factor in the development of her sensitivity and imagination. Sardinia was the matrix of and natural stimulus to Deledda's creativity. Her relative isolation from formal literary and cultural contacts during her youth appeared to set the tone of her creative thought for her entire career. Sardinia, its landscape, traditions, customs, and morality were the constant inspiration for Deledda. Her style of writing corresponded perfectly to her private life, to her innate way of seeing, observing, intuiting, and describing the reality around her.

The fact that Deledda was primarily self-taught may have delayed the maturation of her best qualities. However, she interested herself in the life and customs of her Sardinian people and profoundly loved her native environment. Deledda's ability to watch and interpret, to observe and dream fused the real and imaginary worlds into the productive, sensitive disposition of the author.

Two basic themes recurred in Deledda's narrative writing. The first was regional, that is, the landscape or setting. The second was the dominant moral theme. Each motif had variations within particular stories, but both emerged as the essential foundation of her work.

The regional background of many Deledda novels included extremely accurate details of Sardinian flora and fauna, villages, and houses. The natural details set a nostalgic tone or atmosphere for her stories. Passing from pure description, Deledda used this theme as a counterpoint to the feelings of her characters. There was often a correlation between the setting and the state of mind of the protagonist. It amounted to a fusion of nature and personality that helped her create characters that are emotionally convincing and sharply drawn. Deledda's Sardinia was a poor, rugged country that generated stories and characters as much from its historic and geographic factors as from the author's own particular experiences and memories. There was no novel or short story that did not present a setting transcribed from Deledda's autobiographical reality.

The austere figures of old people were to become a frequent example of the complementary interplay of nature and character. Rugged as the landscape, inspired by the Bible and by Deledda's disposition to cast the nobility and dignity of their character in their physical features, the old people were the bearers of ancient wisdom and tradition. Effix, the old servant of the three sisters in *Canne al vento* (1913), and Dionisio, the aged uncle who represented the continuity of the family in *Annalena Bilsini* (1927), were two such personalities.

The second theme, that of morality, was a basic foundation element of almost all of Deledda's novels. The moral theme became a vital substance in character and setting and generated action and conflict in the stories. The conflict was between good and evil in its various formats of guilt, passion, remorse, punishment, desperation, sin, and redemption. The reality of a character's setting was fixed by factors outside his control: family tradition, fate, and religion. The violation or infringement of the real or perceived restrictions was sinful and accompanied by terror or fear.

Deledda's concept of Divine Providence and Justice for the inevitable wrongs of man was an Old Testament vision of the proud and vindictive God of Moses. As the critic Natalino Sapegno indicated in his preface to the Mondadori edition of Deledda's works (p. xx), the characteristics of this morality were not complex. They were instinctive and primeval, tied to the ethnic background by an elementary concept of existence. More than religious superstition, they were fatalistic and naively pessimistic.

Both prevalent themes, the regional and the moral, tended to be accommodated in the atmosphere of Deledda's stories. They reinforced each other and became the lyric root of her narrative style.

Honesty, simplicity, love, serenity, strength of the natural order, and morality were woven into the fabric of the themes and plots drawn from Deledda's provincial Sardinian background. Her robust style remained faithful to her origins and did not yield to the influence of contemporary literary currents or schools. Deledda's authentic spontaneity and instinctive originality created emotional characters whose stories were related with a simple, instinctive lyricism.

Deledda reached maturity in her style with the publication of her novel *Elias Portolu* in 1900 in serial form in the magazine *Nuova Antologia* ("New Anthology") and as a single work in 1903. (For complete bibliographical citations of her works, see Lombardi, 1979, pp. 115–118.)

Elias Portolu brought together descriptive elements and psychological drama. It was a critically successful analysis of the self-torment created by the weak central character who was unwilling to confront life and his feelings and act resolutely. Elias, a shepherd, returned from prison and fell in love with the fiancée of his brother. Unable to declare his love, Elias decided to become a priest. Maddalena, having married Elias's brother, continued to meet Elias and became pregnant by him. Passion and guilt went hand in hand after their son was born. Yet even after the death of his brother, Elias would not leave the seminary to marry Maddalena. Rejected by the father of her child, Maddalena married a rich relative, who in turn showed great affection for the baby. It was only with the death of the child that Elias was able to feel free from human passions. His weakness created sin and remorse and heroic psychological torment.

Illicit love also moved the story of *Cenere*. The married farmer Anania courted and seduced the young Olì. Before the birth of their son, he sent her into a desperately poor mountain home, where Olì cared for the boy by herself. Unable to carry on, Olì brought her son to the house of his father, where the boy was taken in, raised, and educated by his father's wife. When the son was about to marry a rich young lady, he remembered his mother and went to find her, poor, ill, and alone. He decided to care for his mother at the sacrifice of his own marriage. Olì, who could not convince him to forget her, committed suicide so as not to disturb her son's life. Olì's destiny was classically tragic. Her resignation to a desperate fate was stoic, and representative of the mature writing of Deledda.

The collection of twenty-two short stories in *Chiaroscuro* contained some of her most notable efforts around the motif of good versus evil. The regional theme dominated both in terms of natural phenomena and peasant customs and traditions in carnivals, religious holidays, and processions. Deledda's short story characters allowed her the mixture of regional and moral themes that would represent the best of her literary production.

The plot of the novel *Canne al vento* centered around the biblical figure of Efix, the old servant of the three Pintor sisters, and the motifs of fatalism, loyalty, remorse, and expiation. Years before, Efix had accidentally killed the ladies' father, and his humble dedication to the sisters was his silent atonement for the sin. The appearance of their nephew Giacinto compounded the sisters' financial and personal problems. The relationship of servant to master, the personalities of the women, and the resolution of the problems in an atmosphere of serene resignation to fate, all contributed to the power of one of Deledda's narrative masterpieces.

The entanglement of love and remorse, sin and temptation, fear and scandal motivated the novel *La madre*. Biblical characters contended with the ghosts of evil and sin in a tragedy magnified by the solitude of the setting. Paulo, a young parish priest, was tempted by the love of the rich Agnese. His mother, who had sacrificed much for his education and career, helped arouse her son's conscience so that he was able to free himself from the passion he felt. The tense resolution of the plot during Sunday mass, when Agnese had threatened to reveal all publicly, and did not, and the mother's death in anticipation of the scandal, was loaded with the symbolism that Deledda's narrative adopted so successfully.

The consistent and coherent creativity of Deledda's narrative, based on the fundamental regional and moral themes illustrated briefly above, enabled her to join the pantheon of great Italian writers. She overcame the relative isolation of a provincial background to speak to a national and international audience in terms that everyone could understand and appreciate. Recognition of this with the Nobel Prize in literature in 1926 indicated that Grazia Deledda went beyond descriptive folklore and setting, by means of keen psychological insight and sensitive characterizations, to present the generic spiritual suffering of all men. It was here that readers found her universal value.

RICHARD B. HILARY

Selected Bibliography

PRIMARY SOURCES

Deledda, Grazia. *Romanzi e novelle.* 5 vols. Milan: Mondadori, 1941–69.

———. *Versi e prose giovanili.* Milan: Treves, 1938.

SECONDARY SOURCES

Balducci, Carolyn. *A Self-Made Woman: Biography of Nobel-Prize-Winner Grazia Deledda.* Boston: Houghton Mifflin, 1975.

Convegno nazionale di studi deleddiani, Nuoro—30 settembre 1972, Atti. Cagliari: Fossataro, 1974.

Dolfi, Anna. *Grazia Deledda.* Milan: Mursia, 1979.

Lombardi, Olga. *Invito alla lettura di Grazia Deledda.* Milan: Mursia, 1979.

Miccinesi, Mario. *Deledda.* Florence: La Nuova Italia, 1975.

Petronio, Giuseppe. "Grazia Deledda." *Letteratura italiana - I contemporanei.* Vol. I. Milan: Marzorati, 1963. Pp. 137–58.

Piromalli, Antonio. *Grazia Deledda.* Florence: La Nuova Italia, 1968.

Tobia, Antonino. *Grazia Deledda.* Rome: Ciranna, 1971.

JOSÉ ECHEGARAY Y EIZAGUIRRE *1904*

José Echegaray (1832–1916), born in Madrid on April 19, 1832, was the eighth child of a physician of the same name and Manuela Eizaguirre. Because his father was transferred to Murcia in 1837, the younger José was educated there through the secondary level; he then moved to Madrid, where he completed his engineering degree and where he was to spend most of his life. Echegaray had a multifaceted career that earned him recognition as a civil engineer, mathematician, politician, and, of course, dramatist. He published significant works in all these fields, and at the age of twenty-two he was appointed secretary of the School of Civil Engineering, where he was already on the faculty. He was elected to the Royal Academy of Natural Sciences in 1864, and after the Revolution of 1868, which drove Isabel II to seek asylum in France, he was named director general of public works; thereafter he became secretary of commerce and secretary of the treasury; he was founder of the Bank of Spain and is generally credited with saving Spain from bankruptcy in the 1870s.

At the age of fifty he was elected to the Royal Spanish Academy (but did not actively take his seat until 1894 because he was slow to deliver his own acceptance speech). The Nobel Prize that Echegaray shared with Frédéric Mistral in 1904, then, was but one of many honors bestowed upon a man who has now been forgotten by the public at large. It is remarkable, however, that scholars are turning their attention in increasing numbers to Echegaray the dramatist, who until recently was held in ridicule by critics and even by his literary peers.

The reason for that ridicule is that Echegaray is generally linked to the decadent romantic theater that preceded him. In his works he dwelled on passions and exaggerated sentimentality, developing a type of drama not unlike soap opera. He was hence rejected by the group of writers known as the Generation of 1898, which publicly announced their disapproval of the Nobel award in a newspaper advertisement signed by its most distinguished members (Unamuno, Valle-Inclán, the Machado brothers) as well as by the great Nicaraguan modernist poet, Rubén Darío. The protest was not aimed specifically at the Swedish Academy's choice but, rather, at a royal testimonial planned for the first Spanish Nobel laureate. Ironically, this protest was the cause of a much more elaborate and spectacular celebration of the man than had been planned, with King Alfonso XIII presiding.

The Nobel Prize was awarded to Echegaray in recognition of his rich, inspiring contribution to restoring Spanish drama to the grandeur of the Golden Age. In fact, Echegaray started out under the pen name Jorge Hayaseca, but he was soon recognized by the public. In most of his works he has stripped his romantic models of local color, the legendary and the historical (*La muerte en los labios*, 1880; "*Death in One's Hands*," which deals with Servet, is an exception); he deals with the themes of honor (*El gran Galeoto*, 1881; *The Great Galeoto*), morality, madness (*O locura o santidad*, 1877; *Folly or Saintliness*), and human fate. He even wrote an opera, set to music by Emilio Serrano, *Irene de Orante*, produced in 1894; like most of his plays, it is totally forgotten both as opera and as drama. Between 1874 and 1905 Echegaray wrote sixty-eight plays; he was overshadowed only by Jacinto Benavente, who was awarded the Nobel Prize in 1922.

Echegaray wrote in both poetry and prose, sometimes combining the two. He himself spelled out his poetics in an often quoted sonnet, in which he declares: "I choose an emotion, I take an idea, a problem, or a character; I plant it, like dynamite, within a character that I invent. The plot surrounds the character with numerous puppets that in the real world wallow in mud or bask in the sun."

Realism in Echegaray's work exists only in terms of emotion, carried to the extremes of oratory and pompous verse. One of the major influences in the drama of Echegaray is Ibsen (others, of course, were the Spanish classical masters such as Calderón, Lope de Vega, and the romantics who preceded him). After *El hijo de Don Juan* (1892; *The Son*

of Don Juan), accusations came from all sides that Echegaray had modeled his protagonist, Lázaro, after Oswald, from *Ghosts*. Since *Ghosts* was not performed in Spain until after Echegaray's play was produced, it is clear that the Spanish playwright had at least read, perhaps in French, the Norwegian play, which had been enjoying performance elsewhere in Europe since 1890. Echegaray's drama deals with the tragic discovery just before the marriage of an only child, Lázaro, that he is suffering from tertiary syphilis transmitted through his libertine father (a Don Juan whose past sins are visited upon his son). The last line of the play is, like Oswald's, "Mother, give me the sun." Echegaray defended the originality of his drama by proclaiming it an authentic Spanish work in whose characters heredity played an important role, in which he attacked irresponsible, immoral promiscuity and the consequences that it can inflict upon its innocent victims.

The "honor" plays of Echegaray do not analyze the code of honor the way his classical Spanish models did. *The Great Galeoto*, for example, censures gossip, which succeeds in driving an innocent woman into the arms of the man with whom she is accused of commiting adultery. In Echegaray's plays it is tradition and social circumstances that dictate the protection of honor; neither moral convictions, nor intellectual analysis, nor religious preoccupation are part of Echegaray's theater. His plays are thesis-laden exercises that stirred the emotions of his audiences with flamboyant verse and discourse in which he aired his own moral convictions. Echegaray's plays were popular both in Europe and in the Americas. They attracted the attention of important critics of the day who were divided into two camps: those who proclaimed their dislike of him (Valle-Inclán is said to have locked his actress wife, Josefina Blanco, in her dressing room and thrown away the key when she was to appear in an Echegaray play) and those who admired him, for example, the members of the Swedish Academy and George Bernard Shaw, who said that if Echegaray were British there would be a statue in his honor in every city of Great Britain. The attention that critics and scholars now seem to be paying to the first Spanish Nobelist indicates that his work is about to take its place in the history of Spanish literature as an important transition between romantic theater and the streamlined drama of Benavente.

JOSEPH R. ARBOLEDA

Selected Bibliography

PRIMARY SOURCES

Echegaray, José. *The Great Galeoto.* Translated by Hannah Lynch, with an introduction by Elizabeth Hunt. New York: Doubleday, 1914.

——. *Mariana.* Translated by Federico Sarda and Charles D. S. Wuppermann. New York: Albert and Charles Boni, 1914.

——. *Obras dramáticas escogidas.* 2 vols. Madrid: Imprenta de Tello, 1884.

——. *The Son of Don Juan.* Translated by James Graham. London: T. Fisher Unwin, 1895.

SECONDARY SOURCES

Gergersen, Halfdan. *Ibsen and Spain: A Study in Contemporary Drama.* Cambridge: Harvard University Press, 1936.

Martínez Olmedilla, Augusto. *José Echegaray.* Madrid: Iberoamericana de Publicaciones, 1945.

Mathias, Julio. *Echegaray.* Madrid: EPESA, 1970.

Newberry, Wilma. "Echegaray and Pirandello." *PMLA* 81 (1966): 123–29.

Peak, Hunter. *Social Drama in 19th-Century Spain.* Chapel Hill: University of North Carolina Press, 1964.

Shaw, George Bernard. *Dramatic Opinions and Essays.* 2 vols. New York: Brentano, 1928.

Sobejano, Gonzalo. "Echegaray, Galdós y el melodrama." *Anales Galdosianos* (Anejo), (1978): 435–47.

T. S. ELIOT *1948*

Twenty-five years after the publication of *The Waste Land*, a poem that more than any other defined the spiritual malaise of modernism, T. S. Eliot, in 1948, was honored with the Nobel Prize in literature. With the exception of three late plays and one volume of essays, Eliot had by that time produced the poems, essays, and drama that identified him as a primary chronicler of the modern temperament and a major literary figure.

Thomas Stearns Eliot (1888–1965) was born on September 26, 1888, in St. Louis, Missouri, to Charlotte Champ Stearns Eliot, a writer, and Henry Ware Eliot, a Unitarian minister whose grandfather had emigrated from East Coker, England, to Boston in 1670 and whose identification with England defined family cultural traditions for decades to come. Eliot attended Smith Academy in St. Louis and Milton Academy in Massachusetts before entering Harvard College in 1906. Following the completion, in three years, of his undergraduate degree, Eliot studied for a year at the Sorbonne. After three years of graduate work at Harvard—later to culminate in a dissertation on F. H. Bradley (published in 1964, but without Eliot's having defended it for the doctorate)—Eliot returned to Europe, first to Germany and then to England, where he married Vivienne Haigh-Wood in 1915 and remained for the rest of his life. In London he worked in the foreign department of Lloyd's Bank until 1925, when he joined Faber and Gwyer (later Faber and Faber) publishers. In 1927 he became a British citizen and a member of the Church of England.

Eliot's connections with men of letters during these years included friendships with George Santayana and Irving Babbitt at Harvard, Henri Bergson and Alain-Fournier at the Sorbonne, and Ezra Pound, Wyndham Lewis, and James Joyce. Pound, whom he met in 1914 and whose work was the subject of his *Ezra Pound: His Metric and Poetry* (1917), arranged to have "The Love Song of J. Alfred Prufrock," begun at the Sorbonne in 1910–11, published in *Poetry* in 1915. An interior monologue between the divided selves of Prufrock, one urging action, the other afraid to act, the poem provides a number of indelible images—the evening "spread out against the sky / like a patient etherised upon a table," the yellow smoke that curls catlike, the temperate Prufrock measuring out his life "with coffee spoons"—that track the protagonist's progress and paralysis as he dares "disturb the universe."

Following the publication of Eliot's apprentice work in the *South Academy Record* (St. Louis), the *Harvard Advocate*, and *Poetry* (Chicago), twelve poems appeared in *Prufrock and Other Observations* (1917). That collection of previously published and new poems, with several like "Prufrock" influenced by

French symbolism and particularly by Jules Laforgue, included short satirical and humorous pieces— "Morning at the Window," "The *Boston Evening Transcript*," "Aunt Helen," "Cousin Nancy," "Mr. Apollinax," "Hysteria," "Conversation Galante," and "La Figlia che Piange"—that hardly anticipated the later work. "Portrait of a Lady," on the other hand, a dramatic monologue involving an aging unmarried woman and her silent younger suitor, prepares Eliot's readers for the more influential and successful "Prufrock," recording as it does the dilemma and the consequences of engagement and withdrawal. The later Eliot is also present in seminal form in "Preludes" and "Rhapsody on a Windy Night," the cynical tone of which neutralizes the polite society of the lighter and slighter companion pieces.

A second collection, *Poems*, was published in 1919 by Leonard and Virginia Woolf, later combined with the first volume as *Ara Vos Prec* (1919) and then as *Poems* (1920). Here, too, a number of the pieces are light and satirical—such as "Burbank with a Baedeker: Bleistein with a Cigar," "A Cooking Egg," "The Hippopotamus," and "Mr. Eliot's Sunday Morning Service"—and a number bear French titles—"Le Directeur," "Mélange Adultère de Tout," "Lune de Miel," "Dans le Restaurant." The character of Sweeney (later to appear in *Sweeney Agonistes*) first appears in "Sweeney Erect," a tale of a sexual encounter that mockingly deflates its hero through a piercing image of "Sweeney straddled in the sun,"

clutching a morning razor in a brothel. "Sweeney Among the Nightingales" continues the dehumanization of man through animal images and creates an ironic historicization through placing the lustful Sweeney among the nightingales that sang when Agamemnon was murdered. "Gerontion," the one poem in the collection that is consistently sober in tone, chronicles the final moments in an old man's life as he waits for some sign of renewal: "Thoughts of a dry brain in a dry season." In its vision of sterility and its religious imagery, suggesting a slender but life-renewing hope, the poem is prelude to Eliot's masterwork, *The Waste Land* (1922).

The Sacred Wood: Essays on Poetry and Criticism (1920) was next to appear, the first in a sequence of literary and cultural criticism that established Eliot as one of the most "fecund" (to use Hugh Kenner's word) and influential essay writers of the time. Concerned with the relationship between the Western literary heritage and contemporary poetry, Eliot explored theoretically and specifically the historical interplay that has shaped the twentieth-century mind and twentieth-century art. The centerpiece of *The Sacred Wood* is "Tradition and the Individual Talent," now a classic of literary criticism that speaks of the poet's responsibility to assimilate tradition, even knowing that the reconstructive process necessarily involves historical revisionism and personal surrender. Also influential was "Hamlet and His Problems," in which the term *objective correlative*, later to become common literary parlance for "a set of objects, a situation, a chain of events" that are the formula for a particular emotion, was proposed. A slender volume, with essays on a number of poets including Swinburne, Jonson, Marlowe, and Massinger as well as more general essays, *The Sacred Wood* was followed in 1932 by the more substantial *Selected Essays, 1917–1932.* That volume contains two essays—on the metaphysical poets and on Andrew Marvell—that revalue English poetry and propose a second critical neologism, *dissociation of sensibility*, to suggest the disparity between thought and feeling that Eliot saw in English poetry after Donne and Marvell.

During the 1930s, Eliot delivered a number of lectures on poetry, including *The Use of Poetry and the Use of Criticism*, written while he was professor of poetry at Harvard in 1932. *After Strange Gods: A Primer of Modern Heresy* (1934), a dogmatic argument for Christianity that Eliot, harangued by accusations of anti-Semitism, later withdrew, was originally a series of lectures at the University of Virginia in 1933. Later, he published two volumes of social criticism, *The Idea of a Christian Society* (1939) and *Notes Toward a Definition of Culture* (1948). In 1957 many of his occasional lectures were collected in a volume entitled *On Poetry and Poets*. Eliot published a number of slender books on individual writers as well, including Dryden, Shakespeare, Dante, Milton, and George Herbert. The canon of criticism, only suggested in this catalog, is considerable, consisting primarily of compressed but perspicacious insights that expressed Eliot's traditionalist, Christian position and his intense commitment to the moral, historical, and, finally, religious function of literature.

In 1922 Eliot began a journal, *The Criterion*, devoted to providing a forum for new attitudes and approaches to literature; he remained editor until 1939. *The Criterion* carried the first publication of *The Waste Land*, in the abbreviated version recommended by Pound. Over eight hundred lines long in the original (a facsimile of the manuscript was later published in 1971), *The Waste Land* undoubtedly became not only more compact but more inaccessible after Pound's editing. Elaborately annotated with notes from Jessie L. Weston's *From Ritual to Romance*, the Bible, Ovid, Dante, Shakespeare, Baudelaire, and others, the five-part poem— "The Burial of the Dead," "A Game of Chess," "The Fire Sermon," "Death by Water," and "What the Thunder Said"—relies on vegetation rites and the myth of the Fisher King, mixing pagan and Christian practices to create a scheme within which fertility might finally follow aridity. Beginning with the observation that "April is the cruelest month" and ending with the voice of the thunder from the *Brihadaranyaka-Upanishad*, this intricately designed poem of despair and hope permanently secured Eliot as the poetic voice of a disillusioned postwar Western world.

Other important poems of the period between the wars were *The Hollow Men* (1925) and *Ash*

Wednesday (1930). *The Hollow Men* is a more individualized indictment of spiritual degeneracy, expressed through the voice of one of the hollow men, whose heads are filled with straw. *Ash Wednesday*, spoken as well by a man in despair, records the suffering and hope of one who, struggling for belief, journeys through a process of self-abnegation to a prayerful, penitent vision of hope.

The Ariel poems—"Journey of the Magi" (1927), "A Song for Simeon" (1928), "Animula" (1929), and "Marina" (1930)—signal the increasingly religious imagery and vision of the later poetry. *Four Quartets*, a major sequence published individually between 1935 and 1941 and collectively in 1943, follows a contrapuntal design likened to Beethoven's late quartets. Each of the four poems—"Burnt Norton," "East Coker," "The Dry Salvages," and "Little Gidding"—explores the complex relationship between the timeless and the temporal, the present and the past, seeking the point of intersection.

Throughout his literary career, Eliot had an intense interest in drama. As early as 1927, he wrote *Sweeney Agonistes*, a fragmentary piece that captures the rhythms of jazz, and *The Rock*, a "prose pageant," in 1934. His best-known play, *Murder in the Cathedral*, written for the Canterbury Festival of June 1935, dramatizes the twelfth-century cathedral killing of St. Thomas à Becket. Its chief concern is the spiritual state of the martyr, whose purity is questioned by both state and family. *The Family Reunion*, with links to the *Eumenides* of Aeschylus, appeared in 1939. *The Cocktail Party* (1949), based on the *Alcestis* of Euripides, transferred to drama the two paths to Christian commitment: the way of negation, exemplified by the self-effacing Celia, and the way of affirmation, attempted by Edward and Lavinia, who reclaim their marriage. Commercially successful, the play, like all of Eliot's drama, attempts to revive verse form, an effort that had little impact on the course of the modern theater. After *The Complete Poems and Plays, 1909–1950* appeared in 1952, Eliot wrote two additional plays, *The Confidential Clerk* (1953), a farce based on Euripedes's *Ion*, and *The Elder Statesman* (1958), which dramatized the painful confrontation of its protagonist, Lord Claverton, with the past.

The last of these plays, along with *On Poetry and Poets*, were dedicated to Valerie Fletcher, who became Eliot's second wife in 1957, ten years after the death, following a long illness, of his first wife, Vivienne. The second marriage was to last eight years, until January 4, 1965, when Eliot died.

Eliot left as his legacy a searching and innovative body of literature that has contributed more substantially than any other to defining the first half of the twentieth century.

JUNE SCHLUETER

Selected Bibliography

PRIMARY SOURCES

Eliot, Thomas Stearns. *The Complete Poems and Plays, 1909–1950*. New York: Harcourt, Brace & World, 1952.

———. *The Sacred Wood: Essays on Poetry and Criticism.* London: Methuen, 1920.

———. *Selected Essays.* New York: Harcourt, Brace, 1932.

———. *The Waste Land: A Facsimile and Transcript of the Original Drafts Including the Annotations of Ezra Pound.* Edited by Valerie Eliot. New York: Harcourt Brace Jovanovich, 1971.

SECONDARY SOURCES

Frye, Northrop. *T. S. Eliot: An Introduction.* Chicago: University of Chicago Press, 1963.

Hay, Eloise Knapp. *T. S. Eliot's Negative Way.* Cambridge: Harvard University Press, 1982.

Howarth, Herbert. *Notes on Some Figures Behind T. S. Eliot.* Boston: Houghton Mifflin, 1964.

Kenner, Hugh. *The Invisible Poet: T. S. Eliot.* New York: Citadel Press, 1964.

Matthiessen, F. O. *The Achievement of T. S. Eliot: An Essay on the Nature of Poetry.* New York: Oxford University Press, 1959.

Smith, Grover. *T. S. Eliot's Poetry and Plays: A Study in Sources and Meaning.* Chicago: University of Chicago Press, 1950.

Williamson, George. *A Reader's Guide to T. S. Eliot: A Poem-by-Poem Analysis.* New York: Noonday Press, 1953.

ODYSSEUS ELYTIS   *1979*

Odysseus Alepoudhélis (1911—), the recipient of the Nobel Prize in literature in 1979, was born, the youngest of six children, on November 2, 1911, in Herakleion, Crete, near the ancient Minoan site of Knossos. Both parents originally came from the island of Lesbos in the eastern Aegean. His father had settled in his early youth on Crete, where he became a successful soap manufacturer. In 1914 the family left Crete for permanent residence in Athens. The young Odysseus studied law at the University of Athens, but he left in 1935 without a degree.

Athens has been his home except when he resided in France, for study, 1948–52, and during the regime of the colonels, 1969–71. During his early experiments in poetry he created the surname Elytis. The first element thereof, *el*, is in modern Greek evocative of *Ellas* (Greece), *eleftheria* (freedom), *elpidha* (hope), and of *Eléni*, in Greek tradition the most beautiful of women; the second element, *tis*, is a generic suffix denoting the bearer or exponent of those emblems of the Greek heritage, as in *politis* (citizen): Such is the interpretation of Kimon Friar, long a friend of the poet and his English translator. Others connect his name with Paul Éluard (see below), an *élite* of poetry, and the Greek word *alítis* (wanderer).

Elytis has spent most of his summers on the Greek islands of the Aegean. Lesbos, ancient center of Ionian culture and the land of his ancestry, and Crete, island of eternal mysteries and the land of his birth, have left strong imprints on the poet's psyche and on his intellectual development; the influence of these islands has abided even during Elytis's long residence in Athens and his involvement in its cultural life. But the Aegean realm as a whole, with its azure sky, its blue-green sea, its spare but stunning landscapes, and its beauteous youths, all dazzled by the sovereign sun, have left even a deeper impression on the poet's soul, such that he has long been known as the "poet of the Aegean." The feast of sensuous natural images apprehended by the "sanctity of the perceiving senses" in the Aegean has been at all times for Elytis the locus and, in significant metaphorical transformations, the focus of his poetic vision in the sinuous and palpable vitality of his verse. His perception of the oneness of man and nature produces an unrivaled poetic universe animated by a new "mythology" in which the chief deities are Sky (*ouranós*, which can also mean "heaven" in modern Greek), Sea, Wind, Mountain, Flowers, and Love, over all of whom Sun rules supreme. The Sun, as blazing reality and as radiant metaphor, is Elytis's most powerful, enduring, and affecting image; with it join those of

flame, fire, and light. The luminous purity of the Sun will ultimately exorcise from the world what is dark, rank, and evil and replace that with a new, effulgent reality of light and justice. The Aegean in its lush sensuousness becomes for Elytis the matrix of an autonomous poetic reality suffused with *Eros* (Love). This reality of "lucidity, purity, balance, beauty, newness, youth, and love" (Andonis Decavalles) subsumes in time not only the Greeks, but all of humanity. Even as darker clouds moved into the lucid environment of Elytis's poetry, his basic poetic vision has remained clear in its inspiration and true thereto.

The poet loves the Hellenic language in all of its long and creative history. He is attached, but not enslaved, to the *dhimotikí* (demotic), the speech of his fellow Greeks; he pays respect, but no adulation, to the *katharévousa* (purifying dialect), an artificial stratum based on ancient Attic Greek, devised in the fervor of nationalist struggle. He grafts to the living organism of the *dhimotikí* words, phrases, and images from all of Greek literature, from the ancient Attic to the Septuagint (the Hellenistic translation of the Bible), to the Byzantine hymns, medieval songs and legends, and the poets of the era immediately preceding his own. He has also coined his own words. As Kimon Friar has shown, Elytis, in the manner of a painter or sculptor, shapes and molds language as if it were color or raw material.

The first powerful stimulant to Elytis's poetry was surrealism, mediated through the works of Paul Éluard and the encouragement of

Andreas Embirikos (1901–75), the first exponent of this movement in Greek poetry. In response to the questioning of rationalism and to the loss of scientific and moral certainty, surrealism offered the possibility of a new liberating reality of art and of social revolution. This reality served for Elytis as a counterpoise to the current trends in European poetry, such as neoromanticism, neorealism, and symbolism, which he found unsatisfying, and to his contemporaries' tragic awareness of a glorious past no longer attainable, especially after political and poetic fancies of a Greater Greece to rival the ancient Byzantine Empire had fallen apart. In 1935 Elytis was introduced to the literati of *Nea Grammata* (New Letters), founded that year, who were experimenting with new forms that would soon shape the literary climate in Greece; among these was George Seféris, who would later receive the Nobel Prize (1963). In that year Elytis contributed to *Nea Grammata* his *Prota Poiimata* ("First Poems"). These, together with others published in *Nea Grammata* and elsewhere, appeared in book form as *Prosanatolismi* (*Orientations*) in 1940. Further explorations of this order were published as *Ilios o Protos mazi me tis parallayies pano se mian aktidha* (*Sun the First, Together with Variations on a Sunbeam*) in 1943. These poems make of the intangible phenomena of nature a tangible and palpable poetic reality burgeoning with summer, sun, and light; a mosaic of concrete pictures of nature in its profusion of creations; a

Dionysian revelry of youth, joy, health, and love awakening. "The poet tried to regain this lost land of the heart's desire by creating a clear islandic consciousness, a world of sensual clarity and purity, the mysterious dawn of a new lyrical world opposed to the wasteland around him of decadence and clamor . . . a poetry as natural to him . . . as though it were extensions of the pores of his body" (Kimon Friar).

Nonetheless, Elytis's poetry also reveals darker clouds of youthful melancholy and despair in the sunlit landscape, for his poetic vision of life was always grounded in an acceptance of life as he found it. He wrote: "When reality surpasses the imagination in boldness, then poetic exaggeration becomes useless, and the affectation of pain becomes a mere coarsening of blood and tears. . . . A poet must find those spiritual powers which may counterbalance this drama and this agony. He must aim at such a resynthesis of the fragments of reality that he may pass from 'what is' to 'what may be.'" Elytis strove to re-create a poetic world in his heart's image over against his personal despair and the painful maturity brought on him by the European world at war.

In late 1940 Elytis was mobilized to serve as a second lieutenant in the First Army Corps to defend his country, on the Albanian front, against the attack of the Italian Fascists. After initial successes, which stirred patriotic fervor, Greece suffered attack and defeat, culminating in occupation, which lasted from April 1941, to September 1944. One response to the fear and degradation of this period was *Ilios o Protos*, a final, intense effort to reclaim the beauteous adolescent dream. Another was *Azma iroiko ke penthimo yia ton hameno anthipolohagho tis Alvanias* (*Heroic and Elegiac Song for the Lost Second Lieutenant of the Albanian Campaign*), published in 1945. The "lost second lieutenant," once the adolescent himself, is now come of age and dead on the battlefield, the universal victim of man's malignancy to his fellow. But "Death is that portion of life which man leaves unused," sings Elytis: The youthful victim is transfigured with light, Elytis's symbol of justice, and is resurrected in the Easter of God to become a promise of life itself in its fullness and promise of perfection. In this long poem Elytis turns to the language, symbols, and rites of the Greek Orthodox Church, as he would again do in his acknowledged masterpiece, *Axion Esti* (1959; *The Axion Esti*).

The years 1945–59 were for Elytis a period of poetic introspection and gestation. He struggled inwardly to evolve a new aesthetic that would unite his earlier visions with his increasing notions of responsibility and duty. Between 1948 and 1956 he wrote many poems and aesthetic essays, but he destroyed nearly all of them. He turned to cultural pursuits and to the national service that his growing fame encouraged. He served two terms as director of broadcasting and programming for the National Broadcasting Institute in Athens; he became in 1948 a regular critic of *Kathimerini*, an Athens daily newspaper. In search of a new

site for his creativity, he settled in that year in Paris, where he studied literature at the Sorbonne. During the next four years he traveled widely in Europe and formed friendships with poets and writers (among them Breton, Éluard, Michaux, Ungaretti) and with artists (including Matisse, Picasso, and Giacometti). He wrote many articles on poetic and artistic creation and himself produced gouaches and collages. From 1953, when he returned to Greece, to 1958 he served as a member of the Group of Twelve, a prestigious board of critics that each year recognized and rewarded the best books in poetry, essay, and drama. In the late fifties he held, as well, positions of high responsibility in the administration of Karolos Koun's Art Theater in Athens and of the Greek Ballet.

In 1959 appeared *The Axion Esti*, a vast, symphonic, and architectonic poem that unites the inalienable elements of Elytis's youthful poetic vision with the ineradicable consequences of his mature experience, particularly during World War II. The title, which means "Worthy It Is" (the translators kept the Greek title in the English publication), occurs in the Divine Liturgy of the Greek Orthodox Church and in several hymns thereof in praise of Christ and the Virgin Mary. Of enormous complexity and mathematical precision, the poem is composed of a great variety of language, rhythm, and poetic forms. In Part I, "Ghenesis" ("Genesis"), the poet relates the microcosm of his own experience, from the time he first saw the light of day to his encounter with the evils of the world. With this depiction he interweaves the macrocosm of the world in its creation and passage from "dawn to sudden dusk, from childhood to manhood, from innocence to knowledge of Evil, often equated with war . . ." (Friar).

Part II, "Ta Pathi" ("The Passions"), is composed of three sections, each of which contains six psalms, four odes, and two readings. The psalms are modeled on the Davidic exemplars and on the Byzantine *troparia* (short liturgical hymns); the odes are framed in a complex metrical pattern; the readings, written in simple demotic prose, recall the Gospel sections of the Divine Liturgy. The subject is a graphic, realistic description of the poet's experience as a second lieutenant in the Albanian campaign.

In Part III, "To Dhoxastikon" ("The Gloria"), the sufferings of the war decade are transmuted into Christ's passion as all things, good and evil, "are embraced in an ecstasy of praise" (Friar) and emerge "into the glory of a resurrection in the rebuilding of an earthly, yet spiritual, paradise of justice, freedom, love, and beauty" (Decavalles). The complexity of structure in this section complements grandly the magnificence of the conception. This great work was followed in 1960 by the publication of *Exi ke Mia Tipsis yia ton Ourano* (*Six and One Remorses for the Sky*), some of which had been first written in the 1950s. These are tragic remorses or regrets for the lost azure sky.

The 1960s were a productive period for the poet despite the regime of the colonels, which began in April 1967, and his absence from Greece from 1969 to 1971. He expressed his "solar metaphysics" in *To Photodhentro ke i dhekati tetarti omorphia* (1971; *The Light Tree and the Fourteenth Beauty*), one of four separate volumes of verse he published between 1969 and 1971.

Among his latest works are *Maria Nepheli* (1978; *Maria Nephele*), and *Tria poiimata me Simaia Evkairias* (1982; "Three Poems with Flags of Convenience"), a collection of parallel monologues by a young girl and the poet on the alienation and uncertainty of the modern era, a time from which, nonetheless, the meanings of life and the contributions of poetry thereto may emerge. Elytis has remained popular and influential in Greece and well respected abroad, as recognized by the Nobel Prize in 1979.

HOWARD MARBLESTONE

Selected Bibliography

PRIMARY SOURCES

Elytis, Odysseus. *The Axion Esti*. Translated and annotated by Edmund Keeley and George Savidis. Pittsburgh: University of Pittsburgh Press, 1974.

———. *Selected Poems*. Edited and translated by Edmond Keeley and Philip Sherrard. New York: Viking Press, 1981.

———. *The Sovereign Sun, Selected Poems*. Translated with an introduction and notes by Kimon Friar. Philadelphia: Temple University Press, 1974.

SECONDARY SOURCES

Books Abroad. Autumn 1975. Special Elytis issue.

Friar, Kimon. *Modern Greek Poetry.* Translation, introduction, an essay on translation, and notes. New York: Simon Schuster, 1973. Selections: pp. 590–619. Introduction and notes: pp. 82–88, 695–700.

Ivask, I., ed. *Odysseus Elytis: Analogies of Light.* Norman: University of Oklahoma Press, 1980.

Politis, Linos. *A History of Modern Greek Literature.* Oxford, U.K.: Clarendon Press, 1973.

Trypanis, C. A. *Greek Poetry. From Homer to Seferis.* Chicago: University of Chicago Press, 1981.

RUDOLF EUCKEN   *1908*

It is somewhat ironic that Rudolf Eucken (1846–1926), the second German to win the Nobel Prize in literature, was a professor of philosophy and never wrote any imaginative literature whatsoever. Though he enjoyed worldwide renown during his lifetime and received the Nobel Prize in 1908 "in recognition of his earnest search for truth, and the consistency, rigor, breadth, and humanity of his thought," both his work and his name quickly sank into obscurity after his death in 1926.

Born on January 5, 1846, in the East Frisian town of Aurich, young Eucken already showed a keen interest in questions of theology and philosophy while attending the *Gymnasium* in his hometown. Eucken lost both his father and only brother at an early age, and so his devoted mother, a liberal-minded daughter of a Protestant minister,

nurtured and encouraged her bright son's intellectual interests. Upon completion of his schooling in Aurich, Eucken followed the advice of his religion and philosophy teacher and proceeded to study philosophy and philology at Göttingen and Berlin universities. Perhaps the most influential of his university teachers was the well-known philosopher and philologist F. A. Trendelenberg; under his tutelage in Berlin Eucken devoted himself to the study of classical philology and, most important, to Aristotelian ethics. He was especially attracted to his mentor's historical conceptualization of philosophy and the decidedly ethical character of his philosophical project, which strove to bring philosophy and history into closer relation. Eucken eventually completed his training in Göttingen, where he attained his doctoral degree in classical philology with a dissertation on

Aristotle's use of language. After teaching for several years at a *Gymnasium* in Frankfurt, he accepted a professorship in 1871 at the University of Basel, where he sat on the same doctoral examination committee with Friedrich Nietzsche. In 1874 he moved to the University of Jena, where he taught for the remainder of his career.

Eucken's earliest writing was essentially historical and analyzed various influential philosophical systems from Aristotle to Hegel, while the bulk of his mature work developed a broad-spectrum *Lebensphilosophie* —"a philosophy of life"—that addressed basic issues and problems in religion, ethics, and social theory. An untiring proponent of humanity's spiritual calling, Eucken strove to synthesize a holistic philosophy that would avoid the pitfalls of overintellectualization and professional specializations by embracing the transcendental truth manifest in man's religions, philosophies, and aesthetic creations. He was especially critical of purely abstract systems of thought—various forms of idealism, psychology, and cosmology in vogue at the turn of the century—for they ultimately involved, he believed, a renunciation or denial of their own origins in the lived experience of life. Man, Eucken argued, is neither a purely intellectually nor physically determined being, but rather *the* privileged creature in which spirit and matter converge and evolve. Owing to this privileged position, man thus should always strive to cultivate his full spiritual potential, which involves not only intellect but intuition and free will as well.

Eucken, like many thinkers of the late nineteenth and early twentieth centuries, was troubled by the growing pessimism and cultural skepticism of his time. He was convinced that this spiritual malaise had resulted from the modern overestimation of a scientific or "naturalistic" view of man and world and that this "naturalism" had imposed false limitations upon man's inherent spirituality. Eucken thus worked throughout his career to counter this pernicious reductive view. Although the naturalistic explanation of life was effective in explicating man's biological nature, it could not adequately account for the spiritual realities of truth, beauty, goodness, and free will. Man's destiny is more than a product of natural environment; it is, as he wrote in his central work, *Die Lebensanschauungen der großen Denker: eine Entwicklungsgeschichte der Menschheit von Plato bis zur Gegenwart* (1890: *The Problem of Human Life as Viewed by the Great Thinkers from Plato to the Present Time*), "ruled by spiritual necessities with a spiritual aim and purport" that transcend "the merely natural domain." Thinking, moreover, is itself a manifestation of man's "independent spiritual life"; it is a "transcendence of nature" that had, until the modern era, pushed man beyond the mere material. Western man is thus confused and endangered, Eucken believed, because the advances made by the natural sciences had subtly diverted attention away from the spiritual: Man has lost touch with his transcendental essence, with that creative energy that binds humanity to-

gether in a common spiritual purpose.

Though Eucken always strove
to maintain a critical distance from
individual philosophical systems or
schools, his basic assumption that
man's understanding of life is always
mediated through history clearly
evinces his debt to both Trendelenberg and Hegel. Eucken believed
that history reveals not only the
stages in man's spiritual development but also certain underlying
and eternal truths. "Thought" he
said, "does not drift along with time;
as certainly as it strives to attain
truth, it must rise above time and its
treatment must be timeless." The
treatment of thought in philosophy
is timeless in that it must transcend
the barriers set by specific individuals, cultures, or eras. Since, however, these eternal truths of human
spirituality can only manifest themselves in the concrete experience of
historical consciousness—not in explicit theoretical abstractions—the
practice and study of philosophy
will always be a never ending dialectic between past and present. It is
thus not surprising that Eucken's
first three publications, which appeared between 1870 and 1872, were
historical studies devoted to various
aspects of Aristotelian ethics and
methodology. Within the next five
years Eucken published a history of
philosophical terminology and a
collection of essays on Nicholas of
Cusa, Paracelsus, and Kepler, often
overlooked German thinkers who,
Eucken argued, played a significant
role in the transition from medieval
to modern European philosophy.

In 1878 Eucken published

his first significant philosophical
treatise, *Geschichte und Kritik
der Grundbegriffe der Gegenwart*
("Fundamental Concepts of the Present Day"). This work marks a turning point in his career; though
still historical in basic conception, it
represents his first critical efforts
to address contemporary cultural
problems. It forms, as such, a bridge
between his earlier, more purely historical work and his mature philosophical writing, which culminated
in his most widely read book, *The
Problem of Human Life*. In this
book, Eucken takes up one of his
central concerns, the defect of modern naturalistic thought, by elaborating how the work of various
"great" thinkers of the past actually
lays the foundation for a modern
critique of naturalism. *The Problem
of Human Life* demonstrates, moreover, both in theory and practice,
Eucken's central methodological
precept of historical consciousness:
the work is neither systematic nor
purely theoretical; its polemic thrust
is not explication but rather the
creative transformation and synthesis of what he believed to be man's
eternal intuitive strivings toward
an increasingly self-conscious spirituality.

During his middle and most
productive period, roughly 1888
to 1912, Eucken produced a prodigious amount of writing, including works on Aquinas and Kant
(1901), a philosophy of history
(1907), and four major philosophical works—*Grundlinien einer neuen
Lebensanschauung* (1907; *Life's Basis
and Life's Ideal*), *Einführung in
die Philosophie des Geisteslebens*

(1908; *The Life of the Spirit; an Introduction to Philosophy*), *Der Wert und Sinn des Lebens* (1908; *The Meaning and Value of Life*), and *Erkennen und Leben* (1912; *Knowledge and Life*). It was also during this period that Eucken completed his principal works on religion; the most important were *Der Wahrheitsgehalt der Religion* (1901; *The Truth of Religion*) and *Können wir noch Christen sein?* (1911; *Can We Still Be Christians?*). In these treatises, Eucken argues that Christianity must be revitalized in order to give Western culture the new spiritual grounding it so sorely needs. Western culture's spiritual vacuum—a result of the pervading technological ethos of a modern science whose rational efficacy had undermined the spiritual basis of the Christian value system—must be filled, he proposed, with a new religious idealism. This idealism, he proffered, must supplant an older form of Christianity that was a product, in his words, of a "wearied and faint-hearted epoch," too passive and too willing to put personal salvation entirely into the hands of God. Eucken espoused an enlightened religious tolerance in which all sects and religions would enjoy political equality and complete autonomy from ideological and governmental influence. But he nonetheless felt that Christianity, as opposed to the major Eastern religions, was basically superior, in that it affirmed the significance and spiritual value of each and every individual and thus provided an ethical incentive—also largely absent in Eastern religions—for countering the evils and

inequities of human existence. Though there were also certain Christian rituals and dogma that had, in Eucken's unquestionably Protestant view, outlived their purposes, Christianity's double contribution of spiritual affirmation and universal redemption were the essential ingredients for his religious idealism. Such affirmation and redemption, however, would have to be based on new articles of faith that would complement—not merely counter—the naturalistic drives operating in the modern era.

Concerned about the social upheaval of the tumultuous first decades of the twentieth century and then deeply disturbed by the horrendous effects of World War I, Eucken felt compelled in his later years to address more directly the plight of the individual in the modern technological world. His last two works of note, *Sozialismus und seine Lebensgestaltung* (1920; *Socialism: An Analysis*) and *The Individual and Society* (1923; this book, although written originally in German on commission for the Faith Press in London and translated by W. R. V. Brade was only published in the English translation), though purporting to discuss pertinent social issues, were in actuality often a defensive—and at times reactionary—elaboration of his earlier formulas for the spiritual rejuvenation of Western culture. In his *Socialism: An Analysis*, Eucken elaborated six reasons why socialism, itself a product of the dehumanizing tendencies of naturalistic culture, cannot adequately redress the social woes of modern man. Socialism, Eucken argued, discounts man's spiritual needs and reduces him to a mathematical entity whose value is measured in economic terms and utilitarian purposes. Moreover, in calling for the subordination of individual to community, socialism disregards the spiritual autonomy and integrity of each human being. It thus disregards that which raises man above his physical nature and makes him what he is, the priviledged creature who enjoys the freedom to follow the call of his inner spirituality.

Rudolf Eucken's teaching, though born of an earnest and compassionate humanistic spirit, failed to pass the test of time because his mission was largely retrospective. Although his understanding of the historical character of thinking and consciousness was profoundly modern and even pointed ahead to future developments in existential and hermeneutic philosophy, his answer to the metaphysical and epistemological crisis at the turn of the century involved, ultimately, a nostalgic appeal to the very system of values that had at that time ceased to provide Western man with a spiritual and intellectual foundation.

REINHOLD WOLF

Selected Bibliography

PRIMARY SOURCES

Eucken, Rudolf. *Can We Still be Christians?* Translated by Lucy Judge Gibson. New York: Macmillan, 1914.

———. *The Individual and Society.* Translated by W. R. V. Brade. London: Faith Press, 1922.

———. *Knowledge and Life.* Translated by W. Tudor Jones. London: Williams and Northgate, 1913.

———. *The Life of the Spirit; an Introduction to Philosophy.* Translated by F. L. Pogson. London: Williams and Norgate, 1909.

———. *Life's Basis and Life's Ideal.* Translated by Alban G. Widgery. London: Adam and Charles Black, 1911.

———. *The Meaning and Value of Life.* Translated by Lucy Judge Gibson and W. R. Boyce Gibson. London: Adam and Charles Black, 1909.

———. *The Problem of Human Life as Viewed by the Great Thinkers from Plato to the Present Time.* Translated by W. S. Hough and W. R. Boyce Gibson. New York: Scribner, 1909.

———. *Socialism: An Analysis.* Translated by Joseph McCabe. New York: Scribner, 1922.

SECONDARY SOURCES

Gibson, W. R. Boyce. *Rudolf Eucken's Philosophy of Life.* London: Adam and Charles Black, 1907.

Jones, Abel J. *Rudolf Eucken: A Philosophy of Life.* London: T. C. and E. C. Jack, n.d.

Slosson, Edwin E. *Six Major Prophets.* Boston: Little, Brown, 1917. Pp. 276–310.

WILLIAM FAULKNER   *1949*

William Faulkner (1897–1962), winner of the Nobel Prize in literature in 1949, is one of the major writers of the twentieth century. Faulkner's ability to transform his "postage-stamp of soil," the quasi-legendary Yoknapatawpha County, into an extraordinary saga not only of the American South but of the human condition has led to worldwide recognition and to a critical outpouring unsurpassed in American literature. Though primarily a regionalist, Faulkner transcended provinciality by combining intense, highly imaginative variations on the tragedy of existence with technical mastery of his craft.

Born September 25, 1897, in New Albany, Mississippi, Faulkner, the first of four sons of Murry and Maud Butler Falkner (William added the *u*), grew up in Oxford, some thirty-five miles away. Except for pilot training for the Royal Air Force in Toronto near the end of World War I and brief stays elsewhere (for example, New York City, New Orleans, Europe, Hollywood, Japan, Virginia), he remained in Oxford until his death there on July 6, 1962. In 1929 he married Estelle Oldham Franklin. Fifteen of Faulkner's twenty novels are set in Oxford (renamed Jefferson) and surrounding Lafayette County, the model for Yoknapatawpha.

More than any other major American writer, Faulkner used materials from both his family's and his region's history for his fiction, which makes his work remarkably fruitful as a means of tracing the tangled personal and racial relations among that region's residents. The novelist was certainly conscious of his heritage—his great-grandfather was a pioneer in the area as well as a lawyer, politician, railroad builder, and author—and he was equally ready to defend the region (as in *Intruder in the Dust*) or to be rigorously critical of it (as in *Light in August*).

Faulkner began attending classes at the University of Mississippi after World War I and started writing verse and fiction as well. Following a short stay in New York City and publication of an unsuccessful book of poems, *The Marble Faun* (1924), Faulkner moved to New Orleans, where he met Sherwood Anderson and published his early stories and sketches. With Anderson's assistance, he published *Soldiers' Pay* (1926), but his parody of Anderson's style in the collaborative *Sherwood Anderson and Other Famous Creoles* (1926) resulted in a breach in their friendship. Faulkner's first two novels, *Soldiers' Pay* and *Mosquitoes* (1927), and a group of stories, *These Thirteen* (1931), constitute his relatively short apprenticeship. *Soldiers' Pay*, a minor work, is about the disillusioned postwar generation, with stereotyped characters (a wounded returning serviceman, "flappers"), a derivative plot (Fitzgerald) and style (Swinburne, Housman), and little to suggest Faulkner's later work except for scenes in a black church. The slight *Mosquitoes*, also a derivative effort (Aldous Huxley), satirizes the New Orleans literary world.

Sartoris (1929; uncut version published as *Flags in the Dust*, 1973) is Faulkner's introduction to Yoknapatawpha County. It tells of the brave, unconventional older male generation of the Sartoris clan, an aunt uniquely able to understand and control the family, and the disappointed younger men who find nothing but emptiness following their return from World War I. Bayard Sartoris, whose twin brother was killed in the war, is foolhardy and self-destructive, eventually killing himself in a plane crash. The longer version of the book provides greater detail about other family members, especially the sibling relationships often encountered in Faulkner's work.

During Faulkner's major creative period (1929–36), he produced his four most important works in quick succession, as well as several lesser ones. *The Sound and the Fury* appeared in 1929 (corrected edition, 1984), followed by *As I Lay Dying* (1930; corrected edition, 1985), *Sanctuary* (1931; corrected edition, 1981), *Light in August* (1932; corrected edition, 1985), *A Green Bough* (verse, 1933), *Doctor Martino and Other Stories* (1934), *Pylon* (1935; corrected edition, 1985), and *Absalom, Absalom!* (1936).

Faulkner's absorption of European literary ideas and techniques is clearly evident in *The Sound and the*

Fury, a complex work jumping radically in time and style and presenting the four Compson siblings' accounts of their troubled youth and of their tangled relationships as adults. Caddy, the sexually indiscriminate focal character, names an illegitimate daughter after her oldest brother, Quentin; the daughter eventually steals the savings of a younger brother, Jason, who has treated her cruelly. Caddy's youngest brother, Benjy, an idiot, has been fixated on her since childhood. And brother Quentin is so obsessed with Caddy's sexuality that he believes he has committed incest with her and drowns himself. At book's end, Dilsey, the cook, and Benjy are in church, with Dilsey believing she has seen both the beginning and end of the family. Faulkner's narrative technique, especially his use of interior monologue, is excellent in suggesting the patterns of thinking among the siblings, notably Benjy's confusion of time past and present and Quentin's obsessiveness. This heavily symbolic book reflects a profound sense of personal, familial, and regional loss, with the Compsons' tragedy suggesting, like Eliot's *The Waste Land*, the corruption of a world of innocence and certainty.

Anse Bundren and his five children, a family of poor rural whites, travel through fire and storm in *As I Lay Dying* to bury their wife/mother. Heat and delays result in a decomposing corpse, which Faulkner treats with macabre humor, as when one son drills a hole in the coffin so his mother can breathe. Faulkner again uses interior monologues (for both comic and tragic effect) to suggest the family's nihilistic amorality and absurd indifference to civilized convention. Each of the characters—the seven family members and eight others—narrates one or more sections of the book, with the neighbors providing expository details and the Bundrens primarily commenting on each other. Their journey becomes symbolic as well as literal in serving to reveal each character's true self and attitudes.

Sanctuary was written as "the most horrific tale" Faulkner could imagine, and it remains his most sensational novel. Temple Drake, a college student, is raped with a corncob by one of the author's most evil creations, Popeye, a gangster. Temple then becomes a prostitute for Popeye, who is eventually executed for murder, though ironically not for that of the man he actually killed. Though relatively popular compared with Faulkner's earlier books, *Sanctuary* created a furor, especially in the South.

Light in August is also sensational but more mature. A complicated work in its juggling of several distinct plots, it resembles some of the earlier novels in its focus on characters at points of emotional and ethical extremity. One plot strand tells of Lena Grove, a simple child of nature nine months pregnant, walking down a road to try to find the father of her expected child. Along the way she encounters a variety of people, including Byron Bunch, who tells his friend, Gail Hightower, a guilt-ridden sometime clergyman, of Joanna Burden's murder. Paralleling this plot is the sensational story of Joe Christmas.

Christmas, raised as an orphan thought to be of mixed racial parentage, is later a drifter, lover to Burden (whom he kills the day Lena arrives in Jefferson), then finally victim of an attack by a religious zealot before a sheriff kills and castrates him. The book ends circularly with Lena, now having given birth, continuing her search for her lover and with the journey clearly linking the characters' overlapping stories. Though the novel is relatively uncomplicated stylistically, Christmas, the product of a harsh childhood experience with religious fanaticism, is a complex bundle of frustrations and hatreds, particularly self-hatred.

Pylon is a novel about early pilots; Faulkner was fond of flying (especially stunt flying) and respected pilots' willingness to flirt with death. The book focuses on a tough heroine, the two fliers with whom she is involved, and her ethical turmoil following the death of one of them. It was followed by the writer's most important novel, *Absalom, Absalom!*, a complex work covering several generations and involving four narrators and radical shifts in time. The novel focuses on the dynasty established before the Civil War by Thomas Sutpen, who learned early in life about racial and economic distinctions and who consequently tried to create and control his own dynastic world. Forty years later, Quentin Compson, already seen in *The Sound and the Fury* (and grandson of Sutpen's friend, General Compson), tries to answer his Harvard roommate's question—"What is the South like?"—by telling Sutpen's story as a microcosm of the history of the South. The guilt that passes through each generation makes the characters in the novel incapable of handling the truth, in Quentin's time as in the past, and the novel ends with Quentin's frantic, unpersuasive cry that he does not hate the South. The book's biblical title suggests a father's cry for his dead son, specifically Sutpen's son, who was murdered by his half-brother. The Sutpen legacy parallels Quentin's awareness of the residual effects of slavery on the more modern South as well as on himself. *Absalom, Absalom!* is a compelling analysis of the South's conscience and the sense of rejection, on both national and personal levels, that resulted from its Civil War defeat.

Following this creatively rich period, in which his most significant works were produced, Faulkner published two conventional collections of interrelated stories. The seven parts of *The Unvanquished* (1938) treat the Sartoris family, with Bayard "unvanquished" in terms of having surpassed his father in perception and having therefore become initiated into maturity. The book is a romanticized, sentimental picture of southern life and, with its straightforward style, a contrast both with the previous book and with most of Faulkner's writing. *The Wild Palms and Old Man* (1939) contrapuntally alternates the two stories included, which concern men involved with women who both love and attack them and which reflect degrees of freedom and rigidity in society.

Faulkner's novels during and after World War II are workmanlike

though not so significant as those written in the 1930's. Over a period of seventeen years, Faulkner wrote three interrelated novels about the rise and eventual fall of the Snopes family: shrewd, degenerate, opportunistic, dishonest whites who try to corrupt others. The trilogy—*The Hamlet* (1940), *The Town* (1957), and *The Mansion* (1959)—is ambitious in scope and rich in character portrayal.

Go Down, Moses, and Other Stories (1942), despite its title, is a novel made up of seven stories, notably "The Bear," Faulkner's account of a boy's initiation into adulthood through a hunting trip that provides the opportunity for a mystical identification with the land and with nature. *Intruder in the Dust* (1948), by contrast, is a simple detective tale embellished with moralizing about the South's resistance to civil rights legislation. *Knight's Gambit* (1949), like *The Unvanquished*, is a collection of stories on the same general topic, with material added to tie them together; in this case, the six detective stories constitute less than a coherent novel, though all center on Gavin Stevens, an attorney-sleuth used by Faulkner in a number of his works.

Requiem for a Nun (1951) returns to Temple Drake of *Sanctuary*. A hybrid drama with monologues inserted in which Temple's maid is executed for the death of Temple's daughter, the book melodramatically traces the history of both women as well as of Jefferson itself. Though *A Fable* (1954) won various literary prizes, this book, set in World War I, is stylistically overwrought and simplistically polemical, combining some of Faulkner's familiar themes with explicitly Christian allegory. His last book, *The Reivers* (1962), is a return to the comic tall tale, a nostalgic glance back at Yoknapatawpha County as Faulkner knew it in his childhood; what plot there is centers on a man's auto trip to Memphis to meet his girlfriend in a whorehouse, with various escapades along the way and back. Subtitled "A Reminiscence," the book is effective in showing how a young boy leaves childhood for maturity.

During Faulkner's lifetime, several collections were published in addition to the individual works: *The Portable Faulkner* (Malcolm Cowley, ed., 1946), which did much to establish Faulkner's reputation; *Collected Stories* (1950); interviews from a trip to Japan, *Faulkner at Nagano* (Robert A. Jelliffe, ed., 1956); *New Orleans Sketches* (Carvel Collins, ed., 1958); *Faulkner in the University: Class Conferences at the University of Virginia* (Frederick L. Gwynn and Joseph L. Blotner, eds., 1959); and *Early Prose and Poetry* (Collins, ed., 1962).

Following Faulkner's death, a number of additional works and collections were published, including *Faulkner at West Point* (Joseph L. Fant and Robert Ashley, eds., 1964); *The Faulkner-Cowley File: Letters and Memories, 1944–1962* (Cowley, ed., 1966); *Essays, Speeches and Public Lectures* (James B. Meriwether, ed., 1966); *The Wishing Tree* (1967); *Lion in the Garden: Interviews, 1926–1962* (Meriwether and Michael Millgate, eds., 1968); *A*

Faulkner Miscellany (Meriwether, ed., 1974); *Selected Letters* (Blotner, ed., 1976); *Mayday* (Collins, ed., 1976); *Uncollected Stories* (Blotner, ed., 1979); *The Ghosts of Rowan Oak: William Faulkner's Ghost Stories for Children* (Dean Faulkner Wells, ed., 1980); *A Vision in Spring* (verse, Judith L. Sansibar, ed., 1984); *Novels 1930–35* (revised versions of *As I Lay Dying, Sanctuary, Light in August,* and *Pylon*; Noel Polk and Blotner, eds., 1985); *Letters* (*A Comprehensive Guide to the Brodsky Collection,* Vol. 2; Louis Daniel Brodsky and Robert W. Hamblin, eds., 1984); *The DeGaulle Story* (*Brodsky Collection,* Vol. 3; Brodsky and Hamblin, eds., 1984); *Battle Cry* (*Brodsky Collection,* Vol. 4; Brodsky and Hamblin, eds., 1985); *Country Lawyer and Other Stories for the Screen* (*Brodsky Collection,* Vol. 5; Brodsky and Hamblin, eds., 1987).

Faulkner's prolific output, however, is less important than his masterful exploration of such values as tradition, endurance, and honor as these are reflected in and transcend regional, racial, and class distinctions. His candor regarding vicious behavior and blind ignorance must always be balanced against his persuasive depiction of truly admirable people. Especially in his major creative period, he focuses on violence and shock while simultaneously celebrating the stoical ability to endure or triumph over adversity. In technique he brilliantly explores the individual consciousness through methods of complex and innovative narrative strategies, often employing stream of consciousness to explore the re-

cesses of the psyche. Faulkner's
writing thus reveals a symbolic sub-
text that speaks with force to patterns of belief and behavior. His
originality and accomplishments
put him in the select company of the
world's greatest writers.

PAUL SCHLUETER

Selected Bibliography

PRIMARY SOURCES

Faulkner, William. *The Sound and the Fury.* New York: Jonathan Cape and Harrison Smith, 1929; corrected edition, New York: Random House, 1984.

———. *As I Lay Dying.* New York: Jonathan Cape and Harrison Smith, 1930; corrected edition, New York: Library of America, 1985.

———. *Sanctuary.* New York: Jonathan Cape and Harrison Smith, 1931; corrected edition, New York: Random House, 1981.

———. *Light In August.* New York: Harrison Smith and Robert Haas, 1932; corrected edition, New York: Library of America, 1985.

———. *Absalom, Absalom!* New York: Random House, 1936.

———. *The Hamlet.* New York: Random House, 1940.

———. *Go Down, Moses, and Other Stories.* New York: Random House, 1942.

———. *Collected Stories.* New York: Random House, 1950.

———. *The Town.* New York: Random House, 1957.

———. *The Mansion.* New York: Random House, 1959.

———. *The Reivers.* New York: Random House, 1962.

———. *Essays, Speeches & Public Lectures*, ed. James B. Meriwether. New York: Random House, 1966.

———. *Selected Letters*, ed. Joseph L. Blotner. New York: Random House, 1976.

———. *Uncollected Stories*, ed. Joseph L. Blotner. New York: Random House, 1979.

SECONDARY SOURCES

Blotner, Joseph. *William Faulkner: A Biography.* 2 vols. New York: Random House, 1974.

Brooks, Cleanth. *Toward Yoknapatawpha and Beyond.* New Haven: Yale University Press, 1978.

Hoffman, Frederick J. *William Faulkner.* New York: Twayne, 1961; rev. ed., 1966.

Howe, Irving. *William Faulkner: A Critical Study.* New York: Random House, 1952; rev. ed., New York: Random House, 1952; 3rd ed., Chicago: University of Chicago Press, 1975.

Irwin, John T. *Doubling and Incest/Repetition and Revenge: A Speculative Reading of Faulkner.* Baltimore: The Johns Hopkins University Press, 1975.

Millgate, Michael. *The Achievement of William Faulkner.* New York: Random House, 1966.

Oates, Stephen B. *William Faulkner: The Man and the Artist.* New York: Harper & Row, 1987.

Vickery, Olga W. *The Novels of William Faulkner: A Critical Interpretation.* Baton Rouge: Louisiana State University Press, 1959; rev. ed., 1966.

Wagner, Linda W., ed. *William Faulkner: Four Decades of Criticism*. East Lansing: Michigan State University Press, 1973 (previous eds.: *William Faulkner: Two Decades of Criticism*. Edited by Frederick J. Hoffman and Olga W. Vickery [East Lansing: Michigan State University Press, 1951] and *William Faulkner: Three Decades of Criticism*. Edited by Frederick J. Hoffman and Olga W. Vickery [East Lansing: Michigan State University Press, 1960]).

ANATOLE FRANCE *1921*

Anatole France (1844–1924) French novelist, literary critic, and poet, received the Nobel Prize in literature in 1921. Deeply influenced by the classical tradition, France remained all his life a humanist committed to such values as tolerance and justice.

Born in Paris on April 16, 1844, Jacques-Anatole-François Thibault was the son of Noël-François Thibault, who, after having served in the army until 1830, had become a book dealer specializing in the French Revolution.

In 1855 France enrolled at the Collège Stanislas, and nine years later he obtained his baccalaureate with a solid background in the classical humanities. Very early in life he had developed a taste for books, and he enjoyed spending time at bookstalls. It is therefore not surprising that he worked as a bookseller before becoming a librarian, a literary critic, an editor, and an author.

France decided not to take over his father's business and instead became a reader in the publishing house of Alphonse Lemerre. There he became acquainted with the Parnassian poets, who were to influence him very deeply. In 1868 with his first publication, a study of Alfred de Vigny, the Parnassian group accepted him, and the following year two of his poems appeared in *Le Parnasse Contemporain*.

In 1870 he joined the national guard but in January 1871 was exempted from combat for medical reasons. He then left Paris for a few months until the fall of the Commune. In 1873 he published a volume of verse, *Les Poèmes Dorés*, ("The Golden Poems") and a drama, *Les Noces Corinthiennes*, (*The Bride of Corinth*) that reflect his Parnassian heritage. His style—very classical, sensitive, and precise—already manifested a sense of cynicism about human nature that he would keep throughout his life.

In 1876 he was appointed librarian to the Senate library, a post he held until his resignation in 1890. A year later, he married a twenty-year-old woman from a bourgeois family, Marie-Valérie Guérin de Sauville, with whom he had one daughter. The marriage ended in divorce in 1893.

It was in 1881 with the publication of *Le Crime de Sylvestre Bonnard* (*The Crime of Sylvester Bonnard*) that France became famous. The novel portrays an old scholar in love with books but lost in the everyday business society. Here, in the ironic yet sentimental style that was to characterize his later writings, the author showed his humanistic and skeptical nature reacting against naturalism.

After *Les Désirs de Jean Servien* (1882; *The Aspirations of Jean Servien*) set in the reign of the Commune, France published his first semiautobiographical work, *Le Livre de mon ami* (1885; *My Friend's Book*), a series of childhood memories. From 1887 until 1893, as a literary critic, he wrote a column called "La Vie Littéraire" for the newspaper *Le Temps*. His many articles on such authors as Maupassant, Hugo, Georges Sand, Leconte de Lisle, Pierre Loti, Paul Bourget, and Maurice Barrès, to mention just a few, made him a well-known figure in Parisian literary circles.

Meanwhile, in 1888, he began a liaison with Madame Arman de Cavaillet that inspired two novels: *Thais* (1890; *Thais*) and *Le Lys Rouge* (1894; *The Red Lily*). *Thais*, set in Egypt, is the tale of a courtesan who becomes a saint, while a monk who is in love with her is eventually damned. In this historical novel France again showed his skepticism through an ironic and often sarcastic style reminiscent of Voltaire. *Le Lys Rouge*, which had great success in literary circles, is a contemporary love story in the tradition of the sentimental novel. In it, France provides an interesting display of irony in the descriptions of the city of Florence, where most of the action takes place.

A year before *Le Lys Rouge*, France had published *La Rotisserie de la Reine Pédauque* (1893; *The Queen Pedauque*), a philosophical tale where he introduced the Abbé Jérôme Coignard, a fun-loving monk, sensitive to the pleasures of the flesh and always ready to drink. An epicurean as well as a scholar, Coignard reminds us of Sylvestre Bonnard and the provincial professor M. Bergeret of France's later work *L'Anneau d'améthyste*. That same year, in *Les Opinions de Jérôme Coignard* (*The Opinions of Mr. Jerome Coignard*), France expressed his own opinions of the French Revolution and of the Third Republic. While criticizing the Ancien Régime as well as the fanaticism of the Jacobins, he also criticized the institutions of the Third Republic, which he felt were dominated and ruled by the wealthy for their own benefit. In spite of these criticisms, his sympathies remained with the Republican system, which for him was the only system able to respect political freedom and individual liberties. At the same time, he proclaimed his sympathies for the developing leftist ideas and more specifically for a Socialist regime that, according to him, would really allow each individual freely to assume his own destiny.

The following year, in *Le Jardin d'Epicure* (1894; *The Garden of Epicurus*) France strongly criticized religion—more specifically, Christianity. His pessimism concerning human nature had intensified for two major reasons: he had lost his faith in the Catholic Church and in science. He had become convinced that the church, because of its extremely conservative viewpoints and its political complicity with the Ancien Régime, stood as the main obstacle to the establishment of a democratic society. He also was deeply disappointed with science, which at one point he had thought capable of bringing about social progress. In fact, since for him science was unable to change the moral nature of man, he felt that it was foolish to expect it to provide civilization with a new and better moral order.

In 1896 he was elected to the French Academy, and the following year a major event transformed his life and shaped the rest of his literary career. The Dreyfus Affair, which was dividing French literary circles between right-wing and left-wing writers, offered him a unique opportunity to voice his political ideas publicly. Alfred Dreyfus, a Jewish army captain, had been falsely condemned of high treason in an attempt to protect some important army officials who had been involved in a corruption scandal.

Strongly opposed to social injustice and prejudice, France became one of the most vocal Dreyfusards and joined Zola's campaign for a retrial. Like Zola, he made a strong pro-Dreyfus statement in the daily newspaper *L'Aurore*, and in 1898 he signed Zola's famous "J'accuse" pro-Dreyfus statement. He also showed his support for Zola by testifying at his trial, which grew out of Zola's "J'accuse," and France even returned his Legion of Honor medal when Zola was stripped of his.

In 1899 he joined the daily newspaper *Le Figaro*, and a year later he decided no longer to attend the meetings at the French Academy because of the animosity and resentment of some of his anti-Dreyfus colleagues. He remained, nonetheless, very involved in political matters as a fervent advocate of the Republic and of the separation of church and state. As his belief in social justice grew stronger, so did his criticisms of the bourgeois order. He gave all his support to the Socialist cause, and, at the end of his life, to the Communists.

The Dreyfus Affair inspired his *L'Histoire Contemporaine* (*Contemporary History*), a series of articles published from 1895 to 1900 describing events and characters of the Third Republic. The first three volumes—*L'Orme du Mail* (1897; *The Elm-Tree on the Mall*), *Le Mannequin d'Osier* (1897; *The Wickerwork Woman*), *L'Anneau d'améthyste* (1899; *The Amethyst Ring*)—are an ironic and violent satire of the ridiculous religious and social intrigues of a provincial town. Here France showed again how the church constitutes the main obstacle to the creation of a freethinking society.

The last volume focused upon one character, M. Bergeret, a professor of Latin literature who shared many of France's opinions. Bergeret also supported the Republic, because he felt that even in spite of its weaknesses it was still better than any other political system. Bergeret appeared as a disenchanted fellow who never took the opportunity to involve himself in political life—again, not unlike France himself, who only became involved in politics because of his commitment to support Dreyfus.

With *L'Histoire Contemporaine*, France's social and political preoccupations became more and more prominent as he devoted articles to the cause of the political Left. *Crainquebille* (1903; *Crainquebille*), a story written as part of *L'Histoire Contemporaine*, is an amusing, yet serious comedy in which the author, once again, dealt with the problem of justice, or lack of it. This very popular story tells of the unfair treatment, during his trial, of a small tradesman unable to defend himself against his judges, who would rather believe ridiculous testimony convenient for the authorities than try to find out the truth. In an amusing tone, France again proclaimed his hostility toward the bourgeois order and his support for socialist theories.

In 1904 he started writing for *L'Humanité*, at that time the daily newspaper of the Socialist party. He also gave several public speeches in support of socialism. One year later,

as the Russian Revolution broke out, his political activities increased greatly. The failure of that revolution was a deep disappointment to France. As a result, a very pessimistic tone permeates his subsequent writings: *L'Ile des Pingouins* (1908; *Penguin Island*), *Les Dieux ont Soif* (1912; *The Gods Are Athirst*), and *La Révolte des Agnes* (1914; *The Revolt of the Angels*).

L'Ile des Pingouins is a political fiction as well as a prophecy. It parodies French society with the description of an entire nation where wealthy capitalists exploit a helpless proletariat. In an apocalyptic vision of the future, France imagines this nation destroyed by a succession of explosions whose fumes choke all life. Slowly, however, a new civilization develops, but it turns out to be exactly like the first. That same year France also published *La Vie de Jeanne d'Arc* (1908; *The Life of Joan of Arc*), a violently anticlerical work.

Les Dieux ont Soif, an even more pessimistic novel, appeared in 1912. It is one of France's better-known works. In this work France functions both as a novelist and a historian. Always interested in the revolutionary period, he set his story in the Reign of Terror, with the gods as the leaders of the new order. France had lost all illusions about human nature and its chances for a peaceful and harmonious future. In this work he depicted even the most famous in history as nothing but mediocre men, driven by their selfishness and greed for power. In *La Révolte des Anges* France returned to such topics as God, life, religion, injustice, and intolerance. Although not a very well known work, *La Révolte des Anges* is considered by some as one of France's masterpieces.

During World War I France focused his criticisms on war, violence, oppression, and blind patriotism—which for him led to militarism, fanaticism, and bigotry. Very affected by the war, he became more and more pessimistic and chose to retire to his property in Tourraine. After the war, he became a Communist and remained one for the rest of his life. His literary style took a more biting tone, and he devoted his last years to reminiscences of his childhood. In 1918 he published *Le Petit Pierre* (*Little Pierre*) and in 1922 *La Vie en Fleur* (*The Bloom of Life*).

For the first quarter of the twentieth century, France was one of the most famous figures of French literature, not only because of his talent, but also because of his prominent role in the Dreyfus Affair. At a time when French conservatives were extremely nationalistic and often outright prejudiced, France's ideas appealed to many French liberals and to many foreigners as well. He enjoyed an international reputation, and in 1921 he was awarded the Nobel Prize in literature. When he died in 1924, he was accorded the honor of a national funeral.

If France does not enjoy the same kind of popularity today as he did sixty years ago, it is because he has been the victim of a major evolution of ideas and values. In the years that followed World War I, the surrealists were the first to condemn him for what they considered

his reactionary ideas. In spite of the fact that France was interested in a wide variety of ideas, his style, syntax, and constant striving to perfection made him appear extremely classical and, for that matter, staunchly conservative. He was regarded by the surrealists (and by many others, then and later) more as a representative of the mentality that led to the disaster of World War I than as the liberal who had the courage to denounce the conservative prejudices and bigotries of his time.

JEAN-PIERRE LALANDE

Selected Bibliography

PRIMARY SOURCES

France, Anatole. *Crainquebille, A Comedy in three Acts.* Translated by Barrett H. Clark. New York: Samuel French, 1915.

———. *The Gods Are Athirst.* Translated by Alec Brown. London: The Bodley Head, 1951.

———. *Oeuvres Complètes.* Edited by L. Carias and G. Le Prat. 25 vols. Paris: Calmann-Lévy, 1925–35.

———. *Penguin Island.* Introduction by H. R. Steeves. New York: Random House, Modern Library, 1931.

———. *The Queen Pédauque.* Translated by Joseph A. V. Stritzko. New York: Boni and Liveright, Modern Library, 1923.

SECONDARY SOURCES

Axelrad, Jacob. *Anatole France: A Life Without Illusions 1844–1924*, 3rd ed. New York: Harper & Brothers, 1944.

Chevalier, Haakon M. *The Ironic Temper: Anatole France and His Time*. New York: Oxford University Press, 1932.

Dargan, Edwin Preston. *Anatole France: 1844–1896*. New York: Oxford University Press, 1937.

Jefferson, Carter. *Anatole France: The Politics of Skepticism*. New Brunswick, N.J.: Rutgers University Press, 1965.

Stableford, Brian M. "Anatole France." In *Supernatural Fiction Writers: Fantasy and Horror*. Vol. 1. Edited by Everett F. Bleiler. New York: Scribner, 1985. Pp. 67–72.

Tylden-Wright, David. *Anatole France*. New York: Walker, 1967.

Virtanen, Reino. *Anatole France*. New York: Twayne, 1968.

JOHN GALSWORTHY   *1932*

John Galsworthy (1867–1933) was born in Kingston Hill, Surrey, England, on August 14, 1867, into an affluent family who could trace its ancestry back to the sixteenth century. His father was a wealthy solicitor, and Galsworthy lived in one of the family's mansions until he finished preparatory school at Bournemouth. More interested in sports, especially horse racing, than in academics, he attended Harrow and New College, Oxford, with the knowledge that his family's fortune would provide for him. He nevertheless earned his law degree in 1889, and intended to specialize in marine law. After being admitted to the bar in 1890, he traveled to North America, the South Seas, and Russia, financed by his father, supposedly to conduct business. On the S. S. *Torrens* en route to South America from the Pacific, he met Joseph

Conrad, at that time a mate on a merchant ship. Neither of them had become writers at that point, but they went on to become lifelong friends. Moving into an apartment in London upon his return, he exhibited no proclivity for the serious pursuit of law. Instead, he spent time meandering through the slums of London, collecting rent for his father, observing a level of existence he had never been exposed to. His initial attitude to politics was one of indifference, but as he spent more time circulating in lower-class neighborhoods, he became increasingly aware of the misery, poverty, and social injustices caused by the sharp class distinctions.

He began writing at age twenty-eight, using material from his world voyages as a basis for *From the Four Winds*, a collection of short stories published in 1897 under the pseudonym John Sinjohn. Set in Malaya, Africa, and other ports of call, each contains some sort of moral theme, ranging in subject matter from the supernatural and horrific to the ordinary. His second book, *Jocelyn*, published the following year, again under his pen name, is dedicated to Joseph Conrad. A love story, it draws partly upon his own experience of having become involved with the wife of his cousin Arthur Galsworthy. Ada was the adopted daughter of a physician and three years Galsworthy's senior when they began their ten-year relationship prior to their marriage in 1905, a day after her divorce was granted. Irene in Galsworthy's famous trilogy, *The Forsyte Saga* (1922), is partly derived from Ada, and it is to her that Galsworthy gave credit for his becoming an author. The primary reason he waited so long to arrange for her divorce, despite his devotion to her, was his concern for and loyalty to his father and the implicit repercussions the clandestine affair would have on his inheritance and livelihood.

Villa Rubein, his third book, was published in 1900, again under his pseudonym; however, he reissued it nine years later under his own name. The first book he authored using his own name from the outset was *The Island Pharisees* (1904), a satire on English society and the beginning manifestation of his dedication to social, moral, and economic reform. Two influencing factors in this social awakening were his sisters, Lilian and Mabel, with whom he had minimal contact during his years away at school. Both

sisters were actively involved in intellectual, artistic, and political matters of the time, and as he became reacquainted with them after finishing his education, he came to admire their values. Mabel provided a paradigm for June Forsyte in *The Forsyte Saga*. Lilian, the older, was an enthusiast of German philosophy and was married to a German painter with little fluency in English, whom she met when he was commissioned to paint a portrait of her father. Lilian was not one to conform to the expectations society placed on a lady of her class, and many of her views are included in *The Island Pharisees*. Both of his sisters were discreet and tolerant of his affair with Ada.

He continued the satirical vein in *The Man of Property* (1906), which deals with the wealthy segment of urban society not admitted into the inner circle of the aristocracy. (This subject was revisited in 1917 and developed into *The Forsyte Saga*.) Satire also proved effective in *The Country House* (1907), which probes wealthy landowners' preoccupation with inheritance and their role in the rural hierarchy; in *Fraternity* (1909), a study of class disparity and the failure of "liberal humanitarians'" attempts to provide relief for the poor; and in *The Patrician* (1911), dealing with the governing class and the inheritance issue, the last novel Galsworthy described as a "social study." Most of his satire, which centered around manners and morals surrounding the business, artistic, country, and aristocratic political classes, is marked by a sensitive, lyrical quality.

The next four novels—*The Dark Flower* (1913), *The Freelands* (1915), *Beyond* (1917), and *Saint's Progress* (1919)—moved into a more pragmatic realm of social ideas and the humanitarian concerns that accompany them. Galsworthy's own unorthodox lifestyle freed him from the usual Victorian repression of sexual passion. *The Dark Flower* presents a variation of his and Ada's burgeoning friendship with Margaret Morris, a professional dancer. After they helped her establish the Margaret Morris School of Dance, John and Margaret fell mutually in love, and desired to set up a triangular arrangement. Despite Ada's verbal consent, her distressed attempts to adjust to the relationship were unsuccessful. John's concern for her caused him to end the liaison with Margaret. The conflict in *The Freelands* focuses on various professionals' attempts to temper the effects of traditional Christian morality on a farm worker under their auspices, and *Saint's Progress* addresses the tension between aspects of traditional and idealistic Christianity.

Galsworthy also engaged in writing and producing a number of plays from 1906 to 1917, his interest in drama reaching back to his membership in the Oxford University Dramatic Society. He became an active opponent of censorship, working in conjunction with Fabian socialists (although he was not a Fabian), a group who believed in a gradual, rather than revolutionary, transition of society into socialism. *The Silver Box* (1906) exposes the inequities inherent in the legal system; *Strife* (1909) is a satire directed at the power struggles in labor and industry and their victims; and *Justice* (1910) advocates prison reform and abolition of solitary confinement. Other plays, including *The Pigeon* (1912), *The Fugitive* (1913), *The Mob* (1914), and *The Skin Game* (1920), call attention to anti-Semitism, animal cruelty, the practice of committing indigents to insane asylums with a single doctor's signature, and similar abuses.

The Forsyte Saga trilogy appeared after World War I. It is probably Galsworthy's most outstanding accomplishment. The Forsyte family and their friends and connections appear throughout Galsworthy's other works, covering three generations and providing a framework for satire aimed at the typical Victorian upper-middle-class family. The *Saga* consists of *Men of Property* (1906), *In Chancery* (1920), and *To Let* (1921). A second trilogy *A Modern Comedy* appeared between 1924 and 1928, continuing the saga: *The White Monkey* (1924), *The Silver Spoon* (1926), and *Swan Song* (1928).

Galsworthy went on to speak and publish in favor of expanding women's rights, reforming divorce laws, improving workers' conditions in factories, outlawing vivisection, and upgrading slaughterhouses. He also exhorted banning of the use of airplanes during war. He continued writing plays, sharing a home with his sister and her family.

He wrote a final trilogy, with an even younger generation of the upper class as its subjects. Although his enthusiasm had waned and this

work was not as powerful as his pre-
vious novels, he was awarded the
Nobel Prize in literature in 1932, co-
incidental with the publication of
The Flowering Wilderness in the
United States. Galsworthy died at
Hampstead, London, shortly there-
after on January 1, 1933.

ANN BIDLINGMAIER

Selected Bibliography

PRIMARY SOURCES

Galsworthy, John. *Captures*. St. Clair,
Minn.: Scholarly Press, 1971.
——. *Dark Flowers*. St. Clair, Minn.:
Scholarly Press, 1971.
——. *Ex Libris*. Darley, Pa.: Arden
Library, 1979.
——. *The Forsyte Saga*. New York:
Scribner, 1948.
——. *Fraternity*. St. Clair, Minn.:
Scholarly Press, 1971.

SECONDARY SOURCES

Dupre, Catherine. *John Galsworthy*.
New York: Coward, McCann, &
Geoghegan, 1976.
Dupont, V. *John Galsworthy: The Dra-
matic Artist*. Paris: Cahors, 1942.
Fisher, John. *John Galsworthy, 1867–
1933*. New York: Universe Books,
1976.
Mottram, R. H. *John Galsworthy*. Lon-
don: Longmans, Green, 1953.
Pike, Edgar R., ed. *Human Documents
of the Age of the Forsytes*. London:
Allen & Unwin, 1969.
Pritchett, Victor S. *The Working Nov-
elist*. London: Chatto & Windus,
1965.
West, Anthony, ed. *The Galsworthy
Reader*. New York: Scribner, 1967.

GABRIEL GARCÍA MÁRQUEZ   *1982*

When, in 1982, Gabriel García
Márquez (1928—) won the Nobel
Prize in literature for his 1967 novel,
Cien años de soledad (*One Hundred
Years of Solitude*), the award confirmed his long-standing international reputation for narrative excellence. The novel, like much of his
prose fiction, takes place in the
imaginary small town of Macondo,
which García Márquez patterned
after his birthplace, Arataca, near

the Atlantic coast of Colombia. He
was born on March 6, 1928, and
raised by his maternal grandparents.
After finishing secondary school in a
small town near Bogotá, García
Márquez studied for, but never
completed, a law degree. Writing—
both journalism and fiction—began
to assume an increasingly important
role in his life.

First in the coastal cities of Car-
tagena and Barranquilla, and then

in Bogotá, García Márquez began to work as a journalist. In Bogotá he was a reporter for *El Espectador* ("The Spectator") and then foreign correspondent in Europe. When Rojas Pinilla, then dictator of Colombia, closed down the paper, García Márquez traveled in Europe and then spent two years in Caracas, Venezuela, as a free-lance journalist. After the Cuban revolution, he worked briefly for the official Cuban news agency, first in Bogotá and afterward in Cuba and New York City. Later he moved to Mexico City, where he supplemented his income as a free-lance journalist by writing film scripts and acting as a public relations agent. In 1967 he and his family established residence in Barcelona, Spain. *One Hundred Years of Solitude*, published that year, achieved instant success. Since its publication, the novel has received many awards: Premio Chianciano (Italy, 1969), Prix de Meilleur Livre Etranger (France, 1969), Premio Rómulo Gallegos (Colombia, 1972), and Neustadt International Prize for literature (1972). García Márquez has subsequently been able to devote himself exclusively to writing what he wishes. In 1975 he left Spain for Mexico, where he now spends most of the year, although since 1982, when the president of Colombia invited him back to his native land, he also spends time there.

Gabriel García Márquez is one of the principal contributors to the so-called boom of contemporary Latin American literature. References to his works are a necessity in studies of the unparalleled flourishing of Spanish American writing during the second half of this century. The phrase "magical realism," coined by the Cuban writer Alejo Carpentier in 1949 to describe the narrative representation of Latin American reality, captures one of the primary characteristics of García Márquez's fiction. In his Nobel lecture García Márquez suggested that the originality of Latin American literature may be attributed to the "outsized reality" of the continent and that what appears magical to European eyes is simply the circumstances under which Latin Americans live and create.

An examination of the trajectory of García Márquez's fictional output shows recurring themes and both stylistic continuity and change. The imaginary town of Macondo is the setting of many works; the fictional world demonstrates a continuity similar to Faulkner's Yoknapatawpha county. Although García Márquez's first novel, *La hojarasca* (1955; *Leaf Storm*), takes place in Macondo, and utilizes his typical themes of time, decadence, and solitude, it differs from later works in its presentation of narrative material through the interior monologues of three characters whom the author uses "as mere intermediaries to relate a unified, lyrical account of Macondo's past and present reality" (McMurray, p. 19). The story, "El coronel no tiene quien le escriba" (1958; "No One Writes to the Colonel"), on the other hand, conflates the theme of solitude with that of *la violencia* (the violence) that dominated Colombian public life from 1948 (the assassination of popular leftist politician Jorge Gaitán) into the 1960s. The novella focuses on the apparently absurd hopes of its impoverished protagonist, the colonel, that his pension check, for which he has waited for fifteen years, and which he is owed for his role in completing the inventory of the goods of the rebel forces during their surrender to government troops, will arrive soon. The colonel emerges as a heroic figure who struggles against a violent, implacably corrupt reality to retain human dignity and strength.

The political circumstances—underground forces fighting against governmental repression—and the theme of Colombian violence also emerge in La mala hora (1962; "The Evil Hour"). Using a montage structure to elaborate the moral degeneration of a town caught in the grip of physical and psychological violence, García Márquez dramatically portrays a fictional world that reflects historical reality. This authorial competence is equally highlighted in the eight short stories written between 1955 and 1960 that are collected as Los funerales de la Mamá Grande (1962; Big Mama's Funeral). The title story in particular demonstrates García Márquez's ability to integrate a variety of narrative tones, mixing magical and ordinary realities through hyperbole, enumeration, irony, and absurdity. The result is a rhetorically excellent satire of the political, social, and religious institutions of Colombia.

One Hundred Years of Solitude (1967) is still considered by most readers to be García Márquez's most ambitious and successful narrative. Translated into English barely three years after it was first published in Spanish, the novel appeared on the New York Times best-seller list. It recounts the story of the rise and fall of the Buendía family and of Macondo, the town that José Arcadio and Ursula Buendía found after fleeing the ghost of a man whom José Arcadio had killed because he insulted his macho honor. In the novel, García Márquez offers an ironic critique of Colombian social and political institutions and of North American commercial imperialism. He also lyrically evokes the difficulties of the human condition.

In part, the novel traces Macondo's movement toward Western science and history, and away from its mythic origins in the "enchanted region" that the fictional twentieth-century settlers "discover." Built on the banks of a river "that ran along a bed of polished stones, which were white and enormous, like prehistoric eggs . . ." when "the world was so recent that many things lacked names . . . ," Macondo may be imagined as a paradigmatic site for the beginning of civilization.

A large cast of characters contributes to shaping the complex events described. José Arcadio Buendía, the first patriarch of Macondo and of the family, explores language and especially science. He is aided in this endeavor by the gypsy Melquíades, who brings this knowledge to the town, and who, after many deaths, takes up residence in the Buendía house, where he writes in Sanskrit a chronicle that recounts the story of the Buendía family and that therefore turns out to be the novel itself. The Buendía men are named either José Arcadio or Aureliano, and after a few generations, character traits particular to each name emerge. In general, the Buendía women, and especially Ursula, the matriarch who lives between 115 and 122 years (that is, for most of the novel), keep the household members from starvation. The only other character who lives longer than Ursula (aside from Melquíades) is Pilar Ternera, lover of the second generation of Buendía sons, José Arcadio and Aureliano, and mother of the third, Arcadio and Aureliano José. Complex interactions of other characters, including gringos, corrupt town officials, disillusioned generals, a highly sensitive music teacher, a girl too beautiful to be seen in public, and many others, vivify the pages of the story.

Although treated as fiction, the political history of Colombia plays an important role. Colonel Aureliano Buendía, for example, fights thirty-two battles as a rebel leader, without winning any. Nevertheless, he becomes a national hero. Later, history is rewritten to exclude his feats, just as the massacre witnessed by José Arcadio Segundo Buendía, in which government troops fire on thousands of striking workers on American-owned banana plantations, never appears in official documents. In history textbooks, it never happened.

The language of *One Hundred Years of Solitude* makes the ordinary appear magical and the magical seem ordinary. For instance, an "enormous, transparent block with infinite internal needles, in which the light of the sunset was fragmented into colored stars," turns out to be ice. The attitude of wonder evidenced here—an ordinary object becomes a "miracle"—may be attributed to the innocence and detachment from history of the early inhabitants of Macondo. A converse example—of language that makes the extraordinary ordinary—occurs when José Arcadio Buendía dies: "They saw a light rain of tiny yellow flowers falling. They fell on the town all through the night in a silent storm, and they covered the roofs and blocked the doors and smothered the animals who slept outdoors. So many flowers fell from the sky that in the morning the streets were carpeted with a compact cushion and they had to clear them away with shovels and rakes so that the funeral procession could pass by." The matter-of-fact tone and tools of quotidian life make the flowery precipitation seem normal.

If not the protagonist, time is certainly an essential aspect of the novel's thematic and structural composition. Linear and circular time function in tandem, creating a structure that sometimes follows, but more often challenges, historical chronology. Melquíades's manuscript, in fact, documents past, present, and future moments in coexistence rather than in linear fashion.

There is a fatalistic sense of predetermination in the epigraph of his manuscript, the prophecy that turns out to be true: "The first of the line is tied to a tree and the last is being eaten by ants." The novel ends, and the world of Macondo is destroyed, as the last Aureliano deciphers the last lines of Melquíades's parchments, which describe his death; he simultaneously reads and lives his fate.

After coauthoring a book on the Latin American novel with Mario Vargas Llosa (1968), and publishing several short stories in periodicals, García Márquez collected seven short stories with the title of the longest: *La increíble y triste historia de la cándida Eréndira y de su abuela desalmada* (1972; "The Incredible and Sad Tale of Innocent Eréndira and Her Heartless Grandmother"). None of the stories take place in Macondo, although the protagonist of the title story reminds the reader of a minor character in *One Hundred Years of Solitude*. Colors and visual imagery (usually grotesque) reveal the story's origins as a film script. Set in the desert and on the coast of Colombia, the story develops the theme of human cruelty to and exploitation of others. Eréndira's grandmother requires her granddaughter to become a prostitute in order to pay for the accident that burned down the mansion. Eréndira orders her lover Ulises to kill her grandmother; immediately after he succeeds, she leaves him. Predominantly realistic, there are nevertheless fantastic elements in the story. The grandmother's blood, for instance, is green and oily. Some recurring themes typical of García Márquez are evident: solitude and the corruption possible in human interactions.

The protagonist of *El otoño del patriarca* (1975; *Autumn of the Patriarch*), again a novel of dictatorship, uses absolute power to destroy and maim people, animals, and land. His huge sexual appetite (he is reputed to have fathered five thousand children), flat "elephant-like" feet, and long life (he lives 107 to 232 years) parody the mythic proportions of the archetypal hero. The parody is also emphasized in his infantile attachment to his mother, to his double (whom he uses to prevent being assassinated), and to his wife, an ex-nun. The patriarch embodies both an extreme form of psychological solitude, exemplified in his inability to communicate except through violence, and a more general Latin American sociopolitical reality. Nevertheless, although García Márquez's allusions to corrupt Latin American oligarchs and ecclesiastics and to gringo imperialism abound, the tone is not that of the usual novel of social protest. Time is treated nonchronologically, there are rapid and frequent shifts in narrative voice (dialogue mixes with interior monologue, for example), and grotesque imagery again assumes an important role. *Autumn of the Patriarch* is a dense (sentences can be pages long), highly poeticized critique of human solitude, decrepitude, and cruelty.

Since 1975, García Márquez has published several novels, including

Crónica de una muerte anunciada (1981; *Chronicle of a Death Foretold*) and *El amor en los tiempos de cólera* (1984; "Love in Times of Anger"), written film scripts, and continued to challenge the boundaries of truth and fiction with such works as *Relato de un náufrago, que estuvo diez días a la deriva en una balsa sin comer ni beber, que fue proclamado héroe de la patria, besado por las reinas de la belleza y hecho rico por la publicidad, y luego aborrecido por el gobierno y olvidado para siempre* (1985; "*The Story of a Shipwrecked Sailor who Drifted on a Life Raft for Ten Days Without Food or Water, Was Proclaimed a National Hero, Kissed by Beauty Queens, Made Rich Through Publicity, and then Spurned by the Government and Forgotten for All Time*").

When Gabriel García Márquez was awarded the Nobel Prize, the committee recognized what the world had long known: His writings, and especially the prose fiction, are such skillful depictions of Latin America's "outsized reality" that his name is practically synonymous with the autochthonous literary movement popularly called magical realism.

STACEY SCHLAU

Selected Bibliography

PRIMARY SOURCES

García Márquez, Gabriel. *The Autumn of the Patriarch*. Translated by Gregory Rabassa. New York: Harper & Row, 1977.

———. *Collected Stories*. Translated by Gregory Rabassa and B. Bernstein. New York: Perennial Library, 1984.

———. *One Hundred Years of Solitude*. Translated by Gregory Rabassa. New York: Harper & Row, 1970.

———. *The Story of a Shipwrecked Sailor, Who Drifted on a Life Raft for Ten Days Without Food or Water, Was Proclaimed a National Hero, Kissed by Beauty Queens, Made Rich Through Publicity, and Then Spurned by the Government and Forgotten for All Time*. Translated by Randolph Hogan. New York: Knopf, 1986.

SECONDARY SOURCES

Janes, Regina. *Gabriel García Márquez: Revolution in Wonderland*. Columbia: University of Missouri Press, 1981.

McMurray, George R. *Gabriel García Márquez*. New York: Ungar, 1977.

Miller, Yvette, and Charles Rossman, eds. *Gabriel García Márquez*. Special issue of *Latin American Literary Review*, 13, No. 25 (1985).

Shaw, Bradley A., and Nora Vera-Goodwin, eds. *Critical Perspectives on Gabriel García Márquez*. Lincoln, Neb.: Society of Spanish and Spanish-American Studies, 1986.

Williams, Raymond L. *Gabriel García Márquez*. Boston: Twayne, 1984.

ANDRÉ GIDE   *1947*

André Gide (1869–1951) received the Nobel Prize in literature in 1947, almost at the end of a long and very productive literary life. He was born in Paris on November 22, 1869, into a wealthy bourgeois family. His conservative Protestant parents sent him to the Ecole Alsacienne, a select Protestant school, from which he was expelled several months later because of his "bad [sexual] habits." Subsequently he studied with private tutors, but in a rather disconnected fashion. He studied the piano, perhaps with greatest interest, and was an excellent pianist until his death in 1951. Gide related his youth with complete frankness in *Si le grain ne meurt* (1926; *If It Die*). At eleven, he experienced his first *schaudern*, or trauma, on the death of his young cousin Emile Widmer. Several months later, his father died. Henceforth, as he was growing up, his entourage consisted principally of women who incarnated moral rigor and attempted to teach him to conform to social norms and to fulfill his duties.

In 1882 he and his entire family were traumatized to learn of the love affairs of his aunt Mathilde Rondeaux, the mother of his cousin Madeleine, with whom he fell in love at this time. The episode later helped to inspire *La Porte étroite* (1909; *Strait Is the Gate*).

In 1889 he was readmitted to the Ecole Alsacienne for one year, and the following year he completed his studies at the Lycée Henri IV. During this brief period of formal schooling he befriended the poet Pierre Louys and the literary critic and politician Léon Blum, who remained lifelong friends.

At twenty-one he became unofficially engaged to his cousin Madeleine Rondeaux. The same summer he retired to Annecy to write his first book, *Les Cahiers d'André Walter* (1892; *The Notebooks of André Walter*) which was published the following year, as well as poems and *Le Traité du Narcisse* (1891; *Narcissus*). *The Notebooks of André Walter*, written in the form of a diary, a genre Gide used often, expresses the young man's burning desire to marry his cousin, whom he calls Emmanuelle. He envisaged marriage on an intellectual and spiritual plane as a communion of two souls. At this time he began to frequent literary salons, especially that of Mallarmé, whom he greatly admired. He also met prominent literary figures, including Oscar Wilde, as well as others destined to become great, such as Paul Claudel. During this period he attempted to fulfill his military obligations but received a medical discharge from the army after only one week of service. He traveled extensively in Germany, Spain, and North Africa and wrote several short works. After his mother's death in 1895, and against her advice, he finally persuaded Madeleine to marry him. Prior to the wedding, however, he consulted a physician who mistakenly assured him that, once married, he would see his homosexual preference disappear.

A year after his wedding, he settled on a small estate in Normandy and became mayor of his village, partly out of a sense of responsibility and partly in order to come into closer contact with everyday life while writing his first major work, *Les Nourritures terrestres* (1897; *The Fruits of the Earth*). It was called by some a gospel of joy, for it advocates the abolition of taboos and proclaims the freedom to enjoy life to the fullest in all the opportunities it offers without fear of sin. This proclamation of the emancipation of the individual, who was urged to be concerned only about himself, elicited the admiration of numerous young writers and broadened Gide's circle of friends, which was to include for many years Henri Ghéon, Marcel Drouin, who married Madeleine's sister, and soon afterward Jacques Copeau, Francis Jammes, Jean Schlumberger, and others.

During the following decade Gide continued to travel extensively in Italy, in Germany, and twice in Algeria while writing a number of important essays on literary and philosophical themes. Nietzsche's strong influence on him during this period culminated in the publication of *L'Immoraliste* (1902; *The Immoralist*) and the play *Saul* (1903). *The Immoralist* was Gide's first story that, because of his concern for structural verisimilitude, is narrated in the first person. Michel, the protagonist, tells his friends how he became gravely ill shortly after his

wedding and how in North Africa he not only recovered his health, but also found a new zest for life. He felt morally regenerated thanks to his discovery of a new ethics, which replaced all moral constraints by ideals of self-fulfillment in strength and independence. After his wife, Marceline, dies, in part victim of his new ethics, Michel experiences anguish and doubt. Ultimately, he discovers the limitations of the immorality he had learned in *The Fruits of the Earth*. Thus, in the end, *The Immoralist* qualifies and completes the earlier work while illustrating Gide's development. Although perhaps less evidently so, *Saul* also shows the negative consequences of embracing the doctrine expressed in *The Fruits of the Earth*. It is because Saul, the first king of the Hebrews, followed all his whims and inclinations that he was defeated and killed—or committed suicide.

By 1900 Gide had perfected his art, and his influence had begun to grow, thanks especially to his writings on aesthetic and political issues in several literary publications. In 1909, with his friends Copeau, Drouin, Ghéon, Ruyters, and Schlumberger, he founded *La Nouvelle Revue Française* (*NRF*), which rapidly began to play a very significant role in French letters. Underscoring the importance he attached to the review, Gide published in it *La Porte étroite* (1909; *Strait Is the Gate*) and subsequently almost all his works. After 1919, under Jacques Rivière's able direction, the review played a dominant role in European letters and contributed much to Gide's renown. To a considerable degree, the *NRF* and the literary group Gide formed around it constitute one of his major achievements.

Strait Is the Gate is Gide's second first-person narrative. He made several attempts to write it over a period of almost twenty years. Largely autobiographical, it contains numerous fragments taken from his wife's diary and from letters written prior to their marriage. Following the teaching of their pastor, who urges them to lead an arduous and saintly life, Jérôme and Alissa are shocked at first when they learn that Alissa's mother is adulterous. Although they continue to love each other, they resolve to seek refuge from the world in an exalted spirituality. Jérôme immerses himself in his studies, while Alissa sacrifices herself for her sister and her father. Finally, she is drawn away from her beloved, with whom she wants to be united only spiritually in God. This Protestant asceticism leads her into a frightful solitude and anguish that culminate in her useless death. Jérôme appends to his own account the diary kept by Alissa during this phase of her life. Although Alissa is an admirable character, through her Gide shows how the opposite of Michel's ethics in *The Immoralist* can also be inhuman and destructive.

Just prior to the outbreak of the war in 1914 Gide completed *Les Caves du Vatican* (1914; *The Vatican Swindle* or *Lafcadio's Adventures*). In this *sotie*, or satirical and farcical novel, Gide opted for the conventional structure of the omnipresent narrator whose irony is an important structural factor. The story is based on a hoax. Having been led to believe that the pope had been kidnapped by Freemasons and locked in the cellars of the Vatican, members of the conservative Catholic French establishment attempt to rescue the Holy Father. In the course of this undertaking, one of them, Amédée Fleurissoire, is a victim of the monstrously amoral but charming Lafcadio, the hero of the story, who gratuitously throws him from a moving train and thus kills him. All Lafcadio wanted to accomplish by this act was to prove his freedom, prove that he could do it! Because the crime is gratuitous, it is a perfect crime, and no one can find the criminal. But Lafcadio loathes impunity and is about to turn himself in when he meets Geneviève, Fleurissoire's niece, who falls in love with him. In the end, he is undecided about his crime as well as about Geneviève, for whom his esteem declines as her love increases. Most readers were shocked by Lafcadio's "gratuitous act," by Gide's ridicule of Catholicism, and by the depiction of homosexuality as normal behavior. At the same time, Gide tested the narrative techniques he was to use in *Les Faux Monnayeurs* (1925; *The Counterfeiters).* While *The Vatican Swindle* cost him the friendship of some, including Paul Claudel, it did contribute considerably to his fame as well as to his notoriety on the eve of the war.

During the first year and a half of World War I, Gide did volunteer work to help Belgian refugees, experienced a religious crisis, and carried on an affair with Marc Allégret, the young son of friends. Meanwhile, having finally become convinced of her husband's homosexuality, Madeleine burned their correspondence. Gide was despondent about this loss. In the years following the war, his relationship with several of his closest friends became strained because they had returned to the religious fold, while his friendship with Roger Martin du Gard, Maria van Rysselberghe, and others blossomed. In addition to translations from the works of Conrad, Shakespeare, and Tagore, he published *La Symphonie pastorale* (1919; *The Pastoral Symphony*). In this moving story, Gide returned to the first-person narrative technique. The pastor of a Swiss village takes in a blind adolescent orphan, Gertrude. Thanks to his dedication to her education, the girl makes extraordinary progress. In the meantime, the pastor neglects his own wife and children. Unwittingly, he and Gertrude fall in love with each other. His feelings lead him to the rationalization that restrictive moral Christian teachings came from Saint Paul, whereas Christ had taught love. After a successful operation, Gertrude is able to see. She realizes that in fact she does not love the pastor, but Jacques, his oldest son. Horrified by the grief she caused to all about her, Gertrude throws herself into the river. Moments after she has been pulled out of the stream, she dies, but not before telling the pastor that Jacques had converted her to Catholicism and that he has the intention of taking Holy Orders. While Gide seems to endorse the pastor's view that Christian morality is full of taboos absent from the teachings of Christ, he also shows the pastor to be a tragic example of psychological and moral blindness. *The Pastoral Symphony* has been Gide's most popular work in print and on the screen.

In 1923 Gide published a volume of influential essays on Dostoyevsky, whom he had admired all his life. Intrigued by the idea of paternity, which he had not yet experienced, he had a child, Catherine, by Elisabeth van Rysselberghe, the daughter of his very close friends. Gide adopted his daughter after his wife's death in 1938.

One year after writing an apology for homosexuality, *Corydon*, which appeared in 1924, Gide published *Les Faux-Monnayeurs* (1925; *The Counterfeiters*), which he regarded as his first real novel. Edouard, the central character, is a novelist who keeps a diary while attempting to write a novel about a gang of adolescent counterfeiters. The difficulties he encounters stem from his desire to incorporate into his work his total experience of life and simultaneously contrast it with the reality he is creating. As he presented Edouard pondering on the difficulties he faces with his novel, Gide did not want merely to create the illusion of infinite reflection—the novel in Edouard's diary and the diary in the novel—but to examine all the techniques and possibilities of the genre. In addition to the theme of literary creation, he attacks counterfeiters in the broadest sense of the word—all fakes who emit false values. Gide gives a free rein to his humor and irony. He also satirizes hypocrites and cynics. As Claude Martin most perceptively pointed out, in his polyphonic novel Gide "did not attempt to paint the society of his time; instead he created a moral world and experimented in it with all the stances possible before life as well as with their opposites," for Gide believed that "the novel gives life to the possible; it does not revive reality."

At this point in his life, Gide expressed with increasing clarity his ideas on religion and homosexuality—which, he claimed, were the two most important concerns in his life. He also began to take a stand on the two burning social and political issues of his time: social justice and colonialism. For ten months he traveled in the Congo and Chad, where he was able to observe at first hand the exploitation of the natives and its effects. He gave an account of this trip in *Voyage au Congo* (1927; *Travels in the Congo*).

By then he had written all but one of his major works, *Thésée*, (1946; *Theseus*). Henceforth, he was to spend an increasing part of his time away from his wife, who lived in Cuverville, while he stayed in an apartment in Paris near Maria Van Rysselberghe, known as "la Petite Dame," who would have been his mother-in-law had he married the mother of his daughter. As Eckermann had done for Goethe, she recorded all his activities from 1919 until his death—but without his knowledge. Her extensive *Cahiers*, published in 1970, enjoyed consider-

able success, not only because they are a mine of information on Gide, but for their intrinsic literary qualities.

Until the eve of World War II, Gide was recognized by many as the *contemporain capital*, the dominant literary figure of his time, and widely acclaimed as such around the world. He became committed to the causes of the Left. In addition to campaigning against colonialism, he strongly opposed fascism. He traveled to Berlin with André Malraux to ask Goebbels for Dimitrov's release; he engaged in vast public debates, presided over the International Committee for the Defense of Culture, and protested against the policy of nonintervention in the Spanish Civil War adhered to by Western democracies. This period of commitment culminated in 1936 with his trip to the USSR as an official guest of the Soviet government. Although he was acclaimed there as the greatest living author and showered with the most flattering honors, the little that he did see of the Soviet Union, terrorized by the genocidal famine in Ukraine and by Stalin's purges, dampened his enthusiasm for communism. Above all, he was shocked by the absence of freedom and truth, as well as by the cynicism and brutality of Soviet leaders toward the people. Gide had the courage to recognize his error in supporting communism in his *Retouches à mon Retour de l'URSS* (1937; *Afterthoughts on the USSR*). The profound disillusionment he felt in the Soviet Union was compounded by the attempt of his friends in the French Left, Malraux in particular, to persuade him not to publicize his true impressions for fear that such revelations might hurt the workers' cause. This experience contributed to bring about Gide's political disengagement and to make him turn his full attention again to literary activities, especially to his *Journal*, which he had begun in 1889, perhaps even earlier. Since 1909, he had published occasional excerpts from it in the *Nouvelle Revue Française*. *Journal 1889–1939* (1947–51; *The Journals of André Gide*) exceeds 1700 pages and documents the development of Gide's innermost self as well as an entire epoch as seen by a keen observer who took an interest in all major events and reacted to them. Many readers regard this as his most original and remarkable work.

At the outbreak of World War II Gide went to live with friends in Provence and later in North Africa. Because of his age and circumstances, he did not become involved. A year after the liberation, Gide published his last major work, *Theseus*. Written in Algiers and published in New York, this book recapitulates the major themes of Gide's previous work and seeks to justify his values and actions. The hero, Theseus, with whom Gide can be identified, is serene and regrets nothing. Having written this work, Gide felt fulfilled. The following year, he received the Nobel Prize.

Gide has been one of the most influential French writers of this century, both in France and throughout the world. At the end of his life he legitimately could say with his last hero, Theseus: "It is sweet for me to think that after me, thanks to me, men will realize they are happier, better and freer. For the good of humanity, I have accomplished my work. I have lived."

JEAN-PIERRE CAP

Selected Bibliography

PRIMARY SOURCES

Gide, André. *Journal 1889–1939*. Paris: Gallimard, 1939. In "Bibliothèque de la Pléiade."

———. *Journal 1939–1949. Souvenirs*. Paris: Gallimard, 1954. In "Bibliothèque de la Pléiade."

———. *Oeuvres complètes d'André Gide*. Edited by L. Martin Chauffier. 15 vols. Paris: Gallimard, 1932–39.

———. *Romans, récits et soties, oeuvres lyriques*. Edited by Yvonne Davet and Jean-Jacques Thierry. Paris: Gallimard, 1958.

———. *Le Théâtre complet*. 8 vols. Neuchâtel and Paris: Ides et Calendes, 1947–49.

SECONDARY SOURCES

Boisdeffre, Pierre de. *Vie d'André Gide 1869–1951: Essai de biographie critique*. Paris: Hachette, 1970.

Delay, Jean. *La Jeunesse d'André Gide*. 2 vols. Paris: Gallimard, 1956–57. Abridged and translated by June Guicharnaud as *The Youth of André Gide*. Chicago: University of Chicago Press, 1963.

Goulet, Alain. *Fiction et vie sociale dans l'oeuvre d'André Gide*. 2 vols. Paris: Minard, 1984–85.

Lejeune, Philippe. *Exercises d'ambiguïté. Lectures de "Si le grain ne meurt" d'André Gide.* Paris: Lettres Modernes, 1974.

Martin, Claude. *La Maturité d'André Gide: De "Paludes" à "L'Immoraliste" 1895-1902.* Paris: Klincksieck, 1977.

Martin du Gard, Roger. *Notes sur André Gide 1913-1951.* Paris: Gallimard, 1951. Translated by John Russell as *Notes on André Gide.* London: Deutsch, 1953.

Moutote, Daniel. *Le Journal d'André Gide et les problèmes du moi 1889-1925.* Paris: Presses Universitaires de France, 1968.

O'Neill, Kevin. *André Gide and the "Roman d'aventure."* Sydney, Australia: Sydney University Press, 1969.

Painter, George D. *André Gide. A Critical Biography.* New York: Atheneum, 1968.

Rysselberghe, Maria van. *Les Cahiers de la Petite Dame.* 4 vols. Paris: Gallimard, 1973.

Savage, Catharine H. *André Gide: L'évolution de sa pensée religieuse.* Paris: Nizet, 1962.

Schlumberger, Jean. *Madeleine et André Gide.* Paris: Gallimard, 1956. Translated by Richard H. Akeroyd as *Madeleine and André Gide.* Tuscaloosa, Ala.: Portals Press, 1980.

KARL ADOLPH GJELLERUP 1917

Karl Gjellerup (1857-1919) was born on June 2, 1857, in Roholte, Denmark. His father, the Lutheran pastor Carl Adolph Gjellerup, died when his son was only three years old. In the home of an uncle who was then pastor of the garrison church in Copenhagen, the boy spent his formative years surrounded by the Protestant religiousness of the family and his uncle's literary ambitions. This influence was later reflected in several of Gjellerup's stories whose central theme concerns man's struggle to bring the material, temporal life here on earth into harmony with the doctrine that promises eternal salvation through faith. In 1874 the boy graduated summa cum laude from high school, where he had excelled in all disciplines.

After his graduation, he wrote two dramas in quick succession. Although the works were considered promising for so young a writer, his family felt that it would be better for the young man to get a university education. He fulfilled his uncle's expectations by studying theology. Once again he proved his intellectual abilities when he graduated summa cum laude with a bachelor's degree in divinity in the summer of 1878. Those four years of theological studies and considerable time in the country after his uncle had moved from Copenhagen to South Sjaelland left an indelible impression on Gjellerup and planted the seeds of his subsequent discontentment with the teachings and practices of the church. In view of his growing antipathy toward established beliefs, Karl became gradually aware of the fact that a future as a Lutheran clergyman would amount to abject hypocrisy. He wanted to be a writer.

In the year of his graduation from the university he wrote down his weltanschauung in a novel entitled *En Idealist* (1879; "An Idealist") by using the pseudonym Epigonos. After further intensive readings in Greek, English, and particularly the German classics, the young theologian turned away from his chosen career and prepared himself for a life as a writer of lyrical poetry, dramas, and novels. He became deeply interested in what was then referred to as "modernist doctrines" and soon became a disciple of the naturalist Charles Darwin, the Danish literary historian and critic Georg Brandes, and the British evolutionist philosopher Herbert Spencer. He took up an antitheological battle-ax in a series of short stories and poems that did not so much reflect any profound original thought as they did the disposition and intellectual mettle of a young man whose fiery mind and temperament had yet to be molded. In quick succession he wrote works that reflected the activities and directions of his mind in their titles: *Arvelighed og moral* (1881; *Heredity and Morals*) expostulates Darwin's evolutionary viewpoint; *Germanernes Lærling* (1882; *The Apprentice of the Teutons*) discusses a program for life on earth; and *Aander og tider* (1882; "Spirits and Times") once again reaffirms his support of the thoughts of Darwin.

When Gjellerup inherited a small sum of money in early 1883, he undertook a lengthy journey abroad. This opportunity proved to be fortuitous for the future career of the aspiring writer. For three months he stayed in Rome, where he pursued studies in watercolor painting and stimulated his literary interests through readings about Roman history, philosophy, and art. The short story "Romulus" appeared in 1883 and is a testimonial to his fruitful stay in Italy. On his return home to Denmark, Gjellerup traveled through Switzerland, Greece, Russia, and Sweden. By the end of this yearlong journey Gjellerup's earlier radical theories had become less strident. In fact, he now began to recant much of what he had written earlier about the theories of Darwin and the teachings of Brandes.

Soon after his return home, fully acknowledging that he was not meant to be a clergyman, he declared himself a professional writer. He had, indeed, completed his

Bildungsreise, his journeyman's sojourn to find himself. His natural flair for literature revealed itself in the beautiful short story "G-Dur" (1883; "G-Major"), which treats the closeness and devotion of two people for one another, and in the historical drama *Brynhild* (1884). Both works reflect and affirm an idealism that stands in stark contrast to the dominant naturalistic traits of the times. Gjellerup's affinity for German classicism, his interest in Roman and Greek antiquity, his love for Wagner, his translations into modern Danish of tales of the *Eddas* and Old Norse sagas, all of these rather eclectic intellectual meanderings now contributed to his efforts to reconcile the modern spirit of Christianity with the classical Greek love of beauty. His travel book *Vandreåret* ("Wander Year") published in 1885, reinforced the expectation that Gjellerup's future plays, poems, and stories would have an orientation toward an idealism that sought to reconcile the temporal and the spiritual.

From 1885 to 1887 Gjellerup made Dresden his residence. There he found an artistic and intellectual climate in which he was comfortable and that suited his literary ambitions.

He returned to Denmark in 1887 to marry Eugenia Bendix. Although his years in Denmark after his marriage were productive from a literary point of view—he wrote the plays *Herman Vandel* (1891) and *Windsorn* (1893), the tragic and insightful novel *Minna* (1889), as well as an essay on Richard Wagner's *Nibelungenring*—Gjellerup felt an urge to return to Dresden, where his creativeness had been stimulated so positively during his earlier visit.

In March 1892 Gjellerup moved to the small town of Klotzsche near Dresden. As the turn of the century approached and Dresden experienced a euphoric period culturally, Gjellerup's search for individual fulfillment and salvation led him from the musical drama of Wagner, which was steeped in Germanic tradition and lore, to the philosophical wisdom of an oriental Buddha and the promises of Nirvana, which were firmly rooted in the traditions and lore of India.

Der Pilgrim Kamanita (1906; *The Pilgrim Kamanita*), written in German, is set on the banks of the fictitious River Gunga when the Lord Buddha visits the "City of Five Hills." Kamanita, the rich, well-educated son of a merchant, enters upon his pilgrimage in search of a definition of the world, the secrets of perfection, and the promise of Nirvana. The artistic beauty of this novel, with its brilliantly colorful passages about nature's blossoming gardens, is undeniable. Kamanita's spiritual awakening and subsequent transformation through myriad mutations of Hindu philosophy are portrayed in a fascinating mixture of realism and mysticism.

While writing *Kamanita*, Gjellerup became more and more convinced that the German language was for him the ideal linguistic vehicle with which to advance his art. On a more prosaic level, one could argue somewhat cynically that he had found an audience in Germany that supported him beyond any measure that he had experienced in his native country. Nearly all of Gjellerup's works afterward were written in German and were published by Quelle and Meyer in Leipzig. His dramas *Die Opferfeuer* (1903; "The Sacrificial Fires") and *Das Weib des Vollendeten* (1907; "The Wife of the Perfect One") were very popular productions on the stages of Dresden, Dessau, and Stuttgart and should be considered, along with the poetic novels *The Pilgrim Kamanita, Verdensvandrerne* (1910; "The World Travelers"), *Guds venner* (1916; "The Friend of God"), *Den gyldene gren* (1917; "The Golden Bough"), as part of German literature. One might be tempted to call Gjellerup the foremost Buddhist writer in the German language. As Gjellerup himself remarked, his books had found genuine appreciation only in Germany, perhaps because they were so strongly influenced by German idealism of the eighteenth and early nineteenth centuries.

In awarding Karl Gjellerup half of the prize in literature in 1917, the other half intriguingly enough going to his countryman Henrik Pontoppidan, who was born in the same year as Gjellerup and was also the son of a Protestant pastor, the Nobel Committee of the Swedish Academy cited Karl Gjellerup's accomplishments "for his varied and rich poetry, which is inspired by lofty ideals."

Only two years after receiving the world's most widely known award for literature, Karl Audolph Gjellerup died in Klotzsche on October 13, 1919.

AXEL CLAESGES

Selected Bibliography

PRIMARY SOURCES

Gjellerup, Karl. *Der goldene Zweig.* Leipzig: Quelle und Meyer, 1917.

———. *Minna.* Translated by L. Nelson. London: n.p., 1913.

———. *The Pilgrim Kamanita.* Translated by John E. Logie. London: n.p., 1911.

———. *Romulus.* Translated by Margarete Bottger. Leipzig: Quelle und Meyer, 1924.

SECONDARY SOURCE

Rosenberg, P. A., ed. *Karl Gjellerup, der Dichter und Denker. Sein Leben in Selbstzeugnissen.* 2 vols. Leipzig: Quelle und Meyer, 1922.

WILLIAM GOLDING   *1983*

William Golding (1911—), Nobel laureate in literature for 1983, was born on September 19, 1911, in Cornwall, England, and has lived since 1945 near Salisbury in Wiltshire, where he and his wife Ann Brookfield raised their two children. Pushed in youth by his schoolmaster father to become a scientist, Golding rebelled against this pressure midway through his career at Oxford and took his B.A. in English literature in 1935. After a four-year fling at acting, he married in 1939 and accepted a position teaching English and philosophy at Bishop Wordsworth's School in Salisbury. From 1940 to 1945 he saw considerable combat as an officer in the Royal Navy, an experience that, like Joseph Conrad's Congo journey, darkened his vision of life. At war's end he returned to teaching in Salisbury and began writing fiction in earnest for the first time. Four unpublished novels (not extant) preceded the 1954 publication of *Lord of the Flies*, the novel upon which his worldwide fame still largely rests. Although not an immediate commercial success, by the early 1960s this novel was a best-seller widely taught in British and American universities and high schools. Its success enabled Golding to retire from teaching in 1961 to devote full time to writing and created an audience for the novels that followed it.

Golding is prolific, having published two collections of essays, a play, a travel book, and a volume of short stories in addition to the nine novels that constitute his main work. Following *Lord of the Flies* came *The Inheritors* (1955), *Pincher Martin* (1956), *Free Fall* (1959), *The Spire* (1965), *The Pyramid* (1967), and then, after a twelve-year hiatus during which his reputation declined significantly, *Darkness Visible* (1979), *Rites of Passage* (1980), *The Paper Men* (1984), *Close Quarters* (1987), and *Fire Down Below* (1989). Unquestionably this resurgence of creativity was a major reason why Golding was awarded the Nobel Prize.

In his fiction William Golding is a traditional moralist. Like the ancient Greek tragedians he reveres, as well as such modern writers as Conrad, he is preoccupied with the twin themes of the darkness of the human heart and the necessity that we become aware of this darkness if we are to save ourselves. Related concepts such as original sin, the fall from innocence, the danger of intellectual pride, and the human tropism toward self-deception also inform his work and give it as much a Christian cast (though not a doctrinaire one) as a classical one. Possessed of an imagination seared by the horrors of Auschwitz and Hiroshima, Golding is the intensely serious author of what the Nobel Prize citation accurately describes as "somber moralities and dark myths." What humor exists in his fiction has a distinctly ironic, even sardonic, coloring. In novel after novel he hammers out the message that unless we squarely face the savage impulses within, instead of projecting them onto other men or nature, we are doomed as individuals and as a species.

Although Golding's essential vision is remarkably constant, as is his effort to give it a mythic shape and resonance, he is not a tediously repetitious prophet of doom. Were he merely a Savanarola of contemporary fiction, his work would not have won popular acceptance. The Swedish Academy recognized this when it pointed out that his somber myths "are also colorful tales of adventure which can be read as such, full of narrative joy, inventiveness, and excitement." Invention and sheer storytelling skill do, indeed, characterize most of Golding's novels. At least as impressively, when viewed as a body of work, his novels are a series of fresh starts, of ventures into new settings and different sensibilities, narrative strategies, and prose styles. Although not as radical an experimentalist in fictional form as Joyce or Beckett, Golding rarely repeats himself as an artist.

His imaginative daring and fertility is evident in both major categories of novels he has written—in those more obviously realistic works with contemporary settings as well as those with more imaginary settings in the past or future. Generally, however, Golding's mythmaking powers and his ability to weld moral ideas, plot, and style into a

resonant artistic unity are not as evident when he sets his story amid complex modern sociological realities. *Pincher Martin*, in which the death throes of a drowning World War II sailor are mixed with the sailor's memories of past events that have shaped his nature, shows imaginative intensity and narrative skill, but the novel is too much a monochromatic allegorical portrait of a monster of greed. *Free Fall*, the story of a man's attempt to discover the past moment when he had lost his innocence and freedom is—and this is highly unusual for Golding— too discursive in its treatment of its protagonist's philosophical and theological speculations. In *The Pyramid*, another middle-class hero attempts to understand the shaping influence of his sexual and artistic experience, but while this novel has a nice tragicomic ambiguity and concreteness, its structure is too loosely episodic. *Darkness Visible* is Golding's most ambitious attempt to define the spiritual condition of contemporary England, but despite the powerful strangeness of its plot and style, its two main characters, an ambitious religious prophet and a diabolical young terrorist, are not believably drawn. Even less convincing is this novel's implication that the opposed fanaticisms embodied in these characters are the dominant tendencies of modern English life. *The Paper Men*, the acerbic tale of the relationship between a parasitical scholar and a monstrously egotistical writer, contains more caricaturing than characterization and a bitterness of tone unprecedented in

Golding. Most critics regard it as an embarrassment in the career of a gifted and generous novelist.

Golding's mythic imagination and shaping powers are at their height when he creates fictional worlds remote from, but reflecting, sociological and historical complexities as well as moral problems. The first great case in point is *Lord of the Flies*, where Golding, though limiting himself to the actions of a company of English schoolboys on a remote tropical island, makes their actions dramatize those human tendencies that have plunged the adult world into a nuclear war. Evacuated from England at the outset of the war and forced to land on the island when their plane is damaged, the boys, deprived of adult supervision, initially achieve a stable social organization. Gradually this disintegrates as those assigned to hunting the island's wild pigs regress to a primitive love of killing and, simultaneously, a superstitious terror of a beast who haunts the island. Compelling the allegiance of the majority, the hunters begin to eliminate their still civilized opponents. Their first victim is Simon, a gentle visionary who is killed when he tries to share with them his discovery that the "beast" is only a projection of their own fear and savagery. After next murdering Piggy, the pragmatic intellectual, they begin to hunt down Ralph, the original leader and chief guardian of civilized forms. Saved at the last moment by the appearance of a navy officer, Ralph weeps for "the end of innocence, the darkness of man's heart." The novel ends with grim irony as the officer reproves the boys for not putting up a "good show" and prepares to take them back to an adult world engaged in savagery on a massive scale.

In his next novel, *The Inheritors*, Golding moves from an apocalyptic future back to a time before the beginning of recorded history when a small group of Neanderthals is exterminated by a band of true humans. More boldly inventive than in his first novel, Golding here locates the reader primarily within the quasi-human, almost preverbal consciousness of the last member of the gentle older species to be killed off by the intellectually superior "new people." Although this point of view results in a slower and more opaque narrative, its benefits outweigh its costs: we are afforded an extremely rich experience of the physical texture of life, a believable sense of what it might be like to feel an unselfconscious oneness with nature, and—most thematically significant—the opportunity to view our own species from the outside. The paranoia and violence we witness constitute an ugly but imaginatively convincing vision.

The Spire is set in medieval England and tells the story of an obsessed bishop's building of a four-hundred-foot spire atop his cathedral. Paralleling, but more important than, the actual construction is the bishop's tortuous journey toward awareness of the mixture of spiritual and profane motives within him and toward an agonized understanding that he had sacrificed himself and four other lives to achieve his goal. Although the reader comes to realize with Bishop Jocelin that the spire is as much an expression of his repressed lust for a woman as of a desire to glorify God, the final recognition we are led to is that the spire, like all great civilized achievements, transcends even as it contains its origins in the swamp of human passion and egoism. Rooted in its portrait of an ambiguous but growing character, and emphasizing as much the creative as the destructive potential in man, *The Spire* is Golding's most complex and powerfully symbolic myth.

In *Rites of Passage* Golding shows himself still capable in the twilight of his career of bold new departures in choice of setting and narrative method. Set aboard a British ship sailing for Australia in 1812, this novel concerns the strange and tragic fate of a young clergyman (Colley) who performs a homosexual act in public and then, shattered by the eruption of his repressed passion, takes to his cabin "to die of shame." It is just as much the story, however, of a supercilious young aristocrat's reactions to the humiliation and death of the low-born parson. Although acknowledging with some guilt that his own snobbishness toward the parson and maneuvers for power aboard the ship have contributed to Colley's disgrace and disintegration, Talbot ultimately rationalizes his own failures by persuading himself that others on the vessel were more guilty and, finally, by viewing the tragic chain of events as illustrative of the monstrous depravity of human na-

ture in general. Whether or not Golding consciously intended this evasive conclusion as an ironic comment on his own career-long tendency to comment thus on human nature is interesting, but essentially irrelevant to a judgment of *Rites of Passage* where it works effectively to define the inadequacy of Talbot's response to human suffering. This inadequacy is important, for what Golding does on this novel's symbolic level is to represent through Talbot and Colley a whole cluster of oppositions, chief among which are the rational versus the passional, the romantic versus the neoclassic, the Apollonian versus the Dionysian. The main formal strategy by which he accomplishes this is to revivify two hoary techniques of the English novel, the journal and the letter. He juxtaposes the parson's letter, which passionately conveys his state of mind just before his public disgrace, with the young gentleman's essentially complacent journal. To this journal which is generally complete and comprehensive, Talbot can merely attach the letter, rather than truly assimilate it into his own narrative line and accompanying psychological commentary. Through this disjunction in narrative method, Golding successfully creates a multileveled structural symbol of man's failure to integrate the two sides or tendencies of his nature.

Throughout his distinguished career, but most notably in the novels with settings remote from the literal problems of contemporary life, William Golding has demonstrated that an old and traditional vision of human nature, however somber its cast, can by dint of conviction coupled with artistic originality and skill, be made fresh and compelling. In lauding him "for his novels which with perspicuity of realistic art and diversity and universality of myth, illumine the world of today," the Swedish Academy astutely recognized the timeless quality and high stature of Golding's achievement.

JOSEPH J. MARTIN

Selected Bibliography

PRIMARY SOURCES

Golding, William. *Close Quarters*. London: Faber & Faber, 1987. New York: Farrar, Straus & Giroux, 1987.

———. *Darkness Visible*. London: Faber & Faber, 1979. Reprint. New York: Farrar, Straus & Giroux, 1979; London: Faber Paperbacks, 1980.

———. *Free Fall*. London: Faber & Faber, 1959. Reprint. New York: Harcourt, Brace & World, 1962; New York: Harbinger Books, 1962.

———. *Fire Down Below*. London: Faber & Faber, 1989. New York: Farrar, Straus & Giroux, 1989.

———. *The Inheritors*. London: Faber & Faber, 1955. Reprint. New York: Harcourt, Brace & World, 1962; New York: Harvest Books, 1963.

———. *Lord of the Flies*. London: Faber & Faber, 1954. Reprint. New York: Coward-McCann, 1955; New York: Capricorn Books, 1959.

———. *The Paper Men*. London: Faber & Faber, 1984. Reprint. New York: Farrar, Straus & Giroux, 1984; New York: Harvest Books, 1985.

———. *Pincher Martin*. London: Faber & Faber, 1956. Reprint. *The Two Deaths of Christopher Martin*. New York: Harcourt, Brace & World, 1957; New York: Capricorn Books, 1962.

———. *The Pyramid*. London: Faber & Faber, 1967. Reprint. New York: Harcourt, Brace & World, 1967.

———. *Rites of Passage*. London: Faber & Faber, 1980. Reprint. New York: Farrar, Straus & Giroux, 1980; New York: Playboy Paperbacks, 1982.

———. *The Scorpion God: Three Short Novels*. London: Faber & Faber, 1971. Reprint. New York: Harcourt Brace Jovanovich, 1972.

———. *The Spire*. London: Faber & Faber, 1964. Reprint. New York: Harcourt, Brace & World, 1964; New York: Harvest Books, 1964.

SECONDARY SOURCES

Babb, Howard S. *The Novels of William Golding*. Columbus: Ohio State University Press, 1970.

Crompton, Don. *A View from the Spire: William Golding's Later Novels*. New York: Blackwell, 1985.

Dick, Bernard F. *William Golding*, rev. ed. Boston: G. K. Hall, 1987.

Gregor, Ian, and Mark Kinkead-Weekes. *William Golding: A Critical Study*. London: Faber & Faber, 1984.

Hynes, Samuel. *William Golding*. New York: Columbia University Press, 1968.

Oldsey, Bernard S., and Stanley Weintraub. *The Art of William Golding*. New York: Harcourt, Brace & World, 1965.

KNUT HAMSUN *1920*

Knud Pedersen (1860–1952) was born on August 4, 1860, in Lom, a small town in the Gudbrandsvalley on the Atlantic coast of Norway. His parents, Per and Tora Pedersen, and their seven children (Knud was their third) struggled endlessly to keep the family fed and clothed. When economic circumstances became hopeless in 1862, Per and his family left the valley of their ancestors and moved to the Lofoten Islands, where Tora's brother had settled and had been sending the family letters praising the many opportunities open to those who were willing to endure the harshness of the land and its inclement weather. The Pedersen family rented a small farm, named Hamsund, where young Knut spent a happy life for the next five years. It is during this time that two of the features so prominent in his work find their origins: the character of the strong, brave, sentimental, and shrewd people of the north, solidly rooted in their soil, and the alternating nature of the land between the stark gloominess of winter and the vivid liveliness of summer. Here, at the outer edge of the world, Knud Pedersen spent endless days herding cattle or roaming the woods and fields. The memory of these glorious years remained so strong that later, when he had established himself as a writer, he changed his name to Knut Hamsund and subsequently accepted Hamsun when the final letter was inadvertently left off by the printers on one of his articles about Mark Twain.

The fortunes of the Pedersen family did not materialize along expected lines, and so the boy was sent to the house of his bachelor uncle, where he stayed from 1868 until 1873, until he finished his compulsory education. The peculiar mixture of piousness and viciousness in his uncle's character caused the young boy many a sleepness night and created in him a strong desire to be free to search for his own identity. When his parents gave their permission for his return to his birthplace in the south, the boy rejoiced.

Restless and with an urge to write, he began to drift from one job to another and from one town to the next. During two excursions to the United States (1882–84 and 1886–88), he spent time with Norwegian immigrants in North Dakota, Minneapolis, and Chicago. His efforts to escape the confining spaces of his homeland and to find a world of greater space and larger vision, coupled with his dream of being a writer, however, remained unrewarded. His Norwegian audience in the United States had no use for the dreams and visions of this young man. Those people were too deeply rooted in the traditions of their old country and too firmly fixed on the future in their new land.

Hamsun's first published works, before his journeys to America, are a reflection of his restless mind and his efforts to find a place for himself in a world whose values were changing rapidly from a deep commitment to earthbound traditions to the superficial fancy with quick material gain. The short narrative poem "Meeting Again" (1878) did not reveal artistic promise nor any originality of thought. Only after reading the immensely popular peasant stories by Bjørnstjerne Bjørnson did Hamsun find greater clarity of purpose. His next publication, like its predecessor made possible through a generous stipend from a supportive merchant, seemed to set a new course for Hamsun's goals. *Bjørger* (1879) tells of life in Norway and is one of the first manifestations of Hamsun's boundless compassion for the people and the land of his birth, a theme he entertained throughout his life.

Hamsun's experiences in the United States found expression in some rather unflattering remarks, articles, and lectures dealing mostly with what he perceived to be the country's paucity of culture and intellectual essence and its obsession with crass materialism. The book *Fra det moderne Amerikas Aandsliv* (1889; *Intellectual Life in Modern America*) vents bitter feelings about his sojourn there. He later recanted those remarks as having been the impetuous expressions of a young man in search of himself, which by the turn of the century, he said, no longer represented his opinion of America. Hamsun's literary productivity during his "wander years" was, fortunately, negligible.

In 1888 a Copenhagen magazine, published anonymously several chapters of a book entitled *Sult* (*Hunger*). The reading public was quickly attracted to this naturalistic work depicting the lowest levels of destitution and abject misery. When *Hunger* appeared as a book in 1890 and Knut Hamsun's name was printed on the cover, the author's reputation was established. Although the story is set in Christiania (later renamed Oslo), Hamsun's favorite location in southern Norway for many years, it quickly becomes evident that the location could just as easily have been Chicago or New York. A novel without a plot, it is a compilation of episodes that describe the unspeakable mental and physical sufferings caused by hunger—and it suggests the very difficult years that lay behind the young author. The novel, with an unnamed narrator stringing different episodes together, seems to make a statement concerning the novelist's very own efforts to come to grips with the haunting specter of the past.

In his attempts to demonstrate that man's place is on the land among the trees, lakes, and mountains and not in the world of steel, glass, and concrete, Hamsun created Johan Nagel in the novel *Mysterier* (1892; *Mysteries*) and Lieutenant Glahn in *Pan* (1894), characters much like the unnamed narrator of *Hunger*, who are, to one extent or another, incarnations of the novelist himself. Lieutenant Glahn finds peace and harmony in the forest. The lack of contact with other humans is his good fortune. When this isolation is broken through casual contact with a few other men and his love for a woman, the security of Glahn's existence and its attendant happiness are, literally, blown apart in an accidental rock explosion.

Between *Pan* and his next novel, *Victoria* (1898), Hamsun traveled to Paris and Munich. He completed the drama *Livets Spill* (1896; *Life's Play*) and several short stories, some of which appeared in the German magazine *Simplicissimus*. In 1898 Knut Hamsun married Bergljot Bech. A daughter, Victoria, was born in 1902, but the marriage dissolved in 1906.

Hamsun's prodigious writings continued unabated with the novel *Munken Vendt* (1902)—which treats the life of a harmless drifter and is reminiscent of Hamsun's own years after he left the confines of his uncle's house—and the shorter works *Kratskog* (1903; *Brushwood*), *Dronning Tamara* (1903; *Queen Tamara*), *Sæværmere* (1904; *Dreamers*), the poetry collection *Det vilde kor* (1904; *The Wild Chorus*, *Stridende Liv* (1905; *Struggling Life*), and *Under høstijœrnen* (1906; "Under the Autumn Star"), a collection of novels in five volumes, which was published in English under the title *Wanderers* (1909).

In 1908 Hamsun met Marie Andersen, whom he married a year later. They had two sons, Tore and Arild, and a daughter, Cecilia.

Between the novel *En Vandrer spiller med Sordin* (1909; *A Wanderer Plays with Muted Strings*, part of the *Wanderers* collection) and the novel *Den sidste Glæde* (1909; *The Last Joy*), he finished the play *Livet ivold* (1910; *In the Power of Life*), which once again treated a theme

that had become one of his major thematic occupations—the desperate attempts of an aging woman to retain the attention of men as she fights to stave off the decline of her beauty.

Like Hamsun, his characters acknowledge the advantages of youth over age. The title of "Under the Autumn Star" is in itself an indication of the inevitability of age as winter approaches, the dreary, lifeless, and inhospitable season that is far less prominent in his works than the glorious summer, which is vibrant, active, and comfortable. In *The Last Joy* man's diminishing strength, the loss of his grip on life, reveals Hamsun's conviction that old age is not to be seen as the height of life's maturation, but rather as that stage in life when a comparison with youth reveals the latter's superiority. Time is not capable of adding to man's existence; it only takes away. Age is the time to seek peace and detachment, and where else but in nature's bosom can this solitude be found? In his later works Hamsun increasingly exhorts his audience to return there.

Following the dominant theme of *Wanderers*, in which Hamsun says that "when a wanderer reaches the age of fifty he plays with muted strings," Hamsun now began to find his place in literature. With the appearance of *Børn av Tiden* (1914; *Children of the Times*) and *Segelfoss By* (1915; *Segelfoss Town*), he was ready for what many consider his greatest literary triumph: *Markens Grøde* (*The Growth of the Soil*), published in 1917 and selected in 1920 for the Nobel Prize.

As in nearly all of Hamsun's works, the setting is localized in an isolated region of Norway, but the theme has universal appeal. Isak, convincingly portrayed as one of Hamsun's elemental types who symbolizes man in his inexorable relationship with nature, and Inger, the harelipped, coarse Lapp woman who typefies the basic animal strength and physical nature of the fertile female, are the two Norwegian characters who exemplify, more powerfully than in earlier works, the dominant idea that salvation for the modern world can only be found by getting back to the soil. The novel, whose language, particularly in the early parts, has the cadence and resonance of the Bible's account of creation, is the story of human achievement, of man's struggle for survival without the trappings of civilization. It focuses on the growth of one small seed, reaching for the light, against the odds of survival. The story—despite the many ugly, painful, disgusting passages that reveal those very sides of human nature—is nevertheless full of hope and an optimism that there is room for all kinds of people to live together in harmony and friendship.

Although the events of the war raging through Europe at the time of the novel's appearance do not appear in the narrative, *Growth of the Soil* reminds us that human cruelty far exceeds that of nature. To Hamsun, man is bestial in the environment he has created for himself, which he calls civilization. Nature, on the other hand, though harsh and demanding, is friendly and accommodating in the end.

Hamsun's career suffered as he grew older, much as he envisioned in *The Last Joy*. Although he still spent much time putting down on paper what his creative and artistic urges demanded, he devoted a good deal of his life after 1920 to travels with his wife and children. On both his seventieth and eightieth birthdays Knut Hamsun received congratulations from all corners of the globe.

Hamsun's sympathies for Germany, from an early age through the two wars, forced him into retirement and subjected him to psychiatric observation and subsequent condemnation by a Norwegian court, which sentenced him to the loss of virtually all his property in 1947.

Until his death on February 19, 1952, Knut Hamsun, his sight and hearing totally gone, spent his remaining years with his wife on the Isle of Norholm.

AXEL CLAESGES

Selected Bibliography

PRIMARY SOURCES

Hamsun, Knut. *Growth of the Soil.* Translated by W. W. Worster. New York and London: Knopf, 1921.

——. *Hunger.* Translated by George Egerton. New York and London: Knopf, 1920.

——. *Segelfoss Town.* Translated by J. S. Scott. New York and London: Knopf, 1925.

——. *Shallow Soil.* Translated by Carl Christian Hyllested. New York and London: Knopf, 1921.

———. *Vagabonds*. Translated by Eugene Gay-Tifft. New York: Coward McCann, 1930.

SECONDARY SOURCES
Larsen, Hanna Astrup. *Knut Hamsun: A Study*. New York: Knopf, 1922.

Wiehr, Josef. "Knut Hamsun: His Personality and His Outlook upon Life." *Smith College Studies in Modern Languages*. Northampton, Mass.: Smith College Press, 1922.

GERHART HAUPTMANN *1912*

Gerhart Hauptmann (1862–1946) was born in Obersalzbrunn, Silesia, on November 15, 1862. A leading figure in German literature and life for almost sixty years, he wrote drama, prose, and poetry, but he earned his place in literary history primarily as a dramatist. Although never a doctrinaire adherent of particular literary trends, he was receptive to many, a "seismograph" of his era. Much honored nationally and internationally, he received the Nobel Prize in literature in 1912 and Austria's prestigious drama award, the Grillparzer Prize, three times. Oxford, Leipzig, Prague, and Columbia universities conferred honorary doctorates upon him. During the years of the Weimar Republic he enjoyed unofficial poet laureate status, only to be barely tolerated by the Nazi regime while being denounced by others for staying in Germany. When the Soviet army occupied Silesia at the end of World War II, he was accorded special consideration.

The son of a hotel owner, Hauptmann received limited formal education. At the age of fifteen he tried farming, abandoning it for studies first in sculpture at the Breslau Academy of Art (1880–1902), then briefly in history at Jena University. In 1883 he decided to settle in Rome as a sculptor, but illness forced him to abort his stay. After returning home, he continued his study, first of art in Dresden, and then of history in Berlin, where he also took acting lessons. His marriage to Marie Thienemann in 1885 provided him with financial independence and allowed the couple to settle in Erkner, near Berlin, where he began to write.

The performance of his first play, *Vor Sonnenaufgang* (1889; *Before Dawn*), on October 20, 1889, by the Verein Freie Bühne (Association Free Stage) in Berlin, made the twenty-seven-year-old writer famous overnight. The drama became the symbol of a new literary trend in Germany, naturalism, which claimed Hauptmann as its standard-bearer. Like most of his writings, the drama drew on a mixture of personal and literary experiences (Holz, Haeckel, Ibsen, Zola, Tolstoy). Subtitled "A Social Drama in Five Acts," the play pits the love of a desperate young woman and an idealistic, but ultimately inhuman, social reformer against problems of hereditary alcoholism, female emancipation, and general degeneration of a nouveau-riche Silesian peasant family. Cast in naturalistic style as a crassly realistic "slice of life" with fascinating dramatis personae, victims of heredity and environment and characterized by distinctive dialect speech and pantomime, the drama ends with the heroine's suicide after she has been abandoned by her lover for an abstract cause.

The naturalistic idiom offered Hauptmann new creative possibilities; he made immediate and full use of them in a quick succession of plays. *Das Friedensfest* (1890; *The Coming of Peace*) offers a staggering portrayal of "a family catastrophe" with painstaking attention to psychological detail. Materialistic determinism still limits character development in the work, which scholars see both challenging the naturalist dogma of hereditary and environmental determinism and ushering in "the interiorization or psychologizing of drama." Plot and characters are based upon the writer Frank Wedekind's family secrets, which the latter had confided to Hauptmann. *Einsame Menschen* (1891; *Lonely Lives*), focuses on a progressive idealist too weak to

break with the past, which he ostensibly despises, and too ordinary a thinker to understand the future he professes to proclaim. Caught between traditional duty and progressive challenge, he succumbs to vacillation and suicide after being abandoned by an enlightened female student, the one person on whom he had become dependent intellectually, psychologically, and even physically.

Die Weber (1892; *The Weavers*), a model social drama first conceived as *De Waber* in Silesian dialect, is generally considered Hauptmann's most powerful naturalistic dramatic achievement. A compassionate and moving dramatization of historical subject matter, the 1844 rebellion of the Silesian weavers that had also inspired Heinrich Heine's poem "Die schlesischen Weber," the work presents a variety of characters, each endowed with a unique personality, and all constituting the mass of hungry, exploited humanity that collectively serves as protagonist. Hauptmann would experiment once more with the dramatization of history in the naturalistic mode in *Florian Geyer* (1896), a drama he began before completing *Die Weber*. The latter, embroiled in political turmoil from the start, firmly established his fame as a great dramatist. He, in turn, became a prolific writer. Comedies, tragedies, dream and fairy-tale plays, historical dramas, novels, stories, autobiographical writings, and diaries were to flow from his pen during the ensuing half-century of often intense, albeit uneven creativity.

Kollege Crampton (1892; "Professor Crampton"), Hauptmann's first attempt at comedy, amuses, but suffers from sentimentality. *Der Biberpelz* (1893; *The Beavercoat*), on the other hand, counts as one of only a few great German comedies. Set "somewhere near Berlin," the play features a good-natured, hard-working, but unscrupulously shrewd washerwoman intent on furthering her family's social status through thievery while parading as an honest and upright member of the community and managing to get away with it thanks to dull and inept Prussian officialdom. Humor and undercurrents of seriousness are effectively juxtaposed in this "thieves' comedy," which is rich in characterization (including extensive linguistic individualization), and genuinely hilarious in action. The tragicomedy *Der rote Hahn* (1901; "The Red Cock"), a sequel to *Der Biberpelz*, continues the protagonist's exploits, here focused on her attempt to burn down her own house and collect the fire insurance. But this time she falls from grace, and the fear of the crime being discovered undermines her health and leads to her death. As minor crimes in *Der Biberpelz* become criminal acts in *Der rote Hahn*, comedy gradually yields to tragedy, but the end result is, as with many a sequel, not entirely successful.

Hanneles Himmelfahrt (1894; *Hannele*), the two-act dream play that followed *Der Biberpelz*, is a sympathetic portrayal of the delirious fantasies of a dying child. The drama fused reality and fantasy with touching simplicity, evoking shock among Hauptmann's admirers of the

naturalistic bent. In Russia, where Hauptmann's popularity rested in part on this play, the work offered a common ground for realists and symbolists, providing the latter with a social orientation. Even socialists embraced the play as an example of "humanitarian symbolism." The German fairy-tale drama *Die versunkene Glocke* (1896; *The Sunken Bell*) represents Hauptmann's concession to neo-romantic elements alongside naturalistic characteristics. It was destined to become his greatest popular success. Russia's symbolist avant-garde, for example, saw in the work the rebirth of poetic drama, reveled in its symbolic suggestiveness, and admired what they considered its profound timelessness. Scholars see the five-act verse play variously as a tragedy of the artist who longs for divine inspiration but falls short of his goal, a variation on the naturalist theme of the protagonist's inability to escape the determinism of his milieu; as a social drama of a man between two women representing two competing worlds; as a religious encounter between inadequate Christianity and sun-worshiping paganism; and as a seasonal myth tracing nature's cycle from spring's awakening to winter's rigidity. The emotional struggles of the artist in the drama also reflect Hauptmann's own marital difficulties, which, since 1894, complicated his life and culminated in a divorce in 1904. Later the same year he married Margarete Marschalk, a violinist and actress, twelve years his junior and mother of their four-year-old-son, Benvenuto.

Personal difficulties did not curb

Hauptmann's literary productivity, however. *Fuhrmann Henschel* (1898; *Drayman Henschel*) reverts back to theme (a man between two women) and elements (personal reminiscences; specific social milieu; extensive stage directions; use of dialect) of Hauptmann's naturalistic period, but with tauter structure, greater depth and tension, as well as with detached mastery of tragedy. *Michael Kramer* (1900) returns not only to the problems of an artist, but also to the tragedy of a family as a reflection of the basic human predicament. Carefully crafted scenes delineate the conflict between the ambitious, tenacious, meticulous, but only mildly talented father and his seemingly nonchalant, deformed, shabby, but highly talented son, who squanders his genius on an unworthy waitress and on caricatures of her philistine admirers. In the final act a shaken father stands beside the coffin of his dead son and utters prophetically obscure phrases about sorrow, art, love, and death, implying that the effects of suffering have shown him the way to reconciliation and to the conviction that "death is the most gentle form of life: the masterpiece of eternal love."

In the comic play *Schluck und Jau* (1900) Hauptmann adapts a venerable literary theme, namely, that of a peasant who becomes king for a day. Inspirational sources appear to have been works of Shakespeare, Hofmannsthal, Schnitzler, and Büchner. The dramas *Der arme Heinrich* (1902; *Henry of Aue*) and *Elga* (1905) also have literary roots, the former in a medieval verse epic of the same name by Hartmann von Aue, and the latter in Franz Grillparzer's tale *Das Kloster bei Sendomir* ("The Monastery at Sendomir"). Anchored in direct personal experience (jury duty; marital problems), as well as in the German literary tradition of the "middle-class tragedy" (Bürgerliches Trauerspiel) and the "infanticide" theme (Kindesmörderin), is *Rose Bernd* (1903), the story of the suffering of an unwed, robust young woman abused and degraded to the point of committing perjury and killing her newborn child. Hauptmann successfully reemploys naturalistic techniques here in combination with the social drama of domestic tragedy and his favorite milieu: rural Silesia. *Und Pippa tanzt!* (1905; *And Pippa Dances!*), a "fairy tale" and "quest" play set in the Riesengebirge of Silesia, is an admirable blend of realism, fantasy, and symbolism reflecting Hauptmann's long-standing interest in Silesian folklore and his short-lived but passionate relationship with the young actress Ida Orloff, as well as his experience of the traditional German (i.e., northern) yearning for Italy (i.e., the "magical" south). Other plays of this period—*Die Jungfern von Bischofsberg* (1906; "The Maidens of the Mount"; a comedy of upper-middle-class life centering on the loves of four sisters), *Kaiser Karls Geisel* (1908; *Charlemagne's Hostage*, a stilted blank-verse play dealing with the elderly emperor's supposed infatuation with a young girl), and *Griselda* (1909; a short, fumbling, seven-scene play dealing with love, devotion, and pathological jealousy)—fall outside the realm of

Hauptmann's best work, as do most of Hauptmann's post-1910 dramatic efforts with the exception of the tragicomedy *Die Ratten* (1911; *The Rats*), *Vor Sonnenuntergang* (1932; "Before Sunset"), and *Die Atridentetralogie* (1941–48; "Tetralogy about the House of Atreus").

Die Ratten, today recognized as one of Hauptmann's major achievements, initially enjoyed only limited critical acclaim. Here Hauptmann successfully unravels in the naturalistic mode the basically tragic story of the strong "mother instinct" of a certain Frau John, and parallels it with an essentially comic study of artistic temperaments while offering a symbolic portrayal of the decay of the whole Wilhelminian social structure. *Die Ratten* was followed by *Gabriel Schillings Flucht* (1912; *Gabriel Schilling's Flight*, a rerun of the "artist between women" theme); *Das Festspiel in deutschen Reimen* (1913; *Commemoration Masque*; a poorly received puppet-play in *Knittelvers*—German rhyme scheme—intended to commemorate the centennial of Napoleon's expulsion from Germany); *Der Bogen des Odysseus* (1914; "The Bow of Odysseus," familiar subject matter except for an unfavorable portrait of Penelope); *Winterballade* (1917; *A Winter Ballad*; based on Selma Lagerlöf's story *Herr Arnes Penningar*); *Der weisse Heiland* (*The White Savior*) and *Indipohdi* (both 1920 and both reflecting resignation in tone and a longing for self-sacrifice); *Veland* (1925; a mythical verse tragedy), and *Dorothea Angermann* (1926; a return to natural-

ism and the theme of sexuality; set in Europe and New York).

Vor Sonnenuntergang (1932; "Before Sunset"), with its titular echo of Hauptmann's first play, addresses the questions of old age and erotic attraction, and the "King Lear" theme of ungrateful children. The play contains many reminders of Goethe, to whom Hauptmann felt particularly close. After *Hamlet in Wittenberg* (1935; "Hamlet at Wittenberg"; an intended prelude to Shakespeare's work), *Die Tochter der Kathedrale* (1939; "The Daughter of the Cathedral"; a reconciliation of Christian elements with Dionysian); *Ulrich von Lichtenstein* (1939; an ill-fated attempt at resurrecting the Minnesänger), and the outbreak of World War II, Hauptmann worked primarily on *Die Atridentetralogie*, a powerful cycle of four dramas ostensibly focusing on the fate of Iphigenia and the House of Agamemnon, but also embodying the author's response to the war.

To Hauptmann's representative narrative work belong the novelle *Bahnwährter Thiel* (1888; *Flagman Thiel*), which tells the story of a man who takes a crude, domineering woman as a second wife, only to find his spiritual life destroyed by his passion for her; the travel diary *Griechischer Frühling* (1908; "Greek Spring"), an expression of convictions on the relationships of art, religion, and life inspired by a visit to Greece; the religious novel *Der Narr in Christo, Emanuel Quint* (1910; *The Fool in Christ, Emanuel Quint*), where the religious fervor and naive faith of a simple carpenter clash with modern skepticism; the novelle *Der Ketzer von Soana* (1918; *The Heretic of Soana*), a tale of a priest's surrender to pagan beauty and sensuous love; and autobiographical writings *Das Buch der Leidenschaft* (1930; "The Book of Passion"), *Im Wirbel der Berufung* (1936; "In the Turmoil of One's Vocation"), and *Das Abenteuer meiner Jugend* (1937; "The Adventure of My Youth"). Hauptmann's two epic poems, *Till Eulenspiegel* (1928) and *Der grosse Traum* (1942; "The Great Dream"), like his lyric poetry *Das bunte Buch* (1888; "The Multi-colored Book"), *Die Ährenlese* (1939; "Gleanings"), *Neue Gedichte*, (1946; "New Poems"), found little critical acclaim.

In 1901 Hauptmann had moved into a newly built mansion, Haus Wiesenstein, in Agnetendorf, where, except for absences during his travels and vacations, he resided until his death on June 6, 1946. He was buried on the Baltic island of Hiddensee.

ALBERT A. KIPA

Selected Bibliography

PRIMARY SOURCES

Hauptmann, Gerhart. *The Dramatic Works of Gerhart Hauptmann*. 9 vols. Translated by Ludwig Lewisohn et al. New York: Huebsch, 1913–29.

———. *The Fool in Christ: Emanuel Quint*. Translated by Thomas Seltzer. New York: Viking Press, 1926.

———. *Gerhart Hauptmann. Sämtliche Werke. Centenar-Ausgabe zum 100. Geburtstag des Dichters*. 11 vols. Edited by Hans-Egon Hass, continued by Martin Machatzke. Frankfurt am Main, Berlin, and Vienna: Propyläen, 1966–74.

———. *The Heretic of Soana*. Translated by B. Q. Morgan. Introduction by Harold von Hofe. New York: Ungar, 1958.

———. *The Weavers, Rose Bernd, Drayman Henschel, The Beaver Coat, Hannele: Five Plays by Gerhart Hauptmann*. Translated by Theodore H. Lustig. New York: Bantam, 1961.

———. Hoefert, Sigfrid. *Internationale Bibliographie zum Werk Gerhart Hauptmanns*. Vol. 1. Berlin: Erich Schmidt, 1986.

SECONDARY SOURCES

Behl, C. F. W., and Felix A. Voigt. *Chronik von Gerhart Hauptmanns Leben und Schaffen*. Munich: Bergstadtverlag, 1957.

Cowen, Roy C. *Hauptmann Kommentar zum dramatischen Werk*. Munich: Winkler, 1980.

Guthke, Karl S. *Gerhart Hauptmann: Weltbild im Werk*. Göttingen: Vandenhoeck & Ruprecht, 1961; 2nd rev. ed., 1980.

Hoefert, Sigfrid. *Gerhart Hauptmann*. Stuttgart: Metzlersche, 1974.

Kipa, Albert A. *Gerhart Hauptmann in Russia: Reception and Impact, 1889–1917*. Hamburg: Buske, 1974.

Maurer, Warren R. *Gerhart Hauptmann*. Twayne's World Authors Series 670. Boston: Twayne, 1982.

Shaw, Leroy R. *Witness of Deceit: Gerhart Hauptmann As Critic of So-*

ciety. Berkeley and Los Angeles: University of California Press, 1958.

Sinden, Margaret. *Gerhart Hauptmann: The Prose Plays.* Toronto: University Press, 1957; New York: Russell & Russell, 1975.

Sprengel, Peter, and Philip Mellen, eds. *Hauptmann-Forschung, Neue Beiträge. Hauptmann Research, New Directions.* Frankfurt am Main, Bern, and New York: Lang, 1986.

VERNER VON HEIDENSTAM   *1916*

Carl Gustaf Verner von Heidenstam (1859–1940) was the unopposed leader of an entire generation of Swedish writers and has often been credited with, or accused of, taking Swedish letters in a singular direction that bore the unmistakable stamp of his own passionate, aristocratic, and aesthetic personality.

Heidenstam, who was born on July 6, 1859, was the only son of Lt. Col. Nils Gustaf von Heidenstam, an army officer and aristocrat in charge of building and maintaining Sweden's vast network of lighthouses and pilot stations. His mother, Magdalena Charlotta Rütterskiöld, was also a member of the Swedish aristocracy, and both parents were concerned that their son receive an upbringing consonant with his station. He was educated at the prestigious Beskowska school in Stockholm but spent summers and as much free time as he was able to arrange at Ölshammar, the family estate, near Lake Vättern and the place with which he was to retain the strongest emotional ties all his life.

In 1876 Heidenstam's father, dissatisfied with the progress of his son's education, sent the teenager on a two-year tour of the Orient, a journey that was to prove of seminal importance in the development of Heidenstam's sensibilities. He visited Egypt, Syria, Greece, and the Holy Land, and finally, in 1879, he settled in Rome with the intention of becoming a painter. For a time, he studied with the Swedish artist Julius Kronberg, founder of the so-called Munich School of sensual color and freedom. The following year Heidenstam married his childhood sweetheart, Emilia Uggla, against his father's wishes. The ensuing break between father and son was bitter and permanent and almost from the beginning poisoned the atmosphere of the marriage.

Beginning in 1881, Heidenstam began a frenzied series of trips the length and breadth of Europe: for a time, he studied at the Ecole des beaux arts in Paris, but he was beginning to realize that poetry, not painting, was his calling. Finally, the young couple settled in Switzerland, where Heidenstam met August Strindberg, with whom he quickly became good friends. Strindberg was then the recognized leader of what would be called the "modern breakthrough" in Scandinavian literature—a bold, realistic, even naturalistic, approach to social injustices. Strindberg's avowedly atheistic and Darwinistic boldness impressed the young aristocrat, who admired Strindberg's ability to strike out against hypocrisy and cant. At the same time, however, despite his admiration for the young radicals, Heidenstam's own muse was leading him in quite another direction. Just how different became apparent in 1888 when he published his first volume of verse, *Vallfart och vandringsår* ("Pilgrimage and Years of Wandering").

Swedish poetry had never seen anything like these exotic, colorful verses, redolent with the sensual pleasures of the Orient. Mixed with the exoticism, moreover, was a youthful love of life related in masterly, even mature, diction. A brew this heady was sui generis: The volume was a tremendous public success, and Heidenstam became almost overnight the leader of a countermovement in Swedish letters whose hallmarks came to be fantasy, exoticism, imagination, and a modern, heightened aestheticism. Heidenstam's themes were also exotic, drawn from vivid recollections of his widely traveled youth. The following summer (1889) he published the essay that secured his status as leader of the neoromantic movement and gave it its remarkable

character of rebirth: *Renässans* ("Renaissance"), which stated forthrightly that the new literature would be based on national Swedish characteristics, an earthy realism, and a healthy respect for the freedoms that Strindberg (if not his followers) had won for art. Heidenstam was not yet prepared to distance himself totally from the Strindberg camp because he was still essentially aligned with it philosophically, if not aesthetically.

His first and most stalwart convert was Oscar Levertin, a brilliant, sensitive, and widely read young cosmopolite with a tendency toward the darker side of the neoromantic movement. His intimate acquaintance with French and English literature brought new stars like Baudelaire, Swinburne, Rossetti, and Wilde into the Swedish literary firmament and gained for the Heidenstam movement just a frisson of decadence, although one that was never very prevalent in Heidenstam's own verse.

However, throughout the 1890s Heidenstam's ideals became more and more nationalistic and reactionary, driving him further and further from Strindberg and finally even from his own followers. What had begun as a daring blow struck for artistic freedom and poetic license gradually became a chauvinistic political campaign to revive lost virtues and patriotic zeal. The volume *Ett folk* (1902; One People), spelled out his new program in uncompromising terms: Sweden must heed the call of its mythic ancestors to regain its place under the sun. Unfortunately, the great power and undeniable splendor of much of *Ett folk* and other volumes (*Dikter*, 1895, "Poems," and *Nya dikter*, 1915, "New Poems") has been obscured because of the disturbingly aristocratic and authoritarian tone of the political poetry. But Heidenstam was still one of the greatest lyrical masters in late-nineteenth-century Sweden. A poem like "Tiveden," which is a paean to the great primeval forest at the head of Lake Vättern, where the poet was to spend most of his adult life, is among the finest works of its kind in Swedish. And his increasing absorption in Swedish history did result in some of the finest works of historical fiction ever penned in Swedish. *Heliga Birgittas pilgrimsfärd* (1901; "The Pilgrimage of St. Brigitta"), *Folkungaträdet* (1907; *The Tree of the Folkungs*), *Svenskarna och deras hövdingar* (1908–10; *The Swedes and Their Chieftains*) all attested to Heidenstam's almost mystical affinity with figures from Sweden's distant past. But it was his first novel, written in two parts between 1897 and 1898, that won him future generations of readers. *Karolinerna* (*The Charles Men*) was the story of Sweden's "hero king," Charles XII, and his tragic attempt to restore Swedish hegemony over the Baltic. While few readers today share Heidenstam's view of the doomed king and his loyal warriors, ·*Karolinerna* still has an undeniable appeal as a classic of neoromantic nationalism.

In 1910 Heidenstam became embroiled in a bitter public debate with his former friend and confidant, August Strindberg, over the essential political and aesthetic ideals of the neoromantic movement. The debate, which finally became known as "Strindbergsfejden," or the "Strindberg feud," lasted nearly two years and was won by the Strindberg camp. Although Heidenstam was elected to the Swedish Academy in 1912 and was awarded the Nobel Prize in literature in 1916, his role as a national poet was definitely over. He died on May 20, 1940, his last years marred by a premature senility that led him into a most troublesome flirtation with National Socialism. His last poetic work, *Sista dikter* (1942; "Last Poems"), was published posthumously.

LARRY E. SCOTT

Selected Bibliography

PRIMARY SOURCES

Heidenstam, Verner von. *Christmas Eve at Finnstad*. Translated by M. Sperry. Stockholm: B. Russak for the Heidenstam Foundation, 1950.

———. *Samlade verk*. 23 vols. Edited by Kate Band and Fredrik Böök. Stockholm: Albert Bonnier, 1943–44.

SECONDARY SOURCES

Axberer, Gunnar. *Diktaren och elden*. Stockholm: Albert Bonnier, 1959.

Bang, Kate. *Vägen till övralid*. Stockholm: Albert Bonnier, 1945.

Berg, Ruben G. "Verner von Heidenstam." *American Scandinavian Review* 5 (1917):160–68.

Björk, Staffan. *Heidenstam och sekelskiftets Sverige*. Stockholm: Albert Bonnier, 1946.

Böök, Fredrik. *Verner von Heidenstam*.

2 vols. Stockholm: Albert Bonnier, 1959.

Gustafson, Alrik. "Nationalism Reinterpreted: Verner von Heidenstam." In *Six Scandinavian Novelists.* New York and Minneapolis: American-Scandinavian Foundation and University of Minneapolis Press, 1940.

Kamras, Hugo. *Den unge Heidenstam.* Stockholm: H. Geber, 1942.

Lundevall, Karl-Erik. *Från åttiotal till nittiotal: om åttiotalslitteraturen och Heidenstams debut och program.* Stockholm: Almquist & Wiksell, 1953.

Mortensen, Johan. *Från Röda rummet till sekelskiftet.* 2 vols. Stockholm: Albert Bonnier, 1918–19.

Schoolfield, George. "Charles XII Rides in Worpswede." *Modern Language Quarterly.* 16 (1955):258–67.

ERNEST HEMINGWAY   *1954*

When in 1954 the Nobel Prize in literature was awarded to Ernest Miller Hemingway (1899–1961), he was the most famous and arguably the most artistically influential American writer. The fame grew from the charismatic public persona of "Papa Hemingway," international adventurer; the artistic influence from a style as lean, taut, and disciplined as the hunter, fisherman, war correspondent seemed freewheeling and expansive. Initial recognition of the writer and his work, however, came from neither public image nor craft, though the style was from the beginning distinctive enough to be easily recognized and widely imitated. What early readers of Hemingway's short stories and novels discovered was an original and convincing vision of modern life, unmediated by the usual artifices of literary representation.

Hemingway's vision is pessimistic, tragic—as dour about the hope of earthly felicity as was that of his Puritan predecessors. But in Hemingway's version the "elect" are not foreordained for a better afterlife; they are only those who, recognizing this earth as a vale of tears, accept their condition as best they can and choose for themselves personal values and codes of behavior to allow if not grace, dignity; if not heaven, at least momentary stays against confusion. The characters in Hemingway's world who live most successfully by these codes achieve a kind of herohood; and these code heroes, as they are often called, serve as models for others who strive to emulate them.

Hemingway was born on July 21, 1899, and grew to young adulthood in the comfortable Chicago suburb of Oak Park, Illinois, the son of a successful doctor and a socially active mother. Athletic and outgoing, Hemingway seemed an unexceptional product of his community until, after graduation from high school, he declined further formal education to become a cub reporter for a St. Louis newspaper. When his eyesight kept him from enlisting for service in the American Expeditionary Forces of World War I, he volunteered for the Red Cross as an ambulance driver. Within three weeks of arrival on the Italian front, he was seriously wounded by shrapnel and machine gun fire. He returned to Oak Park a hero, but a displaced person, unable to reacclimate into conventional life.

After marriage in 1920, the first of four, Hemingway resided in Paris, a foreign correspondent for the *Toronto Star*. There among a number of notable expatriates he served his apprenticeship in fiction writing. A small private printing of sketches, *in our time* (1924), was expanded in 1925 into the commercial publication of *In Our Time*, adding fifteen stories to the earlier sketches. Half these stories concern Hemingway's first famous protagonist, Nick Adams, an active, athletic but sensitive youth whose encounters with violence and suffering are all scarring. Like Hemingway himself, Nick Adams has been wounded in war, a correspondence (among many) that led to mistaken readings of the stories as fictional autobiography.

More stories about Nick appeared in *Men Without Women* (1927) and *Winner Take Nothing* (1934), and all would be gathered chronologically in *The Nick Adams Stories* (1972), a posthumous publication. The remaining stories in the first three collections are varied in subject but similar in mood and treatment, and all are written in Hemingway's distinctive narrative style. But if the manner of these stories was recognizable, the point was not so apparent to early readers, who found them slight, almost plotless, until they learned to look beneath the surface of the narrative for the primary conflict and most meaningful action. Among the best are stories of male-female relationships, anatomizing failures through an interior narration that describes the thoughts of characters and, by selective repetition, suggests the primary psychological pressures underlying them. Other stories concern other kinds of failures and a few notable, if short-lived, successes. Collectively, these stories demonstrate Hemingway's mastery of the form, and stories such as "A Clean, Well-lighted Place," "The Snows of Kilimanjaro," and "The Short Happy Life of Francis Macomber" continue to be cited as evidence that the short stories are the acme of Hemingway's artistic achievement.

Popular success came first from the novels, however. Deservedly the best known of these are the first two, *The Sun Also Rises* (1926) and *A Farewell to Arms* (1929), the Pulitzer Prize–winning *For Whom the Bell Tolls* (1940), and *The Old Man and the Sea* (1952). All are in effect contemporary in setting, and in all the principal accomplishment—or failure—of the protagonist is to resist, in the face of repeated disappointments, the seduction of despair.

In *The Sun Also Rises* the first-person narrator, Jake Barnes, lives productively and seemingly comfortably in Paris, more observer than participant in the hedonistic life of British and American expatriates. Physically the most impaired—a war wound has left him with an unnamed sexual dysfunction—Jake understands that all the members of this group are psychologically damaged, though some are better repaired than others. Anyone sharing Jake's understanding of their condition becomes, as Brett Ashley says, "one of us"; but all are separate from conventional life, refusing accepted values and listlessly pursuing immediate pleasures. Truly, as Hemingway reports Gertrude Stein to have said, this is "a lost generation," but they are brilliantly evoked as individual characters who swiftly, surely come to life in sharp descriptions and precise and convincing dialogue.

In *A Farewell to Arms* the narrator, Frederic Henry, describes through his own experiences how the expatriates of *The Sun Also Rises* lost their way. A participant in World War I—as an ambulance driver on the Italian front—Henry is untouched by the experience until a critical injury and the discovery of love change his perspective. Declaring a separate peace for himself and his lover, Catherine Barkley, he escapes with her into the mountains of Switzerland. While they find there temporary sanctuary from the socio-historical trap of a world at war, they cannot escape the ultimate biological trap of their own vulnerable bodies, which they cannot survive. Deeply despairing after Catherine Barkley's death in childbirth, Henry repeats her dying lament, "It's all a dirty trick"—a conclusion that pairs this novel with *The Sun Also Rises* as Hemingway's darkest.

The commercial success of *A Farewell to Arms* gave Hemingway the independent income to pursue a life of travel and adventure, leading to his reputation as a hunter, fisherman, and aficionado of bullfighting. Some of this experience became subjects for nonfiction: in 1932, *Death in the Afternoon*, Hemingway's exploration of the "tragedy" of bullfighting; and in 1935, *The Green Hills of Africa*, essays about his experiences on safari. He also continued to write fiction. In the early 1930s there was a second major period of short story writing, and in 1937 came *To Have and Have Not*, a novel in which Hemingway attempts—with mixed success—to graft onto the story of another code hero, Harry Morgan, a social message suitable for depression times.

Though distrustful of political ideologies, Hemingway was deeply affected by the Spanish Civil War, which he witnessed as a war correspondent. He joined with other American artists to help produce *The Spanish Earth*, a film to solicit international aid for the Loyalist cause. A play about the war, *The Fifth Column*, had a brief run in

New York in 1940. In that same year *For Whom The Bell Tolls*, Hemingway's novel about the Spanish Civil War, was an immediate and overwhelmingly popular and critical success. In this novel Robert Jordan, an American fighting with the Loyalists, has been ordered to blow up a bridge behind enemy lines, an assignment he knows he is unlikely to survive. But Jordan is a Hemingway hero who has grown beyond earlier versions, and he understands that moral responsibility is real, even if self-created, and that some things are worth dying for. Keeping careful control over a mind given to too much thinking, he accepts his duty and follows it uncompromisingly until death. During his three-day wait, Jordan has the good luck to find affirmations for the joys of life—delight in sensuous experience, in nurturing love, in nourishing communion with others. Intended as an epic, the novel recalls others in its presentation of a primary struggle, including heroic adventures related through tales and the celebration of the qualities of a people. It also demonstrated convincingly to Hemingway's detractors, who publicly wondered before its publication if the artist had not been lost in the adventurer, that he was still firmly the master of his craft.

That mastery would only once again so convincingly deliver a completed work, *The Old Man and the Sea* (1952), the story of a Cuban fisherman who daily goes to sea in spite of bad luck stretching so long that it seems a visitation upon him. Persevering, Santiago is rewarded with an extraordinary fish, a huge marlin; but sharks attack and devour it, and Santiago returns to shore exhausted, once again without a catch. The implied biblical connection between Santiago and Job suggests that Hemingway saw this quest in quasi-religious terms: the simple dignity of Santiago, his heroic endurance, his fidelity to a way of seeing and a manner of living, all these create what is Hemingway's most pervasively affirmative vision. In effect, Santiago's unflagging reliance upon his beliefs is the obverse of Brett Ashley's utilitarian description of a personal code in *The Sun Also Rises*: "It's what we have instead of God."

The final decade of Hemingway's life was one of increasingly pressing health problems, including acute depression and repeated physical trauma. He continued to work on "the sea book," of which *The Old Man and the Sea* was originally planned to be the fourth part. Published posthumously from unfinished manuscripts, *Islands in the Stream* (1970), contains much good writing, but it is not the novel Hemingway would have crafted. Less satisfactory yet is *The Garden of Eden* (1986), a novel carved from several incomplete working drafts by commercial editors for commercial reasons. Of the posthumous publications, closest to Hemingway's final intention is *A Moveable Feast* (1962), a nostalgic recollection of his early years in Paris. Under the guise of lessons necessary to be learned in this, his portrait of the young artist, Hemingway portrays friends from those years as writers whose personal defects infect their talent and distort their art. It is unlikely Hemingway himself would have chosen to publish this work.

On July 2, 1961, Ernest Hemingway died of a self-inflicted wound. Behind he left the legends of a remarkable life and the legacy of a life's work of artistic creation. His reputation rests currently on his distinctive and still influential style, which attempts to create true emotion by naming precisely, and without artificial elaboration, the thing evoking it. At his best, Hemingway was able to achieve through simple declaration and repetition the sensations of a heart-gladdening concrete connection between a central consciousness and the natural world. As Wordsworth among the romantics created poetry from intense emotions recollected in repose, Hemingway among the modernists most relied upon immediate feeling to affirm meaning—the sensation of the bent fly rod in the hand holding it, joining emotion and experience.

Less thoughtful attention is given today to Hemingway's subjects and themes, critics preferring discussions of technique to explorations of a pessimistic existential vision that some find too unrelievedly gloomy. But for more than a generation of readers, Hemingway's fiction represented his times more truly and more convincingly than any of his contemporaries; and however dark the perspective, Hemingway's novels assert a prevailing belief that life does matter, at least that humans matter to each other, and that experience itself is life's greatest affirmation that any life lived well is worth living.

DAVID R. JOHNSON

Selected Bibliography

PRIMARY SOURCES

Hemingway, Ernest. *The Collected Short Stories of Ernest Hemingway*. New York: Scribner, 1938, 1966.

———. *For Whom the Bell Tolls*. New York: Scribner, 1940, 1968.

———. *The Old Man and the Sea*. New York: Scribner, 1952.

———. *The Sun Also Rises*. New York: Scribner, 1926, 1970.

SECONDARY SOURCES

Baker, Carlos. *Ernest Hemingway: A Life Story*. New York: Scribner, 1969.

———. *Hemingway: The Writer as Artist*. 4th ed. Princeton, N.J.: Princeton University Press, 1972.

Baker, Sheridan. *Ernest Hemingway: An Introduction and Interpretation*. New York: Holt, Rinehart and Winston, 1967.

Benson, Jackson J. *Hemingway: The Writer's Art of Self-Defense*. Minneapolis: University of Minnesota Press, 1969.

Lynn, Kenneth. *Hemingway*. New York: Simon & Schuster, 1987.

Reynolds, Michael S. *The Young Hemingway*. New York: Oxford University Press, 1986.

Rovit, Earl. *Ernest Hemingway*. New York: Twayne, 1963.

Waldhorn, Arthur. *A Reader's Guide to Ernest Hemingway*. New York: Farrar, Straus & Giroux, 1972.

Williams, Wirt. *The Tragic Art of Ernest Hemingway*. Baton Rouge: Louisiana State University Press, 1982.

Young, Philip. *Ernest Hemingway: A Reconsideration*. University Park: Pennsylvania State University Press, 1966.

HERMANN HESSE　*1946*

Hermann Hesse (1877–1962) was born on July 2, 1877, in the picturesque town of Calw on the edge of the Black Forest. He spent only a few years there before moving to several other towns in Württemberg. Later he settled in Montagnola near Lugano, Switzerland, where he lived for forty-three years until his death on August 9, 1962, at the age of eighty-two. For his novels and poetry Hesse received many prizes and recognitions, the most prestigious of which being the Nobel Prize in literature in 1946. In sending his greetings to the Swedish Academy, Hesse wrote of his hope for "super-nationalism and internationalism" and for "peace and reconciliation" rather than "war and destruction." Although many of his readers were inspired by Hesse's strong moral and social convictions, others, particularly during World War I, attacked the "traitor" Hesse for not backing the German cause. Indeed, he was loved and disliked, understood and misunderstood throughout most of his life.

Hesse's maternal grandfather was a Pietist who had been to India as a missionary, as had Hesse's parents, Johannes and Marie Hesse. They, too, were strict Pietists who attempted to raise their son in a religiously strict and conservative atmosphere. But years later Hesse would describe his religious life more broadly as an unorthodox union of Judeo-Christian, Jewish, Indian, and Chinese religious attitudes. His "universal faith" led him beyond the dogma of one established religion to a personal spiritual life characterized by reverence for life and nature and love of truth, peace, and justice.

During his years as a young student Hesse rebelled against an authoritarian school system that he described best in his novel *Unterm Rad* (1906; *Beneath the Wheel*). Soon after having entered the gymnasium at the former monastery of Maulbronn he escaped. He opposed the harsh and rigid rules of this and of any other educational system that was insensitive to the emotional and personal life of young students like himself. To the end of his life, Hesse would defend the personal right to self-expression and the unhindered discovery and growth of personality. Not surprisingly, many of his readers were the young who cherished Hesse's advocacy of individual rights and freedoms and who rejected being locked into an authoritarian religious, social, and educational system designed to uphold and reinforce outmoded and repressive traditions and beliefs. Indeed, the roots of Hesse's defense of one's concern for self-realization and self-recognition so fervently described in his novels reach back to his agonizing school experiences during the Wilhelminian era.

Hesse found relief by reading works of German literature and philosophy, mostly of the eighteenth century, that he found in his parents' library. This private collection also contained volumes of German romantics, including Novalis, and books on Western and Eastern theology. At an early age he had read "half of the world's literature," including art history, languages, and philosophy. Hesse later said that at the age of thirteen he had decided to become a writer or "nothing at all," marking in this commitment the first turning point of his life. After taking a series of jobs in various towns, Hesse wrote and personally financed his first collection of neoromantic poetry, *Romantische Lieder* (1899; "Romantic Songs"), while employed at a bookstore in Tübingen. This small publication and the appearance of *Eine Stunde hinter Mitternacht* (1899; "An Hour Beyond Midnight"), his first prose vignettes, marked the beginning of Hesse's literary career. Both works contain an abundance of romantic feeling and longing, of human isolation and dreams, a mood Hesse shortly abandoned in his more realistic *Hermann Lauscher* (1901). Despite the title, this latter work is a kind of autobiographical, confessional book in three parts, of which the third, entitled "Diary," is perhaps the most elaborate about some of Hesse's literary and musical influences.

During the next thirteen years Hesse traveled often, to Italy in 1901 and 1903 and to India in 1911; also, he married and had three sons. He resided in Gaienhofen on Lake Constance (1904–12) and in Bern, Switzerland (until 1919). Many friends gathered around him, and he published articles in leading magazines and periodicals (for example in *Simplicissimus* and *Neue Rundschau*) and became well established and recognized as a writer with such works as *Peter Camenzind* (1904), *Beneath the Wheel* (1906), *Rosshalde* (1914), and *Knulp* (1915), to mention the most significant ones.

Peter Camenzind introduces a number of themes Hesse treated again in later novels: a hero's voluntary separation from the place of childhood; worship of and return to nature; love and friendship; yearning to satisfy inner needs; the life of an artist in conflict with society (Peter is a writer); the private life of a nonconformist and outsider; the admiration of women, who seem closer to nature and God than men; and unselfish humanitarian service on behalf of others.

Beneath the Wheel is the emotional story of young Hans Giebenrath's unhappy and bitter years of adolescence and schooling, his brief and intense friendship with Hermann Heilner, his return home and sudden drowning, perhaps by suicide. Hesse's early masterpiece is a satire on authoritarian schools and teachers who, without compassion and feeling, crush sensitive young people in need of understanding and love "beneath the wheel" of a repressive and mechanized system. It is clear that Hesse's own unhappy experiences had served as a model. At the hero's funeral a neighbor tells Hans's father, "Perhaps we failed to do a few things for the boy, don't you think?" Indeed, each person mattered to Hesse, for each is born with unique and precious character traits. But the "teachers apparently regarded a dead student very differently from a living one. They realized for a fleeting moment how irrecoverable and unique is each life and youth, on whom they perpetrated so much thoughtless harm at other times."

The hero of *Knulp* is a good-natured vagabond who experiences an unfulfilled love, lives a lonely life on the road, refuses to settle down, and dies, a sick and lonely man during a snowstorm near his hometown. Knulp had lived outside of but not in total disharmony with the bourgeois, the "established" people, to whom Knulp had brought, so God says to the dying man, a "longing for freedom."

This first phase of Hesse's writings, neoromantic in character, ended in 1914, the first year of World War I. Hesse's pacifism and his hatred for politics and war culminated in an eloquent appeal (essay) "O Freunde, nicht diese Töne" ("Oh Friends, Why Such Rhetoric,") published in November 1914, for Germans to return to "justice, moderation, decency, and humanity" because "love means more than hate, understanding more than anger, peace is more noble than war." These sincere words by the "traitor" Hesse were judged radical and unacceptable even by his patriotic friends who backed the German cause. All but a few abandoned him. One who supported him, however, was the French writer Romain Rolland, without whom Hesse might not have survived the days of agony, despair, and chaos, as Hesse himself confessed later, calling this the second turning point of his life. He sought psychiatric counseling from a Jungian psychoanalyst who helped him discover his "intimate relationship with his own unconscious."

This severe crisis resulted in a quest for true inner life, for a new identity because "the life of each person," as he wrote in his prologue to *Demian*, "is a path to oneself, an attempt to find a way." With new inner strength and a renewed spirit of hope he wrote *Demian* (1919), a mystical, psychoanalytic novel that Hesse published under the pseudonym of Emil Sinclair, which is also the hero's name. It covers the years 1900–14 and ends with Demian's death in the war. In early adolescence young Emil Sinclair is tormented by the knowledge that opposite the light and sheltered world of his parents' home looms a darker and evil side of life. Unable to cope with these extremes that cause anguish and distress, he meets Demian, who liberates him from spiritual and psychological despair. The older Demian is mature, benevolent, wise, and understanding and opens the path toward Sinclair's self-realization. Yet Sinclair returns temporarily to childhood's sheltered world of innocence. It is not until his years at the university that he meets Demian again, who again becomes his intellectual mentor and friend and under whose influence Sinclair begins his quest to find himself. Sinclair reaches a higher form of existence, having found a liberating inner freedom and self-fulfillment, repeatedly symbolized in the novel by a bird breaking out of its shell. Sinclair's realization is that a person's maturity, liberation, and redemption lie within himself, where opposite worlds harmoniously merge into one.

Demian was an immediate success, especially among disillusioned youths returning from war, many of whom took to heart the message that the answers to self-fulfillment lay not in an external world of conflict but in the inner world of redemption and peace. Hesse left Bern and moved to Montagnola in 1919, where he would eventually move into a house (in 1931) put at his disposal by his patron, Hans C. Bodmer, and where Hesse lived until his death in 1962. By 1930 he had become a Swiss citizen and had published several small works, among

them *Klingsors letzter Sommer* (1920; *Klingsor's Last Summer*), an account of a painter's closeness to nature, two reflective studies, *Kurgast* (1925; *At the Spa*), and *Die Nürnberger Reise* (1927; *The Nuremberg Journey*), poetry, and book reviews. But he also finished three novels that are considered to be among his most enduring works: *Siddhartha* (1922), *Steppenwolf* (1927), and *Narziss und Goldmund* (1930; *Narcissus and Goldmund*).

Hesse's lucid, eloquent, and melodious style is nowhere more apparent than in *Siddhartha*, the story of a young Indian leaving home, his trusting friendship with Govinda, and, following a rejection of the Buddha's teachings of self-denial and the doctrine of redemption, his extravagant life as a merchant and lover of Kamala. Growing dissatisfied, Siddhartha leaves the city and meets Vesudeva, the ferryman, in whose presence he discovers the secret of the river: In the eternal sameness and change there is the unity, simultaneity, and totality of all existence. Siddhartha attains a condition of sainthood whose message of love and human service—he becomes a ferryboat attendant—defies adherence to religious dogma. Ironically, the son of Siddhartha leaves his father to begin his own journey toward self-discovery, as the now aging Siddhartha had done years ago. During 1967, when Hesse enjoyed great popularity in the United States, *Siddhartha* sold 100,000 copies. It is still widely read in India, owing in part to Hesse's dependence on the *Bhagavad Gita*, the principal system of the Hindu religion.

It has been said that Hesse's *Steppenwolf* was frequently misread by students in the sixties. They often abstracted from it only ideas to their liking (particularly the use of drugs to counter symptoms of depression and inhibition, as suggested in the "Magic Theater," which the protagonist Harry Haller visits). Less attention was given to the fact that Haller's severe personal crisis ends in hope. Hesse later wrote that Haller's sickness and crisis do not lead to death; it is "not destruction but the opposite: a healing." At age forty-eight Haller contemplates suicide. He is a despairing nonconformist who is alienated from society and conscious of his declining health and vitality. His two souls— one untamed, wild, and lawless, the other bourgeois, orderly, and restrained—create a conflicting aversion to and attraction for the bourgeoisie. Luckily, his own sickness and hellish condition are analyzed for him in a document called "The Tractate of the Steppenwolf" that he finds by chance. At this point, Haller's life begins anew where it may have ended. Life becomes a catharsis for Haller, for he learns to tolerate the opposing realms of spirit, order, and intellect on the one hand and the realm of nature and the senses on the other. Haller must accept both realms, must expand his horizon and introduce into his life what it lacked: sensuality, jazz, and humor (the last one being the message of the Immortals Goethe and Mozart in the "Magic Theater") with which to endure the "great sickness of his time" and to reconcile the tensions of life. Here one finds one of Hesse's great messages: One ought to embrace the sovereign, imaginary world of humor that is bourgeois in origin, "although the genuine bourgeois is incapable of understanding it," to live with humor in this world as if "it didn't exist," and with humor to "respect the law and to stand above it."

Hesse continued his probe of the opposite poles of spirit and nature in *Narcissus and Goldmund.* The spiritual aesthetic thinker, theologian, and seeker of the divine, Narcissus, resides in the monastery Mariabronn, while his nature-oriented friend and artist, Goldmund, leaves him to indulge in sensual pleasures and earthly adventures. In the end Goldmund returns an aged man to die in the arms of Narcissus. The novel, which takes place in the Middle Ages, reinforces the existence of opposite human drives without creating tension, however, or dissonance. They manifest themselves in the different nature of both friends. The sensual Goldmund follows the call of the "Mother" (nature) "for without Mother one can not love, and without Mother one cannot die."

Die Morgenfahrt (1932; *The Journey to the East*) is a symbolic, not easily accessible work that thematically returns to the world of the spirit. Hesse reinforces the concept of service inasmuch as Leo leads other wayfarers or Eastern travelers to a higher intellectual and spiritual existence, the kingdom of the spirit. Thus the journey is not meant or understood as one to the East but rather as an intellectual journey leading within. The work foreshadows Hesse's last novel *Das Glasperlenspiel* (1943; *The Glass Bead Game*), which he dedicated to all Eastern wayfarers.

This lengthy novel falls into three major parts. The first explains the nature and practice of the glass bead game as practiced in the intellectually exclusive, aesthetically oriented elitist Castalian order of which one Josef Knecht becomes spiritual leader. The main part describes Knecht's life and career as Magister Ludi (the one who masters the game), his eventual defection in favor of a commitment to practical service in the larger world outside Castalia, and, finally, Knecht's unexpected drowning in the icy waters of a lake soon after leaving Castalia. The closing part contains Josef Knecht's writings, some poetry including the revealing "Steps," and three fictitious biographies or "Lives," the best-known of which is the "Rain Maker." The novel, told by a Castalian narrator in the year 2400, is not so much one of utopian design as it is a "realistic abstraction" in which ultimately the "rejection of aesthetic abstractionism is the principal theme of the novel."

The game itself is a "symbolic form of the search for perfection . . . an approach to God," a mixture of intellect, logic, and imagination. It is a game of the spirit that incorporates the essence of mathematics, music, and meditation in a secret language. In a larger sense it seeks to unite all disciplines of knowledge into one, revealing their interrelationships and striving toward a common denominator, a "unio mystica of all disparate elements of the Universitas Litterarum." After six years as Magister Ludi, Knecht recognizes the one-sided aspects of the game and the hierarchical structure of the Order and abandons his vita contemplativa for a vita activa, thus rejecting adherence to abstract intellectual pursuits in favor of the existential experience of and full commitment to life. Knecht's decision to become active in society gives credence to the belief that "truth is lived, not taught." As stated in "Steps," one must move from one stage of life to another, for "the world spirit seeks not to tie and confine us but to lift and enlarge us, step by step"; life's mission always calls for new departures and journeys.

Living in his mountain home in Switzerland during the years of Hitler's Third Reich, Hesse remained true to his strong pacifist views, although he refrained from signing political petitions and protests. In his correspondence, however, he assailed the National Socialists' policy of terror, persecution, and war. He wrote thousands of letters, often to troubled youth who sought his advice and admired him as a moralist and teacher. He received numerous awards and prizes, wrote short prose pieces and much poetry; he painted, cared for his garden, and lived a private life until his death in Montagnola in 1962.

Hesse's works enjoyed immense popularity in the United States during the sixties and seventies. Many American youth identified with Hesse's persistent questioning of bourgeois values and his rejection of any authority that restricted or interfered with a person's freedom of self-expression. They took notice of Hesse's spirit of nonconformity, the quiet rebellion of his social outsiders, and his understanding of deep emotional, physical, and spiritual needs. But often Hesse's "reverence for history and tradition" was "either inaccessible or inadequate to them" (Egon Schwarz). His knowledge of the Middle Ages and the Age of Goethe is well documented, as is his love of classical music, the arts, Fyodor Dostoevsky, Novalis, Jacob Burckhardt, E. T. A. Hoffmann, Carl Jung, Romain Rolland, Friedrich Hölderlin, Eduard Mörike, Chinese philosophers, and his beloved Calw. These became lifelong influences on Hesse's life and works.

Despite the inner despair and crises faced by many of his heroes, Hesse left a message of cautious optimism and hope. The pattern is familiar: departure of a person from home and security, separation from others, subsequent trials, anxiety and anguish, vacillation between the polarities of "mother-principle" (nature) and "father-principle" (spirit), between active, worldly experiences and the dedication to asceticism, meditation, and intellectual pursuits. Life may be in the form of an existential encounter with reality, a choice between "romantic resolution and existential acceptance of freedom and responsibility in a meaningless world" (Theodore Ziolkowski). In a lucid and eloquent style he follows the lives of his heroes, reflections of Hesse himself, to

a stage of self-realization and fulfillment. In this there is hope. Strength, reassurance, and optimism also stem from Hesse's uncompromising quest for truth, honesty, dignity, and humanity. These values become a source of comfort not only for unsettled young people but for all people in an unsettling world.

HANS WUERTH

Selected Bibliography

PRIMARY SOURCES

Hesse, Hermann. *Autobiographical Writings*. Edited by Theodore Ziolkowski. Translated by Denver Lindley. New York: Farrar, Straus & Giroux, 1972.

———. *Demian*. New York: Harper & Row, 1965.

———. *Gesammelte Werke—Werkausgabe*. 12 vols. Frankfurt: Suhrkamp, 1970.

———. *Magister Ludi: The Glass Bead Game*. New York: Bantam, 1982.

———. *Narcissus and Goldmund*. Translated by Ursule Molinaro. New York: Farrar, Straus & Giroux, 1988.

———. *Siddhartha*. New York: Bantam, 1982.

———. *Steppenwolf*. New York: Bantam, 1983.

SECONDARY SOURCES

Ball, Hugo. *Hermann Hesse, sein Leben und sein Werk*. Berlin: S. Fischer, 1927.

Boulby, M. *Hermann Hesse. His Mind and Art*. Ithaca, New York: Cornell University Press, 1967.

Mileck, Joseph. *Hermann Hesse and His Critics*. Studies in Germanic Languages and Literatures 21. Chapel Hill: University of North Carolina Press, 1958.

———. *Hermann Hesse and His Critics. The Criticism and Bibliography of Half a Century*. Chapel Hill: University of North Carolina Press, 1958.

———. *Hermann Hesse, Life and Art*. Berkeley: University of California Press, 1978.

Otten, Anna, ed. *Hesse Companion*. Frankfurt: Suhrkamp, 1970.

Rose, E. *Faith from the Abyss, Hermann Hesse's Way from Romanticism to Modernity*. New York: New York University Press, 1965.

Schwarz, Egan. "Hermann Hesse, The American Youth Movement, and Problems of Literary Evaluations." *PMLA* 85, 5 (October 1970).

Ziolkowski, Theodore. *Hermann Hesse*. New York: Columbia University Press, 1966.

———. *The Novels of Hermann Hesse. A Study in Theme and Structure*. Princeton, N.J.: Princeton University Press, 1974.

PAUL HEYSE *1910*

In 1884 Paul Heyse (1830–1914) was awarded the Schiller Prize, which had been endowed in memory of Friedrich Schiller, German literature's most famous writer of ballads and dramatic tragedies. In 1910 Heyse received the Nobel Prize in literature, at which time he was also ennobled. During the Wilhelminian era Heyse had managed to become the leading exponent of the artistic views of those individuals who considered themselves to be the undisputed arbiters of refined literary taste. He devoted what poetic talent he possessed to the composition of verse tragedies, poems, and prose, and most notably to writing novel-

las. The well-bred society that supported his endeavors was even wont to compare its darling man of letters with Goethe. Heyse wrote roughly 120 novellas. However, Heyse's entire opus has now fallen into obscurity with the possible exception of *L'Arrabiata* (1855; *La Rabbiata; The Fury*), an idyllic tale of Lauretta, a young untamed fisher maiden. She is called L'Arrabiata, meaning "angry girl," because of her fierce and unbridled will to determine the course of her own life. Heyse's novellas appealed to the more popular taste of his era, and for years *L'Arrabiata* was cited as the prototype for the perfect novella in European literature. Despite his loss of popularity, Heyse's literary endeavors still can arouse considerable interest in a student of literary sociology.

Paul Heyse was a man of independent means. As such, he never had experienced the problems besetting *Bürgertum*, the middle-class society of his generation, and was able to devote himself exclusively to his aesthetic goal of cultivating a polished literary art. He subscribed to the aesthetic dictum of *l'art pour l'art*, believing that art's essential task was to pursue, capture, and represent ideal beauty and form. Consequently, in addition to his attempt to portray individuals who exude sublime character and reflect psychological beauty and harmony, Heyse strove to inform his works with external beauty, to imbue them with charm through a highly perfected technical virtuosity, yet because he had no established ties to any given social class, this emphasis on technique and excellence of form were never complemented by profound ideas.

Heyse also wrote seven novels, and the sense of form that is apparent to the reader of his shorter prose seems somewhat to have forsaken Heyse whenever he tried his hand at writing larger prose works. Yet the novels, to a certain extent, also succeed in reflecting the tastes and psychological concerns of the upper echelon in Wilhelminian society; for example, its concern about a growing democracy in *Kinder der Welt* (1873; *Children Of The World*); concern about the waxing ultra realism or literary naturalism in *Merlin* (1892; Merlin); or concern about Nietzschean philosophy in *Über allen Gipfeln* (1895; "Over All the Hilltops"). However, since Heyse's peripatetic existence and financial independence prevented him at an early age from acquiring roots in the social forms of bourgeois life, as indeed was the case with his great literary contemporaries Keller, Stifter, and Storm, Heyse thus was never a representative of *Bürgertum*. He does not penetrate beneath the surface of this world, as did those authors whose lives had been conditioned by it. Throughout his life, Heyse remained an aesthete, one who was technically or formally effective as a writer, yet as a thinker, one incapable of elevating his craft of fiction to that of a great literature of intellectual substance. His work is devoid of social criticism. At no point was Heyse an iconoclast like many of his noted contemporaries in literature and philosophy, who hacked away at bourgeois values, the sacred pillars of their society. The problems that Heyse deals with are mere reflections of social and psychological concerns, superficial reactions to the social forces and social conventions of his time.

Paul Heyse's literary production was dominantly in prose; however, he also wrote some fifty dramas. The dramatic productions met with little success, primarily because the stage was undergoing a transition at the time of his work. It had steadily moved away from the classical, idealistic tradition toward a naturalism that deprived man of a free will and focused on him as a creature whose life was determined by his genetic makeup and environment. Within this theoretical context, critics viewed Heyse's aloofness from everyday reality as contrived, and superficial. His detachment from the everyday and concern with the sublime was perceived as an affected fixation on so-called good taste that basically lacked depth and sincerity. Despite the fact that Theodor Fontane, Heyse's most distinguished literary contemporary, was kindly disposed toward Heyse as a man, Fontane nevertheless considered Heyse to be an anachronism. Heyse, however, described himself as a "poet" in the Munich telephone book of 1900, which indicates that as a writer he had never come to realize the extent to which he had been out of joint with the prevailing scientific theories, naturalistic programs, and style of the new literary world.

Heyse was born on March 15, 1830, in Berlin, the son of a notable philologist. He was educated at the Friedrich Wilhelm Gymnasium in Berlin and studied Romance languages at the universities of Berlin and Bonn. In 1851 he embarked on a *Bildungsreise* to Italy, which for him was the land of beauty. When he returned home, he was offered a yearly grant by King Maximilian II of Bavaria, which obligated the writer to do nothing other than to remain in Munich. Heyse was then only twenty-four years old. With his friend Emanuel Geibel, who was also receiving a similar annual stipend from the king, Heyse became a leading figure in the *Münchner Dichterkreis*, a circle of Munich poets whose other members were

like Heyse, namely, advocates of formal beauty. This group of artist epigones were devoted to the preservation of the classical and the romantic values of the earlier part of the century, while simultaneously intent on shunning reality, which they regarded as paltry and unaesthetic. When Geibel's yearly benefaction was revoked, Heyse's popularity and literary success had become so great that he was able to renounce his own monetary grant. Although he continued to live in Munich in the summer, during the winter months he withdrew to his retreat on Lake Garda, where he continued his idealistic quest to write polished aesthetic pieces of prose. Here he also managed to produce translations from Italian into German. Heyse, in fact, did possess considerable ability in this particular area. It can be reasonably asserted that his special talent for translating poetry was indeed his greatest gift. A translation of a book of Spanish poems, the *Spanisches Liederbuch* ("Spanish Song Book"), produced with Geibel, appeared in 1852; his book of poems translated from the Italian, *Italienisches Liederbuch* ("Italian Song Book"), came out in 1860.

Heyse was also a theoretician of the novella. He prided himself on being both a specialist and one of the genre's foremost authorities. He enunciated the most popularly accepted theory of the novella in his "Falkentheorie," based on an allusion to Boccaccio's story of the falcon. Here Heyse demands that each specific story possess a unique quality, differentiate itself from a thousand others, and have a clear "silhouette," a profile that is capable of being delineated in one sentence. Heyse thus emphasizes the need for the central narrative event to be fundamentally significant, the development of the plot to be readily perceptible and strictly compressed. To exemplify what Heyse considered the best and most representative German novellas, he published with Hermann Kurz a good collection of them (*Deutscher Novellenschatz* in twenty-four volumes, 1870–76); a second collection was published with Ludwig Laistner between 1884 and 1888.

"Jungbrunnen," (1849; "Fountain of Youth") was Heyse's first story, and the verse tragedies, starting with the production of *Francesca da Rimini* (1850; "Francisca of Rimini"), were followed by *Meleager* (1854; "Meleager"); *Die Sabinerinnen* (1859; "The Sabine Women"); *Elfride* (1877; Elfride); *Graf Königsmarck* (1877; "Count Königsmarck"); and *Alkibiades* (1880; Alcibiades). Among his plays are *Ludwig der Bayer* (1862; "Louis the Bavarian"); *Elizabeth Charlotte* (1864); *Hadrian* (1865); *Maria Maroni* (1865); *Hans Lange* (1866); *Colberg* (1868); *Die Göttin der Vernunft* (1870; "The Goddess of Reason"); and *Die Weiber von Schorndorf* (1881; "The Women of Schorndorf").

The main collections of his novellas are *Novellen* (1855; "Novellas"); *Neue Novellen* (1858; "New Novellas"); *Neue Novellen* (1862; "New Novellas"); *Meraner Novellen* (1864; "Meran Novellas"); *Fünf neue Novellen* (1866; "Five New

Novellas"); *Moralische Novellen* (1869; "Moral Novellas"); *Das Ding an sich* (1879; "The Thing As It Is In Itself"); *Troubadour-Novellen* (1882; "Troubador Novellas"); *Unvergeßbare Worte* (1883; *Words Never to be Forgotten*); *Himmlische und irdische Liebe* (1886; "Heavenly and Earthly Love"); and *Novellen vom Gardasee* (1902; "Novellas From Lake Garda").

Heyse wrote seven novels, *Kinder der Welt* (1873; *Children of the World*) appeared in three volumes; *Der Roman der Stiftsdame* (1887; *The Romance of the Canoness: A Life History*); *Merlin* (1892; "Merlin") also appeared in three volumes; *Über allen Gipfeln* (1895; "Over All The Hilltops"); *Crone Stäudlin* (1905; "Crone Stäudlin"); *Gegen den Strom* (1907; "Against The Current"); and *Die Geburt der Venus* (1909; "The Birth of Venus").

His *Gesammelte Werke* (1871–1914; Collected Works) are contained in thirty-eight volumes; Whenever reprints are being considered, a fifteen-volume collection, *Gesammelte Werke* (1924; "Collected Works"), edited by Erich Petzet, is the standard edition of Paul Heyse's collected works that is used.

EDWARD R. McDONALD

Selected Bibliography

PRIMARY SOURCES

Heyse, Paul. *L'Arrabiata*. Translated by F. J. Lamport. In *The Penguin Book of German Stories*. Baltimore: Penguin, 1974.

———. *Barbarossa and Other Tales*.

Translated by Levi C. Sheip. London: Low, 1867.

———. *The Dead Lake and Other Stories.* Translated by Ma. Wilson. London: Low, 1870.

———. *A Divided Heart and Other Stories.* Translated by Constance S. Copeland. New York: Brentano, 1894.

———. *Four Phases of Love.* Translated by E. H. Kingsley. New York: Routledge, 1857.

———. *Gesammelte Werke.* 15 vols. Edited by Erich Petzet. Stuttgart: 1924.

———. *The Maiden of Treppi or Love's Victory.* Translated by A. W. Hinton. New York: Hinton, 1874.

———. *Mary of Magdala: A Drama in Five Acts.* Translated by A. I. Coleman. New York: Lederer, 1900.

———. *Novellen.* Introduction (in German) by Manfred Schunicht. New York and London: Johnson, 1970.

———. *The Romance of the Canoness: A Life History.* Translated by J. M. Percival. New York: Appleton, 1887.

———. *The Witch of the Corso.* Translated by W. Ingraham. New York: Munro, 1882.

———. *Words Never to be Forgotten and The Donkey.* Translated by Abbie E. Fordyce. Union Springs, N.Y.: Hoff, 1888.

SECONDARY SOURCES

Helmetag, Charles Hugh. "Love and the Social Morality in the Novellen of Paul Heyse." Princeton University Ph.D. dissertation, 1968. DA 29 ('68–69) 2711 A.

Krausnick, Michail. *Paul Heyse und der Münchner Dichterkreis.* Bonn: Bouvier, 1974.

Martin, Werner. *Paul Heyse. Eine Bibliographie seiner Werke.* Hildesheim and New York: Ohms, 1978.

Michielsen, John Adrian. "Paul Heyse and Three of his Critics: Theodor Fontane, Gottfried Keller, and Theodor Storm." University of Toronto Ph.D. dissertation, 1970. DA 32 ('71–72) 6440 A.

Morgan, Bayard Quincy. *A Critical Bibliography of German Literature in English Translation.* Vol. I, pp. 1491– 1927; Vol. II, pp. 1928– 55. New York and London: Scarecrow Press, 1965.

JOHANNES V. JENSEN *1944*

With no less than sixty-five books, scores of poems, and countless newspaper and magazine articles, essays, and book reviews to his credit, Johannes V. Jensen (1873– 1950) has earned his title as the most prolific Danish writer of the twentieth century. Born on January 20, 1873, in the small town of Farsø in the Himmerland area of Jutland, Denmark, Jensen lived to be seventy-seven, writing and publishing throughout his adult life. His first work, a poem entitled "Korsfareren" ("The Crusader,") appeared in the magazine *Journalen* in 1894, and he completed his last work, an obituary of his friend, Hartvig Frisch, the day before he died on November 25, 1950. Not until 1944, however, did he receive the highest recognition for his literary talent: the Nobel Prize in literature—and he did not officially receive the prize until 1945, after the end of World War II.

Jensen's father introduced him to both of his major interests: science and writing. The elder Jensen had published a number of professional articles in his earlier years in addition to maintaining a demanding veterinary practice. Johannes Jensen's rural upbringing and his father's practice no doubt contributed to his exceptional ability to depict animals realistically and sympathetically, a talent that earned him a reputation as the best animal portrayer in Danish literature. From his mother he learned to question traditional Christianity; yet, like his father, he always sensed a spiritual element in the world, even in modern technology. After several years of tutoring by his mother, a brief stint at school in Farsø, and then more private tutoring at home, he was sent to nearby Louns to prepare for Viborg Cathedral School, a necessary step toward the university. Despite failing the entrance exam, he managed—by making good use of his language skills—to talk his way into Viborg, which changed his life. There he discovered Heinrich Heine, Johannes Jørgensen, and Rudyard Kipling—three authors

who greatly influenced his writing style—and also discovered the "uselessness" of a classical education. In 1893 Jensen began his medical studies at the University of Copenhagen. There he also attended lectures by the nineteenth-century Danish social critic Georg Brandes, who revealed to Jensen the problems with the current neoromantic decadence in fin-de-siècle literature, and Harald Høffding, a nineteenth century Danish philosopher, who introduced him to the modern psychological problems of introspection and skepticism.

In order to support himself at school, Jensen began writing. His first works were cheap serial suspense thrillers published in the weekly *Revuen* between 1895 and 1898. But already by 1896, he had begun his first intellectual novel, *Danskere* ("The Danes"), a critical look at the decadent era he lived in and a realistic depiction of turn-of-the-century Copenhagen. The main theme of longing, which pervades his work, is present even here. After the first of six trips to the United States, he published his second novel, *Einar Elkjær* (1898), and upon its relatively positive critical reception and sales, finally quit medical school. Ironically, these two works both attacked and resembled the neoromantic and decadent style Jensen was attempting to break away from. *Danskere* was criticized for its stylistic inconsistency at first but later was praised for its "truthful, realistic picture of Copenhagen" at that time, while *Einar Elkjær* was immediately praised for its balance of lyrical suggestion and concrete description, which became the basis of his unique writing form, the "myth."

Jensen was strongly influenced by the experiences from his many trips abroad. He traveled for two reasons: to escape what he called "self-absorption" or introspection and to recapture the past, the "lost paradise," by seeking the past of Denmark in more primitive modern societies. Not only did he travel to the United States, but he also completed a world tour (1902–03), a trip to the Middle East (1925–26), numerous trips to Berlin and London, hunting trips to Norway, Sweden, and the Far East, and trips as a newspaper correspondent. His first assignment—with *Politiken*, a paper he wrote for off and on throughout his life—in 1898 sent him to Spain to cover the Spanish-American War over Cuba; he quickly moved away, however, from covering the war to writing "travel letters," sketches that accurately and strikingly captured the essence of the people and places he encountered—elements, like those in *Einar Elkjær*, later found in his "myths." Later that year, his visit to the Ruhr industrial area of Germany reinforced his positive impression of the advantages of technology already developed on his first trip to the great metropolis New York in 1896. Then, in 1900, he covered the World's Fair in Paris, where he once again found reason to extoll the virtues of modern industrial developments—as well as criticize Denmark for lagging behind technologically while "the twentieth century roars above our heads." As a result of his travels, his pessimistic, deca-

dent tendencies gradually were replaced by—in his view—the positive scientific "reality" of the twentieth century and ultimately led him, perhaps, to rediscover his fascination for science, especially the evolutionary theories of Darwin. In modern technology Jensen saw the positive aspects of Darwinism at work—the development of inventions that would benefit man in his progress toward a *peaceful* world.

Jensen's other early works include some of the best he ever wrote. His two early travelogues, *Intermezzo* (1899) and *Skovene* (1904; "The Woods"), are written in an eloquent lyrical style and include mythic moments and lyrical descriptions of machines at work. In 1900 he published *Den gotiske renæssance* ("The Gothic Renaissance"), a collection of reworked travel letters from Spain and Paris (previously published in newspapers) praising the new technology and the return (away from internal "self-absorption") to external "reality." This work helped to reorient Denmark toward a more Anglo-American world view, drawing it away from its preindustrial focus on the past; its compact, strikingly vivid, descriptive style also not only influenced later Danish journalism but also established in part his success as a journalist. Jensen's first works to receive universal critical acclaim, however, were his Himmerland stories: *Himmerlandsfolk* (1898; "Himmerland People"), *Nye Himmerlandshistorier* (1904; New Himmerland Stories), and *Himmerlandshistorier, Tredie Samling* (1910; "Himmerland Stories, Third Collection"). He considered these his first "real" works: "My career as a writer starts with the Himmerland stories; there I began with the beginning," he wrote, for there is where he was born. These works, along with his other realistic fiction, developed parallel with his mythic works and essays. As in all his fiction (and semifiction), the motif of longing pervades these stories, a "lost" feeling caused, in this case, by change as the outside world and modern developments reach the slow-moving rural world of Himmerland. As in all his "realistic" works, the technical optimism is counterbalanced by the sorrowful longing for things lost. The quality of the stories varies; their success lies more in that they are so closely interrelated, depicting a single area and community and reintroducing the same characters in several stories and volumes.

Less successful were Jensen's two "American" novels, *Madame D'Ora* (1904) and its sequel, *Hjulet* (1905; "The Wheel"). Both were dark crime mysteries reminiscent of his earliest works, the serial thrillers, and his first two books. Jensen never succeeded in mastering this genre, perhaps because he developed the stories in a didactic bildungsroman form in which the development of the characters became secondary to the moral, political, or philosophical message he wanted to convey. He was, however, always relatively successful with his poetry, producing several masterpieces, including "Paa Memphis Station" (1903; "At Memphis Station"), a poem both about waiting for a train and the need to keep moving in order to live,

and "Afgang" (1902; "Departure"), a poem about Christopher Columbus, a symbol for Jensen of the longing and lost feeling from which modern man suffers.

Jensen's true talent lay in his myth writing, in the bringing together of nature and time and space in order to find the essence of an experience. While it could be said that myths were an integral part of all his works—not so much a genre as a style—they succeeded artistically only when they dominated and unified the work. As such *Kongens fald* (1900–01; *The Fall of the King*) was perhaps his greatest mythic piece. This novel, originally published in three parts ("The Death of Spring," "The Full Summer," "Winter"), did not enjoy a positive reception with the critics at first, and Jensen himself preferred not to consider it part of his canon. Not until critic Otto Gelsted praised it as a "central masterpiece" in 1913 did it begin to recieve critical and popular attention, and today *The Fall of the King* is the most widely read of Jensen's books. This novel has, and accomplishes, two purposes, which Jensen once accurately described as "an attempt to explain how it came about that, from being a nation of some dimension, we had sunk to a small country" and "a prose work about impermanence—a lyrical product." It is therefore not simply a historical novel—for which Jensen did a great deal of research—but also a myth (or a set of myths) about the "fall" toward death, the return to the earth as the basic law of life and, therefore, about the longing to remain. It is a blend of the historical—

and as such is considered the finest example of a historical novel in Danish literature—and the timeless, with brilliant, realistic, historical descriptions, general observations, and "mythic" moments of pure poetic vision—such as the grinding "Mill Song" of life and death.

Jensen spent years attempting to define the mythic form. Ironically, his first attempt at a definition of the myth was in his book on technology and the future, *The Gothic Renaissance*. He defines it most thoroughly in the essay "The Myth as an Art Form," published is *Aarbog 1916* (Yearbook 1916): "Every description which places a bit of nature in connection with the times is a myth. . . . [it is] the most accommodating of all [modern] art forms . . . every bit of it *true* in so far as it has coherence and resonance and color." Still later, (1929), he attempts to explain its form: "Leave out the plot, concentrate on those short flashes of the essence of things." So the myth has no specific form, but rather a purpose—to capture the essence of things—and a medium—something "real" and concrete, usually nature, plus a little fiction to bring its "essence" out. Eleven collections of myths were published, but only a few selections in each were actually myths. Essays, natural and evolutionary descriptions, fairy-tale-like stories, anecdotes, memoirs, archeological fantasies, and hunting stories were also included in these volumes. Two of his most significant myths were published in *Aarbog 1917* ("Yearbook 1917") and then later incorporated into the last volume of *Den*

lange Rejse (*The Long Journey*), *Christofer Columbus:* "Mog og Barn" ("Mother and Child") and "Den Store Christofer" ("The Great Christopher"). Both have as their main focus characters who personify themes found in many of Jensen's other works: the mother and child as a symbol for the eternal and for the miracle of life, and Columbus as a symbol for human longing, for the "strength" of the "human soul" to endure by searching. "Mother and Child" is an exceptionally beautiful myth (and clearly one of Jensen's best) about a man who, because time has passed him by, yearns after his lost wife and child, who have long since died; Jensen himself considered it "the most valid thing I have ever written."

The year 1906 marked the turning point toward the mature period of Jensen's literary career. That year he began to study Darwin's theories of evolution seriously. Jensen saw the Darwinist theory of evolution as positive progress toward an ideal future, an optimistic view of change that helped him to escape once and for all the decadent pessimism of his earlier years. However, this also marked the beginning of his more shallow, didactic style; as a result, although his later works contain a certain optimistic energy, they lack the depth and richness of his earlier, dark period. The same themes— love, death, impermanence, longing—pervade all his work; only his philosophical world-view changed, from negative nihilist to positive evolutionist. *The Long Journey*, actually a six-volume epic written over fifteen-years (1908–22), was the masterpiece of Jensen's later period. The volumes, neither written nor issued chronologically, survey, in Jensen's own words, "the history of technology and the human spirit, from the earliest prehistoric times up to the discovery of America with which the modern age begins." The epic contains two parallel yet somewhat conflicting elements: the desire to depict the mythic theme of longing and the desire to make Darwinist theory into an epic about man's evolution. Jensen, it seems, never did decide just what the main purpose of his largest work was; consequently, the focus between these two elements shifts from volume to volume, and *The Long Journey* comes across as an uneven blend of fantasy and realism, essay and myth.

Some of Jensen's unique theories are put forth in *The Long Journey*. He believed that Christopher Columbus came from the Nordic culture and that civilization evolved from north to south as a result of the Ice Age. The creation of culture, he claimed, was a direct result of the Nordic race's struggle with the cold. This theory becomes crucial for the unity of the epic, because Christopher Columbus, who for Jensen embodies the Nordic sense of longing—of the desire to find the lost land, the primeval, subtropical pre-Ice Age forests of the North, which compels the Nordic man to migrate in search of it—is the hero of the final volume who finds America, the modern paradise. So in order for him to bring together the theme of longing with the epic on the evolution of man, Jensen was forced to make Columbus into a member of the Nordic race, the originators of culture.

The first volume, *Det table Land* (1919; *The Lost Land*), follows the development of pre-Ice Age man as he becomes *Homo sapiens* by learning to use fire—an act that also separates him forever from a harmonious relationship with nature. As in all of the volumes, there is one main male character; here, he is Fyr ("fire"), a youth who likes to wander and who steals the first fire from the nearby volcano. *Braeen* (1908; *The Glacier*), the first volume written, begins with a snowcap developing over the volcano, signaling the beginning of the Ice Age. Here, the main character is Dreng ("boy"), who chooses to remain behind and battle the oncoming cold as the rest of his group migrates south. The separation from nature becomes the challenge of nature for Dreng who, unlike other animals, learns to protect himself from the cold. *Norne-Gæst* (1919) is a more optimistic work that follows man's progress, represented by the development of the main character, Norne-Gæst, through the Stone and Bronze ages into the Iron Age. Here, the struggle with nature is supplanted by the theme of impermanence as human progress begins to move more quickly. *Cimbrernes tog* (1922; *The Raids of the Cimbri*), the last volume published, still follows Norne-Gæst, who has survived into another age, and his adventures with the Cimbrians, who eventually settle—as slaves—in southern Europe. *Skibet* (1912; *The Ship*) covers the Viking Age, with Germund as the rather briefly present hero. Jensen saw this age as the "adolescence" of the North. The last volume, *Christofer Columbus* (1921), follows its namesake across the Atlantic to establish a new lost land. Despite the conflict of interest in its purpose, *The Long Journey* finds structural unity in the theme of longing and the recurring mythic scenes such as man-meets-woman, the long journey, or the struggle against nature.

Jensen received the Nobel Prize largely for *The Long Journey*, "For the remarkable force and richness of his poetic imagination, combined with a wide-ranging intellectualism and bold, innovative sense of style." This epic shows both sides of his talents—the precise, accurate, scientific analyst and the sensitive, lyrical, original artist. No other author, perhaps, has so successfully attempted to bring together such diverse material in a single work.

SUSAN SWANSON

Selected Bibliography

PRIMARY SOURCES

Jensen, Johannes. "Ann and the Cow." Translated by Victor Folk Nelson. In *Denmark's Best Stories*. Edited by H. A. Larsen. (No city, no publisher.) 1928.

——. *The Fall of the King*. Translated by P. T. Federspiel. New York: Holt, 1933.

——. *The Long Journey*. 6 vols. Translated by Arthur Chater. New York: A. Knopf, 1924–25.

——. "Lost Forests." Translated by Henry Commager. In *Denmark's Best Stories*. Edited by H. A. Larsen. (No city, no publisher.) 1928.

SECONDARY SOURCES

Andersen, Harry. *Afhandlinger om Johannes V. Jensen*. Rødovre, Den.: ROLV, 1982.

Elbek, Jørgen. *Johannes V. Jensen*. Copenhagen: Gyldendal, 1966.

Jørgensen, Aage. *Litteratur om Johannes V. Jensen: en bibliografi*. Aarhus, Den.: Jørgensen, 1985.

Nedergaard, Leif. *Johannes V. Jensen: Liv og Forfatterskab*. Copenhagen: Schønbergske, 1968.

Neilson, Marion L. *Denmark's Johannes V. Jensen*. Logan: Utah State Agricultural College, 1955.

Rossel, Sven H. *Johannes V. Jensen*. Twayne World Author Series. Boston: Twayne, 1984.

JUAN RAMÓN JIMÉNEZ   1956

The poet Juan Ramón Jiménez (1881–1958) is the main representative in Spain of the *modernismo*, a literary movement that originated in Latin America. The *modernismo* represents an attempt to overcome the spiritual crisis of modern society caused by the rapid mechanization of life toward the end of nineteenth century. The modernists searched for new models for the enrichment of poetic expression in the Spanish language. They took the aesthetic creed of "art for art's sake" from the French Parnassian poets, and from the symbolists they adopted the demand for musicality in poetry. Jiménez's verses are, consequently, of an unprecedented musicality in Spanish literature. Jiménez avoids, however, the overdecorated and empty phraseology of other modernists.

Jiménez was born on December 24, 1881, in Moguer, in the province of Huelva, the third offspring of an aristocratic landowner family. Besides their own vineyards and olive groves, the family managed several other lucrative business enterprises in this southern part of Spain. Young "Juanito," as he was then called, received his secondary education from the Jesuits in the nearby town of El Puerto de Santa Maria. At the insistence of his father, Jiménez went to Seville to begin the preparatory courses for law school but soon gave it up, since his interests lay in literature. Back home he became a contributor to the journal

Vida Nueva which was then publishing works by *modernismo* writers. The young poet made a name for himself and was invited to Madrid in April 1900 to meet the literary figure of the day, Rubén Dario.

In June 1900 Jiménez returned to Moguer. In his hometown he finished his two first books of verse, *Almas de violeta* (1900; "Violet Souls") and *Ninfeas* (1900; "Water Lilies"), which were subsequently published. The sudden death of his father affected him deeply, leaving a lasting impression. Young Jiménez became ill, and his concerned family sent him to Bordeaux, in France, to recover from his affliction, a nervous disorder. In 1901, however, he was back in Madrid, where he took up residence in a sanatorium. There he found inspiration for his third book of verses, which bears the title *Rimas* (1902; "Rhymes"). These three works were composed under the influence of Rubén Dario. However, in his collection of 1903, entitled *Arias tristes* ("Sad Airs"), Jiménez's poetry began to acquire its own flavor.

In the subsequent books of verse—*Jardines lejanos* (1904; "Distant Gardens") and *Pastorales* (1905; "Pastorals")—he succeeded in capturing nuances of mood with his peculiar technique of evoking landscapes with their distinct shades of coloring. The poem "El campo duerme temblando" ("The Countryside Sleeps Trembling") in *Pastorales* is a typical example of Vicente Aleixanre's technique:

El campo duerme, temblando
en su celeste tristeza,
a la musica que dan
los grillos y las estrellas.

Translation by Eloïse Roach:
The countryside sleeps, trembling
in its own celestial sadness,
to the music that is made
by the crickets and the stars.

During this period Jiménez widened his education by attending lectures at the famous Institución Libre de Enseñanaza, a progressive center of higher education founded by the pedagogue Francisco Giner de los Rios. It was there that Jiménez became acquainted with Goethe, Schiller, Nietzsche, Schopenhauer, Heine, Carlyle, Shelley, and Browning.

Jiménez returned again to his hometown and remained there from 1905 to 1911. It was during this period—which proved to be his most productive—that Jiménez created the lyrical prose novel *Platero y yo* (1914; *Platero and I*), his masterpiece and best-known work. It represented a break from his connection to the symbolist movement—in which he had been seeking a subjectively conceived invisible reality. On one level, *Platero* deals with the real, everyday life of a donkey and his master, who live in an actual Andalusian village. It is, however, also a work of the highest lyrical mood, proof that poetry can be found everywhere and can be expressed in many forms.

In spite of the poet's tendency to idealize situations and to create an illusory landscape, he never omits the realistic details. There are the whitewashed houses of his native Moguer and the different animals and plain country-folk roaming around in the streets. The animate and inanimate entitites of the story blend together in a harmonious ensemble of universal appeal. Platero, the silver-colored little donkey that accompanies the poet in his daily excursions through the town and out into the fields, is not just a beautiful animal of burden, but also the friend and confidant of his master:

Mira, Platero, qué de rosas caen por todas partes: rosas azules, rosas blancas, sin color . . . Diríase que el cielo se deshace en rosas. Mira cómo se me llenan de rosas la frente, los hombros, las manos . . . ¿Que haré yo con tantas rosas?

Translation by Antonio T. de Nicholas:
Look, Platero, how many roses. . . . It could be said that the sky is melting into roses. Look how my forehead, my shoulders, my hands are being filled with roses. . . . What shall I do with so many roses?

The narrative prose of this work acquires the quality of pure lyrical poetry, an achievement that can hardly be paralleled elsewhere in world literature. The first edition of *Platero*, which appeared in 1914, contained only selected chapters of the book. It had been intended as an edition for children, yet it became an instant success with adults. In 1917 the complete edition appeared, and from 1943 on it began to attain international acclaim with subsequent translations into the major European languages.

Jiménez had returned to Madrid in 1912 and was living at the

Residencia de Estudiantes. Nearby was Miss Huntington's International Institute for Girls. At one of the school's social functions Jiménez met Zenobia Camprubí Aymar from Puerto Rico. He married her in 1916, and they spent a six-month honeymoon in the United States. In New York he was made a member of the Hispanic Society of America. The society honored Jiménez by commissioning the famous Spanish painter Sorolla to paint his portrait, which still hangs in the Gallery of Distinguished Authors of the society. Also, the society organized a luxury edition of selected poems by Jiménez.

After returning from the United States, the couple spent the next twenty years in Madrid. The poet's biographer, Graciela Palau de Nemes, speaks of the ensuing years as a second period in Jiménez's poetic creativity. It began with his book of verse *Diario de un recién casado* ("Diary of a Newlywed Poet") in 1916. During this period the poet's main concern was to achieve what he called *poesía desnuda*, that is, "naked poetry." The titles of two subsequent books of poetry—*Poesías, en verso* (1917; "Poetry, in Verse") and *Belleza, en verso* (1923; "Beauty in Verse")—express quite clearly his belief that poetry and beauty are independent of the mechanics of versification. From then on, Jiménez suppressed the realistic details in favor of metaphorical devices and thus came closer to the concept of *poesía desnuda*. The poem "Desvelo" ("Wakefulness") in *Poesías* in an example of this type of poetry.

Se va la noche, negro toro
—plena carne de luto, de espanto y
   de misterio—,
que ha bramado terrible, inmensa-
   mente,
al temor sudoroso de todos los
   caídos;
y el día viene, niño fresco.

Translation by Eloise Roach:
Night retreats, black bull
—full flesh of mourning, mystery,
   and fright—
that has bellowed terribly, immensely,
to the sweating fear of all the fallen;
and the day comes, fresh child.

In this composition we have no verses, only lines in the poem, and the details of the poetic anecdote have been replaced by expressive metaphors.

In 1936 the Spanish Civil War broke out. Jiménez never took an active part in the political events, but he declared himself in favor of the popular cause, the Spanish Republic. He made his first political speech, "Política poética" ("Poetical Politics"), before he left Spain for the United States as a cultural emissary of the Spanish Republic. The Jiménezes spent the years of World War II as faculty members in the Department of Languages and Literature at the University of Maryland. Outstanding among Jiménez's works written in exile are *Españoles en tres mundos* (1942; "Spaniards of Three Worlds"), *La estación total* (1946; "The Total Season"), *Animal de fondo* (1949; "Animal of Depth"), and *Dios deseado y Dios deseante* (*God Desired and God De-*

siring), not published until 1964. In 1951 the Jiménezes went to live in Puerto Rico, because Zenobia had become ill. In 1953 the University of Puerto Rico dedicated a room in the library to the couple. The Nobel Prize was awarded to the Spanish poet on October 25, 1956, and on October 28 Zenobia, Jiménez's devoted lifelong companion, died of cancer. The poet stayed in Puerto Rico, dying there on May 29, 1958. The bodies of both husband and wife were brought to Spain and buried side by side in the cemetery of Moguer, the beloved hometown of the poet . . . and of Platero.

Juan Ramón Jiménez's striving for poetic perfection made him a leader in the field of Spanish letters during the twentieth century. Even during his early years he cannot be considered a true follower of any literary school, but rather a pathfinder. He became the master for many young authors, especially for the group known as the Generation of 1927. Disciples of his who achieved notoriety include Jorge Guillén, Pedro Salinas, Federico García Lorca, and Rafael Alberti.

ALFRED R. WEDEL

Selected Bibliography

PRIMARY SOURCES

Jiménez, Juan Ramón. *Forty Poems.* Translated by Robert Bly. Madison, Minn.: The Sixties Press, 1967.

———. *God Desired and Desiring.* Translated by Antonio T. de Nicolás. New York: Paragon House, 1986.

———. *Invisible Reality.* Translated by Antonio T. de Nicolás. New York: Paragon House, 1987.

———. *Platero and I.* Translated by Antonio T. de Nicolás. New York: Paragon House, 1986.

———. *Platero and I.* Translated by Eloïse Roach. Austin: University of Texas Press, 1957.

———. *Selected Writings of Juan Ramón Jiménez.* Translated by H. R. Hays. New York: Farrar, Straus & Cudahy, 1957.

———. *Three Hundred Poems, 1903–1953.* Translated by Eloïse Roach. Austin: University of Texas Press, 1962.

SECONDARY SOURCES

Coke-Enguidanos, Mervyn. *Word and Work in the Poetry of Juan Ramón Jiménez.* London: Tamesis Books Limited, 1982.

Fogelquist, Donald F., *Juan Ramón Jiménez.* Boston: Twayne, 1976.

Olson, Paul R. *Circle of Paradox: Time and Essence in the Poetry of Juan Ramón Jiménez.* Baltimore: Johns Hopkins University Press, 1967.

Young, Howard T. *The Line in the Margin. Juan Ramón Jiménez and His Readings in Blake, Shelley, and Yeats.* Madison: University of Wisconsin Press, 1980.

EYVIND JOHNSON *1974*

Eyvind Johnson (1900–76) was born near Boden, in northern Sweden, on July 29, 1900. Due to illness, his father, a railroad worker, could not adequately support his family; thus Eyvind was brought up by foster parents. He finished school in 1913 and left his foster parents in 1914 to work in the timber industry. For the next five years he held various jobs, became a Socialist, and agitated in his places of employment. During these years he was a voracious reader. Reading afforded him not only a means of escaping the daily drudgery, but also a means of developing his mind. In 1919 he moved to Stockholm, where it proved hard to find work. In order to survive, he started to write for the Socialist papers *Brand* and *Vår Nutid*. In 1921 he traveled to Germany and stayed in Berlin, met such figures as Kokoschka and Toller, and gained his first exposure to German expressionism. Back in Sweden in 1924, he published his first literary work: four short stories under the title *De fyra främlingarna* ("The Four Strangers"). His Berlin experiences surface in his first novel, *Timans och rättfärdigheten* (1925; "Timans and Justice"). He spent the next five years in or near Paris, during which time he married Aase Christoffersen. The economic circumstances for the couple were difficult at best, but Johnson's reading and his literary education proceeded steadily. In 1927 and 1928 two more novels appeared, inspired by his north Swedish childhood and by French surroundings: *Stad i mörker* ("Town in Darkness") and *Stad i ljus* ("Town in Light"). *Minnas* ("Remembering"), also published in 1928, was his first attempt to break away from the realistic novel. From then on a mixture of reality and fantasy was his trademark.

Johnson returned permanently to Sweden in 1930. In his writing he experimented with various forms of the novel, publishing one, sometimes even two, annually. His breakthrough as a writer came with a tetralogy *Romanen om Olof* (1934–37; "Novel About Olof"), a novel that delves into childhood memories. In the late thirties Johnson found that he had to express his opinions on the dangers of Nazism and the defense of democracy. His trilogy *Krilon* (1941–43) is an account of man's struggle against evil, the Allies' struggle against Nazism. Johnson called this large prose work his "military service." Besides writing he spent much time raising support for resistance to the invasions of Finland, Denmark, and Norway, to the point where his personal life moved into the background. In 1938 his first wife died. After a period of mourning he married Cilla Frankenhaeuser in 1940.

All of Johnson's postwar works are characterized by a sense of history, that is, history and the present merge. History becomes a means to demonstrate flaws and dangers in contemporary society. Perhaps the best known of these, his topical novels, are *Strändernas svall* (1946; *Return to Ithaca*) and *Drömmar om rosor och eld* (1949; "Dreams of Roses and Fire").

The second part of Johnson's life was punctuated by extended sojourns in Switzerland, England, and Greece, where he researched materials for his novels. In the sixties Johnson's writing slowed down. He was awarded the Nordic Council Literature Prize in 1962. He published a few more novels, addressing contemporary issues but not via the vehicle of history. In 1974 he shared the Nobel Prize in literature with his friend and fellow academician, Harry Martinson. The Nobel Committee cited his "narrative art, far-seeing in lands and ages." Johnson died two years later, at the age of seventy-six.

In 1929 Johnson published the novel *Kommentar till ett stjärnfall* ("Commentary on a Falling Star"). This is, after various experiments, perhaps the first novel in which he started realizing his full potential as a writer. In the story, a cross-section of life in Stockholm in the twenties, several plots intertwine. The main character is an orange dealer, who becomes obsessed with banana peels, ends up in an insane asylum, and finally, after unsuccessfully facing his dominating wife, freezes to death. His tragedy is that he succumbs because he cut himself loose from his humble background—a theme that resurfaces many times in Johnson's novels. Johnson makes clear the sense that bourgeois society and its cultural values are bankrupt

and that money despoils character. The characters themselves are not "round"; they are stereotypes, puppets, who act according to conflicting interests and emotions. But there is also hope; the regenerative powers of nature and childhood memories provide relief. While writing this book, Johnson read Joyce's *Ulysses* and was greatly impressed by the stream-of-consciousness technique, which made it possible to show the psychological and mental complexity of characters and their lives. Obviously, Johnson was also familiar with the works of Freud and Bergson, realizing that "no one can tell the whole truth about himself or another." Gide and Proust were equally important for Johnson's artistic development. Johnson was impressed with Gide's comprehensive view of life and his idealistic passion and by Proust's circuitous method of remembering, by his detailed and exhaustive descriptions.

In the thirties Johnson embarked on a gigantic undertaking; he wrote five novels that all have the same main character, Mårten Torpare: *Avsked till Hamlet* (1930; "Farewell to Hamlet")—Mårten's youth; *Bobinack* (1932)—Mårten has an observer's role in the death throes of bourgeois society; *Regn i gryningen* (1933; "Rain of Dawn")—about a man's attempt to become a middle-class citizen, failing because he becomes unfaithful to his background; *Nattövning* (1938; "Night Maneuvers")—Mårten reappears and calls for resistance to fascism; *Soldatens återkomst* (1940; "The Soldier's Return")—the soldier who fights Nazism is victimized. In these novels the characters are still stereotyped and the plots are linear; ideas and ideals remain the important issue.

The sequence about Mårten Torpare was interrupted from 1934 to 1937, when Johnson wrote the tetralogy, *Romanen om Olof* ("Novel About Olof"). The novel has distinctive autobiographic features. We meet the north Swedish landscape where Johnson grew up, the railroad workers, the simple people, all described elaborately, with warmth and compassion. The characters actually become alive. The first part, *Nu var det 1914* (*1914*) which came out in 1934, is about Olof's childhood. It is worth noting that the author does not transgress the boundaries of the child's realm of experience. World War I is of no interest; neither is social strife, although the povery is tangible. *Här har du ditt liv* (1935; "Here Is Your Life") is dominated by fairytales; there is little action. Olof's intellectual prowess and moral sense develop further. In *Se dig inte om* (1936; "Do Not Look Around"), Olof has a permanent job, his first love affair, his first friend, and all kinds of disappointments. He also is ready now to turn his knowledge and his language into creative endeavors. The next book, *Stutspel i ungdomen* (1937; "Finale in Youth") has Olof leaving northern Sweden and becoming involved in socialist movements. He starts to write, obsessed with the fight for "human dignity," which can only come about with a new social system. *Romanen om Olof* was, and

perhaps still is, one of Johnson's more popular novels. Filled with teeming life, it is lyrical at times, at others dramatic. Johnson seems to settle for himself the issue of being "true to one's background," or to use more modern words, he attempts "to conquer his past."

In the 1800-page *Krilon* trilogy—*Grupp Krilon* (1941; "Group Krilon"), *Krilons resa* (1942; "Krilon's Trip"), *Krilon själv* (1943; "Krilon Himself")—Johnson raises his voice to help defend Europe, freedom, and democracy from fascism. Krilon feels that society without a modicum of freedom has no chance to improve ever. Therefore, he makes the war his war too, although his government clings to a precarious neutrality. The structure of the novel is intriguing, many stories are intertwined, each character is complex and the center of his own story. Thinly disguised, the politicians and the leaders file past. Krilon himself exhibits traits of Churchill, Frank Lind parallels Roosevelt, Jekau (*tjeka - cheka*) resembles Stalin, and Staph (Ge*stap*o) suggests Hitler. Political pacts, e.g., the nonaggression treaty between Hitler and Stalin, have their counterparts in the novel's action. At times Krilon even resembles Christ, but he is not really a Christ figure; he is only an exponent of the Christian idea that spiritual greatness is best achieved in the face of adversity. Johnson himself points out that he "wanted to give a comprehensive picture of the world as I myself saw it and in the form I like best, the novel"; in other words, this is an attempt to show humanity, the human being, as exactly as possible. No doubt, there is much propaganda, the novel is to a certain degree tendentious, yet still very much valid. The phenomena he attacks have by no means been resolved or gone away since World War II.

After the war Johnson channeled his creative energies in other directions. Although man and society still are at the core of his interest, he changes focus: Time becomes an important element. Setting his stories in a historical framework or using historical material has obvious advantages for the author: Distance creates the impression of relative objectivity; historical facts "legitimize" a story, give the writer more authority; contemporary reiterative actions and phenomena underline the general validity of various and sundry human conditions, problems, and concerns. Actually, the "now" and "then" merge; thus in human consciousness no clear separating line can be drawn—moments exist, so to speak, side by side. In his study *Den tidlösa historien* ("Timeless Story") Stig Bäckman presents a very well written and plausible analysis of the issue of time in Johnson's novels.

The first of the historical novels is *Strändernas svall*. It is a retelling of the *Odyssey*. Of course, Johnson takes liberties with the story. For instance, it starts with Odysseus receiving the gods' message that he return from Calypso's island to Ithaca, and there is no triumph at the end. Odysseus is not the Homerian hero; he becomes a soldier in spite of himself, does not want to join the war against Troy, but is forced by circumstances. He is bothered by the killing and the atrocities of war and does not want to kill the suitors of Penelope either, but is urged by Evmaios, his swineherd, to do so because if he does not, slavery and dictatorship might be imminent. Evmaios, incidentally, plays a very important role, and the character of Evrycleia, Odysseus' nurse, is an entirely new invention. The gods are the motors of the story, yet they are strangely neutral and disinterested in the outcome. Other characters, such as Menelaos and Helena and old Nestor, are shown in a satirical light. Johnson sets out conscientiously to tell a story different from Homer's. Whereas Homer glorifies the heroic and spins a "tall tale," Johnson attempts a realistic interpretation of the events. He often finds natural reasons for miracles, discusses variations from Homer. The main characters take a more questioning stance, become conscious of their failings, their guilt. Again Ithaca is the Europe of the forties; force is needed to combat force and to keep a measure of freedom. Odysseus combines again the human elements found in Krilon.

Johnson went back to classical antiquity one more time in his novel *Molnen över Metapontion* (1957; "The Clouds over Metapontion"). This book consists of two parts: the war and postwar experiences of Klemens Decorbie and a part based upon Xenophon's *Anabasis*, the story of a Greek contingent assisting Cyrus against his brother Artaxerxes. In the battle of Cunaxa Cyrus dies and the Greeks have to retreat fighting. Both parts are linked by a thematic parallel—the breaking out of captivity. Again Johnson takes his time with the narration, employing complex characters and a very circuitous style.

Drömmar om rosor och eld (1949; "Dreams of Roses and Fire") takes us to seventeenth-century France. The Catholic priest Grainier makes enemies right and left because of his pride and sarcasm. Prime Minister Richelieu wants to render the city where he lives defenseless by razing the walls. Grainier, in the meantime secretly married, opposes this. Ursuline nuns claim to be possessed by the devil, and an exorcist discovers that the devil really is Grainier. He is burned at the stake. Grainier chooses his martyrdom in order to defeat his enemies. His character has three basic flaws that eventually cause his death: pride, lust for power, and lust for women. Not unlike Odysseus, Grainier too makes an effort to be conscious of his emotions and attitudes; this distinguishes him from his opponents. He seeks his martyrdom in order to stay true to himself. Johnson used historical material for this story; it is different from any of the other historical novels because whereas the protagonists usually are reflective and ironic, there is much wild and untamed passion here.

Hans nådes Tid (1960; *The Days of His Grace*), presents the Europe of Charlemagne. The emperor, just like Richelieu, is described from the point of view of his victims: the Lupigis family from Friuli in northern Italy. Late in the eighth century Charlemagne conquered the kingdom of Lombardy. The Lupigis family has to decide whether to acquiesce in this state of affairs or become involved in an uprising. They decide on the latter, but the revolt is quickly quashed. After imprisonment and escape the three Lupigis brothers pursue various paths: farmer (Warnefrit), soldier (Conald), and scholar (Johannes)—the latter is also the protagonist. Johannes transforms slowly from rebel and subverter to courtier and counselor. He is helped in this transition by the idea that Lombardic identity and culture can be best preserved by studying and teaching Lombard history at the Carolingian court. Thus it eventually might pervade Frankish culture and receive a measure of immortality. A parallel would be the survival of Roman culture in the Middle Ages. Although he is royal secretary, Johannes is passive, but he believes in the future and in the preservation of his people's history. History is studied via sources and memory. But a special process is needed in remembering: Memory has to be purified.

Johnson employs the services of a narrator (a contemporary of Johannes). Frequently either the author himself, the narrator, or one of the characters punctuates the story with digressions and comments. The main stylistic devices are various speech registers, feigned ignorance, and irony. The author researched the material in Berlin and Switzerland; his main source is Charlemagne's vita as told by Einhard.

The last of the historic novels, *Livsdagen lång* (1964; "Life's Long Day") consists of eight different stories. The unifying element is the plot: A man falls in love with a girl who disappears. Pursuing her, accompanied by a servant, he falls into a pit to rise again later to continue the chase. Thus each separate incarnation of the lover dies, but love lives. The second message is that there cannot be masters and servants. A society that tolerates that division is inhumane and leads to tyranny. In structure the novel is faintly reminiscent of Bocaccio's *Decamerone*.

In the sixties and seventies, Johnson published a few more novels in which he again picked up the ideas of the Torpare novels and where he again turned to contemporary Europe: *Favel ensam* (1968; "Favel Alone"), and *Några steg mot tystnaden* (1973; "Some Steps toward Silence"). In the last few years of his life, Johnson was often plagued by illness, and his production virtually ceased. The honor of receiving the Nobel Prize in 1974 was tainted by public reaction in Sweden and abroad, where the Swedish Academy was accused of partiality and nationalism by awarding the prize to one of its own members.

Johnson is, without doubt, one of the best twentieth-century novelists that Sweden produced. His strengths are his style, the virtuosity with which he writes Swedish, his use of irony, and his characterization techniques. He was less successful in inventing stories. But when he found suitable material—*Olof, Krilon, Stränsdernas svall, Hans*

nådes Tid,—he excelled and produced intriguing works of enormous complexity and well formulated ideas. He will be best remembered for his historical novels, two of which have so far been translated into English. That he is not better known in Europe is due largely to the fact that his work is still inaccessible to the non-Swedish speaking audience.

FRITZ H. KÖNIG

Selected Bibliography

PRIMARY SOURCES

Johnson, Eyvind. *1914* (*Nu var det 1914*). Translated by Mary Sandbach. London: Adam Books, 1970.
———. *The Days of His Grace* (*Hans nådes tid*). Translated by Elspeth Harley Schubert. London: Chatto and Windus, 1968; New York: Vanguard Press, 1968.
———. *Return to Ithaca* (*Ständernas svall*). Translated by M. A. Michael. Preface by Mark Van Doren. London and New York: Thames and Hudson, 1952.

SECONDARY SOURCES

Bäckman, Stig. *Den tidlösa historien.* ("The Timeless Story".) Stockholm: Aldus, 1975. English summary.
Meyer, Ole. *Eyvind Johnsons Historiska Romaner* ("Eyvind Johnson's Historical Novels"). Copenhagen: Akademisk, 1976.
Orton, Gavin. *Eyvind Johnson.* New York: Twayne, 1972.

ERIK AXEL KARLFELDT   *1931*

Erik Axel Karlfeldt (1864–1931) was born in the village of Karlbo, Folkärna parish, near the southern boundary of the historic, central Swedish province of Dalarna on July 20, 1864. Reckoned among the select few of the great Swedish poets, Karlfeldt published six volumes of verse at irregular intervals throughout his life. The Nobel Committee offered him its prize in literature in 1918, but he declined the award because he was serving as a member of the Nobel jury and as permanent secretary of the Swedish Academy at the time. The committee repeated its offer in various years but always met persistent refusal. It finally decided to give Karlfeldt the prize after his retirement, but his sudden death in Stockholm on April 8, 1931, prevented this. The academy then proceeded that same year to honor him with its award posthumously "because he represents our character with a style and a genuineness that we should like to be ours" (Österling, 101).

Karlfeldt was born during a time of radical change in Sweden. Industry developing in the cities drew ever more of the population from the land, and these cultural immigrants were wont to recall fondly the life they had left behind. Karlfeldt became the singer and celebrant of this vanishing rural culture, and a surge of nostalgia for the rustic life helped lift his poetry to universal popularity as Swedes left barns and threshing floors in favor of twentieth-century smelters and machine shops. Karlfeldt felt this loss particularly keenly because he was himself an outcast from this paradise, forced by irreversible circumstances to compensate poetically for a stunning reversal of his family's fortunes.

Erik Axel had grown up on the family estate, Tolvmansgården, in Karlbo. His father, Erik Ersson Karlfeldt, was a prosperous landowner and farmer who, as a further mark of local distinction and respect, served as a *nämndeman*, or juror, at the district court. His mother, Anna Jansdotter, from a peasant family, had been married before. Her love and care created the home atmosphere of warmth and safety that served Karlfeldt as a touchstone of emotional stability during the turmoils of his later life. The boy went to school at Vesterås and then entered the University of Uppsala. During Karlfeldt's freshman year his father was ruined by a collapsing grain market. In his attempts to extricate himself, he came into conflict with the law, was handed a stiff jail sentence, and was forced into bankruptcy. Tolvmansgården was sold, and Erik Ersson himself died a short time later of shock and grief.

Although now reduced to poverty, Karlfeldt stayed on at Uppsala for a dozen years. He financed his studies by taking short-term teaching jobs in private and public schools, and eventually completed two degrees. Following graduation in 1898, the young man took positions as a teacher, first in Djursholm and then at the Vermland Folk High School at Molkom. In 1900, he accepted a minor appointment at the Royal Library in Stockholm and then advanced to the position of librarian of the Academy of Agriculture in 1903.

By this time, Karlfeldt had already published three volumes of his poetry: *Vildmarks-och kärleksvisor* (1895; "Songs of Wilderness and of Love"), *Fridolins visor* (1898; "Fridolin's Songs"), and "Fridolin's lustgård" (1901; *"Fridolin's Pleasure Garden"*). These works established his reputation and reflected, in verses of traditional form and increasing poetic skill, the ancient peasant way of life as it had existed for centuries in Dalarna. The poems spoke directly to the need of a Swedish culture in transition. They became widely popular, even revered, the books slipped into jacket pockets to be read aloud during country walks. High literary honors followed. Karlfeldt was elected to the Swedish Academy in 1904 and became a member of the Nobel Committee in 1907. Then in 1912 he left his former position to become the permanent secretary of the Swedish Academy, a post he held until his death.

Karlfeldt continued to publish volumes of poetry, but at ever increasing intervals: *Flora och pomona* ("Flora and Pomona") appeared in 1906, *Flora och Bellona* ("Flora and Bellona") in 1918 and finally, four years before his death, *Hösthorn (The Horn of Autumn)* in 1927. These later works reflect no fundamental change or basic shift in style or point of view. His writing did undergo a maturing process, however, in which "its recurrent motifs and themes took on with time new dimensions, and reached new depths of feeling and of thought. Its form became more subtle, more complex, more richly and finely orchestrated" (Gustafson, 192).

Karlfeldt had announced his intention to retire from the post of permanent secretary when he reached the age of sixty-seven. His colleagues in the academy fully intended to celebrate this event by bestowing finally upon him the award he had so long refused. His unexpected death at home from bronchitis in April surprised and saddened them and awakened deep mourning in Sweden, particularly in Dalarna, which his poems had made immortal. In October 1931, the members of the academy determined to depart slightly from the terms of the Nobel will and grant the prize posthumously. In doing so they felt they were also honoring the wishes of another of their even more recently deceased (July 1931) members, the Archbishop of Uppsala, himself a peace prize recipient in 1930, who had recommended that the award go to Karlfeldt.

The decision drew sharp criticism in Sweden, not because Karlfeldt's stature as a poet was in question, but because, as one of the big Swedish newspapers wrote, "It was never the donor's intention that the Nobel Prizes should fill the coffers of widows and orphans" (Strömberg, 197). (Karlfeldt had married late in life and left a wife nearly twenty years his junior and two daughters.) The academy remained unmoved by such carping. Undoubtedly sentiment and affection for their unofficial poet laureate played a role in this award; but in choosing Karlfeldt, his fellow members clearly were also able to honor their own country and language by celebrating the one poet so particularly and perfectly Swedish that complete understanding of his poems is simply "inaccessible to the foreigner" (Österling, 101).

Karfeldt's poetic images, subjects, and values reflect the intellectual appreciation of an agricultural culture charged with the energy of nature and polarized by the conflicting spiritual forces of Lutheran piety and pagan superstition. The cycle of the seasons, of springtime and harvest, provides a dynamic profusion of subjects from which his verse seeks to distill human significance. The dualism evident in much of his poetry apparently reflects similar characteristics of his personality. A recent critic has spoken of three intertwining strands in Karlfeldt's work: the red thread of eroticism, the black thread of mortality, and the blue thread of the river Dalälven, which flowed both through his childhood village and the poetry of his manhood (Hildeman, 86–88).

Dalarna remained home for Karlfeldt with both the comforting associations of security and mother love and the unsettling consciousness of its traumatic loss. The celebration of this homeland is particularly evident in the early poems, for example, the opening lines of "My Forefathers" (in the translation of Charles Wharton Stork), which formed the introduction to Karlfeldt's first published volume of poems, *Songs of Wilderness and of Love*.

MY FOREFATHERS

On history's page their names do not
    shine,
For humble and peaceful were they,
And yet I can see their long, long line
Stretching back through the ages
    gray.
Yes, here in the ancient iron-rich land
They tilled their fields by the river-
    strand
And smelted the ore in their day.
Neither thralldom nor pomp could
    they understand,
But, dwelling each like a king in his
    house,
They quaffed at their festal carouse.
They kissed their sweethearts in
    springtime's pride,
As husbands their faith they revered,
The king they honored and God they
    feared,
And calmly they died, satisfied.

Virtually all the elements essential to Karlfeldt's work are present in this opening and programmatic elegy. As there is a sturdy homeland with its verities of marriage, husbandry, and death, so there is also the insecure and rootless present with its alarming tensions and temptations as the poet tries to find and articulate a manly ideal appropriate for a different age through contact with nature and recollection of a naïve wholeness.

That a lifelong awareness of

death forms the background of Karlfeldt's writing is evident from the following eerie, mysterious, and powerful text. It might be noted that the wind often symbolizes fate in Karlfeldt's work and that the big white house mentioned here is clearly one of the small churches of his native province.

FIRST MEMORY

Driving far, far from home, we get
    out on the wold
Black and cold,
There is wind, harsh wind.

Someone takes me and pulls me by
    the hand—trees up high
On the sky,
There is wind, harsh wind.

There's a big white house, we go in
    with many more—
Boom and roar,
there is wind, harsh wind.

There's a small white box, it's stand-
    ing on a chair,
We go there,
Still the wind, harsh wind.

Opposing death for Karlfeldt was the life force of an earthy eroticism. The range of his love poems is extraordinary. "It sings about the opposite poles—about the virgin, delicate platonic love and devotion before an unearthly purity; and about the demons of sexuality, the 'mountain tempest' which entangles everyone as an unavoidable menace stronger than commandments, morality and will power" (Hildeman, 86). At first, Karlfeldt's view of love is totally positive—it represents the best in life. Already in the Fridolin books, however, there are hints of an opposite perspective, and in *Flora och Bellona* sexuality is viewed as tyrannical, even damning. The poet's life was apparently not without its emotional complications. Karlfeldt was possessed of powerful desires and an equally powerful sense of propriety. The many-sided poetry "reveals several layers of a complicated personality" (Hildeman, 85).

Karlfeldt's ideal figure was his poetic persona Fridolin. In him Karlfeldt was able to create his image of a successful modern man, in touch with the past, equipped for the future, nimble, quick-witted, confident, and successful with the ladies:

SONG AFTER HARVEST

Fridolin dances free,
And full of sweet wine is he—
Of the berry's juice and the wheat
    field's dower,
And the whirl of the waltz melody.
With the tails of his long coat over his
    arm
He dances full many a partner warm,
Till she leans on his breast like a
    drooping flower,
Overcome by his manly charm.

In contrast to this lusty Fridolin, and appearing already in the Fridolin books, is another figure, the Vagrant (*Löskerkarlen*), a darker and much more vulnerable character reflecting a deep-seated alienation rather than bucolic harmony. The first stanza immediately sets the mood:

A VAGRANT

"Who are you and whence do you
    come?"
    I will not and cannot reply,

I am no man's son and I have no
home,
No son shall I leave when I die.
A stranger from far am I.

Karlfeldt had dreaded old age; in
his final volume of poetry he confronts his approaching death and
works out his final reconciliation
with it. Many critics feel this last
book, *Hösthorn*, contains his finest
pieces. "This book is a farewell to the
life that the author had experienced
up to his last days as filled with the
fragrance of carnations, difficult to
give up, and bitter to lose. But yet
Hösthorn gives an impression of
space and peace" (Hildeman, 87).

... time is a pilgrim; with never a
stay
You push on, you three,* toward the
stern heights afar.
I blow as I march in your festal array,
While your banner flaunts over me
star upon star.
The starlight's adrip from the autumn
horn's rim.
Subduing to earnest its insolent tone,
I at last lay it down, as I hear the deep
hymn
Of the organ swell up round the win-
ter king's throne.

*Refers to the three months of fall.

To assess Karlfeldt's impact on
his profession and on society is to
face the strange situation that although he was Sweden's best-known
and most beloved poet during his
lifetime, he was and has remained
virtually unknown outside his
homeland. In Sweden, Karlfeldt was
the most accomplished of his generation. At least partially true is the
view that he developed a certain tradition of themes and forms to the
point that succeeding generations of
poets had to seek new directions.
Already during his life he had begun to become an anacronism, and
one socialist critic even coined the
term *Karlfeldtfaran* ("the Karlfeldt
danger") to warn younger writers
away from the trap of a traditional
focus.

Charges by Swedish critics that
he was a romantic asocial, shut
away in an ivory tower of nostalgia,
had some validity. While generally
in favor of liberal ideas, he remained
suspicious of attempts to solve social problems politically. He did
support passionately the idea of
world peace but saw World War I
only in terms of individual suffering.
War was a human tragedy forgiv-
able only to preserve human dignity.

Besides verse translations of
some of Karlfeldt's works into German and a prose rendering of several
texts in French, there has been, to
date, but one translation of any of
Karlfeldt's poetry into English. Charles
Wharton Stork prepared and the
University of Minnesota published a
collection entitled *Arcadia Borealis*
in 1938. This was an anthology of
poems selected from all of his works
and grouped by subject. It is no
longer in print. Individual poems
have appeared in poetry magazines,
and a selection from the Stork translation may be found in the Nobel
Library (*Jiménez*, 105–90).

It was Karlfeldt's fate to have
his personal trauma mirror the fate
of millions of his fellow countrymen. His poems were like letters
from home for the first generation
of urban immigrants. He shared

their memories of the land and their feelings of rootlessness and new beginnings in a strange environment. They read him, loved him, and enshrined him in their pantheon of Nobel laureates. Succeeding generations have grown up with other concerns and a different collective experience. Karlfeldt is little read in Sweden today.

JAMES W. SCOTT

Selected Bibliography

PRIMARY SOURCES

Karlfeldt, Erik Axel. *Why Sinclair Lewis Got the Nobel Prize: Address by Erik Axel Karlfeldt, Permanent Secretary of the Swedish Academy, at the Nobel Festival December 10, 1930, and Address by Sinclair Lewis Before the Swedish Academy December 12, 1930.* New York: Harcourt, Brace, 1931.

——. *Arcadia Borealis: Selected Poems of Erik Axel Karlfeldt.* Translated with an Introduction by Charles Wharton Stork. Minneapolis: University of Minnesota Press, 1938.

——. Selections from *Arcadia Borealis.* Translated by Charles Wharton Stork. *Juan Ramón Jiménez, Erik Axel Karlfeldt, Pär Lagerkvist, Selma Lagerlöf.* Nobel Prize Library. New York: Gregory, 1971. Pp. 105–90.

SECONDARY SOURCES

"Dr. Erik Karlfeldt, Swedish Poet, dies." *The New York Times,* April 9, 1931, p. 25.

Gustafson, Alrik. "The Life and Works of Erik Axel Karlfeldt." *Juan Ramón Jiménez, Erik Axel Karlfeldt, Pär Lagerkvist, Selma Lagerlöf.* Nobel Prize Library. New York: Gregory, 1971. Pp. 191–95.

Hildeman, Karl-Ivar. "Erik Axel Karlfeldt: An Evaluation." *Scandinavian Studies* 40 (1968): 81–94.

Kunitz, Stanley S., ed. *Twentieth Century Authors.* New York: Wilson, 1942. P. 746.

Osterling, Anders. "Presentation Address." *Juan Ramón Jiménez, Erik Axel Karlfeldt, Pär Lagerkvist, Selma Lagerlöf.* Nobel Prize Library. New York: Gregory, 1971. P. 101.

Strömberg, Kjell. "The 1931 Prize." Translated by Camilla Sykes. *Juan Ramón Jiménez, Erik Axel Karlfeldt, Pär Lagerkvist, Selma Lagerlöf.* Nobel Prize Library. New York: Gregory, 1971. Pp. 196–97.

YASUNARI KAWABATA *1968*

Kawabata Yasunari (1899–1972), the first Japanese author to be awarded the Nobel Prize in literature (1968), was born in Osaka on June 11, 1899. He was orphaned at an early age, and the last of his close relatives, the grandfather who raised him, died when he was sixteen. Kawabata later said that these early experiences contributed to the generally somber tone of his writing. His college years were spent at Tokyo University, first in the department of English literature and later in the department of Japanese literature. He was thus well versed in both traditions when he began his long literary career.

While still in college, Kawabata attracted the attention of literary critics, and after graduation began a long career as a critic himself. He also served as president of the Japanese P.E.N. Club for seventeen years. In the course of his career he was the recipient of many Japanese literary prizes. In 1944 he was awarded the Kikuchi Kan Prize. In 1954 he received the Japan Academy of the Arts Prize and was also elected to that academy. In the same year he was the winner of the Noma Literary Arts Prize. He was given the Cultural Medal in 1961 and was posthumously granted the Order of the Rising Sun, First Class, thus becoming the first Japanese writer to be so honored. He was active both as an author and literary critic until his death on April 16, 1972.

Kawabata was one of a group of young writers, including Itō Sei (1905–69) and Yokomitsu Ri'ichi (1898–1947), who are often termed modernists and who wrote with an awareness of the work of such Western writers as James Joyce and Marcel Proust. Writers such as Kawabata responded not only to the foreign stimulus but to what seemed to them the sterility of aspects of contemporary Japanese literature. They sought alternatives to the emphasis on social content of the proletarian writers and the confessional novels favored by many writers of the Japanese naturalist school.

Kawabata was among those writers who stressed the importance of portraying the changing perceptions of characters. Psychological states are an important aspect of his work. In 1931 he even wrote an experimental story, "Suishō Gensō" ("Crystal Fantasies"), that showed clear debts to James Joyce's stream-of-consciousness techniques and to Freudian psychoanalysis. Yet this work is not representative of Kawabata, nor was it especially successful. Kawabata wrote consistently about the present, but it is for his expression of Japanese traditions that he was admired by his countrymen, and this aspect of his work was specifically cited when he was given the Nobel Prize in 1968.

It is for this very reason that the Japanese were surprised when he was awarded the prize. They thought that a writer in their literary tradition would probably be inaccessible to readers in other traditions. What the Japanese saw as "Japanese" in his writing, and what Western readers have come to appreciate as one of its special qualities, is a rich and varied use of images well-rooted in the traditions of classical Japanese literature. Comparisons have often been made between his writing and the use of images in the poetic forms of *waka* ("31-syllable poem"), haiku ("17-syllable poem") and *renga* ("linked verse"). What was new with Kawabata, though, was the freedom with which he chose images, the suddenness with which he inserted them in his narrative, and their relevance to contemporary narrative.

The tradition of classical narrative fiction in which Kawabata was well-read often did not demand the strict structuring of plot familiar in the Western tradition. Many of the finest works in this tradition were distinguished by their attention to psychological states and moods, rather than to plot per se. What emerges with Kawabata, then, is a style that is congruent with, aware of, but not strictly derived from, Western modernism. It is this unique blend, and Kawabata's skill in the portrayal of human psychology, that distinguishes his work and sets it apart from his modernist contemporaries in Japan.

Another aspect of the traditional in Kawabata is his sense of deep emotion at the sight of beauty inseparable from sadness at knowing that it is transient. Beauty is always central in Kawabata's works, as is sadness, and in his later years he spoke of "the beauty of nothingness," which might be the supreme beauty since it alone is not evanescent and lies beyond the vagaries of the human world. Here one may see Kawabata's cultural rather than religious links to Buddhism, which informs much of the Japanese tradition with its view of impermanence.

Much of Kawabata's work was published serially in newspapers and magazines before appearing in book form. This form of publication was especially important in Kawabata's early career, when he needed exposure, but the fact that he never really sought other alternatives suggests that it suited Kawabata's style, which favored the subtly rendered vignette over plot and structure. Many of his works were left incomplete. Others often give the impression that they are incomplete or that they could have ended at more than one point. Kawabata often attributed his unfinished works to what he termed "laziness," but this incompleteness seems to stem more from his style than from a lack of self-discipline as a writer.

His first major work to achieve general success was *Izu no Odoriko* (1926; *The Izu Dancer*). In this story, a young man who has been jilted goes from Tokyo to the resort area of Izu and there meets a group of traveling entertainers, among whom is a young female dancer. She is only thirteen, too young to be the object of romantic intentions, and this fact allows the young man to accept her acceptance of him, the stranger. This brief interlude ends with his return to Tokyo. Like many of Kawabata's male protagonists, this one is a sojourner, a transient in the lives of the women he encounters.

Several elements that characterize much of Kawabata's writing are already present in this work. Chief among them are the portrayal of women and the author's views on love. Kawabata did not believe in his capacity for romantic love, although he was deeply aware of human sensuality and feminine beauty. As the result of this dichotomy within himself, many of his female characters are beautiful but virginal. Their beauty is precious by virtue of its purity but always threatened by loss, either to man or to time. This view infuses Kawabata's work with a strong sensual tone and tension because human interaction becomes fraught with the danger of destruction of what is beautiful in human life.

Also typical, even at this early stage, is the sense of Kawabata not only as a detached observer but as one who painfully stands at such a distance from life that even if he would, he can come no closer, although he keenly sees and feels what is going on. Kawabata repeatedly denied that his characters had models in himself or others, although he granted that he often wrote after taking notes about the settings that he was going to use in his stories. If his characters are occasionally like him, it is not because of the infusion of autobiographical elements but rather because of the relevance to both them and Kawabata of such themes as loneliness, longing, loss, mortality, and the burden of memory.

In 1929–30 Kawabata wrote *Asakusa Kurenaidan* ("The Asakusa Crimson Gang"), a dispassionate but evocative look at people living in one of Tokyo's notorious entertainment districts. Apart from the narrator, who is uninvolved in the lives of those whom he describes, the other characters are basically extensions of the place and facets of its moods.

Yukigini (1935–37; *Snow Country*) is one of Kawabata's masterpieces and also one of the most widely read of his works in the West. The story is of a jaded dance critic who visits a hot-spring resort in the snowy north of Japan. There he encounters two geisha, one essentially the virginal type, the other a more strongly sensual woman. Each woman is a different model of perishability. The virginal one apparently dies suddenly, like a moth that is one of the linking images in the story. The other is involved in a more protracted process of destruction, her beauty and enterprise doomed to loss and defeat in the cold mountains. The story breaks off with the man's return to his idle life in Tokyo. This work caught the attention of both critics and readers for its skill in portraying the minds of the two women and for its elliptical style fraught with intriguing shifts of focus and associations of images. Also of interest in the story is the strong presence of nature as the greater background against which the human scene is set.

From his youth Kawabata was deeply interested in the Japanese game of go and in 1938 was asked by a major newspaper to report on a championship match. Kawabata's observations (again distinguished from personal experiences) took on literary form as *Meijin* (1942–54; *The Master of Go*). The account is fictionalized. To the extent that it has a distinct beginning and end, it may seem more straightforward than others of Kawabata's works, but the fundamental aesthetic concern is typical of his oeuvre. The game of go is beautiful because it has no external function. It is an end in itself, pure, like many of the women in Kawabata's stories, and it also entails the inevitability of loss. The tale of the aging master challenged by the younger player who will eventually win also touches on the theme of evanescence.

The Master of Go, begun at the outset of World War II, may be taken as representative of Kawabata's reaction to the political passions and pressures of the time. He was an apolitical writer, and just as he rejected the writing of leftist proletarian literature, so he did not write the overly patriotic literature encouraged by the government during the war years. He was later criticized for joining one of the patriotic literary associations of the day and for a brief wartime visit to Manchuria on assignment from a newspaper, but his writings, which were fewer during this period, reflect no political bias. He later spoke, though, of a deep sense of loss after the war and stated that his remaining years as a writer would be dedicated not to his own pleasure but to manifesting "the tradition of beauty in Japan."

In 1949 Kawabata began two of his postwar novels, *Yama no Oto* (1954; *The Sound of the Mountain*) and *Sembazuru* (1953; *Thousand Cranes*). *The Sound of the Mountain* is an extraordinary work about a man's encounter with forgetfulness, and the restructuring of memory, both harbingers of death. It is distinguished among the author's works not only by its explicit theme of mortality, but also by its strong male protagonist. *Thousand Cranes*, by contrast, is a story centering on female characters, and it derives its imagistic unity from the objects used in the tea ceremony. The characters in this work are basically transients in the scene, whereas the beauty of the tea ceremony will remain. *Nami Chidori* (1953; *Plovers on the Waves*) was intended as a sequel to this work but was left incomplete.

Nemureru Bijo (1960–61; *The House of Sleeping Beauties*) is a tale of a house where men, past the age of sexual activity, spend the night with young women who are in a drug-induced sleep. The protagonist is still potent but forgoes intimacy because of the inevitable loss of beauty that it entails. He is on the fringes of life, and in this strange house the women form a temporary bulwark against the onslaught of mortality.

Despite the increased somberness of tone after the war, Kawabata's literary career continued to flourish, and in 1961 he wrote *Koto* (*The Old Capital*), a work that, along with *The Izu Dancer* and *Snow Country*, was cited by the Nobel Committee in making the award to him. As an evocation of the beauties of Kyoto, the capital of Japan for over a thousand years, it has a certain appeal but is dramatically flat and not one of Kawabata's finer works.

The early 1960s brought serious changes in Kawabata's life. Around this time he began to complain of insomnia, a problem that dogged him to the end of his life, and he became dependent on sleeping pills for relief. This dependency led to several hospitalizations. His works appeared with less frequency and presented the reader with complexities such as those seen in *The House of Sleeping Beauties*. Similar in setting, but even more surreal, is *Kataude* (1963–64; *One Arm*). A woman offers her arm to the man with whom she is sleeping. He replaces his own arm with hers, which is sentient, but later removes it, perhaps seeing a violation of her beauty in his act.

When Kawabata received the Nobel Prize in literature in 1968, he was praised by the Nobel Committee for maintaining the aesthetic traditions of Japan while producing a literature that was individual, distinctive, and contemporary. In his acceptance speech, *Utsukushiki Nihon to Watakushi* (*Japan the Beautiful and Myself*), which was published in the same year as the award, Kawabata spoke of the traditions that he cherished but said little about the personal themes of his literature. His popularity soared, and he traveled in both the United States and parts of Asia after receiving the prize, but his literary production declined further. In 1970, his protégé, the writer Yukio Mishima, committed suicide. Unlike Mishima, Kawabata had never glorified suicide, thus it came as a shock when Kawa-

bata killed himself in 1972. He left no explanation for his act.

Kawabata, from his youth, seems to have been a lonely person, believing in beauty but not romance, accepting the notion of love and happiness but convinced that he was incapable of making another person happy. He was deeply aware of his Japanese tradition, having read extensively both the secular and Buddhist classics of his country. While recognizing these traditions and incorporating them in his aesthetic and philosophical vision, he remained a man of the complex present, both literally and psychologically. It was this complex aesthetic and personal vision, enriched by a lyrical, imagistic, and subtle style, that allowed him to make a unique and enduring contribution to the literature of his nation and of the world.

JACQUELINE MUELLER

Selected Bibliography

PRIMARY SOURCES

Kawabata Yasunari. *Kawabata Yasunari Zenshū*. 35 vols. Tokyo: Shinchōsha, 1980–83.

———. *The Master of Go*. New York: Putnam, 1981.

———. *Snow Country*. New York: Putnam, 1981.

———. *The Sound of the Mountain*. New York: Putnam, 1981.

———. *Thousand Cranes*. New York: Putnam, 1981.

SECONDARY SOURCES

Keene, Donald. "Kawabata Yasunari." Chap. 21 in *Dawn to the West: Jap-*

anese Literature of the Modern Era. Fiction, Vol. 1. New York: Holt, Rinehart and Winston, 1984.

Miyoshi, Masao. "The Margins of Life: Kawabata Yasunari, *Snow Country* and *The Sound of the Mountain.*" In *Accomplices of Silence: The Modern Japanese Novel.* Berkeley: University of California Press, 1974. Chap. 4.

Petersen, Gwenn Boardman. *The Moon in the Water: Understanding Tanizaki, Kawabata, and Mishima.* Honolulu: University Press of Hawaii, 1979.

Ueda, Makoto. "Kawabata Yasunari." In *Modern Japanese Writers and the Nature of Literature.* Stanford, Calif.: Stanford University Press, 1976. Chap. 7.

RUDYARD KIPLING   *1907*

Joseph Rudyard Kipling (1865–1936) was born in Bombay, India, on December 30, 1865. His father, John Lockwood Kipling, was a skilled artist, sculptor, architect, and writer whose appointment to an art school in Bombay earlier in the same year paved the way for his marriage on March 18, 1865, to Alice Macdonald, considered to be his social better. Named for Lake Rudyard, where his parents became engaged after meeting and spending the day together, young Kipling was often called "Ruddy" (his first name was not used). His parents, as was the custom then, left him primarily in the care of Hindu servants. While spoiled, he was not adversely affected later in life by the servants' indulgences. His younger sister, Alice, known as Trix, was born during a trip to London when Rudyard was two, and brother and sister

formed a close bond for the duration of their lives. Kipling quickly learned and preferred to speak in the vernacular of Bombay, a mixture of Hindi, Arabic, and Persian, becoming greatly influenced by the distinctive Indian culture and environment.

Kipling's pleasant early childhood came to an abrupt halt in 1871 when he and his sister were sent, without explanation, to Lorne Lodge in Southsea, England, to be educated and cared for by the Calvinist and callous Mrs. Holloway and her rather ambivalent husband, a retired sea captain who died not long after the children arrived. Although there were relatives with whom the two could have lived, the parents chose this couple, procured through a newspaper advertisement. Kipling rarely referred to these six years, calling the small, dark residence only "House of Desolation," or "Forlorn Lodge," and all signs point to this interim as one of unhappiness. Although his sight began to fail and he disliked the day school he attended, he received adequate schooling in Latin, mathematics, literature, and naval education, the latter providing him with a desire, which never materialized, to join the Royal Navy.

In March 1877 his mother returned to England from India, taking the children to a friend's farm for several months, providing a respite from the restrictive years at Lorne Lodge. They proceeded to London where Kipling cultivated a keen interest in art and literature from the many hours spent in the city's museums. In January 1878, at age twelve, he was sent to United Services College at Westward Ho!, formerly an unsuccessful seaside resort. Established to enable its students to pass the Army Examination, the school was unorthodox in its lack of emphasis on religious practices and its nontraditional curriculum. Kipling's initial term was characterized by harsh discipline and bullying by other boys, but gradually he became accepted as one of a trio of "intellectuals" who also engaged in harmless pranks. Since his poor eyesight prohibited him from partaking in sports, he spent most of his time reading privately and extensively, having an uncommon affinity for American literature. He became a major contributor to the school magazine, secretary of the literary society, and concert composer. However, though the loose curricular format fostered

Kipling's prolific writing and avid reading, the utilitarian rather than academic focus of the college failed to prepare him for admission to either Oxford or Cambridge. Thus, before he reached the age of seventeen, he found himself at the end of his formal education.

His father arranged a newspaper job for him at the *Civil and Military Gazette*, in the ancient Muslim city Lahore, one thousand miles northwest of Bombay, where his family had relocated. *Departmental Ditties*, a volume of satiric verse and his first work, was well received in India upon its publication in 1886. (His father had had a collection of poems printed privately in 1881 [*Schoolboy Lyrics*]). After his transfer to a more prestigious newspaper in a Hindu area, Kipling graduated from reporting to writing documentary and editorial pieces, which were to appear in his first book of fiction the following year. *Plain Tales from the Hills*, published when he was twenty-two, was regarded as a rather shocking account of life in British India.

A year later, in 1889, he returned to England by the way of the Far East and North America, stopping at San Francisco, Vancouver, and Omaha, Nebraska. On this trip he made contacts and cultivated an American audience, despite some travel articles that were critical of American life. *Soldiers Three* (1889) and *Wee Willie Winkie* (1888) drawn from his rich Indian experience, increased his popularity; by 1890 he was regarded as a notable writer in both England and America, impressing critics with his prolific output, which included *Barrack-room Ballads*, (1892), *Life's Handicap* (1891), and the release of eighty other stories published previously in India. A reunion with his first love, Florence Garrard, whom he had met in England when he was fourteen and a half, left him rejected a second time, providing some of the material for *The Light That Failed* (1891). However, he met Caroline Balestier, the sister of close friend and collaborating publisher Wolcott Balestier, who was visiting England from Vermont that fall. "Carrie" was twenty-eight years old, Kipling's senior by three years. She was a petite (Kipling was five feet six inches), aggressive, and capable young woman. The two were married in January 1892, despite his parents' opposition, eight days after Kipling returned to London from a five-month sea voyage to combat the effects of earlier tropical diseases. Henry James served as best man at the couple's wedding, since Carrie's brother had died of typhoid while Kipling was on his trip. Carrie became a protective administrator of her husband's affairs, making it difficult for people to gain access to him. Kipling's ever increasing desire for privacy, however, precluded any obvious objections from him.

Kipling and Carrie embarked on a trip around the world a year after their marriage. After a disastrous stay in Japan, where the failure of a branch bank decimated most of their savings, they continued on to New York and then to Vermont. After they settled on Carrie's family estate near Brattleboro, their first daughter, Josephine, was born, followed by Elsie in 1896. The house they built—named Naulahka after the title of a novel on which Kipling and Carrie's brother Wolcott had collaborated—was designed so that the only access for visitors to Kipling's study was past Carrie's desk. Kipling was able to get a good deal of writing done— it was here that he wrote perhaps his best work, *Many Inventions* (1893)—but his wife's possessiveness gained him a reputation of being somewhat of a recluse. In Vermont he also produced *The Seven Seas* (1896), the two Jungle books (*The Jungle Book*, 1894, and *The Second Jungle Book*, 1895), *Captains Courageous* (1897), the only book with an American setting, and *The Day's Work*, published in 1898 but worked on in Vermont.

In the fall of 1897 the Kiplings returned to England, prompted by a falling out between Kipling and his wife's brother, concern over the territorial conflict in South Africa between England and the United States and how that would affect his status, and the isolation he felt in New England. The subsequent publication of a series of poems in the *Times* seemed to afford Kipling the same recognition as had been accorded to Alfred Lord Tennyson, poet laureate for forty years, but Kipling was not nominated for poet laureate because of his history of turning down other titles. He continued to make speeches and hold public readings, however.

A son was born in 1897, when Kipling was thirty-two. The following winter, to avoid England's inclement weather, the family sailed for Cape Town, South Africa. Kipling developed close friendships there with Alfred Milner, the British high commander, and Cecil Rhodes, who may have been influential in instilling the anti-Boer sentiments he harbored when the South African war broke out. Kipling's political alliances have often been called into question, especially as they have appeared in his work. He believed "the Empire was justified because it fostered virtue in its administrators" and was "attractive because it was an island of security in a turbulent and hostile universe." He preferred to describe himself as "racialist" rather than racist and declared that his belief in the separateness of races was contingent upon the duty of the white man scrupulously to respect other cultures.

The Kiplings returned to the United States to visit Carrie's mother in the winter of 1899. En route, Carrie and their two daughters caught colds; after reaching New York, Josephine died of complications and Kipling contracted pneumonia. He recovered, much to the relief of the throngs outside his hotel, but returned grief-stricken to England with the rest of the family in June never to return to the United States. He went on to spend segments of time in South Africa, working as a war correspondent, visiting the wounded during the Boer War, and writing *Kim* (1901), his valediction to India. He also finished the ever popular *Just So Stories* at Cape Town in 1902.

After the war Kipling moved his family back to Sussex in England. It is thought that this transition marks the end of his most creative years, from 1885 to 1902, during which time his work was most critically acclaimed. During the remaining thirty-four years of his life he resided at Baterman's, a rather dark, cold Jacobean house, where he wrote "The House Surgeon," a chilling tale of the power the atmosphere of a house has over its inhabitants. He became one of the first to own a steam-driven automobile, traveling the region with Carrie. He journeyed overseas to Canada, going farther afield, finding it much to his liking, and visited Egypt as well. In 1907 he won the Nobel Prize. He had refused previous attempts to present him with national honors, including knighthood, but he was accepting of academic bestowments including, in addition to the Nobel Prize, honorary degrees from Duke, Oxford, and McGill universities. During the years prior to World War I he moved from writing to making speeches supporting the right wing of the Conservative party. After the onset of the war both he and Carrie worked with the Red Cross, Kipling going to the front line in France despite increasing health problems. Upon returning to Baterman's, he was notified that his eighteen-year-old son was missing in action in France. He was never found.

After the war Kipling's interest in aeronautical technology heightened, as did a tendency to write about fantasy and the supernatural, a direct contrast to his earlier works revolving around imperialism and tales of soldiers in England's colonies. *Puck of Pook's Hill* (1906) and *Rewards and Fairies* (1910) were historical collections in a more poetic style. His last work, *Limits and Renewals* (1932), centers around the theme of disease and madness and psychological processes of elderly women. This shift in his work may be explained by years of health problems, finally diagnosed in 1933 as duodenal ulcers. On January 18, 1936, he died of complications following a hemorrhage. His ashes are buried in Poet's Corner at Westminster Abbey.

ANN BIDLINGMAIER

Selected Bibliography

PRIMARY SOURCES

Kipling, Rudyard. *Captains Courageous*. New York: Bantam, 1982.
———. *The Jungle Books*. New York: Macmillan, 1964.
———. *Kim*. New York: Doubleday, 1901.
———. *Soldiers Three*. Salem, N.H.: Ayer, 1970.
———. *Wee Willie Winkie*. New York: Penguin, 1988.

SECONDARY SOURCES

Amis, Kingsley. *Rudyard Kipling and His World*. New York: Scribner, 1975.
Birkenhead, Lord. *Rudyard Kipling*. New York: Random House, 1978.
Bodleson, C. A. *Aspects of Kipling's Art*. New York: Barnes & Noble, 1964.
Carrington, Charles. *Life of Rudyard Kipling*. New York: Doubleday, 1955.
Croft-Cooke, Rupert. *Rudyard Kipling*. London: Arthur Barker, 1948.
Manley, Seon. *Rudyard Kipling: Creative Adventurer*. New York: Vanguard Press, 1965.
Stewart, J. I. M. *Eight Modern Writers*. Oxford, U.K.: Clarendon Press, 1963.
Young, G. M. *Victorian England: Portrait of an Age*. Garden City, N.Y.: Doubleday, 1954.

PÄR FABIAN LAGERKVIST *1951*

Pär Fabian Lagerkvist (1891–1974) was born on May 23, 1891, in the old cathedral town of Växjö in the southern Swedish province of Småland. His parents were conservative Lutherans and members of the new middle class; Pär was their seventh, and last, child. He enjoyed a long and productive literary ca-reer, publishing nine volumes of poems, five collections of short stories, fifteen plays, and six novels. Lagerkvist was a well-known writer in Sweden long before the publication of his novel *Barabbas* brought him wide international recognition. He was given the Nobel Prize in literature in the following year, 1951, "for the artistic vigor and true independence of mind with which he endeavors in his poetry to find answers to the eternal questions confronting mankind" (Österling, 201). Shy and retiring, he shunned public appearances and poured his energies into his works. Lagerkvist was a spiritual rebel who could never quite escape his tradition. In seeking to portray the nature of good and evil and question the possibility of redemption, he described himself as "a believer without faith—a religious atheist." At the age of eighty-three he suffered a stroke and died later that same week, on July 11, 1974, in a Stockholm hospital.

A sensitive and imaginative boy, Pär Fabian was born into a narrow-thinking, conservative home. Four centuries of peasant Lutheranism had produced a stolid, suspicious culture steeped in the Old Testament, believing in the status quo as the manifest will of God and in daily Bible reading, a chapter a day, in dogged pilgrimage toward the promised land. Both the boy's father, Anders Johan Lagerkvist, and his mother, Johanna (Blad) Lagerkvist, belonged to this culture, although they had already left the land: Anders supported his family by working as a signalman for the railroad, that powerful symbol of the new industrial age.

The full intellectual consequences of this break with tradition were drawn by young Pär, however. The local school taught Darwin's theory of evolution, and it proved to be heady stuff indeed for an intelligent young man brought up on fundamentalist Christianity. Young Pär

was a misfit. He argued with his teachers about his grades and got as many Fs as As. He kept to himself, was not one of the gang, and decided very early that he wanted to become a writer. With four friends he formed "The Red Ring," which held "anarchist meetings" while the rest of the town attended Sunday worship.

These young radicals were avid readers, devouring books by the astronomer Camille Flammarion, the embryologist Thomas Huxley, the revolutionary Kropotkin, and the Scandinavian writers Ibsen and Strindberg. But it was the *Origin of Species* they particularly venerated, since it was religion with which they had their biggest quarrel. As Lagerkvist later wrote, Darwin's treatise shook "the very foundation of the transcendental view of the world." During his high school years, Lagerkvist wrote for several newspapers. Beginning with a conservative publication, he ended by contributing poems and political songs to *Stormklockan*, a magazine on the political left, and affecting the broad-brimmed hat and flowing bow tie worn by socialists of the period. Lagerkvist later described this period of his life in an autobiographical work entitled *Gäst hos verkligheten* (1925; "Guest of Reality").

In 1910 he entered the University of Upsala to begin the study of art history. By 1912 he had had enough of the academy. In this year of Strindberg's death he published his first literary work, the novella *Manniskör* ("Human Beings"), a fin de siècle work one critic derided as containing 1,200 words and 12,000 dashes. The following year Lagerkvist set out for Paris, where to be young was heaven indeed and an artist might feel at home.

The visit was short, about a month, but enormously important for the young student's intellectual development. He spent hours and days in the Louvre. Somehow he met Gertrude Stein, who showed him her collection of paintings. He was transported by the discipline of the cubists, the vitality of the fauves, and the bold stylization of the naivist painters. He met Cézanne, Gauguin, Matisse, and other radical artists. Lagerkvist returned home after this intoxicating sojourn to unleash a barrage against the Swedish cultural scene in the form of a sixty-page manifesto entitled *Ordkonst och Bildkonst* (1913; "Word Art and Pictorial Art"), with the aggressive subtitle "About the Decadence of Modern Fiction, About the Vitality of Modern Art."

Literature, Lagerkvist argued, should follow the lead of the cubist painters and strive to express "simple thoughts, uncomplicated feelings in the face of life's eternal powers, sorrow and joy, reverence, love and hatred, expressions of the universal which rises above individuality" (Sjöberg, 9). Modern writers should seek renewal particularly in ancient and primitive cultures and study the Old Norse sagas, the *Kalevala*, the Egyptian Book of the Dead, and particularly the Vedic literature of India, not to mention the Bible, the Avesta, and the Koran. Lagerkvist called for a Gauguin of literature and set out to become one himself by publishing a collection of prose poems entitled *Motiv* (1914; *Themes*), contrasting savage effects with hymns and prayers; a book of short stories, *Järn och människor* (1915; Iron and Men), dealing with the recently declared war; and most particularly, a volume of poetry, *Ångest* (1916; Anguish), expressionistic poems with anguish as the main theme.

By this time Lagerkvist had moved to Copenhagen and begun serious study of the drama. In 1918 he married Karen Dagmar Johanne Sörensen, a Dane, and took a job as drama critic for the newspaper *Svenska Dagbladet*. He also published a play, *Den svåre stunden* (1918 "The Difficult Hour"), and an essay, *Teater* (1918; *Modern Theater*). As a critic, Lagerkvist inveighed against the naturalistic style then in vogue and argued for greater stylization to profile a more universal truth. He finished out the decade in Copenhagen, but he left the newspaper in 1919 and published a collection entitled *Kaos* ("Chaos"), containing a "fantasy drama," a short story, and a number of poems. All present a brutal and hopeless vision of life on earth. The play was produced privately in 1919 and 1921 with the young Greta Garbo as a member of the cast.

The publication of *Kaos* began what was to be the first of three rather distinct creative periods in Lagerkvist's career, a period conforming roughly to the decade of the 1920s. Soon after *Kaos* appeared, Lagerkvist began a period of travel through the Mediterranean; Italy, France, and North Africa. The effects of this trip through the warm and sunny lands of ancient culture may be seen in his subsequently published story *Det eviga leendet* (1920; *The Eternal Smile*). In a text that one critic has called Lagerkvist's "first great reconciliation with life" (Linder, 270), the dead tell each other stories about their life on earth. In the end they find God—an old man cutting wood, a simple man, who has worked without wishing anything for himself but only that men should never have to content themselves with nothing. The ordinary people bring forward their children and ask God what he meant by creating them. The old man replies quietly that he meant nothing by them. "Then I was only happy." Death is eternity; happiness is to be sought on this earth.

In the works that followed, Lagerkvist struggled to maintain this humanistic idealism. In this he was not completely successful. The collection of short stories he published in 1924 entitled *Onda sagor* ("Evil Tales") includes one called "Father and I." In this the narrator tells of a walk in the forest he had taken as a ten-year-old with his father. The boy fears the dark, but his father comforts him by saying, "After all, we know that there is a God." As they walk down the railroad tracks, an unscheduled train suddenly rushes out of the night; father and son barely escape with their lives. The boy sees the locomotive as a symbol:

I shivered in my whole body. It was for me, for my sake. I divined what it meant, it was the anguish which was to come, all the unknown, what father did not know

anything of, against which he could not protect me. Such this world, this life was to become for me, not like that of my father's, where everything was secure and safe. It was no real world, no real life. It only dashed, blazing, into the darkness that had no end (Sjöberg, 19).

Increasingly, the way a man endures his unhappiness is the mark of his nobility in Lagerkvist's works.

In 1925 Lagerkvist divorced his wife and married Elaine Luella Hallberg, the widow of the Swedish painter Gösta Sandels. The works he published during the final half of the decade, a book of essays, *Det besegrade livet* (1927; "The Conquered Life"), and the play *Han som fick leve om sitt liv* (1928; *He Who Lived His Life Over*), treated the idea that life is nothing and only "individual men" are worth something, but showed how difficult is the struggle against the impersonal forces of life. In 1930 Lagerkvist moved his family to Lidingö, a small island community outside Stockholm, where he made his home for the rest of his life when not away on one of his frequent travels.

The 1930s and the war years constitute the second important period in Lagerkvist's creative life. Responding to the menace of totalitarianism he perceived growing in Europe, he reacted by writing more directly and forcefully concerning the course of contemporary events. He belonged to a group of very anti-Nazi Swedish writers and sought to mobilize "fighting humanism" against spiritual tyranny and the cult of violence. A flood of poems, prose pieces, plays, and essays poured from his desk until the beginning of the war in 1939.

In the collection of poetry *Vid lägereld* (1932; "By the Campfire"), man's struggle is seen as heroic precisely because it is meaningless. In 1933 he published the powerful story *Bödein* ("The Hangman"). The first attack by a major Swedish author on totalitarian intolerance, it was dramatized the following year and played throughout Scandinavia; it was also given in London in 1935. *Den knutna näven* (1934; "The Clenched Fist") presented his humanist credo in which the ruined Greek Acropolis became a visual symbol of the fight against barbarism. The play *Mannan utan själ* (1936; *The Man Without a Soul*) further expressed Lagerkvist's antipathy toward fascism by presenting the conversion of a political terrorist to humanitarian ideals. A series of prose satires, *I den tiden* (1936; "In Our Time"), ridiculed the cult of violence, and *Genius* ("Genius"), a volume of poetry celebrating the invincibility of the spirit, followed in 1937. In 1939 he finished the ideological play *Seger i mörker* ("Victory in the Dark"), which displayed his basic dualistic philosophy by portraying the struggle between two statesmen: one a democrat, the other a corrupt demagogue.

In 1940 the Swedish Academy invited Lagerkvist to become one of its "Eighteen Immortals" by filling the place made vacant by the death of Verner von Heidenstam. He did so and continued his flow of published works. Two volumes of patriotic poems reflecting the German invasion of Denmark and Norway

appeared in the early 1940s. Then the publication of the major play *Midsommardröm i fatighuset* (1941; "A Midsummer Night's Dream in the Asylum"), which shows how life can mutilate a human soul, brought this period of wartime writing to a close and introduced a brief creative pause.

The short interlude ended emphatically with the publication of the work that was to begin to establish his international reputation, the first of his great novels, *Dvargen* (1944; The Dwarf). The book became a best-seller and heralded Lagerkvist's emergence as a major writer in this genre. Set in Renaissance Italy, *The Dwarf* depicts life at court from the jaundiced perspective of the cynical and yet heroic title figure. The novel investigates the paradox of good and evil coexisting in the same body and concludes, as one critic has written, "that the duality in man's nature is ultimately not defeating, and if there is a dwarf in every man, every man is finally more than a dwarf" (Spector, 63).

Lagerkvist finished the decade by writing two problem plays, *De vises sten* (1947; "The Philosopher's Stone") and *Låt människan leve* (1949; *Let Man Live*). In the second of these, a series of historical and imaginary characters—Socrates, Christ, Joan of Arc, Giordano Bruno, a fighter from the World War II underground, and an American black—find themselves united by their shared fate as victims of hatred and intolerance.

The 1950s saw the beginning of Lagerkvist's third and most important creative period. In the next

twelve years he wrote five major stories. And although they are not necessarily related in characters and
events, they do all ask the same
questions in exploring the idea of
God, the nature of the divine, and
the potential for faith. These were
Lagerkvist's lifelong themes, and
these late works present his most expressive and suggestive set of variations upon them.

The first of these works was the
novel *Barabbas* (1950). Its publication was a major literary event in
Sweden. The work was quickly
translated in eleven foreign countries and became Lagerkvist's most
successful novel. The critical and
commercial success of this work
provided the chief international support for the Nobel Prize awarded
him the following year. The story
itself is a sort of fifth gospel, an eye-
witness account of Christ's passion,
but one written from the point of
view of the nonbeliever Barabbas,
the robber whose place Christ took
on the cross. Following a long life
spent alternately fleeing and pondering the mystery he has witnessed,
Barabbas eventually takes part in
the burning of Rome, for which he is
imprisoned and sentenced to death.
Barabbas is rejected by the Christians at the end, and Lagerkvist describes his crucifixion in a sentence
whose ambiguity avoids a clear resolution of the question of God's presence and goodness: "When he felt
death approaching, that which he
had always been so afraid of, he said
out into the darkness, as though he
were speaking to it:—'To thee I deliver up my soul'" (180).

Man's relationship to God is
also the theme in Lagerkvist's final
book of poetry, *Aftonland* (1953;
Evening Land). The poems in this
collection pursue a problem whose
genesis reaches into childhood. Lagerkvist writes of a young child who
asks about the identity of a figure
who left a message with his thumb in
the swiftly evaporating steam of his
breath on a window pane. "Forever
and ever would not have sufficed to
interpret it," the child remarks, but
he concludes by saying:

> When I got up in the morning, the
>   window-pane was entirely clear,
> and I only saw the world such as it is.
> Everything in it seemed so strange to
>   me,
> and, behind the pane, my soul was
>   filled with loneliness and longing.

Four prose works completed the
pentology Lagerkvist began with
Barabbas. *Sibyllan* (1956; *The
Sibyl*) tells the story of Apollo's oracle, the Pythia of Delphi. This
woman, whose enthusiastic ravings
in the bowels of the temple speak the
divine mysteries, fears that the god
may desert her and seeks security by
making passionate love to a childhood friend. This man subsequently
discovers her identity and abandons
her after witnessing her possession
in the temple. In the shape of a huge
black goat the jealous god then rav-
ishes her "in a love act in which
pain, evil, and voluptuousness were
mingled" (102), and the question-
able product of this dual impregna-
tion is a half-witted child with whom
the outcast Sibyl lives in a mountain
hermitage. Visited by the Wander-

ing Jew, the Sibyl remarks: "The divine is not human; it is something quite different. And it is not noble or sublime or spiritualized, as one likes to believe. It is alien and repellent and sometimes it is madness. It is malignant and dangerous and fatal" (137).

Ahasuerus, the Wandering Jew, is himself the central figure of the following text *Ahasverus död* (1960; *The Death of Ahasuerus*). Condemned to wander for the sin of having failed to recognize God, Ahasuerus eventually comes to recognize Christ as his brother and dies, though rather as one who has been victimized by God rather than saved by him (Sjöberg 41). The remaining works in the pentology, *Pilgrim på havet* (1962; *Pilgrim at Sea*) and *Det heliga landet* (1964; *The Holy Land*) develop the story of the false pilgrim Tobias who eventually comes to the scene of crucifixion and cannot touch the cross of Christ with his bloodstained hand. But he feels drawn to the two robbers and finds that he can touch "the bandit's cross. *My* cross."

Lagerkvist's final novel, *Mariamne* (1967; *Herod and Mariamne*), is a love story that explores the dualistic nature of even this most hopeful human impulse. Herod's love is evil, but at the same time his desire for Mariamne is the only interest beyond himself he has ever known. She is a pure innocent who nevertheless finds some pleasure in her sexual relationship with Herod. In the end, a pathologically suspicious Herod arranges Mariamne's assassination, repents, arrives too late to save his wife, and must live with the question whether her final gesture— that of placing her hand in his— signifies forgiveness or simple ignorance of his role.

Lagerkvist's oeuvre is extensive and substantial. In Sweden he was a writer of major importance who introduced an alternative to naturalism in theater and set high standards of morality and intellectual ambition in his wartime writing and in the spacious architecture of his postwar novels. Translation of his works, most particularly these later works, into at least thirty-four languages is some measure of the impact his writing has had on the larger society. All the major works are available in English translations, and no less a poet than W. H. Auden undertook to render *Aftonland* in collaboration with the literary scholar Leif Sjöberg. Five of the novels and a collection of seven plays are currently in print.

Although hardly known outside of Scandinavian countries when he won the Nobel Prize, Lagerkvist now clearly belongs to that mainstream of authors whose works contribute to the canon of the European literary tradition. In facing his own personal crisis of faith, Lagerkvist attempted to chart the emptiness at the heart of much of human experience in the twentieth century. His succession of tortured, provocative characters warn against a fatuous inclination to substitute sentiment for the bitter contradictions of human relations.

JAMES W. SCOTT

Selected Bibliography

PRIMARY SOURCES

Lagerkvist, Pär Fabian. *Barabbas.* Translated by Alan Blair. New York: Random House, 1951.

———. *The Sibyl.* Translated by Naomi Walford. New York: Random House, 1958.

SECONDARY SOURCES

Flodstrom, Arthur N. "The Early Poetry of Pär Lagerkvist: A Study of the Influence of Cubism." *Dissertation Abstracts International* 32 (1971), 5736 A (Illinois).

Kehl, D. G. "The Chiaroscuro World of Pär Lagerkvist." *Modern Fiction Studies* 15 (1969): 241–50.

Linder, Erik Hjalmar. "The Life and Works of Pär Lagerkvist." Translated by D. D. Paige. *Juan Ramón Jiménez, Erik Axel Karlfeldt, Pär Lagerkvist, Selma Lagerlöf.* Nobel Prize Library. New York: Gregory, 1971. Pp. 268–73.

Österling, Anders. Presentation Address. *Juan Ramón Jiménez, Erik Axel Karlfeldt, Pär Lagerkvist, Selma Lagerlöf.* Nobel Prize Library. New York: Gregory, 1971. Pp. 201–04.

Scobbie, Irene. "Pär Lagerkvist (1891–1974)." *Essays on Swedish Literature from 1880 to the Present Day.* Aberdeen, U.K.: University of Aberdeen, 1978. Pp. 102–24.

Sjöberg, Leif. *Pär Lagerkvist.* Columbia Essays on Modern Writers, no. 74. New York: Columbia University Press, 1976.

Spector, Robert Donald. *Pär Lagerkvist.* Twayne World Authors, no. 267. New York: Twayne, 1973.

Strömberg, Kjell. "The 1951 Prize." Translated by Camilla Sykes. *Juan Ramón Jiménez, Erik Axel Karlfeldt, Pär Lagerkvist, Selma Lagerlöf.* Nobel Prize Library. New York: Gregory, 1971. Pp. 274–75.

Weathers, Winston. *Pär Lagerkvist: A Critical Essay.* Grand Rapids, Mich.: Eerdmans, 1968.

SELMA LAGERLÖF   *1909*

Selma Ottiliana Lovisa Lagerlöf (1858–1940), the author of *Gösta Berlings saga* (1891; *The Story of Gösta Berling*), one of the masterpieces of Scandinavian and world literature, was the first woman of any country and the first Swede to win the Nobel Prize in literature (1909). She was also the first woman to be admitted to the prestigious Swedish Academy (1914), that select group of eighteen authors that has traditionally chosen the Nobel Prize laureates in literature.

Lagerlöf was born on November 20, 1858, at her family's

modest country estate of Mårbacka in the beautiful, forested province of Värmland in central Sweden. She died on March 16, 1940, at Mårbacka, the home that inspired many of her writings.

The first Swedish novelist to achieve international renown, Lagerlöf was the fourth of five children born into an old and cultivated Värmland family. Many of her ancestors had been clergymen. Her brilliant, warm-spirited father, the central figure of her memoirs, served as a lieutenant in the Swedish army before settling down to life as a gentleman farmer. Her rather authoritarian mother was the daughter of a wealthy mine owner. From her earliest years Lagerlöf was surrounded by a lively oral tradition rich in stories and legends about her native region. The Lagerlöf home was a friendly haven for old soldiers and impoverished noblemen. The extended family circle included an unmarried aunt and a cherished grandmother, an entrancing storyteller whose death was keenly felt by the five-year-old Selma.

In her autobiographical works *Mårbacka* (1922) and *Ett barns memoarer. Mårbacka II* (1930; *Memories of My Childhood: Further Years at Mårbacka*) Lagerlöf gives an idyllic account of well-ordered family life on a traditional Swedish homestead, where hard work alternated with festive celebrations. Her whole family delighted in good literature. A year-long paralysis in early childhood left her with a troublesome lameness and may account for her becoming exceptionally well-read at a young age. Sir Walter Scott

and the Icelandic saga-writer Snorri Sturluson were early influences on her development as a writer.

From 1875 on the family's economic situation declined, reflecting the general depression caused by Värmland's failing iron industry. Acting against the expectations of her family, Lagerlöf resolved to get a formal education. With the encouragement of a feminist mentor she borrowed money and moved to Stockholm in 1881. In 1885 she completed her studies at the Higher Teachers' College for Women and began a ten-year career as teacher at a girl's school in Landskrona, a small town on Sweden's southwest coast.

Though the inspiration to write a great epic about Värmland at the height of its glory in the 1820s and '30s first occurred to Lagerlöf in 1881, she struggled with her material for many years before she found the right form. In 1885 her father died, and three years later the ancestral Lagerlöf home had to be sold. It was the loss of Mårbacka, she said, that finally taught her to write—as a way of preserving her home and all the old stories set in the beautiful valley of Lake Fryken.

With *The Story of Gösta Berling* (1891) Lagerlöf achieved a daring and effective break with the spirit of naturalism then dominating Scandinavian literature. A young teacher from the provinces surprised everyone by becoming the first novelist to fulfill Werner von Heidenstam's call for a new Swedish literature in which beauty, imagination, and spontaneity would counteract the pessimistic dissection of character practiced by Strindberg and other harsh realists. In gaining the courage to oppose the literary establishment and write her novel in her own enthusiastic voice, Lagerlöf was inspired by Thomas Carlyle's *Heroes, Hero-Worship, and the Heroic in History.* The brilliant, emotion-charged language of *The Story of Gösta Berling* and its wild, impulsive energy owe much to the influence of the British author.

While the true hero of Lagerlöf's epic romance may be the spirit of Värmland in the days of bold adventurers and great-souled, beautiful women, the loosely structured plot revolves around the power struggle between Gösta Berling and the Major's Wife for control of the great estate of Ekeby and its seven iron foundries. Gösta Berling is a defrocked minister and a drunkard, the best and worst of men, irresistible to women and able to inspire everyone he meets with renewed joy in life. The Major's Wife is the most powerful and richest woman in all Värmland—"courageous as a man, proud as a queen"—a no-nonsense matriarch whose practical wisdom and generosity ensure that where she rules everything is managed for the benefit of everyone. She has saved Gösta from suicide and provided quarters for him and eleven other "cavaliers"—impoverished soldiers and gentlemen—at her well-run estate, Ekeby.

The Major's Wife falls from power through the machinations of the iron-master Sintram, a character from local folklore who is alternately protrayed as the "Evil One" incarnate and as a psychotic human being. His characterization is typical of Lagerlöf's use of figures and events that can be explained rationally but seem to have a supernatural dimension. Possessed by a demonic hatred of all that is beautiful, alive, and good, Sintram persuades the cavaliers that the Major's Wife is a witch who sends men's souls to hell. Gösta and his errant knights pledge themselves to break her power and lay waste to her foundries, the region's economic foundation, by leading a life of idleness and frivolity.

Denounced by those she has helped and loved, the Major's Wife is forced out of her home on Christmas Day and must wander about the countryside as a beggar. Her year of hardship and humiliation is contrasted with the high-spirited adventures of the pleasure-seeking cavaliers. Other figures of Värmland folklore, including the memorable heroine Marianne Sinclair, emerge as protagonists of different chapters of this episodic novel. Behind all the characters the landscape of Värmland is felt as a unifying presence— "the eternal symbol of meditation . . . the keeper of great, serious thoughts." In the end, deep suffering and the true love of a young woman restore Gösta Berling to his better nature. Though the Major's Wife dies, Gösta leads the people of the parish to restore the productivity of Ekeby. The revived morale of a functioning community expresses itself in gratitude and the resolve to continue the good work of the Major's Wife, with each person striving to love his neighbor and help him and believe well of him.

Swedish critics at first did not know what to make of Lagerlöf's novel, finding it too exuberant, naive, and romantic. It was not until 1893, when Georg Brandes—the most influential critic in Scandinavia—praised the Danish edition of *Gösta Berling*, that the startling originality of Lagerlöf's genius was acknowledged in Sweden. From then on her popularity grew quickly.

In 1895 the King of Sweden granted Lagerlöf a fellowship for travel. This recognition and the success of her second book, the collection of short stories *Osynliga länkar* (1894; *Invisible Links*), allowed Lagerlöf to give up teaching and devote herself to writing. Accompanied by her close friend Sophie Elkan, a witty and talented young widow of Jewish heritage, Lagerlöf traveled during the next five years in Italy, Greece, Egypt, and Palestine. The most important result of her stay in Italy was *Antikrists mirakler* (1897; *The Miracles of Antichrist*), a novel that describes the struggle of traditional Christianity with the new teachings of socialism among the Sicilian peasants. To Lagerlöf the work for social justice and reform was in keeping with the true spirit of Christianity. She believed that the alleviation of human misery would require some form of socialism.

Upon her return from Italy Lagerlöf moved from Landskrona to the old mining town of Falun in the province of Dalecarlia, where she lived for most of the next twenty years. The royalties from her books allowed her to establish a home for herself and her mother and unmarried aunt, who lived with her. *En herrgårdssägen* (1899; *The Tale of a Manor*), her first work of this period, takes up the theme of the beloved and abandoned family home, now presided over by Lady Sorrow. A trip to Kungahälla in Norway, the site of royal marriages in ancient Scandinavia, led to a collection of saga-based stories, *Drottningar i Kungahälla* (1899; *The Queens of Kungahälla*). As Vivi Edström has noted, this work can be read as a feminist parallel to Snorri Sturluson's *Heimskringla*, the famous medieval history of the kings of Norway. The transition period between heathenism and Christianity, with all its attendant conflicts, fascinated Lagerlöf, and her sympathies frequently appear divided between heroic values and Christian virtues.

The success of her third novel, *Jerusalem* (2 volumes; 1901–02), secured Lagerlöf's reputation among the critics as well as the reading public. To gather material, she traveled to Palestine in 1899 to meet with a group of Dalecarlian farmers who had joined the Swedish-American religious colony there. *Jerusalem* is a compelling family saga about the Ingmarsson clan. In grand and sober prose the themes of confused love, family honor, guilt, and the acceptance of responsibility are played out in the lives of several generations of Ingmarssons, first in their native parish in Dalecarlia, then in the Holy City. The threat of loss of the ancestral farm becomes a central issue as the religious revivalist movement of the 1880s divides the Ingmarssons and their entire parish. The novel's hero, young Ingmar, remains loyal to the old ways while his sister and fiancé emigrate to the colony in Jerusalem. A simple, practical Christianity rooted in ancient love of the soil and long-held family traditions here confronts religious fanaticism. In its penetrating grasp of peasant life and religious psychology, *Jerusalem* remains unsurpassed in world literature.

Lagerlöf's *Kristuslegender* (1904; *Christ Legends*), a collection of naive tales remembered from childhood and collected on her travels in Italy and the Near East, became one of her most popular works. Her relationship to Christianity, however, was complex and contradictory. Undoubtedly a visionary and a mystic, she sensed that all things were alive and that all beings—humans, animals, plants, lakes, and mountains—were interrelated parts of the one great community of Creation. Her spiritual explorations led her to study theosophy and anthroposophy as well as to practice yoga in her later years. She accepted Freud's theory of the unconscious as well as the belief in life after death and reincarnation. While the redeeming power of love may be her central teaching, Lagerlöf was too good a heathen to accept the Christian doctrine of vicarious atonement. It is the responsibility of each individual, she believed, to atone for his or her own transgressions by making good what has been broken. The central question in all Lagerlöf's works is a moral one: How should human beings conduct themselves in relation to life?

In 1904 Lagerlöf was honored with the gold medal of the Swedish Academy. The same year saw the publication of her most obviously feminist work, the short novel *Herr Arnes penningar* (1904; *The Treasure*). In this chilling tale of "ill-gotten gold," blood lust, and revenge, romantic love wages a tragic struggle with the need for justice. Here, as in other stories, Lagerlöf gives an innocent and emotional young girl the role of moral agent in the pursuit of justice.

Young Elsalill, an orphan who has witnessed the brutal murder of her foster family by three Scottish mercenaries, unsuspectingly falls in love with Sir Archie, one of the murderers. Her dead foster sister returns to her in a vision to reveal the identity of the murderer. In order to break the curse of greed called forth by the treasure of her foster father, Elsalill must deliver her lover up to justice, even though she must sacrifice her own life to do so. Bonnie St. Andrews, in her perceptive feminist analysis of this tightly woven story, characterizes Elsalill as "a plausible balance between the Cinderella aspect of the female who seeks delivery through loving the prince and the Antigone principle in the female which insists on responsible ethical behavior." (*Forbidden Fruit*, 79).

In all her works Lagerlöf is extremely skillful at blending psychological aspects of character with aspects of the landscape, subtly revealing the integration of human life and Nature. In *The Treasure* the sea freezes fast after Elsalill's murder, holding human commerce in a death grip so that Sir Archie cannot escape. Only after he is captured and Elsalill receives the honor of a memorable burial, in which all the women of the community participate, does the ice break up and the natural world return to normal. Nature suffers when humans act cruelly, and Nature frequently comes to the aid of the unfortunate.

At the turn of the century Lagerlöf was invited by the National Teachers' Association to write a textbook for Swedish schoolchildren that would interest them in the geography of their country and its plant and animal life. The result, after three years of preparatory research and travel, was her most successful and best-loved book internationally, *Nils Holgerssons underbare resa genom Sverige* (1906–07; *The Wonderful Adventures of Nils* and *Further Adventures of Nils*). In this unforgettable tribute to her native Sweden, Lagerlöf created an entertaining cultural geography around the story of a farm boy from the southern province of Skania. At the start of his adventures, young Nils Holgersson is a problem adolescent—a trial to his parents, "cruel to animals, and ill-tempered toward human beings." As punishment he is transformed by an elf into a human imp. Ashamed of his miniature size, he avoids humans and turns to the animals for help, for he now has the ability to understand their speech. Riding on the back of a barnyard gander, he joins a flock of wild geese and accompanies them on a year-long tour of Sweden, viewing the various provinces, major cities, and historical landmarks along the way. Nils's airborne journey to Lapland and back becomes a journey in moral development as well. From his wild-animal companions, like a Swedish Mowgli, he learns the value of loyalty, bravery, reciprocity, and generosity. In order to survive, he learns to help others. Transformed from a selfish, indolent boy into a compassionate hero, Nils finally regains his true human form—by refusing to allow his animal friend to be sacrificed for him.

In a poignant chapter of the second volume of this humane bildungsroman for children, Lagerlöf conjures up once again the hardworking, independent, cheerful life her family had lived at Mårbacka and expresses her intense longing to be allowed to return to her childhood home. As if in answer to her deepest wish, Mårbacka was made available to the now world-famous author in the same year her novel appeared. She repurchased the home of her ancestors in 1907 and eventually returned to live permanently on the ancestral farm, taking an active role in its management.

In 1909 Selma Lagerlöf received the Nobel Prize "in appreciation of the lofty idealism, vivid imagination, and spiritual perception that characterize her writings." She was by now Sweden's most popular author, considered by some to be the greatest novelist who had ever written in Swedish. Her celebrity led her to take an increasingly active role in public life. Privately, she was a generous philanthropist, giving away much of her income to needy individuals and important social causes.

A committed advocate of the vote for women, Lagerlöf delivered the widely noticed speech "Home and State" at the World Congress for Women's Suffrage held in Stockholm in 1911. In it she contrasts woman's gift to humanity, the home, with man's gift of the state—including the church, the university, the city, and the industrial world. Though happy homes exist, there has never yet been a state that has satisfied all its members. Pointing to class hatred, oppression, revolution, and emigration, she questions whether man can ever achieve what woman has. She concludes that, just as man has helped woman in the creation of the home, so woman must enter all fields of endeavor in order to help man perfect the state, to make it as beloved as the home. This idea of the state as the people's home became an important concept in the development of Swedish social democracy.

Lagerlöf's writing career continued for nearly thirty years after she won the Nobel Prize. She produced a host of other novels and tales as well as her notable autobiographical writings. *Dagbok. Mårbacka III* (*The Diary of Selma Lagerlöf*), the last of the Mårbacka books, appeared in 1932. Among her later fiction are the profoundly moving Värmland novels *Liljecronas hem* (1911; *Liliecrona's Home*) and *Kejsarn av Portugallien* (1914; *The Emperor of Portugallia*), two volumes of short stories titled *Troll och människor* (1915; 1921; "Trolls and Humans"), the grim pacifist novel *Bannlyst* (1918; *The Outcast*), and the impressive Löwensköld cycle —a planned quartet of novels of which she completed only three. *Löwensköldska ringen* (1925; *The*

General's Ring), the first volume of the Löwensköld trilogy, is a gripping ghost story in which a curse works its way down through successive generations of two families. The title characters of the second and third volumes, *Charlotte Löwensköld* (1925) and *Anna Svärd* (1928), are perhaps the freshest and most independent of all Lagerlöf's heroines.

Though less well known to American readers, Selma Lagerlöf was one of the most popular and highly regarded authors in Scandinavia, Germany, and the Netherlands during the first half of this century. *The Story of Gösta Berling* still ranks among the favorite novels of Swedish readers, and many of her works have been adapted for film and television. Her influence on Swedish writers of prose fiction can be seen most clearly in the works of Hjalmar Bergman and Elin Wägner. Such contemporary Swedish novelists of provincial life as Sara Lidman continue the tradition Lagerlöf helped establish. Her influence may also be seen in the mythic storytelling of American poet Robert Bly and in the poetic vision of Polish Nobel laureate Czeslaw Milosz.

Lagerlöf's personality and her art were a unique synthesis of mystical, romantic, and realist elements. Her long career as an author was dedicated to the creation of novels and tales in which the Swedish landscape and the Swedish people, their spirit and their legends, assume gleaming, mythic life. As Claes Annerstedt, president of the Swedish Academy, expressed it in awarding Lagerlöf the Nobel Prize: She was "one whose soul is deeply rooted in the Swedish earth and who has taken nourishment from its myths, history, folklore, and nature. . . . Few have comprehended the innermost nature of this people with a comparable love."

JEAN PEARSON

Selected Bibliography

PRIMARY SOURCES

Lagerlöf, Selma. *Jerusalem.* Translated by Velma Swanston Howard. Garden City, N.Y.: Doubleday, 1915.

———. *The Story of Gösta Berling.* Translated and with an Afterword by Robert Bly. New York: New American Library, 1962.

———. *The Treasure.* Translated by Arthur G. Chater. Garden City, N.Y.: Doubleday, 1925. Reissued, Plainfield, Vt.: Daughters Press, 1973.

———. *The Wonderful Adventures of Nils.* Translated by Richard E. Ol-denburg. Garden City, N.Y.: Doubleday, 1967.

SECONDARY SOURCES

Edström, Vivi. *Selma Lagerlöf.* Translated by Barbara Lide. Twayne World Authors, no. 741. Boston: Twayne, 1984.

Gustafson, Alrik. "Saga and Legend of a Province." In *Six Scandinavian Novelists.* Princeton, N.J.: Princeton University Press for the American-Scandinavian Foundation, 1940. Pp. 177–225.

Lagerroth, Erland. *Landskap och natur i Gösta Berlings saga och Nils Holgersson.* Stockholm: Bonniers, 1958.

Larsen, Hanna A. *Selma Lagerlöf.* Garden City, NY: Doubleday, 1936.

Pehrson, Elsa. "Glimpses from the Hidden Workshop of Selma Lagerlöf." *The American-Scandinavian Review* 33, 1 (1945): 41–44.

St. Andrews, Bonnie. "Selma Lagerlöf: Ancient Ethics." In her *Forbidden Fruit: On the Relationship Between Women and Knowledge.* Troy, N.Y.: Whitston, 1986.

HALLDÓR LAXNESS 1955

Halldór Guðjónsson (1902—) was born in 1902 in Reykjavík, Iceland, the son of a road construction foreman. Three years later the family moved from the capital to the farm Laxnes, a few miles northeast of town, and took up farming. Even as a little boy Halldór spent his time compiling "loads of scribblings." In 1919 he left Reykjavík High School, traveled to Copenhagen, and published his first novel, *Barn náttúrunnar* (1919; "Child of Nature"), under the pseudonym Halldór frá Laxnesi. His first book was influenced by other Scandinavian novelists such as Bjørnson, Hamsun, and Lagerlöf. Halldór returned briefly to Iceland, but he left again in 1921 and stayed in Germany and Austria, where he was confronted with postwar misery.

In 1921–22 he wrote *Rauða kverið* ("The Red Booklet"). It is philosophical in nature, contrasting medieval Icelandic times and modern technology; there is an awareness of death feelings, but more important is his discovery of prayer and its power. The book was never published. In 1922, with the help of Danish writer Johannes Jørgensen, Halldór moved to the Benedictine monastery of Saint Maurice de Clervaux in Luxembourg. There he was baptized and confirmed in the Catholic faith and named Kiljan Marie Pierre. At the same time he adopted the family name Laxness after his father's farm. His time in the monastery is well documented. His many letters express spiritual turmoil and detail his experience of contemplation and religious routine. In 1923 he published a collection of short stories, *Nokkrar sögur* ("Some Stories"); worked on a manuscript of his stylized autobiography, *Heiman ek fór* ("From Home I Went"), which remained unpublished until 1952; and wrote his second novel, *Undir Helgahnúk* ("Under the Holy Mountain"), which appeared in 1924. This novel, too—published only in fragmentary form—tracing the development of one Atli Kjartansson through childhood, has autobiographic features. When it appeared, Laxness had already left the

monastery, but he wrote the apologetic *Kabólsk viðhorf* ("From a Catholic Point of View") in 1925. His breakthrough as a novelist came in 1927 with the publication of his novel *Vefarinn mikli frá Kasmír* ("The Great Weaver from Kashmir").

During the next five years he traveled, first to the United States and then Canada. In California he met Upton Sinclair and studied the movie scene in Los Angeles. Pre-Depression unemployment and the general economic instability had a strong impact on him. His orientation and his interest changed slowly from religious to social problems. From this time on, Laxness became and remains a socially committed writer. During the thirties he traveled twice to the Soviet Union in order to study social conditions there. In 1930 he returned to Iceland and married Ingibjörg Einarsdóttir, whom he divorced ten years later. In 1945 he married Aubur Sveinsdóttir. In the same year he moved into Gljúfrasteinn, his villa near his parents' farm, where he still lives today.

From the late twenties on Laxness has been an incredibly prolific and hard-working writer. Almost every year has seen the birth of a major novel or other work. In 1955 he was awarded the Nobel Prize in literature. The Swedish Academy cited him "for his vivid epic power, which has renewed the great narrative art of Iceland." Indeed, all of his important books have Icelandic themes and explore political and social issues in Iceland. They also struggle with the issue of Iceland's unique cultural and linguistic heritage.

His first large novel, *Vefarinn mikli frá Kasmír* (1927), is individualistic and antitraditional. It reflects his preoccupation with Catholicism and constitutes a confrontation with non-Icelandic European thought. The work contains a large number of literary allusions, shows the influence of André Breton's *Manifest du surréalisme*, and is stylistically and formally indebted to Strindberg's *Röda Rummet* and Papini's *Un uomo finito*, among others. Steinn Elliði, the main character, is the admired and spoiled offspring of rich Reykjavík merchants who wanders in postwar Europe—a poet errant. After a sojourn in a monastery, he goes back to Iceland and meets his former love, who is now married. She seduces him, wants him back, pursues him, but he rejects her and continues his religious career. Woman appears in this book as the incarnation of everything man must overcome in order to reach God and accomplish something in life. Steinn is torn between God and woman, two irreconcilable principles, and it takes all his willpower to take the straight and narrow path. On the other hand, what Steinn really does is to exchange woman for power and fame. The author tries to reconcile his radicalized views of society with Christianity as he has experienced it. However, no solution emerges. Furthermore, he rebels stylistically against the hallowed Icelandic saga tradition; *Vefarinn* is, as Laxness himself points out, "an experiment in many kinds of form."

The next major prose work is *Alþýðubókin* (1929; "Book of the People"), an essay collection. The texts gather, absorb, and reflect the experiences the author gained during travel in Canada and the United States. The range of topics is wide. Capitalistic exploitation and remorselessness resulting in mass misery in the pre-Depression United States had a lasting impact on Laxness. Issues of personal faith and religion faded into the background, and social issues emerged as the overriding concern as the author himself turned into a loyal socialist. He was fascinated with Spengler's *Decline of the West* but found that it did not concern Iceland. As opposed to the rest of decadent Europe, Iceland was again, he believed, in *statu nascendi* ("state of birth"). Thus he found that he was proud to be an Icelander. He celebrated his newfound national identity in an essay on Jónas Hallgrímsson (1807–45), the Icelandic naturalist and poet par excellence. As far as writing was concerned Laxness underlined the importance of being able to tell a good story. He found bourgeois novelists devoid of the ability to do so and abhorred subjectivistic, psychoanalytical novels dominated by the vanity spawned by capitalism. In Laxness's works everything depends on the author's wish to share his burning convictions with others.

Laxness started immediately to apply his theoretical considerations. In 1931–32, he published, in two parts, the novel about *Salka Valka*, the fishergirl. The novel depicts life in a typical small Icelandic fishing village, Óseyri. Four main characters are juxtaposed: weak, helpless, submissive Sigúrlina, who moves into the community with her daughter, Salka Valka, who evidences the opposite qualities; brutal Steinþór, possessed of animal eroticism; and sensitive and intellectual Arnaldur. Steinþór continuously abuses Sigúrlina, who finds brief moments of respite only in the meetings of the local Salvation Army. She commits suicide when Steinþór, enamored of Salka, leaves on their wedding day. Salka, in love with Arnaldur, tries to organize fishers and workers in order to better their lot. In the end Arnaldur, the cultured struggler for ideals, the bearer of socialism, leaves; but the community has changed. It would have been easy for Laxness to draw in black and white and to agitate forcefully for socialism in this book. But the work is far more multifaceted; the characters, especially Salka and Arnaldur, are subtle. Although the message of social strife and the attack on unmitigated capitalism and the misery it causes are clear and the radicalism of the solution sought is obvious, this is also a book about the dimensions of love and of human solitude. Woman is rendered in a very positive light, almost as the incarnation of uncorrupted life itself. Critics have maintained that many of Laxness's novels are tendentious, engaging in linear political agitation. This is not the case, not in *Salka Valka* nor in later novels. There is always a wealth of themes and formal richness: lyrical descriptions of Icelandic landscape intermingled with pointed and quick dialogue, fine irony with well-reasoned historical or philosophical remarks.

In his novel *Sjálfstætt fólk* (1934; *Independent People*) Laxness explores the second dimension of the Icelandic economy: farming. The main male character is Bjartur, actually a saga character, who is firmly rooted in the soil. Neither the death of loved ones, nor the loss of property, even his farm, can break him. Bjartur is a proletarian of the soil, one link in a thousand-year-long chain, a victim of social conditions that are unjust and inimical to man. His daughter, Sóllilja, is the opposite of Bjartur, a composite of Sigúrlina and Salka, helpless and weak, yet lyrical, full of feeling and insight. It seems to be a strategy of Laxness to bring together characters who are psychologically diametrically opposed or, better yet, to fill the characters with opposing views and feelings. This creates incredible tension on the one hand, while on the other it gives clear signals that life is not black and white but very complex indeed. Peter Hallberg (1971) arrives at the following conclusion: "Laxness's own novels seem to express, first and foremost, a vision of man's condition in life. . . . But perhaps we may notice at times a certain tension between the demands of psychological realism and the desire to rise to the bird's-eye view which the vision offers" (115).

From 1937 to 1940 Laxness wrote his tetralogy about the figure of the parish pauper and folk poet Ólafur Kárason, *Heimsljós* (*World Light*). The novel is a memorial to the Icelandic folk poet through the ages. There exists a real model: the life history of one Magnús Hjaltason, who left his diary in a public library in Reykjavík. Ólafur's childhood is an ordeal. Later he is exploited yet also supported by a strange capitalist, lives with an epileptic woman, works as a teacher, falls in love with a pupil, goes to jail, and finally falls in love with the ideal woman he has searched for all his life. She dies soon after the brief encounter, and he dies while trying to meet her at the mystical glacier. Ólafur's entire life is a search for beauty; nothing else matters. There is remorse and anguish (he finds it impossible to leave his epileptic wife), but he follows his own path. Strangely enough, his longing for beauty is nurtured by a love of fellow man that paradoxically seems to keep this longing alive. In the figure of Pétur Pálsson, the businessman, there are some attacks on Nazism. Within his local limits Pálsson is somewhat of a dictator who forces Ólafur into "inner emigration."

In the forties Iceland was first occupied by the British, then by the Americans for the duration of World War II. At the same time Icelanders discussed national sovereignty and in 1944 declared their independence from Denmark, which was then under German rule. Also, Iceland wanted back her old medieval manuscripts, the foundation of Icelandic cultural and literary life, which were housed in the Arnamagnaean Collection in Copenhagen. Laxness treats many of these topics, such as Icelandic sovereignty, Iceland's occupation, its relationship to Denmark, and the question of the manuscripts in a trilogy *Íslandsklukkan* ("Iceland's Bell"), published between 1943 and 1946. How-

ever, he sets the novel in the late seventeenth and early eighteenth centuries. This allows him to give messages without openly entering the national debate. Laxness himself maintains that *Íslandsklukkan* is no historical novel, that the characters follow the laws of their own actions. On the other hand, he researched the historical period he describes very carefully, and he creates a colorful image of that time. Each part of the trilogy focuses on one of the three main characters. The first volume is about the farmer Jón Hreggviðson, who is accused of murder and—on shaky grounds—sentenced to death. At the last minute he is freed by the lawman's daughter, Snæfríður Eydalín, who sends him to Denmark with a message for Arnas Arnæus, the scholar and collector of medieval vella (modeled on Arni Magnússon), with whom she is in love. Jón, part Quixote, part Sancho, *picaro* in short, arrives via Holland and Germany in Copenhagen, only to find Arnas married. In the meantime, in Iceland, Snæfríður herself marries an impoverished and alcoholic country squire. A few years later Arnas arrives in Iceland as an emissary of the Danish king to fight corruption and to revise legal proceedings. In the course of this he overturns the sentence passed on Jón and in the process ruins Snæfríður's father. Jón himself has to go back to Copenhagen to find justice. Arnas, also back in Copenhagen, is being offered the governorship of the island by German merchants who want to buy Iceland from the Danish king. He declines. The book ends with the burning of Copenhagen. A large portion of Arnas's treasured manuscripts perish in the conflagration.

Jón is the typical Icelandic farmer, part Bjartur, part Ólafur Kárason; he has a stubborn will to endure, is completely unsentimental, and possesses a grim sense of humor. At the same time he is firmly rooted in Iceland's literary traditions, singing, at opportune and inopportune moments, *rímur*, from which he seems to draw tremendous inner strength. Snæfriður is a character from the saga age, the bright maid, fiercely proud, longing for the highest values life has to offer and strangely disconnected from the grim realities of daily life. Arnas sacrifices his love for Snæfriður, i.e., his personal happiness, for the sake of trying to save Iceland's literary heritage. The characters operate on several different levels: First, they are caught in the ageless web of relationships, determined by love and hate and the social framework; second, they are, all three of them, themselves exponents of saga-age values and literary traditions; third, they are influenced by and influence themselves the national fate of Iceland. This is Laxness's first historical book. Together with the new, historical dimension, Laxness deployed a new style. Whereas he spurned the saga style in his early works, he now adopted it. He was helped along in this direction by his translation of Hemingway's *Farewell to Arms*. Hemingway's style of writing—short, concise sentences, and much dialogue—is not unlike saga prose. Because of the large dialogue segments, it was fairly easy to drama-

tize the book. The resulting play, *Snæfriður Íslandssól*, was performed at the inauguration of the National Theater in Reykjavík in 1950.

In 1945 World War II was over, and Icelanders expected the American military to leave. But the confrontation between the United States and the Soviet Union became stronger and more dangerous, and the Americans wanted to hold on to bases on Iceland. The new republic joined NATO in 1946, and after secret negotiations and much public debate, Parliament voted to grant the United States the continued use of the military airport at Keflavík. This issue was hotly debated in Iceland at the time and caused a polarization of the population, pro and con, a condition that, to some degree, still exists today.

This situation is the background for Laxness's novel *Atómstöðin* (1948; *The Atom Station*). It is Laxness's first novel in which the action is contemporary and where he participates directly in the public debate; it is a sarcastic reaction to the foreign policy of Ólafur Thors, Iceland's prime minister at that time. Thors actually appears as a character in the novel. Not only as far as content is concerned does Laxness proceed along new lines, but formally as well. The story is narrated by a fictitious character named Ugla. She is also the protagonist. Ugla, from Eystridalur, a small rural community, arrives in Reykjavík to work in the house of a rich merchant and member of parliament. She takes this position in order to study organ music with a well-known organist. The organist receives in his house members of a criminal urban subculture. With one of them, a corrupt policeman, Ugla has an affair and later gives birth to a child. She does not want to marry the policeman at first because of obligations to the child, and she does not want to marry the merchant because she does not want to be bought with material things. She wants to be free, a human being in her own right. In this respect she seems related to Salka Valka. Ugla is not the naive country bumpkin lost in fashionable urbanity but a purposeful and resourceful person. The humane, tolerant organist, an artist of high caliber, provides Ugla with possibilities of articulation, artistic encounter, and, last but not least, mental and sentimental growth. Social issues are implicit in this novel, too: the exploiting, insensitive capitalist and the female narrator who comes from a precapitalist agrarian background. But there is no actual clash; rather, there is distance, or at best a merging of elements of both worlds in Ugla. The novel does discuss the role of woman and concludes that woman ought to be able to mold her own destiny. Aldo Keel (1981) sees in Ugla's personal story an ironic counterpart to the political development of the country: While Iceland is in the process of changing from self-sufficiency to foreign domination, Ugla struggles to achieve the opposite effect (57).

In the decade from 1950 to 1960, the decade in which he received the Nobel Prize, Laxness published three major novels. In the first one, *Gerpla* (1952; *The Happy Warriors*), by using saga material (actually the *Fóstbrœðra saga*), as a model, he ignored an Icelandic taboo. The main theme is the heroic, the role of the hero, and hero worship, issues that were very appropriate after World War II and during the Korean War. But the novel seems to imply that heroic posturing and hero figures tend to cover up reality, that heroes live in a dreamworld. On the lighter and more entertaining side, *Gerpla* is somewhat of a spoof on *Fóstbrœðra saga*. Þórgeir, one of the protagonists, dies, simply because he finds himself in a physical position that is favorable for killing. To his sworn brother, Þormóður, the act of revenge that must be undertaken comes somewhat as a burden. The king (Holy Ólafur) is the prototype of a fat, conniving politician who does not even want to receive the poem Þornóður composed in his honor. Again the message—but military heroism was slightly outmoded even then. In *Brekkukotsannáll* (1957; *The Fish Can Sing*) the themes are similar to some of those in *Atómstöðin*. Again economic systems, countryside, and petit bourgeois in the city are confronted; the discussion of art, begun in *Atómstöðin*, is continued. *Paradísarheimt* (1960; *Paradise Reclaimed*) is the story of an Icelandic farmer who goes to Utah, converts to Mormonism, and acquires worldly possessions, but he returns to Iceland and starts again to build his old farm, which by now has fallen in disrepair. The farmer does not leave Iceland because he is thirsting for religious deliverance but merely for the sake of economy and adventure, and he does not return as a glowing missionary but mainly because he found the Mormon society too intolerant, too narrowminded.

It has been mentioned earlier, in connection with the discussion of *Íslandsklukkan*, that because of extensive use of dialogue it is not too difficult to dramatize Laxness's novels, which, incidentally, grew closer and closer to "naked drama." In 1965 Laxness published a collection of essays and articles, *Upphaf Mannúðarstefnu* ("The Beginning of Humanism"), in which he expounds some of his ideas on the novel. He demands artistic "objectivity," which he finds absent both in modern(ist) novels and in the French *roman nouveau*. In these, he asserts, a character, "Plus X"—i.e., the writer himself, with his undesirable subjectivity—who cannot disconnect himself from the narrator, is always present. Although this statement seems somewhat absurd, it probably ought to be interpreted as a call for more artistic discipline and control. In this context, Laxness finds that the drama, less encumbered by "Plus X," exhibits more density and conciseness than the novel. During the sixties Laxness published three major plays, perhaps the best known of which is *Dúfnaveislan* (1966; "The Pigeon Banquet").

In his memoirs, *Skáldatími* (1963; "A Writer's Schooling"), Laxness made it clear that he was no longer the socialist firebrand he had been. Travel to many countries after receiving the Nobel Prize had made him skeptical of rigid ideologies, just as he had become skeptical of inflexible religious convictions years earlier. He apologizes for idealized reports from the Soviet Union in the thirties: "The gibberish of Freud competed with that of Marx to cripple the language of my youth." His concerns at this stage—as expressed eloquently, for instance, in *Paradísarheimt*—were the rights of the individual; consequently, he demanded religious and political tolerance.

Less politically engaged and intent on avoiding subjective description of psychological developments, Laxness again started writing novels. In 1968 a novel appeared that is perhaps, from the reader's point of view, the most difficult one Laxness ever wrote: *Kristnihald undir jökli* ("Christianity in Snæfellsnes"). The content is basically about a church supervisor, Umbi, who is sent by the bishop with a set of instructions to report on a certain church and its minister. (Laxness had used the technique of putting the story in the mouth of a narrator before, e.g., Ugla, in *Atómstöðin*, formulated the story and sorted it out for the reader—and at the same time, was one of the dramatis personae.) Umbi, although expressly given a narrative mandate, does not really function as a narrator. The entire novel follows a strategy of reader disorientation, of alienation. Umbi, who in his report has to document, or try to document, the world he encounters, fails because it eludes documentation. Events keep piling up that

Umbi cannot interpret. There is no causal connection. The one traditional character in the book, the minister, is also the one who does not strive to find the truth anymore, nor does he believe in words. He maintains an artistic, poetic stance in life, which means that he is quiet, does not use words. His life and his surroundings are manifest in abounding metaphors that, in the end, conquer the narrator, who finds himself enveloped in the minister's Taoist mysticism. In commenting on Laxness's pessimistic stance in this novel, Aldo Keel noted: "Icelandic reality of 1968 is not poetic and humane, the future is death" (118).

Two years later, in 1970, Laxness presented his next "experiment," *Innansveitarkronika* ("A Parish Chronicle"). He set the novel in his own surroundings, Mosfellssveit. The story is about an old church that people decided to tear down in the 1880s but finally agreed to rebuild because it is supposed to contain the skull of Egil Skallagrimsson, one of the famous saga characters. Laxness spends much time describing the rural background, the work of the farmers, et cetera. The picture he evokes is idyllic. Gone are the hunger, the sweat, the struggle for survival that he so vividly described in earlier novels such as *Sjálfstætt fólk*. In this novel it is as if the historical dimension turned the farm scenery into a gigantic, static painting. Tradition is conjured up time and time again but remains strangely inadequate for orienting the reader. The symbolism is tangible, yet what message comes across? The church is restored, the spire points skyward—is that the future?

In *Guðsgjafaþula* (1972; "The Game of Chance") Laxness deployed yet another narrative strategy, that of the "keyhole narrator," who more or less accidentally observes events but soon finds himself deeply involved. This is Laxness's novel about herring, one of the cornerstones of the Icelandic economy, and it hones in on the central problem of that very economy, namely, its dependency on fishing—a game of chance.

During his long life as a writer Laxness seems to have undergone several metamorphoses. From his search for God, his struggle for faith, he turned to social issues, fought for social justice. He involved himself in political issues, in the debate around national sovereignty and independence. After he received the Nobel Prize, he entered a period of retreat from social and political discussions and agitation. This change of focus brought in its wake an artistic crisis that engendered aesthetization and his experimentation with drama and various forms of the narrative, which he is still conducting today. Laxness's contribution to Icelandic political and cultural life is enormous. It might be debated whether he helped shape his nation's political fate, but it is certain that Icelandic literature in the twentieth century without Laxness's decisive role is unthinkable.

FRITZ H. KÖNIG

Selected Bibliography

PRIMARY SOURCES

Laxness, Halldór. *The Atom Station.* Translated by Magnus Magnusson. London: Methuen, 1961.

———. *The Fish Can Sing.* Translated by Magnus Magnusson. London: Methuen, 1966; New York: Crowell, 1967.

———. *The Happy Warriors.* Translated by Katherine John. London: Methuen, 1958.

———. *Independent People.* Translated by J. A. Thompson. London: George Allen & Unwin, 1945; New York: Knopf, 1946; New Delhi: People's Publishing House, 1957.

———. *Paradise Reclaimed.* Translated by Magnus Magnusson. London: Methuen, 1962; New York: Crowell, 1962.

———. "A Quire of Seven." Translated by Alan Boucher. In *Icelandic Review*, Reykjavík, 1974.

———. *Salka Valka.* Translated by F. H. Lyon (from Gunnar Gunnarsson's Danish translation of the original Icelandic). London: George Allen & Unwin, 1936; Boston: Houghton Mifflin, 1936.

———. *World Light.* Translated by Magnus Magnusson. Madison and London: University of Wisconsin Press, 1969.

SECONDARY SOURCES

Hallberg, Peter. *Halldór Laxness.* Translated by Rory McTurk. New York: Twayne, 1971.

Keel, Aldo. *Innovation und Restauration, Der Romancier Halldór Laxness seit dem Zweiten Weltkrieg.* Basel and Frankfurt am Main: Helbing and Lichtenhahn, 1981.

SINCLAIR LEWIS   *1930*

Harry Sinclair Lewis (1885–1951), the first American to win the Nobel Prize in literature (1930), dominated American fiction between the world wars with his social satire, which neatly skewered virtually every important form of hypocrisy, every pompous, pretentious institution of his day. Before most Americans were even aware of such issues, he dealt with women's rights, religious opportunism, and the business world's mendacity, as well as with racism, fascism, and other insidious forces. Lewis satirized an array of recurring characters (both specific persons and types), including physicians, con men, bigots, clergymen, Rotary Club members, xenophobic Americans, and others.

Lewis was born on February 7, 1885, in Sauk Centre, Minnesota (the small frontier town that became the model for *Main Street*), the third and youngest son of Edwin J. and Emma Kermott Lewis. His mother died, after a long illness, when Lewis was six; his father, a physician, remarried a year later. Lewis's father valued hard work for its own sake— and young Lewis, a loner, learned that those who work hard, though perhaps dull and unexciting as subjects for fiction, nonetheless reflected frontier principles of steadfastness, determination, and commitment.

In 1898 Lewis tried without success (because of his age) to enlist for the Spanish-American War, in 1902 he attended Oberlin Academy to prepare for college, and in 1903 he entered Yale University, where he wrote for school and local newspapers. He sailed on a cattle boat for Liverpool in the summer of 1904, where his naive ideas about British superiority, especially literary, were dispelled. When he went home to Sauk Centre the following summer, he realized how limited small-town life was. He again visited England (in 1906), but then suddenly left Yale as his senior year began. He spent a month with Upton Sinclair in a socialist community in New Jersey, free-lanced as a writer in New York, traveled to Panama, and returned to Yale to graduate. He then worked as a journalist in Iowa, California, and Washington, D.C., eventually returning to New York, where he stayed for five years. Lewis married Grace Livingstone Hegger in 1913; they were divorced in 1928, the same year he married journalist Dorothy Thompson, from whom he was divorced in 1942. In the 1940s he moved to Duluth to try to recover his heritage, but after two years he moved to Massachusetts and continued traveling throughout Europe. He died in Rome January 10, 1951, and is buried at Sauk Centre.

Despite his lifelong traveling, in his writings, Lewis continually returned psychologically and fictionally to the small midwestern towns he knew as a child. His life and career are usually divided into conventional periods of apprenticeship, maturity, and decline. The first forty years (through World War I) reflected major changes in virtually all aspects of American life and in Lewis's own convictions. His first book, a boys' novel, *Hike and the Aeroplane* (1912), written under a pseudonym, is undistinguished and conventional, but *Our Mr. Wrenn* (1914) is more mature both in skill (garnered from the dozens of stories he began selling to major magazines) and in subject. It deals with a clerk who travels to Europe for excitement only to return home, contrite and eager to settle down as a decent, dignified American. *The Trail of the Hawk* (1915) shows growth in technique, though the subject matter—about an aviator who moves from small-town anonymity to fame—merely combines the emphases of his first two books. *The Job* (1917) focuses on a woman who succeeds in the man's world of business and reflects Lewis's growing sense of structure and erotic candor. *The Innocents* (1917), though, is a sentimental throwback, an idealistic tale of a poor-but-happy couple. *Free Air* (1919) is based on travels Lewis and his first wife took to the Pacific Northwest.

All these apprentice efforts, though useful in introducing typical Lewis character types and (especially in *The Job*) a glib, facile style reflective of actual speech patterns, were small preparation for his 1920 blockbuster, *Main Street*, which marked the beginning of Lewis's mature career.

Though other writers (e.g., Hamlin Garland, Sherwood Anderson) had also written critically and satirically about American small-town life, the disillusionment younger writers felt after World War I led to an identification of such communities with the naive, self-righteous hypocrisy and smug religiosity that defended both the war and Prohibition. *Main Street* captures the emptiness of the village, the Philistine tastes, the lonely, unfulfilled, and hopeless lives that cannot escape, the crying out for emotional and intellectual security. Carol Kennicott, an idealistic librarian one year out of college, marries a physician and moves to Gopher Prairie, intending to remedy the town's faults. In particular, she hopes to bring "culture" to the gossiping, biased, insular townsfolk who are preoccupied with civic boosterism and unthinking acceptance of religious and political truisms. Kennicott discovers that she cannot overcome the dullness of the town and leaves for Washington, D.C., only to return permanently a year later, chastened and reconciled to the empty routines she had previously criticized. The impact of *Main Street* was far-reaching and controversial, with Lewis accused on the one hand of having slandered America's heartland and values and on the other of having provided a needed exposé of small-town mendacity and shallowness.

The success of *Main Street* enabled Lewis and his family to travel to Europe, and in 1922 he published *Babbitt*, generally considered his best book. The sharp contrast between idealism and reality is again present, as a middle-aged real-estate man realizes the limitations and inconsistencies of his conformist behavior. Despite Babbitt's efforts to break away from conventionality, he returns to middle-class respectability and family; he is at least aware of what his life lacks even if he cannot make any major changes. Lewis explores virtually all of Babbitt's bourgeois attitudes—sex, religion, family, politics, money, civil liberties, business, labor relations—through extensive documentation (used in most of his subsequent books as well) and a fine ear for dialogue, with the result that Babbitt is a target of both satire and sympathy.

Arrowsmith (1925) similarly satirizes middle-class values but in the process depicts a genuine hero, a bacteriologist (based on Paul de Kruif, noted researcher in bacteriology and writer of popular books on science) devoted to pure research who gradually loses his scientific innocence through commercial realities. Arrowsmith is close to discovering an antitoxin for a plague devastating a Caribbean island. This could result in scientific recognition and financial rewards, but his single-mindedness and carelessness lead to his wife's death and the invalidation of his experiments. Devastated, he retreats to an isolated laboratory where, incapable of introspection, he devotes himself to research. Lewis was awarded the Pulitzer Prize for *Arrowsmith* but declined the honor because of resentment over the award's not having been given to *Main Street* or *Babbitt*.

After writing a slight book, *Mantrap* (1926), about a naive New York lawyer's disillusioning expedition into the wilderness where he discovers that "roughing it" offers little genuine pleasure, Lewis published one of his most controversial books, *Elmer Gantry*, in 1927. Though Lewis had dealt with organized religion before, his preparation for *Elmer Gantry*—which included speaking in churches, meeting with clergy, and immersing himself in works of popular theology— enabled him to write with documentary authority about the definitive hypocrite. Gantry is expelled from a seminary, becomes an associate to (and lover of) a woman evangelist (modeled on Aimee Semple McPherson), then becomes a superficially respectable, prominent clergyman wholly lacking in conviction or principle in his search for money, sex, and status.

The Man Who Knew Coolidge (1928), another slight book, is a series of monologues focusing on a bigoted Babbitt type who rambles about Prohibition, sports, salesmanship, marriage, and politics. The excellent *Dodsworth* (1929), unique for Lewis in that it is not overtly satiric, depicts a well-meaning man's difficulty in choosing between two women, with a trip to Europe serv-

ing—as it did for Henry James and others—as a catalyst for the sympathetic character's reasoning and choices. Dodsworth, a manufacturer, is able to experience for himself the contrast between the New World and the Old and reluctantly, but with conviction, changes his life, his goals, and his wife—as Lewis did at the same time.

Lewis's acceptance speech upon winning the Nobel Prize in 1930— for which he was cited for his "vigorous and graphic art of description and his ability to create, with wit and humor, new types of characters"—addressed the decline of the image of the United States as a genteel, pastoral society, citing other worthy American writers as well as important younger ones (Faulkner and Hemingway among them). Though Lewis's post-prize books were often popular, they tended to repeat his earlier techniques and subjects and in some cases dealt with trivial issues. The sensational *Ann Vickers* (1933) is a cry for penal reform, but the protagonist's sex life (including an abortion and illegitimate child as well as several lovers) overrides the social import of the work. By contrast, the ineffectual *Work of Art* (1934) praises a man's calling in the hotel business.

It Can't Happen Here (1935), though, has become increasingly relevant in recent decades. Written to support Franklin Delano Roosevelt's reelection in 1936 and loosely based on the life of Louisiana politician Huey Long, the novel describes the rise of a populist American fascist who is elected president and turns the United States into a dictatorship complete with martial law, concentration camps for political opponents, and racial and gender restrictions intended to lead to "Victory for the Forgotten Men." A small-town editor who opposes the president joins the underground resistance. Lewis concludes with an equivocal statement about the survival of ordinary people and the relative merits of the president. *The Prodigal Parents* (1938), by contrast, is a minor, sentimental attempt to expose communism through the microcosm of a family's disputes.

None of Lewis's last books is memorable, despite some topical, even propagandistic touches. *Bethel Merriday* (1940) follows a woman's stage career from adolescence to minor success, and *Gideon Planish* (1943) exposes philanthropic excesses through a Gantry-like con man's rise. *Cass Timberlane* (1945), the best of the later works, tells of an introspective judge's second marriage to a younger woman, her abandonment of him for one of his friends, and her repentant return to the judge when she is deathly ill. Lewis's perceptive analysis of marriage (he was by this time divorced from his second wife and involved with a young woman) is heightened by numerous "interchapters" about other unhappy marriages among Timberlane's friends. *Kingsblood Royal* (1947) tackles race prejudice, especially miscegenation, resulting from a racist banker's discovery that he has a small percentage of "black blood."

The God-Seeker (1949) was intended as the first part of a historical trilogy, a saga following several generations as they try to build the wilderness and contend with each other. *World So Wide* (1951), written while Lewis was dying, again presents an American seeking substance in Europe that he cannot find in America. In 1952, *From Main Street to Stockholm: Letters of Sinclair Lewis, 1919–1930* was published, and in 1953 *The Man from Main Street*, a selection of essays, reviews, and college writings—he had previously published *Selected Short Stories* (1935), as well as several plays, some based on his novels. *I'm a Stranger Here Myself and Other Stories* appeared in 1962. Lewis's collaboration with director Dore Schary on an allegorical screenplay about World War II, *Storm in the West*, appeared in 1963.

In addition to becoming self-parodistic and dated, Lewis's works after the Nobel Prize showed other slippage. The exposés of the 1920s changed to generally tepid explorations of safer subjects in the 1930s and 1940s, and the realism became irrelevant. Worse, the satire that enlivened the early books became the bitter denunciations of an old man. Yet at its best, Lewis's work presents character types that exist as commonly today as before, and his artistry and care in researching his characters and their worlds enable his best books to appeal to successive generations. His skill at simultaneously satirizing and creating sympathy for specific targets, even opportunistic quacks, is unmatched, and his picture of American life in a particular era remains the typical one for many readers, American or foreign. Most important, Lewis's brilliant depiction of stultifying, repressive environments, whether in small towns or conformist professions, is still pertinent.

PAUL SCHLUETER

Selected Bibliography

PRIMARY SOURCES

Lewis, Sinclair. *Ann Vickers.* Garden City: Doubleday, Doran, 1933; London: Cape, 1933.

———. *Arrowsmith.* New York: Harcourt, Brace, 1925; London: Cape, 1925.

———. *Babbitt.* New York: Harcourt, Brace, 1922; London: Cape, 1922.

———. *Cass Timberlane.* New York: Random House, 1945; London: Cape, 1946.

———. *Dodsworth.* New York: Harcourt, Brace, 1929; London: Cape, 1929.

———. *Elmer Gantry.* New York: Harcourt, Brace, 1927; London: Cape, 1927.

———. *It Can't Happen Here.* Garden City, N.Y.: Doubleday, Doran, 1935; London: Cape, 1935.

———. *Kingsblood Royal.* New York: Random House, 1947; London: Cape, 1947.

———. *Main Street: The Story of Carol Kennicott.* New York: Harcourt, Brace and Howe, 1920; London: Hodder and Stoughton, 1921.

SECONDARY SOURCES

Dooley, D. J. *The Art of Sinclair Lewis.* Lincoln: University of Nebraska Press, 1967.

Grebstein, Norman. *Sinclair Lewis.* New York: Twayne, 1962.

Griffin, Robert J., ed. *Twentieth Century Interpretations of "Arrowsmith": A Collection of Critical Essays.* Englewood Cliffs, N.J.: Prentice-Hall, 1968.

Lewis, Grace Hegger. *With Love from Gracie: Sinclair Lewis, 1912–1925.* New York: Harcourt Brace, 1955.

Lundquist, James. *Guide to Sinclair Lewis.* Columbus, Ohio: Merrill, 1970.

———. *Sinclair Lewis.* New York: Ungar, 1973.

Schorer, Mark. *Sinclair Lewis: An American Life.* New York: McGraw-Hill, 1961.

———. *Sinclair Lewis.* University of Minnesota Pamphlets on American Writers, No. 27. Minneapolis: University of Minnesota Press, 1963.

———. ed. *Sinclair Lewis: A Collection of Critical Essays.* Englewood Cliffs, N.J.: Prentice-Hall, 1962.

MAURICE MAETERLINCK   *1911*

The Belgian writer Maurice Maeterlinck (1862–1949) was born in Ghent, the capital of Flanders, on August 29, 1862, into a very old family of Flemish stock. His father was a retired notary whose only occupations were gardening, bee tending, and paying attention to his investments. His mother, the daughter of a wealthy lawyer, had some sympathy for literature.

Maeterlinck showed a precocious predisposition for literature. By the age of ten he had written adaptations of Molière's plays. Fearing such activity might lead to dissipation, his father decided to put an end to his son's literary bent and sent him, at age twelve, to the Jesuit College of Sainte Barbe in Ghent. For the seven years he was there Maeterlinck received a good education, but all the while he intensely disliked the school. There, Charles Van Lerberghe, the future author of *La Chanson d'Eve* (1904; "The Song of Eve"), was his friend. Although Maeterlinck was strongly attracted to poetry and a literary career, his father, who regarded business as the only worthy occupation, insisted that he study law at Ghent University for four years. As early as 1883, however, he published his first poem in the literary review *La Jeune Belgique* ("Young Belgium"), which had just been founded. After graduation from law school, he went to Paris, where he established contact with literary circles, especially the symbolists. Among them, Villiers de

l'Isle Adam had the greatest influence upon him.

Soon, however, Maeterlinck had to return to Ghent and begin the practice of law, which he found totally boring. In 1886 he founded a literary magazine, *La Pléiade*, in which he soon published a short story, "Le Massacre des Innocents" ("The Massacre of Innocents") and poems. In his first short story he broached the problem of evil, which he was to treat again in future works. In the meantime, he continued to practice law. In 1889 he published *Serres Chaudes* (*Warm Greenhouses*), the poetry he had been writing in his spare time. Before the end of the year, he had also published his first play, *La Princesse Maleine* (1889; *Princess Maleine*). It is the first of Maeterlinck's symbolist plays to be acclaimed as a masterpiece by the prominent French critic Octave Mirbeau. Like all his early symbolist plays, this one is the spontaneous expression of feelings, moods, and obsessions. The action takes place in a gloomy atmosphere in northern Flanders. *Princess Maleine* is typical of Maeterlinck's dramaturgy: hallucinating characters shrouded in mystery wander like shadows in a natural environment that helps doom the love of the princess and the prince. Maleine, one of the gentlest and sweetest characters Maeterlinck created, suffers a mysterious and tragic destiny, as do other victims in Maeterlinck's plays. Three major characteristics of symbolist theater already appear in this play: a sense of timelessness, vagueness in the drawing of characters who seem to be weak, and the presence of symbols that affect the drama and the spectators.

Mirbeau's excellent review of *Princess Maleine* so encouraged Maeterlinck that the same year he published two more plays: *L'Intruse* (1890; *The Intruder*) and *Les Aveugles* (1890; *The Blind*). In both plays the characters are the pawns of invisible fatal forces.

In *The Intruder* a woman recovering from childbirth is visited by death (the Intruder) while her family (her husband, brother-in-law, three daughters, and a blind grandfather) try to dissipate their anguish by talking. The blind man is alone in having felt the presence of the Intruder. Soon, a nun emerges from the sick woman's room to announce her death. Too many symbols obscure the meaning of this one-act play and detract from its poetry.

The symbolism is clearer in *The Blind*. The action takes place in a northern forest under a clear sky sparkling with stars. Twelve blind men and women are groping to find their way, thinking that their guide will return. Finally, they discover that he has died of old age, leaving them defenseless in the face of great danger. This allegory represents humanity having lost faith, its only guide. These two plays, regarded by many contemporaries as the best expression of the spirit of the time, brought immediate international renown to Maeterlinck and were translated into most major languages.

The following year Maeterlinck published *Les Sept Princesses* (1891; "The Seven Princesses"), which has been regarded as inferior to his previous plays by most, including its author, and as a mere interlude prior to *Pelléas et Mélisande* (1892; *Pelleas and Melisande*). Written in prose, the play has a simple plot. Lost in a forest, prince Golaud, a mature man and a widower, encounters a tearful girl, Mélisande, who is also lost. Golaud brings her to his castle and later marries her. However, his younger brother Pelleas is irresistibly attracted to Mélisande, and they fall in love. Golaud kills Pelleas and wounds Mélisande, who dies soon after. All major characters are the pawns of fate to the extent that even love is experienced by them almost unconsciously. The fairy tale structure contributes to an ambience in which symbols can abound. A year later, Claude Debussy began to set *Pelléas and Mélisande* to music. It was to become his greatest opera and was to contribute much to Maeterlinck's fame.

Sharing Schopenhauer's view that man has no control over his will, the cause of his unhappiness, Maeterlinck began to feel that puppets were ideally suited to represent the archetypal characters with which he wanted to people his theater. Thus, in 1894 he published three plays for marionettes: *Alladine et Palomides* (*Alladine and Palomides*), an extension of *Pelléas and Mélisande*; *Intérieur* (*Interior*), as a meditation on death; and *La Mort de Tintagiles* (*The Death of Tintagiles*), another meditation on the futility of man's will in the face of destiny. These plays completed a body of work Maeterlinck produced between 1889 and 1894—eight plays and a book of poetry—that gave the French symbolist movement its quintessential language and form.

In 1895 Maeterlinck met the French actress Georgette Leblanc, who was to be his companion and inspiration for twenty years. She was able to help him discover the more positive aspects of the human condition. Her influence on him was considerable in *Douze Chansons* (1896; *Twelve Songs*) which became *Quinze Chansons* ("Fifteen Songs") in 1900. In these poems he gave up some of the trappings of symbolist poetry in favor of popular rhythms to express not only anguish but also serenity, absence, and death. The play *Aglavaine et Sélysette* (1896; *Aglavaine and Selysette*) marks a transition from symbolism into a new literary phase. In it, the characters no longer seem unconscious. They actively try to react against their fate, although unsuccessfully.

In 1896 Maeterlinck also published *Le Trésor des humbles* (*The Treasure of Humble Folks*), a series of essays that are indicative of the sources of his thought—Ruysbroeck, Novalis, Emerson, Carlyle, and Plotinus—as well as of his reactions to positivism and pragmatism. Claudel and Bergson had similar attitudes and reactions toward the dominant ideology of the time—they felt that the creative spirit was repressed by a rationalism and pragmatism debasing for the soul. The work enjoyed immense success. After 1898, influenced by Georgette Leblanc, Mae-

terlinck broke with his family, who disapproved of his choice of a career, and lived mostly in France. His literary production continued to be abundant, and it was generally well received. *Sagesse et Destin* (1898; *Wisdom and Destiny*) was a philosophical synthesis marking a substantial departure from Shopenhauerian pessimism, in part because of Georgette Leblanc's influence.

Maeterlinck was interested not only in human nature, but in all aspects of nature. He tried to discover similarities and analogies between the life of humans and that of animals, as in *La Vie des Abeilles* (1901; *The Life of Bees*), which is a scientifically accurate essay on bee culture. Later he wrote *L'Intelligence des Fleurs* (1907; *The Intelligence of Flowers*), an essay on horticulture. In 1901 Maeterlinck also published *Ariane et Barbe Bleue* (*Ariane and Bluebeard*). In this play he focuses on Bluebeard's last wife, the one who, refusing to be dominated by anyone, escaped and forged her own destiny. She did so by disobeying, because "whatever is permitted teaches one nothing." *Ariane and Barbe Bleue* presents the point of view of a liberated woman and is regarded as one of the first feminist plays. It received high critical acclaim and enjoyed great success. In *Sœur Béatrice* (1901; *Sister Beatrice*), inspired by a medieval miracle play, Maeterlinck remains outside the gloomy atmosphere of his earlier symbolist plays. This new type of theater was designed to involve primarily the minds of the spectators and only secondarily their feelings.

For *Monna Vanna* (1902), Maeterlinck also sought his inspiration in the Middle Ages. Writing this play like a classical historical drama, he abandoned his earlier style. *Joyzelle* (1903), inspired by Shakespeare's *Tempest*, marked a departure from his early approach, but, philosophically too complex, it failed, as did two other minor plays.

Less than two years later, however, Maeterlinck enjoyed one of his greatest theatrical successes with *L'Oiseau Bleu* (1905; *The Blue Bird*). Like most of Maeterlinck's early symbolist dramas, it was inspired by several fairy tales, and more particularly by J. M. Barrie's *Peter Pan*. It is a fantasy in five acts and twelve "tableaux" in which the two children of a poor woodsman, Tytyl and Mytyl, have nothing to look forward to on Christmas Eve. In their sleep, however, they dream of a fairy who takes them on a search for the Blue Bird, the harbinger of happiness. She gives them a diamond that enables them to see the true nature of things. In their travel to the land of memories (Memory Lane), they see dead members of their family merely asleep. Death is presented as another state of life. Then they travel through the Palace of the Night, the Garden of Happiness, and the Kingdom of the Future, where they meet children yet to be born. In the morning a neighbor asks for Tytyl's bird for her sick daughter. That is when the boy notices he had been holding the Blue Bird all along. Maeterlinck borrowed many traditional motifs but modernized them at will and set them in an optimistic context, in sharp contrast with the gloomy symbolist stories of his earlier period. This work was first performed in Moscow in 1908 and has had enormous success throughout the world ever since. With *Pelléas and Mélisande*, it contributed to earning Maeterlinck the Nobel Prize in literature in 1911 as well as everlasting fame.

In the years immediately preceeding World War I, Maeterlinck continued to try to find psychological and philosophical balance. He began to express his concern for social problems, and during the war he attempted to enlist and fight for his country. However, this evolution from a fantasy world to the real one had an adverse effect on his creative genius. After the war, he left Georgette Leblanc and married a very young actress, Renée Dahou. He traveled extensively in the United States and around the Mediterranean, continuing to write plays, including *Le Bourgmestre de Stilmonde* (1919; *The Burgmaster of Stilmonde*), *Les Fiançailles* (1922; *The Betrothal*), a sequel to *The Blue Bird*; and several works on nature—*La Vie des Termites* (1926; *The Life of White Ants*), *La Vie de l'Espace* (1928; *Life of Space*), *La Vie des fourmis* (1930; *The Life of Ants*), and *Le Grand Secret* (1921; *The Great Secret*. He also published numerous volumes of essays on mysticism, science, and psychometrics. It has been said, however, that his writings after 1914 have not enhanced his stature as a world literary figure. While they are not nearly as important as those of his symbolist period, they should not be dismissed as lightly as they usually are.

In 1939 Maeterlinck settled in Portugal, and in 1940, because of the war, moved to the United States, where he stayed for seven years. In 1947 he returned to his home in Nice, where he died two years later. In the last year of his life he wrote *L'Abbé Sétubal* ("Father Setubal"), *Les Trois Justiciers* ("The Three Justices"), and *Le Jugement dernier* ("The Last Judgement"), which were not published until 1959.

The plays Maeterlinck wrote prior to World War I established him indisputably as the prominent symbolist dramatist, just as *Serres Chaudes* had confirmed his position as a leading poet. His influence was considerable on French and world literature. His deep spiritual inclination; his probing of man's inner world of dreams, desires, and anguish; and his ability to use fairy tale structure and motives, rather than classical myths, to express the collective unconscious have had a major impact on the artistic imagination in the twentieth century. Maeterlinck's often mentioned eclipse from the critical limelight may not be an accurate indicator of his lasting contribution, especially in view of the fact that it corresponds to the falling from favor after World War I of the entire symbolist movement.

BIRUTA CAP

Selected Bibliography

PRIMARY SOURCES

Maeterlinck, Maurice. *Ariane et Barbe-Bleue*. Brussels: Paul Lacomblez, 1909.

——. *Le Grand Secret*. Paris: Fasquelle, 1919.

——. *Œuvres*. Brussels: Jacques Antoine, 1980. (*Serres Chaudes, Quinze Chansons, Les Aveugles et l'Intruse*).

——. *L'Oiseau Bleu*. Paris: Fasquelle, 1909.

——. *La Sagesse et la Destinée*. Paris: Charpentier, 1902.

——. *Les Sept Princesses*. Brussels: Paul Lacomblez, 1891.

——. *Théâtre complet*. Geneva: Slatkine, 1979. (Contains the symbolist plays from 1889 to 1901 except *Les Sept Princesses*.)

——. *La Vie des Abeilles*. Paris: Charpentier, 1902.

SECONDARY SOURCES

Doneux, Guy. *Maurice Maeterlinck, une poésie, une sagesse, un homme*. Brussels: Palais des Académies, 1961.

Halls, Wilfred [sometimes William] Douglas. *Maurice Maeterlinck. A Study of His Life and Thought*. Oxford, U. K.: Clarendon Press, 1960.

Hanak, Miroslav John. *Maeterlinck's Symbolic Drama*. Louvain: Peeters, 1974.

Postic, Marcel. *Maeterlinck et le Symbolisme*. Paris: Nizet, 1970.

NAJĪB MAḤFŪẒ *1988*

Najīb Maḥfūẓ (1911–) (also translit-
erated as Naguib Mahfouz), the
1988 Nobel laureate in literature, is
the first Arab author ever to win the
Nobel Prize. The award therefore
represents one of those intermittent
gestures whereby this Western institution recognizes the achievements
of a non-Western culture and invites
a worldwide readership to explore
the unfamiliar through the works of
its Laureate. In the case of Najīb
Maḥfūẓ, we are dealing with an
Egyptian novelist who over a period
of five decades had devoted himself
assiduously to the task of perfecting
and transforming the fictional craft
in Arabic in order to make of the
novel genre both a mirror of Egyptian—and, by extension, Arab—society and a catalyst for change.
Many of the Arab novelists who
have participated in the burst of fictional creativity during the last two
or three decades have acknowledged
the pioneer role that Maḥfūẓ has
played in the development of the
novel genre in Arabic. Building
upon earlier examples of historical
and romantic fiction and initial attempts at reflecting present realities
in novelistic form, Maḥfūẓ has
taken it upon himself to read examples from the various traditions of
world fiction, to master the various
aspects of the craft, to develop a
style that will serve as an accurate
and artistic vehicle for his creative
vision, and to reflect the problems
and aspirations of several generations of his fellow countrymen. With
him, the novel has indeed within the
Arab world context become, in Lio-
nel Trilling's words, "a most useful
agent of the moral imagination."

Maḥfūẓ was born in Cairo,
Egypt, on December 11, 1911. He
has lived in that city all his life, depicting its quarters and people in a
vast outpouring of fiction in both
novel and short-story form. The few
"plays" that he has published have
been essentially short stories cast in
a dialogue form. He has left his native city and country only on rare
occasions. Apart from the Egyptian
capital, his other home locale is the
Mediterranean resort city of Alexandria, the favorite of most Egyptians during the sweltering summer
months. Maḥfūẓ is married and has
two daughters, now in their
twenties. He lives in a relatively
modest apartment in ᶜAgūza, a suburb within the city limits of Cairo
situated on the west bank of the
Nile. He is an extremely organized
person, one who plans each of his
works carefully in advance and then
proceeds to compose them within a
rigid time schedule made necessary
in no small part by an eye condition
that makes him intolerant of bright
light and thus restricts his writing
time to certain periods of the day.
Thursday of each week finds him
heading for the building of *al-Ahrām*,
the Cairo daily newspaper, in order
to write the weekly column that he
has contributed for a number of

years. The same evening in the week he will often frequent the cafe that he currently favors, discussing current affairs and cultural issues with a circle of friends. One immediately becomes aware of his disarming humility and his gift of a copious wit, a national trait. This was illustrated when he was asked what he would do with the Nobel Prize money; without pausing for breath, he announced that he would, of course, be handing it over to his wife!

Maḥfūẓ's schooling was an Egyptian one, beginning in primary and secondary schools in the quarters where his family resided and thereafter at the University of Cairo, where his major focus was on philosophy. While still a student in the early 1930s, he began to write stories, and it was while commencing work on an M.A. program in philosophy that he decided to concentrate on writing fiction. As he began his long career in fiction, Maḥfūẓ acknowledged the inspiration of a number of twentieth-century pioneer Arab figures, including ᶜAbbās Maḥmūd al-ᶜAqqād, Tawfīq al-Ḥakīm, Yaḥyā Ḥaqqī, (b.1905) and Ibrāhīm al-Māzinī. He found particular encouragement from renowned Egyptian Fabian socialist Salāma Mūsā. Mūsā shared with the young Maḥfūẓ an interest in ancient Egypt and in the writings of such Westerners as Tolstoy, Shaw, and Ibsen, and he published several of Maḥfūẓ's earliest stories in his journal, *Al-Majalla al-jadīda*. The local nature of Maḥfūẓ's formal education and his distaste for travel should not lead to the assumption that the themes, techniques, or ap-

peal of his most famous works are in any way "local." In addition to the Western literary giants just mentioned, Maḥfūẓ has read widely in Western literature, and in particular the writings of Camus and Kafka, interest him. The consequences of his extensive readings are abundantly evident in the way in which his own fictional oeuvre has developed over the course of the past five decades.

Much of Maḥfūẓ's career was spent as a civil servant working as a staff member of the Ministry of Culture. Following the Egyptian revolution of the early 1950s, he devoted a great deal of his administrative and creative energy to the cinema, including the writing of original scenarios for films and the adaptation of the works of other authors. The award of the Egyptian State Prize for Literature in 1957 for his monumental three-part novel generally known as The Trilogy led to an increased interest in his published novels, not only in Egypt but throughout the Arab world. During the 1960s Maḥfūẓ, while retaining his position in the ministry, published a flood of distinguished works of fiction. Then came the June War of 1967 with Israel, which provided a traumatic disruption to the creative activities of litterateurs across the Arab world. In that Maḥfūẓ was no exception. But, whereas many Arab authors resorted to silence or blind anger, Maḥfūẓ's response was couched in a series of short stories in which he examined the issues of moral and political responsibility. In Egypt the death of President ᶜAbd al-Nāṣir in 1970 and the advent of the presidency of Anwar al-Sādāt led to a period of so-called liberalization, at least in the economic sphere, and a period of retrospect and recrimination. Mahfūz contributed to this process of reassessment in a number of works, and his lack of enthusiasm for the social mores that accompanied the process of economic "opening-up" of markets (called *infitāh* in Arabic) was abundantly evident in his writings. For a period he and a number of other prominent Egyptian writers and critics (including Tawfīq al-Hakīm and the great short-story writer, Yūsuf Idrīs) were banned from the official Writers' Union and thus officially unable to publish. Fortunately, the order was soon rescinded.

Since his retirement from government service in the early 1970s, Mahfūz has written his weekly column for the widely read newspaper *al-Ahrām* and also continued his career in fiction. The works of the latter 1970s and the 1980s have tended to reflect a wider political phenomenon, a period in which the heady aspirations of postrevolutionary pan-Arabism and Nasserism have been replaced by a focus on more local concerns. Egypt, with its crushing problems of population growth, agricultural and economic development, and bureaucratic stagnation, certainly has more than an adequate supply of such issues. Thus, while many other novelists throughout the Arab world have built upon the foundations that Mahfūz laid earlier in his career and have expanded the themes, structures, and style of the novel genre in

Arabic in radical ways, Mahfūz has continued to focus the lion's share of his attention on Egypt and its urban, bureaucratic middle class. In the wake of World War II that societal subset could provide a paradigm with which the entire Arab world's reading public could easily identify. Since that time, however, political, economic, and social developments have made it merely one in a whole host of possible venues and subjects for fictional treatment. Mahfūz thus remains the foundation builder, but the house now has many wings.

In surveying Mahfūz's colossal output in fictional form, it is possible to identify certain distinct phases in his development, although one should immediately sound the customary note of caution that such categories should not be allowed to impede a view of his works as a continuum. As noted above, Mahfūz showed an interest in the ancient history of his homeland early in his career, to the extent of translating into Arabic a work on the subject by James Baikie. We learn from interviews with the author that he had plans for a series of novels on the topic; indeed three were published between 1939 and 1944. However, the events of World War II and its impact on Egyptian society in particular were to provide Mahfūz with a more pressing contemporary agenda. During this period he began work on a group of novels set in the older quarters of Cairo, and in the process he provided modern Arabic fiction with its first fully developed examples of social-realist novels.

Zuqāq al-Midaqq (1947; *Midaq Alley*), an alley in one of the older quarters of Cairo, paints a brilliant portrait of a microcosm of the larger Egyptian society. Maḥfūẓ clearly relishes the opportunity to describe the scene in intimate detail and to provide his reader with a set of characters, some of whom could well be part of medieval Arabic prose narratives, such as Zayṭa who specializes in making beggars appear misshapen (the traditional craft called *mushaᶜᶜib* in Arabic). The relationships among this set of characters are masterfully handled, and no more so than in the ever-so-polite but utterly duplicitous encounters between the mother of Ḥamīda, the alley's beauty, and Mrs. ᶜAfīfī, the marriage arranger.

His descriptive ability and character portrayal are carried over and multiplied in abundance into Maḥfūẓ's enduring masterpiece, *Al-Thulāthiyya* (1956–57; The Trilogy, a group of three novels named after quarters of Cairo, *Bayn al-Qaṣrayn*, *Qaṣr al-Shawq*, and *Al-Sukkariyya*). In a work that took five years of research and writing and that was completed *before* the Egyptian revolution of 1952, Maḥfūẓ adopts as his temporal frame the interwar period in Egyptian history (1917–44), years of political and cultural ferment, and traces events on the larger scale through the careers, relationships and crises of the ᶜAbd al-Jawwād family. Citing the famous literary theoretician Georg Lukacs, "we might almost say that the entire inner action of the novel is nothing but a struggle against the power of time" (*The Theory of the Novel* [1971 trans.], 122); the remark certainly applies to Maḥfūẓ's portrait

of Egypt and one of its families. The struggle of the paterfamilias takes the form of an inexorable reduction of his traditional authority over the members of his household, beginning with his wife and culminating in a furious discussion with his son, Kamāl, over the relative roles of religion and science in modern life. In the third volume, *Al-Sukkariyya*, the increasing polarization of the society itself is tragically reflected in the activities of the younger generation. One grandson becomes a member of the Muslim Brethren, a fundamentalist religious group, while another joins the Communist party. It is an appropriate symbol of the social and political unrest of prerevolutionary Egypt that, as this huge work concludes, both are in prison.

In the heady days immediately preceding the establishment of the United Arab Republic (between Egypt and Syria) the publication of this huge novel caught the historical moment exactly. Readers throughout the Arab world were able to find their recent political and social malaise reflected in a work that was utterly realistic in both time and place and that, following the lead of the great European novelists, provided the revolution with a clear societal agenda by showing the miseries of immediate past history in considerable detail. Not only were Maḥfūẓ's previous works now studied with increasing scrutiny, but great things were anticipated. Maḥfūẓ's preoccupation with his position in the Ministry of Culture was at least partially responsible for the fact that his readership had to wait until 1959 before the appearance of his next and most notorious work, *Awlād Hāratinā* (1959, in newspaper article form, 1967, in book form; *Children of Gebelawi*). This highly allegorical work in five sections shows the fate of a "quarter" (which has now become far more of a symbol than in previous novels) at the hands of a group of "leaders." The names of these leaders are clearly evocative of key figures in the history of the great monotheistic religions; for example, the first, Adham, is not that far removed from Adam, and the second, Jabal ("mountain"), is a fairly obvious reference to Moses. The last leader is named ᶜArafa (from the verb meaning "knowledge" and therefore "scientia"). The ensuing events are such that the reader is left to assume that science has supplanted religion in the minds of the "people of the quarter." The work was immediately banned in Egypt and in several other Arab nations, but was later published in Lebanon. While *Awlād Hāratinā* is clearly a major milestone in Mahfūz's continuing search for vehicles through which to express his own intellectual concerns, it has to be admitted that it is only a limited success as a work of fiction, due in no small part to the inconsistency of the allegorical layering of the story.

After the initial successes of the Egyptian revolution under ᶜAbd al-Nāsir's leadership, the 1960s were to prove a period of painful adjustment to new realities and responsibilities; this was a period when many Egyptian writers were deprived of basic rights and suffered both intellectually and personally. Mahfūz catches the mood of this period in a series of novels and short stories that sound an increasingly obvious note of disillusion. The first to be published was *Al-Liṣṣ wa-al-Kilāb* (1961; *The Thief and the Dogs*), in which a released prisoner, Saᶜīd Mahrān, seeks revenge on his wife and her lover for framing him but kills innocent bystanders instead. Spurned in his attempts to get help from his former supporters, he finds temporary shelter with the prostitute Nūr; he is eventually cornered in a cemetery. Here already the theme of "fair-weather socialism" and opportunism are raised. It is seen from the opposition side in *Al-Summān wa-al-Kharīf* (1962; *Autumn Quail*), here the downfall of a senior governmental official from the prerevolutionary period is explored. The same theme is painted with sneering relish by many characters from the thoroughly alienated cultural sector in *Tharthara fawq al-Nīl* (1966: "Chatter on the Nile").

Mīrāmār (1967; *Miramar*) may well be the best-known work of this set, in no small part because its criticism of the Egyptian socialist establishment is scarcely concealed. Making skillful use of the multinarrator technique, Mahfūz takes his readers into the microcosm of an Alexandria pension where a group of disparate characters from different classes and generations of Egyptian society gather, talk, squabble, and fight; the frequent focus of these interactions is a lovely peasant girl, Zahra, whose trustful simplicity and determination to succeed make her an obvious symbol of Egypt itself. The main event of the novel is the suicide of Sirhān al-Buḥayrī, a senior figure in the Arab Socialist Union, whose plans to rob a truck loaded with fabric end in failure. Such is Mahfūẓ's view of the course of his country's revolution immediately before the event that was to transform the Middle East in radical ways, the June War of 1967.

In the series of short stories that Mahfūẓ wrote in reaction to this conflict, the use of symbolism often seems to reach the level of cryptography. During this period of anger, recrimination, and intense self-examination, Mahfūẓ invited and even challenged his readers to penetrate the often cyclical symbolic maze of his stories and to establish thereby the nature of his concerns. One of them was clearly the need to establish a sense of individual and corporate responsibility, as can be deduced from such stories as *"Tahta al-mazalla"* (title story of *Tahta al-Mazalla*, 1967; "Under the Bus Shelter") and *"Nawm* (1967; "Sleep"). With the presidency of Anwar al-Sādāt, a reexamination of the immediate past became a national passion, and Mahfūẓ's contribution to the process was an unusual work, *Al-Marāyā* (1972; *Mirrors*), a series of alphabetized vignettes in which a narrator (whose life runs exactly parallel to that of the author) provides a series of interlinked portraits of Egyptians and thereby a telling commentary on the course of Egyptian history in the first half of this century.

The primary topic of Mahfūẓ's output in novel form has thus been an apt reflection of the earlier development of the Western fictional tra-

dition, in that the author has chosen to focus on the life and problems of Egypt's urban middle class and in particular the segment of that social grouping with which he is himself intimately acquainted, intellectuals and civil servants. Whereas other modern Arab novelists have been motivated by political and literary concerns to venture outside the environs of the modern metropolis in order to portray the harsh realities of the life among the rural peasantry, Mahfūẓ has consistently set his works in the city and among the class he knows best. In using his novels to portray this class and to reflect the values of his generation, he has honed a writing style of great symbolic power and nuance. During the course of his long career he has clearly taken great pains to develop a prose style that, in its clarity and directness, can both describe and suggest. An important stylistic issue of debate regarding the development of the Arabic novel has revolved around the question of the language of dialogue. While other writers have sought to lend an element of authenticity by introducing conversation in the colloquial dialect of their region, Mahfūẓ has preferred to remain with the syntactic structures of the standard Arabic language, occasionally peppering his character's comments with individual words and phrases that evoke colloquial discourse. This rich stylistic medium has served as a vehicle not only for the wide variety of atmospheres and scenarios to be found in his works, but also for the often sardonic witticisms that his Egyptian characters, reflecting a well-known national trait, hurl at each other. The fictional world into which the reader is thus drawn is created in a style that describes and characterizes with great subtlety.

Najīb Mahfūz continues to write fiction, and as such he remains a participant in a cultural enterprise that, in its geographical scope and generic variety, owes much to his pioneering role. Only temporal perspective will allow for a critical judgment of his total oeuvre. Meanwhile, the award of the Nobel Prize acknowledges the debt that modern Arabic fiction owes him, one that, thanks to the award, should now be shared with a much wider readership.

ROGER ALLEN

Selected Bibliography

PRIMARY SOURCES

Mahfūz, Najīb. Awlād Hāratinā. Published in the Cairo newspaper al-Ahram, 1959; in book form, Beirut: Dar al-Adab, 1967. Translated by Philip Stewart as Children of Gebelawi. London: Heinemann, 1981; Washington, D.C.: Three Continents Press, 1981.

———. Bayn al-qasrayn. Cairo: Maktabat Misr, 1956.

———. al-Liss wa-al-kilāb. Cairo: Maktabat Misr, 1961. Translated by Trevor Le Gassick and Mustafa Badawi as The Thief and the Dogs. Cairo: American University in Cairo Press, 1984.

———. al-Marāyā. Cairo: Maktabat Misr, 1972. Translated by Roger Allen as Mirrors. Minneapolis: Bibliotheca Islamica, 1977.

———. Mīrāmār. Cairo: Maktabat Misr, 1967. Translated by Fatma Moussa-Mahmoud as Miramar. London: Heinemann, 1978.

———. Qasr al-shawq. Cairo: Maktabat Misr, 1957.

———. al-Sukkariyya. Cairo: Maktabat Misr, 1957.

———. al-Summān wa-al-Kharīf. Cairo: Maktabat Misr, 1962. Translated by Roger Allen as Autumn Quail. Cairo: American University in Cairo Press, 1985.

———. Tharthara fawq al-Nīl. Cairo: Maktabat Misr, 1966.

———. Zuqaq al-Midaqq. Cairo: Maktabat Misr, 1947. Translated by Trevor Le Gassick as Midaq Alley. Beirut: Khayat, 1966; reprinted in London: Heinemann, 1974, and Washington, D.C.: Three Continents Press, 1974.

SECONDARY SOURCES

Allen, Roger. The Arabic Novel: An Historical and Critical Introduction. Syracuse: Syracuse University Press, 1982.

———. Modern Arabic Literature. Library of Literary Criticism Series. New York: Ungar, 1987.

Moussa-Mahmoud, Fatma. The Arabic Novel in Egypt (1914–1970). Cairo: General Egyptian Book Organisation, 1973.

Peled, Mattityahu. Religion My Own: The Literary Works of Najib Mahfuz. New Brunswick, N.J., and London: Transaction Books, 1984.

THOMAS MANN *1929*

Thomas Mann (1875–1955) is one of the greatest and most widely read authors of the twentieth century. He sometimes is given the credit for bringing the German novel back to a leading position in world literature. Intellectually deep and stylistically formidable, Mann's novels, short prose, and essays present difficulties to the reader. In addition, the works often contain little plot in the ordinary sense. Despite the complexity of his fiction, Mann gained wide popularity and an appreciative audience in both Europe and in the United States. During the sixty years of his literary career Mann received numerous literary honors, including the Nobel Prize in literature (1929) and the Goethe Prize (1949).

Mann is primarily known for his voluminous novels, in which he shows little regard for an impatient reader's expectation of shallow entertainment. These books can be fully appreciated only by a patient and contemplative reader who is willing to recognize the well-balanced interplay between pessimistic metaphysical ideas and epically serene descriptions. The reader has to take time to follow the careful and thorough presentation of the conflict of opposing values. In superficial reading one may miss the intellectual irony that is so distinctively Mann's style.

An innovative stylist and synthesizer of the intellectual trends of his time, Mann exerted much influence on modern fiction not only in Germany but in Europe and in both Americas as well. His perceptiveness as an interpreter of Western cultural heritage and his skill as a cosmopolitan teacher of democratic and humanistic values earned him recognition as a "mirror of his age" and a "citizen of the world."

The second of five children, Mann was born in the Hanseatic city of Lübeck in 1875. His father, the city senator Thomas J. M. Mann, was a wealthy and respected wholesale grain merchant. His mother, Julia da Silva Bruhns, was born in Brazil, the daughter of a German father with family ties in Lübeck and a Portuguese-Creole Brazilian mother. Mann's older brother, Heinrich, later also a well-known writer, was born in 1871; his sisters, Julia and Carla, in 1877 and 1881; and his younger brother, Viktor, in 1890.

In 1891 Mann's father died at the age of fifty-one, and the family business was dissolved. The family moved shortly afterward, in 1893, to Munich. There, Mann worked at first for an insurance company and then, in 1894, as a staff member of the satirical journal *Simplicissimus*. At the same time he took courses, mostly in literature, history, and economics, at the University of Munich, and he began to write short stories. In 1898 he published his first book, the novella *Der Kleine Herr Friedemann* ("Little Mr. Friedemann") in S. Fischer Verlag (S. Fischer Publishing House), which has subsequently published all of his works.

As a free-lance writer, Mann traveled in 1893 with Heinrich to Rome and spent the next two years in Italy, mostly in Rome and Palestrina. There he started writing his first novel, *Buddenbrooks*, which was published in 1901 (English translation, 1924) and which made him famous. Later he received the Nobel Prize, primarily for this novel. Back in Munich Mann served in 1898 and 1899 as the editor of *Simplicissimus* before he was inducted into the imperial army in 1900. In 1905 he married Katharine ("Katja") Pringsheim, the daughter of a well-known Munich mathematics professor. The couple lived in Oberammergau, Bad Tölz, Davos (Switzerland), and from 1914 to 1933 again in Munich. The Manns had six children; three sons—Klaus (1906), Golo (1910), Michael (1919) —and three daughters—Erika (1905), Monika (1910), and Elisabeth (1918). The oldest son, Klaus, who committed suicide in 1949, followed the example of his father and also became a writer.

As far back as the early 1890s. Mann had started to read Nietzsche; before the turn of the century he discovered Schopenhauer. He later said they provide the "critical-metaphysical" content for his novels, especially for *Buddenbrooks*. Mann gives Leo Tolstoy, the great Russian novelist, credit for influencing the structure of his work which he calls "the great composition." Young Mann not only loved to pattern his writing technique after Tolstoy— e.g., the leitmotif method with atten-

tion to detail—but he also strove to achieve Tolstoy's ability to present his personal artistic self in the literary work. Tolstoy's portrait, which stood on Mann's writing table, always reminded him of his ambition.

Richard Wagner's music, known to Mann since his school days, also became a major force in the author's literary compositions. The theme of the emerging relationship between the bourgeois life of the nineteenth century and the precarious modern sensibility of the artistic temperament, already masterfully presented in *Buddenbrooks*, continued to be the central issue in Mann's early works. This is shown in the verse drama *Fiorenza* (1906; *Florence*), and the stories "Tonio Kröger" (1903) and "Der Tod in Venedig" (1912, "Death in Venice").

Mann's happy married life is reflected in the rather lightweight novel *Königliche Hoheit* (1909; *Royal Highness*), a comedy with a happy ending in the form of a novel. In 1911 Mrs. Mann had to be hospitalized at a sanatorium in Davos, Switzerland, for pulmonary trouble. The author's visits gave him new impressions, which he used later in *Der Zauberberg* (1924; *The Magic Mountain*).

After the onset of World War I Mann gradually became more preoccupied with contemporary social and political issues. His ultraconservative and nationalistic views, which can be read in the *Betrachtungen eines Unpolitiscken* (1918; *Meditations of a Non-Political Man*), led him to a painful break with his brother Heinrich, who held more international and pacifist values. After the war Mann moved steadily away from his defensive, nationalistic position, and in "Die Forderung des Tages" (1930; "The Challenge of the Day") and other essays he expressed faith in democracy and the Weimar Republic. He also took a firm stand against fascism, as seen in the story *Mario und der Zauberer* (1930; *Mario and the Magician*). With the advent of the Third Reich in 1933, Mann chose, during a lecture trip abroad, not to return to Germany and settled in Switzerland. In Germany his property was confiscated and his books were condemned.

Mann stayed away from Germany for sixteen years. In 1936 the Nazis revoked his German citizenship and Mann took Czech citizenship. He edited the literary journal *Mass und Wert* (*Measure and Value*) in Switzerland, where he and his family remained until 1938. All through the 1930s Mann worked on his crowning achievement, the tetralogy *Joseph und seine Brüder* (*Joseph and His Brothers: Die Geschichten Jaakobs* [1933; *The Tales of Jacob*]; *Der junge Joseph* [1934; *The Young Joseph*]; *Joseph in Ägypten* [1936; *Joseph in Egypt*]; *Joseph, der Ernährer* [1943; *Joseph, the Provider*]). This tetralogy shows the influence on Mann of Freud's theories about the manifestations of the subconscious.

In 1938 Mann emigrated to the United States, where he became a visiting lecturer in humanities at Princeton University. Later he moved to California and settled from 1942 to 1952 in Pacific Palisades. Three years after becoming a United States citizen in 1944, Mann published the symbolic and social novel *Doktor Faustus, Das Leben des deutschen Tonsetzers Adrian Leverkühn, erzählt von einem Freunde* (1947; *Doctor Faustus, The Life of the German Composer Adrian Leverkühn, as Told by a Friend*), a modern treatment of the Faust theme that combines the life of Friedrich Nietzsche with the evils of Nazism and war against the background of the innovative twelve-tone music system of the Viennese composer Arnold Schönberg.

In 1947, for the first time after the war, Mann traveled to Europe, and in 1949, on the occasion of the bicentennial of Johann Wolfgang von Goethe's birth, he visited both East and West Germany. He refused to settle in Germany again and, distressed by the oncoming McCarthy era in the United States, moved to neutral Switzerland. There he lived in the small town of Kilchberg near Zürich until his death in 1955. One of his last works was a story, "Die Betrogene" (1953) translated into English as "The Black Swan," which reflects Mann's critical assessment of the American character. In the last three years of his life Mann visited Germany regularly, and shortly before his death he became an honorary citizen of his native city, Lübeck.

Buddenbrooks (1901), the first of Mann's major novels, is based partially on the history of his own patrician family of grain merchants in the Hanseatic city of Lübeck. It deals with the decline of a once proud, influential, and energetic merchant family through four generations. The prosperity and vitality of the family is threatened and gradually undermined by a fascination with arts and learning. The fall is prompted not by any outside circumstances but by psychological forces. In each successive generation, with the growth of an antibourgeois spirit, the decadance of aestheticism increases. The self-confidence and the will to live weaken. Ultimately, the last representative of the family line, a delicate and sensitive "artist," dies of typhus. The family business is liquidated and the Buddenbrooks name becomes extinct.

The central theme of this powerful social novel is the conflict between the nineteenth-century bourgeois life and the precarious modern sensibility of the artistic temperament, a theme that can also be found in several of Mann's other works, such as *Florence*, "Tonio Kröger," "Death in Venice," *The Magic Mountain*, and *Doctor Faustus*. The conflicting claims of the bourgeois and the artist's worlds fascinated Mann and can be seen as an expression of the author's own personal problem. Mann himself was an artist, but in the world of the Buddenbrooks there was no place for the artist.

In *Buddenbrooks* Mann demonstrates the highest perfection of the milieu technique, which was introduced by the French naturalists. The minute descriptions of life and customs in Lübeck, the small autonomous city-state on the Baltic Sea, are presented with great care. The large number of major and minor characters found in the novel are part of the traditional objective nineteenth-century social novel. *Buddenbrooks*, however, is much more complex than the traditional naturalistic novel. Mann analyzes his characters with sensitivity and understanding instead of employing the simplistic theories of hereditary determinism. He does not present unpleasant details merely for their shock value, but describes illness and death in a dry, clinical, and detached manner. The complexity of symbols and interlinking motifs elevates *Buddenbrooks* above the ordinary naturalistic prose. When Mann received the Nobel Prize in literature in 1929, it was primarily for *Buddenbrooks*, which was at that time the best known and most popular of his works.

The other monumental novel that contributed to Mann's fame and eventual selection for the Nobel Prize was the symbolic novel *The Magic Mountain*. Mann began this characteristically German bildungsroman in 1912 during a three-week visit to his sick wife at a sanatorium in Davos, Switzerland. Twelve years later, with World War I intervening, the long novel was published. Against the background of the Swiss Alps, symbolizing the world of pure aestheticism, the physical and mental ills of modern society are thoroughly scrutinized. On the eve of World War I, Hans Castorp, the initially healthy, ordinary but impressionable hero of the novel, visits his cousin at a tuberculosis sanatorium. He remains there for several weeks, and in the hothouse atmosphere of luxurious living and lovemaking he is drawn into many baffling relationships. He is surrounded by exponents of every conceivable human attitude, such as Settembrini, who represents humanism and liberalism, Peeperkorn, who embodies strong vitality and animal sensuality, and Naphta, a Jewish convert to Catholicism, who is a fanatical believer in violence and despotism.

Typical of Mann's antithetical structure, there are two poles between which Castorp finds himself. On one hand, there is the ordinary, respectable life of Castorp's prosperous middle-class family in Hamburg, where he was trained as a maritime engineer. On the other hand, by falling in love with the bohemian Russian Claudia, who has faintly oriental features, Castorp is introduced to the more instinctive world of the East. He also has to choose between the views of his two self-appointed teachers, the humanist Settembrini and the right-wing extremist Naphta. Hans Castorp finally finds enough strength to escape the extremes of the Western spiritual heritage by balancing the aesthetic and the practical sides of human nature. He leaves the upper-middle-class world of the refined idlers and presumably will perish in the tragic World War.

The Magic Mountain is a novel of ideas; it is also a social and political novel. The sanatorium is an intellectual microcosm, and the sickness is symbolic of the sickness of Europe. By the end of his stay Castorp has been exposed to every aspect of European culture and has become a synthesis of opposing forces. In the tradition of the German apprenticeship novel, *The Magic Mountain* is also a psycho-

logical novel tracing the formation of a young man's character. The mood of the novel is generally ironic. The study of sanatorium life can also be viewed as entertaining and the analysis of tuberculosis as naturalistic.

Mann was very surprised that *The Magic Mountain*, despite its length and complexity, became an instant best-seller. Eventually it became Mann's most famous and, according to many critics, his best novel. The depth of its intelligence, the precision of its descriptions, and the breadth of its arguments make it one of the finest contributions to novelistic literature.

The tetralogy *Joseph and His Brothers* (1933–43), which is based on the second half of the book of Genesis, is Mann's most ambitious literary undertaking. Mann published essays on Freud, and he was interested in the theories of recurring myths in world history. He also knew Jung's definitions of the archetype. These particular theories gave him the inspiration to write the story of Joseph as an archetypical situation. Young Joseph sees the biblical world more and more perceptively as he is learning and he matures. As a story of education, *Joseph and His Brothers* is also an apprenticeship novel. The mood of the novel is serious but never tragic. Even in death Joseph emerges as a conqueror; the efforts of human undertaking are affirmed.

Among Mann's many well-written works of short fiction, "Death in Venice" (1912), a novella based on Mann's impressions during his stay in Venice, is the most famous. It was made into a successful film. Typically for Mann, the novella deals with the problem of the unhappy, sick artist, Gustav von Aschenbach, who envies the healthy and "normal" people of the bourgeois society. The conflict is further complicated by the theme of homosexuality.

Reading Mann's works, even his early ones, is difficult. His style is highly artistic, cool, analytical, and sometimes ironic, but the plot tends to be amorphous, with little action in the traditional sense. Most of his work is taken up by involved discussions of aesthetic, philosophical, social, and theological issues. Several motifs recur throughout Mann's work and can be traced back to Nietzsche's concepts of existence, Schopenhauer's pessimism, and Wagner's music. The major theme, the conflict between life and spirit, is usually presented in the context of illness and decadence. Mann's cultured, cosmopolitan, overly refined, sensitive, but also decadent heroes lack the stamina for survival in the modern world. They suffer from some kind of disease, and in their hearts they carry a romantic yearning for death. The artists find themselves hopelessly isolated in the bourgeois society.

Mann's works are sometimes described as "styled symphonies in words." Indeed, his style contains similarities with a musical composition: the recurrent leitmotifs, lyrico-philosophic intermezzi, and contrapuntal devices. The antithesis, also part of a musical composition, is used by Mann in various forms. Concepts are often personified by antithetical characters. In *The Magic Mountain*, for example, Settembrini personifies the rational, Naphta the demonic. In *Doctor Faustus* Zeitboom personifies the bourgeois world while Leverkühn is demonic.

Mann's strength lies in sketching the sick, demonic, and artistic geniuses. These eccentric artists are divinely touched, and they achieve the highest and most ecstatic pleasures of creativity. Yet they cannot partake in the simple bourgeois happiness; they are denied the comfort of a home, the love of a woman, and the tranquility of a happy, everyday life. The bohemian artist is painfully aware of his separation from the rest of mankind.

For Mann, illness is somehow mystically associated with creativity. The sick artists are often musicians, and music is connected with illness. So, for example, Leverkühn in *Doctor Faustus* reaches his highest musical expression only after he has contracted syphilis. The setting of *The Magic Mountain* is a fashionable Swiss sanatorium, and in this milieu Mann investigates the various physical and mental ills of the society and the role of aesthetics in the modern world.

Mann is successful in creating strange and frightening atmospheres, as in "Death in Venice." He is also interested in Jungian "archetypes" and in universal and timeless myths. "Tonio Kröger" is a good example of Mann's masterful depiction of a despairing young man. Satirical portraits can be found in most of his novels and stories, and although not typical of Mann's writing, *Bekenntnisse des Hochstaplers Felix Krull* (1922, 1936, 1954;

Confessions of Felix Krull, Confidence Man) is a good example of the ironic picaresque novel. Mann's numerous essays on literary, philosophical, political, historical, and cultural topics show the same creative insight and originality as his fiction. The only negative criticism of Mann's work is that his fiction at times tends to be too pedantic, verbose, and superfluous.

RADO PRIBIC

Selected Bibliography

PRIMARY SOURCES

Mann, Thomas. *Death in Venice and Seven Other Stories.* New York: Vintage Books, 1963.

———. *Gesammelte Werke.* Frankfurt am Main: S. Fischer, 1960.

———. *Joseph and His Brothers.* New York: Knopf, 1934.

———. *The Magic Mountain.* New York: Knopf, 1958.

SECONDARY SOURCES

Altenberg, P. *Die Romane Thomas Manns. Versuch einer Deutung.* Bad Homburg: Gentner, 1961.

Brennan, Joseph G. *Thomas Mann's World.* New York: Russel & Russel, 1962.

Eichner, Hans. *Thomas Mann. Eine Einführung in sein Werk.* Bern: Franke, 1961.

Feuerlicht, Ignace. *Thomas Mann.* New York: Twayne, 1968.

Hatfield, Henry. *Thomas Mann. A Collection of Critical Essays.* Englewood Cliffs, N. J.: Prentice-Hall, 1964.

Hollingsdale, R. *Thomas Mann. A Critical Study.* Lewisburg, PA.: Bucknell University Press, 1971.

Kahler, Erich. *The Orbit of Thomas Mann.* Princeton, N. J.: Princeton University Press, 1969.

ROGER MARTIN DU GARD   *1937*

Roger Martin du Gard (1881–1958) was born in Neuilly-sur-Seine, near Paris, on March 23, 1881, into an upper-middle-class family. After completion of rather average secondary studies, he earned a degree in paleography and history at the Ecole des Chartes at the Sorbonne. Thanks to his personal wealth and that of his wife, he was able to dedicate his entire life to writing. In 1908 he abandoned his first work, *Une vie de saint* ("A Saint's Life"), after having written two volumes of it, and he wrote and published his first novel, *Devenir* ("Becoming"), which he soon considered to have been a mere exercise. In 1913 he published his first major work, *Jean Barois*, a novel consisting of dialogues and documents on a man's evolution from traditional faith to a faith in science within the historical context of the turn of the century. The work is dominated by the Dreyfus Affair, which Martin du Gard strives to describe accurately. The hero, who has become a liberal positivist and a socialist, is dedicated to Dreyfus's cause. In the end, however, he becomes dissatisfied with the reasons for his rejection of religion and is drawn back to the religious fold. Despite this ironic ending inspired by Martin du Gard's desire to be equitable, the work is a strong attack on Catholicism and the anti-Dreyfus forces. For these reasons and owing to its artistic merits, *Jean Barois* was welcomed by the *La Nouvelle Revue Française*—the influential journal founded in 1909 by André Gide and others—and its circle. Martin du Gard became a close friend of Gide's group.

Immediately after *Jean Barois*, Martin du Gard wrote an excellent farce, *Le Testament du Père Leleu* (1920; "Daddy Leleu's Will"), which Jacques Copeau performed in 1914 in the Vieux-Colombier, an avant-garde theater he had founded in 1913. Martin du Gard became fascinated by the theater, and, even during World War I, which he spent in the transportation corps, he longed for a resumption of his collaboration with Copeau. In 1920, however, he left the Vieux-Colombier in order to dedicate himself to a novel he had just begun, *Les Thibault* (1922–40; *The Thibaults*). This masterpiece was to occupy him for the better part of two decades. After his parents' death he moved to Le Tertre,

an estate he acquired in Normandy, where he spent most of his time until World War II.

From the beginning Martin du Gard envisioned *Les Thibault* as a roman-fleuve, a vast multivolume novel recounting the lives of two brothers who, though superficially dissimilar, are "deeply marked by hidden similarities which a powerful common heredity creates between two beings of the same blood." The story is set against an extremely well-informed historical background. The two principal characters live in a society torn by powerful conflicting forces and headed toward a catastrophic war. The author's keen interest in various ideologies and his preoccupation with the challenging problems of his time are woven into the fabric of the novel.

The work is divided into eight parts of uneven length, covering periods of varying duration starting ten years prior to the outbreak of World War I. The author focuses on certain events and scenes within rather brief periods of time, separated by long intervals connected by narrative. The numerous characters are inclined to self-study and are strongly individualized, yet they are realistic representatives of society.

The first volume of *Les Thibault, Le Cahier gris* (1922; *The Gray Notebook*), presents the diary of the younger of the Thibault brothers, Jacques. It narrates a short crisis lasting a week, caused by Jacques and his friend Daniel de Fontanin. The two adolescents had run away from home. Whereas Daniel is welcomed back by his understanding and loving Protestant mother, Jacques's bigoted, Catholic, self-righteous, and authoritarian father sends him to reform school. This punishment pushes him deeper into rebellion against the oppression of his family and society in general.

The second volume, *Le Pénitencier* (1922; *The Penitentiary* or *The Reformatory*), describes the harsh treatment Jacques receives in reform school. Thanks to the intercession of the Abbé Vécard, a priest who is a friend of the family, Antoine, Jacques's older brother, a practicing physician, obtains his sibling's release into his custody. As their life together is described, the two brothers are contrasted. Antoine is mature, practical, and leads a purposeful life, whereas Jacques remains moody, idealistic, and uncertain about his future. Antoine's reasonable and humane attitude, which derives from his faith in science, contrasts with his father's harshness and blind acceptance of religious dogma.

La Belle Saison (1923; *The Springtime of Life* or *High Summer*) is the longest volume prior to the epic-length *L'Eté 1914* (1936; *Summer 1914*). It focuses on two families, the Thibaults and the Fontanins. The three youngest men, Antoine and Jacques Thibault and Daniel Fontanin, have the leading roles. In their "beautiful season"— their youth—which holds great possibilities restricted only by their heredity and conditioning, the young men broaden their exploration of society. Daniel's artistic talent is limited only by his strong inclination to philander like his father. Jacques is admitted to the presti-

gious Ecole Normale Supérieure, but he neglects to pursue a brilliant academic career because he becomes interested in socialism, as his father had been in philanthropy. He is attracted to Daniel's sister, Jenny, who rejects him. Antoine emerges as a liberated positivist who greatly enjoys the practice of his profession. Influenced by the literature of the times, which advocated rejection of bourgeois values, and by the example of their fathers, none of these young men will found families.

Antoine, the medical doctor, is at the center of *La Consultation* (1928; *The Consulting Day*), in which Martin du Gard focuses on the activities of the physician on a typical day. As he ministers to his father in the final phase of a terminal illness, Antoine faces the question of whether to hasten death or to wait for it to come in the midst of useless suffering. Disregarding the dictates of religion and even of medical ethics but in conformity with his philosophy and professional views, he is prepared to resort to euthanasia. Throughout this crisis, one of his major concerns is Jacques's disappearance. As he observes the world about him, he catches glimpses of the harsh economic conditions faced by the working class, and he becomes aware of the intensifying international tension about to culminate in World War I.

The next volume, *La Sorellina* (1928; "The Little Sister") relates the events of the week following *La Consultation*. Quite by chance, Antoine discovers a short story, "La Sorellina," written by Jacques, and learns that his brother has not committed suicide as he had been led to believe. He learns that Jacques is in Lausanne and brings him back to their father's deathbed.

Upon their return, the two brothers discover that their father's condition has worsened. This is the beginning of *La Mort du père* (1929; "Death of the Father"). Reflecting the increased precision of language in our scientific age, Martin du Gard gives a technical description of Thibault's illness and treatment. The fear of death becomes the focal point of the father's thoughts and the preservation of his life his overriding concern. He does not accept death and rejects the consolation of religion. Rather than letting their father suffer "like an animal," his sons agree to resort to euthanasia. As Antoine reads his father's personal papers, he discovers—too late—that he could have understood and loved him. On the other hand, Jacques continues to hate his father and, in general, his sentiments remain violent and nihilistic.

As they travel back to Paris after the funeral, Antoine and Abbé Vécard engage in a discussion on faith. Strong arguments are advanced on each side. In the end, however, Antoine, reflecting the author's view, simply admits that he may lack a religious sense as some lack a musical sense. After three decades of reflection on the subject, Martin du Gard seems to have concluded that religious belief was more a matter of temperament than one of reason.

While working on the next volume of *Les Thibault, L'Appareillage* ("Casting Off"), Martin du Gard had a severe automobile accident. During his recovery he decided to scale down his roman-fleuve by ending it with a masterful last part on World War I. The first casualty of his new plan was *L'Appareillage*, which he not only abandoned but subsequently destroyed. Before undertaking *L'Eté 1914* he published "Confidence africaine" (1931; "African Confession"), a short story on the theme of incest, and wrote *Un Taciturne* (1932, revised edition 1948; "A Taciturn Fellow"), a play on the subject of homosexuality, and *Vieille France* (1933; *The Postman*), a volume of sketches of country life loosely connected by the activities of a character. Between 1932 and 1937 he published three volumes of *L'Eté 1914*. His huge novel, on the scale of Tolstoy, his model, was complete but for the *Epilogue*, which he finished in 1939. In the meantime, he received the Nobel Prize in literature in 1937 in recognition especially for *L'Eté 1914*. Thereupon, he took a cruise with his wife in the Caribbean, at the end of which he spent three weeks in the United States.

L'Eté 1914 deals in detail with events that took place between June 28, 1914, the date of the assassination of Austrian Archduke Ferdinand in Sarajevo and August 1914, when the actual fighting began. For all the major characters, the outbreak of World War I is a climactic event, as indeed it was for all Europeans. Although Martin du Gard wrote at least a decade after the war, the perspective of his characters is historically credible.

At the beginning of *L'Eté 1914*,

the reader resumes contact with Jacques, who lives in Geneva in a cosmopolitan socialist milieu. He and his fellow revolutionaries are developing various plans to bring about the advent of socialism. In June 1914 Jacques is sent on a mission to Paris where he sees Antoine. He finds his brother rather out of touch and unconcerned with the alarming political situation threatening Europe. Furthermore, out of temperament and habit Antoine opposes socialist ideals. While in Paris, Jacques also sees Jenny, whom he had left abruptly four years earlier. At first resentful toward him, Jenny soon comes to share his idealism and his commitment to socialism.

As the political situation worsens, Jacques's clandestine liaison missions with socialist leaders in several European capitals reveal the lack of a unified view among socialists. Antoine's faith in reason and science is as futile in the face of the war movement as Jacques's hope to bring about an agreement between French and German socialists to organize a general stike to prevent the war. Martin du Gard succeeds in re-creating the tension and the confusion of the days preceding the declaration of war.

On the day Germany declared war on Russia, Jacques tells Antoine of his love for Jenny. During that night Jacques and Jenny consummate their love, although not very happily. Jenny's mother prevents her from accompanying Jacques, who returns to Geneva determined to do all he can to stop the war. In a last and desperate attempt

to persuade French and German soldiers at the front not to fight, Jacques and a fellow revolutionary try to drop a million leaflets from an airplane. However, their plane crashes, the leaflets are burned, the two revolutionaries are killed, and the war continues. In spite of his useless death, Jacques appears heroically to embody an ideal of justice and a vision of a better world.

Les Thibault could have ended with Jacques's death, as it begins with his misadventure. However, there is an additional volume, *Epilogue* (1940; *Epilogue*). Almost four years have elapsed. Antoine is being treated for toxic gas inhalation in a hospital in southern France. During a brief stay in Paris, he visits the Fontanin family. He sees Jenny and Gise, both of whom are caring for Jean-Paul, Jenny's child by Jacques, and the only hope for survival for the two families. Daniel, completely transformed by a castrating wound, has lost all interest in life and contemplates suicide. And Antoine, upon visiting his doctor, realizes that he will not recover.

Epilogue ends with letters and the diary kept by Antoine during the last four months of his life. Through it we learn of his anguish and solitude. In his despair, he imagines Jean-Paul's future in a world of peace. He offers to marry Jenny in order to give her son his name, but she, being a true revolutionary, refuses. In the end, Antoine rejects the consolation of religion and hastens his own death. In spite of his cruel faith, he dies believing in human progress. The novel ends with the words "Jean-Paul"—the last words written by Antoine before his death.

A number of critics have claimed that Martin du Gard did not possess the talent of other authors of vast novels, such as Romain Rolland and Jules Romains. Yet readers continue to find his characters compelling and their world interesting. Martin du Gard's themes have sharpened our sensitivity and raised crucial questions. His novels are regarded as uniquely authentic socio-historical documents concerning the first two decades of our century. Some fifty years after its publication, the language of Les Thibault remains astonishingly fresh.

In 1940 Martin du Gard undertook another vast novel, Le Lieutenant-colonel de Maumort (1983; "The Lieutenant Colonel de Maumort"), which he left unfinished at his death in 1958. Colonel de Maumort is an old military man living alone in a wing of his house, which has been occupied by the Germans during World War II. Martin du Gard wanted to evoke the entire life of a man who had lived through the Dreyfus case, the war in Morocco, World War I, and the turbulent twenties and thirties. His hero simultaneously observes and experiences the daily reality of life under the German Occupation, which inspires the colonel to reflect on the vagaries of French and European history. Martin du Gard succeeded in completing only the first chapters of Le Lieutenant-colonel de Maumort, which was published posthumously in 1983. The remainder of this large volume, which Martin

du Gard did not consider entirely finished, contains numerous extensive passages of considerable stylistic and documentary value.

Martin du Gard's personal Memoirs and much of his correspondence have been published. The latter has received especially high acclaim.

In spite of reservations expressed by some critics, Les Thibault has enjoyed enduring success worldwide, and its author's position in twentieth-century French literature seems assured.

JEAN-PIERRE CAP

Selected Bibliography

PRIMARY SOURCES

Martin du Gard, Roger. Le Lieutenant-colonel de Maumort. Edited by André Daspre. Paris: Gallimard, 1983.

———. Oeuvres complètes. 2 vols. Paris: Gallimard, 1955.

———. Summer 1914, Enlarged edition. Translated by Stuart Gilbert. New York: Viking, 1941. (Includes L'Eté 1914 and Epilogue).

———. The Thibaults. 2 vols. Vol. 1 translated by Stephen H. Guest; vol. 2 translated by Stuart Gilbert. London: Lane, 1933, 1934. (Includes Le Cahier gris, Le Pénitencier, La Belle Saison, La Consultation, La Sorellina, and La Mort du père).

SECONDARY SOURCES

Daspre, André, and Jochen Schlobach, eds. Roger Martin du Gard. Études *sur son oeuvre*. Paris: Klincksieck, 1984.

Savage, Catharine. *Roger Martin du Gard*. New York: Twayne, 1968.

Sicard, Claude. *Roger Martin du Gard. Les Années d'apprentissage littéraire (1881–1910)*. Lille: Atelier Reproduction de Thèses, Université de Lille III, 1976.

Taylor, Michael John. *Martin du Gard: Jean Barois*. London: Arnold, 1974.

Wehrmann, Renée Fainas. *L'Art de Roger Martin du Gard*. Birmingham, Ala.: Summa, 1986.

HARRY MARTINSON *1974*

Harry Martinson (1904–78) was born in the parish of Jämshög, province of Blekinge, in Sweden, on May 6, 1904. His father, Martin Olofsson, a seaman, died of tuberculosis in 1910, and his mother emigrated to the United States in 1911, leaving her children behind. Thus Harry and his siblings were "orphaned." Harry lived in the parish, staying on various farms where he was to help with the chores. He ran away several times; his only respite was school. In 1919 he joined the Boy's Naval Training Corps in Karlskrona and in 1920 he went to sea. For seven years he was a sailor. His travels took him first to Scotland, Ireland, France, and England; he was wrecked off Gotska Sandön in the Baltic. Eventually he came to North America, survived a cyclone in the West Indies, and spent two years in South America. He worked on a sheep farm in Uruguay, then hiked to Brazil, where he found himself pressed into a revolutionary guard, but he finally deserted because "he was not interested as to whether the Governor in Rio Grande was called Goles or Dias." From Brazil he went to South Africa on a British ship, from there to India, China, and Siberia (Vladivostok). In 1925 he did his military service in Sweden, left again for West Africa, and returned to Sweden in 1927 in order to stay at a sanitorium during a bout with tuberculosis. One year later he made his way to Stockholm and started publishing poems and short prose pieces in local papers, later in the press of the capital. In Stockholm he fell in love with the somewhat temperamental writer Moa Johansson, fourteen years his senior, whom he married in 1929. In the same year he had his first collection of poems published, *Spökskepp* ("Ghost Ship"). But his real breakthrough did not come until the following year, when his second collection of poetry, *Nomad*, came out.

After his success with *Nomad*, Martinson concentrated on his life at sea and the experiences of his difficult youth, creative endeavors that resulted in four prose volumes. In the late thirties, with the rapidly changing cultural and political scene, he became more issue-oriented and published three collections of essays and short prose in rapid succession from 1937 to 1939. The year 1940 marks a caesura in his personal life; he participated in the Finnish-Russian War as a mail carrier and liaison on the Finnish side, divorced Moa, and again spent time in a sanitorium. From 1942 on, his ship seems to have sailed in calmer waters. In 1942 he married Ingrid Lindcrantz, and the following era of domestic bliss was paralleled by a period of renewed creativity.

In 1945 a new collection of poems appeared, *Passad* ("Trade Winds") and in 1948 the prose work *Vägen till Klockriket* (*The Road*). These two books were very well received and made it possible for Martinson to be elected in 1949 to the Swedish Academy—the organization that annually awards the Nobel Prizes. From the fifties on, Martinson, with the exception of one play and one small volume of short prose, wrote only poetry, increasingly cosmic and pantheistic in outlook, culminating in *Aniara*, a book-length space-age poem about mankind. In his subsequent poetic works Martinson reverted to the microcosm as manifest in earthy natural and nature phenomena. In 1962 he circled the globe one more time writing articles for a large Swedish daily newspaper. Martinson shared the Nobel Prize in 1974 with his friend and fellow Swedish writer, Eyvind Johnson, for, as the Academy expressed it, "writings that catch the dewdrops and reflect the cosmos." Since Martinson was not very well known outside Sweden, the Academy, in awarding this prize to one of its own, was accused of nationalism. Martinson felt victimized. This disillusionment, combined with rapidly deteriorating health, caused him to withdraw from public life and to stop publishing. He died on February 11, 1978.

In *Nomad*, the ocean and nature in its cosmic dimensions are the chief sources of inspiration; childhood memories also play a certain role. Nature is described via sexual images and symbols. Typical are poems such as "Dröm" ("Dream") and "Utsikt" ("View"). The poems are fairly traditional in form. They derive their distinction from Martinson's preoccupation with the individual word, its sound and shades of meaning. Many of the poems exhibit naive traits (Martinson had seen naive art in several museums). His early poetry evidences influence by other poets, such as Ferlin, Fröding, Karlfeldt, and Kipling. As a typical autodidact, he was a voracious, albeit haphazard, reader. Due to his extensive travel, his interest in Darwin, Alexander von Humboldt, and Hugo Grotius was natural. Later on he read Bergson, Freud, and Spengler. He liked D. H. Lawrence, Sherwood Anderson, Carl Sandburg, and Edgar Lee Masters, as well as Finland's Swedish modernist poetry. Of his contemporaries in Sweden, he admired Asklund,

Kjellgren, Lundkvist, and Sandgren, with whom he was represented in an anthology as early as 1929. The years 1932 and 1933 saw the publication of two impressionistic and sketchlike volumes of prose: *Resor utan mål* ("Voyage Without Aim") and *Kap Farväl!* (*Cape Farewell*). In these two books Martinson talks about his experiences at sea. His utopia is a "dynamically organized nomadic life on earth," lived by "an individual who is mentally and emotionally universal." He believes in humanity and humaneness, tolerance and liberalism, He occasionally takes up the cause of the economically and racially exploited. The books were extremely well received.

Two more prose volumes came out in 1935 and 1936: *Nässlorna blomma* (*Flowering Nettle*) and *Vägen ut* ("To the End of the Road"). In these works Martinson goes even further back in time, describing his childhood. He demonstrates sensitivity and psychological insight. The books detail his escape as a youth from a harsh reality to nature and daydreaming.

In the late thirties and the early forties Martinson published five books of essays. The first three volumes—*Svärmare och harkrank* (1937; Insect Swarms and Waterbugs"), *Midsommardalen* (1938; "Midsummer Valley"), *Det enkla och det svåra* (1939; "The Easy and the Difficult")—basically deal again with nature in all its aspects, especially descriptions of middle-Swedish landscape as found around Ösmo Torp, where he lived, outside Stockholm. The fourth, *Verklighet till döds* (1940; "Reality to the

End"), gives an account of his life on the Salla front during the Finnish-Russian War. He cannot understand that Sweden will not come to the aid of a Scandinavian sister nation. He attacks communism, but identifies the real enemy as modern technology, a "Machine civilization." In 1941 he published *Den förlorade jaguaren* ("The Lost Jaguar"); Cassandra calls about the negative influence the cinema has on Swedish youth, and a continuation of the cultural debate that was already evident in some of the "nature" books.

Decisive changes in Martinson's lifestyle seemed to bring about a change in his work as well. After maturing fully as a writer, having conquered his past with the "sailor" novels and the books about his youth, he struggled with the issues of his own time. His magnum opus, a volume of poems entitled *Passad* ("Trade Winds"), was published in 1945. Fittingly enough the book opens with the poem "Till mognadens sång" ("To Maturity's Song"), which sets the basic tone and is a calm prelude, a poem that with summerly warmth contemplates life's potential. A cultural exposé entitled "Passader" follows. In the second and third section the discussion started in *Verklighet till döds* is continued. In the third, but especially the fourth, section nature takes over. The fifth is a lyrical necrology about priests and priestesses of dreams and beauty. The sixth is aphoristic in a Chinese setting. The last poem, "Besök på observatorium" ("Visit to the Observatory") opens the view to the stars and eternity. Maturity bears fruit; the trade winds escape into the cosmos.

In the meantime Martinson also continued to write prose. *Vägen till Klockriket* (*The Road*) is the title of a volume of tales published in 1949. It is a book about vagrants in Sweden around the turn of the century. Martinson could draw from many European models: Villon, Eichendorff, Hamsun, and, last but not least, the cavaliers in *Gösta Berlings Saga*. The various chapters in the book are only loosely connected, held together by the main character, Bolle, a decent man, friendly, polite, good-humored with an almost Buddhist view of life. Although he is not quite as comical as Chaplin, he shares many of the great comedian's character traits and misfortunes. Social problems (unemployment, emigration, suicide) are discussed. Yet this is not a novel about social injustice; rather it is one about the superiority, the adaptability of the individual, and human potential. Lyrical descriptions change with philosophical dialogue. The characters, with the exception of Bolle, are presented in vignettes: the fatalist, the glutton, the philosopher, et cetera. The most fascinating part of the book is Bolle's dreamlike transmigration from this life to the next. If Martinson gave first glimpses of the cosmos, *his* cosmos, in *Passad*, his poetic work of the fifties—*Cicada* (1953; "Cecada") and *Aniara* (1956) (*Cicada* contains the first twenty-nine songs in *Aniara*)—develop entire cosmic systems and invent space adventure. *Aniara* is the story of 8,000 people on the "goldonda Aniara," a space ferry that flies to and fro between radiation-poisoned Earth and Mars. A jammed rudder sends Aniara past Mars toward Lyra, a fictional distant solar system and on into the void. At a certain point, the crew has to share the dreadful secret with the passengers who, in the end, accept their fate. An intricate computer with endless creative possibilities, named Mima, conjurer of dreams, provides escapist reveries for the passengers. Mima, the universal conscience, has an almost divine function; the poet acts as a priest. Martinson invents dozens of new words, words that evoke objects beyond the reader's imagination. These new words are vague enough to allow for individual speculation. In this intriguing, highly technical setting such themes emerge as the pantheistic structure of the cosmos and the indeterministic character of present-day science. Tord Hall points out in his preface to the English-language edition of *Aniara* that the second law of the thermodynamics states that the cosmos moves unhesitatingly from order toward chaos. Martinson applies this to man himself. The entropy of evil is continuously expanding in our souls, and the dark instincts of destruction point the way to death and chaos. Hall goes on to compare *Aniara* to a poetic nuclear explosion where science and poetry become organically fused. The message is also that giant steps forward in science are not paralleled by mankind's ethical gains. Ethical developments have lagged behind and eventually man will not be able to control the destructive weapons produced by science. In 1959 *Aniara* was made into an opera.

In 1964 Martinson wrote his only play, *Tre Kvinnor från Wei* ("Three Women from Wei"). Ingemar Bergman, who was then director of the famous Stockholm theater Dramaten, helped Martinson to turn it into a playable piece. With his health deteriorating, Martinson found the creative process lengthy and difficult in the sixties. There is a small volume of nature prose, *Utsikt från en grästuva* (1963; "View from a Tuft of Grass"), and an even smaller volume of poetry, *Vagnen* (1960; "The Vehicle"), which was not well received.

But Martinson made one last great effort to create poems, and to rewrite some earlier ones and put them in order. The result is the large collection *Dikter om ljus och mörker* (1971; "Poems About Light and Darkness") and the smaller volume *Tuvor* (1973; "Tufts of Grass"). These two books contain Martinson's best poems. There are several categories: philosophical-reflective poems, childhood memories, symbolist poems, myths, but above all nature poems. Nature poems are the core, the soul of Martinson's work. In them we find an idyllic, sentimentalized nature, and few romantic elements. Yet nature for Martinson is clearly an expression of the divine, and we as human beings are part of nature, but a part that has not learned yet to live in harmony with the rest.

From 1973 until his death in 1978, Martinson did not publish, which does not mean that he was not creative. He left a large number of unpublished works.

Martinson, although a Nobel Prize winner, is not very well known outside of Sweden. The lack of international recognition probably has several causes. On the one hand, he is mainly a poet, and it is difficult to translate poetry, especially from one of the so-called minor languages. On the other, he does not belong to any identifiable school of writers. He is neither modernist nor postmodernist, not political nor socially very engaged. And finally, "nature" poetry does not seem to be very much in demand these days.

FRITZ H. KÖNIG

Selected Bibliography

PRIMARY SOURCES

Martinson, Harry. *Aniara*. Translated by Hugh McDiarmid and Elspeth Harley Shubert, with an introduction by Tord Hall. New York: Knopf, 1963.

———. *Cape Farewell*. Translated by Naomi Walford. New York: Putnam, 1934.

———. *Flowering Nettle*. Translated by Naomi Walford. New York: Cresset, 1935.

———. *The Road*. Translated by M. A. Michael. New York: Cape, 1955.

SECONDARY SOURCES

Encyclopedia of World Literature in the Twentieth Century. Vol. 2. Pp. 387–88. New York: Ungar, 1964.

Svensson, Georg. *Harry Martinson— som jag såg honom*. Stockholm: ALBA, 1980.

Ulvenstam, Lars. *Harry Martinson*. Stockholm: Bouviers, 1950.

FRANÇOIS MAURIAC 1952

François Mauriac (1885–1970) was one of the most prolific French writers of the first half of the twentieth century. He tried his hand at virtually every genre but is known chiefly as a novelist. His fictional world is a refraction of the provincial, Catholic, and bourgeois milieu of his native region, transformed by his sensitivity, his psychological insights, and his Catholic faith, and expressed in a dense, poetic style, which is more suggestive than explicit. It engages the reader to see Mauriac's world through the mind of his protagonists. Like Dostoyevsky, whose literary technique he greatly admired, Mauriac believed in the mystery of the soul. It is the exploration of his characters' psyche that reveals their universality.

Born in Bordeaux on October 11, 1885, he was the youngest of the five children of Jean-Paul and Claire Coiffard Mauriac. His father, the son of a wood importer, had shown a predilection for study and literary ability by winning school prizes, but was obliged to continue the family business, which was soon liquidated, forcing him to continue earning his family's livelihood as a bank employee until his early death in 1887. François's Uncle Louis, who had studied law and never married, became the guardian of the Mauriac children. All the men on François's paternal side—his grandfather, father, and uncle—were anticlerical; his mother, grandmother, and aunts, on the other hand, were staunchly devout. Their lives were organized around religious practices, from daily devotions through formal education. Religious values were expounded, if not always observed. The family's social world was circumscribed by Catholic circles, in which the family circle was most important.

After her husband's death, Claire Mauriac found it necessary to move her family to her mother's house, occupying the top floor there. François's grandmother, a lady of means whose husband had done well in the textile business, exercised her matriarchal powers over the families of her daughters, truly holding court at family reunions like a dowager queen.

When François was five, he began attending kindergarten, and at seven his mother enrolled him in the Marist school of their neighborhood. During his early school days François seems to have lived in terror of his teachers and was taunted by his classmates who maliciously called him *Coco-bel-oeil* ("handsome droopy-eye") because of his drooping eyelid, incurred in an accident during play. At ten he began his studies at the Marist *collège* Grand Lebrun, where his stay was brightened by the inspiration of an outstanding teacher, Abbé Péquignot, who aroused François's interest in literature. After graduating from Lebrun, he continued his studies at the University of Bordeaux and earned his *licence* (the equivalent of an M.A.) in 1904. In the fall of 1906 he went to Paris to prepare for the prestigious Ecole des Chartes. He did study there from 1908 to 1909, but soon realized that he wanted to devote himself entirely to writing, and published his first book, a volume of poetry, *Les Mains jointes* (1909; "Folded Hands"). Although it was praised by Barrès, who at the time was the most prominent French writer, Mauriac decided that fiction was his true medium, and the following year published his first novel, *L'Enfant chargé de chaînes* (*Young Man in Chains*), in the most respected literary periodical, *Mercure de France*, and two years later in book form. This autobiographical, rather harsh self-criticism was followed by a more indulgent look upon his recent past, *La Robe prètexte* (1914; *The Stuff of Youth*). Upon arriving in Paris, Mauriac had immediately joined Catholic groups and was elected president of the Catholic student union. He returned to Bordeaux for vacations, and in 1912 met Jeanne Lafont, the daughter of a Bordeaux banker, who became his wife in 1913.

The events of World War I, during which he served in the Red Cross, as well as personal ones—his marriage and the birth of his first son, Claude, who was to become a novelist as well—interrupted Mauriac's literary flow. Soon after peace returned, he resumed writing and published his third novel, *La Chair et le sang* (1920; *Flesh and Blood*) followed by a fourth, *Préséances* (1921; *Questions of Precedence*), a

year later. Both were autobiographical, written in the first person. However, it was only his fifth novel, *Le Baiser au lépreux* (1922; *The Kiss to the Leper*), written when Mauriac was already thirty-seven, that brought him instant success and fame.

Like all his subsequent masterpieces, *Le Baiser* is set in his native Bordelais. Jean, puny and ugly, leads a lonely existence with his hypochondriac father, Jérôme, in a small village in the pine forests of the Landes. In order to keep the inheritance of their lands from the anticlerical side of the family, the father and the village priest hatch the plan to marry Jean to the robust and attractive peasant girl Noémi, whose parents are pleased to see their progeny's fortunes rise. However, Noémi is so repulsed by Jean that she starts to waste away. In the face of physical evidence of his effect on her, Jean finds pretexts to spend prolonged periods of time away from home. When he decides to keep a vigil at the bedside of a friend consumed by tuberculosis, Jean contracts the disease himself. His illness brings a young and handsome doctor to the house. He and Noémi soon share an inevitable attraction to each other. Although Jean would acquiesce to their union after his death, the father insists that Noémi will become heiress to their lands only if she vows to remain a widow. Sensitive to Jean's sacrifice for her liberation, she does indeed renounce her love and enters upon perpetual widowhood, which confers upon her a certain dignity in the eyes of the townspeople.

The story is told in the third person, with sparse description, which nevertheless conjures the particular atmosphere of the setting most vividly by intense and well-suited figures and correlations. Likening his terse and precise evocations to those of Racine and Flaubert, critics were almost unanimous in their praise of *Le Baiser.*

A year later, after the not-so-successful *Le Fleuve de feu* (1923; *The River of Fire*), Mauriac published another masterpiece. *Génitrix* (1923; *The Family*). Félicité Cazenave is a possessive mother who has kept her son, Fernand, a bachelor until the age of fifty. When he marries a young teacher, Mathilde, Mme. Cazenave lets her die after a miscarriage in order to repossess her son. Through this episode, Fernand finally understands his mother's domination and rebels, undermining his delicate health. To nurse her son back to health again, Mme. Cazenave serves meals that are fatal to her own heart condition. This stark drama takes place almost entirely in the Cazenave's house and garden, and the house itself has an important role in the story. The juxtaposition of the rooms and their particular decor give a special meaning and concreteness to the feelings of their occupants.

In his next masterpiece, *Le Désert de l'amour* (1925; *The Desert of Love*), Mauriac, in full mastery of his talent, depicts a whole family in a closely intertwined double plot. Dr. Courrèges, a conscientious and overworked doctor whose family relationships have deteriorated, falls in love with one of his patients,

Maria Cross, a young widow in financial difficulty who has become the mistress of the businessman Larousselle. Dr. Courrèges cannot express his love for her because she venerates him. On her daily streetcar rides to the cemetery to visit the grave of a son who had died as a small child, she meets Raymond Courrèges, the doctor's son, who takes the same streetcar to commute to the university. Because of Raymond's timidity, she mistakes him for naïve. When she invites him to her house, he reveals his true, cynically passionate nature by trying to seduce her brutally, whereupon she orders him never to approach her again. Sometime later, when Dr. Courrèges is summoned from home to treat Maria after an accident, Raymond realizes that both he and his father love the same woman. After her recovery, Maria is sent to live in Paris. Eighteen years later, Raymond, who has never overcome Maria's rejection of him, meets her in a Paris bar accompanied by Larousselle, who has married her. When Larousselle succumbs to a stroke, he is taken home by Maria with Raymond's help. Raymond calls on his father, in Paris for a conference, for help, and both men realize at Larousselle's deathbed that they had unsuccessfully loved the same woman, who has found an object for her maternal affections in her stepson, Bertrand. This novel differs from the previous ones somewhat in that the descriptions are more detailed, and in the use of the flashback technique.

Two years later, in 1927, Mauriac was to make the most felicitous use of flashback in *Thérèse Desqueyroux* (*Thérèse*), which is now considered his foremost masterpiece. Thérèse is the daughter of a local politician and the wife of an owner of pine forests, to which she has joined her own properties. The book opens with Thérèse's return from a trial in which she has been acquitted, in order to avoid scandal, of the accusation of having poisoned her husband, Bernard. Thérèse mentally composes her confession to him, explaining the events and half-conscious motives that led her to this act. This *examen de conscience* occupies two-thirds of the book. Although Thérèse is prepared to ask for Bernard's forgiveness, upon her return home he sequesters her and treats her like a prisoner, then leaves. Losing all desire for life, Thérèse refuses to eat, chain-smokes, and becomes weak and emaciated. As recompense for her acquittal, she is asked to put up a display of family harmony in church and especially toward the Deguil-hem family, whose son is engaged to Bernard's half-sister, Anne. After Thérèse fulfills this duty and Anne marries, Bernard liberates Thérèse and allows her to live in Paris.

Since the novel ends when Thérèse is still a young woman embarked on a new life in the city, Mauriac was obsessed with this character for many years to come. In 1933 he wrote two short stories, *Plongées* (1938; "Descent") about Thérèse's sordid love affairs, and in 1935 another novel, *La Fin de la nuit* (*The End of the Night*). Thérèse, now forty-five, is living a lonely life in Paris when her seventeen-year-old daughter Marie, to whom she had renounced all maternal rights, visits her. In reality, Marie's reason for coming to Paris is to follow George, whose family will not permit their marriage because Marie's dowry is insufficient to finance George's business. Thérèse generously offers the remains of her own dowry to Marie so that the union can take place. In the meantime, George has fallen in love with the more sophisticated Thérèse. Although flattered by his overtures, Thérèse realizes the folly of such a liaison and tries to reconcile George with Marie. Although the novel drew praise from contemporary critics and the portrayal of Thérèse is psychologically deep and more compassionate than in the earlier novel, *La Fin de la nuit*, which is set almost entirely in Paris, lacks the poetic quality of Mauriac's novels set in Bordeaux, and readers find the last third of the story contrived and theatrical. In fact, Mauriac had difficulty writing its conclusion and tore up his first version.

While thinking about the new, contrite Thérèse, Mauriac wrote another masterpiece, *Le Noeud de vipères* (1932; *Vipers' Tangle*), a diptych consisting of a long letter and a diary, both written by the protagonist, Louis, a sexagenarian who had been a brilliant lawyer, and, despite his peasant origins and unattractive appearance, had married the aristocratic Isa Fondandège. However, being oversensitive to his weaknesses, he is alienated from his wife upon discovering that before her marriage she had been attracted to another man of her own class. The rift between the spouses is accentuated by Isa's doting on their children, which Louis resents, and her fear that Louis's atheism will have a bad influence on them. Because of Louis's miserliness, the family resorts to plotting against him, and when he discovers this, he dispossesses them altogether, leaving his property to an illegitimate son. In the end, through an exchange of letters by his children and grandchildren, his complex and contradictory character is revealed more fully. If in this family drama Louis stands out far above the other characters, it is because Mauriac's purpose in writing this novel was to show the redemption of a cynical miser.

The last of Mauriac's great novels is *La Pharisienne* (*Woman of the Pharisees*), in which the complex intertwined plots of two love stories are subordinated to the hateful domineering of Brigitte Pian, a self-righteous matriarch who plays God. A counterpoint to her starkly dark character is the loving Abbé Calou, one of her victims. Although this novel's more complex structure and frequency of tragic events have been perceived by some critics as flaws, *La Pharisienne* is more ambitious than Mauriac's other novels in that it creates a world beyond the family's microcosm. Well received in Scandinavia, the book contributed to Mauriac's winning the Nobel Prize in 1952 over Graham Greene and Menendez Pidal.

The characterization of Mauriac's unforgettable protagonists is marked not only by deep psychological searching, but also by an impenetrable mystery attributable to his religious upbringing. Like his mother, François Mauriac held Jansenist-like views about man's salvation. Moreover, his characters possess observed traits of Mauriac's own family members and often his own, which explains the recurrence of certain character types, such as physically diminished, sensitive young men with great souls —priests, lawyers, philanderers, anticlerical misers—and among women, the domineering matriarch. Likewise, the bourgeois landowners and industrialists of Bordeaux are depicted in the contradictions of their values and carnal desires against the concrete background of the places of Mauriac's childhood. The more positive aspects of his youth are found in the fictionalized autobiography, *Le Mystère Frontenac* (1933; *The Frontenac Mystery*).

While Mauriac was chiefly a novelist, during his long and very productive literary life he also wrote poetry, essays, literary criticism, plays, short stories, and memoirs, and engaged in journalism and polemics for his causes. As was customary at the time, he began his career as a writer with two volumes of poetry, *Les Mains jointes* (1909; "Folded Hands") and *Adieu à l'adolescence* (1911; "Farewell to Adolescence"). His essays parallel his novels. Of special interest is *Ce qui était perdu* (1930; *That Which Was Lost*), which reflects his religious crisis after a confrontation with André Gide. Mauriac tried his hand at theater after his reputation as novelist was firmly established, and obtained considerable success with *Asmodée* (1937; *Asmodée* or the *Intruder*), followed by *Les Mal Aimés* (1945; "The Unloved Ones"), *Passage du Malin* (1948; "The Passing of the Devil"), and *Le Feu sur la terre* (1948; "Fire on Earth"). His polemic writing was considerable. He was committed to liberal Catholic politics, to de Gaulle's campaign to liberate France during World War II, to anticolonialism, and opposed to the excesses of the anticollaborationist purge. The Christian and patriotic values of his upbringing resulted in a moderate-liberal stance, and engaged him actively to condemn policies and acts that oppressed the individual or the group. *Le Cahier noir* (1943; *The Black Notebook*), published by the underground and expressing opposition to the German occupation, was perhaps the most noteworthy and the most influential of Mauriac's polemic writings.

After he received the Nobel Prize in 1952, Mauriac published his last novel, *L'Agneau* (1954; *The Lamb*). He devoted his remaining years to journalism, writing his weekly column *Bloc Notes* (1958–1961; "Note-pad") on literary topics for *Le Figaro Littéraire*. During de Gaulle's campaign for Algerian decolonization, Mauriac rallied to his cause, continuing to publish his denunciation of colonialism in *L'Express*. During the last decade of his life he also wrote three volumes of memoirs.

While Mauriac's fictional work is set in the narrowly circumscribed world of the bourgeois Bordeaux of his youth, and develops from sordid family quarrels and local scandals he had witnessed, his characters are modern equivalents of major mythical figures of classical Western literature. A master of characterization, Mauriac also excelled in the poetic recreation of the world of his childhood, which he never lost but reproduced in many variations. Although the universality of his characters may seem paradoxical in their precise and limited setting, as Mauriac explained himself in his acceptance speech of the Nobel Prize in literature in 1952, "The gift of the novelist goes back precisely to the power of making evident the universality of his narrow world, in which we have learned to love and to suffer." A moralist and critic, Mauriac ranks with major European novelists such as André Malraux, Georges Bernanos, Thomas Mann, and Boris Pasternak.

BIRUTA CAP

Selected Bibliography

PRIMARY SOURCES

Mauriac, François. *Oeuvres complètes.* 12 vols. Paris: Fayard, 1950–56.

———. *Oeuvres romanesques et théatrales complètes.* 3 vols. Edited by J. Petit. Paris: Gallimard, 1978–81.

SECONDARY SOURCES

Goesch, Keith. *François Mauriac: Essai de bibliographie chronologique, 1908–1960.* Paris: Nizet, 1965.

———. *François Mauriac.* Paris: Editions de l'Herne, 1985.

Jarett-Kerr, Martin. *François Mauriac.*

Cambridge, Mass.: Bowes & Bowes, 1954; New Haven: Yale University Press, 1954.

Jenkins, Cecil. *Mauriac*. Edinburgh and London: Oliver & Boyd, 1965; New York: Barnes & Noble, 1965.

Kushner, Eva. *François Mauriac*. Paris: Desclée de Brouwer, 1972.

Lacouture, Jean. *François Mauriac*. Paris: Seuil, 1980.

Smith, Maxwell A. *François Mauriac*. New York: Twayne, 1970.

CZESLAW MILOSZ   *1980*

Czeslaw Milosz (1911—) is a great writer who combines remarkable breadth of vision and power of expression with a young boy's need for privacy—very like a Polish-Lithuanian Huck Finn. The combination of vision and squint-eyed peevishness, the linking of those historically loaded adjectives, *Polish* and *Lithuanian*, provide an opening into the Miloszian labyrinth that must be entered if we are to find our way through the historical half-lights and wounded privacy of his works.

Milosz manifests, despite numerous disclaimers, attitudes of exclusivity and hauteur that have been characteristic of some representatives of the Polish well-born intelligentsia. All of this and more we must consider, even in a brief essay, if we are to get a hold on this poet who, perhaps more than any other, speaks for our age and whom the Russian Nobel Prize winner Joseph Brodsky has called "perhaps the greatest poet in the world"—this self-described thoughtful rustic who has emerged from the mists of an idealized "Lithuania" to become a planetary spokesman in Polish.

Czeslaw Milosz was born on June 30, 1911, in Szetejnie, Kiejdany* District, of the Lithuanian part of the erstwhile Polish-Lithuanian Commonwealth, then (in 1911) under czarist Russian rule. His family was of Polish and Lithuanian (and other) ancestry, still strongly consciously Lithuanian on his mother's side, but Polish in language, social standing, and general culture. From 1918 on, young Czeslaw combined schooling in Wilno (ethnically a Polish and Jewish city) with immersion in the predominantly Lithuanian (and Belorussian, often still pagan) countryside: primeval

---

*Since Milosz is a Polish poet, the biographer has used Polish orthography throughout for place names. A strong case could be made for using Lithuanian names, where appropriate, to preserve the localness so important to Milosz's memory systems.

forests, bogs, still fresh streams and lakes—an urban-bucolic-cultural mix that proved formative for his later poetry. Many of his themes and postures, problems of personal and cultural identity, the need for "distance," the persistent need to escape the past by constantly re-stirring the cauldron of the past, hark back to these years.

He attended the Zygmunt August High School in Wilno (named for a Polish king who was also grand duke of Lithuania), then the Stefan Batory (another king) University in the same city, where, while studying law, he was active in the Polish Studies Literary Club.

Literary activity became dominant with publication in 1930 of his first poems in the university periodical *Alma Mater Vilnensis* and his cofounding of the literary group *Żagary* ("Kindling"), part of what was later called the Second Avant-Garde or "catastrophist" group of poets in interwar Poland. Milosz's early antiaestheticism (still in place in 1988) and attraction to Marxism (no longer in place) are evident during this period.

During trips to Western Europe he met his cousin Oskar de Lubicz Milosz, who grew up considering himself a Pole, became a Lithuanian in response to official Polish antipathy toward a separate, independent Lithuania after World War I, and also became, while serving in the Lithuanian diplomatic service, a leading French poet. This concatenation of "identities" represented by his older cousin-mentor had a profound effect on young Czeslaw's emerging view of himself as Pole,

Lithuanian, European, and eventually (few others so qualify for the term, although he would reject it) "Earthling."

Milosz's reputation as a poet began in earnest with the publication of his first independent volume, *Poemat o czasie zastyglym* (*Poem on Frozen Time*), in 1933. He also began his career as editor and social critic with the publication of *Anthology of Social Poetry*; Zbigniew Folejewski, who later achieved international fame as a literary historian and linguist, was coeditor.

The poet-editor grudgingly completed his law studies (master of law degree) in 1934. In the same year he achieved significant recognition for his poetry, an award from the Union of Polish Writers and a grant from the National Cultural Fund, with which he financed a year's stay in France. He resumed his formative contacts with Oskar Milosz (in 1935), while studying at the Alliance Française and the Institut Catholique, where he attended lectures on Thomism. While thus broadening his Catholic base and struggling with the narrowly focused version he had been exposed to in Poland (much like the young James Joyce in Ireland), Milosz wrote two important early poems, "Hymn" and "Bramy arsenala" ("Gates of the Arsenal").

On his return to Poland, Milosz worked for Polish Radio in Wilno. He soon lost his position because of his leftist views, which were not acceptable to the Polish government in the late '30s. With the help of the Union of Polish Writers, he nevertheless published his second volume of poetry, *Trzy zimy* (1936; *Three Winters*).

After leaving Wilno in 1937 and traveling to Italy, he worked for Radio Warsaw. His struggle to work, to publish, to *locate* himself in a society with which he was intensely involved yet within which he felt himself to be an outsider (much as he does today in the United States) persisted right up to the outbreak of World War II. He returned to Wilno in time for the outbreak of the war in 1939.

Poland suffered a double invasion in 1939 from the then two most potent tyrannies known to history: Nazi Germany and Soviet Russia. We may get at once a characteristic glimpse of modern Polish history and of the response of Czeslaw Milosz by quoting from the recent (1987) translation of *Conversations with Czeslaw Milosz* (from which much of this biographical material is drawn): "1940—Milosz escapes from Soviet-occupied Wilno to Nazi-occupied Warsaw. . . ." Can the comfortable American reader imagine that? That *choice*? (Milosz gives details of how that choice was made, and its ramifications, in his autobiographical *Rodzinna Europa*, translated as *Native Realm: A Search for Self-definition*.) What seems important to stress here is the poet's decision to move to the Polish center, where he well knew when he made the choice that conditions were far more hellish than at the admittedly brutal Soviet periphery. This choice is not only important for confirming Milosz's bona fide credentials as what is usually called a "hero" (again, despite his disclaim-ers), but speaks volumes about his commitment to Polish civilization.

During he war he worked within the socialist arm of the resistance (the Polish Socialist party, PPS, a powerful, democratic, national but not chauvinist movement dating from the 1890s through the Occupation). Obtaining a relatively "safe" sinecure as "janitor" at the Warsaw University Library, Milosz illegally and clandestinely wrote, took part in poetry readings, and published. He worked and drank with many later famous Polish literati, among them Jerzy Andrzejewski, eventual author of *Popioł i diament* (*Ashes and Diamonds*), made into a classic film of the post-World War II "Polish Wave" by Andrzej Wajda. He witnessed the destruction of the German-built Warsaw Ghetto (April 1943) and experienced the general Warsaw Uprising of August–October, 1944.

With the establishment of Soviet Russian power in Poland (see *The Seizure of Power*, below), Milosz decided to join the Polish client government of Boleslaw Bierut—in the poet's view, the only "clean" and sane choice at the time. He was quickly assigned (December 1945) to the Polish consulate in New York City, and he remained abroad until the summer of 1949. This is critical, for during this time the entire Mikołajczyk tragedy was acted out.

Stanisław Mikołajczyk was the prime minister of the wartime London-based Polish government-in-exile who, at the urging of the British and American governments, went to Poland to participate in a coalition government and in "free and unfettered elections." The elections were a fraud, conducted under repressive conditions; in 1947 Mikołajczyk, having learned that he was on an official "hit list," fled to the West. Subsequently, Mikołajczyk's Peasant Movement and the Polish Socialist party were absorbed at gunpoint into the Red Army–supported Communist (minority) party to form the Polish United Workers party, and all pretense of a "coalition" government was jettisoned— all this, as it were, behind Milosz's back. When Milosz returned to Poland in that fateful summer of 1949, he was shocked to recognize the face of totalitarianism, the presence of that abstract-yet-palpable fear that he had learned to recognize under both the Soviets and Nazis. Now it was established as "normal" in Poland, as an aspect of a system he had supported. He was stunned.

In 1950 he was sent to Paris as the first secretary of the Polish embassy there. When, later that year, he went to Warsaw and his passport was temporarily taken away, he recognized that his government had become aware of his disaffection with it; he had become suspect. He returned to Paris in early 1951, at which time he decided to ask for political asylum. Thus began his career as emigré Polish ex-diplomat, poet, scholar, and geopolitical whistle blower. This culminated in his publication of *Zniewolony umysł* (1953; *The Captive Mind*), still the most sophisticated, satisfying discussion of Marxism's appeal for sincere and otherwise intelligent European intellectuals—moreso than, for example, the explanations of Arthur Koestler.

Milosz's break with the Polish government in 1951 marks the beginning of his truly international career, sealed in 1953 by publication of *Captive Mind* by the Instytut Literacki (Kultura) in Paris. Ever since Milosz has retained his association with this most prestigious and significant Polish publishing center outside Poland (excepting, perhaps, *The Polish Review* in New York). In 1953 also *Zdobycie władzy* (*The Seizure of Power*), his first novel, received the Swiss *Prix Litteraire Européen* and Instytut Literacki published his first volume of poetry as an emigré, *Swiat o dzienne* (*The Light of Day*).

The year 1955 saw the publication of *Dolina Issy* (*The Issa Valley*), perhaps Milosz's most satisfying and moving evocation of his Lithuania-cum-adolescence mythos. Though in *Native Realm* he more explicitly spells out the myriad ethnic, geographic, cultural, religious, and political *connotations* of the terms *Lithuania* in general and *Poland* in particular. Here, too, he began to emerge more strongly as a scholar (the eventual University of California professor) with his translation of Jeanne Hirsh's *Politics and Reality*. Here, too, we may mention his strong response to various women writers, most notably the Franco-Jewish mystic, Simone Weil.

During this period of his French domicile (1951–60) it seems fair to say that Milosz fully emerged as an international literary figure. Key professional events of this period include 1957, *Traktat poetyckie* (*A Treatise on Poetry* [Instytut Literacki]) and *Kultura's* annual literary prize; 1958, publication of *Native Realm Kontynenty* (*Continents*), a volume of essays and translations of Simone Weil's *Selected Writings* (Milosz's translation), and an award from the Union of Polish Emigré Writers.

Surely in our century, the "permanent" move (1960) to the United States of an author of such international repute is bound to have an impact on that individual: liberating, perhaps traumatic—who knows? For Milosz, it seems, to this writer, to have been integrative; a maturing experience, in the uninsulting sense. Here in America, he has emerged as a truly grand figure. His thought has matured, his formulations have become more penetrating, although, related to his lingering Litho-Huck-finnism, he still has to guard against extra-cute "protections," sudden claims to the right to privacy, et cetera. I am reminded of Joseph (Korzeniowski) Conrad's annoying habit of taking the reader to the brink of disclosure only to turn away with a muttered (in print) claim that the reader wouldn't be interested in that, or that it doesn't matter.

From 1960 to 1980, when he was "to everyone's surprise" awarded the Nobel Prize, Milosz quietly, persistently mined west-of-the-Atlantic culture with Polish-Lithuanian implosives. His influence on young American scholars and poets will manifest itself in their works for years to come.

In 1962 he published *Król Popiel i inne wiersze* (*King Popiel and Other Poems*) and a study of the Polish philosopher, critic, and novelist Stanisław Brzozowski, *Człowiek wśrod skorpionów: studium o Stanisławie Brzozowskim* (*Man Among Scorpions: Studies on Stanislaw Brzozowski*). Brzozowski remains one of Milosz's meta-poetico-philosophical passions. In 1965 the Institut Literacki in Paris published *Gucio zaczarowany* (*Bobo's Metamorphosis*) (poems), and, elsewhere, in English, *Post-War Polish Poetry: An Anthology*.

Prizes began to pile up: in 1967 the Marian Kister Literary Award in New York and in 1968 the Jurzykowski Award, a distinguished Polish-American recognition of international standing. In 1967 also the (Polish) Poets' and Painters' Press of London published a collection of his *Poems*.

The twelve years between 1968 and the award of the Nobel Prize in 1980 were years of undiminished productivity and growing fame outside the confines of emigré and specialist groups. In particular, his relaxed yet masterful *History of Polish Literature* (1969), used as a text in Polish studies courses throughout the United States, became, if not a "best" at least a good seller, attracting readers from well beyond the specialist-student market. Milosz began becoming broadly known and appreciated among many in the large population of Polish-Americans who, while not professional scholars, show a keen interest in their Polish heritage. Proof of its popularity is the fact that the University of California Press in 1983 issued a second edition of Macmillan's 1969 first edition. Clearly, the publishers were drawing on Milosz's new post-Nobel notoriety; nevertheless, the history of the text demonstrates that from the early '70s on Milosz began to emerge from the self-imposed attitudinal cocoon of the exile-poet-scholar.

Further milestones on the way to the Nobel Prize were the publication of *Widzenia nad Zatoka San Francisco* (1969; *Visions from San Francisco*) (essays), *Miasto bez imienia* (1969; *City Without a Name*) (poems), and *Selected Poems* (1973); a Guggenheim Fellowship in 1976; the publication of *Ziemia Ulro* (*The Land of Ulro*), a major reexamination of his life and his relation to Polish and world culture, *Utwory poetyckie* (*Collected Poems*), and *Cesarz ziemi* (*The Emperor of the Earth*), all in 1977; in 1978 the Neustadt International Literary Prize, the University of California (Berkeley) Citation, and publication of the great anthology, *Dzwony w zimie* (*Bells in Winter*); and, finally, in 1979, the Zygmunt Hertz award for Milosz's translations from Hebrew to Polish.

The Nobel award in 1980 permanently wrenched Milosz from his private musings. The prize plus events in Poland prevented him from withdrawing from the public scene. In 1978 Karol Wojtyla, Cardinal Archbishop of Krakow, had been elected pope as John Paul II; in 1979 he had visited his homeland, a visit that focused the world on Poland and that strengthened those processes already underway that emerged in 1980 as the powerful, creative socio-cultural movement called Solidarity. Milosz's works, which had circulated underground in Poland, after the Nobel Prize were openly published, and in 1981

Milosz went to Poland, where to his amazement, but with profound emotional effect, he was received as a bona fide Polish hero—if not "the voice of the Diaspora" (which he denies), surely the leading voice of Polish culture on the world stage. He was particularly touched by his reception by Lech Walesa, the workerleader of Solidarity, who would receive a Nobel Prize (peace) in 1983. The Polish government even officially honored the poet by issuing in 1982 a Milosz postage stamp.

Since returning from Poland, Milosz has remained active as poet, translator, scholar, and public figure, participating in symposia and other events, e.g., Polish-Jewish discussions involving reevaluation of the Holocaust. Milosz sees the Holocaust as a general Polish disaster, which includes Polish and non-Polish Jewish victims as a major subset, but rejects the impression of the Holocaust as an exclusively Jewish tragedy. He knows what has not been sufficiently publicized: about the three million Polish Gentiles, predominantly civilians, killed as a result of the German occupation, mostly outside of combat situations, e.g., in camps, street roundups, medical experiments, etc. The threemillion figure does not include victims of Russian action in Poland during and just after World War II, nor does it include civilian victims of other nationalities, separate issues that also remain on Milosz's agenda.

His recent publications include *Świadectwo poezji* (*The Witness of Poetry* [his Harvard lectures of 1981]), *Osobny zeszyt: przez galeria luster* (*The Separate Notebooks: A*

Mirrored Gallery), Nieobjęta ziemia (*Unattainable Earth*), both in 1984 in their original forms, and, most recently, the already mentioned *Conversations with Czeslaw Milosz* which is an English translation and merging of two earlier Polish works by Aleksander Fiut and Eva Czarnecka.

Czeslaw Milosz shows no public signs of slowing down or running out of private or public history to process. His poetry, even in translation, has great evocative power. This is partly because of the poet's application of severe discipline to the dyonysiac, yet simple and concrete impulses that drive his muse; partly due to the unflinching honesty that imparts an apollonian cast to the finished poem. And it has not hurt that Milosz, who is fluent in English, can participate in the translating of his own works.

Perhaps Milosz's appeal derives mostly from the recognition that he combines in one person the romantic's passion for the past with having experienced, survived, and built beauty on the most horrendous challenges a human being may be asked to face; that he has not only emerged from the defining evil of our century but has preserved and developed the remarkable intelligence and power of artistic engagement with which he started.

In his Nobel lecture he characterized his work-behavior as a process of "leaving behind books as if they were dry skins, in a constant escape forward from what has been done in the past . . ."

In the summer of 1981, he said, "One leaves Poland today with the impression that the most beautiful flowers sometimes bloom on the edge of the abyss."

Perhaps his readers feel that he has provided them the means for that constant escape forward, that he has given them the power to see those flowers blooming on the edge of the abyss.

ROBERT P. PULA

Selected Bibliography

PRIMARY SOURCES

Milosz, Czeslaw. *Bells in Winter.* Translated by Czeslaw Milosz and Lillian Vallee. New York: Ecco Press, 1978.

———. *The Captive Mind.* Translated by Jane Zielonko. New York: Alfred A. Knopf, 1953. New York: Vintage Books, 1955; 2nd edition, 1981.

———. *Emperor of the Earth: Modes of Eccentric Vision.* Berkeley: University of California Press, 1977.

———. *The Issa Valley.* Translated by Louis Iribarne. New York: Farrar, Straus & Giroux, 1978.

———. *The Land of Ulro.* Translated by Louis Iribarne. New York: Farrar, Straus & Giroux, 1984.

———. *Native Realm.* Translated by Catherine S. Leach. New York: Doubleday, 1968.

———. *Nobel Lecture.* New York: Farrar, Straus & Giroux, 1981.

———. *The Seizure of Power.* Translated by Celina Wieniewska. New York: Criterion Books, 1955.

———. *Selected Poems.* Translated by Czeslaw Milosz and others. New York: Ecco Press, 1980.

————. *The Separate Notebooks.* New York: Ecco Press, 1984.

————. *Unattainable Earth.* Translated by Czeslaw Milosz and Robert Hass. New York: Ecco Press, 1986.

————. *Visions from San Francisco Bay.* Translated by Richard Lourie. New York: Farrar, Straus & Giroux, 1975.

————. *The Witness of Poetry.* Cambridge: Harvard University Press, 1983.

SECONDARY SOURCES

Blejwas, Stanislaus A. "The Prejudice of Polish Intellectuals." *Polish Heritage Quarterly* XXXVIII, 3 (Fall 1987):2, 11.

Czarnecka, Ewa, and Aleksander Fiut. *Conversations with Czeslaw Milosz.* Translated by Richard Lourie. New York: Harcourt Brace Jovanovich, 1987.

"Czeslaw Milosz: A Special Issue." *Ironwood 18.* Tuscon, Ariz.: Ironwood Press, 1981. Translations, biographical data, and criticism.

Michailovich, Vasa D. et al., eds., "Czeslaw Milosz," in *Modern Slavic Literatures.* Vol. II. New York: Ungar, 1976. Pp. 340–47.

"A Tribute to Czeslaw Milosz." *The Polish Review* XXXI, 4 (1986):257–84.

FRÉDÉRIC MISTRAL   *1904*

Frédéric Mistral (1830–1914), the son of a well-to-do farmer, was born, lived, and died in Maillane, a small village in Provence, in southern France. When he was sent to school in Saint-Michelle-Frigolet, and later in Avignon, he was shocked and deeply hurt to discover that Provençal, his mother tongue, was the object of derision and regarded as a patois to be used only by peasants and shepherds. This experience had a traumatic effect on the adolescent and determined the orientation of his life and his career. As he avidly studied the causes and history of the cultural subjugation of Provence, he discovered that the intellectuals had been the principal collaborators of the dominant power. "Let us not forget," he wrote, "that for four hundred years, all the forces and the malice of the human mind have been used to deprovençalize us. The most horrible thing is that all the intellectuals and all the prominent people of Provence have helped with all their influence this movement contrary to nature" (M. André *La Vie harmonieuse de Mistral*, Paris: Plon et Nourrit, 1928, p. 136).

While a student in Avignon, Mistral was encouraged to learn that one of his teachers, Joseph

Roumanille, also wrote poetry in Provençal. Soon they became friends and later, with Théodore Aubanel, they formed "the Félibrige trinity." The purpose of the Félibrige movement was to restore Provençal to literary dignity and, more generally, to preserve Provençal culture from annihilation by French political and cultural domination. The only language taught in the schools and used by the administration on all levels in Provence was French. Mistral was convinced that only in the context of a federalist system could the language and culture of Provence be reborn and have a chance for normal development. Although he never advocated the abrogation of the 1484 treaty of union of Provence with France, his position was misunderstood, and he was suspected of being a separatist—especially by those who subscribed to the Jacobin tradition and pursued relentlessly the goal of a centralized France in which only one language and one culture would exist. According to their scheme, all regional languages and cultures were to be tolerated as mere patois with the full expectation that in time, they would disappear completely. This form of intolerance of minority culture prevailed in all countries with cultural minorities. It is an aspect of imperialism. As a result of this situation, Mistral's enormous success had not merely a regional but a worldwide impact. (In 1913 the Chilean writer Lucila Godoy y Alcayaga chose the pseudonym Gabriela Mistral.) Wherever people struggle for the preservation of their language and culture, Mis-

tral's achievement and ideas often become an inspiration. Throughout Europe, ethnic leaders, especially the Catalan leader Balaguer and the Romanian Alecsandri, became Mistral's friends. The influence he had on them has been well documented. His relationship with other leaders will only slowly come to light since his archives, including his enormous correspondence, became accessible to scholars only in 1964.

While Victor Hugo was urging Europeans to unite and form one state, unification respecting ethnic identities has been a more attractive option for oppressed minorities. Like the founders of the Brotherhood of Cyril and Methodius, who proposed the creation of a confederation of the Slavs, Mistral wanted to unite Latin peoples, to form a Latin fraternity within which all minorities would enjoy equal rights and possibilities for cultural development. Thanks to the generally benevolent attitude of the French government, due in part to Mistral's extraordinary success and his oft repeated reassurances that his provincial patriotism was in no way antagonistic to patriotic allegiance to France, he was allowed to have a considerable influence in southern France. The fact is, he envisaged his Latin fraternity to be built around France, "the elder daughter of the Latin race, the shining light of modern civilization upon humanity."

The Félibrige movement had a considerable influence on European literature in general, and it contributed to the emancipation or cultural development of numerous peoples. Indirectly, its influence continues to

be felt. Félibrige aesthetics emphasize creative spontaneity—especially
by nonprofessional artists, by peasants and workers—or the adaptation and modernization of folkloric
works of the distant past in the restored and natural language of the
people. In France, such principles
caused a modest shift in literature
from aristocratic and bourgeois
styles, themes, and tastes toward
populist ones. Rooted in a traditional and Catholic rural society, the
movement had obvious artistic and
political limitations. Nonetheless, its
impact was considerable from the
beginning of Mistral's success in
1859 to World War I.

Mistral attained almost instan-
taneous fame in 1859, at the age of
twenty-nine, with his first work,
Mirèio, or Mireille in French, thanks
in part to the enthusiastic article by
the aging but still extremely popular
poet and former statesman Lamar-
tine, published in his Cours familier
de littérature ("An Informal Course
in Literature"). Merely three years
later, in 1862, Gounod wrote an immensely popular opera based on
Mireille, which contributed to the
poet's reputation in France and
abroad.

Mirèio is a pastoral epic poem
in twelve cantos, in which Mistral at
once displayed the full range of his
poetic imagination and a complete
mastery of the resources of the Provençal language, which he simultaneously enriched and elevated.
The plot, romantic in its inspiration,
is quite simple. A basket maker,
Ambroise, and his son, Vincent, are
received ьy Ramon, the master of

the wealthy Micocoules farm. Ramon's daughter, Mireille, is enchanted
as she listens to Ambroise sing old
songs and Vincent tell stories. Soon
Vincent and Mireille fall in love with
each other. The heiress to Micocoules rejects three suitors. The last,
Ourrias, who has discovered Mireille's secret love, challenges Vincent to a fight. Vincent manages to
have the upper hand, but as he
generously releases him, Ourrias
treacherously strikes and gravely
wounds Vincent. The young man is
brought to Micocoules. After Vincent is healed by a witch, his father
asks Ramon to allow Mireille to
marry his son. When he refuses, Mireille flees her father's house to
go and pray for the intercession
of the saints of Saintes-Maries-de-la-
Mer. As she rushes there, she suffers a sunstroke, and she is found in
time only to embrace Vincent and
die. In all its aspects, this masterpiece complies with the aesthetics of
the Félibrige movement, its poetic
qualities have inspired universal
admiration.

After Mirèio, Mistral published
a major work approximately every
seven years. In 1867, it was Calendau,
or Calendal, his second epic poem,
for which he sought inspiration in the
rich Provençal heritage of the trouba-
dours. The purpose of this work was
to express the needed struggle by
Provence against centralization in
order for its culture to survive.
Calendau is the best symbolic expression of the Félibrige ideal.

Calendal, a fine fisherman, tries
in vain to win Estérelle's love.
Touched, she finally tells him why

she cannot accept his love. She is the descendant of an illustrious troubadour family and is married to Count Séveran. She fled her husband, however, because of his rudeness and immorality. He is the leader of a band of brigands. Calendal challenges Séveran and performs numerous valorous deeds. When Séveran lures him into his castle where he tries to corrupt him, Calendal destroys everything in sight and flees to join Estérelle. Finally, he triumphs in love and glory. Estérelle is Mistral's only heroine who does not die, because she symbolizes Provence in her struggle for survival. Probably because it is more symbolic and abstract, *Calendal*'s popularity was never comparable to *Mirèio*'s.

The next work is *Isclo d'or* (1875; *Les Iles d'or*, "The Golden Isle"). It is a monumental collection of poems of various genres and on numerous themes, exemplifying the poetic possibilities of the Provençal language. Especially noteworthy is the allegory entitled "La Comtesse" ("The Countess"), which expresses Mistral's federalist concepts, and "La Coulpe" ("Guilt"), which became the Félibrige anthem.

In *Nerto* (1884; or *Nerte*), again a long love poem, Mistral uses a Faustian mythical structure set in fourteenth-century Avignon. A gambling lord sells his daughter Nerte's soul to the devil. When faced with the need to deliver his part of the bargain, he sends her to the pope for help. As she arrives at the castle, she meets Rodrigue de Luna, a young debauched adventurer who

happens to be the pope's nephew. After various vicissitudes, remembering the fate that awaits her, Nerte becomes a nun. Rodrigue comes to abduct her, but has to fight to reach her. When he is able to reach his beloved, she has disappeared. In despair he calls on Satan and presents to him the cross of his sword. Finally, Nerte and Rodrigue are saved and can enter into the kingdom of God.

Lou Pouèmo dou Rose or *Le Poème du Rhône* (1897; *Anglore: The Song of the Rhône*) is the love story of Guillaume, a Dutch prince of the House of Orange who while traveling on an ancient riverboat down the Rhône River in quest of his ancestors meets the beautiful Anglore, who is looking for gold. Their romance is ended when a steamboat causes their boat to sink. The crew of the ancient boat is saved, but the lovers are swallowed up by the Rhône, or the river dragon. In his quest of a mythical past, the prince stumbles on the prosaic but very real present, which sweeps all illusions away, including the poet's.

Mistral's poetic technique progressed significantly with his adoption of free verse in *Calendau*, which was to stir such interest a decade later among poets in France and elsewhere. Together with *Mirèio* and *Calendau*, *Lou Pouèmo dou Rose* constitutes the summit of Mistral's poetic achievement.

Les Oliviades (1912; "The Olives"), the last of Mistral's poetic works, has even less formal thematic unity than *Les Iles d'or*. Although it does not increase his prestige as a poet, several of the poems it contains are masterpieces. They express the poet's melancholy wisdom and constitute his literary and philosophical legacy.

Mistral's most autobiographical work, however, *Moun espelido; memóri e raconte* (1906; *Mes origines. Mes Mémoires et Récits* (English translation 1907; *Memoirs of Mistral*), are not strictly personal memoirs. His dignity and modesty would not have permitted him such direct outpouring. Instead, Mistral dwells on the leadership he exercised over the Félibrige movement for over fifty years and the role he played in the renaissance of Provençal culture.

To Mistral's poetic works one needs to add the three volumes of *Prose d'Almanach* (1926–30), and above all, *Lou Tresor dòu Félibrige; dictionnaire provençal—français embrassant les divers dialectes de la langue d'oc* (1876–86; "The Treasury of the Félibres"), which is a treasure of philological science so remarkable that its author received the Nobel Prize in 1904, in part for this work. He used the proceeds of the prize, which he shared with José Echegaray, to develop and enrich the ethnographic museum he had created in Arles.

While Mistral was deserving of the prize for his literary achievements alone, the Swedish Academy seemed to recognize and support all his efforts in defense of his threatened culture. Thanks in large part to Mistral, Provençal has survived and Provençal literature has continued to develop, albeit on a more modest

scale than the poet had wished because of the political and social upheavals of the past half century.

JEAN-PIERRE CAP

Selected Bibliography

PRIMARY SOURCES

Mistral, Frédéric. *Mémoires et récits. Correspondance* (choisie). Vol. 3. Aix-en-Province: Is ed. R. Berenguié, 1969.

———. *Oeuvres poétiques complètes de Frédéric Mistral.* Edited by Pierre Rollet. 2 vols. Aix-en-Provence: Is edicion Ramoun Berenguié, 1966.

SECONDARY SOURCES

Aldington, Richard. *Introduction to Mistral.* Carbondale: Southern Illinois University Press, 1960.

Bayle, Louis. *Grandeur de Mistral, essai de critique littéraire.* Toulon: Ed. de la Targo, 1964.

Boutière, Jean. *Lis Isclo d'or, édition critique.* 2 vols. Paris: Didier, 1970.

Decremps, Marcel. *Mistral, Mage de l'Occident.* Paris: La Columbe, 1954.

Jouveau, René. *Histoire du Félibrige 1870–1914.* Nîmes: Imprimerie Benel. Vol. 1, 1970; Vol. 2 (1914–41), 1977.

Lafont, Robert. *Mistral ou l'Illusion.* Paris: Plon, 1954.

———, and C. Anatole. *Nouvelle histoire de la littérature occitane.* Paris: Presses Universitaires Françaises, 1970.

Place, Georges. *Bibliographie de Frédéric Mistral.* Paris: Editions de la Chronique des lettres françaises, 1928–76.

Ripert, Emile. *Mireille des amours.* Paris: Editions Spes, 1930.

Scheludko, Dimitri. *Mistrals Nerto. Literarhistorische Studie.* Halle: Niemeyer, 1922.

———. *Lou Pourtoulan dòu pouémo dòu Rose.* In *Calendau.* t. 84. Montpellier: L'Auteur, 1940.

Talvart, Hector, and Joseph Place. *Bibliographie des auteurs de longue française (1801–1967)* etc. Vol. XVIII, 1968, pp. 69-221.

Teissier, Léon. *Calendau. Introduction au poème de Mistral.* Montpellier: l'Auteur, 1959.

GABRIELA MISTRAL 1945

In 1945 Lucila Godoy Alcayaga (1889–1957), known as Gabriela Mistral, became the first Latin American writer, and one of a handful of women, to win the Nobel Prize in literature. She had been born in Vicuña, in the northern part of Chile on April 6, 1889, but spent her adult years traveling almost continuously beyond the borders of her native land. She dedicated her life to education, to poetry, and to service to her country until her death in 1957. Mistral's pedagogical activities and governmental service did not prevent her from publishing several books of poetry, one collection of readings, two other prose works, and many journal articles. The poetry collections include *Desolación* (1922; "Desolation"), *Ternura* (1924; "Tenderness"), *Nubes blanca* ("White Clouds") and *La oración dela maestra* ("The Teacher's Prayer," published without the author's permission in 1926), *Tala* (1938; "Felling"), and *Lagar* ("Wine Press"). The prose anthology is entitled *Lecturasas para mujeres* (1924; *Readings for Women*); the other two prose works are *Recados* (1957; "Messages") and *Cantando a Chile* (1957; "Singing to Chile").

A career in teaching motivated most of Gabriela Mistral's life until 1925, even though in the rural Andean town where she spent her first years she had received little formal education. When Lucila was three years old her father deserted the family, and her mother and half-sister supported the household as teachers. Determined to prepare Lucila for teaching, they gave her instruction from the primary grades through normal school. In 1908, after experimenting with other pseudonyms, Godoy published a poem, "Del pasado" ("Of the Past") in the newspaper *El Cuquimbo Diario Radical* under the name Gabriela Mistral. By 1910 she was teaching high school, and after 1912, she made her home in Santiago, where she not only taught, but also continued to write and to seek an

appropriate spiritual path. The suicide in 1909 of a former lover had
saddened her, and she transformed
the incident into a literary monument. Her eleven "Sonetos de la
muerte," probably written in 1911
appeared in various newspapers and
journals. In 1922 the three most
famous appeared in her book
Desolatión.

In 1922 José Vasconcelos, secretary of education for the new postrevolutionary government of Mexico,
asked Mistral to participate in organizing the reform of the Mexican
national educational system. She accepted, in part in order to distance
herself from another unsatisfactory
love relationship. For two years she
lived and worked in Mexico, where
she became particularly interested in
teaching rural Indians and where
her Americanist view of the world
was strengthened.

After leaving Mexico, she traveled throughout Europe and visited
the United States, Puerto Rico,
Cuba, the Dominican Republic,
Panama, Guatemala, and El Salvador. Upon her return to Chile, she
became a member of the Chilean
diplomatic corps, serving in consu-
lates in Spain, Portugal, Brazil, and
the United States. Her travels also
took her to several South American
countries. In 1943 her nephew,
whom she had adopted as her son,
died under mysterious circumstances, probably a suicide. This
event contributed to the deteriora-
tion of her health. Two years later,
she accepted the Nobel Prize in literature. In 1953 Mistral served as
Chile's delegate to the United Nations, until illness forced her to re-

tire. In January 1957 she died of
pancreatic cancer in Long Island,
New York, where she had lived with
her friend Doris Dana since 1954.
Although Gabriela Mistral wrote in
several genres to friends, students,
colleagues, and readers around the
world, she is primarily remembered
as a poet.

Chronologically, Gabriela Mistral is part of the generation of poets
who wrote during the years after the
apex of Latin American modernism
and who borrowed meter, some
topoi, and experimentation with
form from the modernist poets, but
rejected their legacy of artifice and
exoticism. The lyrical, interiorizing
poetic voice they utilized was characteristic of post-modernist poetry.
Mistral is the most widely remembered woman of this generation,
which also included Delmira Agus-
tini (1886–1914), Juana de Ibarbou-
rou (1895–1979), and Alfonsina
Storni (1892–1938). She is best
known for her poems concerning
love, maternity, and death and for
her contemplative verses about God
and nature. Almost always, the first-
person-singular poetic voice speaks
to the poetic subject or to the reader.
Critics have sometimes read her
poetry as melodramatic autobiography in which love and death are
inextricably intertwined and in
which a maternity realized through
teaching and writing compensates
for the poet's real-life frustration.
Most agree, however, that she contributed in a fundamental manner to
the development of contemporary
Latin American poetry through the
use of creole and archaic vocabulary
from rural Chile, a refined lyrical

voice, descriptions of American landscapes and peoples, and sparsely adorned poetic forms.

Though she had been well-known in Chile, it was not until *Desolación* was compiled and published by the New York Hispanic Institute in 1922, that the poet's international reputation was established. Many of the themes developed in *Desolación* were reiterated and elaborated in later volumes of poetry, although the meter and rhythm of the first collection is more varied. Divided into several parts—subtitled "Vida" ("Life"), "La Escuela" ("School"), "Dolor" ("Sorrow"), "Para niños" ("For Children"), and "Naturaleza" ("Nature") —the volume also contains some prose poetry and four lullabies. Many critics argue that *Desolación* contains Mistral's greatest poetry. Certainly, several of her most widely quoted and anthologized poems appear in this volume, including "Los sonetos de la muerte."

The three "Los sonetos de la muerte" combine several of Mistral's typical themes: human love expressed through maternity, the consolation of nature, a religious sense of life and death. The pretext for writing these verses enables the poet to meditate on human communication, life, and death. She expresses anger, sadness, and existential fatigue in moving, lyrical verses that metaphorically evoke nature. In the first sonnet, she speaks to a dead person: "From the icy niche in which men put you, / I will lower you to the humble and sunny ground." In the third, she addresses God: "His little boat pushes the black wind of a storm. / Return him to my arms or you reap him as he flowers."

The Spanish American landscape, frequently admired and praised in Mistral's poems, becomes a symbol of Americanist sentiments, and may be associated with America's indigenous heritage. In *Tala* ("Felling"), for instance, in a section entitled "America," the palm trees of Puerto Rico express hope for a better future, "Mar Caribe" ("Caribbean Sea"); the importance of corn to Mexican cultures poeticizes history, "El maiz" ("Corn"); the Andean mountains, especially in Chile, become a maternal symbol of unity, "Cordillera" ("Mountain Range"). Mayan and Incan cosmology, whose center is the "mature American sun," form the basis for a description of the land, "Sol del tropico" ("Tropical Sun"). "Recado a Victoria Ocampo" ("Message to Victoria Ocampo"), in the section called "Recados" ("Messages"), ends with a farewell to the Argentinian literary luminary Ocampo and asks that she take care of "the American lands."

In her concern that a poetry worthy of the Spanish American landscape be written, Mistral shares a place in literary history with Pablo Neruda. "One misses," she said, "when looking at the indigenous monuments or the Andes, a complete voice that has the courage to approach those formidable materials." However, the variety of personalized tones with which she writes about the Latin American landscape avoids the epic quality of, for example, Neruda's "Machu Picchu." Instead, the author expresses deeply felt spiritual communication with natural surroundings.

The poetic rendition of the Chilean mountainous terrain, fueled by nostalgic memories of childhood, is intensely personalized. In the poems of "Tierra de Chile" ("Land of Chile") and in the long narrative "Poema de Chile" ("Poem of Chile") places and scenes are evoked through the author's perceptions and thoughts. The reader becomes, in a sense, a companion on this journey of remembrance in which the repeated use of the first-person singular emphasizes the emotive quality of the verses.

God is a frequent interlocutor in the nature poems, in the children's verses, and in the poems about everyday objects and events. There are also many explicitly religious poems. As Cáceres discusses in the introduction to the *Poesías Completas* (1966; *Complete Poems*), Mistral's humanistic Catholicism, tempered with anguish, is influenced by Maritain. "Credo" ("Credo") and "Nocturno" ("Nocturne") (in *Desolación*) draw upon and personalize standard Catholic prayers. A section of *Lagar* ("Wine Press"), entitled "Religiosas" ("Religious Ones"), includes poems on a variety of subjects, from a European cathedral to an Indian Christmas. Although Mistral occasionally rails at the divine being, she elaborates a surely felt Christianity and places her faith in God, especially in his manifestation as Jesus Christ. Hers is a God, like Saint Teresa of Avila, who "walks among the pots and pans"; that is, he exists everywhere, even in factories "Patrón de los telares" ("Patron of Cloth Mills").

Some overtly religious poems treat female biblical characters. In the first section of *Lagar* entitled "Locas mujeres" ("Crazy Women"), a poem about Martha and Mary expresses Mistral's parallel vocations: activity and contemplation. A sonnet sequence from *Desolación* rewrites the story of Ruth and Boaz. Each of the three poems in this series re-creates one moment of the narrative, but as Mandlove has pointed out, the shifts in emphasis highlight Ruth's equality with Boaz, as well as her autonomy.

An experiential (not political) sense of identification as a woman, based on the stages of life, may be perceived in many of the poems of (*Tala*) which begins with the section "Muerte de mi madre" ("Death of My Mother"). In "Todas íbamos a ser reinas" ("We Were All Going to Be Queens"), a poem set in the Elqui valley where Mistral grew up, she evokes childhood through an apocryphal game sung by a group of girls. "Vieja" ("The Old Woman") personifies death, but the poem ends with a reference to a trio of female saints who "could not die": Clare of Assis, Catherine of Siena, Teresa of Avila.

Mistral privileges maternity throughout her poetry and glorifies the mother-child relationship in *Ternura* ("Tenderness"), her book of children's poems. Included are lullabies, rounds, other games, stories, and hymns. Although the tone is sometimes sad, a religious view of life again emerges. These poems are highly concrete; they use highly visual and aural rhyme schemes and vocabulary. The alternating shorter and longer lines of the lullaby "Meciendo" ("Rocking"), for instance, imitate the rhythmic, soothing sounds of a rocking chair. Some poems evoke the local flora and fauna of the rural mountainous region in which Mistral was raised. Others are sentimental evocations of motherhood, in which the child speaks, such as "Caricia" ("Caress"): "Mother, mother, you kiss me/but I kiss you more,/and the swarm of my kisses/doesn't let you even look. . . ."

Throughout Mistral's active life as a pedagogue, an educational reformer, and a diplomat, she wrote poetry. Mistral, a very self-conscious writer, was sensitive to critiques of her treatment of poetic form. Before they were published, she repeatedly polished and rewrote almost all her poems, choosing meter, syntax, and lexicon with great care. Although the reader is not privy to the revisions in the finished product, her concern with the process of writing, and with literary production, appear as poetic themes. In a section of *Tala* titled "Historias de loca" ("Stories of a Crazy Woman"), for instance, the poem "La flordel aire" ("Flower of the Air") personifies poetry as a female spirit who leads the speaker through mountainous terrain; the author's note calls the poem her "adventure with poetry."

Gabriela Mistral's compassion for others and holistic view of the world moved her to write poems on many topics, from human suffering to the orindary aspects of daily life: about the Jewish people, the Indians, a prisoner's wife, salt, water, bread. There are no verses by Mistral in which the substance of things, as Valéry has said, is not present. In general, hers is a sparingly ornamented poetry; she prefers "voluntary prosaicisms," as she has said. Serene in its spiritual certainty and its compassionate recognition of all living creatures, her poetry evokes for her readers the dignity and warmth with which she lived.

STACEY SCHLAU

Selected Bibliography

PRIMARY SOURCES

Mistral, Gabriela. *Selected Poems of Gabriela Mistral.* Translated by Langston Hughes. Bloomington: Indiana University Press, 1959, 1962, 1966, 1972.

――――. *Poesías completas.* Edited by Margaret Bates. Introduction by Esther de Cáceres. 3rd ed. Biblioteca Premios Nobel. Madrid: Aguilar, 1966.

――――. *Crickets and Frogs: A Fable in Spanish and English.* Translated and adapted by Doris Dana. Illustrated by Antonio Frasconi. New York: Atheneum, 1972.

――――. *Index to Gabriela Mistral Papers on Microfilm (1912–1957).* Washington, D.C.: Organization of American States, General Secretariat, Department of Cultural Affairs, Department of Cultural Affairs, 1982.

SECONDARY SOURCES

Algería, Fernando. "Notes Toward a Definition of Gabriela Mistral's Ideology." In *Women in Hispanic*

Literature: Icons and Fallen Idols. Edited by Beth Miller. Berkeley, Los Angeles, London: University of California Press, 1983. Pp. 215–26.

——. *Genio y figura de Gabriela Mistral.* Buenos Aires: Editorial Universitaria de Buenos Aires, 1966.

Arce de Vasquez, Margot. *Gabriela Mistral: The Poet and Her Work.* Translated by Helene Masslo Anderson. New York: New York University Press, 1964.

Castleman, William J. *Beauty and the*

Mission of the Teacher: The Life of Gabriela Mistral of Chile: Teacher, Poetess, Friend of the Helpless, Nobel Laureate. Smithtown, N.Y.: Exposition, 1982.

Preston, Mary C. *A Study of Significant Variants in the Poetry of Gabriela Mistral.* Washington, D.C.: Catholic University of America Press, 1964.

Taylor, Martin C. *Gabriela Mistral's Religious Sensibility.* Berkeley: University of California Press, 1968.

THEODOR MOMMSEN *1902*

Historian Theodor Mommsen (1817–1903) was the first German writer ever to receive the Nobel Prize in literature. He was born on November 30, 1817, in Garding (Schleswig) and died almost eighty-six years later, on November 1, 1903, at Charlottenburg near Berlin. The Nobel statutes declare that any literature other than belles lettres may be awarded this prize as long as it is distinguished by excellence in both content and form. It was primarily Mommsen's comprehensive, widely translated *Römische Geschichte* (1854–56; *History of Rome*) for which the Swedish Academy awarded him the Nobel Prize in 1902.

Mommsen was the son of a Protestant pastor. He and his two younger brothers—Tycho, with whom he would later carry on a productive and revealing correspondence, and Albert—developed a deep interest in classical studies at an early age. They were gifted and diligent students who dedicated themselves to serious studies in and out of school. The Mommsen family soon moved from Schleswig, then a part of Denmark, to Oldesloe, and from there to Altona, where Theodor attended the gymnasium until 1838. At the age of twenty-one he entered the university at Kiel, where he studied philology, history, and law, especially Roman, which would arouse Mommsen's lifelong interest in antiquities.

His doctoral dissertation dealt with "The Secretaries and Marshals of the Roman Magistrates." It initiated a long and rich career of scholarship and teaching that spanned some sixty years and dealt with Roman history, chronology, life, coinage, inscriptions, and law. Mommsen's thorough and precise research, his determination to gather new evidence, his vast knowledge of the subject matter, and his mastery and eloquence of literary style and expression soon made him one of the most respected and productive German scholars of the nineteenth century.

Mommsen's acceptance of a Danish scholarship to study in Italy from 1844 to 1847 was a significant event in his life. He traveled throughout Italy, learned to speak and write the Italian language, and started the ambitious project of collecting and recording Latin inscriptions, most of which had remained unread and unrecorded. His objective was to prepare complete and accurate copies of all discovered texts that had been recorded on bronze, iron, or stone. He would eventually make these inscriptions available in a spectacular and immense collection entitled *Corpus Inscriptionum Latinarum* (1863 and after). Mommsen became the editor in chief of this colossal work, endorsed and sponsored by the Berlin Academy of Sciences. Its publication and success would have been unthinkable without Mommsen's flawless scientific approach, rare organizational skills, untiring dedication, and iron will.

In the revolutionary year 1848 Mommsen received his first professorship at Leipzig. At the same time the tumultuous political events in Germany activated his interest in politics. Earlier in his life, he had opposed the Danish rule over Schleswig by advocating the region's integration into a unified German nation. Although a liberal at heart, he favored rule by monarchy as long as it ensured basic human rights and freedoms. His political outspokenness and criticism of Saxony's government resulted in his being prosecuted in court and dismissed from the university. Mommsen fled to Switzerland, where he became professor in Zurich in 1852. When he returned to Germany two years later, he received a law professorship at the University of Breslau. In 1858 he moved to Berlin, where he lived until his death.

During his Breslau years three volumes of Mommsen's monumental and celebrated work, *The History of Rome*, appeared. Volume four, a history of the emperors, was never written, but volume five was published in 1885. This last work covered the Roman rule of the provinces from the time of Caesar to Diocletian. *The History of Rome* clearly established Mommsen's fame as one the greatest scholars and writers of the nineteenth century. It was read by specialists and nonspecialists alike and earned for its author high marks for brilliant style, lively imagination, and vast knowledge of the history of Rome and Italy, as well as for Mommsen's tendency to compare events in Roman history with certain major political developments and attitudes in nineteenth-century Germany.

Mommsen's work is foremost a comprehensive reference work that ranges from the first settlers in Italy to the first decades of Rome, from the unification of Italy to the defeat of Carthage and the Greek states, from arts, literature, and religion to sciences, laws, economy, and commerce. He documented the times from the Romans' modest beginnings to their domination of the ancient world; he traced the increasing demands of a growing empire to Rome's disregard of legal restraints imposed by the old constitution; and he described in great detail the prolonged and fierce political struggles that led to the fall of the republic. His account reflects intuition and insight and frequently rivals the force, eloquence, and realism of a mid-nineteenth-century German novel. He displayed an extraordinary gift for describing battles with poetic flair and the confidence of an astute historian; and he never failed to show at length the roles played in these battles by their victorious or humiliated architects, generals, and warriors. In reflecting on major decisive developments and decisions of the past as well as on the achievements or follies of Roman statesmen and leaders, he presented the course of history as being a continuous struggle between freedom and necessity.

His portrayals, both positive and negative, of such men as Sulla, Pompey, Hannibal, Cicero ("a journalist in the worst sense of the word"), C. Gracchus ("a political incendiary"), Mommsen's idol and absolute protector of the decaying Republic, Caesar ("the complete and perfect man"), and numerous others were drawn with power of the word and passion of judgment. Mommsen was criticized for often abandoning his objective narration in favor of subjective judgments, and for allowing his feelings and emotions to interfere with an otherwise rational detachment from events and the actors in them. It was said that Mommsen never loved or hated things by halves and that he was quick to judge from feeling and prejudice. But it was this side of his writing that made Mommsen popular with the educated and uneducated alike, both of whom learned about their present while reading about a past long gone. "How miserable and small is the world," he wrote "in the eyes of a man who sees in it only Greek and Latin authors, or mathematical problems." The study of history, Mommsen believed, sheds light on problems of the past that remain unresolved to this day. Thus, unsettled conflicts and issues of the past may become challenges and opportunities of the future. For example, in the three hundred years that lay between the age of Augustus and Diocletian, Mommsen claimed, the hope and need of Jews and non-Jews to live together peacefully became but an illusion. Instead, hate, arrogance, and contempt destroyed the hope for mutual respect, understanding, and a peaceful coexistence. "The legacy of these times," Mommsen sadly stated, "still burdens mankind to this day."

In his *History of Rome* Mommsen clearly revealed his personal understanding of history. He did not glorify the Roman past, idealizing and glamorizing its grandeur and achievements as had been done in the eighteenth century. Rather, he clearly saw both the empire's greatness and decay, its struggle for freedom and its necessary submission to the powers of fate, the struggle of the empire for distinction and progress and its inevitable fall and final defeat. Like a plant, the Roman Empire was born, blossomed, and perished. In a larger sense, he said, "the history of mankind is a continuous step ahead and a step back." As natural as is a people's march toward greatness is the necessity of its inevitable collapse. History repeats itself, empires rise and fall, but life goes on. "A new dawn is not possible," he claimed in his third volume, "until the world first lies in darkness." But the new day surely comes, handing over to those who survive the educational tools with which to build and shape a new future. History is "our teacher," it is like a "Bible," to whose better understanding Mommsen would dedicate his life and career.

His total dedication to scholarship culminated in an avalanche of publications. He had more than 900 items published before his seventieth birthday, and more than 1,500 when he died at the age of eighty-five. Three other works that received much attention were his *Geschichte des Römischen Münzwesens* (*History of the Roman Coinage*), published in 1860, *Römisches Staatsrecht* (*Roman Constitutional Law*), published in three volumes between 1871 and 1888, and the last of his major works, *Römisches Strafrecht* (*Roman Criminal Law*) in 1899.

Mommsen was particularly proud of his *Roman Constitutional Law*. He did not attribute much legal authority to the Roman Senate, for in strictly legal terms it played a lesser role than the popular assembly and the magistrates. In Mommsen's view, the Roman state was a legal order; its legal provisions constituted the essence of the state. He examined very closely the constitutional roles played during the republic by the popular assembly and the magistrates on one hand, both of which were institutions of law, and the Senate on the other, which he saw at the center of the state but only de facto. Although one task of the Senate was to prevent the disobedience of the magistrates, Mommsen made it clear that any decision made by the Senate was inconsequential, for only the legal aspects of the state were, according to Mommsen, the essential ingredients of a legal order. Mommsen paid less attention to other aspects of the state, such as its economy, sociology, and philosophy, which he considered less important or irrelevant. Of course, modern scholars have since gone beyond Mommsen's narrow boundaries of research as they examined essential economic and social factors in the development of the Roman state, as, for example, Marxist historians have done. Nevertheless, Mommsen's gigantic effort led to a better understanding of Roman constitutional law, which he brilliantly codified, systematized, and clarified and which covers the period to the end of the third century.

It is remarkable that Mommsen found time to pursue activities other than research and writing. He and his devoted wife raised a large family that included sixteen children. It is probable, however, that his children received less of their father's attention than his personal library and the scholarship to which he dedicated most hours of the day and night. Sunday was not a day of rest but of continued work. He worked at a furious, disciplined pace, missing hardly one day due to illness his life long. During his last forty or so years he had become one of the best-known personalities in Germany. He was the embodiment of the learned scholar whose presence had furthered the image of the German university throughout Europe. Mommsen, a rather tiny man with piercing eyes and generously thick, long white hair, became a living monument of intellectual greatness and respectability.

Another activity demanding much of his time was politics. Mommsen, the historian, never hesitated to express himself forcefully and emotionally on decisive events and leading politicians of his day. Some 150 of his publications reflect his political views and include recommendations for change and reform. As early as 1848 he had pleaded for German unity and the establishment of a constitutional monarchy that would protect fundamental human rights and freedoms, including academic freedom. Although he remained a historian foremost, he became so involved in politics that he was elected to serve in the Prussian Landtag from 1863 to 1866 and from 1873 to 1879 and to a seat in the German Reichstag from 1881 to 1884. But numerous critics, Chancellor Bismarck included, were more complimentary of Mommsen the historian than the politician. When Mommsen dared call Bismarck's economic policy a "swindle" since it seemed to serve special-interest groups more than sponsor education and welfare programs for the old and poor, Bismarck brought Mommsen to court for libel. The liberal Mommsen never cared for the Iron Chancellor's autocratic leadership.

As he became older, Mommsen frequently expressed his concern over Germany's illusion of greatness and power. He warned his listeners and readers of the inherent danger of rising nationalism, militarism, and anti-Semitism. He became embroiled with noted historian and colleague Heinrich von Treitschke, whose anti-Semitic essays from 1878 angered Mommsen into publishing his *Auch ein Wort über unser Judentum* (*My Word about Our Jewry*). The rising anti-Semitism at the end of the nineteenth century was not yet racial in character but cultural and economic. Mommsen attacked Treitschke for demanding that his "Jewish fellow citizens" become Germans. "They are Germans," Mommsen replied, "as much as he and I." He called Treitschke's articles "miscarriages of national feeling," particularly since Treitschke seemed to have spoken for most of his colleagues. Mommsen cut off all ties with his equally famous colleague. He became more troubled over Germany's conspicuous plan to gain greater political power. In light of various ominous developments not many years after his death in 1903, some of his prophetic last writings on the social, academic, military, and political trends in Germany at the turn of the century warrant greater study today.

With his death, the German universities lost perhaps their most skillful, meticulous, patient, and knowledgeable historian, whose works became masterpieces in both content and literary grace. He had worked tirelessly—writing, lecturing, and acting as the editor of the monumental *Corpus Inscriptionum Latinarum*, while serving as the long-time secretary to the Berlin Academy. He should also be remembered as one who advocated strong educational programs, who defended the truth in all things written and taught, and who cherished those human freedoms without which a society could not hope to survive, grow, and prosper.

HANS WUERTH

Selected Bibliography

PRIMARY SOURCES

Mommsen, Theodor. *Abriss des römischen Staatsrechts.* 1899. Darmstadt: Wissenscheftliche Buchgesellschaft, 1982.

———. *The Provinces of the Roman Empire: The European Provinces.* 1888. Edited by T. Robert Broughton. Chicago: University of Chicago Press, 1968.

———. *Römische Geschichte.* 1854–56. Munich: Deutscher Taschenbuch Verlag, 1976. English edition: *The History of Rome.* Glencoe, Ill.: Free Press, 1957.

SECONDARY SOURCES

Bekker, E. J. *Ein Philosoph der Tat, Theodor Mommsen.* Berlin: Archiv für Rechts- und Wirtschaftsphilosophie, 1911.

Fowler, W. Warde. "Theodor Mommsen: His Life and Work." In *Roman Essays and Interpretations.* Oxford, U.K.: Clarendon Press, 1920. Pp. 250–68.

Hartmann, Judo Moritz. *Theodor Mommsen: Eine Biographische Skizze.* Gotha: F. A. Perthes, 1908.

Heuss, Alfred. *Theodor Mommsen und das 19. Jahrhundert.* Kiel: Ferdinand Hirt, 1956.

Liebeschütz, Hans. "Treitschke and Mommsen on Jewry and Judaism." In *Year Book VII.* London and New York: Secker & Warburg for the *Leo Baeck Institute of Jews from Germany*, 1962. Pp. 153–82.

Mommsen, A. *Theodor Mommsen im Kreise der Seinen.* Berlin: E. Ebering, 1936.

Wickert, Lothar. *Theodor Mommsen: Eine Biographie.* 4 vols. Frankfurt: V. Klostermann, 1958–80.

Wucher, Albert. *Theodor Mommsen. Geschichtsschreibung und Politik.* Berlin: Musterschmidt-Verlag, 1956.

EUGENIO MONTALE   *1975*

Eugenio Montale (1896–1981) was born in Genoa, Italy, on October 12, 1896, the last of five children. His father was a successful businessman, dealing in chemicals and paint-related products. Montale's schooling, undertaken entirely in his native city, ended on account of his poor health as he was completing the third year of technical school. Ironically, his first preference was not literature, but music—voice, in particular. This great love was to prove long-lasting and was to manifest itself not only in the musicality of his verse but in the position that he later held as music critic for Milan's *Corriere d'Informazione*. His formal music training—begun in 1915 and interrupted on account of the war—ended abruptly in 1923 with the death of his mentor, Ernesto Sivori, one of the most renowned baritones of that period.

In this same period Montale widened his literary knowledge by studying the Italian classics and such foreign authors as Shakespeare, Milton, Eliot, Cervantes, Bergson, and Bourtroux (all of whom he later translated), as well as contemporary Genoese poets such as Boine, Ceccardi, and Sbarbaro.

The fruits of this intense formative period were evident in his first major publication, *Gli Ossi di seppia* (1925; *The Bones of Cuttlefish*). Most of these poems had already appeared in some of the finest literary journals of the time. As the title suggests, the poems were to be sim-ilar to the cuttlefish bones that can be seen scattered throughout the rugged, arid land- and seascape of his Ligurian region. In this desolate "waste land," Montale attempted to answer some of the universal thematic questions confronting mankind. He felt that man is doomed to hardship and suffering and that escape is difficult if not impossible, especially in his own case. This does not mean, however, that man should lower his head in total submission to his fate, as he explained in one of the last compositions of this collection. Montale shows that even though a chain-link barrier imprisons man, somewhere an opening might exist. It is this opening that man ought to desperately seek if he wishes to leap through to "safety." The "illusion" of escape remains the single most positive element throughout the volume.

Through the use of real images, like the continuous wall, the scale-like infinite sea, the dry and split earth, the glaring sunlight at midday, the vegetable and fruit gardens, and finally, the chain-link barrier, Montale offers understandable real barriers and obstacles that man must face throughout his lifetime and eventually learn to cope with. Life moves on relentlessly toward the abyss of oblivion, and it is useless for man to attempt to stop its course or to offer plausible explanations. In the end, man's fate is like the sistrum sounds of the cicada, which will soon vanish into nothingness as summer ends. As a consoling force, Montale offers a redeeming grace in the form of "love," which man ought to learn to cherish since it alone can help him to turn the "illusion" into a possible reality.

On April 30, 1925, Montale signed Benedetto Croce's antifascist cultural manifesto. The person who previously had always shunned active political participation felt morally compelled to take a stand. On this, he stated that culture has the moral obligation to defend its rights and to free itself from politics. That same year he also published an important critical essay on the Italian writer Italo Svevo, which proved extremely influential in the discovery of this previously unknown great writer.

In 1927 Montale, "intellectually stifled" by the Genoese lifestyle, moved to Florence, accepting employment with the Bemporad publishers. Although not greatly satisfying, this position did offer him the opportunity to meet many of the leading literary figures of his time.

In 1929 Montale succeeded Bonaventura Tecchi, another well-known Italian writer, as director of the "Vieusseux Cabbinet," the leading Italian intellectual professional state honorary society. A decade later, however, he was forced to resign because of his antifascist political ideology and because he refused to become a member of that party.

In 1931 he was awarded the literary prize for the best Italian poetry of the year, the "Antico fattore," for his *La Casa dei doganieri e altri versi* (*The Customshouse and Other Verses*), which later became

part of his second volume, *Le Occasioni* (1939; *The Occasions*). The latter marks the beginning of what most critics have called "Montale's second poetic season," as it presents a considerable shift in the thematic as well as syntactic makeup of his compositions. While his first book had offered a picture of the barren landscapes of his Ligurian region and presented the innumerable hardships and vicissitudes facing mankind as a whole and himself in particular, this collection shifted his attention to the area of Tuscany and of Florence in particular, where he was residing at the time. Now the "occasion" inspired him to create a particular composition, and "woman" became his primary inspirational force. Compared with his first volume, *The Occasions* represents Montale's more mature contribution. While the languid Crepuscular poets had been the predominant stylistic influence on his earlier compositions, it is to the Hermetic school that he looked for his new poetic directions. His new work featured a reduction of adjectives and other modifiers, the use of the "analogy," and the use of the "pure" meaning of the word. Thematically, the collection reveals an even greater feeling of tragic expectation in life than *The Bones of Cuttlefish*. Moving from the premise that man stands alone in the universe, Montale concluded that quite often it is vain even to hope for consolation. His final message, one of desolation and despair, emphasizes that there is no hope and no escape possible from the net that encircles us. The move from his native shores to the region of Florence also brought a noticeable shift in the landscape and imagery in this work. Montale himself once acknowledged in his diary that the twenty years spent in Florence proved to be the most important ones toward his maturation. Montale's poetic introduction and development of "the woman figure" qualifies as a great symbolic addition to his literary accomplishments. Becoming a most powerful and poetic force, "the woman figure," revealed as "Clizia," "Iride," or "Volpe" in this collection, and identified in subsequent works as "Annette," or "Adelheit," actually achieves a status of poetry itself. Montale's literary use of "the woman figure" will ultimately inspire and influence man to engage in the universal search for the ultimate "Good."

His collaboration with the Milan newspapers *Il Corriere della Sera* and *Il Corriere d'Informazione* influenced Montale to move to that city, where, in 1956, he published his third volume of poetry, *La Bufera ed altro* (*The Storm and Other Things*). The first part of this volume contained poems that had been published clandestinely at Lugano, Switzerland, in 1943 under the title *Finisterre*. *The Storm*, which began Montale's third poetic "season," also catapulted him into international fame. The University of Rome was the first to recognize his greatness when it conferred on him the university degree "honoris causa" in 1961. During this period he made numerous trips abroad, beginning with his travels to England and Syria in 1946 and followed by those to Switzerland, New York,

France, Spain, Portugal, Greece, Palestine, and finally to Israel in 1964. Most of these experiences he later reported in *Fuori di Casa* (1969; *Abroad*).

Although Montale consistently shunned direct involvement in the politics of his troubled nation, in 1967 then-president of the republic Giuseppe Saragat granted him an honorary appointment as senator for life. In December 1975 the Royal Swedish Academy conferred upon him the Nobel Prize for his poetic contribution to the literary world. In accepting the prize, Montale addressed the issue, "Is poetry still possible?"

Unlike his Italian predecessor Salvatore Quasimodo, Montale's active literary career did not end with the Nobel award. After receiving the prize, Montale published three more volumes of poetry: *Satura* (1971), *Diario del '71 e del '72* (1973; *Diary of 1971 and of 1972*), and *Quaderno di quattro anni* (1977; translated as *It Depends: A Poet's Notebook*), his final collection.

These new works again showed noticeable changes in his style and themes. Even though *The Storm* continued to use the imagery of destruction and desolation, and retained almost throughout the same background of violence and of human solitude, it also revealed the positive development of Montale's imagery of woman. In *The Occasions* Montale, because of the ruling fascist power, had removed himself from an active participation in life's events. *The Storm*, on the other hand, reversed that trend. With the fall of the fascist state, Montale felt a desperate need to participate again in the vital life flow of events. *The Storm* was for him the creative work that vividly would reflect a part of life itself. In this endeavor, woman was to become the redeeming grace not only for the poet, but for humanity as a whole. Unquestionably, *The Storm* constitutes Montale's most tormented production. Although Clizia remains the poet's inspirational and guiding force throughout the volume, Montale's efforts to negate the existence of God are complicated by his ironic attempts to reach His realm. The impossibility of this quest undoubtedly demonstrates his tormenting unrest.

In *The Diary of 1971 and of 1972*, Montale began to shift to a proselike style. Striking are the author's evaluations of the postwar years and the delusions they brought him.

A Poet's Notebook portrays a writer who has left the loftier heights of poetry that he had previously known. Most of these compositions, written in conversational style, describe everyday events. Interestingly, with the single exclusion of despair, the word *death* and the sentiments related to this phenomenon become a current theme throughout this work.

In order to summarize Montale's work, one should perhaps return to his *Intenzioni: Un' Intervista Immaginaria* (1946; "Intentions: Imaginary Interview"), which the author used to create a specific concept of what constituted an exemplary poet based on his social experience. Holding the great Ugo Foscolo as his poetic model, Montale stated that a poet ought not "waste" his voice in numberless repetitive compositions but ought to captivate the "occasion" and sing it. The poet has the final obligation and duty to sing of "man's conditions" and not so much the particular historic event.

Eugenio Montale died in Milan on Saturday, September 12, 1981, exactly one month before his eighty-fifth birthday.

ERASMO G. GERATO

Selected Bibliography

PRIMARY SOURCE

Montale, Eugenio. *L'Opera in versi*. A cura di Rosanna Bettarini e Gianfranco Contini. Turin: Einaudi, 1980.

SECONDARY SOURCES

Almansi, Guido, and Bruce Merry. *Eugenio Montale. The Private Language of Poetry*. Edinburgh: Edinburgh University Press, 1977.

Barile, Laura. *Bibliografia montaliana*. Milan: Mondadori, 1977.

Brandeis, Irma. "Eugenio Montale." *Saturday Review of Literature* LXVI (July 18, 1963): 1–32.

Cambon, Glauco. *Eugenio Montale: A Critical Study of His Poetry, Prose and Criticism*. New Haven and London: Yale University Press, 1973.

Caprioglio, Giuliana. "Intellectual and Sentimental Modes of Rapport with Reality in Montale's 'Ossi' and 'Occasioni.'" *Italian Quarterly* LIX (1969): 50–66.

Martelli, Mario. *Eugenio Montale.* Florence: Le Monnier, 1982.

Pipa, Arsi. *Montale and Dante.* Minneapolis: University of Minnesota Press, 1968.

Rebay, Luciano. "I diaspori di Montale." *Italica* 46 (1969): 33–53.

Singh, Ghanshyam. *Eugenio Montale: A Critical Study of His Poetry, Prose and Criticism.* New Haven and London: Yale University Press, 1973.

West, Rebecca J. *Eugenio Montale: Poet on the Edge.* Cambridge, Mass., and London: Harvard University Press, 1981.

PABLO NERUDA *1971*

Chilean poet Pablo Neruda (1904–73) was awarded the Nobel Prize in literature in 1971, but long before he was accorded this honor, Néruda was one of Latin America's most famous writers.

Neruda's writings reflect the unique situation of the Latin American people, which was recognized by the Swedish Academy when it cited his works as "poetry that with the action of an elemental force brings alive the continent's destiny and dreams." His poetry illuminates the reality of Latin American—and, more specifically, Chilean—life. The poet's strength is rooted in his ability to express the everyday occurrences and anguish of the Chilean people.

Neruda was born Neftali Ricardo Reyes Basoalto (changed to Neruda in the 1920s) in Parral, Chile, on July 12, 1904.

His mother died shortly after his birth, and his father, a train conductor, moved the family to Temuco, in southern Chile, and later remarried. Neruda lived in Temuco for fifteen years, where he came to admire Chile's Indian culture and identified with the country's oppressed peasants. The family lived a modest life in Temuco, and Neruda occupied his time reading and writing poetry for hours. As a young student, he was constantly mocked for his love of poetry by his fellow students and his proletarian father, but he found a friend in Gabriela Mistral. Mistral, a Nobel laureate herself, recognized Neruda's talent and supported his thirst for knowledge by supplying him with many books.

By 1921 Neruda had won many literary prizes in Temuco. The time had arrived for him to expand his horizons. The young poet moved to the capital, Santiago, where he continued his studies and became a French teacher. His writing flourished and in 1923 at the age of nineteen he published his first work, *Crepusculario*, a collection of poems. *Crepusculario* coincided with the ascension to power of Arturo Alesandri, who was inaugurated as president of Chile with grand illusions, supported by the middle class, and considered almost demigodlike. It was a time in Chile when university education was flourishing, and Neruda's first work reflected this. It is enriched with romanticism, enthusiasm, and liveliness, but it also depicts an open sensitivity to the social uneasiness and problems that plagues his contemporary Chile. *Crepusculario* and most of the poet's early works were of the symbolist-"modernista" genre.

While his poetry was a literary success, it did not provide Neruda a steady income. Thus, to earn a living, he was forced to write newspaper articles and act as a translator. He, however, was neither happy with himself nor his poetry. He needed to escape Santiago and move about the world in search of new experiences. Neruda in 1927 was appointed honorary consul to Rangoon in Burma, and it was from there that he journeyed throughout Europe seeking new adventures and happiness. During his time abroad, however, he experienced poverty, disorientation, and loneliness. In 1930 Neruda accepted the post as consul in Batavia, the capital of the Dutch West Indies, where he fell in love with and married a Dutch girl. In 1932 he returned to Chile and published *El hondero entusiasta* ("The Ardent Slingsman") and *Residencia en la tierra* (1925–1931; *Residence on Earth*), both of which

dealt with his travels abroad. Once again his poetry could not support his family, and he was forced to take a government position. An unhappy Neruda was appointed consul to Barcelona in 1934. In Barcelona, and a few months later when he moved to Madrid, Neruda's success mounted. After separating from his wife in 1936, Neruda fell in love again, befriended Federico García Lorca (the great Spanish poet), and became an ardent supporter of the Spanish Republicans. In 1936 too, he became intimately involved in radical politics and the communist movement, and he founded the review *Los poetas del mundo defiencien al pueblo español* (*Poets of the World Defend the Spanish People*). In 1937 he co-published *España en el coruzón* ("Spain in My Heart"), which signified the end of Neruda's loneliness, for now he had become politicized and had found a cause worthy of his time and energy.

Neruda returned to Chile in 1940 to work on *Canto General* ("General Song"), but he could not remain sedentary for very long. He traveled extensively through Latin America and compiled poems based on his experiences while traveling. In 1945, back in Chile, Neruda was elected senator in the provinces of Tarapaca and Antofagasta. In July of the same year he joined the Communist party, but his election and political allegiance came at a time when the Left was losing support. Neruda in 1946 supported a leftist candidate for president who surprisingly won the election, but soon he began to persecute his people and crack down on the labor unions, the

Communist party, and intellectuals. In Chile strict censorship became the norm. Neruda was removed from his Senate seat and forced underground. During this period Neruda finished *Canto General*, which deals with the indignation, anger, and repression that he felt while living in repressive Chile. Neruda left in 1949 and made his way to Mexico, where he met and fell in love with Matilde Urrutia. His vehement love for her produced some of his best love poems.

In 1950 *Canto General* was published in Mexico, and quickly it became a success throughout the world, including the Soviet Union. Back in his native Chile, however, Neruda's works were outlawed and *Canto General* appeared in only secretly published magazines. While in exile, Neruda traveled and sought refuge in France, Mexico, Italy, and Guatemala. In 1952 he published *Los versos del capitán* (*Captain's Verses*).

The political situation changed in Chile that year and Neruda was allowed to return home. He was received with great acclaim and settled down to write his *Odas Elementales* (*Elemental Odes of Pablo Neruda*), which clearly represented a new poetic adventure for him. Although his *Elemental Odes* dealt with everyday life and common objects and attitudes, Neruda managed to bring dignity and liveliness to them. In 1954 *Elmental Odes* and *Las uvas y el viento* ("The Grapes and the Wind") were published in Buenos Aires and met with great success. In 1956 *Nuevas odas elementales* ("New Elemental Odes") and in

1957 the *Tercer libro de las odas* ("Third Book of Odes") were received with great acclaim. Neruda's popularity continued to increase, and in spite of his reputation as an ardent Communist, he was widely read throughout the world. His *Obras Completas* (*Complete Works*) were also published in 1957 and translated into almost every language. By now, Neruda no longer needed to concern himself with government positions. The royalties from his books permitted him to travel, to collect antique objects, and to build houses, the most memorable one on the Isla Negra, where he spent the last years of his life.

The late 1950s saw a marked change in Neruda's style. No longer did he write about political problems and oppression; his attention turned to love, inspired by his new wife, Matilde. In 1958 he published *Estravagaria*, in 1959 *Cien sonetos de amor* (*One Hundred Love Sonnets*), and later, in 1967, *La Barcarole* ("Barcarole"), all of which expressed his love for Matilde. By 1962 Neruda was ready to settle down. Although he did travel, he spent more and more time at his island retreat on the Isla Negra. From there his poetry began to reflect the peace and tranquility that he enjoyed, and in 1964 he wrote the five-volume set *Memorial de Isla Negra* (1970; *Isle Negra: A Notebook*). Neruda continued to lecture and read his poetry, and in 1967 he moved into the realm of theater with his *Fulgor y muerte de Joaquin Murieta* (1972; *Splendor and Death of Joaquin Murieta*), which was based upon the life of a Chilean bandit. In

1968 Neruda returned to both poetry and politics. He had once again become active in Chilean politics and concerned with the everyday needs of the Chilean people. He wrote *Las manos del dia* (*"The Hands of Day"*) in 1968 and *Fin de mundo* (*"The World's End"*) in 1969, both of which were based upon the sadness, pain, hunger, and universal suffering of Latin American people.

In 1969 Pablo Neruda became the Communist party's candidate for the presidency of Chile. However, he renounced this honor in favor of his friend Dr. Salvador Allende, who was the sole candidate for all leftist parties. In 1970 Allende was swept to victory, becoming the first Marxist president of Chile, and Neruda expressed hope that social injustice and poverty would be abolished. That same year Allende appointed the poet as ambassador to France, where he remained until 1972. On October 8, 1971, Pablo Neruda received word that he was the recipient of the Nobel Prize in literature. In his acceptance speech in Stockholm, he expressed his utopian hopes and dreams for the world, but back in Chile the political situation was worsening. Already dying from cancer, Neruda returned to Chile in 1972. Remarkably, he continued to publish and was in the midst of writing his memoirs and eight books of poetry when he received the news that President Salvador Allende had been killed. Twelve days later, on September 23, 1973, Pablo Neruda succumbed to the cancer that had plagued him for nearly three years.

Immediately after Neruda's death, his eight books of poetry were published and in 1974 his memoirs, *Confieso que he vivido: Memorias* (1977; *Memoirs*). The timeless words of Pablo Neruda still live today. His dream for a new life for Latin Americans, and in particular for his own Chilean people, has never died. Neruda remains the voice of the working class and the peasants. For nearly seventy years his poetry depicted the reality of Chile and all of Latin America. In *Canto General* Neruda's vision of life is quite harsh:

Ha quedado un olor entre los
   cañaverales
una mezcla de sangre y cuerpo, un
   penetrante
pétalon nauseabundo. Entre los co-
   coleros
las tumbas están llenas de huesos de-
   molidos,
de estertores callados.

(A stench remains among the sugar canes: a mixture of flesh and blood, a penetrating petal that brings nausea. Between the coconut palms the graves are full of crushed bones, of speechless death-rattles.)

Today, the situation that Neruda depicted remains the same. In Chile the political system is quite repressive and the works of Neruda are censored. But Neruda's greatness will live on forever in the hearts and minds of all Chileans, and perhaps someday they will win the peace and tranquility that was Neruda's on the Isla Negra.

RADO PRIBIC AND
SCOTT C. SCHWARTZ

Selected Bibliography

PRIMARY SOURCES

Neruda, Pablo. *The Captain's Verses.* Translated by Donald D. Walsh. New York: New Directions, 1972.

——. *Estravagaria.* Translated by Alastair Reid. New York: Farrar, Straus & Giroux, 1974.

——. *The Heights of Macchu Pichu.* Translated by Nathaniel Tarn. New York: Farrar, Straus & Giroux, 1966.

——. *Isla Negra: A Notebook.* Translated by Alastair Reid. New York: Farrar, Straus & Giroux, 1981.

——. *Splendor and Death of Joaquin Murieta.* Translated by Ben Belitt. New York: Farrar, Straus & Giroux, 1972.

——. *Twenty Poems.* Translated by James Wright and Robert Bly. Madison, Minn.: Sixties Press, 1967.

SECONDARY SOURCES

Belitt, Ben, ed. *Pablo Neruda: Five Decades, A Selection.* New York: Grove Press, 1974.

Bizzarro, Salvatore. *Pablo Neruda: All Poets: the Poet.* Metuchen, N.J.: Scarecrow Press, 1979.

Bly, Robert, ed. *Neruda and Vallejo, Selected Poems.* Boston: Beacon Press, 1971.

Costa, René de. *The Poetry of Pablo Neruda.* Cambridge: Harvard University Press, 1979.

Lowenfels, Walter, ed. *For Neruda, for Chile: An International Anthology.* Boston: Beacon Press, 1975.

EUGENE O'NEILL   *1936*

When Eugene O'Neill (1888–1953) received the Nobel Prize in literature in 1936, he became the first, and to date the only, American playwright to receive this distinguished award. Curiously, in 1936 O'Neill had yet to write some of the dramatic works for which he is best known, and *Long Day's Journey into Night*, his autobiographical account of the Tyrone family, would not be published or produced for twenty years.

O'Neill was born on October 16, 1888, in a New York City hotel room on the corner of Broadway and 43rd Street. Sixty-five years later, on November 27, 1953, he died of a degenerative disease in a hotel room in Boston, an irony he thought appropriate for one who never felt a sense of home. O'Neill's young life was nomadic, necessitated by his father's profession; for thirty years and six thousand performances, James O'Neill toured the United States as the lead in Dumas's

The Count of Monte Cristo.
O'Neill's feeling of rootlessness was exacerbated by a troubled childhood: An older brother, Edmund, died from the measles just prior to O'Neill's birth; his mother, Ellen Quinlan O'Neill, enduring guilt occasioned by her infant son's death, public embarrassment occasioned by an alcoholic, free-spirited husband, and the pain of giving birth to Eugene, who weighed over ten pounds, welcomed her physician's decision to give her morphine. She eventually became an addict, which O'Neill learned about only after her attempted suicide when he was in his teens. He received the traumatic news with a deep sense of responsibility and guilt.

After attending a number of boarding schools, O'Neill went to Princeton University for one year, until he was expelled in 1907 by university president Woodrow Wilson over a window-breaking incident. He spent time in Honduras prospecting for gold, but a bout with malaria forced him to return to the United States. For a time, he worked as actor and stage manager with his father's company, then signed on as a seaman and traveled to South America and elsewhere, returning to New York's taverns when he was in port. When he was twenty-four, he worked as a reporter for the New London (Connecticut) *Telegraph*, but his fragile health forced him to stay for six months in a tuberculosis sanatorium in Wallingford, Connecticut, where long hours and unresolvable emotional conflicts prompted avid reading, partic-

ularly Greek tragedy and Strindberg, and a growing desire to write.

Though he produced some undistinguished poetry, O'Neill's preferred genre even in these apprentice years was drama. After leaving the sanatorium and writing his first play, *A Wife for a Life* (1913), he developed skill in the form through attending, in 1914, George Pierce Baker's Harvard University playwriting course, which a number of writers, theater people, and journalists have acknowledged as a shaping influence in their careers. O'Neill's early dramatic efforts (1913 through 1920) were primarily one-act plays, such as *The Web, Thirst, Warnings, Fog, Recklessness, The Sniper, The Movie Man, Servitude, Abortion, Bound East for Cardiff, Before Breakfast, The Moon of the Caribees, Now I Ask You, In the Zone, The Long Voyage Home, Ile, Where the Cross Is Made, Shell Shock, The Rope, The Dreamy Kid*—mostly naturalistic pieces in a tragic tone, many with a sea setting. After moving to New York's Greenwich Village, then to Provincetown, Massachusetts, then back to New York, O'Neill joined a group of writers and artists and found a forum for production in the Provincetown Players and, between 1923 and 1927, in the Greenwich Village Theatre, which he, Kenneth Macgowan, and Robert Edmond Jones ran.

In 1920 O'Neill's first full-length play, *Beyond the Horizon*, was mounted on Broadway, winning the young playwright the first of his four Pulitzer prizes. In that play, the Mayo brothers allow their love for the same woman to reshape, unhappily, their lifestyles: Robert, the poetic sibling, becomes a farmer, while Andrew, the more practical, goes to sea. *The Emperor Jones* (1920) appeared in London shortly afterward and, later, in New York, with Paul Robeson in the title role. Borrowing some of the expressionistic techniques of between-the-war German dramatists, the play follows the final moments of Brutus Jones, a black American outcast who has become ruler of a West Indian island. O'Neill uses the depths of the tropical forest to reflect the man's psyche. *Anna Christie* (1921, but unsuccessfully produced the year before as *Chris Christopherson*) challenges the conventions of the nineteenth-century theatrical fallen woman and of naturalism as an informing principle as it dramatizes human action against the backdrop of "dat ole davil, sea"; the play won O'Neill a second Pulitzer Prize.

In *The Hairy Ape* (1922) O'Neill worked further with expressionistic techniques, again focusing on an outcast who, unlike the Emperor Jones, cannot find a place in society or achieve a sense of personal identity. Having failed to belong in the human world, Yank, a worker of limited intelligence and intense pride, turns to the apes in the zoo, his quest for identity metaphorically reflecting modern alienation. Other plays produced in the 1920s, with varying degrees of success, included *Exorcism, Diff'rent, Gold, The Straw, The First Man, Welded, All God's Chillun Got Wings, The Fountain, The Great God Brown, Marco Millions, Lazarus Laughed,* and *Dynamo*; most represent deviations from the naturalistic form, experiments in romanticism, symbolism, and expressionism.

O'Neill won a third Pulitzer Prize for *Strange Interlude* (1928), a lengthy drama that voices not only dialogue but thoughts, freezing the action as characters deliver their uninflected interior monologues. This novelistic analysis of character, also attempted in *Days Without End* (1934), was a radical departure from the naturalistic dramatic form. Nina Leeds, the play's central character, is a woman whose relationships with several men and the psychological subtexts of those relationships clearly preoccupied O'Neill.

These and ensuing years saw productions of three major plays: *Desire Under the Elms* (1924), *Mourning Becomes Electra* (1931), and *Ah, Wilderness!* (1933). *Desire Under the Elms* is an intensely personal working out of a man's relationship with his mother, who appears in the play in two forms: the spirit of Eben's dead mother, who must sanction her son's sexual relationship with his father's new, young wife, and that young wife as passionate whore and surrogate mother. The play dramatically records the pressure of the puritanical on the liberal spirit, a conflict that O'Neill, himself an Irish Catholic living in New England, understood. A variation on Oedipal conflict reappears in *Mourning Becomes Electra*, where Lavinia's love for her father and hatred for her mother finally condemn her to a lonely, austere life. Lavinia's brother's love for his mother contributes to familial antagonisms, none of which can be resolved without calamity. A reworking of Aeschylus' *Oresteia*, the play's three major parts correspond to the Greek trilogy, but the external forces of fate are replaced by psychological determinism. *Ah, Wilderness!*, which explores the adolescent romances and rebellions of Richard Miller, is O'Neill's only full-length comedy, but the playwright's greater comfort with more somber drama is hinted at through Miller's developing sense of guilt.

When O'Neill, brooding and ill, began a twelve-year hiatus from the theater in 1934, he was married to Carlotta Monterey, his third wife. Before he entered the sanatorium in 1912, he and his first wife, Kathleen Jenkins, whom he had married secretly in 1909, had divorced. In 1918 he married Agnes Boulton Burton, with whom he had two children: Shane, who committed suicide in 1977, and Oona, whom O'Neill disowned when she married the much older Charlie Chaplin. His first son, Eugene, by Kathleen Jenkins, ended his career as classics professor through suicide in 1950. O'Neill's 1929 marriage to Carlotta lasted until his death; as both wife and mother, she provided O'Neill with a strong if sometimes tumultuous marriage.

It was, ironically, during his absence from the theater that O'Neill won the Nobel Prize. Cited for the "power, honesty, and deep-felt emotions of his dramatic works, which embody an original concept of tragedy," O'Neill, too ill to attend the ceremony, accepted the award with modesty, acknowledging his debt to Swedish playwright August Strindberg, "the greatest genius of all modern dramatists," and crediting his colleagues in America with having contributed to this recognition by Europe of the "coming-of-age of the American theatre."

When O'Neill came out of hibernation in 1946, having worked intensely on *A Tale of Possessors Self-Possessed*, an ambitious nine-play cycle dealing with several generations of an American family, it was with *The Iceman Cometh*, a long, tedious, insightful exploration into the nature of "pipe dreams." In it, the habitués of Harry Hope's bar, modeled on the dockside Jimmy-the-Priest's that the young O'Neill had frequented, wait with empty hope, finding solace and safety in illusion.

The following year (1947), *A Moon for the Misbegotten* became the last of the plays to be performed during O'Neill's lifetime. Prompted by the story of an Irishman and a New England aristocrat that Jamie, in the yet unpublished *Long Day's Journey Into Night*, relates, the playwright dramatizes the confessional relationship between the alcoholic Jamie and Jose, a farm woman. Nine years later, *Long Day's Journey Into Night* appeared. Though completed in 1941, the play was withheld, at O'Neill's request, from stage and publication; in 1956, less than three years after his death, Carlotta permitted its mounting in Stockholm and, under the direction of José Quintero, later that year in New York. The play, which won O'Neill a posthumous Pulitzer Prize, follows a day in the life of the troubled Tyrone family. James, an actor, is frugal and drinks too much; Mary is addicted to morphine; one of the sons is an alcoholic; the other son suffers from consumption. The most directly autobiographical of O'Neill's plays, this was, for O'Neill, an expression of both pain and purgation.

A Touch of the Poet, written during O'Neill's hiatus and the only completed testimony to the expansive work he had planned, was produced in Stockholm in 1957, the following year in New York; and *More Stately Mansions,* also written in the late thirties, was staged in Stockholm in 1962 in a five-hour version that was half the length of the text. *A Touch of the Poet* dramatizes the tensions between an Irish immigrant father, Cornelius Melody, reduced from his pretended aristocratic status to New England pubkeeper, and his daughter, Sara, determined to marry a poet. Unproducible in its original form, the play, like much of O'Neill's earlier work, is an indictment of materialism. An unfinished part of the proposed cycle, *More Stately Mansions* presents Sara Melody of *A Touch of the Poet* as married to Simon Harford, whose poetic impulses yield to materialism and, finally, to a mental breakdown.

The last of O'Neill's plays to appear posthumously is *Hughie,* written in 1941 and published in 1959. A two-character, one-act naturalistic play, *Hughie* admirably sustains the near monologue of Erie Smith as he speaks to the night clerk at a budget New York hotel. The idiom recalls the colloquial language of a number of O'Neill's early plays, in which characters master New England, Irish, and other dialects and capture the verbal patterns of the working class.

The lengthy, even epic works of O'Neill's later years suggest the range of this uncommon playwright, who was as capable of creating a tightly framed one-acter as he was a tenhour play. O'Neill's writing reflects his skill at creating both the realistic drama that has dominated the American theater and the more innovative European forms. Behind O'Neill's consistently somber if not tragic vision is the need to articulate insistent personal conflict and pain. Once asked whether he would ever write a play with a happy ending, O'Neill wryly replied that he would if he saw the need for one. That vision, combined with the recognition that modern drama needed to reflect the special anxieties of an emerging modernism within a distinctive and accommodating form, has secured O'Neill's position as the seminal shaper of modern American drama.

JUNE SCHLUETER

Selected Bibliography

PRIMARY SOURCES

O'Neill, Eugene. *Complete Plays of Eugene O'Neill.* 12 vols. New York: Scribner, 1934–35.
———. *The Plays of Eugene O'Neill.* 3 vols. New York: Random House, 1941, 1951.

SECONDARY SOURCES

Floyd, Virginia, ed. *Eugene O'Neill at Work: Newly Released Ideas for Plays.* New York: Ungar, 1981.

Gassner, John, ed. *O'Neill: A Collection of Critical Essays.* Englewood Cliffs, N.J.: Prentice-Hall, 1964.

Gelb, Arthur and Barbara. *O'Neill.* New York: Harper & Row, 1962.

Martine, James J., ed. *Critical Essays on Eugene O'Neill.* Boston: G. K. Hall, 1984.

Raleigh, John Henry. *The Plays of Eugene O'Neill.* Carbondale: Southern Illinois University Press, 1965.

Shaeffer, Louis. *O'Neill: Son and Playwright* and *O'Neill: Son and Artist.* Boston: Little, Brown, 1968, 1973.

BORIS PASTERNAK   *1958*

Boris Leonidovich Pasternak (1890–1960) was born on February 10, 1890, in Moscow. His father, Leonid Osipovich Pasternak, was a well-known painter who taught at and eventually became the director of the Moscow School of Painting, Sculpture, and Architecture. His mother, Rosa Isidorovna, was a talented pianist who gave her first public performance in Odessa at the age of eight. When she married Leonid, however, she gave up her career in music for her husband and four children: sons Boris and Alexander and daughters Josephine and Lydia. She often played at home entertaining such guests as Leo Tolstoy, the Russian painter Nikolai Ge, the famous singer Fëdor Chaliapin, and other prominent figures from the world of Russian and European culture. Besides the Tolstoys, the Pasternaks counted among their friends the prominent Russian pianist and composer Anton Rubinstein, the Russian composer Aleksandr Scriabin, and the Austrian poet Rainer Maria Rilke.

The atmosphere of creativity and art that surrounded young Pasternak could not fail to have a tremendous impact on him. In an autobiographical work later in life Pasternak would remember a night when his "consciousness was set into motion, henceforward without any great gaps and interruptions, as with grown-up people." On that night in 1894 the Tolstoys were visiting and Rosa Isidorovna and two other musicians performed Tchaikovsky's Trio. The music and the sight of the great writer were forever impressed in Pasternak's memory.

He also remembered a man the family met on the train who spoke to his father in German. This was in 1900 and the man was Rilke. Later, Boris found in his father's library a collection of Rilke's poetry—a Christmas present from the author. This early acquaintance with Rilke and his art was another powerful influence on the boy.

In 1903 Pasternak met and heard Scriabin. The Pasternaks

were staying at a dacha near Moscow that summer, and Scriabin rented a neighboring dacha. Pasternak would often accompany his father and Scriabin on long walks in the beautiful countryside, listening to their discussions of life and art. Recalling his youthful years, Pasternak wrote: "More than anything else in the world I loved music; more than anyone else in music, Scriabin."

The great impact that Scriabin's music had on him encouraged Pasternak to consider a career as a composer. He started to take music lessons from the prominent composer Reinhold Glière, who also taught Sergei Prokofiev and after the Revolution became the director of the Moscow Conservatory. In 1909, when Pasternak had already graduated from a classical gymnasium and enrolled at the law school of Moscow University, he summoned the courage to show his compositions to his idol, Scriabin. The maestro was very pleased with his work and assured him that it showed Pasternak's great potential and originality. Scriabin went on to advise Pasternak to leave the law school and to study philosophy.

For the young Pasternak this period was a time of seeking his real calling. Despite the encouragement he received from Scriabin, he decided not to pursue further a career in music. He studied philosophy at Moscow University, and in the summer of 1912, when his mother presented him with a modest sum for a trip abroad, he decided to take a summer course from the German philosopher Hermann Cohen at the University of Marburg. His studies there were so successful that Cohen invited him to a private dinner at his residence—an honor that only a very few students were granted in recognition of their progress. The day before the dinner, however, Pasternak proposed to his friend Ida Vysotskaya, who was visiting him in Marburg. She refused him, and the resultant turmoil and shock that he experienced made him alter the direction of his life once again. He abandoned philosophy, and right there, in Marburg, began writing poetry, which would remain his primary occupation for the rest of his life.

Perhaps music, philosophy, or poetry could have provided an adequate means of expression for Pasternak's complex inner world. His choice of poetry, however, was not accidental. The beginning of the twentieth century in Russia witnessed a cultural explosion in all the arts. The composers Scriabin, Stravinsky, Rachmaninov, Prokofiev, and later Shostakovich; the painters Vrubel, Chagal, Kandinsky, Larionova, Serebriakova, Petrov-Vodkin, Malevich, and Tatlin; the dancers Nijinsky and Fokin—these and many other giants of culture won for this period of Russian history the designation of the Russian Renaissance.

This era, however, is also referred to as the Silver Age of Russian poetry—a short, unsurpassed period of flourishing poetic schools, movements, and individual poets, a period that boasts no fewer first-rate poets than the so-called Golden Age of Russian poetry, that is, the Pushkin period. In 1912, when Pasternak was in Marburg, the symbolist poets Blok and Balmont could still attract huge crowds to poetry readings, although the symbolist movement had already passed its zenith. For several more years Blok would remain the idol of the Russian reading public, but new poets of no less talent were already crowding out the symbolists. The acmeists Gumilev, Gorodetsky, Mandelstam, and Akhmatova had already challenged the symbolist tenets. Toward the end of 1912, the futurists Mayakovsky, Khlebnikov, Kruchenykh, and D. Burliuk would demand that the entire culture of the past, including Pushkin, Tolstoy, and Dostoyevsky, "be thrown overboard from the Ship of Modernity." The ego-futurist Igor Severianin was "singing" his *poésas*. Two books of poetry by Innokenty Annensky had recently been published. The older poet died in 1909, but his newly discovered poetry made a profound impression on the younger generation. Esenin, Tsvetaeva, Kuzmin, and Khodasevich had either won or were winning public recognition.

At the beginning of his career as a poet, Pasternak joined a futurist group, Lirika, later renamed Centrifuge. After the Revolution, in the 1920s, he also associated himself with the futurist movement LEF (Left Front of Art) for a short period. But he was too original and independent to be fettered by any preconceived tenets; therefore, he quickly left these groups, although traces of futurist poetics are easily discernible in his early poetry. Like his futurist colleagues, Pasternak did not hesitate to introduce prosa-

isms, colloquialisms, and even bureaucratisms into his poetry. Meaning in his early poems was often sacrificed to the sound of the word; startling rhymes, a repetition of the same morphemes, and other technical innovations figured as independently valuable verse elements. Comprehension was additionally hampered by an overabundance of metaphors and remote associations. Indeed, when one reads a poem or two from Pasternak's early writings the first impression is usually one of complete incomprehensibility; yet Pasternak has always been one of the most admired poets in Russia.

Pasternak's poetry presents a unique world, one that becomes accessible only after readers take the time and effort to acquaint themselves with it, to get used to its powerful stream of sounds and images. The main property, of Pasternak's early poetry is a surplus of energy. That is why there are so many thunderstorms, downpours, whirlwinds, passions, abrupt bursting movements, and the like in his poetry. In most cases the poems are oversaturated with images and metaphors, not because the poet wants to astonish us with some technical trick, but precisely because he is striving to express in a small unit of text the tremendous vital force that overflows his entire being. This force is so great in Pasternak's early poetry that it often rends a poem's fabric.

Pasternak often writes about nature. Nature in his poetry, however, does not play its traditional literary role of symbolizing the inner state of the persona, serving as a vehicle of metaphor, or simply making a beautiful picture. A keen critic of Pasternak's poetry, Andrey Sinyavsky, has remarked: "A landscape in Pasternak is not just the object of description but the subject of the action, the main hero and the mover of events." There is no borderline between man and nature, between nature and the objects surrounding man and constituting part of his life. In the poem *Sestra moiazhizn* (*My Sister—Life*), the poet addresses life as "my sister" and life responds in a sisterly way: the setting sun sympathizes with him—this is not the station where the poet wants to be; the bell also feels guilty and apologizes: "sorry, not here." In another poem, "Stars in the Summer," "the wind tries to lift a rose on request from the lips, hair, shoes, skirts, and nicknames." In "With Oars at Rest" willows, stooping down over the boat sailing by, kiss collarbones, elbows, and oarlocks. People, things, and nature coexist and interact within the same world as partners, on an equal footing.

Another inhabitant of this world is art. Poetry may be defined through nature:

It's the snapping of compressed ice,
It's the night, freezing the leaves,
It's the duel of two nightingales.

On the other hand, nature can become a literary work:

"The book of the storm burst through the window.
I opened it without getting dressed."

The whole universe, along with gardens and ponds, appears in the poem "A Definition of Creativity" as products of man's creativity, which, as though with checkers, plays with "sleep and conscience, and night, and love."

The gardens, and ponds, and fences,
And the universe bubbling with white howls
Are only the discharges of passion
Accumulated by human hearts.

From 1914 through 1932 Pasternak published several collections of poetry—*Bliznets v tuchakh* (1914; *Twin in the Clouds*), *Poverkh barerov* (1917; *Over the Barriers*), *Sestra moia-zhizn* (1922; *My Sister— Life*), *Temi i variatsii* (1923; *Themes and Variations*), *Vtoroe rozhdenie* (1932; *Second Birth*)—as well as a few short prose pieces—*Detstvo Liuvers* (1925; *The Childhood of Liuvers*), *Appellesova cherta* (1915; "Apelles' Mark"), *Vozdushnye puti* (1924; "Aerial Ways"), *Okhrannaia gramota* (1930; "Safe Conduct"). These works established Pasternak as a leading figure in Soviet literature.

In his prose one finds the same fresh, childlike perception of the world, the same exuberance and enhanced emotionality, and the same anthropomorphosis of nature and inanimate objects as in his poetry. "His poetry strove toward prose, and his prose, toward poetry," the prominent Soviet scholar Dmitry Likhachev wrote. Those who missed this crucial property of Pasternak's prose would later completely misinterpret and misunderstand *Doctor Zhivago*.

In the 1920s Pasternak also wrote several narrative poems, such as "Vysokaia Bolezn" ("High Malady"), "Leitenant Schmidt" (1926; "Lieutenant Schmidt"), "Deviatsot piatii god" (1927; "The Year 1905") and a novel in verse, *Spektorsky*. In them the poet attempted to add a fourth member, history, to his harmonious triumvirate of life, nature, and art. If in his lyric poetry Pasternak wrote about man in nature and man and nature, these long poems deal with the theme of man in history; in particular, man and revolution. This theme would become an important thread in the complicated texture of Pasternak's novel *Doctor Zhivago*. It is not surprising therefore that many themes, motifs, and images from *Spektorsky* recur later in the novel.

Pasternak himself was displeased with these poems. In one of his letters to the poet Marina Tsvetaeva he wrote: "*Spektorsky is definitely bad. . . . In it and in Deviatsot piatii god* (with the exception of several recent chapters of *Schmidt*) I got myself into terrible boredom and arrhythmia."

With Stalin's reign of terror, the 1930s were tragic years in Soviet history. Millions died in camps or were executed as "enemies of the people." These years were also very difficult years for Pasternak, although he was luckier than many of his friends, including Boris Pilnyak, Osip Mandelstam, and Georgian poets Titsian Tabidzè and Paolo Yashvili who did not survive the era. From 1932, when his fifth book of poetry, *Vtoroe Rozhdenie*, was published, until the publication of his sixth book, *Na rannikh poezdakh* (*On Early Trains*), in 1943, Pasternak wrote very little original work and practically no poetry. He characterized this period as the years "when

all poetry had ceased to exist, when literature had stopped." To make a living, he worked on translations, producing remarkable Russian renderings of Georgian poetry, works by Kleist, Byron, and Sandor Petöfi, tragedies and historical dramas by Shakespeare, and, later, Goethe's *Faust*.

The war with Germany brought temporary relief from the nightmare of arrests and persecutions. The country was no longer torn by the incessant struggle with "enemies of the people" but was united against the real and deadly enemy. During World War II Pasternak returned to writing poetry. His style, though underwent a considerable change. In his last three books *Na rannikh poezdakh*, *Zemnoi prostor* (1945; *The Breadth of the Earth*) and *Kogda razguliaetsa* (*When Skies Clear*; completed in 1959), as well as in the poems from *Doctor Zhivago*, Pasternak, without abandoning "the kinship with all that exists," reached that naturalness and simplicity that is, in his words, characteristic of only "great poets." His style became clear and simple. His poetry lost the abundant energy and sparkling exuberance of his youthful works, but, in Victor Erlich's words, "in the best poems of that period, most notably in the best 'poems of Yury Zhivago,' the richness and intricacy of the imagery are all the more effective for being brought under stricter control and placed in the service of a clearly articulated moral vision."

Toward the end of the war Pasternak began *Doctor Zhivago*. His work on it was interrupted by ailments, including several heart attacks, periodic persecution, and tribulations in his personal life. The manuscript was completed in 1955 and sent to the journal *Novy mir* for publication. In 1956 *Novy mir* rejected the novel because the editorial board had found that its spirit is "that of nonacceptance of the socialist revolution"; but a contract was signed with the State Publishing House for the publication of an abridged version. Another Soviet journal, *Znamya*, published several poems from the novel. At the same time Pasternak arranged to have the manuscript given to the Italian publisher Feltrinelli. In 1957, when it became clear that the publication of the novel in the Soviet Union would not take place at any time soon, Feltrinelli went ahead and printed the novel in Italian. It was immediately translated into many other languages. The official Soviet press ignored the novel for almost a year, until the news reached the Soviet Union in October 1958 that Pasternak had been awarded the Nobel Prize in literature. Only then did the novel's title appear in the Soviet press—unfortunately not in congratulatory articles but in a most vicious campaign against Pasternak. The book was called "a libel on the October Revolution, the people who made the Revolution, and the building of socialism in the Soviet Union." Pasternak was expelled from the Union of Soviet Writers, and his colleagues asked the Soviet government to throw "the traitor" out of the country. Scores of Soviet people who had never before heard of the novel or even of the author himself wrote letters to newspapers

in which they condemned Pasternak and demanded the most severe punishment for him. In this atmosphere the persecuted writer renounced the Nobel Prize and in his letters to Khrushchev and *Pravda* recanted his mistakes and asked not to be exiled from the Soviet Union. He wrote to Khrushchev: "A departure beyond the borders of my country would for me be equivalent to death, and for that reason I request you not to take that extreme measure in relation to me." He lived for little more than a year after that campaign, dying of lung cancer on May 30, 1960.

Even many of those who loved Pasternak and detested the campaign against him considered the novel a failure. One of his admirers, the Soviet dramatist Aleksandr Gladkov, remarked that "all the conversations of the characters are either a naive personification of the author's ideas, poorly masked as dialogues, or a weak imitation. The language in all the scenes involving simple people is almost always false. Plot elements are also naive, conventional, and artificial. . . . There is not a broad and multifaceted picture of the time, which is characteristic of epic works." The fallacy of this similar criticisms lies precisely in the fact that Pasternak's novel is not an epic work and, strictly speaking, not a novel at all. To accuse Pasternak of not writing a good novel is the same as to accuse Dostoyevsky of not writing good detective stories. In his work Pasternak hardly intended to present a broad picture of life in turn-of-the-century Russia. Nor should one look to his novel for an epic depiction of the Revolution in the manner of Aleksey Tolstoy or Mikhail Sholokhov. Gladkov, however, is right in one respect: it is the author's voice that we hear in the characters' conversations. With this in mind, one can see in Lara's farewell words at Yuri's deathbed an accurate statement of what the novel is and is not about.

The riddle of life, the riddle of death, the enchantment of genius, the enchantment of unadorned beauty—yes, yes, these things were ours. But the small problems of practical life—things like the reshaping of the planet—these things, no thank you, they are not for us.

Pasternak's novel is a lyrico-philosophical work that presents the same world that we observe in his poetry. Everything and everybody is merged in a harmonious unity in this world, everything and everybody—man, nature, things, history, and God—live, love, and die in the same cyclical order: birth, life, death, and resurrection. It is preposterous, therefore, to call the novel counterrevolutionary—in it the October Revolution and its aftermath simply constitute death in a particular cycle of Russian history; likewise, winter constitutes death in nature and Zhivago's end is death of this particular man and his art.

The last chapter of Pasternak's own life story—the "resurrection"—is being written now, during Gorbachev's era of perestroika and glasnost. A commission headed by the poet Andrei Voznesensky was established in 1987 to study Pasternak's literary heritage. A biography of Pasternak by his son Evgeny was announced for publication. On the twenty-seventh anniversary of the poet's death, May 30, 1987, a symposium on Pasternak's works took place at the Moscow Literary Institute, where sixty papers were read—five of them on *Doctor Zhivago*. In 1988 the novel itself appeared in installments in *Novy mir*—the same journal that thirty years earlier had rejected the manuscript and accused Pasternak of slandering the Revolution. There are plans to turn the poet's dacha in Peredelkino into a museum dedicated to his life and work. And, finally, he was posthumously reinstated in the Union of Soviet Writers—an honor he might have had doubts about accepting had he been alive today.

KONSTANTIN KUSTANOVICH

Selected Bibliography

PRIMARY SOURCES

Pasternak, Boris. *Collected Short Prose.* Translated with an introduction by Christopher Barnes. New York: Praeger, 1977.

———. *Doctor Zhivago.* Translated by Max Hayward and Manya Harari. New York: Pantheon, 1958.

———. *I Remember; Sketch for an Autobiography.* Translated by David Magarshack. New York: Pantheon, 1959.

———. *My Sister—Life and A Sublime Malady.* Translated by Mark Rudman with Bohdan Boychuk. Ann Arbor, Mich.: Ardis, 1983.

———. *The Poetry of Boris Pasternak.* Selected, edited, and translated by George Reavy. New York: Putnam, 1959.

————. *Selected Poems*. Translated by Jon Stallworthy and Peter France. New York, London: Norton, 1983.

SECONDARY SOURCES

Conquest, Robert. *The Pasternak Affair: Courage of Genius*. London: Collins & Harvill, 1961.

Davie, Donald, and Angela Livingstone, eds. *Pasternak. Modern Judgments*. London: Macmillan, 1969.

de Mallac, Guy. *Boris Pasternak. His Life and Art*. Norman: University of Oklahoma Press, 1981.

Erlich, Victor, ed. *Pasternak. A Collection of Critical Essays*. Englewood Cliffs, N.J.: Prentice-Hall, 1978.

Hingley, Ronald. *Pasternak. A Biography*. New York: Knopf, 1983.

Nilsson, Nils Ake, ed. *Boris Pasternak. Essays*. Stockholm: Almqvist & Wiksell, 1976.

Saint-John Perse   *1960*

Saint-John Perse (1887–1975), the French poet and diplomat, was born May 31, 1887, on the small private island of Saint-Leger-les-Feuilles, near Guadeloupe in the French West Indies. He was a descendant of a French aristocratic family whose ancestors had migrated to the then prosperous French islands in 1682. They changed their name from Léger Saint-Léger to Saint-Léger Léger. His father, Amédée Saint-Léger Léger, an attorney, married Françoise-Renée Dormoy, with whom he had four children. Alexis, who would later adopt the pseudonym Saint-John Perse, was their only son. He had three sisters, the youngest of whom died when he was eight.

In the tropical setting of the island, a cross-roads of races and cultures, the young Alexis spent many happy hours studying the infinite variety of flora that surrounded him and establishing close ties with various animals. His family and friends were often bewildered by the "animal magnetism" the gifted child possessed. Whenever he rode his horse, he felt that together they formed one single being. Nature always moved him, and he was not afraid of the natural calamities— such as volcanic eruptions—that struck the island. At one point, when his parents were absent, a beautiful Hindu servant initiated him into the cult of the Hindu deity Shiva, who is said to have made the universe arise from the primordial chaos. This was an experience that would mark him personally and reappear in his poetry.

Fascinated by the ships arriving from all corners of the world, he spent most of his free time at the port and he soon began writing his impressions which were collected in "Mouvement du Port" ("Movement of the Port"). As a consequence of managerial problems and devastations caused on their estates by volcanic eruptions the family was forced to return to France in 1899. The young boy, who reacted with dismay at having to leave behind his horse and the corner of Eden where he had spent so many happy hours, was overwhelmed by a feeling of exile.

The family settled in Pau, a fairly cosmopolitan city where he met his first genuine *compagnons*, the poet Francis Jammes, twice his age but also of Antillean ancestry; Paul Claudel, a friend of the Jammes family; and Valéry Larbaud, French author and translator. His first major poem, "Images à Crusoé" ("Pictures for Crusoe"), was started in 1904 but not published until 1909. An outcry of a young man in exile, it contains some striking parallels with Claudel's "Les Muses."

Alexis's early dreams of a carefree life in the timeless paradise of his childhood had been shattered by the family move, and in 1907 he suffered another blow—the death of his father. However, the same year while sojourning in the Pyrenees to help offset his disappointment and sorrow, Alexis started to give shape to his first luminous poem "Pour fêter une enfance" ("To Celebrate a Childhood"), which would later be included in the collection *Eloges* (*Praises*), first published in *La Nouvelle Revue Française* (1909–10), thanks to André Gide's friendly support, and later in book form (1911).

This poem continues the style of a regal sacred discourse used in "Images." *Eloges* already contains the essence of Alexis's poetic vision: a vast celebration of life forces in the unending cycle of destruction–creation in the universe.

After receiving his baccalaureate with honors, he completed in 1908 his law studies started in 1904. In 1911 he decided to prepare for the French foreign service examination, inspired no doubt by the example of Claudel, whose diplomatic career had taken him to the United States and China. After passing the necessary examination, he entered the French diplomatic service in 1914.

Two years later, in the fall of 1916, he was selected for a mission to China. In Peking he felt alien and solitary but was fascinated by the Chinese. He took long rides on horseback outside the city, thus reestablishing a symbiotic contact like the one he had during his youth.

In the summer of 1917, after the quickly aborted coup d'état of General Tchang-Hsiun and the installation of President Li in Peking, Léger decided to spend most of his free time in the disused Taoist temple of Tao-Yu nestled in the hills that dominate Peking, away from the numerous social obligations of a diplomat. It was in this retreat that *Anabase* (1924; *Anabasis*) was conceived and written in a few weeks. In the spring of 1920 Léger had the opportunity to carry out one of his fondest dreams: to go on an expedition into central Asia on horseback. This adventure and his subsequent visits to Japan, Polynesia, and America provided him with a rich stock of images that later appeared in his poetry.

Anabase is a "descente vers la mer la commune mer" ("a descent toward the sea, the communal sea") and is of a much larger scope than preceding works. It is a narrative poem, in ten cantos, that vividly describes a migration of epic proportion made by nomadic horsemen. Written in language that seems to come out of a sacred book, it contains allusions to mysterious ancient rites and somehow transcends history placing the reader in a kind of immemorial time. The poem, unfolding in worldly images, is also a defiant affirmation of life and a celebration of man, who lives in a perpetual state of tension, lonely in his action but constantly exploring the paths and the endless horizons of a world against which death cannot prevail.

Saint-Léger Léger published *Anabase* under the pseudonym Saint-John Perse. There is however, no clear relationship between Xenophon's work and his poem, and some critics have explained his choice of Perse as nom de plume by saying that, together with Tacitus and Racine, the Latin satirist Perseus was his most admired literary model.

For the next twelve years he played an active political role in France, working closely with Aristide Briand, minister of foreign affairs and "Apostle of Peace," whom he greatly admired. However, all the dreams of peace he had entertained with Briand were shattered with the advent of World War II, although the idea of human brotherhood remained an active theme of his poetry.

After Briand's death in 1932, Léger (he used the pseudonym Saint-John Perse only for his poetry) served under a number of foreign ministers. However, in 1939 his enemies in the foreign service began to conspire against him and in 1940 he decided to leave France after having refused the position of ambassador to Washington offered to him by Daladier, minister of foreign affairs to Marshal Pétain. A very lonely Léger took a British freighter to London and then proceeded to the United States. When he arrived in Manhattan, he was informed that the Vichy government had stripped him of his nationality, his Legion of Honor, and his possessions. Early in 1941 he moved to Washington, D.C., and accepted the position of consultant in French literature at the Library of Congress.

The period 1941 to 1948 was a period of intense creativity for the poet. *Exil* (1942; *Exile*), which develops the theme of creation in the midst of emptiness and is a hymn to the eternal return of being manifesting itself in poetic creation, was followed by *Poème à l'Etrangère* (*Poem to a Foreign Lady*) in 1942, *Pluies* (*Rains*) the same year, and *Neiges* (*Snows*) in 1944. These four poems are linked by a common theme: The ordeal of exile is a purifying ritual that reopens to man the kingdom where the sacred reveals its presence.

Perse wrote *Pluies* during a trip to Savannah, Georgia. The poem contains nine sections and describes the purifying and liberating role of the rains. The rains bring fertility, wash the face of the living and the dead, of those who doubt and those who have knowledge. In his exhortation the poet asks the rains to purify poetry itself. The true celebration of the rains finally takes place in a Mallarméan silence.

Neiges, written during the winter in New York, was a gift to his mother, who had been alone in France for the preceeding four years. The poet is divided between his awareness of human suffering and the ecstasy brought by the pure splendor of the snow. He is searching for the revelation hidden in the ultimate source of language itself.

After the liberation of France, Perse was fully reinstated as a French citizen and as an ambassador *en disponibilité* (unassigned) with full rights and privileges. The four preceeding poems, collected under the title *Les Quatre poèmes* (*1941–1944*), were published in Buenos Aires and sold for the benefit of the Comité Français de Secours aux Victimes de la Guerre (French Committe for Aid to Victims of the War).

Resisting the urgings of old friends in the French diplomatic corps, he decided to stay in America and devote himself to poetry. In the summer of 1945 Saint-John Perse completed *Vents* (*Winds*) and published a short poem "Berceuse" ("Lullaby") in New York. Perse saw the winds as life itself—unruly but fecund, unpredictable but powerful. The poem is like a cosmogony, the principle of which is perpetual movement in a cycle of destruction and creation. As in the myth of Shiva, what indolent nature allows

to reoccur becomes a law of nature—to which language itself is subjected. The poet becomes the winds and as such must constantly renew himself. Illuminated by his poetic vision, he attains a state equivalent to lightning, a superhuman dimension from which he must return to live among men. At the time, *Vents* was the poet's grandest work. Even Claudel praised him.

Next he began writing *Amers* (1957; *Seamarks*), which was to be his most ambitious work and is considered by many critics as his masterpiece. The first fragments appeared in 1948. In this long poem (180 pages) the sea is a symbol of the unceasing quest of the human spirit. The march of man to the sea is "the exaltation of life, in the active mystery of its strength and the great unrevealed order of an eternal race." Seamarks literally mean the limits reached by mankind in the pursuit of its goals. The ninth canto, "Etroits sont les vaisseaux" ("Narrow are the Vessels") is the most celebrated. It has been compared with the "Song of Songs" and is considered the greatest erotic poem in the French language. The lovers' bed becomes a ship sailing over a limitless ocean. Man and woman become one in a ceaseless flow of being. The desire of the woman is depicted as a tide rising. The union of man and woman is a *hiérogamie*, a sacred and ritual marriage. The lovers consequently usurp a condition that belongs to the Godhead. These words: "la mer, l'amour, la mort" ("the sea, love, death") sound like an echo that suggest both an analogy, phonetically, and also a conflict, semantically. Poetry is another alien presence that takes hold of the human soul. But the sea is one, it resolves all the contradictions. It symbolizes the mystery of universal being, which transcends all the distinctions created by man.

In 1957 a group of friends and admirers made Perse a gift of a house on the peninsula of Giens in Provence, where he spent his first summer in France in seventeen years. Henceforth, he spent five months of each year in France (late spring to late fall) and the rest of the year in the United States.

In the summer of 1959, he felt ready to write another poem to celebrate the mythic "great age" of humanity. *Chronique* (1959; *Chronicle*) is another affirmation of the poet's faith in the creative aspects of life and the continuity of the cosmos. The speaker, trying to identify with the reader by using the "nous" ("we") form uses autobiographical reminiscences to symbolize the progression of man toward the "great age," the achievement of his life in the universe. Life is compared with the voyage of a sailor who brings home a treasured catch. For the speaker death is not the absolute limit of human life. A cluster of positive archetypal symbols express the ultimate victory of life. A new future is in sight for mankind beyond the troubled times and the prophecy of apocalyptic doom which surrounds us. The great round of being will triumph. The celebrant at the end of the poem raises his arms to present his praise for all he has acquired in riches before his departure.

In 1960 the great voyager visited Patagonia, Tierra del Fuego, and Cape Horn as a guest of the Argentinian government. He met Jorge Luis Borges, Marcos Victoria, and several other writers in Buenos Aires. Upon his return to North America, he explored the American Northwest on horseback.

Back in France, he received more honors and prizes: the Grand Prix National des Lettres, the International Grand Prix de Poésie, honorary membership in the American Academy and National Institute of Letters, and a similar membership in the Bavarian Academy. However, his greatest honor came in the winter of 1960: the Nobel Prize, which he received in Stockholm. His acceptance speech, "Poésie" ("Poetry"), praised poetry and described it as an integral mode of life, an irreductible part of man.

The peaceful years that ensued between 1960 and 1970 were divided between the villa in Provence and a quaint house in the Georgetown section of Washington, D.C. Many men of letters and artists visited him at both places. He spent time traveling: cruises to the British Antilles, to the Camargue, to northern Italy. In France his collected works were published in a new edition, in two volumes, and many bilingual editions followed.

He then began a joint project with the French painter Georges Braque: *L'Ordre des oiseaux* (*The Avian Order*), which was published in 1962. This edition "de grand luxe" contained twelve etchings by Braque. In 1963 it was followed by an edition of the text alone *Oiseaux* (*Birds*). The bird, at ease in the three elements—the earth, the air, and the water—ambiguous but unique, is like the poet. It is even more: poetry itself. The bird-poet, always flying to greater heights, eventually reaches the sacred center where the never ending cosmic cycle originates. The final words convey the message that the birds preserve something of the dream of creation for us.

In 1968 Perse wrote a shorter poem, "Chanté par Celle qui fut là" ("Sung by the One Who was There"), expressing love and sorrow through the voice of a woman who helps her beloved to continue to live by returning, in memory, to his origin. Henceforth, Perse, feeling the first symptoms of illness, would not leave Provence. This gave him time to assemble all the texts he wanted to see published in the definitive edition of *Oeuvres complètes* (1972; *Collected Works*).

Three years after "Chanté par Celle qui fut là," he wrote another short poem, "Chant pour un équinoxe" (1971; "Chant for an Equinox"). It is again a celebration of life, returning, this time, to its point of origin. The dying poet knew that his art would be reincarnated. After addressing himself to the familiar elements of rain and snow he turned to the maternal earth. For him, poetry was an eternal song, a passage like the equinox, between man and the earth.

Another poem followed in 1972: "Nocturne," full of anguish and despair. However, it announced the passage from death to new life. Saint-John Perse's very last poem, "Sècheresse" ("Drought"), was written one year before his death. In it drought is the mark of the "chosen," the poet, who by announcing the destruction of the dry earth by fire, will prepare the advent of a rebirth. Rebirth is imminent, and human and mortal time will finally be replaced by the Godhead's eternal and regenerative time. Total union with the Divine will follow annihilation.

Saint-John Perse died on September 19, 1975, the day of the autumn equinox, in Giens. He was buried not far from the sea he loved so much.

ANTOINE SPACAGNA

Selected Bibliography

PRIMARY SOURCE
Perse, Saint-John. *Oeuvres complètes.* Paris: Gallimard, 1972.

SECONDARY SOURCES
Charpier, Jacques. *Saint-John Perse.* Paris: Gallimard, Bibliothèque Idéale, 1962.

Galand, René. *Saint-John Perse.* New York: Twayne, 1972.

Guerre, Pierre. *Saint-John Perse et l'homme.* Paris: Gallimard, 1955.

Henry, Albert. *AMERS de Saint-John Perse. Une poésie du mouvement.* Neuchâtel: Editions de la Baconnière, 1963.

Horry, Ruth. *Paul Claudel and Saint-John Perse.* Chapel Hill: University of North Carolina Press, 1971; London: Oxford University Press, 1971.

Knodel, Arthur. *Saint-John Perse: A Study of his Poetry*. Edinburgh: Edinburgh University Press, 1966.

Levillain, Henriette. *Le rituel poétique de Saint-John Perse*. Paris: Gallimard, 1955.

Loranquin, Albert. *Saint-John Perse*. Paris: Gallimard, 1963.

Murziaun, Christian. *Saint-John Perse*. Paris: Editions Universitaires, Classiques du XXe siècle, 1960.

LUIGI PIRANDELLO   *1934*

The Italian author Luigi Pirandello (1867–1936) was born June 28, 1867, near Girgenti (modern Agrigento), Sicily, and died December 10, 1936, in Rome. He was awarded the Nobel Prize in literature in 1934.

As a writer of poetry, short stories, novels, essays, and drama, Pirandello's career is marked by change, evolution, and development of concepts and themes that anticipated and influenced much of twentieth-century drama. His contributions include several of the absolute hallmarks of the modern stage. Pirandello's total production, published in six volumes in the complete Mondadori collection, includes 7 novels, 246 short stories, 44 plays, and 4 critical essays. There are seven collected works of poetry.

One of the keys to a greater understanding of this prodigious production is found in Pirandello's personal life and academic-professional background. There are decisive events in his childhood and cultural development that provide an insight into the sociological and psychological basis of his mature work.

Luigi Pirandello was the second of six children of Stefano Pirandello and Caterina Ricci Gramitto. His father, who managed rented sulfur mines, has been described as tall, violent-tempered, indifferent, and overbearing. The children were raised by a peasant maid servant, Maria Stella, whose language, religion, superstition, and mystical tendencies clearly influenced the sensitive young man. Pirandello loved to read. He admired Cellini, Bruno, Goldoni, and the poet Arturo Graf. The family moved to Palermo in 1882 followiong his father's bankruptcy. Pirandello studied law at Palermo, then moved to Rome in 1887 and on to Bonn in 1889, where he took a degree in Romance philology in 1891. Although the experience in Germany marked an important moment in his life by bringing him into contact with a broader, European culture, Pirandello's Sicilian temperament, with its formality and inflexible attitude toward the family and women, was to remain a fundamental characteristic.

Pirandello moved to Rome in 1891 and plunged into the capital's literary and artistic circles. He met Ugo Fleres and then Luigi Capuana, who advised the novel as a medium of expression, and helped launch Pirandello with his publishers.

On January 27, 1894, Pirandello married Antonietta Portulano of Agrigento. They had three children. The couple lived off her dowry and an endowed income, and after a financial crisis in 1897, his salary as professor of stylistics at the Magistero in Rome, a position he held full time between 1908 and 1924. This second phase of his career is marked by literary success (including the writing of twenty-eight plays between 1916 and 1924) and his wife's progressive illness. Antonietta's latent psychic instability, which began as a mild nervous breakdown, became a persecution complex combined with extreme jealousy. Pirandello attempted to treat his wife at home, but eventually he had to have her committed to an asylum in 1919. She died there in 1959.

Antonietta's madness was an essential part of Pirandello's vision of the absurdity of the world. Critical success and literary fame seemed haunted by the ghost of his personal family tragedy. After 1921 and the renewed enormous success of *Sei personaggi in cerca d'autore* (*Six Characters in Search of an Author*) and *Enrico IV* (Henry IV), Pirandello immersed himself in literary activity. He wrote constantly, renewed and fostered literary contacts, wrote for the *Messaggero* literary supplement, and enjoyed the critical debate he caused. Pirandello joined the Fascist party in 1924, and although he supported the regime early, he later became disenchanted. His politics were superficial, and his contributions essentially cosmetic, but the government nominated him to the Italian Academy in 1929 and subsidized the Teatro d' Arte that he founded in Rome in 1925 with the actress Marta Abba and the great actor-director Ruggero Ruggeri. Marta Abba became his inspiration and interpreter, and their relationship lasted the rest of his life.

Pirandello's most intense artistic activity was between 1910 and 1930, and he received the Nobel Prize in 1934. Pirandello's final drama, *Giganti della montagna* ("Mountain Giants") remained incomplete at his death in 1936.

The character and personality of Luigi Pirandello the man, apparent in many of his works, were the evident composite result of his personal and professional background. He loved to be around people and was a cordial, friendly person, but he also loved solitude. He had a brilliant mind with an innate capacity to observe, remember, and analyze incidents in general and specific detail. He sought out opinions but was always independent in judgment and approach. The seminal nature of his creative genius reflected his unique personality.

Pirandello is best known today for his drama, but he came to drama later in his career, having established a literary reputation with his short stories and novels. His first collection of poetry, called *Mal giocondo* ("Troubled Joy"), was published in 1889. Because of his natural sensitivity and ability to analyze psychologically and express his observations descriptively, Pirandello was able to move easily from poetry to prose and to theater. His narrative and dramatic works were parallel but autonomous developments of his writing, often with plots in common. But as Emanuele Licastro points out (in his *Luigi Pirandello dalle novelle alle comedie*), the short stories are complete in themselves and not sketches for later theater. "Verismo" (realism) is very important in Pirandello's prose, through the influence of Verga and Capuana, while in his theater the concepts of personality, symbolism, and dialectic are dominant.

One critic, Anne Paolucci (1974), deals with Pirandello's drama as a total unit with a continuity of interrelated themes.

Pirandello's poetry, prose, and theater share common themes, and the autobiographical aspect of his works is a common thread at all levels. Pirandello insulated himself from contemporary Italian and European literary and artistic movements and thereby achieved an intellectual independence that conferred a particularly pertinent freedom on his observations on the world and life.

The dramatic themes of Pirandello's works are the relativity of truth, multiple personality, and the different levels of reality. His drama is intellectual. Pirandello challenges his audience to participate in the self-criticism and self-analysis that his characters struggle with. His themes are not abstract philosophical problems, but instinctive, real drama, the heart of contemporary ideas and modern anxieties and pessimism.

Some of the best-known works illustrate the viability and comprehensive application of Pirandello's themes in prose and drama. The novel *Il fu Mattia Pascal* (1904; "The Late Mattia Pascal") is the first-person story of a modest provincial librarian who abandons his family and seeks to establish a new life for himself. Having won a fortune at Monte Carlo—and mistakenly considered dead in his hometown—Pascal takes the name Adriano Meis and tries to create a new life in Rome. Delusions and solitude overwhelm him, and Pascal decides to feign the suicide of Adriano and return home to his former life. But his wife has remarried, Pascal is officially dead, and Adriano never was, so Pascal remains a shadow of himself, without name, place in the world, or personality.

Il fu Mattia Pascal, written at the time of the first manifestations of Pirandello's wife's madness, clearly marks the first step of Pirandello's art. It presents an early demonstration of the themes of multiple personality and the relativity of reality.

A number of dramas, some taken directly from his short stories, indicate the overall significance of Pirandello's Sicilian background. *La giara* ("The Jar"), a one-act play of 1917, taken from the short story published in 1912, and *Liolà* (1916, in Sicilian dialect; in Italian text, 1928) emphasize the traditional Sicilian interest in family, property, honor, and peasant shrewdness.

The question of the relativity of truth is the central idea of the play *Così è (se vi pare)* (1918; "Right you are [If you think you are]") taken from a short story published in 1916. The plot concerns Signor Ponza and his mother-in-law, Signora Frola. Ponza lodges his wife and his mother-in-law in separate houses and refuses to let them meet. Colleagues and neighbors seethe with curiosity. Ponza claims that Signora Frola is mad, believing that he forbids her to see her daughter who, he claims, died in an earthquake. Signora Frola states that Ponza is mad and that his delusion consists in believing that his wife had died. Each argues convincingly, and any documents that could have given proof have been destroyed by the earthquake.

What is the truth? It exists, according to Pirandello, only as an illusion to each individual, relative to himself and the representation each one makes of it.

Perhaps the most famous and most typical drama of Pirandello is his *Sei personaggi in cerca d'autore* (1921). Pirandello highlights the creative evolution of a character from the author's first conception to final presentation in the theater. The fantastic reality of these phantom characters, who have been sketched out but not completed by their author, is thrust onstage during a rehearsal of another play. The characters insist on presenting the drama within them, but they cannot conclude their tragic story without an author. Their incomplete drama torments each character, as well as members of the company in re-

hearsal, as they strive to fulfill the partial reality only they themselves live and recognize. The variation of levels of reality becomes irresolvable.

Pirandello's concern with the question of identity and reality always involves his drive for truth and his concern with the difficulty of communication, a dilemma of complex proportions. It is the same idea found in *Enrico IV* (1922).

The tragedy *Enrico IV*, written by Pirandello for Ruggero Ruggeri, is often considered the masterpiece of Pirandello's theater. It employs all of Pirandello's dramatic themes in a startling examination of the protagonist's creative madness. Masks, mirrors, and portraits are the functional symbols of the drama. The protagonist assumes the mask of the eleventh-century emperor of Germany for one evening's masquerade, but by accident of fate he is crystallized in that mask by madness. As the result of a fall from a horse, Enrico becomes insane. Since he is wealthy, he is allowed to keep up his illusion. Friends, servants, and doctors are forced to accommodate his madness by continually appearing in his presence in costume as historic figures. For twelve years the madness endures, and then suddenly Enrico is cured. But he realizes, like Mattia Pascal, that his life has passed him by: His love, Matilde, has married his rival, Belcredi. Enrico withdraws into a conscious madness for another eight years, watching life as an outsider. The action of the play revolves around a final attempt to jolt Enrico into reality by means of the pictures of himself and Matilde painted for the masquerade party twenty years ago. Matilde's daughter Frida, costumed as her mother was twenty years earlier, is to stand in the place of the portrait in the throne room, and both she and her mother will confront Enrico with the reality of time past. The chilling confrontation in the throne room results in the death of Belcredi, stabbed by Enrico in a fit of revenge, and the definitive retreat of Enrico into the mask that drove him to murder.

The reversals of personality in *Enrico IV* are the most complex and suggestive in the entire Pirandellan repertory. The author's extraordinary skill keeps the puzzle of Enrico's sanity before the audience. The true tragedy of *Enrico IV* is the antithesis of identity and reality, the antagonism between life and form.

The fantastic and the real become a compelling dramatic contrast in the works of Luigi Pirandello.

RICHARD B. HILARY

Selected Bibliography

PRIMARY SOURCE

Pirandello, Luigi. *Opere. I classici contemporanei italiani.* 6 vols. Milan: Mondadori, 1956–60.

SECONDARY SOURCES

Boschiggia, Elisabetta. *Guida alla lettura di Pirandello.* Milan: Mondadori, 1986.

Giudice, Gaspare. *Pirandello, A Biography.* Translated by Alastair Hamilton. London: Oxford University Press, 1975.

Leone de Castris, Arcangelo. *Storia di Pirandello.* Bari: Laterza, 1962.

Licastro, Emanuele. *Luigi Pirandello dalle novelle alle comedie.* Verona: Fiorini, 1974.

Macchia, Giovanni. "Luigi Pirandello." *Storia della letteratura italiana.* Edited by Emilio Cecchi and Natalino Sapegno. Vol. IX. Milan: Garzanti, 1969. Pp. 441–92.

Munafò, Gaetano. *Conoscere Pirandello.* Florence: LeMonnier, 1981.

Nardelli, Federico Vittorio. *L'uomo segreto. Vita e croci di Luigi Pirandello.* 2nd ed. Milan: Mondadori, 1944.

Paolucci, Anne. *Pirandello's Theater. The Recovery of the Modern Stage for Dramatic Art.* Carbondale: Southern Illinois University Press, 1974.

Starkie, Walter. *Luigi Pirandello 1867–1936.* 3rd ed. Berkeley: University of California Press, 1974.

Virdia, Ferdinando. *Invito alla lettura di Luigi Pirandello.* 2nd ed. Milan: Mursia, 1976.

HENRIK PONTOPPIDAN 1917

Henrik Pontoppidan (1857–1943) was born on July 24, 1857, in Fredericia on the Jutland peninsula of Denmark and raised in his father's parish in Randers. His father was one in a long line of Pontoppidans who had been influential members of the Danish Lutheran church. Much of Henrik's work addressed and often assailed this religious heritage and its deep ties to nineteenth-century bourgeois values. Such criticism is especially prominent in his longest and greatest piece, *Lykke Per* (1898–1904; *Lucky Per*), the work that ultimately won him the Nobel Prize in literature in 1917— an honor Pontoppidan shared that year with a fellow Dane, Karl Gjellerup. This occasion marked only the middle of Pontoppidan's literary career, for he lived to write another twenty-six years, publishing his last work shortly before he died on August 21, 1943. Yet, even though he has become firmly established in the Danish literary canon as one of the greatest writers of his time, Pontoppidan has remained little known outside of Denmark, and many of his most famous works have never been translated. Very little criticism and only part of one of his major multivolume works *Det Forjættede land* (1891–95; *The Promised Land*) has been translated into English.

The sixteen children in the Pontoppidan family were variously talented, with several achieving prominence in such fields as medicine and politics as well as in the Lutheran ministry. Henrik showed a natural talent for mathematics, and, encouraged by a math teacher, he took and passed the entrance examination for the polytechnical institute in Copenhagen to study engineering. In 1873, at the unusually young age of sixteen, he moved to Copenhagen to begin his studies. However, a short trip to Switzerland in 1876 completely changed the direction of his life. This trip abroad inspired him to travel more and learn about the world, if not directly, then vicariously, through reading and the theater. He soon began to attempt plays of his own, and he became increasingly dissatisfied with his technical studies. He finally left the polytechnic in 1877 to take a position teaching technical subjects at his brother's rural Grundtvigian folk high school (named after the founder of the nineteenth-century Danish adult education movement, Nikolaj F. S. Gruntvig) in Frerslev. Here he found time to broaden his literary horizons while getting to know those people he was writing about, the Danish peasants. Pontoppidan would later include sympathetic sketches of these people, especially the poor and outcast, in all of his works.

Pontoppidan's critical view developed during his stay at the folk high school through reading the works of such influential thinkers as nineteenth-century Danish social critic Georg Brandes and Danish philosopher Søren Kierkegaard (and later, Friedrich Nietzsche). He also read much nineteenth-century fiction, including the Danish authors who came to influence his own style most, Steen Steensen Blicher, Sophus Schandorf, and Meir Goldschmidt. With their help, he became a writer in search of the truth, always socially critical but never committed to a single political stance; instead, he created his own. As one critic put it, he strove to "hold up a mirror" to his people and culture "in such a way that a multitude of faults was exposed." As a result, Pontoppidan has been called "the castigator of Denmark." Yet he remained popular, perhaps because the Danes realized his criticisms were not only accurate but also the result of his deep and abiding concern for his people.

In 1881, Pontoppidan published his first work, a short story entitled "Et endeligt" ("The End of a Life") in the journal *Ude og Hjemme*. "Et endeligt" depicts the plight of an unlucky poor family. After the grandfather dies, his wife and granddaughter are forced from their home, finding sympathy neither with the local doctor nor the grandfather's employer nor even the local minister, all of whom represent the social system to which the grandfather had always been faithful while he was alive. Although the story is carefully objective, relying on crisp, clear description rather than didactic narration to present its social criticism—how the poor are mistreated by society simply because they are poor—the criticism of bourgeois snobbery could not be more effective. Since it was favora-

bly received by critics, Pontoppidan published it and three other short stories in his first book, *Stækkede vinger* (1881; "Clipped Wings"), later that year, and with the honorarium from it he finally quit teaching and moved to a rural area north of Copenhagen to launch his full-time career as a writer.

His early works reflect this setting, focusing on daily life in rural Denmark, and make up his more realistic writing. In these works he idealizes the Danish rural landscape without depicting the life there as ideal, but rather as strenuous and demanding. These stories include realistically portrayed individual characters who are presented as victims of heredity and environment, a naturalistic theme that was to become a main focus in much of Pontoppidan's later work. Already in "Et endeligt" we see this and related themes, such as society's intolerance of the poor and other forms of social injustice. His second book and first novel, *Sandinge menighed* (1883; "Sandinge Parish"), about a poor country girl who is subjected to the hypocritical charity of a bourgeois Copenhagen family, contains still other major themes of Pontoppidan's. Here he examines the conflict between country and city, particularly the discord between idealized "natural" country life and "real" city life and the problems with Grundtvigianism, a uniquely Danish folk high school movement, as a means of unifying the two. In *Sandinge menighed*, we see his desire to find a way to bring urban and rural culture together, but Grundtvigianism (Gruntvig's principle of adult education), because of its conservative religious foundations—especially its sentimentalism and its simplistic world view—was not a way. Stylistic elements that Pontoppidan later came to master, such as social satire, caricature of human weaknesses, and the symbolic use of landscape, are all tested in this novel. The book's strengths lie in its use of irony and realistic descriptions, but it ultimately fails because it attempts too much, too many different stylistic techniques as well as themes. One critic of the time observed that "there lies in the plan of this narrative doubtless . . . raw material for an entire social novel of no little interest," but Pontoppidan, he felt, "had not yet learned to construct a work of art."

The acceptance of Pontoppidan's next collection of stories, *Landsbybilleder* (1883; "Village Sketches") by Gyldendal, the leading publishing house in Denmark, confirmed his position as a promising young writer. His talent for vivid, realistic description—especially of the rural Jutlanders—combines with subtle irony in these stories to point up, among other things, the myth of the ideal rural life and the consequences of human greed. His work here is more clearly naturalistic, as these sketches focus less on the plights of individual characters and more on the characters' symbolic values as exemplars of general social problems. The stories in his subsequent collection, *Fra hytterne. Nye landsbybilleder* (1887; "From the Huts. New Village Sketches") are even more socially critical; these stories have as a result been called "intentional contributions to the literature of social con-

sciousness." Several have as their main themes class differences, society's unfair treatment of the poor, and the power of money. Others contrast the uneducated rural population with the highly educated urban population to show the social evils of ignorance and superstition as well as hypocrisy. Such socially critical works, according to some literary theorists, helped to make Denmark one of the most socially conscious countries in the world today.

Skyer (1890; "Clouds"), Pontoppidan's third collection of short stories, is considered his most significant as well as his most widely read collection. Rather than the plight of individuals, or of the lower classes in general, this work has as its main focus the political climate of the 1880s and its effect on all of Denmark. In these stories he attacks the passivity of his countrymen, who allowed a provisional government that bordered on a dictatorship to run Denmark in the late 1870s and early 1880s. Here he mixes irony and satire with eloquent description and subtle metaphors to create a dialectical-dramatic criticism of the times and the people. *Skyer* includes "Ilum galgebakke" ("The Gallow Hill at Ilum"), now considered a classic in Danish political satire.

Pontoppidan's talent for conveying social criticism through objective description culminates in his first multivolume work, *The Promised Land*, a trilogy about a man at odds with his environment. The first two volumes of this work, *Muld* (1891; *Sod*) and *Det Forjættede land* (1892; *The Promised Land*, same title as for the whole trilogy), are more a psychological character study, or bildungsroman, than "A Picture of the Times," as the works' subtitle would suggest. Emanuel Hansted, an enthusiastic clergyman from Copenhagen sent to work in a rural parish, causes his own downfall when he tries to abandon entirely the urban culture from which he came. After attempting to become one of the rural folk by supporting the folk high school movement and marrying a peasant girl, he finds himself drawn to the intellectual circle of the city-educated doctor in town. He eventually goes mad—as his mother had before him—when he comes to believe that God has forsaken him. This work depicts country life more naturalistically than any of Pontoppidan's previous pieces, relying more on realistic dialogue and description of daily activities in the country than caricature or satire to convey his criticisms, and proves him to be a master of nineteenth-century Danish prose. The simple, short sentences produce a clarity that even Pontoppidan's unusual choice of imagery and metaphors cannot cloud. The third volume, *Dommens dag* (1895; *Doomsday*), is, however, "a picture of the times," as Hansted's failure and subsequent return to Copenhagen has already occurred before the volume begins. While it details Hansted's fate, this part also contains philosophical discussions on the problematic state of religion in Denmark—in particular, the effects of the Grundtvigian movement on the church as well as the church's general decline in the nineteenth century.

After publishing several minor novels, Pontoppidan began his longest and most significant work, *Lucky Per*, perhaps also the most important novel in Danish literature. His own religious upbringing comes through here even more than in *The Promised Land*. This eight-volume work, which was first revised to three volumes (1905), then finally to two (1918), is also a bildungsroman, tracing the life and spiritual development of Per Sidenius, a clergyman's son, from his youth, when he turns his back on his family and religious upbringing, through all his failures—the result of his self-centered desire for material success—to his self-awareness in old age. Sidenius typifies the optimist of the late nineteenth century; his faith in industrialization and technology as a means of bettering the world carry him away from conservative Lutheranism and agrarian-based culture to the modern twentieth-century world of machines. After a happy childhood in a rural town in Jutland, he goes to Copenhagen to study engineering, only to quit a short while later so that he can pursue his ambitious plans to build a canal system throughout Denmark. His lust for success, however, leads him to take advantage of several people, including his fiancée, the wealthy Jewish woman Jakobe. Per's unrealistic plans and his attempts to realize them by dubious means force him into a spiritual void. As a result, he loses interest in his project, becoming absorbed instead in a search for a tenable life philosophy. His search takes him back to his Jutland hometown, where he tries, like Emanuel Hansted, to become part of the peasant world by marrying a local girl. But this, too, does not last, because he cannot escape the spiritual values of his upbringing, and so he ends his days in lonely isolation from people and God but freed from the obsessions of wealth and power. Although the work demonstrates Pontoppidan's masterful use of language, especially his talent for naturalistic description—the book is replete with difficult and painful situations in which a modern reader might also find himself—it is perhaps best known and appreciated for its historical interpretation. He shows how complex historic events and developments of the late nineteenth century are interrelated by condensing them into the fictionalized context of Per's life. Historic figures also appear—most notably Georg Brandes, thinly veiled as Dr. Nathan and the main topic of conversation in the cosmopolitan Jakobe's house. The work's ultimate unifying element is its philosophical message, which extends beyond Per and Denmark and history: "To thine own self be true." While early criticism of the novel focused on and praised this ethical message, the exceptional clarity and simplicity of Pontoppidan's style drew praise in later criticism. Although certain weaknesses in the work's characterization and critical argumentation have been pointed out in recent years, its status as a masterpiece of Danish literature remains unquestioned.

De dødes rige (1912–16; "The Realm of the Dead") is perhaps Pontoppidan's most profound book, full of the pain of existence and what it means to be human. This five-volume work differs somewhat from his other multivolume pieces in that it has no single protagonist and is therefore more truly "a picture of the times," focusing on a time period (the turn of the century) and a place (Denmark) rather than on the development and experiences of a single character. Two characters, however, provide a connecting link: Torben and Jytte, whose unsuccessful courtship becomes the main focus of the first volume. The next three volumes describe the careers of Tyge Enslev—a once powerful politician and newspaper owner—and his nephews, while the last volume ties the work together by tracing the outcomes of all the main characters' lives. Like *Lucky Per*, *De dødes rige* addresses the life philosophy "to thine own self be true." The lust for power and the inability to be oneself can ruin people's lives, so they must find a life philosophy that works for them, and though they may never actually find one, it is the attempt that can lead to a meaningful and fulfilling existence. But *De dødes rige* receives its title from another theme: "the heavy hand of the dead." Like Per and Hansted, the characters in this novel cannot escape their heritages; they are trapped by the influence of their forebears.

Pontoppidan's last novel, *Mands himmerig* (1927; "Man's Heaven"), returns to the "life philosophy" theme. This work is about two journalists, one who succeeds because she is true to herself, and another who fails because he seeks power and neglects himself. The laureate's last work, a detailed and penetrating autobiography in four volumes (1933–40), was later completely revised and condensed into one volume, entitled *Undervejs til mig selv* (1943; "Underway to Myself"). Only his second nonfiction piece (the first was a 1914 essay against the clergy, "Kirken og dens mænd"—"The Church and its Men"), it is carefully objective and, ironically, avoids information about his private life. Instead, Pontoppidan chose to focus on the sources of his literary interests. His autobiography shows him to be a rationalist for whom "neither solace nor help can be found any place outside myself." In the final version of the autobiography, he contradicts some of what he had written earlier, revealing this work to be more fiction, perhaps, than fact. But what was important was conciseness combined with clarity, and so, by tempering the figurative and rhetorical aspects of his writing, he achieved a smooth and clear style that left more to the reader's imagination. Pontoppidan revised all of his works, sometimes so much so that the revision seemed more like a new work. This compulsion to revise was, perhaps, the most notable aspect of his writing.

Henrik Pontoppidan was, in the words of Thomas Mann, "a born epic poet" and a great "critic of life and society." He was an artist who had an eye for the picturesque as well as for the ironic, and a Danish patriot who only criticized his people because he loved them.

SUSAN SWANSON

Selected Bibliography

PRIMARY SOURCES

Pontoppidan, Henrik. *Emanuel; or, Children of the Soil*. Translated by Mrs. Edgar Lucas. London: Dent, 1896.

——— . *The Promised Land*. Translated by Mrs. Edgar Lucas. London: Dent, 1896.

SECONDARY SOURCES

Ahnlund, Knut. *Henrik Pontoppidan. Fem Huvudlinder i Författerskapet*. Stockholm: Norstett, 1956.

Andersen, Poul Carit, ed. *Digteren og Mennesket. Fem Essays om Henrik Pontoppidan*. Copenhagen: Published by the editor, 1951.

Astrup Larsen, Hanna. "Pontoppidan of Denmark." *American-Scandinavian Review* 31 (1943):231–39.

Mitchell, P. M. *Henrik Pontoppidan*. Twayne World Author Series. Boston: Twayne, 1979.

Woel, Cai M. *Henrik Pontoppidan*. 2 vols. Copenhagen: Ejnar Munksgaards, 1945.

SALVATORE QUASIMODO *1959*

Salvatore Quasimodo (1901–68), born at Modica, a tiny town in the Sicilian province of Syracuse (today, Ragusa) on August 20, 1901, spent an itinerant childhood because of his father's numerous transfers of employment. As a railroad station chieftain, his father, Gaetano, was transferred to Roccalumera first and later to Gela, Acquaviva, Trabia, and finally to Messina. It was in this city, which had been the site of a most destructive earthquake in 1908, that the youthful Quasimodo experienced the atrocities of that natural calamity, which had left thousands of people dead or maimed and the city itself a shambles. The tragic memory of man's helplessness and powerlessness against such superior forces, tied with the natural beauty of his land, would later become themes that recurred in his poetry throughout his lifetime.

From Messina, he moved to Palermo, where he succeeded in receiving the diploma as a geometrician. In 1919 he enrolled in the polytechnic at Rome but never received the final degree. While in Rome, Quasimodo was forced to undertake a score of employments, some of them menial, in order to sustain his livelihood, and it was here that he began his literary experiences and his initial ties with the Florentine intelligentsia of the *Frontespizio* journal. This group, whose members expounded the ideas of the young hermetic poetic school of thought,

would influence the youthful Quasimodo and would become an important part of his formative literary career.

He joined the civil engineer corps and moved for a brief period to Reggio Calabria, where he met often with the literary elite of Messina and where he strengthened ties with influential men of letters such as Giorgio La Pira, Salvatore Pugliatti, Glauco Natali, and Salvatore Pella, who constituted the "humus" of Sicilian humanism. Quasimodo moved back to Florence, where in 1930 he published his first collection of poetry, *Acque e Terre* (*Waters and Lands*).

The exquisite reminiscing themes of his beautiful Sicily, the idyllic mythological ties with a classic Greek world that he relived through the numerous ancient Greek ruins preserved throughout the island, and human love and camaraderie are thematic elements that are born in this collection but that reappear throughout his prolific lifetime production. Quasimodo also sang the melancholy feeling of his "exiled" state and his constant yearning to return to his land one day.

Transferred by his Florentine office, he moved on to Imperia in the Ligurian region, and later to the island of Sardinia, to Sondrio and finally to what would later become his beloved Milan. In this period he published *Oboe Sommerso* (1932; *Sunken Oboe*), *Odore di Eucalyptus*

ed *Altri Versi* (1932; *Eucalyptus'
Scent and Other Verses*), *Erato and
Apollyon* (1936), and *Poesie* (1938;
Poems). All of these collections continued the major themes already
found in his first volume of poetry:
the remembrance of years past, the
recollection of the breathtaking Sicilian landscapes and seascapes, a
mythical reevocation of primitive
yet innocent times when the poet
was indeed in unison with his surroundings. His "exile" became, at
times, so burdensome that it forced
him to find solace in the illusory
escape of his creative mind. The
above collections present a remarkable prelude to the greater poetry of
the postwar period.

Feeling ever more the burden of
literary notoriety and the determination to expound further his lyric
message, in 1938 he abandoned his
position with the civil corps of engi-
neers, which was literally taking up
his "precious creative time," and accepted an appointment as editorial
correspondent for the weekly journal *Tempo* of Milan. Shortly thereafter, he also accepted a post as professor of Italian literature at the
Giuseppe Verdi Conservatory of
Music in that same city.

With the publication of his
translation of the *Lirici Greci*
(*Greek Lyrics*) in 1940, Quasimodo
reached a high point in his poetic
powers. His assiduous yet loving efforts spent in studying his mythological "ancestors" culminated in the
creation of one of his poetic masterpieces, *Ed è Subito Sera* (1942; *And
Suddenly It's Evening*). In this work
mythological entities abound. The
poet feels a genuine tie to that an-

cient classic culture and civilization
which is manifested by the sadness
of his reminiscence. It is with this
publication that Quasimodo's verse
attained a classic universality.

With the publication of *And
Suddenly It's Evening*, Quasimodo
concluded the first phase of his poetic career. As it did with many
other writers, the inhumanity of
World War II temporarily silenced
his muse. When he did return, a new
writer was disclosed to the reader.
The atrocities and catastrophic
manifestations of a long and horrendous war that he personally experienced as an active member of the
Italian resistance movement would
change significantly his creative
spirit and poetic directions. His future collections of poetry would reflect this change in a most striking
fashion. He abandoned earlier emphasis on childhood reminiscences
and autobiographical elements and
began to address the civil and social
bewilderment of postwar society,
calling for a panhumanism that
transcended national boundaries. It
was a prolific period, during which
Quasimodo would publish what
many critics regard as his best and
most striking work, filled with love,
compassion, and a deep concern for
humanity: *Giorno dopo Giorno*
(1947; *Day After Day*), *La Vita non
è Sogno* (1949; *Life Is not a Dream*),
Il Falso e Vero Verde (1954; *The
False and True Green*), and *La
Terra Impareggiabile* (1958; *The In-
comparable Earth*).

During this time he also made
frequent and extensive journeys
throughout the European continent,
visiting Russia a number of times.

These trips, which later inspired him to write much of his new poetry, also brought him the international recognition that led to several Italian literary prizes awarded for poetry (San Babila, 1950; Etna-Taormina, 1953; Viareggio, 1958) and eventually the Nobel Prize in literature in 1959.

The "new" collection of poems, *Day After Day* opened with a striking composition titled "On the Willow Branches," whose initial verses have become recognized as truly classic: "And how could we have sung/with the foreigner's foot upon our heart,/among the dead abandoned in the squares/on the grass hardened by ice." These lines not only attest to the poet's tremendous desire to sing out to the world once again, but remind us that a cold and senseless war had silenced his muse. There is in this and other poems of this collection a constant lament for the suffering of man, a description of the atrocities of war, and of the "vanity of joyous times," the changed landscape that has become "barren" and "gray," and the universal vanity of man's past strivings when reflected in the harshness of the current reality. Moreover, the poet abandoned the subjective "I" and the soliloquy and began to address all of humanity for the first time. Quasimodo concluded that what seemed to have once been his pain and sorrow has now become the pain and sorrow of all mankind.

After receiving the Nobel Prize, Quasimodo, tired and physically afflicted, began to exhibit a decline in both the volume and quality of his work. He seemed to have already given his best and to have shared his central poetic message. Many contemporary critics have interpreted his works quite negatively, viewing Quasimodo as no longer a Neoclassic writer, nor even a true symbolist or languid Crepuscular poet. Stripping him of his appellation as a true Hermetic poet, Carlo Bo lowers him to the rank of a mere "road companion of Hermetic writers" since he conveniently used the stylistic devices of that movement during a time when that form was in vogue. Critic Elio Gioanola believes that Quasimodo was fortunate to have enjoyed a popularity much superior to his own worth. Quasimodo should remain a champion of the new classicism between the wars and a neorealist in the postwar period and not a "creator or originator of new forms of poetic expressions."

Salvatore Quasimodo's last official literary function was the signing of a document while presiding over a special committee in the city of Amalfi. This document, which awarded the prize for the best poetry of the year, was presented to two aspiring young writers. Struck by a brain hemorrhage shortly after, Quasimodo was rushed to a clinic in Naples, where he died on the afternoon of June 14, 1968.

ERASMO G. GERATO

Selected Bibliography

PRIMARY WORKS

Quasimodo, Salvatore. *The Selected Writings of Salvatore Quasimodo.* Edited and translated by Allen

Mandelbaum. New York: Farrar, Straus & Cudahy, 1960.

———. *Tutte le Poesie*. With a preface by Sergio Solmi and Carlo Bo. Milan: Mondadori, 1972.

SECONDARY SOURCES

Beall, Chandler. "Quasimodo and Modern Italian Poetry." *Northwest Review* IV (1961):41–48.

Cambon, Glauco. "A Deep Wind: Quasimodo's 'Tindari'." *Italian Quarterly* III (1959):16–28.

Dego, Giuliano. "Quasimodo: 1903–1968. A Last Visit." *London Magazine* 8 vi (1968):5–18.

Donini, Filippo. "Quasimodo and the Nobel Prize." *Italian Quarterly* III (1959):3–8.

Genot, Gérard. "Salvatore Quasimodo ou la Quête du Dialogue." *Revue des Etudes Italiennes* II (1965):269–82.

Gigante, Marcello. *L'ultimo Quasimodo e la Poesia Greca.* Naples: Guida, 1970.

Jones, Frederic J. "The Poetry of Salvatore Quasimodo." *Italian Studies* XVI (1961):60-77.

McCormick, C. A. "Salvatore Quasimodo and the Struggle Against Silence." *Meanjin* XX (1961):269–74.

Rossi, Louis R. "Salvatore Quasimodo: A Presentation." *Chicago Review* XIV (1960):1–23.

Tedesco, Natale. *Quasimodo e la Condizione Poetica del Nostro Tempo.* Palermo: Flaccovio, 1960.

WŁADYSŁAW REYMONT *1924*

Władysław Stanisław Reymont (1868–1925) was born in the village of Kobielie Wielkie, Poland, in the province of Piortków on May 7, 1868. In 1869 his family emigrated to a settlement called Tuszyn near the city of Łódź in central Poland, where young Reymont spent most of his childhood. He died in Warsaw on December 5, 1925, one year after being awarded the Nobel Prize in literature for his national epic, *Chłopi (The Peasants)*, written between 1902 and 1909.

His family, of lower-middle-class origin, owned a small piece of land on which his father operated a mill; his father was also the village organist. As the only male child in the family, Reymont was kept busy with farm chores; yet he managed to read every book in the home library. His parents enrolled him in several schools and apprenticed him to a few trades, but Reymont felt himself unable to become involved in formal education. In essence he was a self-educated man. Intermittently, he was a novice in a religious order, a wandering actor, a tailor, and a railroad worker. He also traveled to England, France,

Italy, and twice to the United States to gather material and then, just prior to his death, once again to the United States to raise funds on behalf of Poland.

During his vagabond years, Reymont wrote poetry; but his true vocation was prose. He wrote numerous short stories, documentary stories, and several major works based to a large extent on his life experiences and impressions. He first became known in Poland when a Warsaw weekly published a number of his short stories, such as *Śmierć* (1893; *The Death*), *Wigilia Bożego Narodzenia* (1893; *Christmas Eve*), and *Pielgrzymka do Jasnej Góry* (1895; *Pilgrimage to Jasna Gora*). These stories describe religious events and peasant life.

Reymont's classic statement on peasants and peasant life is his four-volume, Nobel Prize epic *The Peasants*. Set in the Polish village of Lipce, then under czarist rule, the novels details the "toils and pleasures and customs and the drama of human loves and hates" in the daily life of the tillers. Therein lies its universal appeal. Yet, the work is unmistakably Polish in its vivid description of the local countryside and in its perceptive characterization of the inhabitants in late-nineteenth-century Russian Poland.

Each of the four volumes is given the name of a season, deliberately following the order of the rural year: *Jesień* (1902; *Autumn*); *Żima* (1902–09; *Winter*); *Wiosna* (1902–09; *Spring*); *Lato* (1909; *Summer*). Reymont thus underscores the development of his main

characters, namely, Yagna, old Bornya, and Antek. The human dramas proceed slowly and with increasing tension from the first page to the last: from the wedding of old Bornya and Yagna in autumn to the awakening of passion between Yagna and her stepson, Antek, in the winter; from the bitter fight between father and son, husband and stepson-lover of Yagna and the tragic and cruel death of the father in the spring to the mob-attack on Yagna in the summer. In addition, it is Yagna as well as the Bornya family into which she marries together with their associates whose way-of-life is being transformed by the loss of forest lands and by the oncoming industrialization.

In this agrarian novel, Reymont interrelates the community with its individual members and interweaves the personal with the historical: the unsuccessful uprising of the peasants against the manor-folk and its resultant dire consequences for each household with the tragedy of the Bornya in a son's rivalry with his father over his stepmother. Reminiscent of Sophocles' *Oedipus Rex* and Shirley Jackson's *The Lottery*, one person in the Polish village is held responsible for all the ills that befall the community of Lipce. That person is Yanka.

Another major work, but of lesser significance stylistically, is his first novel, *Ziemia Obiecana* (1899; *The Promised Land*). This work deals with the world of industry and business and the problems of industrial expansion. Reymont was one of the first in Europe to document industrialization, specifically in its early stages.

The "promised land" is the city of Łódź where Reymont had spent several years as a young adult. Often referred to as the Polish Manchester, Łódź had developed into a major textile manufacturing center and a modern urban metropolis in the 1880s.

In the novel interest is focused on the city's main ethnic groups and the single unifying force between them, i.e., the pursuit of business. The virtues and vices that each ethnic group manifests in this pursuit are vividly portrayed by Reymont in their characteristic speech patterns. Initially, the contribution to the industrialization of Łódź by each group reflects its traditional role within the broader Polish society: the Jew—capitalist; the German—technician; the Pole —laborer. With time, each group attempts to secure for itself new advantages and the drive to riches becomes ruthless. In the process, "city life becomes mechanized and man dehumanized."

All the "Lodzers" are constrained by the laws of the jungle. Those who refuse, as well as the lazy, the weak, and the incompetent, are otherwise destroyed. Yet some successfully resist the change and are able to preserve their honor and their principles.

The Promised Land details the impact of social change on Łódź's main ethnic groups, the crowds, and the "Lodzer-Mensch," but devotes little attention to the plight of the worker. In later works Reymont does explore man's relationship to the machine. Especially noteworthy is the short story "On a Certain Day" (1900) in which he relates the process by which the working man becomes passive. The working man in this story has been compared to the little man as portrayed by Charlie Chaplin who is overcome by the fear of things to come. In yet another short story, "Tomek Baran" (1890), Reymont explores how a worker survives unemployment, hunger, and poverty.

Reymont's treatment of the world of the artist draws upon his own youthful experiences in the theater. He wrote several short stories and novels whose main theme is the conflict existing between the artist and the society. None of the works was particularly well received, partly because they were written at the beginning of his career when Reymont was still unsure of his writing style. The best-known work that has been recently adapted as a movie is *Komediantka* (1896; *The Comedienne*), a tale of Janka who is drawn to the theater by its external glitter. Ignoring what she sees—the conflicts among the theater people, the actors' struggle for mere survival—Janka dreams of becoming a beautiful and famous actress, but the dream never materializes. Alone and pregnant by a lover who has deserted her, Janka attempts suicide. To her friends, Janka is, in the true sense of the word, a comedienne.

Reymont's works have been translated into English, French, and German. A few of the English translations may be found in the Oxford University Press world classics series and in the *Anthology of Modern Slavonic Literature*. It was not until the Nobel Prize was awarded that any real interest was shown in Reymont outside Poland. Today, he remains relatively unknown as a man and an artist.

Reymont is classified as a representative of the *Młoda Polska* (Young Poland) literary movement that emerged in the 1890s. The two main literary methods of the movement—positivism and naturalism—characterized his earlier style of writing. His works reflect his keen observation of social life and his fine ability to record with scientific exactness the details of what he observed. But Reymont was also influenced by the tradition of realism that eventually dominated his thinking and his style of writing. He was especially interested in the real life of people and situations to which he could relate his experiences. This interest is evident, for example, when he sets down the peculiarities of speech of the peasant, the city dweller, and the actor. While he always insisted on great detail in his writing, Reymont differs in one important respect from the literati to whom he has been compared, such as Emile Zola, Frank Norris, and Theodore Dreiser. Although influenced by the literary trends of his time, Reymont's style of writing was

very personal; he remained his own man—independent and self-reliant.

JOSEPHINE WTULICH

Selected Bibliography

PRIMARY SOURCES

Reymont, Władysław. *The Comedienne*. Translated by Edward Obecny. New York: Putnam, 1920.

——— . *The Peasants.* 4 vols. Translated by Michael Dziewicki. New York: Knopf, 1924–25.

——— . *The Promised Land.* 2 vols. New York: Knopf, 1927.

——— . "Tomek Baran." Translated by G. R. Noyes. In *Great Stories of the World*. B. B. Clark, ed. New York: Putnam, 1920.

SECONDARY SOURCES

Borowy, Waclaw. "Reymont." *The Slavonic Review* XVI (1938):439–48.

Boyd, Ernest. Władysław Reymont." *The Saturday Review of Literature* I, 18 (November 29, 1924):317–19.

Hughes, Hubert. "Poland's Peasant Novelist." *The New York Times Magazine*, July 18, 1919, pp. 10, 25.

Krzynanowski, Jerzy R. *Władysław Reymont*. New York: Twayne, 1972.

Stender-Paterson, Adolf. "Reymont, Winner of the Nobel Prize." *The Living Age* 324, 4202 (January 19, 1925).

ROMAIN ROLLAND *1915*

French playwright, novelist, essayist, biographer of great musicians, professor, polemist, and pacifist, Romain Edmé Paul Emile Rolland (1866–1944) was born on January 29, 1866, in Clamecy, in the department of Nièvre, central France, of an old bourgeois Burgundian family. His father, Emile, was a *notaire* (notary) tracing his descent from a family of five generations of *notaires*. His mother, Antoinette-Marie Courot, was the daughter of local farmers and *notaires*. A neglected childhood illness after birth left Rolland with a lifelong pulmonary infirmity. Two years after his birth a sister was born who was named Madeleine. She died at age three, and a second sister, born in 1872, was given the same name. Rolland received his secondary education at the Collège de Clamecy (now named after him) until the "seconde" (last class before the baccalaureate).

In 1880, when the boy was fourteen, his father sold his *étude* (office) and the family moved to the Latin Quarter in Paris so that the young Rolland might continue his education. Rolland's father consequently accepted an unimportant position in a bank. Between 1880 and 1882 Rolland studied at the Lycée Saint-Louis. In September 1882 his health caused him to go to Allevard, a spa famous for treatment of bronchial disorders. The proximity of Allevard to the French Alps enabled Rolland to visit Switzerland for the first time. While on summer vacation in August 1883 he met Victor Hugo and was deeply moved by "the old Orpheus."

During his years of preparation for the difficult and competitive entrance examination to the Ecole Normale Supérieure, he attended many concerts with Paul Claudel, his classmate. Both were Richard Wagner enthusiasts. In July 1886 Rolland was accepted at Ecole, where he would study until 1889. There André Suarès became his best friend. He obtained his *licence-ès-lettres* at the end of the first year and at first seemed to be interested in philosophy. However, discouraged by the "paper spiritualism" he found in this discipline, he decided to pursue history and read the Russian writers who had recently become popular in France. Tolstoy in particular fascinated him, and in 1887 Rolland began corresponding with the Russian writer. In August 1889 Rolland passed the *agrégation d'histoire*, ranking eighth, and was appointed a member of the French Archaeological School of Rome for two years. While at the Farnese Palace, seat of the French Embassy and the French School in Rome, Rolland developed his piano skills considerably and wrote his first plays: *Empédocle* (never completed) and *Orsino* (1890). In addition, he started *Les Baglioni* which he finished in Paris in 1891. There he wrote a play in verse, *Niobé*, and started a fifth drama, *Caligula*. Despite his efforts he was never able to have these plays performed.

Still suffering from his chronic infirmity, he soon asked for a year's leave of absence from teaching. Invited one day to the home of his professor of classical philology at the Collège de France, he met the professor's daughter, Clotilde Bréal. The young lady shared his interest in music, and Romain fell in love with her. They were married in October 1892. In November the young couple moved to Rome. Here Rolland gathered, in four months, the material for an essay on the origins of opera. Back in Paris during Easter 1893, Rolland completed his documentation and wrote his dissertation while teaching a course in art history at the Lycée Henri IV, then at Louis-le-Grand (1894–95). He was subsequently appointed to teach a course in art history at the Ecole Normale Supérieure.

Between 1895 and 1897 he continued to write plays within the framework of a projected cycle, *The Divine Tragedy*. The first of these, *Saint-Louis*, was completed in 1895 and published by Jules Lemaître in the *Revue de Paris* (1897). *Jean de Piennes* (1896) was never published. In the summer of 1896 he spent two months in Germany and started writing another play, *Aërt*, simultaneously with his monumental saga novel, *Jean-Christophe*. *Aërt* was published in 1898 by the *Revue d'art dramatique* and staged by Lugné-Poë at the Théâtre de l'Oeuvre in May 1898.

Caught in the climax of the Dreyfus Affair, Rolland wrote another play, *Les Loups* (1898; *The Wolves*), in two weeks under the pseudonym of L. Saint-Just, a revolutionary theoretician of the Reign of Terror (1793–94) whom he much admired. At first Rolland did not completely believe in the innocence of Dreyfus. His wife and his best friend, Suarès, who were both Jews, were able to influence him, and he later changed his mind but never became personally involved. This attitude of intellectual support without active participation was a characteristic for which Rolland was often criticized by his friends. *Les Loups*, which angered both the pro- and anti-Dreyfus parties and did not satisfy the Jewish community, was the first of another cycle of plays, *Le Cycle de la Révolution*.

Between 1898 and 1904 Rolland wrote reviews and articles for the *Revue de Paris* and the *Revue d'art dramatique*. The articles would later be collected in *Le Théâtre du Peuple* (1903; *The People's Theater*). He also published *Le Triomphe de la Raison* (1899; *The Triumph of Reason*), a play on the fall of the Girondins, and *Danton* (1900), which was performed at the end of the year and published the following year in the *Cahiers de la Quinzaine* (1901; *Fortnightly Notebooks*). At this point, his father-in-law began to criticize Rolland for his interest in the revolution, which probably precipitated his separation from Clotilde that same year, followed shortly thereafter by an official divorce. Undaunted, he wrote two more plays, *Le 14 juillet* (1902; "The Fourteenth of July"), published by Péguy, and *Le Temps viendra* (1903; "The Time Will Come"), inspired by the Boer

War. Between 1901 and 1904 he also wrote for the *Revue d'histoire et de critique* (later entitled *Revue musicale*) and taught, after May 1902, courses in the history of music at the Ecole des Hautes Etudes Sociales (until 1911). In 1903 Rolland published *Vie de Beethoven* (*Life of Beethoven*) in the *Cahiers de la Quinzaine* as the beginning of a new and unfinished cycle, *Vies des Hommes Illustres* ("Lives of Famous Men"), heroes whose lives provide lessons in courage. His health was still delicate. He was poor and lived a solitary life in a small apartment on the Boulevard Montparnasse. Hard work was his only consolation.

The period of most intense creativity for Rolland was the decade 1903–12. He was occupied by the writing of his major work, the saga of an imaginary musician, Jean-Christophe Krafft, who shared many traits with Beethoven. The narrator wanted the readers to feel "the heroes' breath" in a monument to "Divine Music." The protagonist lives a life full of energy in a trying world of turmoil. A period of history was unfurled, and important moments in the life of an emerging musical genius were explored: childhood, adolescence, friendship, and love. It was an act of faith in traditional qualities such as moral strength, brotherly love, the musical beauty of the world around us, personal generosity—life in its infinite diversity.

Before its Paris publication in ten volumes by Ollendorff (1905–12), *Jean-Christophe* appeared in the *Cahiers de la Quinzaine* in installments. An English translation

by Gilbert Cannan appeared in three volumes (New York: Holt, 1910, 1911, 1913). During the same period Rolland wrote several other works: *Michel-Ange* (1905), translated in 1915, and *La Vie de Michel-Ange*—the second volume of his cycle, "The Lives of Famous Men" published in *Cahiers de la Quinzaine* (1906)—later translated as *The Life of Michelangelo*. He also gathered his articles on music criticism and musicology and in 1908 published them in two volumes, *Musiciens d'aujourd'hui* (*Musicians of Today*) and *Musiciens d'autrefois* (*Musicians of Former Years*). *Handel* (1910) was also published during the same period as his collected dramas *Théâtre de la Révolution* (1909; "Theater of the Revolution") and *Tragédies de la Foi* (1913; "Tragedies of Faith"). In 1905 he was awarded the Vie Heureuse literary prize, and in 1909 he received the Legion of Honor. On October 20, 1910 he was run over by a car. This accident left his left arm and leg half paralyzed. While convalescing, he re-read Tolstoy, and developed an article he had written into the third biography of "The Lives of Famous Men," *Vie de Tolstoï* (1911; *Life of Tolstoy*), published in Paris and in English in New York. His biography was approved by the family of the Russian writer.

After two years of leave from the Sorbonne for health reasons, he resigned in July 1912 to concentrate on his writing. Between April and September 1913, he rested in Switzerland, having completed *Jean-Christophe*. In June of that year the French Academy bestowed upon him the Grand Prix de Littérature.

He was again in Switzerland a year later when World War I broke out. At forty-eight, too old and unfit for military service, he remained in Switzerland. On September 2, 1914, he published his *Lettre ouverte à Gerhardt Hauptmann* ("Open Letter to G. H.") blaming him for the destruction of Louvain. This began a series of pacifist articles in *Le Journal de Genève*, collected and published in 1916 under the title *Au-dessus de la mêlée* ("Above the Battle"), the most famous of the series. This article was addressed to the youth of the world ("O jeunesse héroïque du monde") on September 15, 1914, and it caused much controversy and misunderstanding in France, where some did not hesitate to call him a traitor. Essentially, the article advocated stopping the killing of innocent young men and to rise above nationalism and chauvinism to build a world free from the injustice and prejudice of individual nations. These articles and many others were collected and published in book form in Paris in November 1915. The book helped make Rolland a leader of pacifism among the young intellectuals of his time despite the storm of protests raised among the general public. The volume was sold for the benefit of the Agence Internationale des Prisonniers de Guerre (International Agency for War Prisoners), to which Rolland devoted his total energy between October 1914 and July 1915.

The year 1916 was an important one for Rolland. He went back to creative writing and conceived a new type of hero, Clérambault, a pensive, quiet man whose battlefield was in the mind. This was also a new form of novel: a "roman meditation," a mix of novel and reflections. The original title he had in mind was *L'un contre Tous* ("One Against All"), but afraid of raising more controversy, he settled for *Clérambault: histoire d'une conscience libre pendant la guerre* (1921; *Clerambault: The Story of an Independent Spirit During the War*). Rolland also collaborated with Henri Guilbeaux, who had just founded the journal *Demain*. His articles published between 1916 and 1918 would be later gathered in *Les Précurseurs* (1919; "The Precursors"). On November 13, 1916, the Swedish Academy bestowed upon him the Nobel Prize in literature. He divided the money between the Red Cross and several French charitable organizations.

On May 1, 1917, Romain Rolland expressed his hope that free Russia would bring peace to Europe, and on March 15, 1918, he advocated the creation of an "Internationale de l'Esprit" (International Union of Minds) to propagate humanism. He finished his essay "Empédocle d'Agrigente," which was published in Switzerland. He wrote another play, *Liluli*, an allegorical farce. In it, a character who had escaped death on the battlefield was buried under an avalanche. God was powerless, and many critics interpreted this as an indication of Rolland's loss of faith.

When the Versailles Treaty was signed on June 23, 1919, Rolland felt quite pessimistic about the future. On June 26 his manifesto "Déclaration d'Indépendence de l'Esprit" ("Declaration of Independence of the Mind") appeared in *L'Human-ité*, signed by a thousand intellectuals. It advocated universal brotherhood. On August 26 he wrote to Rabindranath Tagore expressing his hope that India and the Orient would help to save Europe. *Pierre et Luce*, a tragic idyll inspired by the war, was published a year later (1920).

In 1919 Henri Barbusse founded an international association, Clarté, based more or less on ideas expressed by Rolland. Although sympathetic to the group, Rolland, as usual, remained aloof, following his principle of noninvolvement. A polemical exchange of correspondence ensued. He criticized the "Rollandistes" and the infallibility of the "social geometry" asserted by Clarté. In April 1921 he left again for Switzerland with his father and his sister, Madeleine. Exactly one year later they settled in the Villa Olga in Villeneuve (Vaud Canton), where they remained until 1937. The same year Rolland started to write the serial novel that he had been thinking about for nine years, *L'Ame enchantée* (1922-33; *The Soul Enchanted*). It is the feminine counterpart of *Jean-Christophe*, the saga of a woman, Annette Rivière, described through an overview of "the generation born between 1895 and 1880."

Concerned by the frequent symptoms of his deteriorating health, Rolland began his spiritual testament, *Le Voyage Intérieur* ("Journey Within"), in 1924, a poetic portrait of his origins and his soul. It would remain unfinished although several chapters were published in 1942 under the same title.

Others were issued posthumously. Between his various activities Rolland found time to take up his former project, the *Théâtre de la Révolution*. He wrote several works simultaneously, as was his habit. In January 1926 an international homage to Rolland appeared in *Europe* on the occasion of the writer's sixtieth birthday.

From 1927 to 1931, Rolland undertook an ambitious musicological study that resulted in *Beethoven: Les Époques créatrices* (1928-43; "Beethoven: The Creative Years"). Between 1929 and 1933, Rolland finished *L'Ame enchantée* (*The Soul Enchanted*). The fourth volume, *L'Annonciatrice* ("The Messenger"), was published in two volumes in 1933.

In 1929 he met a young Russian widow, Marie Kodachova, and she became his companion and secretary. They were married in 1934. On June 16, 1931, Rolland's father died. In December of the same year Gandhi visited Rolland in Villeneuve. Invited to preside over the World Congress against War in Amsterdam in 1932, Rolland was unable to attend because of poor health. The Academy of Science of Leningrad elected him an honorary member shortly thereafter. The following April Rolland refused the Goethe medal presented to him by the German government under Hitler. In May 1933 he started a polemic with the *Kölnische Zeitung* concerning the Reichstag fire. He wrote several articles in *L'Humanité* and *Europe* condemning the actions of Hitler's government. They were later collected into two volumes.

Quinze ans de combat, 1919–1934 (translated as *I Will Not Rest*) and *Par la révolution, la paix* ("Through Revolution, Peace"). Both were published in 1935 and impounded during the Occupation of France in World War II.

Rolland's faith in Russia and his enthusiasm for its vitality led him to take a trip there between June 23 and July 21, 1935. Accompanied by his wife, he visited Maxim Gorky and stayed with him. Rolland felt that the political direction of the U.S.S.R. represented the hope of civilization. In 1936 he published *Compagnons de route* ("Fellow Travellers"), which contained several literary essays expressing his aesthetic and ideological position.

The following year was one of change. After publishing the third volume of his *Beethoven, Le Chant de le Résurrection* (1937; "The Song of the Resurrection"), Rolland decided to return to France to stay permanently, and he bought a house in Vézelay, the region of his birth.

In July 1939, *Le Jeu de l'Amour et de la Mort* (1925; *The Game of Love and Death*) was placed in the repertoire of the Comédie-Française on the occasion of the 150th anniversary of the French Revolution. The day of the Franco-British declaration of War (September 3, 1939), Rolland wrote to President Daladier to express his "complete dedication to the cause of democracy and France, in danger today," as it was 150 years earlier at Valmy.

During the war, between 1940 and 1944, Rolland, while keeping his house in Vezelay, took a small apartment in the old section of Paris he liked best, Montparnasse. He became seriously ill, and on December 30, 1944, he succumbed to tuberculosis at his home in Vezelay. He was buried in Clamecy, then transported to Brèves, ten kilometers away.

A very prolific writer, Rolland coined the term *Roman fleuve* (serial novel) to describe *Jean-Christophe*, his vast fresco or saga presenting the life of an artist against the background of a period. This fictionalized life, published in installments, contained biographical elements of the life of a real artist, like Beethoven, and autobiographical details of the author's life. This new genre was to dominate the literary scene for the next forty years.

Today Rolland's lyricism and spontaneous style—using frequent ellipses, repetitions, and hesitations—as well as his ideas concerning illegitimacy, feminism, revolution, freedom, and universal peace seem outmoded, although they were considered avant-garde during his lifetime and attracted both enemies and emulators. Romain Rolland is, to some extent, the victim of a historical literary evolution. His works are not much read today, although his place in the history of literature is secure and *Jean-Christophe* is always mentioned in literary manuals and encyclopedias.

ANTOINE SPACAGNA

Selected Bibliography

PRIMARY SOURCES

Rolland, Romain. *Colas Breugnon.* New York: Holt, 1919.

———. *Clerambault, the Story of an Independent Spirit during the War.* New York: Holt, 1921.

———. *The Soul Enchanted.* 5 vols. New York: Holt, 1925–34.

———. *Jean-Christophe.* New York: Holt, 1910–13; Modern Library Giant, 1938.

SECONDARY SOURCES

Arcos, René. *Romain Rolland.* Paris: Mercure de France, 1950.

Barrère, Jean-Bertrand. *Romain Rolland par lui-même.* Paris: Seuil, 1955.

———. *Romain Rolland, l'âme et l'art.* Paris: Albin Michel, 1966.

March, Harold. *Romain Rolland.* New York: Twayne, 1971.

Robichez, Jacques. *Romain Rolland.* Paris: Hatier, 1961.

Starr, William Thomas. *Romain Rolland and a World at War.* Evanston, Ill.: Northwestern University Press, 1956.

Wilson, Ronald A. *The Pre-War Biographies of Romain Rolland and Their Place in his Work and the Period.* London: Oxford University Press, 1939.

Zweig, Stefan. *Romain Rolland: The Man and His Work.* Translated by Eden and Cedar Paul. New York: Seltzer, 1921.

BERTRAND RUSSELL   *1950*

Bertrand Arthur William Russell, 3rd Earl Russell (1872–1970), mathematician, philosopher, and social reformer, was born at Ravenscroft, the younger son of Viscount Amberley and his wife, Kate, daughter of the 2nd Baron Stanley of Alderley. An orphan before the age of four, Russell and his older brother, Frank, were the objects of an unsuccessful attempt by his progressive and unconventional guardians—his godfather, T. J. Cobden-Sanderson, and scientist D. A. Spalding—to wrest custody of the children from his grandparents, reformist Prime Minister Lord John Russell (died 1878) and his wife, the former Lady Francis Elliot. Thus, the desire of the freethinking, nonreligious Amberleys to ensure that their children would not suffer from the rigidity of Victorian moral principles, from the shadow left by the fame of Lord John Russell, and from the sterile emotional darkness of Pembroke Lodge, his grandparents' estate, was defeated.

Frank and Bertrand Russell were entrusted primarily to the care of their grandmother Lady Russell, who lived with an overpowering sense of the past. Realizing that she had lost control of Frank, then a student at the distinguished public school Winchester, Lady Russell determined that a different educational pattern must be created for Bertrand. As George Santayana recalled, "Lady Russell demanded that Bertie at least must be preserved pure, religious, and affectionate; he must be fitted to take his grandfather's place as Prime Minister and continue the sacred work of Reform." Russell was tutored at home, inculcated with his grandmother's puritan notions of correct behavior, and imbued with self-discipline and responsibility. Lady Russell created a self-contained, isolated world for him to grow up in, one that completely subverted the Amberleys' ideals.

The unemotional atmosphere of Pembroke Lodge shaped his social and intellectual development. Seeking "certainty in an uncertain world" led Russell first to mathematics and then to philosophy. Only by entering Trinity College, Cambridge, in 1890 to read mathematics was Russell freed from his grandmother's regimen of aggressive idealism.

At Cambridge Russell's intellectual qualities were quickly recognized, and he received an invitation to become a member of the Apostles. This self-selected group of students and dons, including such gifted individuals as J. E. M'Taggart, D. L. Dickinson, the Trevelyan brothers, and G. E. Moore, comprised Cambridge's intellectual elite. The group met to discuss current political and philosophical questions, examining, for example, notions of Oxfordian idealism. Russell remained at Cambridge an addi-

tional year after finishing the math tripos to pursue moral sciences (philosphy).

After Cambridge Russell served for a short period at the British embassy in Paris. Returning from France, despite family opposition, he married on December 13, 1894, Alys Whitall Smith, the sister of Logan Pearsall Smith and the sister-in-law of Bernard Berenson. The daughter of a wealthy manufacturing family of Philadelphia Quakers who settled near the estate of Russell's Uncle Rollo, Alys Whitall Smith was considered by Lady Russell to be "no lady, a low-class adventuress, a designing female, a person incapable of all the fine feelings." Lady Russell's assessment that the marriage would be unsuitable later proved to be correct.

In 1895 Russell was elected to a fellowship at Trinity. The following year he published a study of political economy, *German Social Democracy*, evaluating principles of Marxism. Russell's first philosophical book, *An Essay on the Foundations of Geometry* (1897), was a crisply written reassessment of his dissertation evaluating a Kantian conception of geometry to the emergence of non-Euclidean geometries. At this time, he and his wife traveled to the United States, visiting Johns Hopkins University, Bryn Mawr College, and Harvard University, where they were the guests of philosopher William James, before returning to Britain.

By 1898 Russell realized the necessity of moving away from idealism if he were to develop a new structure for mathematics, one that did not require the acceptance of postulated axioms and concepts. In addition, he needed to pierce through the monadist core of Leibniz's philosophy, resulting for Russell in a deeper appreciation of the analytical process, in his distrust of the subject-predicate form, and in the belief of knowledge based on experience. Russell set out his objections to idealism and to Leibniz in *A Critical Exposition of the Philosophy of Leibniz* (1899) and developed by 1900 the first draft of *The Principles of Mathematics*, which forms the basis of his work with Alfred North Whitehead.

Stimulated by his inquiry into the grammar of logic, Russell published his influential article, "On Denoting," in *Mind* in 1905. Of this article, which sets forth his "theory of descriptions," Russell writes: "What was of importance in this theory was the discovery that, in analyzing a significant sentence, one must not assume that each separate word or phrase has significance on its own account" ("My Mental Development"). Driven by the same creative energy needed to produce his theoretical work, Russell sought a way to apply his intellectual skills to the world of practical politics, thereby approaching family notions of social responsibility. Therefore, in 1907 Russell unsuccessfully contested a parliamentary seat as a women's suffrage candidate. Although denied a place in the House of Commons, Russell the following year was elected a fellow of the Royal Society, ensuring acceptance into the British intellectual establishment.

The year 1909 found Russell spending most of his time estranged from his wife, working at Trinity in collaboration with Alfred North Whitehead on *Principia Mathematica* (1st vol., 1910; later vols. 1912 and 1913). The work produced by Russell and Whitehead was an effort to reconstruct mathematics on a new logical foundation and to provide existing mathematical beliefs with a superstructure of logic, producing a basis for the language of symbolic logic. Russell and Whitehead's inquiry into the "mathematical treatment of the principles of mathematics" aimed at developing a framework for "diminishing to the utmost the number of undefined ideas and undemonstrated propositions (called, respectively, primitive ideas and primitive propositions)," for setting out "precise expression, in its symbols, of mathematical propositions" in the most convenient notation, and for solving "the paradoxes which, in recent years, have troubled students of symbolic logic and the theory of aggregates." Recognized as a seminal achievement, *Principia Mathematica* assured Russell's position as a major philosopher.

Elected president of the Aristotelian Society in 1911, Russell finally separated from his wife, took Lady Ottoline Morrell as a mistress, and, most important, met Ludwig Wittgenstein, who became his student. Soon Russell discovered that Wittgenstein was not just a brilliant student but a catalyst leading him into new directions of philosophical inquiry. Their work together concerned Russell's application of the techniques of formal logic to major assumptions of traditional notions of empiricism. During this prewar period, Russell gave several important lectures elaborating his ideas on the nature of philosophy and epistemology and published significant philosophical essays, which were later gathered in *Mysticism and Logic* (1918). The Lowell lectures, which he gave at Harvard, were published in *Our Knowledge of the External World* (1914). *Problems of Philosophy* (1912), written for the Home University Library, set out the current direction of his research.

In 1915 Russell joined the pacifist No-Conscription Fellowship, and the next year he lost his lectureship at Trinity. In June he met Dora Black, later to be his second wife, and fell in love with Colette O'Niel, later Lady Constance Malleson. Russell published a political book, *Principles of Social Reconstruction* (1916), resigned from the No-Conscription Fellowship (1917), and gave a series of lectures, "The Philosophy of Logical Atomism" (published in *Monist*, 1918–19), reflecting Wittgenstein's influence on his intellectual development. His 1918 article on strike breaking led to a six-month prison sentence for sedition, during which time he wrote *Introduction to Mathematical Philosophy* (1919).

After World War I Russell was unemployed and had limited financial resources. To earn money, he published *Roads to Freedom* (1918) and his London School of Economics lectures as *The Analysis of the Mind* (1921). Restored to Trinity in 1919, Russell then traveled with Dora Black to Russia, publishing *The Practice and Theory of Bolshevism* (1920; reprinted 1949), an indictment of Bolshevik cruelty and political machinations. Next Russell and Black went to China, after which Russell published *The Problem of China* (1922), got his divorce from Alys (1921), and immediately married Dora, who gave birth to a son two months later. He resigned from his Trinity lectureship.

Russell spent the period until the beginning of World War II for the most part writing journal articles and publishing books popularizing his social and philosophical ideas. Two serious reflexive philosophical works, *The Analysis of Matter* (1927) and a new edition of *Principia Mathematica* (1925), maintained his intellectual respectability. However, works such as *The Prospects of Industrial Civilization* (1923), *On Education* (1926), *ABC's of Atoms* (1923), and *Relativity* (1925) are merely popular accounts of developments in social and scientific thought. *Marriage and Morals* (1929), *The Conquest of Happiness* (1931), *Education and the Social Order* (1932), and *Religion and Science* (1935) deal with current issues of permissive social thought. His essay collections *Sceptical Essays* (1928) and *In Praise of Idleness* (1928) are still somewhat readable.

Russell was politically active, standing as a Labour candidate in the general elections of 1922 and 1923. In 1927 he and Dora founded a progressive school, Beacon Hill. Several lecture tours in America brought additional funds for the Russells. He and Dora divorced in

1935, and in 1936 he married Peter (Patricia) Spence, née Marjorie Helen Spence. On the death of his brother in 1931, Russell inherited the earldom.

Returning to academic and intellectual prominence, Russell published his 1938 Oxford lectures, "Words and Facts," as *An Inquiry into Meaning and Truth* (1940). He wrote that this book was an attempt "to combine a general outlook akin to Hume's with the methods that have grown out of modern logic." In 1939 Russell assumed a visiting professorship at the University of California at Los Angeles but became embroiled in a conflict with that university's right-wing president. He was subsequently offered a chair at City College of New York, but, as it turned out, he was not to assume this professorship because a powerful attack led by Bishop Manning fomented a wave of hysteria based on objections to ideas set out in *Marriage and Morals*. The anti-Russell group's successful interference in university governance so threatened the free flow of ideas that *The New York Times* wrote their actions strike "at the security and intellectual independence of every faculty member in every public college and university in the United States." City College of New York, a public institution under the control of the City Board of Higher Education, was sued by Manning supporter Mrs. Jean McKay, outraged that public funds would be used to employ "an alien atheist and exponent of free love." In a highly political and emotional decision, New York State Supreme Court Justice McGeehan, castigating Russell's

appointment as "in effect establishing a chair of indecency," upheld the suit. The administration of Mayor LaGuardia, bowing to political pressure, foreclosed any appeal by withdrawing budget support from City College. Fortunately, public outcry from Americans interested in academic freedom encouraged Harvard to invite Russell to Cambridge to give the William James Lectures.

Still facing financial problems, Russell was rescued by Dr. Albert Barnes, eccentric inventor and art patron of Philadelphia. His foundation hired Russell to give lectures on the history of philosophy. However, Barnes, under a contractual clause prohibiting Russell from giving outside lectures, found a pretext for dismissing Russell in 1942. Russell's countersuit for wrongful dismissal was successful in 1943, and he was awarded a year's salary in damages. Invited to nearby Bryn Mawr College, Russell continued the work begun at the Barnes Foundation before returning to Trinity in 1944.

In 1945 Russell published *A History of Western Philosophy*, the work that occupied him in America. Russell's lively prose, interesting biographical insights, and broad historical sweep made this book an immense financial success. Now in addition to financial security and the prestige of being back at Trinity, Russell gained widespread fame as a member of the BBC's Brain Trust radio program. Both the publication of *A History of Western Philosophy* and being a panelist on radio raised Russell to the status of celebrity.

Enjoying this new level of public acceptance and respect in Britain,

Russell focused his attention on the effects of the atomic bombings on Japan. Although an ardent pacifist in World War I, Russell saw the necessity of fighting Hitler; however, he did have some misgivings about atomic warfare. He justified his reluctant acceptance of the use of the bomb on Japan as graphic deterrent to any further thoughts of war. In 1947 he thought that the threat of the atomic bomb could coerce Russia into accepting international agreements on the control of nuclear power. It was not until later that Russell became a fervid antinuclear advocate and thus had to deal with the embarrassment of this position.

However, at this time revered and honored, Russell made a worldwide tour and gave the first in a series of lectures named in honor of BBC founder Lord Reith. These lectures, broadcast on radio, were published in 1949 as *Authority and Individual.* A year later Russell was awarded the 1950 Nobel Prize in literature "in recognition of his varied and significant writings, in which he champions humanitarian ideals and freedom of thought." During this period his relationship with his third wife, Patricia, soured and led to a divorce in 1952. In the same year he married Edith Finch, whom he had first met at Bryn Mawr.

Human Knowledge (1948), his last major philosophical book, was not well received, since it appeared to be merely a restatement of his earlier positions. He continued writing, publishing *Portraits from Memory* (1956), *My Philosophical Development* (1959), *Autobiography* (3 vols., 1967, 1968, 1969), *Common Sense* *and Nuclear Warfare* (1959), *Has Man a Future?* (1961), and *Unarmed Victory* (1963).

During this last period of his life, Russell became a vigorous opponent of nuclear weapons. His 1954 radio broadcast, "Man's Peril," his 1955 press conference at Westminster, which produced his antinuclear weapons manifesto, his 1957 participation in the first Pugwash Conference (an international conference of distinguished scholars and politicians invited to discuss world problems), and his 1958 election as president of the Campaign for Nuclear Disarmament, all attest to the depth and vigor of his commitment. In 1960 he formed the more militant Committee of 100, dedicated to using civil disobedience. In 1960 Ralph Schoenman, a militant American postgraduate student at the London School of Economics, attached himself to Russell. This young man exerted an unfortunate and discrediting influence on Russell. Under Russell's name Schoenman issued silly and hostile political statements attacking the United States, especially its action in Vietnam, while condoning Russian imperialism. These statements of Schoenman made Russell appear foolish. Finally, in 1969 Russell, heeding the advice of friends, disowned Schoenman and many of his antics. Shortly before his death, Russell wrote an account of his relationship with Schoenman.

On February 2, 1970, Lord Russell died at his home, Plas Penrhyn, in Wales.

JAMES REIBMAN

Selected Bibliography

PRIMARY SOURCES

Russell, Bertrand. *The Autobiography of Bertrand Russell, 1872–1914.* Vol. 1. Boston: Little, Brown, 1967.

——. *The Autobiography of Bertrand Russell, 1914–1944.* Vol. 2. Boston: Little, Brown, 1968.

——. *The Autobiography of Bertrand Russell, 1944–1969.* Vol. 3. Boston: Little, Brown, 1969.

SECONDARY SOURCES

Clark, R. W. *The Life of Bertrand Russell.* London: J. Cape, Weidenfeld, and Nicolson, 1975.

Egner, R. E., and L. E. Denonn, eds. *The Basic Writings of Bertrand Russell.* New York: Simon & Schuster, 1961.

Wood, Alan. *Bertrand Russell—The Passionate Sceptic.* London: St. Martin's Press, 1957.

NELLY SACHS   *1966*

The poetess Nelly Sachs (1891–1970) only narrowly escaped almost certain death in a Nazi concentration camp in 1940 when she was allowed at the last possible moment to emigrate from Germany to Sweden. Having received on the same day both her emigration papers and her orders to prepare to leave for a "work camp," Sachs and her mother immediately flew with neither money nor possessions to Stockholm, where they both spent the rest of their lives. It is an ironic twist of fate that this major twentieth-century German poet, who would later be hailed "the poetess of the Holocaust" or "the prophetess of German-Jewish reconciliation," should have known as a schoolgirl neither the synagogue nor the evils of turn-of-the-century anti-Semitism.

Born in Berlin on December 10, 1891, the only child of prosperous and completely assimilated German Jewish parents, Leonie (Nelly) Sachs grew up in a protected and cultured milieu of Wilhelminian Germany and was only superficially aware of her Jewish heritage. After less than three years of public education, she withdrew from school in 1900 on account of poor health and received private instruction until 1903, when she entered a private school for the girls of well-to-do Berlin families. Her interests in this early period ranged from dance and music to watercolor painting and poetry. On her fifteenth birthday she received a book—the *Göste Berlings Saga* by the Swedish Nobel laureate Selma Lagerlöf—which may well have saved her life. Moved by the book, she began sending her verse to Lagerlöf, who years later was instrumental in securing her permission to emigrate to Sweden. In 1966, on her seventy-fifth birthday, she shared the Nobel Prize with the Israeli novelist Samuel Joseph Agnon. She died three and a half years later in 1970, a naturalized citizen of Sweden.

Nelly Sachs received no further education upon completion of her schooling in 1908 and, as did most young women of her social position, embarked upon a life of cultivation in cosmopolitan Berlin. Though she continued to read and write, she seems to have had little interest in the active intellectual scene of early-twentieth-century Berlin. She preferred Dostoyevsky, Hölderlin, and the German romantics to revolutionary movements of the early modernist period. In 1921 she published her first book, a small volume of Nordic legends and tales written in the style of her Swedish mentor, Selma Lagerlöf; in 1929 she first published some of her verse, which, like the poetry of the next eight years or so, was in form and content essentially a neoromantic reflection of the secure world of upper-middle-class Europe. It was not until 1943 at the age of fifty-two, when the reports of the unspeakable horrors of the "final solution" began to reach the world and she had the news of a former lover, who in her words "suffered a martyr's death," that Nelly Sachs first wrote the poetry that established her as a major European poet. "I wrote as if in flames," she later reported. "Images and meta-phors were my wounds and death was my teacher. I wrote in order to survive."

If one were to choose an emblem for Nelly Sachs's life and work after 1943, it would almost certainly have to be the flame. Through her survival, the flame of concentration camp crematory ovens was transfigured into the eternal flame of poetry: She eluded the conflagration of the death factories in order to speak for the millions of anonymous victims for whom there was no intervention by a Nobel laureate. Her poetry had saved her life, and from 1943 on its flame was the flame of the Holocaust. "I will not stop following step by step the path and flame of our people," she wrote to a fellow exile in 1946, "and I will bear witness with my poor being." And this she did. Living for years on the fringes of destitution, she continued until her death to write and bear witness with her "poor being." Symbolic of this selfless mission was the fact that she never moved from the one-room apartment that she had shared with her mother from the earliest days in Stockholm. There she lived and wrote even after her mother's death in 1950 and even when the financial security and renown of her last years would have allowed her to find more comfortable accommodations.

Her mission was not easy and the price high; often on the brink of psychological collapse and haunted by visions of paranoia, Sachs spent considerable time in Swedish sanatoria. Nevertheless, she never ceased to search for new words and images to express the horror that was always greater than any linguistic formulation: "I plunge into fire," she wrote, "to find the words for the unsayable," words that would illuminate and objectify but also transfigure the enigma of all human suffering. And this was Nelly Sachs's great talent: Without sentimentalizing her personal anguish or reducing it to the sterility of abstraction, she was able to transform it into vivid interpersonal images whose concrete detail never lost sight of the reality of its horrific origins.

Published by the Aufbau Verlag in East Berlin in 1947, Sachs's first postwar collection of poetry, *In den Wohnungen des Todes* (*In the Habitations of Death*) went almost totally unnoticed by the German readership. Written essentially in her first breakthrough phase of 1943–44 and attributed to her recent discovery of the mysticism of Jewish Hasidism, the volume revealed that Sachs had found the vocabulary and courage to pay tribute to her "dead brothers and sisters." The book is comprised of four groups of poems, poetry that contains the central imagery of dust, stones, smoke, and stars that is characteristic of her work as a whole. The first group, entitled "Your Body in Smoke Through the Air," contains one of the most powerful yet representative poems of this period, "O the Chimneys." Begun with an epigraph from the book of Job: "And after my skin has been thus destroyed, then without my flesh I shall see God," the poem vascillates between unmistakably concrete imagery—"chimneys / On the ingeniously devised dwellings of death"—and characteristi-

cally enigmatic turns: "When Israel's body drifted as smoke . . . Was welcomed by a star, a chimney sweep,/ A star that turned black/ Or was it a ray of sun?" Exemplary also of this early period is the exact and poignant semantic reversal of basic words such as *dwellings*. These "dwellings of death" speak of an era when there is no shelter, no refuge from the "ingenious" inventions of insidious ideology.

Her second collection, *Sternverdunkelung* (1949; *Eclipse of the Stars*), experienced a similar reception. Unable to find a German publisher, Sachs had to turn to a Dutch firm, Bermann-Fischer Querido of Amsterdam, to get this book into print. That nobody appeared to take note of her verse did not slow her poetic production. It did, in effect, free her from the pressures of the literary marketplace so that she could allow her increasingly dense and idiosyncratic mode of expression to follow its own course of development. Like *In the Habitations of Death*, *Eclipse of the Stars* consists of a series of poem cycles and is likewise dominated by the theme of the Holocaust. The paradoxical image of a star—earth—that has become dark is another typical semantic reversal of a concrete entity and relates as such the cosmic darkness of the epoch to the putrid black cloud of the crematoria, "the blossoms of death in the clouds."

Nelly Sachs's well-known scriptural drama, *Eli. Ein Mysterienspiel vom Leiden* (1951; *Eli: A Mystery Play of the Sufferings of Israel*), was, like the preceding two books, also published in obscurity. It was printed privately in Malmö, Sweden, in 1951 and only first produced, as a radio play, ten years later. Composed of seventeen brief episodes and set, significantly, in a small Polish town—Poland was the country in which Hasidism originated—the play takes as its theme the historical plight of the persecuted Jewish people. The plot revolves around the murder of an eight-year-old Jewish boy who had the audacity to play his "pipe to God" in order to prevent soldiers from abducting his parents. Eli stands not only for the one million children murdered in concentration camps, but also for the innocence of the Jews who throughout history have been attacked for their religious conviction. Though the Holocaust looms in the background of this play, Sachs typically mentions neither "Germany" nor "German." When Eli's murderer is eventually found, he disintegrates under the weight of his guilt, not the sword of secular justice. Here, as in all of her work, Sachs refrains from indictment of the Germans. Her words know no hate, vengeance, or accusation, and for this reason it was easy for Germans to later honor her as the "poetess of German-Jewish reconciliation."

There are a number of reasons for the poor reception of her work in the early postwar years. The most decisive factor was the uncomfortable topic of her writing: Germany was not ready to deal with the poetry of death camps. Under the conservative way of the Adenauer Restoration, the West German readership exhibited a guarded if not skeptical stance toward "exile literature," regarding it pejoratively, as did one celebrated twentieth-century German poet, Gottfried Benn, as a kind of "emigrant literature"—literature written by authors who only viewed the German situation from outside and who had not remained in Germany to endure the trauma and hardships of life in Nazi Germany. This problem of reception was complicated by Sachs' eclectic and somewhat isolationist poetic stance. She willfully held herself at a distance from the main currents of twentieth-century literature. What and how she wrote was dictated, she felt, by inner compulsion, not by the styles of the day. Her poetry became difficult and incomprehensible, she once remarked, "when my language began to express my real self." Sometimes characterized as an epigonic avant-gardist, she created verse in the early postwar period that was a curious mix of the exalted language reminiscent of Friedrich Hölderlin—she has been called the "sister of Hölderlin"—and the abstract obscurity of the visionary expressionists.

Both strange and not readily accessible, her works attracted little attention until the socio-political mood changed in the late fifties as West German intellectuals began to take a critical look at the deeper implications of the Adenauer Restoration. In a political climate that now allowed for the literary exploration of the inhumanity of the Third Reich in the works of such authors as Rolf Hochhuth, Günther Grass, Heinrich Böll, or Uwe Johnson, Nelly Sachs, now nearly seventy years of age, finally achieved recognition in her German homeland. The year 1957 marked the first publication in West Germany of a book of her verse, *Und niemand weiß weiter* (*And No One Knows How to Go On*). This book marks the beginning of her middle period. Whereas her first breakthrough (1943–44) is closely linked to the immediate events of the Holocaust and her discovery of the Hasidic mysticism of the eighteenth century, this change in direction is likewise tied to two events: the crisis brought on by the death of her mother and the subsequent overcoming of this crisis through her study of Jewish mysticism, this time the thirteenth-century Spanish Cabbala. Moving beyond the plight of Israel per se, the poetry of her middle period—which also includes the volume *Flucht und Verwandlung* (1959; *Flight and Metamorphosis*)—encompasses a wider spectrum of the human condition. From now on, the Holocaust takes on a more universal symbolic value that joins the victims of the extermination camps, through the mystery and redemption of all human suffering, to those who perished in Hiroshima and the other mass annihilations of human civilization.

Hailed in 1959 by Hans Magnus Enzensberger as "the foremost poetess writing in the German language," Sachs then received in the next seven years an impressive series of awards, prizes, and public tributes: In 1959 she received the Poetry Award from the National Federation of German Industry; in 1960 the Meersburger Droste Prize; in 1961 the Culture Prize of the City of Dort-

mund; in 1965 the German Book Trade Peace Prize; and finally, in 1966, the Nobel Prize in literature "for her dramatic and poetic writing, which interprets with moving intensity the fate of the Jews."

This pronouncement, and the assertion that her work "reconciles German and Jew without contradiction" (from the Peace Prize citation), contributed, unfortunately, to a somewhat limited appreciation of Nelly Sachs as the "poetess of the Holocaust" or the "prophetess of German-Jewish reconciliation." Such epithets, however, completely disregard her powerful quasi-mystical later poetry, which includes *Fahrt ins Staublose* (1961; *Journey into a Dustless Realm*) and *Glühende Rätsel* (1964; *Glowing Enigmas*). This poetry, which is yet another step removed from the Holocaust, becomes increasingly self-conscious and reflexive. Language has become not so much a medium of expression as a vehicle for touching the "enigmatic" pantheistic oneness of an eternally changing cosmos. Though she has become patently mystical, Sachs does not take refuge in this later verse in the comforting embrace of a transcendent *unio mystica*. The veil of smoke that rose from the death-camp chimneys remains an impenetrable enigma whose "crooked line of suffering/ Gropes fumblingly after the divinely lit geometry/ Of the universe."

Perhaps even more pernicious than the one-dimensional reception of her work that immediately followed her Nobel Prize was the critical backlash to her sudden ascendancy to the status of cult figure in the mid-sixties. Though it is certainly true that her rather sudden German popularity is subliminally connected to the collective guilt of the Germans and that this popularity and guilt was then manipulated by the culture industry for less than altruistic motives, the cynical disregard for her work in the late sixties and early seventies seems now to have been a short-sighted critical reaction (or overreaction) to her popularity, not to her poetry.

ERIC WILLIAMS

Selected Bibliography

PRIMARY SOURCES

Sachs, Nelly. *O the Chimneys: Selected Poems, Including the Verse Play, "Eli."* Translated by Michael Hamburger [and others]. New York: Farrar, Straus & Giroux, 1967.

——— . *The Seeker and Other Poems.* Translated by Michael Hamburger, Ruth Mead, and Mathew Mead. New York: Farrar, Straus & Giroux, 1970.

SECONDARY SOURCES

Bahr, Ehrhard. *Nelly Sachs.* Munich: Beck, 1980.

Berendsohn, Walter A. *Nelly Sachs: Einführung in das Werk der Dichterin jüdischen Schicksals.* Darmstadt: Agora, 1974.

Dodds, Dinah. "The Process of Renewal in Nelly Sachs's 'Eli.'" *The German Quarterly* 1976 (49):50–58.

Holmquist, Bengt, ed. *Das Buch der Nelly Sachs.* 2nd ed. Frankfurt am Main: Suhrkamp, 1977.

Syrkin, Marie. "Nelly Sachs—Poet of the Holocaust." *Midstream* 13 (1967):13–23.

JEAN-PAUL SARTRE   *1964*

Philosopher, novelist, playwright, essayist, literary critic, and political activist, Jean-Paul Sartre (1905–80) became the most widely known existentialist philosopher in the world after World War II. He was the intellectual leader of an entire generation, committed not only to a literary and philosophical career, but also to various social and political activities.

Jean-Paul Sartre was born into a bourgeois family in Paris on June 21, 1905. Having lost his father at the age of two, he was raised by his mother and his maternal grandfather Carl Schweitzer, who was the uncle of Albert Schweitzer and a professor of German at the Sorbonne. As a child, he led a very quiet and protected life, free from the discipline of a father. His grandfather taught him his love for books and his respect for intellectual activities. During these years, however, the child developed a feeling of rejection and became acutely aware of a "difference" between him and other children his age. In his autobiographical work, *Les Mots* (1964; *The Words*), Sartre mentioned this complex and explained how, from an early age, he saw the act of writing as the only form of justification and salvation.

In 1917 he moved to La Rochelle with his mother, who had just remarried. Three years later he went back to Paris, and in 1924 he was accepted at the prestigious Ecole Normale Supérieure. There he became a friend of Paul Nizan and Raymond Aron and met Maurice Merleau-Ponty and Claude Lévi-Strauss, among others. He also met Simone de Beauvoir, who was going to remain his companion for the rest of his life. They both received their "agrégation" in philosophy in 1929 and went on to become "the existential couple." They shared the same ideas and convictions, but Sartre, as a philosopher, concentrated on the development of a theory of existentialism; whereas Simone de Beauvoir was more interested in trying to apply her existential principles to the various problems of life.

After the completion of his degree Sartre served for sixteen months in the army before being appointed professor of philosophy at the Lycée of Le Havre, where he remained for two years. In 1933 he spent a year at the French Institute of Berlin, where he studied the philosophy of Husserl and Heidegger.

Upon his return to France, he resumed his teaching, first in Le Havre, then in Laon and Neuilly near Paris. In 1939 he was drafted to serve in World War II. Captured by the Germans in 1940, he spent some time in a prisoner-of-war camp before being released for health reasons. In 1941 he returned to Paris and taught at the Lycée Condorcet until 1944, when he decided to devote himself entirely to writing.

His first works, philosophical and known to only a few specialists, include: *L'Imagination* (1936; *Psychology and Imagination*), *La Transcendance de l'Ego* (1936-37; *The Transcendence of the Ego*), *L'Imaginaire* (1940; *The Psychology of the Imagination*), followed in 1943 by *L'Etre et le Néant* (*Being and Nothingness*). It was only with the publication of his first novel *La Nausée* (1938; *Nausea*) that Sartre started to become popular. Considered very controversial at the time, it was nonetheless the most celebrated novel of that period. By far Sartre's most philosophical work of fiction, it departed from the traditional novel of adventure and action by introducing most of the existential themes that the author was to develop later. As a novel, it advocated a literature of commitment, a commitment that stemmed from Sartre's existential doctrine.

La Nausée is the diary of Roquentin, a solitary man, who lives in Bouville (Le Havre) while working on the biography of an eighteenth-century marquis. Thirty years old and single, Roquentin is unable to enjoy his freedom; he leads a dull and solitary existence and feels empty. Each time he comes into contact with the external world he experiences a feeling of alienation and a sensation of nausea. The more he tries to understand the true nature of this reaction, the more the surrounding world becomes oppressive. Material objects seem sticky and invading, as if they were having an existence of their own. Soon Roquentin is overwhelmed by a feeling of repulsion toward his environment (the world of concrete matter, the world of others, and even his own body). One day as he is sitting on a bench in a city park in Bouville, he has an apocalyptic vision that eventually leads him to some understanding of his situation. Suddenly everything appears to him as monstrous; he sees matter growing everywhere, invading everything in a completely irrational way. In the midst of this unexplainable proliferation of matter, he feels not only trapped but also quite superfluous, with no reason to exist, "de trop." The city is "de trop," the trees in the park are "de trop," his body is "de trop," *he* is "de trop." He now understands that his nausea comes from his awareness that existence itself is "de trop." It cannot be justified, it is simply *there*, for no reason.

As Roquentin realizes that the world around him cannot be justified or explained, he also understands that existence itself, including his own, cannot be justified or explained either. It follows no rule, it has no purpose, it is absurd. Everything that exists is absurd, Roquentin is absurd, the universe is absurd. But by the same token it is also free. Freedom is possible within the very nature of existence; therefore Roquentin is free, even free to find a justification for his existence, which so far has been absurd.

Finally, as he tries to free his consciousness from the concrete world, he discovers that the only justification for his own existence would be the creation of a work of art. It would give a meaning to his life because it would transcend matter and existence itself. Roquentin then decides that he must write a novel and not a history book about someone who has existed because "one existent can never justify the existence of another existent."

The moral of *La Nausée* is that every individual must find his own reason to live, and for Roquentin the creation of a work of art points the way toward salvation. In the novel, Sartre introduced the main themes of his existential philosophy, which he later developed in a more theoretical manner in *L'Existentialisme est un Humanisme* (1946; *Existentialism and Humanism*)—freedom and salvation. In a universe without God, nothing can be predetermined, man cannot be a creature of circumstances. He exists, free and responsible. He is responsible for his actions, which determine what he is. Sartre says: "Existence precedes essence." Man is nothing but what he chooses to make of himself during his life. Hence the ever present anguish of the inevitable free choice. The existentialist philosopher teaches that man is free and "condemned to be free," condemned to choose a course of action while he can because there is no resurrection from death.

Sartre's second work of fiction,

Le Mur (1939; *The Wall and Other Stories*), is a series of short stories. It also created a scandal but constituted nonetheless a powerful masterpiece. After 1940, Sartre, who was still mostly known as a philosopher, tried to give to his literature of commitment a more popular appeal by writing a novel focusing on contemporary events, i.e., the war.

Les Chemins de la Liberté (*Roads to Freedom*) remained unfinished, only three volumes out of four were published: *L'Age de Raison* (1945; *The Age of Reason*), *Le Sursis* (1945; *The Reprieve*), *La Mort dans l'Ame* (1949; *Troubled Sleep*). After *La Nausée*, where the concepts of freedom and salvation remained metaphysical, Sartre wanted to write a novel expressing the concerns of the war period with characters actively involved in current events. It is fair to say however that in general *Les Chemins de la Liberté* constituted a relative failure insofar as the author did not introduce any notions that were not already in *La Nausée* or *Le Mur*. As a result, Sartre abandoned the novel as a genre to concentrate on drama.

Sartre came to the theater during World War II with the intention of reaching a wider public while remaining faithful to his literature of commitment. Quite traditional in its forms, his theater owes its originality to the nature of the situations that it stages. The themes are the same—freedom and salvation—but they are now presented in very concrete situations. In fact, Sartre's theater has been called a theater of situations. Characters are seen either as free individuals at the moment of a crucial choice that commits them and determines the rest of their life or as individuals of bad faith who, unable to face their freedom and responsibility, try to blame fate or others for their failure.

One very successful play is *Huis-Clos* (1944; *No Exit*), which was performed for the first time in Paris in 1944. The drama takes place in one room between three characters: Estelle, Garcin, and Inès, and it quickly appears that they are dead and in hell. There is, however, no instrument of torture nor any appointed torturer. Instead the room is furnished with three sofas and a few utensils, apparently useless, but there are no windows and no mirrors. It turns out that the three characters do the torturing themselves, each one being the others' torturer as well as victim.

Garcin and Estelle are cowards and hypocrites who try to lie about why they are in hell, but Inès, who laughs at their stories, eventually forces them to acknowledge their weaknesses while admitting herself why she has been condemned. Once they have confessed, Garcin, who wants everybody to have a good opinion of him, suggests that they should try to help each other, but Inès refuses and keeps asking questions. Garcin, who feels more vulnerable now that the others know the true nature of his personality, wants to leave, but he must first convince Inès that, even though he has committed cowardly acts, he is not a coward. He argues that he just died too soon and was not given enough time to show his real self. At that point, Inès takes upon herself to teach him the existential lesson that Sartre wants to convey. She says to Garcin: "One always dies too soon—or too late . . . and yet . . . you are your life, and nothing else." She insists that he is a coward because his deeds are those of a coward and now that he is dead, his life is nothing but the sum of those cowardly deeds. Garcin is furious and tries to seek comfort with Estelle, who is ready to believe anything he says. He would like to make love to her and she would like to make love to him too, but once again there is no escape. Garcin and Estelle cannot satisfy their desire because they cannot escape Inès's contemptuous look. She keeps repeating to Garcin that he is a coward. Finally, Estelle tries to kill Inès but to no avail since she is already dead. The three are doomed to stay together and torture each other for eternity. Garcin then understands that "Hell is other people" because, in one's own consciousness, it is impossible to escape from the opinion and the judgment of others.

In Sartre's other plays, freedom and salvation are tied more closely to the idea of individual and social responsibility. In 1943 Sartre published *Les Mouches* (*The Flies*). Even though it was not a very popular play, it is still one of his best works insofar as the notions of freedom, choice, and responsibility are woven into a situation that sets man against God in a conflict of rare intensity. Sartre uses the Greek myth of Orestes to show how man, in the process of asserting his freedom, inevitably comes in conflict with God's authority, which he must eventually reject. At the same time,

the play points very distinctly to major contemporary problems. The theme of national guilt in Argos obviously refers, at least partially, to the cowardly attitude of the Vichy government and its followers during the German occupation of France. The allusion is so obvious that the production of the play was eventually censored.

Orestes returns from exile to his native Argos as a young man with no obligations and no memories. The city is guilt-ridden because ever since his murder of Agamemnon, Aegisthus, with the complicity of Jupiter, has carefully perpetuated a sort of national repentance that reinforces his power over his people. Because he feels completely free, Orestes does not partake in the repentance and remains an outsider in his own town. In order to feel that he exists, he needs to do something that will make him a citizen of Argos. He wants to commit his freedom and himself. After having accomplished his (existentialist) *act*, i.e., having avenged his father Agamemnon's murder, he shows no remorse and comes in direct conflict with Jupiter, who condemns his disobedience and orders him to repent in exchange for forgiveness. Orestes rejects the request as he realizes that God is powerless as soon as man is free. He has chosen to act, and he has become his act. No one, not even a god, can do anything about it. A formidable argument follows and Orestes decides to leave the city whose guilt he has now taken upon himself to assume.

In *La Putain Respectueuse* (1946; *The Respectful Prostitute*),

Sartre for the first time sets the action of the play in a real social context to focus on the insidious consequences that oppression can exercise on the consciousness of its victims and its perpetrators. With *Morts sans Sépultures* (1947; *The Victors*), torture becomes the main theme. Political oppression and dictatorship set the stage for *Les Jeux sont Faits* (1947; *The Chips are Down*). Here the drama focuses on the distance that separates, in spite of themselves, two individuals who belong to two opposite social classes. *Les Mains Sales* (1948; *Dirty Hands*), which is a sort of modern version of *Les Mouches*, presents another political conflict in the form of the struggle of a few individuals trying to organize the proletariat in order to achieve a successful revolution. In *Le Diable et le Bon Dieu* (1951; *The Devil and the Good Lord*), Sartre staged the period of the civil wars in Germany at the beginning of Luther's reformation to denounce the shortcomings of such notions as morality and sanctity. His last play, *Les Séquestrés d'Altona* (1959; *The Condemned of Altona*), is the richest and most complicated of all. Here Sartre asked again the question that he could not answer as a philosopher and a novelist: Can modern man assume responsibility for the collective crimes of his society?

After World War II Sartre also became more and more involved in contemporary social and political matters. Commitment was more important than literature. From a metaphysical concept, freedom became for him a weapon for political struggle. In 1945 he founded *Les Temps Modernes*, which he directed. At first it was a literary review; as the years went by, it concentrated more and more on socialist studies. In the early '50s, even though he never joined the Communist party, Sartre had become an admirer of the Soviet Union, and he remained so until the invasion of Budapest by Soviet troops. He then strongly condemned Moscow's policy as well as the French Communist party, which kept supporting that policy.

In 1964 he was awarded the Nobel Prize in literature, but he refused it. Two years later, at the invitation of Bertrand Russell, he joined a commission of investigation on the war in Vietnam, which he strongly condemned. In May 1968 he supported the students' riots in Paris, and the same year he publicly condemned the Soviet intervention in Prague. In the '70s he became the first director of *Liberation*, a liberal daily newspaper. He also sympathized with the French Maoist movements and was occasionally active in the promotion and sale of some of their publications, such as *La Cause du Peuple*. Finally he took an active part in the making of two films: *Sartre par lui-même* ("Sartre by Himself"), 1976 and *Simone de Beauvoir*, 1978.

As an essayist and literary critic, Sartre goes again beyond literature, which he often sees as a compensation on the part of the author in his attempt to overcome a failure to live. For this reason, Sartre's literary criticism has often been looked upon as an "existential psychoanalysis" of the writer that he studies. He applied the same method and attitude to his analysis of himself in his autobiography *Les Mots*, where he tried to justify his literary vocation. His critical works include *Qu'est-ce que la Littérature?* (1948; *What Is Literature?*), where he argued that literature must be a literature of "extreme situations" and replace what he called a bourgeois literature of consumption. The same year he published *Baudelaire*, then *Saint Genet, Comédien et Martyr* (1952; *Saint Genet, Actor and Martyr*), his masterpiece of literary criticism, and finally *L'Idiot de la Famille* (Vols. 1 and 2, 1971; Vol. 3, 1972; *The Family Idiot, Gustave Flaubert*), a huge sociological, philosophical, and biographical study devoted to Flaubert. Different essays and articles written between 1947 and 1976 also appeared in a series of ten volumes entitled *Situations*.

Sartre died on April 15, 1980, and his funeral was attended by thousands of people, old and young, who saw him as the intellectual leader of the '40s, '50s, and even the '60s, as well as the indefatigable advocate for freedom in all its forms and aspects.

JEAN-PIERRE LALANDE

Selected Bibliography

PRIMARY SOURCES

Sartre, Jean-Paul. *Being and Nothingness*. Translated by Hazel Barnes.
New York: Philosophical Library, 1956.
———. *Nausea*. Translated by Lloyd Alexander. New York: New Directions, 1949.
———. *No Exit*. Translated by Stuart Gilbert. In volume with *The Flies*. New York: Knopf, 1947.
———. *The Wall and Other Stories*. Translated by Lloyd Alexander. New York: New Directions, 1948.
———. *The Words*. Translated by B. Frechtman. New York: Braziller, 1964.

SECONDARY SOURCES

Champigny, Robert. *Sartre and Drama*. Columbia, S.C.: French Literary Publications, 1983.
Cranston, Maurice W. *Jean-Paul Sartre*. New York: Grove Press, 1962.
Danto, Arthur C. *Jean-Paul Sartre*. New York: Viking Press, 1975.
Goldthorpe, Rhiannon. *Sartre*. Cambridge: Cambridge University Press, 1984.
Greene, Norman N. *Jean-Paul Sartre: The Existentialist Ethic*. Ann Arbor: University of Michigan Press, 1960.
Jeanson, Francis. *Sartre par lui-même*. Paris: Le Seuil, 1955.
Suhl, Benjamin. *Jean-Paul Sartre: The Philosopher as Literary Critic*. New York: Columbia University Press, 1970.
Thody, Philip. *Jean-Paul Sartre: A Literary and Political Study*. London: Hamilton, 1960; paperback, 1964.

GEORGE SEFERIS   *1963*

George Seferis (1900–71), poet, essayist, and critic, was born Giórgios Seferiádis on February 29, 1900, in Smyrna, Asia Minor, a preeminently Greek city, then part of the Ottoman Empire, now Izmir, Turkey. He first wrote poetry at the age of fourteen and adopted the pen name Seferis, in his first published collection, *Strophi* (1931; *Turning Point*). His father, Stylianos Seferiádis, an authority on international law and professor thereof at the University of Athens from 1919 on, dabbled in poetry and verse translation. In 1914, at the outbreak of World War I, the family settled in Athens, where Seferis finished his secondary studies at the First Classical Gymnasium in 1917. From 1918 to 1924 he studied law and literature at the Sorbonne in Paris. Upon receiving his law degree in 1924, he lived in London for a year in order to enhance his command of English as he prepared for a career in the Greek diplomatic service. He served first at the Ministry of Foreign Affairs in Athens and subsequently held many diplomatic posts, beginning as vice-consul in London, 1931. Thereafter, he served as consul in Koritsa, Albania, 1936–38. Following the German occupation of Greece in 1941, Seferis and his new bride, Maria Zannou, served with the government-in-exile in Egypt, South Africa, and Italy. After the liberation of Greece he returned to Athens, where he remained until 1948. Subsequently he was counse-

lor at the Greek embassies in Ankara and London, and, between 1953 and 1956, ambassador to Lebanon, Syria, Jordan, and Iraq; during these years he also visited Cyprus twice. From 1957 to 1962 Seferis served as ambassador to England in London, whereupon he retired. His oeuvre in poetry was honored first with the Palamàs Prize of the Academy of Athens in 1946, then with an honorary doctorate at Cambridge in 1960, and finally with the Nobel Prize in literature in 1963, the first such honor to a Greek national. Following this came honorary degrees at Oxford, Thessaloniki, and Princeton and an honorary fellowship from the American Academy of Arts and Sciences. In 1969, he exerted his enormous national prestige in dramatic denunciation of the dictatorial regime of the colonels in Greece. At his death on September 20, 1971, his fame as poet and his passionate defense of freedom drew thousands to the funeral.

Seferis's extensive study, travel, experience and service abroad (1918–25 and many periods between 1931 and 1962) brought him into fruitful engagement with contemporary intellectual and poetic experiments. The *poésie pure* of the French symbolists, chiefly Stéphane Mallarmé and Paul Valéry, resonates in its technical and stylistic effects throughout his early work, notably in *Strophi*. His long encounter with England, early and late, is felt in the evident influences of Ezra

Pound and particularly of T. S. Eliot. Seferis's homage to Eliot is manifest in the mythic-historical panorama of *Mythistorima* (1935; "Mythical Story"), a kind of Hellenic *Waste Land*; in *Kichli* (1947; "Thrush"), which is reminiscent of *Four Quartets*; in his translations of *The Waste Land* and *Murder in the Cathedral*; and in probing critical essays on Eliot.

Seferis's long and painful absences from his homeland also powerfully shaped a recurrent theme in the personal mythology of his verse: the persona of the modern Odysseus alienated from the tragic decay of his own time and longing to return to the splendors of a lost, distant world. As Seferis wrote, "Wherever I travel, Greece wounds me" (cited by Andonis Decavalles in a standard handbook of European writers). This persona, which is the central figure of "Mythical Story," was also developed in Stratis Thalassinos ("Stratis the Sailor") of the three *Logbooks* (1940–65). The context of his tormented alienation is particular, Hellenic, and universal: With the defeat of the Ottoman Empire, Greek forces held Smyrna in 1919, and the Treaty of Sèvres in 1920 established Greek presence on the west coast of Anatolia. But by 1922 the Turks under a new nationalist regime recaptured Smyrna and expelled the Greek populations from Asia Minor in what came to be known as the Asia Minor Disaster. For Seferis the loss of his native city, long redolent of Ionian Greek culture, became "a wound that was never to heal" (C. A. Trypanis, 1981). For him the Hellenic reality is "the grief of Greekdom," which is one "with the ancient monuments and the contemporary sorrow" (quoted in Linos Politis, 1973). On a universal and symbolic plane, moreover, the destruction of Smyrna united with the horror and tragedy of two world wars to become for Seferis an emblem of life as "a crumbling edifice, a condemned structure destined to fall into ruins, a pitiful memorial to a beautiful, mythical past" (Trypanis). From this world Seferis felt in permanent exile both literal, because of his itinerant career, and metaphorical.

Such "exile" notwithstanding, Seferis's poetry, like his soul, is rooted in the soil of postclassical Greece and in its long poetic tradition. Folk songs and ballads, the fifteen-syllable verse of folk literature deriving from the Byzantine era, the literature of sixteenth- to seventeenth-century Crete, including the highly influential *Erotokritos* of Vitzentzos Kornaros (c. 1650), and the poetry of the modern Greek revival in the works of Solomos, Kalvos, Palamas, Sikelianos, and Kavafis (Cavafy)—all profoundly inform the poetry of Seferis. To the infamous "language problem" of the Greeks, whether to use the *dhimotiki* ("demotic," i.e., vernacular) or the *katharévousa* (a modern, artificial, classicizing dialect), Seferis, like all great Greek writers of the twentieth century, responded with firm use of the demotic in "natural, proselike verse, predominantly dramatic, tragic in essence, compact and highly suggestive in its apparent simplicity and directness" (Decavalles). For Keeley and Sherrard

(1967), Seferis's most eminent translators, it is a language of "density and economy." To this vital postclassical tradition of language and literature Seferis grafts ancient myths, images, and characters. His poems are studded both with ancient allusions and with quotations from Greek authors as early as Homer. As Keely and Sherrard have noted, the literal and poetic landscape of Greece, always present in the poet's mind, offers the most natural setting for the classical heritage, such that it is not a case of "Teiresias on the Thames or Prometheus in Pennsylvania. . . ." Further, "before he [Seferis] attempts to carry the reader to the level of myth, he earns his sympathy and belief by convincingly representing the present reality sustaining his myth—and it is a contemporary, Greek reality always . . . the ancient and modern worlds meet in a metaphor without strain or contrivance as we find the legendary figures moving anachronistically onto the contemporary stage that the poet has set before our eyes." As Decavalles has noted well, "the present is always bending under the weight of past memories"; conversely, the legendary figures of the past must respond to the burdens of the present: In particular, "the deserted, arid, repetitive land and the calm, embittering sea . . . are symbolic of Odysseus's frustrating voyage, of his failure to realize the island paradise he longs for" (Keeley and Sherrard).

As preeminently a Greek poet as he is, Seferis is "wholly rooted in the anxieties of our time and those of contemporary man" (Politis). He seeks no antiquarian escape from such reality. His grief, melancholy, and pessimism derive not only from his direct encounter with the tragedy and suffering of his own era, but also from the *depth* of his reflection, as a Greek, on the history of achievement, failure, and despair in his people and nation. His greatness as a poet is his ability to transform particulars into universals, to seize upon an event, or a personal matter, or a myth, and to render it a metaphor and an emblem for the condition of mankind in our time. His enduring value as a poet remains "in offering insights that carry with them the weight of universal truths and that thus serve to reveal the deeper meaning of our times" (Keeley and Sherrard).

Seferis's early oeuvre, epitomized in *Strophi*, promised both to revolutionize and to modernize Greek poetry, as the poets of the "generation of 1880" had done for their era. The poems of this collection are new in language, tone, and lyric power. The most important of them, "Erotikos Logos" ("The Discourse of Love"), written in four-line rhyming stanzas of the fifteen-syllable verse, is at once an homage to the *Erotokritos*, a Greek form of *poésie pure*, and a culmination of lyricism. Its subject is the thoughts and feelings of lovers upon their separation. *I Sterna* (1932; "The Cistern"), a long, philosophical, and pessimistic poem, concludes the era of experimentation and prepares the terrain for Seferis's mature work, beginning with *Mythistorema* (1935; "Mythical Story").

Mythistorema, a free-verse poem in twenty-four parts, manifests what Seferis had absorbed from the Greek demotic tradition—and, importantly, from Pound and Eliot—about the need to find a direct, "quasi-prosaic" (Trypanis) voice unhindered by rhetorical embellishment or suffuse lyricism. The major subjects of the poem are images and thoughts on the Greek world following World War I and the Asia Minor Disaster, as mediated by a *modern* Odysseus deeply sensitive to the condition of this world as a metaphor, in the mode of *The Waste Land*, for that of modern man: "dry rocks, naked islands, old, disused harbours, broken oars, battered wrecks washed ashore . . . low-backed mountains, a scarcity of water, a longing for coolness, dried-up wells, mutilated statues, solitary hovels under a sun that empties the eye sockets and strips the face down to the bone . . ." (Trypanis). These images become powerful symbols of fatigue, frustration, and despair as the ancient and the modern world face each other. This "rhapsody of bitterness" becomes the leitmotif of all of Seferis's subsequent work.

The year 1940 proved an important one for Seferis. In March, as war enveloped Europe, he published in *Tetradhio Gymnasmaton* (*Book of Exercises*) poems of 1928–37 that had not yet been collected; in April, *Imerologhio Katastromatos A'* ("Logbook I"), which had been written mostly in Albania; and in May, all of his previously printed poems as *Poiimata* ("Poems"). In *Imerologhio Katastromatos A'*, the selection "O Vasilias tis Asinis" ("The King of Asine"), set in ancient Mycenae, is a haunting evocation of the meaning of death-in-life and life-in-death as the poet confronts the golden death mask of the King of Asine and reflects on the loss caused by death. *Imerologhio Katastromatos B'* (1944; *Logbook II*) is largely a record of the places of his exile poetically transformed into reflections on life and death, freedom and subjugation. "Telefteos Stathmos" ("The Last Stop") at the end is a profound record of Seferis's growing disillusionment with life as, in an Italian harbor, he embarked on the ship that would bring him home to Greece.

Seferis's first postwar poem, and in the view of many critics his most self-revelatory, is "Kichli" ("The Thrush"), written in 1947 on the peaceful island of Poros. There the *Kichli*, a ship sunk by the Germans in the harbor of the island, parts still visible, becomes the focus of intense reflections on life and death, on life that becomes death, and on light "angelic and black." Arising from the famous epigram "It is better not to know and not to feel," the poem in three parts moves through memories of childhood and home, to those of youth and erotic pleasure, to those of "the coarsening of body and soul" (Trypanis).

Seferis's trips to Cyprus between 1953 and 1956, at the time of the Cypriot struggle for independence, proved to be of lasting impact on his poetic vision. *Imerologhio Katastromatos C'* (1965; *Logbook III*), dedicated to the people of Cyprus, is a powerful vindication of the "Greekness" of the land and of its struggle for freedom. But topicality as such yields in Seferis to powerful universals, such as "the experience of the human drama" (in his words).

Although Seferis edited major collections of his works in 1950 and in 1961, he was silent from 1955 until 1966, at which time he published *Tria Krifa Poiimata* ("Three Secret Poems") in a voice now more austere and esoteric.

Apart from his impressive poetic oeuvre, Seferis devoted much time to translation and criticism. He did translations of Eliot *in primis*, Pound, Gide, MacLeish, Eluard, Michaud, and others, all collected in *Metagraphes* (1965; *Transcripts*). His literary essays, chiefly in the editions of *Dokhimes* (1944; revised edition, 1962; *On the Greek Style: Selected Essays in Poetry and Hellenism*) are among the most penetrating in all of modern Greek criticism.

HOWARD MARBLESTONE

Selected Bibliography

PRIIMARY SOURCES

Seferis, George. *George Seferis: Collected Poems, 1924–1955.* Translated and edited by Edmund Keeley and Philip Sherrard. Princeton, N.J.: Princeton University Press, 1967; 3rd ed., 1982. Bilingual edition.

——. *Poems by George Seferis.* Translated by Rex Warner. Boston: Little, Brown, 1960.

——. *A Poet's Journal: Days of 1945–1951.* Translated by Athan Anagnostopoulos. Cambridge: Belknap Press of Harvard University Press, 1974.

SECONDARY SOURCES

Friar, Kimon, trans. and ed. *Modern Greek Poetry.* New York: Simon & Schuster, 1973. Pp. 66–72, 740–47.

Politis, Linos. *A History of Modern Greek Literature.* Oxford, U.K.: Clarendon Press, 1973.

Sherrard, Philip. *The Marble Threshing Floor: Studies in Modern Greek Poetry.* London: Valentine and Mitchel, 1956. Pp. 185–231.

Trypanis, C. A. *Greek Poetry from Homer to Seferis.* Chicago: University of Chicago Press, 1981.

Warner, Rex. *On the Greek Style.* Selected essays from Seferis's *Dokhimes.* Boston: Little, Brown, 1966.

JAROSLAV SEIFERT 1984

The poet Jaroslav Seifert (1901–86) is the first Czech to be awarded the Nobel Prize (1984). He was born into a blue-collar family in Prague's proletarian quarter, Žižkov, on September 23, 1901, and except for a short stay in Brno, he lived in his native city until his death on January 10, 1986. Prior to World War II, Seifert traveled extensively, visiting Italy, Austria, Switzerland, France, and the Soviet Union. Memories of these trips are masterfully captured in many poems.

Seifert was not a militant person, yet he never hesitated to speak out when freedom and human dignity were at stake. He considered it the duty of a writer to stand up for justice, for, in his view, "remaining silent meant lying." In 1929, together with six leading Czech writers, Seifert signed a manifesto revealing the incompetence and unscrupulousness of the Czech political hierarchy. For that he was expelled from the Communist party and the literary association *Devětsil*, which he had helped found in 1920. In 1956, at the Second Congress of Czech Writers, Seifert vigorously condemned the crimes and harassments during the Stalin era and demanded restitution. When in 1968 the hopes of the Czech people for a more human socialism were crushed by Warsaw Pact troops, the ailing poet accepted the chairmanship of the Writers' Union and continued the struggle against oppression and persecution. Finally, in 1977, the poet supported the protest declaration known as *Charter 77*. The Czech authorities responded to Seifert's defiance by treating him as a persona non grata. For more than a decade the poet was allowed to publish selections of his poetry or republish older works, but his new collections had to be distributed in typescript by the underground *Petlice* ("Padlock") or had to be printed abroad.

When in 1984 the Nobel Prize in literature was conferred on Seifert "for his poetry, which, endowed with freshness, sensuality, and rich inventiveness, provides a liberating image of the indomitable spirit and versatility of man," the Czech daily press conveyed the news in a short note on the second page, and the mass media mentioned it merely at the end of the evening news. Yet, when Seifert passed away a year later, he was eulogized by the Ministry of Culture as the greatest Czech poet. The poet Jan Pilař gave an impressive survey of Seifert's literary work, and President Husák in his condolence letter extolled the poet's love for his native country, his involvement with the working class, and his struggle for peace and progress.

Although a very prolific and publicly acclaimed writer, Seifert made his living until 1949 predominantly as a journalist and editor of numerous newspapers and periodicals of different political orientations. He edited selected poetry by Karel Toman, Stanislav Kostka Neumann, Vítěszlav Hálek, Jan Neruda, and Jaroslav Vrchlický, published Czech fairy tales, and translated Verlaine, Apollinaire, and Blok.

Seifert's first collection of poetry, *Město v slzách* (1921; "The Town in Tears"), mirrors the mood and the style of Proletarian Poetry, a literary trend prevailing in the early twenties. In free verses and in an exuberant style, the poet evokes the horrors of war and writes about the hopes and the fears of the working masses. He believes in the success of the great revolution that will change the world into a better place for everyone. Seifert is less aggressive and more conciliatory than the other poets of this group: He will hurl the first stone, but he will also be the first to dress the wounds.

Seifert's next collection, *Samá láska* (1923; "Nothing but Love"), heralds Seifert's withdrawal from poesie engagée and its blaring rhetoric. Personal feelings begin to blend with revolutionary ideals, and "the beauties of the world" are now the technical achievements of the twentieth century.

Seifert's shift to the aesthetics of the avant-garde Poetism, founded by the poet Karel Teige, is best manifested in the collection *Na vlnách TSF* (1925; "On the Waves of TSF"). Exotic settings, extraordinary situations, erotic and increased sensuality, absurd imagery and bizarre metaphors mark the poems of this collection. In *Slavík zpívá špatně* (1926; "The Night-ingale Sings Poorly") and in *Poštovní holub* (1928–29; "The Carrier Pigeon") Seifert's poetry intensifies and assumes a slight meditative character. Nostalgic sadness supersedes the hedonistic mood, questions of existence, death, and dying become recurrent motifs. The poet leaves behind the world of dreams and hallucinations, he gives up the play with words, forms, and concepts, and, like the carrier pigeon, he returns to his native land, to a vast range of everyday concerns. Seifert's style becomes transparent; his verse takes on an almost classical form. As the critic F. X. Šalda put it, "Seifert is creating something of nothing." The new aesthetic approach is best displayed in the collections *Jablko s klína* (1933; "The Apple from the Lap") and *Ruce Venušiny* (1936; "The Hands of Venus"). For the latter the poet was awarded the State Prize for literature.

In 1936 Seifert published a collection of witty satires, *Zpíváno do rotačky* ("Singing into the Printing Press"), which relate to various social and cultural affairs. In autumn of 1937 he mourned—in a set of melancholic poems, *Osm dní* (*Eight Days*)—the death of President T. G. Masaryk, whom he had held in high esteem. The last collection before World War II, *Zhasněte světla* (1938; "Extinguish the Lights"), captures the Czech nation's grief and despair after the arbitration of Munich. The poems radiate love and compassion for the mutilated and suffering country and express, at the same time, hope for survival.

During the German occupation Seifert becomes the true bard of his nation, especially of his beloved Prague. The collections *Vějíř Boženy Němcové* (1940; "The Fan of Božena Němcová"), *Světlem oděná* (1940; "Clad in Light"), and *Kamený most* (1944; "The Stone Bridge"), extol the beauty of Prague and its glorious past. They are richly imbued with confidence and optimism—"Everything time has taken away, time will bring back again." The collection *Ruka a plamen* (1943, enlarged 1948; "The Hand and the Flame") is a vivid recollection of various Czech artists and writers. Seifert also prepared selections of his poetry that he entitled *Jaro sbohem* (1942, enlarged 1944, final version 1947; "Good-bye Spring") and *Jabloň se strunami pavučin* (1943; "The Apple Tree with Strings of Cobweb").

After World War II Seifert became quite productive. Despite two lengthy interruptions due to illness (1956–66) and the political situation after 1968, Seifert prepared various selections of his older poetry and published a series of new collections in which his poetic talent peaked. Except for the lovely poems in *Šel malíř chudě do světa* (1949; "Poor Went the Painter into the World") accompanied by drawings of M. Aleš, Seifert's poetry now shows a strong meditative tendency. This mood distinguishes the collection *Píseň o Viktorce* (1950; "The Song about Viktorka"), which centers on a tragic figure from B. Němcová's novel *Babička* ("Grandmother"), as well as the rondels *Mozart v Praze* (1951; *Mozart in Prague*). It is even more conspicuous in the collection *Maminka* (1954; "Mother"), which

presents a fascinating variety of moods and memories from the poet's childhood. The collection earned Seifert the K. Gottwald Prize in literature.

Love, death, and the instability of everything in life are the central motifs in the collections *Koncert na ostrově* (1965; "The Concert on the Island"), *Odlévání zvonů* (1967; *The Casting of Bells*), and *Halleyová kometa* (1967; "Halley's Comet"). The same motifs in a rich set of variations prevail in the last two collections, *Morový sloup* (1977; *The Plague Column*) and *Deštník z Piccadilly* (1979; *An Umbrella from Piccadilly*). By this point, Seifert had developed an extremely concise style, his language had become crystal clear, and the flow of his verse resembled rhythmical prose. Both collections as well as Seifert's graceful and relaxed memoirs, *Všechny krásy světa* (1981; "All Beauties of the World"), were first published abroad.

Despite Seifert's engagement in public life, his poetry remained essentially unpolitical. As he stated, "Searching for beautiful words is more important than killing and murdering." Seifert always remained a very subtle poet; even when he responded to the most tragic moments in the life of his nation, he did it in an unobtrusive way. And his poetry is distinguished by saturation with emotional intensity. In the poet's own words, besides love, "Music and poetry are the most beautiful things in the world."

ELISABETH PRIBIĆ

Selected Bibliography

PRIMARY SOURCES

Seifert, Jaroslav. *The Casting of Bells.* Translated by Paul Jagasich and Tom O'Grady. Iowa City: The Spirit That Moves Us, 1983.

———. *Dílo.* 7 vols. Edited by A. M. Píša. Prague: Československý spisovatel, 1953–70.

———. *Eight Days: An Elegy for Thomas Masaryk.* Translated by Paul Jagasich and Tom O'Grady. Iowa City: The Spirit That Moves Us, 1985.

———. *Mozart in Prague; 13 Rondels.* Translated by Paul Jagasich and Tom O'Grady. Iowa City: The Spirit That Moves Us, 1985.

———. *The Plague Column.* Translated by Ewald Osers. London, Boston: Terra Nova Editions, 1979.

———. *The Selected Poetry of Jaroslav Seifert.* Edited and translated by Ewald Osers. New York: Macmillan, 1986.

———. *An Umbrella from Piccadilly.* Translated by Ewald Osers. London: London Magazine Editions, 1983.

GEORGE BERNARD SHAW *1925*

George Bernard Shaw (1856–1950) after accepting the 1925 Nobel Prize in literature but refusing the cash award, beset with requests from impecunious writers, commented: "I can forgive Alfred Nobel for having invented dynamite. But only a fiend in human form could have invented the Nobel Prize." This sardonic observation not only sums up Shaw's attitude toward conventional honors, but also introduces us to his wit, his iconoclasm, and more generally to his personality, which had as much to do with his winning the Nobel Prize as did his voluminous dramatic and critical works. During most of the first half of the twentieth century Shaw was the dominant figure on the British stage, and he exploited this popularity to convey his ideas on politics, economics, and the reform of English orthography and phonetics.

Yet Shaw was no prodigy, no Mozart of the stage bursting upon the world with youthful genius. He was born in Dublin on July 26, 1856, into a family who were members of the city's petit bourgeoisie. He began his career as a junior clerk and then as cashier for a Dublin estate agency. His early artistic ambitions to be a painter and later to be a novelist were thwarted by a conspicuous lack of talent. Between

1876, when he left Dublin for London (he was not to return to Ireland for twenty-nine years), and 1883 Shaw wrote five novels: *Immaturity, The Irrational Knot, Love Among the Artists, Cashel Byron's Profession,* and *An Unsocial Socialist* (all of which were published many decades after they were written). Despite these failures, the last two decades of the nineteenth century shaped Shaw's political and aesthetic views and prepared him for a career that would resurrect British drama and drag it at least partially into the modern era. Influenced by the lectures of Henry George, an American economist and social-welfare advocate, and by the writings of Karl Marx, Shaw developed a lifelong interest in politics that led him to join the newly formed Fabian Society (which advocated evolutionary socialism) in 1884, to be a vestryman and borough councillor in London from 1897 to 1903, and to become a prolific writer of political treatises. Among these political works are *Fabian Essays in Socialism* (1889), *The Common Sense of Municipal Trading* (1904), "Common Sense About the War" (1917), *The Intelligent Woman's Guide to Socialism and Capitalism* (1928), "The Adventures of the Black Girl in Her Search for God" (1932), and *Everybody's Political What's What?* (1944). Throughout his life Shaw would capitalize on the immense popular appeal of his plays to promote his social, economic, and political views by developing the polemics of his plays in long prefaces. As he put it, he had the "simple desire to give [his] customers good value for their money

by eking out a penniesworth of play with a pound of preface," and he was not joking; the preface to *Major Barbara* runs 50 pages, to *Heartbreak House*, 48 pages, to *Saint Joan*, 67 pages, and to *Getting Married*, 129 pages.

The 1880s also brought Shaw together with William Archer, English dramatist, critic, translator, and promoter of the works of Henrik Ibsen. Archer not only introduced Shaw to Ibsen's work, but also helped launch Shaw's successful career as music, art, and theater critic. For the rest of the decade and into the '90s, Shaw wrote for daily papers and monthly journals such as the *Pall Mall Gazette, The World, The Star,* and *The Saturday Review.* Though an attempt by the two men to write a collaborative play failed, the effort eventually led to Shaw's *Widowers' Houses*, first performed in 1892. The previous year Shaw achieved a degree of fame and notoriety with his book-length essay *The Quintessence of Ibsenism*, which revealed more about Shavian philosophy and aesthetics than about Ibsenism. Shaw saw Ibsen's early verse plays as an "intellectual analysis [and condemnation] of idealism" and the later prose plays as models of rationalism and realism, the revelation of the hypocrisy of conventional philistine and idealist moral strictures. Though there is more of Mozart's joy and playfulness in Shaw's plays than of Ibsen's gloom and tragedy, Shaw embraces and emulates what he sees as Ibsen's iconoclasm and his honest, "anti-idealist," "modern" view of the world. As Shaw puts it, "the destroyer of ideals, though denounced as an enemy of the society, is in fact sweeping the world clear of lies."

In his first three plays, *The Widowers' Houses*, *The Philanderer*, and *Mrs. Warren's Profession*, all completed in 1892 and 1893 and later published together as *Plays Unpleasant*, Shaw demonstrates his debt to Ibsen's anti-idealist world view, but he also demonstrates a debt to nineteenth-century melodrama, to the witty one-liners of Oscar Wilde's plays, to the "well-made" plays of Eugene Scribe (though Shaw condemned the Scribean formulas), and to the tragicomic chatter of Chekhov's characters. The first play was admittedly "propagandist" and "didactic," a "topical farce" about a widower who owns slum property; in an apologia cum social critique Shaw claims that the play was a reaction to "modern commercialism," which, he says, is "squalid, futile, blundering, mean, ridiculous," pretending to be "wide-minded" and "humane." The philandering protagonist of his second play (which takes place in the library of "The Ibsen Club") comically justifies his infidelities when he asks Grace, an "advanced woman" and object of his fleeting affection, "Does Julia belong to me? Am I her owner—her master?" After evoking the response that he intended— "Certainly not. No woman is the property of a man. A woman belongs to herself and to nobody else"—he concludes, "Quite right. Ibsen forever!" *Mrs. Warren's Profession*, with its Ibsenian hint of incest and its frank and sympathetic presentation of a member of the

world's "oldest profession," was banned from public performance until 1925 (though it was presented privately by the Incorporated Stage Society in 1902). This interest in Ibsen continued with *Candida*, which Shaw called "a counterblast to Ibsen's *Doll's House*, showing that in the real typical doll's house it is the man who is the doll." Here, as well as in *Arms and the Man*, *The Man of Destiny*, and *You Never Can Tell*, published together with *Candida* as *Plays Pleasant* (1898), Shaw takes on an antagonistic role against critics, the established theater, and the general public, attacking romantic misrepresentations of war, hero worship, politics, religion, and love. Though these plays at first brought little success, they demonstrated the playwright's virtuosity as a dramatist for the Ibsen-inspired New Independent Theatre, his mastery of comic timing, his facility with natural and fast-paced dialogue, and his development of unconventional characters, such as Captain Bluntschli, Candida, and his Napoleon. Through these early plays, his voluminous dramatic criticism, his fictional "interviews" with himself, and his letters to editors, Shaw was creating a public persona as the cynical, eccentric, brilliant wordmonger known simply as G.B.S., and at the same time he was creating and educating an audience who would eventually hail him as the most influential and most popular playwright of his time.

The production of *The Devil's Disciple* (1896), the publication of this play along with *Caesar and Cleopatra* and *Captain Brass-*

bound's Conversion in *Three Plays for Puritans* (1901), and the staging of eleven of Shaw's plays in the repertory season at the Court Theatre from 1904 to 1907 were among the first high-water marks of Shaw's popularity. "I have advertized myself so well that I find myself, whilst still in middle life, almost as legendary a person as the *Flying Dutchman*"; with this sardonic comparison of himself to the unlucky, perpetually wandering ghost ship, Shaw demonstrates his uncanny understanding of the success that greeted *The Devil's Disciple*. Much of his preface to his "Puritan" plays attempts to answer the question, "What is wrong with the theatre that a strong man may die of it?" The answer had to do with the "pleasure-mongering" audience and stage management who have, in their demand for sensuality, wish fulfillment, and immediate gratification, transformed the theatrical profession into Mrs. Warren's. Shaw ironically calls on the Puritans to rescue the theater from the obsession with romantic plays that, in Shaw's view, gratifies the public's desire while keeping "real" matters of love and sex off the stage. Enter Dick Dudgeon, the Dickensian defrocked Puritan hero of *The Devil's Disciple*. Answering American reviewers' praise for "the audacious originality" of this play, Shaw pointed out that if this epithet "'original' applies to the incidents, plot, construction, and general professional and technical qualities of the play, it is nonsense: for the truth is, I am in these matters a very old-fashioned playwright."

Shaw's originality lies partly in his personality, the public persona so carefully cultivated, and more significantly in the irreverent, sardonic, anachronistic, and iconoclastic matter of his plays. By the end of the '90s audiences were ready to see villains as heroes, heroes defrocked, priests sell their gods for five talents, history and literature's most famous femme fatale presented as a spoiled child, and even the English language subverted and modernized. Shaw brilliantly exploited nineteenth-century theatrical methods to inculcate twentieth-century ideas, doing more to popularize European thinkers such as Ibsen and Nietzsche than any other Irish or English playwright. When Apollodorus addresses Caesar at the climax of *Caesar and Cleopatra*, he sums up Shaw's view of the interrelationship between art and life: "What you say has an Olympian ring to it: it must be right; for it is fine art."

The first decade of the new century brought Shaw his own Olympian stature with *Man and Superman*, an overtly Nietzschean exploration of the individual's "life force" with its potential to revitalize Europe's decaying civilization; *John Bull's Other Island*, an examination of British stereotypes of the Irish; *Major Barbara*, a satirical comparison of the ineffective philanthropy of the Salvation Army with the pernicious but more humane munitions industry; *The Doctor's Dilemma*, a tragicomic diatribe against the excesses of the medical profession; *Getting Married: A Disquisitory Play* without act or scene breaks, obeying the ancient "unities" of time and place and exposing the British marriage law as "inhuman and unreasonable to the point of downright abomination"; *The Shewing-Up of Blanco Posnet*, which Shaw himself called "a very simple and even crude melodrama" and which was banned as sacrilegious. This unremarkable play, like *Mrs. Warren's Profession* before it and *Press Cuttings* after, provided Shaw with a forum through which to attack British censorship.

Androcles and the Lion (written in 1912) and its massive preface provided another discussion of Christianity, and together with the immensely popular *Pygmalion*, written the same year, showed Shaw again drawing on his theatrical success to convey views on religion, the class system, and language. As in the earlier "historical" plays, much of the humor of *Androcles* results from Shaw's anachronistic language, the colloquial twentieth-century English spoken by these first-century Christians. Language becomes the focus of *Pygmalion*; its preface tells us that "the English have no respect for their language, and will not teach their children to speak it. They cannot spell it because they have nothing to spell it with but an old foreign alphabet of which only the consonants . . . have any agreed speech value." Until the end of his life Shaw argued again and again for the abolition of "abominable Frenchifications" such as *programme* and *cigarette*; for a simplified phonetic spelling: e.g., *labor* for *labour*, *Renascence* for *Renaissance*, *advertize* for *advertise*; for the end to the apostrophe—"the ugly and silly trick of peppering pages with these uncouth

bacilli"; and for a total reform of the alphabet. A note to *Pygmalion* provides a specific example: "In the dialogue an *e* upside down indicates the indefinite vowel, . . . for, though it is one of the commonest sounds in English speech, our wretched alphabet has no letter."

Although Shaw's strong stand against British involvement in World War I undermined his popularity from 1914 to 1918, by 1919 the public looked back on the war with horror rather than with patriotic fervor and greeted a revival of *Arms and the Man* with great enthusiasm, acknowledging *Heartbreak House*, an indictment of the bankrupt society that led to the war, as one of Shaw's greatest achievements. A few years later Shaw's five-play *Back to Methuselah* (published 1921, performed 1922) extended this criticism and warned against future wars. Shaw would continue to write plays through the 1930s and to write polemical prose until his death in 1950, but his last great play would be *Saint Joan*, first produced in the United States in 1923 and in England in 1924. Once again tragedy and comedy come together in this humanization of Saint Joan, which demonstrates the impossibility of idealism in this world of realpolitik. Shaw found it odd that the Nobel committee chose to award him the prize for 1925 when he had published nothing that year, but it is fitting that the award came so soon after *Saint Joan*, the play that Shaw considered to be his best.

Bernard Shaw has influenced playwrights as diverse as Noel Coward, Bertolt Brecht, John Osborne,

Peter Weiss, Jean Anouilh, and Eugene O'Neill. Film versions of many of the plays, including *Caesar and Cleopatra*, *The Devil's Disciple*, *Major Barbara*, *Saint Joan*, and *Pygmalion* (later popularized still further as *My Fair Lady*) gave Shaw new popularity (and wealth) in the 1930s and 1940s, and his plays continue to draw popular and critical praise the world over.

STEVEN D. PUTZEL

Selected Bibliography

PRIMARY SOURCES

Shaw, [George] Bernard. *Bernard Shaw: The Diaries*. Edited by Stanley Weintraub. University Park: Penn State University Press, 1986.

——. *Bernard Shaw. Early Texts: Play Manuscripts in Facsimile*. Edited by Dan H. Laurence. 12 vols. New York: Garland, 1980–81.

——. *Bernard Shaw's Nondramatic Literary Criticism*. Edited by Stanley Weintraub. Lincoln: University of Nebraska Press, 1972.

——. *Collected Letters*. Edited by Dan H. Laurence. 4 vols. London: Reinhardt, 1965–86.

——. *Collected Plays with Their Prefaces*. Edited by Dan H. Laurence. 7 vols. New York: Dodd, 1975.

——. *The Portable Bernard Shaw*. Edited by Stanley Weintraub. New York: Viking Press, 1977.

——. *Practical Politics: Twentieth-Century Views on Politics and Economics*. Edited by Lloyd J. Hubenka. Lincoln: University of Nebraska Press, 1976.

——. *Shaw and Ibsen: Bernard Shaw's Quintessence of Ibsenism, and Related Writings*. Edited by J. L. Wisenthal. Toronto: University of Toronto Press, 1979.

——. *Shaw's Dramatic Criticism (1895–98)*. Selected by John Matthews. Westport, Conn.: Greenwood Press, 1971.

——. *Shaw's Music: The Complete Musical Criticism*. Edited by Dan H. Laurence. 3 vols. New York: Dodd, 1981.

——. *Shaw on Language*. Edited by Abraham Tauber. London: P. Owen, 1965.

SECONDARY SOURCES

Bloom, Harold, ed. *George Bernard Shaw*. New York: Chelsea, 1987.

Crompton, Louis. *Shaw the Dramatist*. Lincoln: University of Nebraska Press, 1969.

Gibbs, A. M. *The Art and Mind of Shaw: Essays in Criticism*. New York: St. Martin's Press, 1983.

Mills, John. *Language and Laughter*. Tucson: University of Arizona Press, 1969.

Whitman, Robert. *Shaw and the Play of Ideas*. Ithaca N.Y.: Cornell University Press, 1977.

MIKHAIL SHOLOKHOV   *1965*

Mikhail Aleksandrovich Sholokhov (1905–1984) was born May 24, 1905 in Krughilin, USSR, in the Don Cossack region. (The Don is one of the major rivers in European Russia.) His mother, Anastasiia Danilovna Chernikova, was from Ukrainian peasant stock and worked as a maid for the Sholokhovs, a Russian merchant family. Mikhail's father, Aleksandr Mikhailovich Sholokhov, fell in love with Anastasiia and wanted to marry her. However, when she became pregnant his family (since she was their servant) married her off to an unknown Cossack. Thus, Mikhail was officially born into the Cossack status. Eventually, in 1912, after Mikhail's Cossack "father" died, Anastasiia and Aleksandr were married, and Mikhail lost the Cossack status. He became a member of the lower middle class.

Aleksandr wanted his son to have a good education, and he sent Mikhail to elementary school in Kargin. Around 1914 or 1915 Mikhail continued at a private secondary school in Moscow, where he studied for about two or three years. He then studied in Boguchar and Veshenskaia until 1918, when he was forced to end his education due to the continuous fighting of the spreading civil war.

During the war Mikhail lived in Pleshakov, which was very near, and sometimes in, the battle zone. The sights and sounds of battles made lasting impressions on Sholokhov, which would be useful to the author later in his career.

Sholokhov held several small jobs for the new Soviet government until 1922, when he was sent to Bukanovskaia. There he was placed in command of the regional food-requisitioning project. However, many people resisted the policies he instituted, and he was forced to deal with brutal uprisings, which were just as brutally suppressed. On two separate occasions he was almost executed. These events, too, made a lasting impression upon him and provided themes for many of his early stories.

Sholokhov began to write short stories and plays in 1920, but all of his writings between 1920 and 1922 were lost. In October 1922 Mikhail moved to Moscow hoping to continue his education and to become a professional writer. He worked in several occupations (as a laborer, longshoreman, stonemason, accountant) and was unable to publish until 1923, when he joined a group of Komsomol (Communist youth) writers called Molodaia Gvardiia ("Young Guard"). He published his first articles in *Iunosheskaia Pravda* ("Youth Truth").

Later that same year Sholokhov went back to the Don region to marry Maria Gromoslavskaia, a food inspector he had met while in Bukanovskaia. After the wedding, they settled in Moscow and raised four children.

Sholokhov published his first book, *Raskazi* (*Tales of the Don*), a collection of short stories, in 1925, soon to be followed by *The Azure Steppe* (1926). But he gained recognition as an exceptional writer only when he began publishing the first parts of the epic novel, *Tikhii Don* (1928–40; *The Quiet Don*). This work would become the best-selling novel not only in the Soviet Union but also in many other countries. It would bring Sholokhov the Nobel Prize in literature in 1965. It also brought Sholokhov worldwide fame, being translated in more than forty languages in over thirty countries.

All of his writings to this point deal with the lives of the Cossacks during the Revolution, the civil war, and the early 1920s. Most critics praise Sholokhov for his knowledge of the Cossack life, use of language, and imagery; yet he has been criticized for lack of characterization. Rumors of plagiarism also spread. However, there is little evidence to support these rumors.

As a Communist party member in good standing, Sholokhov interrupted the writing of *The Quiet Don* in the 1930s so he could write the Five-Year Plan novel *Podniataia Tselina* (1931; *Virgin Soil Upturned* also translated as *Harvest on the Don* and *Seeds of Tomorrow*). Although the novel is to a large extent ideologically motivated, it can be considered a literary success. Party critics held it as a model of socialist realism. Eventually, Sholokhov became a member of the party's Central Committee, deputy of the Supreme Soviet, and recipient of Stalin and Lenin prizes in literature.

Politics continued to affect his writing career. Censorship, as well as duties for the party, interfered with his writing. Several of his works remained unfinished for as long as ten years. World War II also took Sholokhov away from his novels and sent him to the front as a reporter for Soviet newspapers. He published only one short story and several sketches during this time. The author admitted that he did not enjoy journalistic reporting, for his natural tendency was to write slowly and at great length. However, he did begin to write the novel *Oni srazhalis' za rodinu* (1943–45; *They Fought for Their Country*) during this period.

From 1946 to 1953 he contributed political commentaries to newspapers. Through these, on one hand, he admonished Western leaders and dissident Soviet writers; on the other hand, he praised the Soviet people and the party's policy, which he avidly followed.

Privately, Sholokhov was a simple man who enjoyed being outdoors. Hunting, fishing, and answering the mail he received filled most of his last days in Veshenskaia.

Mikhail Sholokhov has been praised as a writer of the people. More specifically, Sholokhov has become known for his realistic depictions of the Cossacks. His short stories and novels describe real people, mostly the Cossacks just as they were, as peasants tied to the soil or as soldiers wandering the land. The author possessed a keen knowledge of the Cossack dialect and humor. He reveals their passions and temperaments by describing their labor and love for the land. He rarely created characters as political statements. The Cossacks were not revolutionary or anti-Soviet; they were ordinary men and women struggling with human problems.

One of Sholokhov's most common themes is man's cruelty to man. He often depicts man as a violent being with little hope for a change. Tragedy and violence were integral parts of human nature, yet Sholokhov describes them in a detached and calm manner. He uses descriptive details and imagery to convey a mood or scene. Nature is a primary background to human disasters in his works. The author reproduces nature to an exact image, then draws a relationship between the Cossacks and their environment. Sentiment for the land and the people's involvement with it were strongly reflected in Sholokhov's work.

Sholokhov's concern with man and nature is the main theme of his novel *Virgin Soil Upturned*. It is both an artistic and a propagandistic novel about the collectivization of agriculture. It deals with life in a Soviet village and the struggles of its characters. Sholokhov exposes both the good and evil in his characters, regardless of their political convictions.

Nature is an important element in Sholokhov's most famous work, *The Quiet Don*. He deftly emphasizes the unity that men, particularly the Cossacks, share with nature and nature's effect upon the lives of various characters in the novel. Sholokhov's love for the land is quite obvious in *The Quiet Don* through his careful and attentive descriptions of the landscape and seasons. In many of his descriptions Sholokhov compares nature with man's actions and

stresses the superiority of the former over the latter, implying a higher regard for nature than for man. Sholokhov emphasized the eternal, seasonally changing landscape, which is more fundamental to life than man's struggles. Nature is constant and self-perpetuating, whereas man could perish by his own destructive tendencies.

Sholokhov often uses nature to reflect the spirit of man. Seasons foreshadow the lives and events of his characters. For instance, much of the action during the war and Revolution take place during the harsh months of winter, while Gregor (the novel's hero) returns home from the front during spring. Moreover, conditions of the Don River also reflect human emotions and occurrences. Either the Don is peaceful and serene during moments of reflection for Gregor, or it swells in a stormy rage as he struggles with his feelings for his love, Aksinia. He knows that she is married, but Gregor cannot control his passion for her. Aksinia also has feelings for Gregor, yet she makes it difficult for him when they are together. The Don River is a metaphor for the struggle between the two. Gregor's lack of control over Aksinia and the anxiety she causes for him are similar to the uncontrollable and dangerous waters of a stormy Don.

For Sholokhov, elements of nature are often similar to the lives of the Cossacks in that they are interrelated. He uses many metaphors and similes in his prose to describe the Cossacks and their natural environment. Land was very important to the Cossacks since it was the primary setting for their labors. For most Cossacks, working the land was all they had in life. They were hearty, strong people who toughened themselves through their labor.

The Quiet Don has been described as a tragedy of the Cossacks as a group, not just of one man. The pain and conflict that arise with each Cossack's personal decision about the Revolution make life difficult for all the Cossacks. There is an increased tension between farmers and traders, poor and rich Cossacks, and between rank-and-file soldiers and landowning officers. Although taken as a whole they are a unified people, the war forces them to fight each other. Historical events such as World War I, the Revolution, and the civil war are confusing to the Cossacks, and they lose control of their own destiny.

The Quiet Don has been noted as the oustanding historical novel in Soviet literature. Sholokhov has been praised as the first Soviet author to write a novel for and about the people. The novel is a commentary not only on the war and the Revolution, but also on the effects that these had on the Cossacks. The political doubts Gregor experiences are reflective of the conflicts that most Russians felt.

Some critics say that the novel lacks form or placement. Sholokhov involves too many characters in his attempt to cover so much history. The novel has also been criticized for having a loose construction and lack of characterization. Sholokhov does incorporate many characters into the novel; however, they all represent various important elements of Russian society. It is obvious that Sholokhov tries to follow in the footsteps of Tolstoy's *War and Peace*. He, however, failed to bring Tolstoy's psychological depth and careful character development to bear on the work. *The Quiet Don* is prominently written from a sociological and ethnographic point of view. But without a doubt, the novel is both a literary and social success for Mikhail Sholokhov.

Sholokhov died at the age of seventy-nine on February 21, 1984.

RADO PRIBIC
AND LORI SCARPA

Selected Bibliography

PRIMARY SOURCES

Sholokhov, Mikhail. *Seeds of Tomorrow*. Translated by Stephen Garry. New York: Alfred A. Knopf, 1935.

————. *Virgin Soil Upturned*. Translated by Stephen Garry. New York: Putnam, 1935.

————. *They Fought for Their Country*. Moscow: Foreign Languages Publishing House, 1959.

————. *Harvest on the Don*. Translated by H. C. Stevens. New York: Alfred A. Knopf, 1961.

————. *The Don Flows Home to the Sea*. Translated by Stephen Garry. New York: Vintage Books, 1966.

————. *And Quiet Flows the Don*. Translated by Stephen Garry. New York: Vintage Books, 1966.

SECONDARY SOURCES

Ermolaev, Herman. *Mikhail Sholokhov and His Art*. Princeton, N.J.: Princeton University Press, 1982.

Grinberg, Joseph. "Mikhail Sholok-hov." In *International Literature*. Moscow: State Literary Publishing House, 1945. Pp. 52–57.

Medvedev, Roy, A. *Problems in the Literary Biography of Mikhail Sho-*

lokhov. New York: Cambridge University Press, 1975.

Stewart, David H. *Mikhail Sholokhov: A Critical Introduction.* Ann Arbor: University of Michigan Press, 1967.

HENRYK SIENKIEWICZ   *1905*

Henryk Sienkiewicz (1846–1916), the first Polish writer to be awarded the Nobel Prize in literature, was born into an impoverished family of noble heritage in 1846. He was educated in Warsaw and studied law, medicine, history, and literature at the university, which he left in 1871 without completing his examinations in order to embark upon a career in journalism. He became co-owner of the biweekly *Niwa* ("The Field"), editor of *Slowo* ("The Word"), and contributed regularly to the prestigious *Gazeta Polska* ("Polish Gazette"). Even though he later adopted fiction as a career, Sienkiewicz maintained an active relationship with newspapers and often utilized them to express his views.

Disturbed by the cultural life of Warsaw and eager to expand his horizons, Sienkiewicz arranged for a trip to the United States in 1876 financed by *Gazeta Polska*. He reported on American life in regular dispatches for more than a year and also covered the visit of the popular Polish actress Helena Modjeska, who was most anxious to leave what she considered the jealousies and cultural intrigues of the Polish capital. A further purpose of Sienkiewicz's visit was to locate a suitable site for a colony where these cultural exiles could settle. A location near Anaheim, California, was selected, but the small group found itself poorly suited for manual labor, and the romantic aura of tilling the soil fell victim to more practical considerations. The author returned first to Western Europe and subsequently to Poland, having produced *Listy z podróży do Ameryki* (1876–78; *Letters from a Trip to America*), which established him as something more than a news reporter. The letters were somewhat critical of aspects of American life, particularly of the large cities, but the author was willing to note the positive as well, and he demonstrated a commendable balance in reporting. This balance was later to be very evident in his fiction.

Sienkiewicz's extensive writing may be broadly said to be a product of his journalistic bent and his patriotic feelings stimulated by the fall of the Polish-Lithuanian Commonwealth to Prussian and Russian domination. The journalist demanded honesty and some authorial distance, but the patriot was not averse to portraying heroism, victorious military engagements, and chivalrous romance. In the atmosphere of political oppression the patriot looked to history for solace and the memory of national grandeur, while the journalist found that his most comfortable and successful reportage was in the form of chronicles of events with a twist of humor. These factors produced a novelist of striking proportions and broad significance.

Although it is as a novelist that Sienkiewicz is known, he also produced short stories and sketches throughout his writing career. These works typically deal with social and political issues—the brutish Polish nobility, the plight of the peasants, the evils of Prussian domination, the lack of Polish efforts to free the nation, the misery of Polish exiles. The stories are told with an irony and understatement that produce authorial distance, but the effect is nonetheless powerful and intimate. Several short works were mentioned in the Nobel citation, including the collection *Szkice weglem* (1877; *Charcoal Sketches*), *Janko muzykant* (1879; "Janko the Musician"), *Latarnik* (1882; *The Light-House Keeper*), and *Pojdzmy za Nim* (1892; "Let Us Follow Him"), which introduced his examination of the early Christian era. These tales unite psychological subtlety with social consciousness and individuals with a sense of history.

Sienkiewicz gained international acclaim in the 1880s with the publication of a novelistic trilogy dealing with seventeenth-century Poland. Throughout his career and after his death these novels formed the core of his popularity. The trilogy includes *Ogniem i mieczem* (1883–84; *With Fire and Sword*), which centers on the Cossack rebellion of 1747–51; *Potop* (1884–86; *The Deluge*), which tells the story of the war between Poland and Sweden in the 1650s; and *Pan Wolodyjowski* (1887–88; *Pan Michael*), which begins with the election of King Michael Wisniowiecki in 1669 and examines the clashes of Poland with the Tatars and Turks. The trilogy portrays a positive view of the Polish-Lithuanian Commonwealth as being a generally useful and productive entity. Each volume concludes with the description of a Polish military victory, and the trilogy was intended to be a boost in morale to a country under foreign domination in the 1880s.

It is in the historical novels that Sienkiewicz blossomed as a writer of fiction. Colorful and exciting plots, vivid narrative with a successful attempt at reproducing the language of the past, effectively drawn pictures of nature, careful and clear characterization, romance, intense and vivid battle scenes, and good humor characterize the works. The proportions are truly epic in quantity and quality, and the Nobel Committee specifically cited "his outstanding merits as an epic writer" in their 1905 presentation. Each of the long novels was serialized in Polish newspapers, and this factor contributed in no small way to their broad popular appeal.

Even though the trilogy was written with the intent of buoying the national spirit, Sienkiewicz does not hesitate to portray his characters with balance. His Polish patriots have flaws, the enemies sometimes exhibit ability and courage, yet it is ever clear where the author's sentiments lie, and true virtue is found on the Polish side. Not surprisingly, the novels provoked disagreements over Sienkiewicz's historicity and interpretation of events, but the weight of both history and scholarship supported his fiction, to which he invariably devoted considerable study and research. Like many writers of historical fiction, and consistent with his own artistic views, Sienkiewicz reserved the major roles in his trilogy for those not typically highlighted in official histories. Kings and generals are present, but it is those of lesser stature who contribute most to the flow of events. It is the lives of these people that are examined against the backdrop of dramatic national events.

Following the substantial success of his historical fiction, the author turned to the arena of contemporary problems, which afforded the opportunity to add considerably more psychological depth to his characters. *Bez dogmatu* (1891; *Without Dogma*) was his first effort in this vein and is considered by many to be his most important contribution to fiction. Ploszowski, the central male protagonist, is endowed with wealth and considerable abilities, but he has no guiding idea or set of values. He is sophisticated, worldly, and skeptical of religious and moral values. His life ends in suicide as an authorial warning against the agnostic intellectual decline of man and the morbid mood of the end of the century, yet many of the younger generation adopted Ploszowski as a model because of his analytical and introspective approach to life. The novel became much more popular abroad than in Poland because of the character's inability to address current internal social and political issues. Sienkiewicz was held in such respect abroad because of this novel and his historical trilogy that he was elected to the Russian Imperial Academy of Arts and Sciences in St. Petersburg as an expert in psychology and history.

Without Dogma was followed in 1893–94 by *Rodzina Polanieckich* (*The Polaniecki Family*, or as it is sometimes translated *Children of the Soil*), which was greeted by a Polish reading public anxious for positive solutions to the dreary and intense world of Ploszowski. Polaniecki is practical, hard-working, and considers himself to be a man of action. Despite the fact that he too is not guided by dogma or values, he attains substantial worldly success, and he provided some degree of hope for society. This hope could not fulfill all needs, however, since positivist values and business success could not satisfy the spiritual dimension of man.

Since his youth Sienkiewicz had possessed a fondness for antiquity, regularly read the Greco-Roman classics, and even memorized verses from Horace. When he turned his journalistic and historical eye to the era of the classics and visited Italy and Greece, the result was *Quo Vadis* (1895–96), which became an astounding commercial success and solidified his worldwide reputation. The novel is set in the time of Nero and depicts the moral floundering of Roman culture in juxtaposition to the moral strength of the emerging Christian movement. The plot is filled with adventure, intrigue, and lively characterization and can be read as a historical romance, yet the novel stands as a profession and defense of faith as well. Nero and his courtiers are uniformly inferior to the humble practitioners of the new faith, and the fact that there are those who convert and become part of the movement illustrates the author's sentiments. With this novel Sienkiewicz again demonstrated his capacity as a historian, his journalistic accuracy, and his deep sense of humanity.

Sienkiewicz next turned to Polish medieval history and serialized *Krzyzacy* (1897–1900; *The Knights of the Cross*), in which he examines the interaction of the Teutonic knights and local nobles in fifteenth-century Poland. The knights have lost their moral and religious purpose and exhibit deceit, hypocrisy, and debauchery. The fact that the knights were a source of the future Prussian state that partitioned and dominated nineteenth-century Poland was not lost on Polish readers, nor was the saintly behavior of a Polish count whose actions make the knights appear truly bestial.

It was this body of fiction that resulted in the Nobel Prize in literature in 1905. The prize was accepted with a brief speech in which Sienkiewicz emphasized that the award actually recognized the achievements and genius of Poland, which even though under foreign domination was not exhausted and enslaved as some would profess. The two novels that followed the prize seemingly built upon the author's acceptance speech. *Na polu chwaly* (1905; *On the Field of Glory*) portrayed events prior to the Polish defeat of the Turks at Vienna in 1682–83, and *Wiry* (1909–10; *Whirlpools*) contended with the socialist and revolutionary fervor of the first decade of the twentieth century and expressed concern that society not disintegrate over the fervor but remain unified and capable of regeneration.

Sienkiewicz added one new dimension to his work after the award with the publication of *W pustyni i puszczy* (1911; *In the Desert and Wilderness*), his only children's tale. The story stems from his trip to Africa in 1890–91, which also produced *Listy z Afryki* ("Letters from Africa") in the Polish newspapers. The work is full of adventure and excitement and was a product of the author's opinion that every writer should produce at least one work for children.

As World War I unfolded Sienkiewicz left Poland for his safety and moved to Switzerland, where he was active in organizing relief for Polish war victims and promoting the cause of Polish independence. This tireless work took its toll and combined with arteriosclerosis, with which he had long suffered, to end his life in 1916. Sienkiewicz left behind a large body of writing that was eminently popular, as witnessed by the fact that his work has been translated into well over forty languages. As a tribute to this popularity and the quality of his work, Sienkiewicz was recognized by the Polish government following World War II as one of the twelve outstanding Polish writers whose works were placed under the patronage of the government.

RICHARD L. CHAPPLE

Selected Bibliography

PRIMARY SOURCE

Sienkiewicz, Henryk. *Dziela* (*Collected Works*). 60 vols. Warsaw: Panstwowy Instytut Wydawniczy, 1947–55.

SECONDARY SOURCES

Baculewski, Jan. *Henryk Sienkiewicz.* Warsaw: Wiedza Powszechna, 1958.

Curtin, Jeremiah. *Memoirs.* Madison: State Historical Society of Wisconsin, 1940.

Femelidi, A. M. *Genrikh Senkevich, ego literaturnaya epokha, zhizn', trudy i mysli.* Petersburg, Russia: Vol'f. 1912.

Gardner, Monica. *The Patriot Novelist of Poland, Henryk Sienkiewicz.* London: Dent, 1926.

Giergielewicz, Mieczyslaw. *Henryk Sienkiewicz.* New York: Twayne, 1968.

———. "Henryk Sienkiewicz's American Resonance." *Antemurale* (Rome) 10 (1966):256–354.

Lednicki, Waclaw. *Bits of Table Talk on Pushkin, Mickiewicz, Goethe, Turgenev, and Sienkiewicz.* The Hague: Martinus Nijhoff, 1956.

———. *Henryk Sienkiewicz: A Retrospective Synthesis.* The Hague: Mouton, 1960.

FRANS EEMIL SILLANPÄÄ   *1939*

Frans Eemil Sillanpää (1888–1964) was born on September 16, 1888, in the rural village of Kierikkala, parish of Hämeenkyrö, in southwestern Finland, then part of the Russian Empire. A writer of prose, Sillanpää's reputation rests chiefly on several novels published during a creative spurt in the early 1930s. Awarded the Nobel Prize in literature in 1939 "for his deep comprehension and exquisite art in painting the nature of his country and the life of its peasants in their mutual relations" (Nobel Citation), Sillanpää became the first Finnish writer to be so honored.

To be born a Finn in the nineteenth century usually meant to be born a peasant. The future laureate's ancestors had been independent landowners in the province of Satakunta, where farming lore and traditions were the rich heritage of generations. Debts, however, had brought the family down in the world, and Frans Eemil was born as the third and only surviving child of landless peasants. His father, Frans Henrik Koskinen, worked as a day laborer and owned a small cabin near the millrace in Kierikkala. His mother, Loviisa Vilhelmiina Mäkelä, sold a few basic items from a corner of the cabin to supplement their meager income. Following Finnish village tradition, Frans Eemil took his surname from the land on which he lived and thus became Sillanpää ("bridgehead").

Although his parents were poor, they made every sacrifice to provide the best for their only child. There was, as yet, no compulsory education in Finland. The village primary school, however, was good, and Frans was an able pupil. He was sent to the nearby town of Hankijärvi, where he gained admittance to a newly founded grammar school. The family then moved to Hankijärvi along with their son and were so encouraged by his academic progress that they resolved to make the heavy sacrifice of another move to Tampere, Finland's chief industrial city, for the sake of the superior educational opportunities available there.

Thus in the fall of 1886, eight-year-old Frans began a new life, one that permitted him to experience a much broader range of Finnish society. The country lad now discovered the city with its very different horizons and tempo. The family first lived among the working class in rooms rented from a carpenter. As money ran short, the principal of the Lyceum Tampere secured a position for Frans as tutor to the son of a wealthy local industrialist, and he soon moved into this home with its very different milieu. The student continued to show great promise and, with the help of classmates and borrowed money, matriculated in 1908 at the Imperial Alexander University Helsinki.

Sillanpää spent five years at the university studying the natural sciences, particularly biology. At this time Darwinism provided the intellectual foundation for the discipline, and this view of man as the product of evolutionary forces undoubtedly contributed much to the writer's subsequent attitude of fatalism regarding the laws governing life processes. The university also provided Sillanpää with new acquaintances, one of whom introduced him to a life more stimulating than that offered by the curricula of biology and zoology.

Eero Järnefelt was a painter, prominent aristocrat, and an important figure in the history of Finnish art. At the university, Sillanpää became good friends with his son and through him was introduced to the circle of artists at Tuusula outside Helsinki. This group, among other artists and intellectuals, included the painter Pekka Halonen, the writer Juhani Aho, and the composer Jan Sibelius. These members of the Finnish cultural elite welcomed the bright young man warmly, and the excitement of his association with this stimulating group contributed substantially to his growing unhappiness with the academic regimen.

On December 24, 1913, the twenty-five-year-old Sillanpää returned for the traditional Christmas sauna to his parents' very humble cabin, Töllinmäki ("Shanty Hill"), in Heinijärvi. He had come home to stay. At the university he had taken no exams and had no degree to show for the years of work and sacrifice. A complex of factors contributed to produce this break. His official biographer, Toivo Vaasikivi, spoke of his dissatisfaction with city life and his need to return to his roots. He himself cited the impatience of his creditors. An unmistakable mental instability certainly contributed to the crisis; the first signs of agoraphobia had appeared as early as his freshman year. In any case, the hopes his parents had cherished for their talented son seemed to come to nought.

The following summer, 1914, he chanced to meet a seventeen-year-old servant girl, Sigrid Maria Salomäki, the daughter of a poor tenant farmer. Their marriage in 1916 only seemed to confirm his decision to reject any life apart from the land. But to blossom, Sillanpää's creativity apparently required the warmth of a stable and encouraging relationship, and he found it first in this happy union.

Sillanpää's first literary efforts followed his return to Töllinmäki and the beginning relationship with Sigrid Salomäki. These were a series of sketches and stories published under the pseudonym E. Syväri in the influential Helsinki newspaper *Uusi Suometar.* These pieces attracted the attention of the publishing house of Werner Söderström at Provoo, which obtained the author's name and wrote in 1915 asking Sillanpää to contact them. Sillanpää had always been a voracious reader and had greatly admired the works of Maurice Maeterlinck, Knut Hamsun, and Johan August Strindberg. Praise from a publisher for his own writing was all the encouragement Sillanpää needed to complete his determination to make literature his career. As his courtship progressed, so did his first large-scale work, and it was as a newly married man that he published his first novel *Eläma ja aurinko* ("Life and Sun") in the fall of 1916.

Elämä ja aurinko is a love story set in the freshness of the Finnish countryside. It was well received and even caused a bit of a stir. Sillanpää's biographer, Olof Enckell, characterized the subject of the work as "the rapt bewilderment of young life following its instincts in the open air, on the warm, steaming earth. . . . Moral principles simply lapse in this lover's world; only impulse and the elemental force of natural ties hold sway and act on each other" (Enckell, 290f.). The erotic intensity of some scenes disturbed conservative readers but marked the arrival of a fresh and frank new voice.

One year later the Russian Revolution broke out in St. Petersburg and provoked in Finland the brutal conflict between the "Whites" and the "Reds," known variously as the War of Independence, the Civil

War, and the Red Rebellion. After three months of bitter fighting, the Finnish nationalist Whites led by Baron Mannerheim defeated the Finnish Bolshevik Reds and their Russian supporters. In the eyes of the victorious bourgeoisie, the Finnish workers appeared as rebellious, bloodstained rabble. Sillanpää, of course, had lived with members of both classes and had remained neutral in the conflict. In February 1919 he published his reflections upon the new social and psychological situation in the form of the novel *Hurskas kurjuus* (*Meek Heritage*).

Hurskas kurjuus had a tremendous impact in Finland. Immediate translation of the work into Swedish continued to spread Sillanpää's reputation beyond national boundaries. The story itself looked with sympathy and compassion, but without sentimentality, upon the fate of an orphaned cotter as representative of the downtrodden working class. In recounting the wretched fate of this hapless individual from his birth in the "hungry sixties" to his death before a White firing squad in 1918, Sillanpää described the struggles of his people without taking sides, but rather challenging and condemning both sides for forgetting the humanity of their fellows. While conservative readers were offended by the sympathetic treatment of an old Red, the book established Sillanpää at one stroke as the foremost Finnish author of his day and gained him a state pension for authors.

The reading public, hungry for the emergence, finally, of the Great Finnish Writer, entertained the most extravagant expectations for Sillanpää. These expectations were to be disappointed in the decade of the 1920s. Instead of producing substantial novels, he published shorter works and collections of essays and autobiographical pieces. One of these, *Ihmislapsia elämän saatossa* (1917; "Children of Mankind in the March of Life"), had already appeared in 1917 and contained stories written before the publication of *Elämä ja aurinko*. Other similar works followed: *Rakas isanmaani* (1919; "My Dear Fatherland"), a short story collection; *Hiltu ja Ragnar* (1929; *Hilda and Ragner*), a novella of unhappy love and suicide; *Enkelten suojatit* (1923; "Wards of the Angels"), stories about children; *Omistani ja omilleni* (1924; "Of and to My Own"), an essay on the writer's ethos; *Maan ta salta* (1924; "On Ground Level"), realistic vignettes of village life; *Töllinmäki* (1925; "Cottage Hill"), a collection of fables; and finally, *Rippi* (1928; "The Communion"), a novella.

Although these works added to his reputation in Finland and Scandinavia, Sillanpää's affairs were otherwise in disarray: he had built a cabin he could not afford near his parents at Töllinmäki, his family had already grown to include six of his eventual eight children, bills mounted, and income was inadequate. The electric company finally cut off service to the house. His publisher, Söderström, offered him the editorship of a new literary journal, *Panu*, and in 1924 the family moved to Porvoo. Three years of steady office routine did not really enable him to untangle his financial situation; he left after 1927 and spent an unsettled year drifting between Hämeenkyrö and Tampere. An urgent appeal to Söderström for an advance brought less than he had hoped for. In the early spring of 1929, he wrote in desperation to the rival publishing firm Otava and received an immediate and gratifyingly generous response from the owner and director, Professor Alvar Renqvist.

The new arrangement marked a turning point in Sillanpää's creative life. As part of the agreement, the new publisher assumed full responsibility for managing Sillanpää's business affairs and moved him and his family to Helsinki. The writer began afresh with the confidence of a secure income, and the years 1930–36 were to become the most productive of his career. He published six books, including three major novels, more than fulfilling the hopes raised by his earlier work. In 1930 a volume of essays on moral and intellectual subjects appeared, *Kiitos ketkistä, Herra* . . . ("Confession and Thanks for the Moments, Lord"). And beginning already with the publication of his long novel *Nuorena Nukkunt* (*The Maid Silja*) in 1931, Sillanpää's name appeared on the list of writers under consideration for award by the Nobel Foundation.

The Maid Silja, the tale of the decline and extinction of a peasant family, was an immediate and triumphant success. The following year Sillanpää published *Miehen tie* (*A Man's Way*), a novel describing a young farmer's growth from youth to maturity. The book was filmed in 1940 with great success. In 1934 *Ihmiset suviyössä* (*People in the Summer Night*) appeared, a novel that synthesized the author's experiences to that point: "Youthful arrogance is shattered by the disappointments of the grown man; love-smitten melancholy is succeeded by the unthinking brutishness of hard drinking; the mystery of childbirth is counterbalanced by a violent death" (Enckell, 294). With the publication of an extensive collection of short stories, *Viidestoista* ("The Fifteenth") in 1936, this period of extraordinary creativity came to an end. The writer was exhausted and had begun to drink heavily.

The remaining years of the decade brought a further decline in Sillanpää's personal fortunes. He wrote two more novels, but withheld their publication because he was not satisfied with them. In the fall of 1939 his wife Sigrid died, and he lost in her his chief moral and emotional support. His self-control failed, and it was a sick man and confirmed alcoholic who received the news in November that the Nobel Committee had awarded him the prize in literature. His mood may be judged by his comment at a press conference following the announcement of the award: "The Prize is due my country as much as to me."

Sillanpää was the only laureate to make the trip to Stockholm that year. He returned home in March 1940 to enter a short-lived marriage with his former secretary. A short time later he was admitted to a psychiatric hospital. He emerged in the mid-1940s as a broken man and spent the final twenty years of his life living quietly with his eldest daughter outside Helsinki. In the meantime, another publisher had issued the two novels he earlier rejected under the titles of *Elokuu* (1941; "August") and *Ihmiselon ihanuus ja kurjuus* (1945; "The Beauty and Misery of Human Life"). During the 1950s the occasional volume of personal reminiscences appeared under his name: *Poika eli elämäänsä* (1953; "A Boy and His Life"), *Kerron ja kuvailen* (1955; "Telling and Describing"), and *Pävivä korkeimmillan* (1956; "The High Moment of the Day").

Following his release from the mental hospital, Sillanpää began consciously to play the role of "Taata," an old diminutive for "grandpa." A great bear of a man with a flowing beard and single tooth, he appeared in the Helsinki park near his home in a black skullcap to the delight of neighborhood children. And in a favorite Christmas tradition, Finns would gather around the TV or radio to hear Taata tell stories of Christmas long ago at Hämeenkyrö. Seventy-five years old, Sillanpää suffered a brain hemorrhage and died a week later on June 4, 1964, in a Helsinki hospital.

The Nobel Prize in literature awarded to Sillanpää in 1939 was not uncontroversial. Historians agree that the Nobel Foundation was using the award to indicate Swedish support for Finland, then fighting to preserve its independence from its powerful Soviet neighbor. Sweden itself had historical ties to Finland; and while the ruling coalition remained officially neutral, popular sentiment was clearly with the Finns. In responding to such talk, Rafael Koskimies, professor emeritus of modern literature at the University of Helsinki, replied that Sillanpää had been worthy of the Nobel in 1919, the year he published *Meek Heritage*. Nevertheless, although it is true that Sillanpää had been nominated for the prize every year since 1930 and surely would have received it sooner or later, the particular condition of European politics in 1939 had as much to do with the timing of his award as the publications that justified its presentation to Finland's greatest living writer.

Literature in Finnish really only begins with Lönnrot's collection of folktales first published under the title of *Kalevala* ("Land of Heroes") in 1835. This text presents an essentially animistic view of a brutal and beautiful nature to which human characters must respond in their struggle to endure. It apparently provided Finnish writers through the 1930s and 1940s with accepted major perspectives and motifs. The result was a style that has been called "lyric realism," a style that "interweaves landscape and character, romantic optimism and Darwinian determinism" (Kinneavy, p. 206).

Most Finnish critics find Sillanpää to be the clearest example of this national tradition. His settings are the humble farms and villages in which even today over half the population lives. To an often severe and implacable nature he opposes characteristic Finnish *sisu*, "a kind of physical and moral hardiness which allows, even demands, the Finn to bear the snow and icy waters after sauna" (Kinneavy, p. 207). For Sillanpää the trace of this essential human dignity was sooner to be found in the long peasant tradition of involvement with the land than in the intellectual cultivation of city life.

In spite of its evident literary quality and wide translation (*The Maid Silja* into seventeen languages, *A Man's Way* and *People in the Summer Night* into eight, and *Meek Heritage* into six), it is fair to say that Sillanpää's writing has not made much of a lasting impression outside Scandinavia. Of the major novels, thus far only three have been translated into English; of the fifteen volumes of short stories, nothing. Critical interest in Sillanpää, too, has been slight, to judge by the number of studies published on his work. Still, this may yet change, for readers continue to find Sillanpää's texts.

People in the Summer Night, which has been called his most finished and poetic novel, was first translated into English as recently as 1966. The fine Matson translations have never gone out of print; *Meek Heritage* was last reissued in 1972 and *The Maid Silja* in 1984. It is probably unfortunate that the short stories have remained inaccessible to English readers. By some accounts they are equal or superior in quality to the longer works and could well hope to find a place in anthologies of world literature. Perhaps the Nobel Prize will continue to work its magic to bring this writer to a wider public. This, at least, was Sillanpää's hope when he remarked upon learning he had won the award: "I feel deep joy that I can render my country the greatest service an old author can render it . . . that of increasing the world's respect for Finnish culture and helping to make the voice of the Finnish spirit heard in the world."

JAMES W. SCOTT

Selected Bibliography

PRIMARY SOURCES

Sillanpää, Frans Eemil. *The Maid Silja: The History of the Last Offshoot of an Old Family Tree.* Translated by Alexander Matson. New York: Macmillan, 1933.

——. *Meek Heritage.* Translated by Alexander Matson. New York: Knopf, 1938.

——. *The Maid Silja.* Translated by Alexander Matson. Dunwoody, Ga.: Berg, 1974.

——. *People in the Summer Night: An Epic Suite.* Translated by Alan Blair, Nordic Translation Series. Madison: University of Wisconsin Press, 1966.

SECONDARY SOURCES

Beck, R. "Sillanpää: Finland's Winner of the Nobel Prize." *Poet Lore* 46 (1940):358–63.

Enckell, Olof. "The Life and Works of Frans Eemil Sillanpää." Translated by James Emmons. *Nelly Sachs, Jean-Paul Sartre, George Bernard Shaw, Frans Eemil Sillanpää, René Sully-Prudhomme*, Nobel Prize Library. New York: Gregory, 1971. Pp. 287–95.

"Frans Eemil Sillanpää, 75, Dies; Finland's Nobel Prize Novelist." *The*

New York Times, June 4, 1964, p. 37.

Kinneavy, Gerald. "Sillanpää." *Scandinavica* (1981):205–12.

Rothery, Agnes. "Novels from Finland." *Virginia Quarterly Review* 16 (1940):296–99.

Strömberg, Kjell. "The 1939 Prize." Translated by Dale McAdoo. *Nelly Sachs, Jean-Paul Sartre, George Bernard Shaw, Frans Eemil Sillanpää, René Sully-Prudhomme*, Nobel Prize Library. New York: Gregory, 1971. Pp. 297–99.

Tarkka, Pekka. "The Nobel Pursuit." Translated by Hildi Hawkins. *Books from Finland* 14 (1980):13–16.

Viljanen, L. "Sillanpää." *American Scandinavian Review* 28 (1940):49–53.

CLAUDE SIMON   *1985*

Claude Simon (1913–) was born of French parentage in Tananarive, Madagascar, in 1913. He was educated in France and began writing in the 1940s, having trained originally as a painter. His narratives, which are highly experimental in nature, reflect this earlier training. By his own admission, the fusion of these two traditionally opposed artistic categories is of fundamental importance to him in his writing: "J'écris mes livres comme on ferait un tableau. Tout tableau est d'abord une composition." ("I write my books as one would create a painting. Any painting is above all a composition.") The originality of his novelistic technique has received widespread attention, and in 1985 he was awarded the Nobel Prize.

Simon experienced many of the significant political, social, and artistic events of his time. He was in Spain during the Spanish Civil War. During World War II he served France in a cavalry regiment and in 1940 was imprisoned in a German camp, from which he escaped that same year. He owns a vineyard in the Roussillon, a province in the south of France, where he currently lives and writes.

Simon belongs to a group of French authors of what has become known as the New Novel. The members of this school include Alain Robbe-Grillet, Nathalie Sarraute, Marguerite Duras, Michel Butor, and Jean Ricardou. Like most of the New Novelists, Simon is reluctant to discuss his life, but he is eager to expound upon his literary experimentation.

In order to better understand the originality and the importance of a writer like Simon, it is not only necessary to be familiar with his literary heritage, but also the tenets of the New Novel school to which the author loosely adheres. The reasons for this lie in the New Novelists' overriding concern with novelistic theory. The New Novel is first and foremost a rejection of the realistic tradition of nineteenth-century narrative. It is a reaction against fiction representing a real or historical social context outside of the novel (Zola's working class, Balzac's Paris, Dostoyevsky's czarist Russia). The context represented should be inherent in the text and created by it.

If reality is created by the text itself, the world represented will most often be impersonal and devoid of any but the most banal distinguishing signs. The object becomes the primary signifier, as the narrative eye, similar to that of the moving camera lens, attempts to seize it from all possible angles. The most mundane, innocuous objects are described in elaborate detail by what appears to be a coldly scientific and objective observer. The object is perceived as pure existence without meaning. Alain Robbe-Grillet, the major theoretician of the group, has stated its main premise succinctly: "Le monde n'est ni absurde, ni signifiant, il *est*." ("The world is neither absurd nor meaningful, it simply *is*.")

The notion of characterization, eminently important in the realistic novel, is destroyed through a process of immobilization and reification. Characters are viewed geometrically, as moving objects with no inner dimensions. The anatomical figure is viewed as a series of dissected and fragmentary parts. Human action is presented not as a flow of movement, but as a series of "still shots."

The narration is disconnected and divided into static scenes, or tableaux. A favorite process is to describe a painting and to have the events portrayed alternately come alive and freeze, forcing the reader to accept the similarities between pictorial representation and the other levels of reality within the text. Narration is replaced by description, and the past preterit by the eternal present.

The world represented becomes impersonal, as the author avoids interpretation, hypothesis, or judgment. The narrative eye conveys a feeling of uncertainty and neutrality in its perception of what is real. The attempt to avoid influencing the reader's reception of the text provokes the latter's more active participation in the act of reading. This active participation can be termed a game of reconstruction. It can be seen as similar to the task of a detective attempting to impose his logic, order, and explanations on a number of disorienting clues. The attempt to reestablish causality to the reading process is, however, frustrated at every turn of events, as the writer leads the reader on a wild goose chase.

The New Novel is self-referential, hermetic, and autonomous. The reader, in turn, is discouraged from taking into account anything but the work itself. Unlike the previous generation of politically committed existentialist writers, the New Novelists have no message to convey other than their own exploration of the boundaries of writing.

If, then, the New Novel has no meaning to convey beyond its own reality and if it allows for no causality, no artificial chronological order to help the reader along on his or her course of discovery, how is the latter able to sustain interest in the difficult reading process? More than any other of the New Novelists, Claude Simon has emphasized the power of repetition with infinite variations and the superimposition of images. He refutes the traditional notion of chronological ordering on the basis that human thought never proceeds in a direct linear manner. The word itself has an almost magical power of generation, leading the author himself through the tortuous convolutions of his own memory. This process is, however, not to be confused with automatic writing, for the writer makes a conscious effort to discover experienced time by returning to individual images, rearranging and recombining them with new perceptions, thereby fusing past into present in an ever-changing dynamic structure. The dynamics of this multitude of interconnected moments are what gives significance to the aesthetic experience.

Claude Simon has, in the course of his numerous writings, established himself as a writer with a method of his own. His most flagrant interest is in the analysis of characters grappling with fluctuating perceptions of time, who find themselves at the crossroads of past, present and future. Inextricably entangled, temporal perceptions become superimposed, giving the bland characters caught up in banal

situations an illusion of substantive existence. Convoluted sentences attempt to capture in their repetitions and backtracking the most minute evolutions of human understanding trying to conjure up the very essence of reality and its aberrations due to the imperfections of memory. Each of Simon's novels is a *"tentative de reconstruction"* (an attempt at reconstruction) of the world as it is without the mediation of language: a language that is, nonetheless, the only possible means of communication for a writer. Simon's more recent novels are less concerned with telling a story than with describing the traces left by certain events on an individual impressionable memory. His works have received critical acclaim for the sincere attempts of an ever-vigilant eye at mastering and surrounding a living and moving reality.

The preceding remarks may give some clue as to why it is nearly impossible to give a coherent synopsis of Simon's texts. *La Route des Flandres* (1960; *The Flanders Road*), which is considered to be one of the author's finest works, and perhaps one of the more readable, will serve as an example. It must, however, be understood that the corpus of Simon's writings presents a constant evolution and reevaluation of the writing process and that each novel takes a further step away from the traditional story with its cause and effect rationality and psychological depth.

La Route des Flandres retraces the memories of one central "character," whose name is Georges. His narrative eye, or narrative "I" (for the events are recounted in the first person, although the narrator occasionally refers to himself in the third person, as a "he"), attempts to reconstruct a series of historical events (the defeat of France during World War II) and his own past desire for a woman whom he had never met: the wife of his commander, Captain de Reixach. His imaginary fantasies about de Reixach's wife, Corinne, are heightened during his stay in a prison camp where he converses with a certain Blum and Iglésia, a jockey who professes to have been Corinne's lover. Past fantasies fuse with present reality as Georges has now (after the war) become Corinne's lover. Simon rigidly eschews any testimonial other than that of the main witness of events; however, the multiplicity of perspectives is not thereby eliminated, as the narrator grapples with the uncertainties of his recollections and is forced restlessly to revise and reshuffle his perceptions.

Simon's stated intention was to write a novel whose narrative structure would resemble that of a cloverleaf, with the image of a dead horse (which the French soldiers pass on the Flanders Road) in "dead" center. Scenes are carefully ordered about generative points, and the four circles in the cloverleaf represent the circular, revolving projections of the active world of the imagination around certain pivotal signs. The dead horse itself is not motionless, but undergoing decomposition and transmutation. Linear narration has been abolished, as the development of the novel depends entirely on an ever denser proliferation of images about a generative axis. Ac-

cording to Simon, such horizontal paradigmatic layering lies closer to the essence of reality than the syntagmatic approach, which sees events as dots on a linear continuum. One cannot disturb any element without altering the entire structure, for all perceptions are tightly interwoven and interdependent. What emerges from all of this is not an explanation but a composition (Simon's early training as a painter comes to the fore here) that signifies the mind's failure at attributing conceptual meaning to essential reality and at imposing a logical order on events.

Other major works by Simon include: *Le Palace* (1962; *The Palace*), *Histoire* (1967; *History*), *La Bataille de Pharsale* (1969; *The Battle of Pharsalus*), *Les Corps conducteurs* (1971; *Conducting Bodies*), *Leçons de choses* (1976; *The World About Us*), and *Géorgigues* (1981; *Georgies*).

ROXANNE DECKER LALANDE

Selected Bibliography

PRIMARY SOURCES

Simon, Claude. *The Battle of Pharsalus.* Translated by Richard Howard. New York: Braziller, 1971.

——— . *Conducting Bodies.* Translated by Helen R. Lane. New York: Grove Press, 1987.

——— . *The Flanders Road.* Translated by Richard Howard. New York: Riverrun Press, 1985.

——— . *Histoire.* Translated by Anthony Cheal Pugh. London: Grant & Cutler, 1982.

———. *The Palace*. Translated by Richard Howard. New York: Braziller, 1963.

———. *Triptych*. Translated by Helen R. Lane. New York: Viking Press, 1976.

SECONDARY SOURCES

Birn, Randi, and Karen Gould, eds. *Orion Blinded: Essays on Claude Simon*. Lewisburg, Pa.: Bucknell University Press, 1981.

Britton, Celia. *Writing the Visible*. Cambridge: Cambridge University Press, 1987.

Evans, Michael. *Claude Simon and the Transgressions of Modern Art*. New York: St. Martin's Press, 1988.

Loubère, J. E. A. *The Novels of Claude Simon*. Ithaca, N.Y.: Cornell University Press, 1975.

Mercier, Vivian. *The New Novel from Queneau to Pinget*. New York: Farrar, Straus & Giroux, 1971.

ISAAC BASHEVIS SINGER *1978*

Isaac Bashevis Singer (1904—) received the Nobel Prize in 1978 for his literature about Jewish life and culture in Europe, a world that had been annihilated in World War II, and for books written in Yiddish, the language of that lost world, itself faced with imminent extinction. The award was ironically bestowed upon him as a citizen of the United States, his adoptive home, and he became the only American laureate whose work was not written in the English language. Born into a pious home in Poland on July 14, 1904, Isaac Singer was the son of a Hassidic rabbi and a religiously observant but rationalistic mother. Both the mystical and rational strains that he inherited from his parents are evident in all of his writings. As testimony to his indebtedness to his mother's legacy, he signed his Yiddish works with her name, Bashevis (Bathsheva), while only the translated published works bear the full name Isaac Bashevis Singer. Singer emigrated to America in 1935, becoming a regular contributor to the Yiddish daily *Der Forverts* (*The Forward*), where his popular journalism ran under the name of Isaac Warshofsky and where all of his books first appeared in serial form under the signature Isaac Bashevis. In 1964 he was elected to the National Institute of Arts and Letters. When he received the National Book Award in 1974, he characterized himself as a "Jewish writer, a Yiddish writer, an American writer."

Thus, Singer's recognition as a Nobel Prize laureate challenged the norms of homeland and national language as commonly accepted categories of literary identification. The Yiddish language had never been associated with a homeland, although it was spoken by more than eleven million Jews before the destruction of European Jewry in World War II. In his Nobel acceptance speech, Singer saw the honor bestowed upon him as also "a recognition of the Yiddish language—a language of exile, without a land, without frontiers, not supported by any government, a language which possesses no words for weapons, ammunition, military exercises, war tactics; a language that was despised by both Gentiles and emancipated Jews." Despite the social and demographic evidence that Yiddish is rapidly becoming a dead language, Singer continued, "Yiddish has not yet said its last word."

Steeped in the Jewish tradition and liturgy, in the sacred texts of the Bible, Talmud, Midrash, and Kabbalah, Singer writes of that lost world of Eastern European Jewry as if it had never been destroyed. He himself has admitted that Vaihinger's philosophy of "As if" has shaped his work, for he believes that every man lives with the same philosophy. "He behaves as if he will never die." This consciously sustained illusion at the heart of his works coexists, however, with a sensibility of hindsight, so that the texts in which he evokes that lost community are haunted by the author's and reader's knowledge of its subsequent extermination.

The mystical unworldly universe of Singer's father is evident in his first major work, *Der Sotn in Goray* (1934; *Satan in Goray*), a macabre account of the ecstatic behavior of a community obsessed with reports of imminent apocalypse, which recasts their own grotesque sufferings of the pogroms and massacres of 1648 as birth pangs of the messianic age. Rooted in the history of the Sabbatian movement, which saw masses of Jews hailing the charlatan Sabbatai Zevi as the messiah and interpreting his apostasy to Islam as a paradoxical and mystical stage in the process of the end of days, *Satan in Goray* chronicles a community's hysteria and submission to the forbidden, seeing these phenomena as the effects of their sufferings and as their conscious acceleration of the process leading to the apocalypse. The grotesque events of the novel are infiltrated by the supernatural, by a whole repertoire of demons, imps, and spirits.

Singer's fiction is marked by the influence of the Kabbalistic text, the Zohar, and by the Gothic works of E. T. A. Hoffmann, Edgar Allan Poe, and Knut Hamsun. And Singer's immersion in a world of bizarre superstitions and medieval demonology is precisely what has earned him recognition as a modernist writer, for in the surrender to the forbidden as a form of redemption and in the torment brought about by fanatical adherence to false saviors, critics have seen a parable about the modern age with its sanctification of libidinal desires and its dangers of charismatic leaders and false ideologies. Ironically, within the Yiddish literary world, which has tended to be humanistic and moralistic, Singer is treated with skepticism for his use

of folkloristic and mystical materials. He has admitted that he identifies himself more as a Jewish than as
a Yiddish writer.

Satan in Goray was made available to English readers in 1955, two
years after the publication of one of
Singer's major stories in a similar
mystical vein appeared in Partisan
Review in a translation by Saul Bellow. "I am Gimpel the Fool," begins
the story by that name, "I don't
think myself a fool. On the contrary.
But that's what folks call me." Gimpel is considered a fool because he is
a believer; he believes what anyone
tells him: that his parents are resurrected from the dead, that the rabbi's wife gave birth to a calf, that the
cow jumped over the moon. "Who
really knows how such things are?"
asks Gimpel. "I believed them, and I
hope at least that did them some
good." When Gimpel discovers that
his wife had been deceiving him all
of the days of their marriage, he is
visited by the Spirit of Evil, who
tells him that there is no God, only a
"thick mire." Yet Gimpel resists the
temptation to take revenge on those
who have ridiculed him because it is
better to be foolish than to be evil.
He leaves the town for the life of a
traveling storyteller. Gimpel chooses
to remain a "fool" and to remain a
believer, despite the evidence to the
contrary because he believes in a
world beyond the visible.

Many other stories in Singer's
prolific canon depict a detailed sensual world that points obliquely to
an invisible world of supernatural
powers. Among his novels Der
kuntsnmakher fun Lublin (1960;
The Magician of Lublin) falls into

the same category. Yasha Mazur, an
acrobat and magician, leads a life of
sensuality, decadence, and crime;
when he sees the "hand of God," he
retreats from the world to live in a
permanently locked hut as an as-
cetic, who, in turn, is worshipped by
others as a miracle worker. His acknowledgment of the existence of a
god does not alter his struggles in
life nor does it prevent him from
being tormented by sexual fantasies.
Like "Gimpel the Fool," The Magician of Lublin raises questions
about the fine line between saints
and fools, between madmen and
holy men.

Singer's more realistic fiction,
such as Di familye Mushkat (1950;
The Family Moskat) and Der Houf
(written serially 1953-55 as Part
One of a larger work of the same
title for Der Forverts—1962; The
Manor), records the family histories
of several generations of Jews in
Eastern Europe, thereby chronicling
the history of an era without the
infiltration of the supernatural and
the demonic that marks the rest of
his corpus. Yet the two dramatically
different styles do share certain features, among them very concrete
and vivid descriptions and characters driven by strong sensual desires
and by sensitivity to evil forces in
their environment. Although both
The Family Moskat and The Manor
take place before World War II,
they are pervaded by the hindsight
of both the author and the reader
that they are doomed communities.
The Family Moskat, for example,
takes place from the turn of the century to 1939 in Warsaw, a city one-
third of whose population was Jew-

ish by the advent of World War II. In the case of this novel Singer is reconstructing a lost world "as if" that world were still alive. In a *New York Times Magazine* interview in 1978 Singer said of this book, "Let's say in *The Family Moskat* I said to myself, 'Warsaw has just now been destroyed. No one will ever see the Warsaw I knew. Let me just write about it. Let this Warsaw not disappear forever.'"

The Family Moskat is in the tradition of European family sagas that cover several generations. Singer traces the decline of faith in the Moskat family, and in the various stages of the central character, Asa Heshel, he recounts the transformation of a community. Asa leaves his traditional calling as a Talmud scholar for the secular pursuits of the city, where he turns to competing ideologies embodied by other characters, only to finally become a nihilist marked for annihilation himself in the Warsaw ghetto. The city of Warsaw threatens the Jewish community's ability to maintain its Jewishness, and Singer demonstrates ironically how the threat of assimilation is overtaken by the threat and real destruction brought on by the Third Reich. The many trains and stations in this work have a haunting quality about them as they acquire menacing connotations retrospectively, for Singer draws on images that are charged with Holocaust associations. At the end of the work, Asa Heshel remarks that "all of humanity is caught in a trap. No going forward to no going backward. We Jews will be the first victims." In a strange echo of *Satan in*

Goray, the messianic spirit is mocked at the book's end when a character in the ghetto who has been characterized by his spiritualism throughout the book recognizes that he is experiencing the end of days, "Death is the Messiah. That's the real truth."

Although Singer has written short stories and a novel, *Sonim: Di geshikhte fun a libe* (1972; *Enemies: A Love Story*), about actual survivors of the Holocaust living in America, his works set in the past capture more compellingly the traumatic scale of the annihilation of a world. This is particularly forceful in his most autobiographical work of fiction, *Shosha* (1978). In the novel the narrator, Aaron Greidinger, is a promising young writer, vegetarian, and redhead much like Singer himself in Warsaw in 1939, with one major exception—he chooses to remain in Poland despite the opportunity to leave. The novel seems to weave together Singer's two writing styles—the realistic evocation of Warsaw's Krochmalna Street, reminiscent of *The Family Moskat*, and the mystical and allegorical dimension of *Satan in Goray*. The latter is embodied in the character of Shosha, the young bride for whom Aaron Greidinger remains in Warsaw and endures the war. Unlike the seductive women who tempt Greidinger with alternative fates, such as flight into Russia and Communist ideology or immigration to America, Shosha is a childlike woman, a mere waif, whose very name in Hebrew suggests that she is the rose of Jacob, the people of Israel. In her innocence, provincialism, and love of stories, Shosha takes on the qualities of the Yiddish language and culture of Eastern Europe, toward which Greidinger demonstrates his loyalty. By having his character choose to marry Shosha instead of seeking escape for himself, and then survive her death in Israel, Singer can reenact his history of having left Poland early enough to escape death. But he has added the risk that Greidinger takes, a risk that demonstrates his devotion to a culture that was destroyed and, like Shosha, left no progeny. Singer creates a narrative, then, that is a version of his own life, that is the imaginative experience of the road not taken. Greidinger recalls that in his childhood in Poland he was an anachronism, enveloped in an ancient culture and studying dead languages. Singer himself has continued that tradition of being anachronistic as he creates Yiddish fictions in New York City for an ever smaller group of readers. And just as Greidinger is a widower at the end, mourning his child bride, Shosha, who was a victim of the Nazis, so Singer is a lone storyteller in Yiddish, mourning the premature demise of his culture and re-creating in story after story that vanished world.

HANA WIRTH-NESHER

Selected Bibliography

PRIMARY SOURCES

Singer, Isaac Bashevis. *Satan in Goray*. Written under the name Isaac Bashevis. Translated by Jacob Sloan. New York: Noonday Press, 1955; reprinted, New York: Farrar, Straus, 1979.

——— . *The Family Moskat*. Translated by A. H. Gross. New York: Alfred A. Knopf, 1950; reprinted, New York: Fawcett Books, 1975.

——— . *The Magician of Lublin*. Translated by Elaine Gottlieb and Joseph Singer. New York: Noonday Press, 1960; reprinted, New York: Fawcett Books, 1979.

——— . *The Manor*. Translated by Elaine Gottlieb and Joseph Singer. New York: Farrar, Straus, & Giroux, 1962.

——— . *The Estate*. Translated by Elaine Gottlieb, Joseph Singer, and Elizabeth Shub. New York: Farrar, Straus, & Giroux, 1969.

——— . *Enemies: A Love Story*. Translated by Aliza Shevrin and Elizabeth Shub. New York: Farrar, Straus, & Giroux, 1972.

——— . *Shosha*. New York: Farrar, Straus, & Giroux, 1978.

——— . *The Collected Stories of Isaac Bashevis Singer*. New York: Farrar, Straus, & Giroux, 1982.

——— . *The Death of Methuselah*. Translated by the author. New York: Farrar, Straus, & Giroux, 1988.

SECONDARY SOURCES

Alexander, Edward. *Isaac Bashevis Singer*. Boston: Twayne, 1980.

Miller, David Neal, Ed. *Recovering the Canon: Essays on Isaac Bashevis Singer*. Leiden: E. J. Brill, 1986.

ALEXANDR SOLZHENITSYN   *1970*

Alexandr Isaevich Solzhenitsyn (1918—) was born on December 11, 1918, in Kislovodsk, a resort town in the south of Russia. His mother, Taisia Shcherbak, was a daughter of a wealthy, self-made farmer. Solzhenitsyn's father, Isaaky, did not come from as rich a family, yet they earned enough money—also by farming—to run an independent, profitable farm and to send Isaaky to Moscow University before World War I. Both families, however, lost all their possessions during the Revolution, so, by the time Solzhenitsyn was born, there was nothing left to sustain a dignified living. To make matters even more difficult, six months before Solzhenitsyn's birth his father was fatally wounded in a hunting accident.

Taisia had to move to a larger city, Rostov, where it was easier to find a job and to hide the damaging truth about her social origins: Not only did her father belong to the "exploiting class," but her husband had been an officer in the czarist army. The word *officer* at that time carried the same ominous meaning as the word *counterrevolutionary*. Solzhenitsyn remembered how he and his mother buried his father's medals because they feared a house search and subsequent punishment. Such little tricks did not help much, however, and, despite her very high qualifications as a typist and stenographer, Taisia could not obtain a well-paying job in a government office or receive a room from State

Housing. She had to pay double or triple rent for a room in a privately owned rundown shack without running water or adequate heating in the winter. To provide an absolute minimum of food and clothing for her son and herself—barely enough to survive—she always worked overtime and often took work home.

Both the Solzhenitsyns and Shcherbaks were practicing Christians, and his mother and their relatives, with whom Alexandr sometimes stayed, had taken him to church on the main holidays. The continuous indoctrination in school, however, proved to be a stronger influence on him; he became first a "young pioneer" (a member of the children's Communist organization) and later joined the Komsomol (Young Communists' League). He grew up a devout believer in the Revolution and Marxism-Leninism.

Solzhenitsyn developed a passion for writing unusually early, at the age of nine. He started with short stories and science fiction; later he and his childhood friends enthusiastically worked on homemade journals. When he was eighteen, he decided to write a long novel about the Revolution and actually started to work on it—a work to which he returned thirty years later after having fought in a war, spent ten years in camps and exile, and become a world-renowned writer. When the time came for him to choose a profession, he nevertheless enrolled in the Department of

Mathematics and Physics at Rostov University. There was not a good literature department at Rostov, but Solzhenitsyn did not want to transfer to Moscow and leave his mother, who had developed tuberculosis. For the time being, literature became "a consolation of the spirit" rather than his main occupation, but in 1939, while still a student of mathematics at Rostov University, he also enrolled in a correspondence course at the Moscow Institute of Philosophy, Literature, and History. In 1940 he married Natalya Reshetovskaya, a student of biochemistry and his junior by one year.

The month Solzhenitsyn graduated from Rostov University—June 1941—Germany invaded the USSR. Solzhenitsyn wanted to become an artillery man, like his father, and entered an artillery school for officers. After graduating, he served at the front and by 1945 was decorated and promoted to the rank of captain.

Although a faithful Leninist and a diligent student of Marxism, Solzhenitsyn nevertheless proved to be a shrewd observer of the real political situation in the 1930s. The Stalinist show trials and the incessant hysterical incantations against "enemies of the people" and about ever-increasing "class struggle" sharply contrasted with his idea of the first socialist state twenty years after the Revolution. Even more unacceptable for the young man with a very strong ego was the virtually religious worship of "the Father of All Peoples," Josef Stalin. Hence the growing loathing not for the regime—for many years to come Solzhenitsyn remained a convinced advocate of the socialist system—but for the cruel and inept ruler.

Solzhenitsyn shared his opinions about Stalin and plans for postwar political discussions in letters to his childhood friend, also an officer in the Soviet army. The letters were intercepted, and in February 1945 Solzhenitsyn was arrested and charged with anti-Soviet propaganda and with founding a hostile organization. He was sentenced to eight years of hard labor, without a trial, by an NKVD (now KGB) Special Board. Later he learned that the second charge, founding a hostile organization, automatically entailed "perpetual exile" in remote areas of the Soviet Union after serving the main term in labor camps.

Thus began Solzhenitsyn's ten years of jails, camps, and exile—the years that completely transformed his political views, philosophical orientation, and concept of his own mission in life. He started serving his term in a camp near Moscow, where he dug clay for a brick shop. Given meager food rations, high production quotas, inadequate clothing and housing, and practically no medical help, few inmates managed to survive "general works," that is, actual production, whether it was felling trees, working at a construction project, or digging clay for bricks. Political prisoners sentenced on the basis of the infamous Article 58 suffered the worst. Both the camp administration and common criminals treated them as scum—at best, scorning and harassing them as fascists, but often robbing them of their last belongings, beating them up, or even murdering them.

The youthful decision to pursue studies in physics and mathematics proved providential for Solzhenitsyn and saved him from the afflictions of the "general works" and maybe from death. In the fall of 1945, he was transferred to a special prison research institute near Moscow. The Soviet state strove to use slave labor with the highest possible efficiency, not wasting precious scientific cadres. "*Sharashkas*"—the slang name for such prison institutes—were organized, and talented scientists brought in, including the famous airplane designer Andrei Tupolev and the father of the Soviet space program, Sergei Korolev.

Solzhenitsyn worked in one such institute, located in the little town of Marfino, until the spring of 1950. Food and living conditions here were much better, the work made much more sense, as scientists conducted research in their fields; and the atmosphere was much less hostile than in the general camps. The inmates even felt as though they had more freedom in the *sharashka* than they had had outside before their incarceration. Indeed, here they could discuss topical political questions and exchange their opinions on virtually any question of interest, from the purity of the Russian language to the personality of "Cockroach" or "the Boss," as the prisoners called Stalin. These discussions immensely enriched Solzhenitsyn, broadened his horizons, and made him reconsider and reappraise many of his values. In particular, the discussions of the Russian language served as a stimulus to further his interest in this subject.

He acquired and then never parted with the dictionary of the Russian language by Vladimir Dal—a nineteenth-century dialectologist, ethnographer, and writer. The dictionary, besides giving definitions, also contains many examples, including Russian proverbs and folk expressions.

In May 1950, Solzhenitsyn's peaceful life in the *sharashka* came to an aburpt end. His behavior had grown too independent for the administration to tolerate, and he was sent packing to a general camp in Kazakhstan. He worked there as a bricklayer and later as a smelter's mate in the foundry.

While serving his term, Solzhenitsyn never lost his inclination for writing, even in the harshest conditions. He wrote a long autobiographical poem, "Shosse entuziastov" ("The Way"), and a play in verse, *Pir pobeditelei* (*The Feast of the Victors*), describing the violent march of Soviet troops through eastern Prussia at the end of the war. Given the subject matter of his writings, it was out of the question to keep them amidst his belongings. Their discovery by the guards during a search would necessarily entail a severe punishment and a prompt relocation to a camp in the northeast. The solution to the problem was to memorize the whole text: One of the reasons why Solzhenitsyn switched to poetry was that verses were easier to memorize than prose.

One year before the end of his term, Solzhenitsyn developed cancer. In February 1952, in the crude conditions of the camp hospital, he underwent an operation that lasted for half an hour. Surprisingly, he recovered quickly and without complications and in two weeks was sent back to work. In March 1953, his eight-year term expired, and on March 3, two days before Stalin's death, he came to a little Kazakh town, Kok-Terek, the place of his perpetual exile. He had left Rostov at the beginning of the war as an average Soviet youth, just having graduated from the university, an idealist prepared to defend his fatherland—and now he stood, a thirty-four-year-old man with four years of war and eight years of camps behind him, with a deadly disease that he probably brought with him, and the prospect of living and dying in that godforsaken place that was not even in his Russia.

With difficulty he managed to get a job in a local school as a teacher of mathematics, physics, and astronomy. The work gave him immense pleasure and satisfaction. He loved teaching, and the students were fond of him.

Although pleasant and rewarding, teaching remained only a means for earning a living and a screen for Solzhenitsyn's main occupation, which was conducted in deep secrecy and with all possible precautions. He was at last able to transcribe the thousands of verses he had created and memorized in the camps. He was also writing new works; and, with the privations of his prison years still fresh in his memory, free to write, free from fear of starvation, freezing, and violence, Solzhenitsyn spent perhaps the happiest and most carefree period in his life here, until the fall of 1954, when his cancer recurred. He went to Tashkent and there underwent intensive X-ray treatment and chemotherapy, and took some folk medicine clandestinely. Again he was cured. Perhaps it was this miraculous remission—considering the time and the conditions in a provincial hospital thousands of miles away from Moscow—that finalized Solzhenitsyn's conversion to Christianity, which had started back in the camps, where surviving each day had been a little miracle.

Another miracle in Solzhenitsyn's life also had its beginning in Tashkent. Rumors were spreading of an imminent amnesty for political exiles, but he had to wait for another year before his "perpetual exile" was terminated and he was allowed to return to Russia. In 1957 he was completely "rehabilitated."

He settled in central Russia, first in a small town in Vladimir Province, later in Ryazan, a city about a hundred miles from Moscow. He continued working as a teacher and writing. During the late 1950s Solzhenitsyn wrote his first novel, *V kruge pervom* (1968; *The First Circle*), based on his experience in the Marfino *sharashka*, the short story *Matrenin dvor* (1963; *Matryona's Place*), and *Odin den' Ivana Denisovicha* (1962; *One Day in the Life of Ivan Denisovich*). The Khrushchev "thaw" was sweeping through Moscow and Leiningrad and all cultural centers of the Soviet Union. Writers, artists, theater and movie directors and actors were reveling in the sensation of freedom, unheard of in more than twenty-five years, and in the expectation of even greater freedom, and nobody knew that a modest Ryazan teacher had already written the works for which, ten years later, he would receive the Nobel Prize.

Why did Solzhenitsyn not try to publish his works for six years after his return from exile? Having spent ten years in camps and exile for a couple of careless remarks about Stalin, he could hardly imagine that his writings could appear in the official press. Indeed, virtually all of them described injustices suffered by good Russian people because of the very system that controlled not only all the publications, but the lives of those who published and who were published. He was convinced that if they even learned about the existence of his works, they would drag him right away back to the places he wrote about, if not in fact shoot him on the spot.

Only in 1961, after the 22nd Congress of the Communist Party of the Soviet Union, did he gather enough courage to send—through friends, without a return address, and signed with a pseudonym—his story of Ivan Denisovich to Aleksandr Tvardovsky, the editor in chief of the best and the most liberal Soviet literary journal at the time. Tvardovsky's judgment was similar to that of the nineteenth-century Russian poet and publisher Nikolai Nekrasov when he finished reading Dostoyevsky's first novel, *Poor Folk*: A great new writer had appeared in Russia. To publish the novella, however, was a different matter. It took nine months of clever scheming on Tvardovsky's part,

Khrushchev's support, and a special meeting of the Politburo to get it published in the November 1962 issue of *Novy mir*.

One Day in the Life of Ivan Denisovich was a shock, an explosion, and a revelation. Its publication seemed as much a miracle to readers as it had to its author. After so many years of lies, falsifications, or, at best, feeble half-truths, Soviet readers could find, at long last, a vivid picture of the injustices, persecutions, and sufferings they had experienced. For the first time a literary work published in the Soviet Union showed the Soviet system as the culprit and people as its innocent victims.

Merely dealing with a forbidden topic would not have been adequate reason for many critics to rate the novella as a great work of world literature or to compare the author with Tolstoy and Dostoyevsky. It was bringing literature back into the realm of the ultimate questions of life and death, elevating it from the mundane to the eternal, that won Solzhenitsyn recognition on the order of that granted these great writers. During the "thaw" many liberal writers turned to sharp social conflicts as the subject matter of their works. The castigation of cynical careerists and bureaucrats, the unbearable situation in the Soviet village, the young generation in search of new paths—these became popular themes at the time, important, topical, yet transient. Solzhenitsyn, like Tolstoy, asked not what man ought to do in this or that concrete social conflict, but what man should live for. And, like Tolstoy, he was inclined to look for the answer in the Christian call to love one's neighbor, live for others, live by truth—or, in Solzhenitsyn's reemphasized moral appeal: "Don't live by lies." Also like Tolstoy, Solzhenitsyn looked for his ideal in the simple Russian peasant, finding folkways purer, more natural, and therefore more truthful than mores contrived by reason, the mores of the *obrazovanshchina* (intellectuals lacking morality and spirituality).

In Solzhenitsyn's writings one finds a similarity with Dostoyevsky in the notion that without a great deal of suffering man cannot attain complete happiness and cannot become a fully developed spiritual being. Solzhenitsyn tests the moral strength of his characters or exposes their spiritual poverty by placing them into situations where they have to face constantly the choice between life in servility and self-abasement and a possibly cruel but dignified death. The polyphonic character of his works, in which the authorial voice and point of view are suppressed and the characters are presented through their own consciousness and speech (indirect interior monologue), is also a feature traced by the critics back to Dostoyevsky.

Perhaps Solzhenitsyn's most important artistic achievement lies in the area of language. Like many other Soviet authors who, during the post-Stalin period, took up the task of revitalizing the Russian literary language in order to replace the emasculated discourse of Socialist Realism with living speech, Solzhenitsyn liberally interspersed the nar-

rative with dialectisms, slang words, and thinly disguised profanities. But he went even further: He created a unique language in his works by enriching the text with maxims, structured in the manner of Russian proverbs, and numerous neologisms that he built by using the Russian language's derivational morphemes. His infatuation with Dal's dictionary and a collection of proverbs by the same author proved invaluable for this work. The word is a very important unit in Solzhenitsyn's texts. He savors each word the way his hero, Ivan Denisovich, savors rare bits of real food that he fished out from a thin camp soup. One can also note Solzhenitsyn's careful modifications of syntax, especially the use of inversions, which often gives his texts an epic character.

The 1960s was a fruitful decade for Solzhenitsyn. He completed a "publishable" version of *The First Circle*; wrote another novel, *Rakovyi korpus* (1968; *The Cancer Ward*), based on his trip to Tashkent for cancer therapy; several short stories; a play, *Svecha na vetru* (*Candle in the Wind*); and the three-volume *Arkhipelag Gulag* (1973; *Gulag Archipelago*), "an experiment in literary investigation" dealing with the huge network of Soviet labor camps. He considered the latter his duty to the millions of those who forever remained in the frozen "islands" of the Gulag. Out of this voluminous production, however, only four short stories were published by the same faithful Tvardovsky in his journal. In 1963 *Novy mir* nominated Solzhenitsyn for the Lenin Prize, the highest Soviet prize in the arts; but after two days of behind-the-scene intrigues and despite Solzhenitsyn's obvious superiority over the other candidates, the prize was awarded to someone else. More and more critical and outright hostile articles started to appear in the Soviet press. This marked the beginning of the official ten-year campaign against Solzhenitsyn. The reason for his decline from the status of a national celebrity to an outcast was twofold: the waning of the liberalization process in the Soviet Union and the acclaim Solzhenitsyn had won in the West. The notion that the West is seeking to destroy the first socialist state in the world has been one many Soviet people strongly believe, and government propaganda makes sure that the idea will not die. Writers whose works are published in the West without an official approval and discussed in an anti-Soviet context are automatically considered accomplices in hostile actions against the Soviet Union and are dealt with accordingly.

In 1965 Solzhenitsyn's archive was seized by the KGB; in 1969 he was expelled from the Union of Soviet Writers; and in 1970, after he was awarded the Nobel Prize in literature, the campaign against him assumed an especially vicious character. Official propaganda even tried to cash in on popular anti-Semitic sentiments and circulated the rumor that his real name was Solzhenitsker and that he was a Jew. After the KGB got hold of a copy of the *Gulag* in 1973, Solzhenitsyn decided to release it to the West for publication. This perhaps was the last straw. In February 1974, Solzhenitsyn was arrested and

taken to Lefortovo prison. On the next day he was officially stripped of his Soviet citizenship and flown to West Germany. His second wife, Natalia Svetlova, their three children, her mother, and a son from his wife's first marriage followed him abroad soon afterwards.

While still in the Soviet Union, Solzhenitsyn had written several articles expounding his views on Russia's past and present, its relations with the West, its problems and ways of overcoming them. Many critics noted that his ideological positions often resemble those of the nineteenth-century Russian Slavophiles. Indeed, there are quite a few similarities. Solzhenitsyn believes, as did the Slavophiles, that the Russian nation has a unique character and that it ought to be allowed to develop along its own historic path. For both, then, the reforms of Peter the Great, which brought Russia closer to the West, were ruinous for the Russian people. In these articles, and later in speeches and articles he wrote in the United States, Solzhenitsyn denounces Western-style democracy as unsuitable for Russia. Moreover, he avers, with its emphasis on legality as opposed to morality, with its striving for material happiness rather than for spiritual perfection, the Western democratic system has already brought the West to the brink of a very profound social and political crisis. According to Solzhenitsyn, an authoritarian system based on morality, Russian Orthodoxy, and the unique national character of the Russian people would be an ideal arrangement for the Russian state. He could accept even the present Soviet regime, as he writes in his "Letter to the Soviet Leaders," if those leaders would abandon the obsolete and erroneous Marxist ideology that has begotten only lies and violence on Russian soil. He suggests that they concentrate on internal, purely Russian goals, instead of squandering the national wealth on Africa, Latin America, and Arab countries. He also suggests that they curtail the space program and reduce the size of the army, asserting that the West is weak, torn by its own internal crises, and therefore does not present a serious threat to the Soviet Union.

After having stayed for two years in Zurich, Solzhenitsyn moved to the United States and settled in Vermont. His current life there has been outwardly uneventful. His main project in the 1980s has been his magnum opus, *Krasnoe koleso* (*The Red Wheel*), a multivolume, fictional history of the Russian Revolution. Solzhenitsyn has already completed the first three books of this epic: a new version of *Avgust chetyrnadtsatogo* (1971; *August 1914*), *Oktiabr' shestnadtsatogo* (*October 1916*), and *Mart semnadtsatogo* (*March 1917*). He conceived this work before the war when he was a young man of eighteen, but his views have drastically changed since then. He is no longer trying to show that Stalinism was a distortion of and deviation from Leninism. On the contrary, he believes that there is in principle no difference between them, that Stalin was a faithful, if "less than brilliant," follower of Lenin, and that the cruel "Stalinist" methods of suppression and persecution were in fact introduced by Lenin and Trotsky.

Despite his ardent anti-Leninist and anti-Communist convictions, Solzhenitsyn has never lost faith that one day they will no longer be an obstacle to his return to Russia. One of his prophesies has already come true. He wrote in the third volume of *The Gulag Archipelago*: "Soon, soon there will come to Russia an epoch of glasnost." It is dubious, however, that Solzhenitsyn will be able to go back any time soon. But, as his biographer Michael Scammell writes, "if Solzhenitsyn himself does not return to Russia, his books undoubtedly will."

KONSTANTIN KUSTANOVICH

Selected Bibliography

PRIMARY SOURCES

Solzhenitsyn, Alexandr. *August 1914*. 2 vols. Translated by Harry Willetts. New York: Farrar, Straus & Giroux, 1986. (First version published 1972.)

————. *Cancer Ward*. Translated by Nicholas Bethell and David Burg. New York: Farrar, Straus & Giroux, 1969.

————. *The First Circle*. Translated by Thomas Whitney. New York: Harper & Row, 1968.

————. *The Gulag Archipelago*. Vols. 1, 2, 3. Translated by Thomas Whitney. New York: Harper & Row, 1974, 1975, 1978.

————. *One Day in the Life of Ivan Denisovich*. Translated by Max Hayward and Ronald Hingley. New York: Praeger, 1963.

SECONDARY SOURCES

Dunlop, John B., and Alexis Klimoff eds. *Aleksandr Solzhenitsyn: Critical Essays and Documentary Materials.* Boston: Nordland, 1973.

Dunlop, John B., Richard S. Haugh, and Michael Nicholson, eds. *Solzhenitsyn in Exile: Critical Essays and Documentary Materials.* Stanford, Calif.: Hoover Institution Press, 1985.

Feuer, Kathryn, ed. *Solzhenitsyn: A Collection of Critical Essays.* Englewood Cliffs, N.J.: Prentice-Hall, 1976.

Labedz, Leopold, ed. *Solzhenitsyn: A Documentary Record.* Enlarged Edition. Bloomington: Indiana University Press, 1973.

Scammell, Michael. *Solzhenitsyn: A Biography.* New York and London: Norton, 1984.

WOLE SOYINKA   *1986*

In the past four decades African literature has gradually come of age. When the 1986 Nobel Prize in literature was awarded to the Nigerian Wole Soyinka (1934—)—the first African so honored—it finally signaled what most people in this field had known for some time; that is, that African literature had been assured a place in the community of world literature. In its citation, the Nobel Committee hailed Soyinka as one who "in a wide cultural perspective, and with poetic overtones, fashions the drama of existence." For nearly thirty years Wole Soyinka has been a dominant literary influence in Nigeria (and Africa), exposing the structural contradictions in his society and sounding the caution that civilization in Nigeria and elsewhere in Africa stands imperiled by tyrannical abuses. The award thus climaxed not only the full international acknowledgment of African literature as a literary art form, but also the recognition of its significance for the African culture and society that are so powerfully evoked by Soyinka.

Some have wondered why the Nobel was not awarded to the Kenyan Ngugi wa Thiong'o, whose political commentary is more incisive than Soyinka's, or to the Senegalese humanist Leopold Senghor, another nominee. While we cannot delve into the minds of the Nobel Committee members, we cannot doubt that Soyinka's immense artistic production and influence may have both been factors. At heart a playwright, Soyinka has wrestled with practically every literary genre, including the novel, drama, poetry, and autobiographical prose. He has also written a major work of literary criticism, *Myth, Literature and the African World* (1976), which embodies his philosophy of the interrelationship of myth, culture, literature, and world view. His principal publications include fifteen major plays, two novels, two autobiographical narratives, four volumes of poetry, and the book of literary criticism. He has produced a film, an album, and several revues, and has been featured as an actor, a director, and a producer. It is a mark of his literary stature that well over three hundred articles, books, features, and dissertations as well as countless reviews have been written about him. Soyinka writes exclusively in English. However, his works have been translated into numerous languages, including German, French, Finnish, Swedish, Japanese, and Russian.

Though the Nobel Prize is an award for individual distinction, Soyinka himself viewed it in collective terms as an honor bestowed on all of Africa: "I believe that we have won it. I merely have been lucky to be chosen. It is not a personal award. . . . It's for what I represent. I'm part of a whole literary tradition."

Akinwande Oluwole Soyinka was born on July 13, 1934, a member of the Yoruba-speaking people of western Nigeria. He grew up in the Yoruba traditional town of Abeokuta. His father, Ayo, and his mother, Eniola, were both teachers. Early childhood influences appear to have made an indelible impression on the author-to-be's life. The strict discipline for which his family

was noted may have created a countereffect in the young Wole in producing in him rebellious attitudes commonly associated with the *enfant terrible* type. In his autobiographical work *Ake* (1981), in which he reminisces on his childhood up to about ten or eleven years and provides insights into his family background, Soyinka suggests that he may have developed very early in life a deep distrust for a world in which he saw "neither justice nor logic." Equally significant for the later development of Soyinka's imagery were some of his other childhood experiences. For example, images of deities at the court of the Oba (chief) must have nurtured in him his motifs of the supernatural and the whole rich tradition of Yoruba mythology, anchored in the imagery of the god Ogun, that permeate much of his writing.

After his primary schooling at Abeokuta, Soyinka received his high school education at Government College, Ibadan (forty-eight miles away), and subsequently attended University College in Ibadan (now the University of Ibadan), majoring in English, history, and Greek. After his graduation in 1954, he furthered his education at the School of English, University of Leeds, an institution that was then active in the theater, and received a B.A. honors degree in English in 1957.

Soyinka's literary talents were already beginning to show even as a student at Leeds when he wrote "The Other Immigrant," a satirical poem about a pretentious student who returns home to become the one-eyed king. The parallels in Shakespearean dramatic symbolism and the ritual symbolism in Yoruba tragedy that were to become much evident in Soyinka's later works have also been attributed to the influence at Leeds of the British dramatist George Wilson Knight.

Following his graduation, Soyinka became a substitute teacher in London. It must have been during this period that he wrote *The Swamp Dwellers*, which recalls rural underdevelopment in the swamps of the Niger Delta, and *The Lion and the Jewel*, one of his most popular plays, for both were staged in London in 1958. In the fall of the same year, Soyinka started working as a script reader at the Royal Court Theatre in London, where he acquired invaluable skills in stage management. By this time, his publication of "Telephone Conversation," a satire, and *The Invention*, a one-act, witty play commenting on apartheid in South Africa, were already gaining him recognition as one of the new generation of dramatists to come out of the newly independent Africa. And reviewers of his works wasted no time in recognizing his gift for words and imagery and his "remarkably deep penetration of humanity."

After eighteen months at the Royal Court, Soyinka returned home in 1960, and, supported by a Rockefeller fellowship, traveled extensively in Nigeria, deepening his insights into Nigerian festivals, rituals, and masquerades and continuing his career as a dramatist. Within the first year of his return, he had written and produced the radio plays *Camwood on the Leaves* and *The Tortoise*; the television play, *My Father's Burden*; and the farcical (stage) play *The Trials of Brother Jero*. In the same year (1960) he founded his first acting company, The 1960 Masks. Simultaneously, the recently opened Arts Theatre in Ibadan was filling its halls with highly successful productions of *The Swamp Dwellers* and *The Lion and the Jewel*. In addition to writing a weekly radio series ("Broke-Time Bar"), Soyinka wrote and produced *A Dance of the Forests* as part of the activities commemorating Nigeria's independence in 1960. As evidence of his commitment to African drama beyond his own productions, Soyinka directed plays by other African dramatists, such as the Sierra Leonean Sarif Easmon's *Dear Parent and Ogre* and the Nigerian poet John Pepper Clark's *Song of a Goat*. With his own plays being staged in Nigeria, Europe, and the United States, Soyinka, by the tender age of twenty-seven, had quickly acquired recognition as one of the most talented dramatists not only in Africa, but also in the entire English-speaking world.

Two fundamental themes that were to pervade much of Soyinka's writings surfaced very early in *A Dance of the Forests*: first, the Yoruba (and African) world view, which sees life in a cyclical chain linking the living with the dead and the unborn and which recognizes the coexistence of humans and gods; and second, the author's condemnation of his society's maladies—political repression and corruption. With censorship increasing, Soyinka resorted to satire and drama as vehicles for attacking societal evils. He therefore assumed an increasingly visible and public role as a champion of political freedoms. It is in this light that *Kongi's Harvest* (1965), which ridicules political aggrandizement of power symbolized by a yam harvest, and *Idanre and Other Poems* (1967), which deplores the 1966 massacre of Igbos by Hausas, have to be seen.

Inevitably, Soyinka's political involvement led him into two run-ins with the Nigerian authorities. In 1965 he was arrested (but later released) on charges associated with pirate radio broadcasting. Two years later he was arrested again and this time held incommunicado for twenty-seven months. He was charged with conspiring with secessionist Biafra (against the Nigerian federal government), although in reality he was attempting to mediate in the civil war. A man of tremendous internal fortitude, Soyinka not only survived the months of incarceration but came out of prison with an amazingly substantial collection of prison notes that were written literally in between the lines of books that were smuggled to him, on the inside of cigarette packs, and on toilet paper. It was these notes that later became the basis of five major publications: two volumes of poetry, *Poems from Prison* (1969) and *A Shuttle in the Crypt* (1972); a novel, *Season of Anomy* (1973); a play, *Madmen and Specialists* (1974); and the notes themselves, *The Man Died* (1972).

A powerful dramatic indictment set in the context of the Nigerian civil war and its aftermath, *Madmen and Specialists* is highly critical of the excesses of power exhibited by a "corrupt militarism and a rapacious Mafia" that dehumanized Nigerian society. In the fictional work *Season of Anomy* the author engages in, through the use of allegory and myth, a quest for social justice, a moral alternative to the condition of anomie. The quest for justice reappears in *Shuttle*, in which Soyinka likens his prison cell to a crypt and himself to a shuttle. In two of *Shuttle*'s poems, "Conversations at Night with a Cockroach" and "And What if Thus He Died," he laments the failure of his ideal of a Third Force as a vehicle for effecting a moral solution to Nigeria's crises. The moral quest reemerges in *The Man Died*, in which Soyinka demonstrates a deep concern for moral issues: "Justice is the first condition of humanity," he affirms. Incorporating his prison experiences into fictionalized representations of people and places, *The Man Died* presents a visualization of social transformation by men of integrity through the instrumentality of Third Force. In this powerful work, Soyinka lashes out against the political and economic power of the state symbolized, satirically, by the Cartel that is driven solely by profit motivation.

From 1970 to 1975 Soyinka lived for the most part in voluntary exile, largely in Europe. In addition to the works just discussed, he also published during this period three major plays: *The Bacchae of Euripides* (1973), modeled after the Greek;

Jero's Metamorphosis (1974); and *Death and the King's Horsemen* (1975). In 1976 Soyinka returned home to take up the position of professor of comparative literature at the University of Ife. His later works include *Ogun Abibiman* (1976), *Myth, Literature and the African World* (1976), *Opera Wonyosi* (1977), *Ake* (1981), *Requiem for a Futurologist* (1983), and *A Play of Giants* (1984).

In the seventies and eighties Soyinka has held visiting professorships at universities in Great Britain, the United States, and Ghana. He has at the same time lectured extensively throughout the world. His long list of awards and honors includes honorary doctorates from Yale and Leeds universities, the *New Statesman* John Whiting Award, an Amnesty International Prisoner of Conscience Award, and the prestigious title of Commander of the Federal Republic of Nigeria that was conferred on him by President Ibrahim Babangida in recognition of the Nobel award. His plays have been staged in New York, New Haven (Connecticut), Chicago, Washington, D.C., London, Paris, Stockholm, Dakar, Accra, Kampala, Nairobi, Kingston (Jamaica), and a host of other cities throughout the world. At home, Soyinka has been actively involved in road-safety work as the chairman of the Oyo State Road Safety Corps. He has served as secretary general of the Union of Writers of African Peoples and is the current president of the International Theater Institute. Despite these immense accomplishments and the high acclaim, Wole

Soyinka is a very private man who loves solitude. His principal hobby is hunting.

Yoruba world view is based on a holistic conception that integrates the metaphysical with the human worlds in a relationship of interdependence. Two elements that are central to Yoruba world view are important for an understanding of Soyinka's writings: the interrelationship between the living, the dead, and the unborn, and the dominating influence in the Yoruba cosmic realm of the supreme deity, Ogun, the god of metal (iron). Ogun's multiple manifestations and contradictory nature make him simultaneously a master craftsman and a warrior, the dual essence of creativity and destruction.

These images pervade, in symbolic and metaphorical forms, much of Soyinka's writings. His ritual archetypes, therefore, have to be understood in this paradigm of experience. The actor in Soyinka's drama has to prepare himself mentally and physically for his symbolic disintegration and re-creation. Indeed, for Soyinka, traditional drama originated from ritual activities. Thus the Yoruba gods of Ogun and Sango are not only deities but primordial ritual archetypes. The stage, then, is a symbolic representation of the earth and universe, with the actor enacting the relationship between humans and the cosmic world.

Thus in Soyinka's first major play, *A Dance of the Forests*, the forest becomes in metaphorical terms the arena where human drama and transformations from one being (physical) to another (spiritual) are enacted. Though Forest Father's intervention in human follies is ineffective, the richness of this modern African drama is quite evident. In an intricate interplay of idioms such as ritual, dance, mime, and masquerade, Soyinka defies static time and takes his play back and forth from the present to the past, echoing the interrelation between the living, dead, and unborn in Yoruba world view. The totem, a tall flagpole, symbolizes man's criminal history, which is anchored in the past but is at the same time linked to the present and the future.

The ever present force of Ogun, Soyinka's personal muse, reappears persistently in his poetry. *Idanre* and *Ogun Abibiman* are in fact epics that celebrate Ogun's indomitable force as the archetype of change, in Nigeria in the former, and in all *abibiman* ("Black Africa") in the latter. In *Idanre*, which is heavily based on Yoruba mythology, Ogun, as the god of harvest, descends on earth through a cosmic deluge to fertilize it, while in the long poem *Ogun Abibiman*, we see Ogun, not as god of harvest, but of metal (i.e., war), whose moral force sets him on a course of liberation in southern Africa, a mission for which the invincible Zulu warrior Shaka is the forerunner. Soyinka's poetry is replete with parallels of Ogun's attributes: *The Road* (1965), symbolizing the hazards of travel, is dedicated to Ogun as the god of the road; "Of Birth and Death," recalling the stages of life, exemplifies Ogun's dualism of creativity (birth) and destruction (death); "October '66," which was inspired by the 1966

disturbances that precipitated the Nigerian civil war, reaffirms Ogun as god of war.

Indeed, the metaphor of destruction and re-creation is omnipresent. In *Shuttle*, for example, Soyinka parallels his prison ordeal and hope for survival with that of Ogun and his ultimate triumph. Often, ritual functions not only as the symbolic bond and the communicative medium between the human celebrant and nature, but also as the revitalizing rite necessary for re-creation. Thus in the *Shuttle's* "Chimes of Silence," Soyinka and other victims of injustice undergo a rite of passage preparatory to rebirth, while in *The Bacchae of Euripides*, Dionysus is the ritual archetype who suffers death and disintegration as a condition for regeneration.

The political and social relevance of Soyinka has to be seen less in his writings embodying Yoruba world view and more in his works of political satire, in which he wields a double-edged sword against, first, the corrupt bourgeoisie of Nigeria, and, second, despotism in Nigeria and Africa generally. Thus *The Interpreters* (1965) has to be seen as an indictment against the hypocritical bourgeoisie of intellectuals and professionals, the apostates who, while lacking moral courage themselves, have arrogated to themselves the right to set moral standards for society. But it is against the agents of tyranny that Soyinka unleashes much of his rage through the medium of a satirist's pen, especially in the highly evocative plays, *A Play of Giants* and *Opera Wonyosi*. In these works Soyinka lashes out against the perpetrators of "crimes committed by a power-drunk soldiery against a cowed and defenceless people," not just in the corrupt Nigeria of the oil-boom seventies, but also elsewhere in Africa, and singles out such "repellent and vicious dictators" as the then "President-for-Life" Idi Amin Dada of Uganda, "Emperor-for-Life" Jean-Bedel Bokassa of the Central African Republic, and "President-for-Keeps" Macias Nguema of Equatorial Guinea. Equally impassioned as a political satirist is Soyinka's prison quartet: *The Man Died*, in which the victim of injustice envisions himself as a truth-seeking moralist on a direct collision course with the perpetrators of injustice; *Season of Anomy*, in which the fictionalized just community of Ayero is presented as an alternative to the corrupt and tyrannical soldiers-cum-politicians alliance; *Shuttle*, which decries repression; and *Madmen and Specialists*, in which the devastations of the civil war are abhorred in near cannibalistic allegory.

Soyinka as a satirist goes beyond bitter denunciations of despotism and corruption. He is himself the conscience of a society pursuing a moral mission against not only the dictators themselves but also against lesser officials—all whose "active connivance and mutual protection games" make possible the perpetuation of injustice. It is in this light, for example, that the Dentist in *Season* operates as the "extractor" of evil. Similarly, he regards it a "moral task" for one to seek the power to destroy his

Kaduna prison wardens, whom he characterizes as "the pus, bile, original putrescence of Death in living shapes." Indeed, for Soyinka, "the man dies" in whoever acquiesces in or condones tyranny. It is in this context that *Ogun Abibiman* was dedicated to Soweto's "maimed and wounded" victims of injustice.

Soyinka's writings defy easy categorization along classical dramatic lines. Like his world view, his drama is a holistic theater that exploits to the full the fusion of music, dance, mime, and masquerade. His imagery and themes are complex because he eschews linear or sequential development of character or story line. To Soyinka, literature represents "extracts and summations of various experiences." Therefore, he celebrates life as much as he condemns life, combining the mythic with the comic and the tragic. And all this is possible because Soyinka is the personification of unlimited creativity, ingenuity, and versatility. He is not only multidimensional; he took after no models.

Behind the dense imagery and symbolism is a language that is equally dense, so complex that he has been accused of "linguistic obscurity" and verbal mystification. It might not, however, be altogether incidental that, like that used by the orator in Yoruba rites, the language of Soyinka's ritual drama is equally charged, or that mystic experiences defy easy articulation, or that epic energy is sustained by linguistic dexterity.

Despite the fact that injustice emerges as a theme in a number of his publications, the social relevance of Soyinka's literary works has been called into question. The criticism against him is that he does not go far enough. Nigerian leftists like Biodun Jeyifo, Femi Osofisan, and Chimweizu and non-Nigerian writers like the Kenyan Ngugi charge that Soyinka lacks a clearly identifiable commitment to political activism, which they view as the supreme responsibility of the artist in contemporary Africa, and that his preoccupation with cosmic values is irrelevant and in fact obscures the urgent realities facing the writer today. The critics also charge that even though Soyinka uses Yoruba (African) symbolism, he comes across as a Western writer, and, above all, that his choice of language makes him an elitist writer who is out of touch with the majority of his people. To these charges Soyinka responds that a commitment to a solid class perspective inhibits the "fluid operations of the creative mind." In "Who's Afraid of Elisin Oba?" (1977), he defends the freedom to write without ideological labels and argues that myth and ritual are relevant to people's spiritual needs. In Soyinka's view, the writer only complements but does not usurp the role of the politician, technocrat, and worker as upholders of morality.

Granted that Soyinka is not attuned to the struggles of the masses à la Ngugi's *Petals of Blood* (1970) or Ayi Kwei Armah's *Two Thousand Seasons* (1973), a thread of social realism and moral commitment runs through much of his works whether seen through Bandele, who, in *The Interpreters*, lashes out in the voice of

thunder against the violators of the moral code, or through the Dentist, who, in *Season*, aligns himself with the forces of good against evil. Indeed, the Dentist as well as Ofeyi are presented in clearly socialist perspectives. Perhaps the relevance of the whole debate over the social relevance of Soyinka's works is a debate over the wider and more complex question as to what should be the role and function of the writer in contemporary African society.

Despite these criticisms, Soyinka's impact cannot be doubted. He has been one of the most compelling literary voices on the African scene. At home he has been the dominant influence on Nigerian theater since the 1960s. He has influenced or helped to launch the careers of a long line of dramatists that include Ola Rotimi, Dapo Adelugba, Wale Ogunyemi, Odia Ofeimun, Fumsa Aiyejina, Femi Osofisan, Barry Record, Sarif Easmon, and J. P. Clark. Though rejecting overt identification with political activism, Soyinka has forged for himself a distinct role of political engagement, one in which he shares with Chinua Achebe, Sembene Ousmane, Mariama Ba, Ayi Kwei Armah, and a host of other West African writers the role of the publicist against injustice, repression, and corruption. The challenge he represents to the West is in his firm exposition of an African world view that, in its holistic conception, is diametrically antithetical to the compartmentalized views of life in the West. The greater challenge that Wole Soyinka presents is for younger African writers to follow his hard act. For while some may quarrel with his individual style and approach, all, nonetheless, recognize his mastery of technique, language, and style and, above all, the need for the continuation of the African literary tradition in whatever form at its highest levels.

JOSEPH K. ADJAYE

Selected Bibliography

PRIMARY SOURCES

Soyinka, Wole. *Ake: The Years of Childhood.* London: Collings, 1981.

———. *Myth, Literature and the African World.* London: Cambridge University Press, 1976.

SECONDARY SOURCES

Gibbs, James, ed. *Critical Perspectives on Wole Soyinka.* Washington, D.C.: Three Continents, 1980.

———. K. H. Katrak, and Henry-Louis Gates, Jr. *Wole Soyinka: A Bibliography.* Westport, Conn.: Greenwood Press, 1986.

Maduakor, Obi. *Wole Soyinka: An Introduction to His Works.* New York: Garland, 1986.

Moore, Gerald. *Wole Soyinka.* London: Evans, 1971.

CARL SPITTELER   *1919*

Carl Spitteler (1845–1924) was born in Liestal, Switzerland near Basel, on April 24, 1845. A Swiss national who wrote in German and the author of epics, novels, essays, and poems, Spitteler received the Nobel Prize in literature in 1919. The son of a civil servant, he studied law at Basel and theology at Zurich and Heidelberg, before rejecting a parsonage (1871) in favor of spending eight years as a private tutor in Finland and Russia. Upon his return to Switzerland in 1879, he turned first to teaching (Bern, Neuveville) and then to journalism (Basel, Zurich) to earn a living. His stint as literary section editor of the prestigious *Neue Zürcher Zeitung* (1890–92) gave him the opportunity to try his hand at a variety of literary forms. In 1892 an inheritance enabled him to settle in Lucerne and to devote himself entirely to writing, and Lucerne remained his home until his death on December 29, 1924.

Deliberately unorthodox, Spitteler rejected literary tendencies (realism, naturalism) of his day and attempted to adapt a venerable but exhausted form, the epic, to contemporary concepts. His first work, the mythical epic *Prometheus und Epimetheus* (1880–81; *Prometheus and Epimetheus*), appeared under the pseudonym C. F. Tandem. The work anticipated Friedrich Nietzsche's *Also sprach Zarathustra* (*Thus Spoke Zarathustra*). In rhythmic prose and through figures of classical mythology Spitteler contrasts the rise of the human soul to its fullest potential (Prometheus) with its fall into barren routine (Epimetheus). During the last years of his life he recast the work in rhymed iambic hexameter and entitled it *Prometheus der Dulder* (1924; "Suffering Prometheus"), portraying Prometheus as an artist engaged in an intense struggle against rampant subjectivism. Neither version found much favor with the critics or the public. An exception was the Swiss writer Gottfried Keller. He praised "the inherent power and beauty of the depiction of dark images" but simultaneously admitted that he did not fully understand their symbolic significance.

Spitteler's second poetic epic, *Der olympische Frühling* (4 vols.; 1900–06; revised 1910; "Olympian Spring"), still regarded as his best work, earned him the Nobel Prize. Cast in rhyming couplets and in mythological terms, it is a bold, imaginative, at once simple and complex tale of divine and human fate reflecting the pessimistic philosophy of the author's idols Jacob Burckhardt and Arthur Schopenhauer. Earth and Mt. Olympus face a change. Cronos has been deposed, and Hera's era begins. Anankes orders Hades to awaken the Olympians, the gods of the new era. Zeus, Apollo, Hermes, and Poseidon compete for Hera. Apollo wins, but Anankes interferes, and Zeus becomes Hera's spouse, obtaining dominion over the world. Zeus and Apollo are reconciled, earth is opened to the gods, and a "golden age," which Aphrodite's wantonness soon ends, begins. Finally Zeus summons all the gods to their duty. He himself, at odds with Hera, heads for earth where he assumes the role of a judge, but is incarcerated by man. Angered at first, then brought to reason by Gorgo, he delegates his son Heracles to earth. In spite of Hera's plans to destroy Heracles, one senses that the "olympian spring" shall be followed by an earthly one.

Spitteler's prose stories of the 1890s, especially *Gustav* (1892) and *Conrad, der Leutnant* (1898; "Conrad, the Lieutenant"), reflect the narrative realism of his predecessors Jeremias Gotthelf (1797–1854) and Gottfried Keller (1819–90). In his employment of the *Sekundenstil* technique in *Conrad, der Leutnant*, Spitteler makes a concession to naturalism, a literary movement he otherwise loathed.

In 1906 Spitteler published his autobiographical novel *Imago*, a story of sexual obsession sublimated in devotion to art, with perceptive, original psychoanalytic elements. The work attracted the attention of Sigmund Freud's circle. The psychoanalysts saw the novel as a model for psychoanalytic theories and subsequently named their journal after it. (*Imago. Zeitschrift für Anwendung der Psychoanalyse auf die Geisteswissenschaften.*)

Other works by Spitteler include seven original cosmic myths that appeared in verse under the title *Extramundana* (1883); volumes of poetry: *Schmetterlinge* (1889; "Butterflies"), *Balladen* (1896; "Ballades"), and *Glockenlieder* (1906; "Bell Songs"); two insignificant comedies; the story *Gerold und Hansli, die Mädchenfeinde* (1907; "Gerold and Hansli, the Misogynists"), an idyll based upon childhood experiences; a touching autobiographical work, *Meine frühesten Erlebnisse* (1914; "My Earliest Experiences"), and numerous stimulating essays, including *Lachende Wahrheiten* (1898; "Laughing Truths"), *Meine Beziehungen zu Nietzsche* (1908; "My Relationships to Nietzsche"), and *Unser Schweizer Standpunkt* (1914; "The Swiss Position"), aimed at defusing the tension evoked by World War I between the German- and French-speaking regions of Switzerland. Spitteler's support of Swiss neutrality and his questioning of German war propaganda led to calls for a boycott as well as burning of his works in Germany. Ultimately, along with the support of Romain Rolland, these became deciding factors in his selection for the Nobel Prize in literature.

ALBERT A. KIPA

Selected Bibliography

PRIMARY SOURCE

Gesammelte Werke. 11 vols. Edited by G. Bohnenblust, W. Altwegg, and R. Faesi. Zurich: Artemis-Verlag, 1945–58.

SECONDARY SOURCES

Beriger, L. *Carl Spitteler in der Erinnerung seiner Freunde und Weggefährten.* Zurich: Artemis-Verlag, 1947.

Faesi, R. *Spittelers Weg und Werk.* Frauenfeld, Switz., and Leipzig: Huber, 1933.

McHaffie, Margaret, "Prometheus and Viktor: Carl Spitteler's *Imago.*" *German Life and Letters* 31 (1977); 67–77.

Pender, Malcom. "From *Imago* to *Stiller*: Aspects of the German-Swiss 'Künstlerroman'." In *Modern Swiss Literature: Unity and Diversity.* Edited by John L. Flood. New York: St. Martin's Press, 1985. Pp. 93–109.

Rommel, Otto. *Spittelers "Olympischer Frühling" und seine epische Form.* Bern: Francke, 1965.

Schmidt-Henkel, Gerhard. "Mythos und Mythologie in Carl Spittelers *Olympischem Frühling.*" In *Mythos und Mythologie in der Literatur des 19. Jahrhunderts.* Edited by Helmut Koopman. Frankfurt: Klostermann, 1979. Pp. 307–20.

Stauffacher, Werner. *Carl Spitteler: Biographie.* Zurich: Artemis, 1973.

Wetzel, Justus H. *Carl Spitteler. Ein Lebens- und Schaffensbericht.* Bern: Francke, 1973.

JOHN STEINBECK *1962*

John Ernest Steinbeck (1902–68) was awarded the Nobel Prize in literature in 1962, the sixth American writer to be so honored, in recognition of his "sympathetic humor and sociological perception" and his "instinct for what is genuinely American, be it good or bad." In his speech accepting the prize, Steinbeck spoke of the "high duties and the responsibilities of the makers of literature," who are "charged with exposing our many grievous faults and failures . . . for the purpose of improvement," and equally charged to "declare and celebrate man's proven capacity for greatness of heart and spirit"; above all, he declared, writers must "passionately believe in the perfectibility of man. . . ." Coming at the acme of a life dedicated to writing, these comments are a fitting summary of the intent and the achievement of Steinbeck's work.

Born on February 27, 1902, in Salinas, California, in the farming country and near the coastal areas that were to become the settings for many of his novels and stories, John Steinbeck was the third of four children, the only son, in a middle-class family. His parents encouraged his reading—notably Milton, Dostoyevsky, Flaubert, Hardy, and Malory's *Morte d'Arthur*—but discouraged his aspiration to become a novelist. Nevertheless, quite early he decided upon writing as a vocation, and in 1919 he enrolled at Stanford University with this in mind. He attended intermittently, choosing courses in English, writing, and science, until 1925, when he left without a degree. After an unsuccessful attempt at newspaper reporting in New York City, Steinbeck returned to California as caretaker of a Lake Tahoe estate, a job giving him time to pursue his writing. In 1930 he married Carol Henning, and soon after the couple moved to the summer cottage of his parents in Pacific Grove, where his wife worked as a secretary while Steinbeck wrote. During this time Steinbeck met and became closely associated with Edward F. Ricketts, a marine biologist whose thinking was to influence him profoundly.

Three book-length works were published during these years of apprenticeship. *Cup of Gold*, a novel based on the life of the pirate Henry Morgan, was published in 1929. Though the manner of representation is more allegorical than realistic, this novel demonstrates that Steinbeck understood something of the wasteland themes of his expatriate contemporaries, Eliot, Fitzgerald, and Hemingway. *The Pastures of Heaven* (1932) followed, a sequence of stories about the residents of a California farming valley who are victimized by misunderstandings and by their own self-delusions. *To a God Unknown* (1933) shares with *Cup of Gold* Steinbeck's interest in common people who rise to something like heroic stature. None of these works attracted many readers or significant critical attention.

With *Tortilla Flat* (1935) Steinbeck combined the picaresque with local color and naturalistic fiction to achieve his first popular success. In these stories about the *paisanos* (ethnically mixed Mexican-Indian-Caucasians) of the Monterey Peninsula, readers found an inviting escape from dreary Depression times. Though dismissed by some as sentimental comedy, *Tortilla Flat* offers an early instance of Steinbeck's social criticism: while given to petty theft and chicanery, the reprobates and social dropouts of Tortilla Flat live more contentedly and do less harm than their more affluent neighbors on the other side of the gulch.

The social criticism of *In Dubious Battle* (1935), a novel about a California fruit pickers' strike, in the genre of proletarian fiction, led to the first of several public controversies about Steinbeck's politics. Siding neither with the California agribusinessmen nor with Marxist union organizers, Steinbeck drew fire from both. Less overtly, the novel does choose, as Steinbeck's writing consistently would, affirming the critical importance of respect for life and denying arguments for the necessity of either economic exploitation or dehumanizing ideology.

More deeply imbedded is the social criticism in *Of Mice and Men* (1937), a novella (and a play, in collaboration with George S. Kaufman) that brought Steinbeck into literary prominence. In the spare, poetic language that would become a hallmark of Steinbeck's style, the narrator tells of simple farmhands, George and Lennie, whose dream of a small farm of their own is doomed by imperfect nature and an exploitative economic system. As in several earlier works, Steinbeck is at once naturalist—compassionately depicting his characters as victims of instinct, environment, and chance—and social critic—contrasting the simple friendships of ranch hands to the self-imposed isolation of materialists. Similarly evocative and often naturalistic are the stories of *The Long Valley* (1939), which contains the repeatedly anthologized "Chrysanthemums" and "Flight" and the four stories comprising *The Red Pony* (1953).

In retrospect, the considerable accomplishment of these early works seems preparation for *The Grapes of Wrath* (1939); for this masterwork, Steinbeck drew from his earlier writing the subjects and many of the narrative methods for a style that is at times spare, reportorial, at others rich, subtle, poetic. *The Grapes of Wrath* combines sympathetic observation of simple life and pointed social criticism into a novel of epic proportions about the Joads, Oklahoma farmers driven from their land by crop failure and mortgage foreclosure. Their journey to the false promised land of California becomes both an exposé of the woeful conditions endured by migrant workers and a pilgrims' progress toward redemption. At first isolated from others by the strength of their family bonds, the Joads are forced by the experience of shared suffering to enter into the lives of others. Though hardship and death threaten to disintegrate what family identity remains, the Joads come to understand, though imperfectly, that all life reveals a wholeness and holiness, and from this knowledge they are able to draw renewed hope for the family of humankind.

Both a critical and popular success, winning the 1940 Pulitzer Prize for fiction after months atop bestseller lists, *The Grapes of Wrath* focused national attention on the plight of migrant workers, creating a public controversy that led to governmental investigations and even to book bannings and burnings. Steinbeck escaped some of the public attention by joining his friend and mentor, Ed Ricketts, on an expedition to gather marine life. From this voyage came *The Sea of Cortez* (1940), a collaborative effort in nature writing and essays on ecology, elaborating what Steinbeck and Ricketts described as a nonteleological explanation of life, seeking interrelationships rather than analyzing causation. Recent critical commentary of Steinbeck's fiction has drawn upon these essays.

During World War II Steinbeck contributed to the war effort as a correspondent and as a writer for the Air Force. During this time he also wrote *The Moon Is Down* (1942), a war novella (and also a play) about the Nazi occupation of an unnamed Scandinavian country. Publication of this novel brought a decoration from the king of Norway, but also embroiled Steinbeck in a third controversy, many readers finding his depiction of the Nazi occupiers insufficiently damning to be patriotic. Before war's end Steinbeck turned, perhaps for relief from his experience as a correspondent, to a series of lighthearted stories

about social misfits and dropouts in a California coastal town. Like their precursors from Tortilla Flat, the residents of *Cannery Row* (1945) are primitives, hunters and gatherers loose in a world of private property. But while the humorous portraits of Mack and the Boys, the "Virtues, Graces, Beauties" of the Row, did offer welcome respite from the war, readers found as well typical Steinbeck moral instruction in the contrast of the boys with "people who tear themselves to pieces with ambition and nervousness and covetousness." Notable in this work is a fictional portrait of Ed Ricketts as Doc, the owner of a marine biology station who, in his sympathetic acceptance of an imperfect world—including, if cautiously, the denizens of the Row—lives as successfully as man can.

Steinbeck's first marriage ended in divorce during the war. In 1945 Steinbeck and his second wife, Gwyndolen Conger, took up permanent residence in New York, bringing to a symbolic end his long if intermittent residence in California. The change also signaled the end of his period of greatest artistic achievement, though there were yet to be popular and critical successes. In 1947 came the parable-like novella, *The Pearl*, which continues to be a staple in school curricula, and *The Wayward Bus*, equally moralistic but less convincing in character portrayal. Steinbeck wrote entertainingly of his travels in the Soviet Union in *A Russian Journal* (1948), and attempted to conquer Broadway again with *Burning Bright* (1950), notable primarily for the brevity of its run. In 1948 his second marriage failed.

In 1950 came both his third marriage, to Elaine Scott, and publication of *East of Eden*, a novel interrelating two California families, the Hamiltons and the Trasks. Believed by Steinbeck to be his best work, his most mature and developed vision of life, this novel argues more forcefully than earlier works for the possibility of free will, the ability of the mature, thinking person to choose and to accept the consequences of choice. But the attempt to interrelate the two families never achieves artistic unity; while perhaps Steinbeck's most ambitious effort to demonstrate the perfectability of mankind, for most readers the novel fails to create vital characters or convincing philosophy.

During the remaining years of his life, Steinbeck engaged himself increasingly in journalistic writing, much of it excellent except when compared with the best of his fiction. There were several notable additions to the fiction: *Sweet Thursday* (1954), a visit to postwar Cannery Row; *The Short Reign of Pippin IV* (1957), a social satire set in France; and *The Winter of Our Discontent* (1961), the publication of which occasioned the 1962 Nobel Prize. A cross-country excursion with his poodle became the material for Steinbeck's meditation on America, *Travels with Charlie* (1962), a popular success after the announcement of the Nobel Prize, and in 1966 Steinbeck returned to the subject in *America and Americans*. Though a private man throughout most of his life, after the Nobel Prize John

Steinbeck was active in politics and public life until failing health restricted him in his final year. He died of a heart attack on December 20, 1968.

The best stylist and most effective social critic of the Great Depression's proletarian writers, Steinbeck grew beyond the literary limits of naturalism and class criticism. He sought not only to serve as society's conscience, dramatizing the human consequences of its failings and thereby spurring correction, but also to communicate through his art a conception of humanity's individual and collective relationships to the natural world, a nonteleological vision celebrating the interconnectedness of all that is. His most notable qualities are his spare but richly expressive style, through which is communicated an intimate regard for all life, and his compassionate understanding of simple, untutored, even primitive humanity. His was a versatile talent, and his art experimental in both subject and narrative technique. Though the quality of work is mixed, and though moral zeal led at times to sermonizing, the high achievement of his best, most notably *The Grapes of Wrath*, *Cannery Row*, and *Of Mice and Men*, is unassailable.

DAVID R. JOHNSON

Selected Bibliography

PRIMARY SOURCE

Steinbeck, John. *The Portable Steinbeck*. New York: Viking Press, 1971.

SECONDARY SOURCES

Benson, Jackson J. *The True Adventures of John Steinbeck, Writer.* New York: Viking Press, 1984.

Fontenrose, Joseph. *John Steinbeck: An Introduction and Interpretation.* New York: Barnes & Noble, 1963.

French, Warren. *John Steinbeck.* Boston: Twayne, 1975.

Kiernan, Thomas. *The Intricate Music: A Biography of John Steinbeck.* Boston: Little, Brown, 1979.

Levant, Howard. *The Novels of John Steinbeck.* Columbia: University of Missouri Press, 1974.

Lisca, Peter. *The Wide World of John Steinbeck.* New Brunswick, N.J.: Rutgers University Press, 1958.

McCarthy, Paul. *John Steinbeck.* New York: Ungar, 1980.

RENÉ-FRANÇOIS-ARMAND SULLY PRUDHOMME *1901*

René-François-Armand Prudhomme (1839–1907), known as Sully Prudhomme, was the first recipient of the Nobel Prize in literature. Though once considered a major poet of the nineteenth century, he rarely is read now and most of his works have been forgotten by all except historians of French literature and culture.

Sully Prudhomme was born in Paris on March 16, 1839. Having lost his father (from whom he inherited the nickname Sully) at the age of two, he was raised by his mother with the help of an aunt and uncle. He attended various Parisian boarding schools and the Lycée Bonaparte (now the Lycée Condorcet), where he was required to specialize either in letters or in the sciences; he opted for the latter. Though afflicted by ill health, he successfully obtained the degree of *bachelier ès sciences* (bachelor of science) and began preparing to compete for admission to the prestigious Ecole Polytechnique. He was forced to abandon these plans after he contracted an eye illness as a result of intensive reading.

Sully Prudhomme left the Lycée Bonaparte in 1857 and went to stay in Lyons with relatives whose Catholic piety marked him deeply; for a time he considered taking monastic orders. His religious convictions dissolved upon his return in 1858 to Paris, where he obtained the baccalaureate degree in letters. After a period of employment in the Creusot factories, he attended law school, at the same time clerking in a notary's office. None of these occupations proved to his liking. When he came into an inheritance, he was able to devote himself to poetry, which he had been writing since childhood, and to such philosophical and scientific meditations as those that appear in the lengthy preface to his translation of Canto I of Lucretius's *De rerum natura* (*On the Nature of Things*), published in 1869.

Sully Prudhomme's first book of verse, *Stances et poèmes* ("Stanzas and Poems"), appeared in 1865 and met with considerable success, being praised by Sainte-Beuve and by a number of other critics. It contains "Le Vase brisé" ("The Broken Vase"), Sully Prudhomme's most famous and most frequently anthologized poem, which compares a broken vase and the desiccated flower inside it to a broken heart in which love has withered. This piece, like several others in the collection, reflects one of its author's greatest disappointments in life: around 1864, a girl whom he had loved throughout much of his youth and whom he had hoped to marry became engaged to another man. Sully Prudhomme never recovered from the blow, which casts a dark shadow throughout his lyrical poetry, and he remained a bachelor for the rest of his life.

A number of the *Stances et poèmes* convey an enthusiastic belief in beauty and goodness and in the redemptive power of poetry that faded from Sully Prudhomme's verse as he was assailed by feelings of loneliness and of metaphysical anguish. Like so many of his contemporaries, Sully Prudhomme was a convert to positivism—a materialistic, deterministic philosophy, which held that the only valid source of knowledge was scientific observation and experimentation—yet he yearned for a sense of moral certainty and purposiveness that positivism could not provide. The conflict between his spiritual aspirations and the materialistic views that undermined them is movingly expressed in his second book of poems, *Les Epreuves* (1866; "Trials"), in a section entitled "Doute" ("Doubt") that contains two especially interesting sonnets: "La Grande Ourse" ("The Great Bear") and "Le Doute" ("Doubt"). At least some of the poems in *Les Epreuves* and most of those in the roughly contemporaneous *Croquis italiens* (1872; "Italian Sketches"), written in 1866–67, express more mundane concerns; the latter collection, which Sully Prudhomme composed during a tour of Italy, reveals a sensuous delight in beauty unparalleled elsewhere in his writings.

In 1869 Sully Prudhomme published *Les Solitudes* ("Solitude"), poems in which his thwarted love and his metaphysical torment are significant themes. The work excited considerable interest, being acclaimed among positivists as a lucid exercise in psychological self-analysis. Soon after it appeared, Sully Prudhomme was shaken by the deaths of his mother, his aunt, and his uncle and by the outbreak in July 1870 of the Franco-Prussian War. He volunteered and was accepted for active service despite his frail health, which deteriorated so badly during the German siege of Paris that he was discharged from military duty. While convalescing outside of the city, he wrote *Impressions de la guerre* (1872; "Impressions of the War"), poems in an elegiac, patriotic vein that anticipate the ones he published a few years later under the title *La France* (1874). The war left the author of *Les Solitudes* a partly paralyzed invalid who felt more convinced than ever of his aloneness and of the impossibility of his finding any solace in life, feelings that pervade his last book of lyric verse, *Les Vaines Tendresses* (1875; "Futile Caresses").

During Sully Prudhomme's later career, his poetry changed. Inspired by Lucretius's *De rerum natura* and by André Chénier's imitations of that poem, *L'Hermès* and *L'Amérique*, Sully Prudhomme undertook to write verse that would serve as a vehicle of philosophical and scientific knowledge. This ambitious scheme is realized with varying degrees of success in *Les Destins* (1872; "Destinies"), a didactic poem concerning the creation by rival spirits of two worlds—one good and one evil—that turn out to be virtually identical; in *Le Zénith* (1875; "The Zenith"), a paean to modern science celebrating the exploratory balloon ascent of three aeronauts; in *La Justice* (1878; "Justice"), which initially argues that the Darwinian struggle for survival precludes justice but then recoils from this harsh conclusion, asserting that the ideal of justice genuinely exists in the human heart; and in *Le Bonheur* (1888; "Happiness"), a long and for the most part tedious symbolic epic that Sully Prudhomme took some ten years to complete. It concerns the interplanetary adventures of two lovers united in death whose search for happiness follows the three paths defined in the poem's three major sections: "Les Ivresses" ("Intoxica-

tions"), "La Pensée" ("Thought"), and "Le Suprême Essor" ("The Supreme Flight"), which deal respectively with sensuality, intellection, and virtue. The lovers ultimately achieve perfect bliss through self-sacrifice. Sully Prudhomme's spirit of philosophical and scientific inquiry also manifests itself in a variety of prose works that he wrote toward the end of his career and that seriously interested contemporary professional philosophers: *Que sais-je?* (1896; "What Do I Know?"), *Le Crédit de la science* (1901; "The Authority of Science"), *Le Problème des causes finales* (1902; "The Problem of Final Causes"), written in collaboration with Charles Richet, *La Vraie Religion selon Pascal* (1905; "True Religion according to Pascal"), and *Psychologie du libre arbitre* (1907; "The Psychology of Free Will"). Sully Prudhomme's other prose works include a treatise on aesthetics, *L'Expression dans les beaux-arts* (1883; "Expression in the Fine Arts"), and a volume of collected poetry criticism, *Testament poétique* (1901; "Poetical Testament"), which includes the previously published *Réflexions sur l'art des vers* (1892; "Reflections on the Art of Versification").

Sully Prudhomme usually is classified as a member of the Parnassian school, whose principal writers he met and frequented in the 1860s and with whom he maintained good relations in later years. He acknowledged the merits of Parnassian poetry, which influenced some of his own verse (a fine example is "Le Cygne" ["The Swan"], one of the poems in *Les Solitudes*); he admired

Leconte de Lisle and was a friend of Hérédia and Coppée; and he contributed to the famous anthology of poetry entitled *Le Parnasse contemporain* ("The Contemporary Parnassus"), published in three series in 1866, 1871, and 1876. Yet Sully Prudhomme's lyricism set him apart from the Parnassians in the period preceding 1875, and he explicitly denied being a member of their school afterward. He vigorously rejected the Parnassian doctrine of art for art's sake and effectively inverted it, arguing that art is a second-rate activity. "Works of science," he once wrote, "are far superior in my eyes to works of imagination; I do not know a literary work that comes close in my estimation to the discoveries of Newton. . . . The *Iliad* and the *Odyssey* seem to me nothing but children's games compared to the discovery of the square of the hypotenuse and of the rotation of the earth." He believed that poetry should seek to convey scientific and philosophical truth. Though Sully Prudhomme has a superficial affinity with those Parnassians who neglected art for art's sake to dabble in scientific poetry, he differs from them in the seriousness of his commitment to the natural sciences, to mathematics, and to philosophy—disciplines that he studied assiduously throughout his life. The philosopher Camille Hémon in 1907 described him as the "creator" and "sole representative" of French scientific poetry, a claim that no doubt is greatly exaggerated but that indicates the uniqueness of Sully Prudhomme's accomplishments as they were perceived by his contemporaries.

Sully Prudhomme's lesser poetry includes *La Révolte des fleurs* (1874; "The Revolt of the Flowers") and the collections *Le Prisme* (1886; "The Prism") and *Les Epaves* ("Flotsam and Jetsam," published posthumously in 1908). He was elected to the French Academy in 1881, received the Nobel Prize in 1901, and died on September 7, 1907. If he ever regains more than a vestige of his past fame, it will probably be owing to a renewed appreciation of his place in intellectual history and to a revival of interest in his lyrical poems, which are some of the saddest in French literature.

GEORGE M. ROSA

Selected Bibliography

PRIMARY SOURCES

Sully Prudhomme, René-François-Armand. *Journal intime. Lettres. Pensées.* Edited by Camille Hémon. Paris: A. Lemerre, 1922.

——. *Lettres à une amie (1865–1881).* Paris: Le Livre contemporain, 1911.

——. *Œuvres de Sully Prudhomme. Poésies.* 6 vols. Paris: A. Lemerre, 1925–26.

——. *Œuvres de Sully Prudhomme. Prose.* 2 vols. Paris: A. Lemerre, 1904–08.

Translations

Boni, Albert, ed. *The Modern Book of French Verse.* New York: Boni & Liveright, 1920. Pp. 181–85.

Carrington, Henry, ed. *Anthology of French Poetry, 10th to 19th Centuries.* New York: Frowde, 1900. Pp. 276–79.

SECONDARY SOURCES

Charlton, Douglas G. "Positivism and the Parnassians (2). The Philosophy of Sully Prudhomme." In *Positivist Thought in France during the Second Empire, 1852–1870*. Oxford, U.K.: Clarendon Press, 1959. Chap. 9, pp. 190–223.

Estève, Edmond. *Sully Prudhomme, poète sentimental et poète philosophe*. Paris: Boivin, 1925.

Flottes, Pierre. *Sully Prudhomme et sa pensée*. Paris: Perrin, 1930.

Hémon, Camille. *La Philosophie de M. Sully Prudhomme*. Paris: Alcan, 1907.

Morice, Henri. *La Poésie de Sully Prudhomme*. Paris: Téqui, 1920.

Zyromski, Ernest. *Sully Prudhomme*. Paris: Colin, 1907.

RABINDRANATH TAGORE *1913*

Rabindranath Tagore (1861–1941), the first Asian writer to be awarded the Nobel Prize in literature, was born into a well-to-do Hindu land-owning family in Calcutta on May 7, 1861. He died in Calcutta on August 7, 1941. From his youth he strongly disliked formal education and was taught mostly at home by tutors. He was precocious, however, and made his first attempts at writing poetry in 1869, when he was only eight, and his first work was published in a literary magazine in 1875. He spent a year abroad at college in Britain in 1879 but returned to India without earning an academic degree. In 1883 he was married to Mrinalini Devi.

The 1880s were primarily years of literary experimentation for Tagore and also saw his first attempts

at writing drama, publication of his first collections of songs, as well as publication of his first collection of critical essays. His activities in the 1890s were more diverse. He left Calcutta to supervise family estates and there developed a deep appreciation of the rural scene and nature that was to inform much of his later writings. He started his family, and in 1898 brought his children to the country so that he might educate them himself. He believed strongly in learning from nature, and this belief took further form in 1901 when he founded a school called Santiniketan ("Abode of Peace"). The school was radical, not so much in its educational philosophy, which drew on the model of the *asram*, as in its social philosophy, which did not restrict students to a particular ethnic group or espouse strictly religious education. It became Visva-Bharati University in 1918.

The first decade of the twentieth century was a trying time for Tagore. In 1905 the British partitioned Bengal between the Hindu and Moslem populations, a move opposed by many who supported Bengali nationalist aspirations. Tagore was sympathetic to these goals and was involved for a time in protests against the partition order. In 1907, however, he withdrew from political activity and concentrated instead on his educational enterprises.

The events of the 1910s in Tagore's life revolve primarily around the award of the Nobel Prize in 1913 and the vogue for his writings in the West. In the wake of the Nobel Prize he was awarded an honorary doctorate by the University of Calcutta in 1913 and a knighthood by the British in 1915. He resigned the latter in 1919, however, to protest the British massacre at Amritsar. Much of this decade and the beginning of the next centered around the preparation of manuscripts in English, and Tagore also embarked on several lecture tours abroad. After 1920, however, public interest in his works in the West declined. Tagore had consistently used the royalties from his publications and lectures to support his educational enterprises, and when the inflation of the 1930s seriously cut his income, he had to increase his fund-raising efforts. Although chronically ill through much of the last decade of his life, he continued to support various liberal causes, including Margaret Sanger's campaign for birth control in India.

He died on August 7, 1941, at the age of eighty, a respected figure in his own country but largely forgotten in the West.

Tagore emerged as a writer at a time of cultural change in Bengal. At the beginning of the nineteenth century, Bengal was still very much under the influence of the Hindu religious and Sanskrit literary traditions. In 1828, however, a Hindu reform movement called Brahmo Samaj emerged. It was aimed at moving the practice of Hinduism away from the worship of images and blind ritual toward a form of monotheism or unitarianism along broad secular and humanistic lines. Among the Bengali intellectuals for whom this movement had appeal was Tagore's father, Debendranath (1817–1905), and the influence of this secular and liberal Hinduism can be clearly seen in Tagore's lifelong commitment to progressive causes of which his literary works are an aspect.

Sanskrit had long been viewed as the language of literature and scholarship, and most privileged young people of Tagore's generation studied Sanskrit and English in school but not their vernacular language. One of Tagore's early and most enduring contributions was to champion vernacular Bengali, as opposed to its classical or heavily Sanskritized form, as a worthy literary language as well as the language for the education of Bengali youth.

When Tagore began to write, he found that there were few vernacular literary genres on which he could draw and for the basis of his verse turned to nonliterary forms. One of these was the *kirtan*, a form of anti-phonal song associated with the Hindu Vaishnava movement. The substance of these songs was the enduring quest of man for union with the divine, often expressed through the metaphor of human love. Tagore drew on elements of this form for both the language and themes of much of his poetry.

The process of transformation from this popular tradition to an individual and literary voice in poetry was not a simple one. While Tagore drew on a rich resource, he had to develop his own tools and refine the tradition by working out problems of prosody, diction, theme, and tone. The young Tagore was influenced not only by the philosophy of the Brahmo Samaj movement but by his exposure to Western romantic poets. His early verse was strongly romantic in tone and filled with juvenile lucubrations, but with *Prabhat Sangit* (1883; "Morning Songs"), Tagore had struck a characteristic theme by recognizing that all parts of life, even its minute aspects, are part of a greater, universal whole, and that the individual poet is congruent with that whole. Later poetic works show further developments. *Ksanikā* (1900; "Ephemera") was an experiment in the use of more colloquial language. Tagore was criticized by literary conservatives in Bengal, but this collection is an example of Tagore's ongoing effort to find a contemporary literary expression freed of the bonds of classicism.

Gītāñjali (*Song Offerings*) was published in 1910. Here, Tagore's thematic debts to the tradition of Vaishnava lyrics is apparent, and the image of man as the sojourner and quester appears frequently. *Gītāñjali* is important not only in terms of Tagore's development as a poet, but because this is the collection that brought him to the attention of the West and for which he was awarded the Nobel Prize. It is also representative, in tone and theme, of much of the verse that was published in English.

Later collections by Tagore showed further developments and the range of his poetic voice. Even as late as 1932 Tagore was still involved in experimentation. That year saw publication of *Punascha* ("Postscript"), which was an experiment in free verse or prose poems in Bengali. Tagore was a prolific writer of poetry to the end of his life, and this form comprises the greater part of his works.

Tagore's roots in vernacular traditions can also be seen in the area of drama. In Bengal there had long been popular dramas that told in verse stories from the Indian classics. Tagore drew on this tradition, although he was never content simply to retell a classical story and pursued his experiments in language in this area as well. An example of this is the early play, *Raja o Rani* (1889; *The King and the Queen*), which tells the story of a king so consumed by love that when his queen disturbs his fantasy, his love turns to hate and results in her death. The experiment in this play was the use of prose, since many of Tagore's dramas were in verse.

Several of Tagore's lyric dramas were also adapted into English.

These were primarily serious, often allegorical dramas in contrast to several social comedies he wrote for a popular Bengali audience. An example of the first sort is *Chitrangada* (1891; *Chitra*). The story elements come from the *Mahabarata*. Chitrangada, an only child, a girl who has been raised like a man, meets the hero Arjuna and in order to win him gets from the gods the gift of perfect womanhood for the space of a year. Initially, the two are enraptured by love, but each becomes dissatisfied, and Arjuna begins to ask about the other woman, Chitrangada, of whom he has heard. Chitrangada finally rejects the gift of perfect womanhood and it is only then that she accepts, and Arjuna discovers, her true and complete self.

Occasionally Tagore essayed social commentary in the form of a drama, as with *Dak-Ghar* (1912; *The Post Office*). A frail young boy is kept in a darkened room by his guardians for fear that he would be exposed to illness if allowed outside. Thus the world he knows is only that which he can see from his window. He believes the postman, who says that he will bring him a letter from the king, and dies imagining the arrival of the king himself. The play may be seen as critical of Hindu conservatism in the face of modernizing influences.

At the beginning of the nineteenth century there were in effect no Bengali prose genres. The first to attempt a Bengali novel was Bankimchandra Chatterji (1838–94), who wrote historical novels in Sanskritized Bengali. Tagore picked up and continued his work, using increasingly vernacular language and contemporary themes, and paved the way for later Bengali writers. Among them is Bibhutibhushan Bannerji (1899–1950), whose stories, such as *Pather Panchali* (1929; *Pather Panchali: Songs of the Road*) and *Aparajita* (1932; *Unconquered*), are perhaps best known in the West as rendered in film by Satyajit Ray (b. 1922).

Tagore's novels display the same diversity of tone and theme as many of his other works. *Nouka-Dubi* (1906; *The Wreck*), was an early but popular work that told a story of mistaken identities leading to an inadvertent exchange of wives. The story might be slight, but it was well told in a lively vernacular, and this work became the most widely translated of Tagore's novels. Far more topical was *Gora* (1910; *Gora*), the story of an Irish boy orphaned in the Sepoy Mutiny of 1857. He is raised by a Brahman woman and grows up to be a Hindu extremist. When the secret of his true birth is revealed, he realizes that there is no place for him at all in the Hindu scheme of things and resolves to work for an India that will accommodate people of all backgrounds united by their broader identity as Indians.

Similar concerns appear in more subtle forms in *Ghare-Baire* (1916; *The Home and the World*). Portrayed here is the potential conflict between social idealism and political activism. An idealistic husband and his sheltered wife are manipulated by a political organizer for the strongly anti-British Swadeshi movement. Disaster is averted by the husband's exercise in common sense and the wife's eventual understanding that political rhetoric will not necessarily bring her the freedoms for which she yearns as a woman.

Tagore broke new ground by establishing the short story as a genre in Bengali literature, and it is here in particular that one can see his articulation of several highly topical and contemporary themes. Chief among them are the gap between the rural poor and the urbanized elite, the conflict between traditional values and those imported from the West, the problems of Bengali nationalism, and the problems of Bengali women within traditional Hindu society.

An example of this form is "Rajtika" (1898; "We Crown Thee King"). It is the story of two brothers-in-law, each uncertain about how to react to British domination at a time of Indian nationalism. One of the men earns an academic degree in England, where he becomes alienated because of the demeaning way in which the British treat Indians. The other thinks that he can serve "patriotism" by making financial contributions to nationalist political parties and yet seek token honors bestowed by the British. The Indian National Congress itself is portrayed as foolish for believing that membership lists and financial contributions are the same as true patriotism.

More subtle, but nevertheless telling in its criticism, is the 1910 story "Rashmonir Chele" ("Rashmoni's Son"). Kalipada, the son of the title, is raised by an indulgent father who lives on dreams of past status and wealth and a strict mother who has to deal not only with her husband but a large number of relatives from both sides of the marriage. The son, initially critical of his mother, comes to realize that it is she who is holding the family together through her hard work and self-discipline and determines to make his own way in the world by earning a college degree. He sacrifices greatly to this end but is abused at college by the sons of the new elite and finally dies as the result of their mistreatment. In the end it is revealed that, because of a will forged by a dishonest relative, the property controlled by the father is worthless. Examined here are the problems of the old elite being pushed aside by a ruthless new elite catering to colonialist values, the capacity of human beings for exploitation, and the disproportionate burden of fiscal and social responsibility placed on the shoulders of the woman in a Bengali marriage.

Tagore came to worldwide attention with the award of the Nobel Prize in 1913 at a time when many in Western intellectual circles were concerned with the future of Western culture, which to some seemed mired in utilitarianism and materialism and devoid of spiritual values. Many sought spiritual experiences outside of the orthodox institutions. This took many forms, including theosophy, occultism, and the study of Eastern religions. As presented in the West, Tagore's writing, lyrical and resounding with the theme of the love for a universal God, had understandable appeal to these people. William Butler Yeats, the Irish poet and dramatist who was involved in the Celtic revival, was very much taken with Tagore and instrumental in his introduction in Europe and America.

The process of expression for this audience on Tagore's part, and reception on the part of the West, was, however, fraught with problems. First of all, those who gave him literary recognition in the West were largely unaware of the nature of Tagore's literary and linguistic roots. Linked with this unawareness was a widespread belief that Tagore was writing with the specific intention of interpreting his spiritual and cultural traditions for the West. This was a cornerstone of Tagore's vogue in Europe and America and led to his being seen by many as a spiritual leader, which he was not. Where Tagore's verse generally struck readers as having universal appeal in its lyricism and humanism, opinion was less unified about his novels. A minority of Western readers saw them as incisive, insightful portraits of real life in Bengal, while the majority felt that the genre of the novel was too "foreign" for a Bengali whose "natural" form of expression was more diffuse and "spiritual." An additional criticism was that they held little interest or relevance for Western readers beyond their "exotic" setting. Tagore's plays were appreciated primarily as forms of lyrical expression and not as workable drama, because they were rooted in a performance tradition different from that of the West. Critics also observed that Western actors were not convincing in their roles as Indians.

Inextricably linked with these problems was the way in which Tagore's works were rendered into English. Tagore himself knew a fair amount of English but did not have total fluency, and the language of original composition for him was almost always Bengali. Tagore's early editors, such as Yeats, knew no Bengali. Tagore himself was diffident about his abilities in English and also convinced that some of the things he had to say in the original would not be understood by his Western readers and so made omissions as he edited some of his works for publication in English. Several of Tagore's works were translated by others, of course, but neither in Bengal nor in England did Tagore have a competent literary translator. Moreover, he was not always a careful preparer of manuscripts and sometimes withdrew from active participation in the English language versions when he was upset with translator or publisher or distracted by other matters. An extreme result of this situation was that one of his novels was published in the West with no indication that it was a translation and Tagore was castigated for the shortcomings of the English.

The English *Gītāñjali*, for which Tagore won the Nobel Prize, is an example of how his works were transformed when they were rendered into English. The principals in this effort were Tagore himself and Yeats, his first English editor. The English version, for instance, contained only a fraction of the poems in the Bengali *Gītāñjali*, augmented by selections from other works by

Tagore. The prosody of the Bengali original, marked by complex meter, rhyme, and numerous rhetorical devices, became free verse in English. It may be argued that *Gītāñjali* was still a poem, and not prose, but there were cases, too, where Tagore's works changed genres as they changed languages. This is particularly true of the plays, which were sometimes adapted as short stories in English.

One unintended benefit of these English language adaptations of Tagore is that his works became accessible to non-Bengali-speaking Indians and so made Tagore part of the larger Indian literary scene. Some of these readers criticized Tagore for dissipating his energies in the West, but others greatly admired Tagore for literary, social, and political reasons. Some younger Bengali writers found themselves smothered by Tagore's immense presence at home and attacked both the man and his writings, but the overall judgment of critics of Indian literature has been kind. Tagore was, if not a complete writer, nevertheless a gifted one who did much not only to develop modern vernacular Bengali literature but also to encourage the development of similar literatures elsewhere in India as well. Part of Tagore's literary endeavors were linked with educational and political goals. One of Tagore's great contributions was to press for the use of vernacular Bengali in basic education, an endeavor in which he was successful. Tagore's status in the world of Indian nationalism may be judged by the fact that Mahatma Gandhi, who was some years his junior, was among his acquaintances.

Tagore's popularity declined sharply in the West after World War I, partly as the result of the general sense of disillusion that arose in the wake of the war. The present situation is that Tagore's works, to the extent that they are known in the West, have aged badly, partly because the manner of their presentation was so inadequate by modern standards. The tone of much of his verse, while distinguished by imagination and beautiful imagery, sometimes seems maudlin, and other works, acceptable in their time, now seem marred by didacticism or an excessive use of irony. Tagore's image as a spiritualist and guru does not compel belief anymore. Yet there remains among his works available in English a core of stories that are beautifully narrated and distinguished by workable characterizations, lively dialogue, and keen insights not only into particularly Bengali realities but into the human condition in general. There are few good translations of Tagore's work and only a limited number of critical studies of modern Bengali literature. When better translations and more critical works become available, it will be possible to reevaluate his works in a clearer light.

JACQUELINE MUELLER

Selected Bibliography

PRIMARY SOURCES

Tagore, Rabindranath. *The Broken Nest*. Columbia: University of Missouri Press, 1971.

————. *Collected Works.* New York: Gordon Press, n.d.

————. *Gītāñjali (Song-Offerings).* New York: Macmillan, 1971.

————. *The Housewarming, and Other Selected Writings.* Edited by Amiya Chakravarty. Westport, Conn.: Greenwood Press, 1977.

————. *A Tagore Reader.* Edited by Amiya Chakravarty. Boston: Beacon Press, 1966.

SECONDARY SOURCES

Kripalani, Krishna. *Rabindranath Tagore: A Biography.* New York: Grove Press, 1962.

Lago, Mary M. *Rabindranath Tagore.* Boston: Hall, 1976.

SIGRID UNDSET *1928*

Sigrid Undset (1882–1942) was born on May 20, 1882, in Kalundborg, Denmark, the eldest of three daughters. Her mother was Danish, her father, the well-known archeologist Ingvald Undset, came from the Trondheim area in Norway. In 1884 the family moved to Christiania (the Norwegian capital, named Oslo since 1925). Sigrid had a happy childhood, but her father died in 1893. Four years later she took the middle school exam and enrolled in Christiania Commercial College, from which she graduated in 1898. During the next decade she worked as a secretary in an office and helped support her family. Conversations with her father and the atmosphere in her home had instilled in her an interest in history and in literature. While doing work in the office, which was not very much to her liking, she read extensively, which afforded a measure of escape and con-

tinued education. At the same time came the first creative attempts. She sent a historical novel to Gyldendal Publishers in Copenhagen, which was returned with the advice to stick to contemporary issues. She heeded this counsel and was more successful with a novel in diary form, *Fru Marta Oulie* ("Mrs. Marta Oulie"), published by Aschehoug in 1907. In 1908 her first collection of short stories appeared, *Den lykkelige alder* ("The Happy Age") and a year later historical fiction, *Fortellingen om Viga-Ljot og Vigdis* ("Story of Viga-Ljot and Vigdis"). Being thus established as a writer, she received a government grant for study and travel. Via Germany she went to Rome where she stayed until 1910. In Rome she met the Norwegian painter Anders C. Svarstad, with whom she fell in love and whom she married the same year.

After the couple's return to Oslo

Undset became acquainted with fellow writer Nini Roll Anker, who exposed her to the suffrage movement and issues of women's rights. In 1911 her first full-length novel, *Jenny*, a tragic love story, was published. This work soon became both popular and controversial, and Sigrid Undset became an integral part of the Norwegian literary scene. After *Jenny*, Undset conducted various structural and stylistic experiments in her prose works. The themes, however, varied little; she remained concerned with woman's role, the importance of the home as the nucleus of society, and marriage as the focal point.

During the decade from 1910 until 1920 Undset felt an increasing need for religion as a stabilizing factor in her life and also a need for spiritual growth. Her writing evidenced more and more religious overtones. In 1919 she moved with her children to the city of Lillehammer on Lake Mjøsa, where she bought an old farmhouse. In 1924 she converted to Catholicism and had her marriage to Svarstad annulled. She was to spend most of her life in Lillehammer. Here, close to the open-air museum of Maihaugen with its samples of ancient farms and thousands of medieval artifacts, she wrote the two large historical novels *Kristin Lavransdatter* and *Olav Audunssøn* in the twenties, an achievement for which she was awarded the Nobel Prize in 1928, "mainly in view of her splendid descriptions of Scandinavian life in the Middle Ages," as the Swedish Academy stated. In the thirties Undset became engaged in religious

debate and polemic. She published several articles that constituted an apology for Catholicism, in addition to some attacks on Lutheranism, but especially on modern paganism and materialistic doctrines such as communism and fascism. In 1929 and 1930 two novels appeared that outline the story of a man who is received into the Catholic Church— there are clearly autobiographic aspects. She followed these with two that again homed in on marriage problems: *Ida Elisabeth* and *Den trofaste hustru* (*The Faithful Wife*).

Undset was in the middle of writing another historical novel, *Madame Dorthea*, this time set in the eighteenth century, when she had to flee Hitler's invading armies. Via Sweden, the Soviet Union, and Japan she arrived in the United States, where she stayed until 1945. As a refugee in America, she did not find the necessary calm and the creative resources to continue with her work as a writer. Instead she became "mobilized"—as she said of herself—and worked for the Norwegian Information Service, aiding Norwegian resistance at home and the fight against the Nazis in general. She returned to Lillehammer after the war and started writing again, but was plagued by poor health. She died in 1949, survived by a son, Hans. Her other son, Anders, had died fighting the Germans, and a mentally retarded daughter had also died earlier. A collection of some of her articles, as well as her biography of Catherine of Siena, were published posthumously.

Sigrid Undset's first novel, *Fru Marta Oulie* (1907), starts with the ominous line "I have been unfaithful to my husband." This is quite a confession, considering the time it was written in, but outspokenness is Undset's trademark. There is no false romantization, rather a cool, detached presentation. The main character, Marta, is revealed through the skillful use of flashbacks as a student equally interested in women's rights and in happiness in love and marriage. When the dull housewife routine becomes too much to bear, she has an affair but later finds her way back to her husband. Although love means everything to Marta, she lacks guiding principles, is self-centered, and is morally adrift. Her husband finds support and strength in religion; Marta sees this, finds it logical, yet cannot bring herself to accept Christianity.

This first novel of Undset's is symptomatic of the type of prose that she turned out for the ensuing decade. The main theme is woman caught in the struggle to provide for the family, to find happiness in love and marriage, and to grow spiritually by accepting God and the conceptions of contrition and mercy. The latter is the sine que non without which the former pursuits never succeed. Tragedy looms for the woman who is caught in narcissistic attitudes, who does not take a commitment to marriage and family seriously, who is one-sidedly career-bound. The characters typically belong to the educated middle class, i.e., they have backgrounds similar to Undset's.

Her next book, *Den lykkelige alder*, appeared in 1908. It contains sketches and short stories about the married life of young women, similar to the ones she met daily in the office. The characters are fully developed and traced with great psychological sensitivity. *Fortellingen om Viga-Ljot og Vigdis* (1909; translated into English as *Gunnar's Daughter*), is her first attempt at working with historical material. It is a somewhat grim medieval romance, set in the eleventh century. Ljot violates Vigdis and is cursed by her. She wants to use her son by Ljot to kill him. The plan works and tragedy unfolds, although both Ljot and Vigdis know that they really love each other. The work tries to imitate the spirit and style of the saga, yet fails. The emotions expressed and the subjectivity, the obvious woman's point of view, all are alien to the saga.

Without any doubt, the most successful and readable book Undset produced during the first thirteen years of her authorship was *Jenny* (1911). Jenny, the main character, is a young, gifted artist, self-assured, someone who has learned to run her own life and knows how to survive economically. She believes in love, yet wants to wait until the right man comes along, so that she can give herself passionately and without holding back. While developing her artistic skills in Rome, living with her insecure, fickle girl-friend, Francesca, she meets Helge, a young Norwegian archeologist. They are attracted to each other and drift into a relationship. But back in Oslo, it becomes obvious that she does not really love Helge and they break up. It is difficult for Jenny to start working again; she feels emotionally unbalanced and very much alone. At that point Gert, Helge's father, steps forward and offers support and understanding. They fall in love and soon Jenny is expecting his child. She leaves Norway and struggles to separate from Gert because she understands that he cannot be her future either. The child is born and dies soon afterward. Jenny arrives in Rome completely burnt out and emotionally drained. Her creative spirit is gone. At that point Gunnar, an old friend, offers his love, but Jenny cannot respond. When Helge also appears on the scene, the situation becomes too much for her and she commits suicide in a strangely unreflective manner.

The message is clear: Woman must assert herself; she has an innate right to love and happiness. The career cannot be a substitute for the fulfillment and the happiness encountered in love. A. H. Winsnes (1953) points out that Jenny is intensely religious, longing to serve someone she sets higher than herself, but she does not believe in God. Her ideal of purity is no camouflaged dread of sex; it springs from her unconscious religious feelings. Her tragedy is that she does not find this missing piece of the puzzle. In the end she is not as strong as she thought she was, and when offered love, has nothing to return. The strong points of the novel are the characterization techniques and the description of background and setting. Darkly haunting accounts of the oppressive middle-class society in Oslo alternate with bright and lyrical passages where Rome and its surroundings are pictured. The weak points are that the novel frequently borders on the melodramatic, and the nature of Jenny's relationship to Gert is somewhat bewildering. And Vinde (1930) talks of a "congenital weakness" that all of Undset's novels exhibit: always the same point of observation, namely, her inner self. Thus the perspective is falsified. Her portraits are not realistically exact because only the dark side of reality is being reproduced. There is little humor in her work.

There are four more books, more or less in the same vein as *Jenny*: *Fattige skjebner* (1912; "Poor Fortunes"), is a collection of short stories. The novel *Vaaren* (1914; "Spring"), is a love story too but this time an idyll—a young, idealistic couple after a difficult period of adjustment are able to save their marriage because they become less self-centered. Marriage for Undset is a binding arrangement that requires limitless loyalty and dedication. It is devoid of romantic notions and wild passion. The third book, *Splinten av troldspeilet* (1917; "Images in a Mirror"), contains two short stories, once more about young women who seek pleasure and gratification in marriage and are not willing to make sacrifices. Finally, another collection of short stories, *De kloge jomfruer* ("The Wise Virgins"), appeared in 1918.

In 1871 the critic Georg Brandes demanded that literature show its vitality by "submitting problems to debate." In other words, realism and contemporary life were called for.

Undset largely follows suit and puts herself in the mainstream of Scandinavian realism. Yet she raises social and religious issues only in a very roundabout way. It is her basic belief that each human being is responsible for his own fate, but that he can master this fate successfully only with Divine help.

In the twenties Undset published her great novels on the Middle Ages in Scandinavia. These novels were an instant success, far more so than the earlier works, and were translated into many languages. The first one is the trilogy about *Kristin Lavransdatter*, set in the first half of the fourteenth century. The first part, *Kransen* (*The Bridal Wreath*), was published in 1920. Kristin grows up at Jørundgaard in Gudbrandsdal. She has a happy youth. At fifteen she is betrothed to Simon, son of Andres Gudmundssøn. While staying at Nonneseter Monastery in Oslo, she meets Erlend Nikulaussøn at the fair and falls in love with him. Erlend already has a mistress and children, but neither Kristin nor Erlend have much regard for decency and proper behavior. Simon confronts them in Oslo, but wants to spare her father's feelings. Kristin is blinded by passion, and in the end, the marriage of Kristin and Erlend is brought about with much deception. The wedding is splendid, but there is no triumph of love. Erlend's mistress commits suicide, and Kristin is left with the gnawing knowledge that she has sinned against her father and God. In the second volume, *Husfrue* (1921; *The Mistress of Husaby*), Kristin is a good manager of Erlend's estate at Husaby. Erlend is

carefree, his world consists of affairs of state and arms. After the birth of their first child, Kristin makes a pilgrimage to Nidaros (Trondheim) to atone; she feels true contrition. Kristin gives birth to six more children over the years, but tensions build up because Kristin lacks gentleness and tolerance. Erlend is suddenly imprisoned and charged with treason. Simon intercedes; Erlend is released but forfeits Husaby. In the third part, *Korset* (1922; *The Cross*), the family moves back to Jørundgaard. Erlend, who has no friends, roams the woods with his sons. Again the tensions build up, and Erlend moves to an outlying farm. Kristin follows him; an attempt at reconciliation fails. Back home, Kristin gives birth to the eighth child, and people accuse her of infidelity with a servant. Erlend returns to protect Kristin but is himself killed by an angry mob. After his death Kristin becomes more peaceful; when she sees that Jørundgaard is in her son's good hands, she makes a second pilgrimage to Nidaros and joins a convent there. In 1349 the Black Death sweeps through the country. Kristin looks after the victims, but finally succumbs herself.

Undset researched the material for this novel extremely well, yet what she produced is not really a historical novel. The historical framework, and many historical facts and figures are there, but all they provide is a backdrop and framework for the action. On the other hand, the cultural information brought to life yields a picture of amazing depth and breadth. The themes from Undset's earlier novels are still with us: love, marriage, loyalty, sin, contrition, and the like. But there are no liberals now, no freethinkers; these are medieval men and women who have no doubt about God, about right and wrong, or about the steps they must take to put their house in order. It takes Kristin an entire lifetime to turn away from selfishness, passion, and other sinful ways, to show true remorse and the will to sacrifice everything. Undset chose the fourteenth century probably because it was then that Norway had become Christian and thus part of Europe. People were Christians, yet encumbered by remnants of paganism (e.g., the lust for revenge). She used the tension that results from conflict between God's will and the self-will of man. The time was a period of transition, and people were turning *toward* Christianity—difficult as it was—and not *away* from it, as often is the case in the twentieth century.

Her second large novel about the Middle Ages is *Olav Audunssøn i Hestviken* (1925; *The Master of Hestviken*) and its second part, *Olav Audunssøn og hans børn* ("Olav Audunssøn and His Children"). The action takes place a generation earlier than in *Kristin Lavransdatter*; the protagonist this time is male. Olav commits two basic sins: He sleeps with the girl betrothed to him before the wedding, and later he kills his wife's seducer clandestinely. Again Undset produced a novel about marriage, loyalty, sin, and contrition. Olav, like Kristin, also needs his entire life in order to save himself. Both figures are not so much the product of their age and

milieu; rather they reveal, like the figures in all other Undset novels, the basic struggle between external, material elements and internal, spiritual ones. The historicity does not matter because fiction has a justifiable life of its own.

After receiving the Nobel Prize in 1928, Undset returned to the contemporary mode of novel writing. In 1929 she published the novel *Gymnadenia* (*The Wild Orchid*) and the following year *Den brennende busk* (*The Burning Bush*). Both books deal with the conversion of one Paul Selmer to Catholicism. There is much Catholic propaganda manifest here as well as attempts at satire; the Protestant clergy and the liberal theologians come under attack. Whereas the "medieval" novels were theologically Augustinian in nature, the "contemporary" ones tend to be Thomist. Selmer needs the Catholic Church as catalyst without which spiritual development and fulfillment would be impossible. These novels are not among Undset's better works; at best, one might consider them works of religious edification, frequently tedious and doctrinaire.

In 1932 Undset published *Ida Elisabeth*, a realistic treatment of the problem of marriage and loyalty, without too many religious overtones this time, but the role that religious impulse plays in human relationships is the central topic in *Den trofaste hustru* (1936; *The Faithful Wife*). In 1939 Undset delved one last time into history and started work on the novel *Madame Dorthea*, which remained uncompleted because of her flight from

Norway at the onset of the German occupation. The novel is set in the Age of Enlightenment in the eighteenth century. The action is limited to half a year. While the plot seems fairly thin, the individual characters show promise. Undset's creative life, unfortunately, was shortened considerably by the war.

During her lifetime and afterward Undset has been extremely popular, both at home in Scandinavia and abroad. Her two "medieval" novels, in particular, have received much acclaim. Rarely has cultural history been presented with so much vivid detail. And not many writers in this century have had such a secure grip on the psyche of their characters or have demonstrated such sensitivity to and so much insight into internal struggles of the human soul. Sadly, Undset's own life exemplified her writing, or vice versa. Human existence appears dreary and cumbersome; there is little light and little joy. Suffering is required because through suffering we gain strength and become part of a divine system.

F<small>RITZ</small> H. K<small>ÖNIG</small>

Selected Bibliography

PRIMARY SOURCES

Undset, Sigrid. *The Burning Bush.* Translated by Arthur G. Chater. New York: Knopf, 1932.

———. *The Faithful Wife.* Translated by Arthur G. Chater. New York: Knopf, 1937.

———. *Ida Elisabeth.* Translated by Arthur Chater. New York: Knopf, 1933.

———. *Jenny.* Translated by W. Emmë. New York: Knopf, 1921.

———. *Kristin Lavransdatter. The Bridal Wreath.* Translated by Charles Archer and J. S. Scott. New York: Knopf, 1923.

———. *Kristin Lavransdatter. The Mistress of Husaby.* Translated by Charles Archer. New York: Knopf, 1925.

———. *Kristin Lavransdatter. The Cross.* Translated by Charles Archer. New York: Knopf, 1927.

———. *Madame Dorthea.* Translated by Arthur G. Chater. New York: Knopf, 1940.

———. *The Master of Hestviken.* I. *The Axe*; II. *The Snake Pit*; III. *In the Wilderness*; IV. *The Son Avenger.* Translated by Arthur Chater. New York: Knopf, 1934.

———. *The Wild Orchid.* Translated by Arthur G. Chater. New York: Knopf, 1931.

SECONDARY SOURCES

Bayerschmidt, Carl F. *Sigrid Undset.* New York: Twayne, 1970.

Vinde, Victor. *Sigrid Undset, A Nordic Moralist.* Seattle: University of Washington Chapbooks, No. 45, 1930.

Winsnes, A. H. *Sigrid Undset, A Study in Christian Realism.* Translated by P. G. Foote. New York: Sheed & Ward, 1953.

PATRICK WHITE *1973*

Patrick Victor Martindale White (1912—) was born in London, on May 28, 1912, while his wealthy Australian parents were traveling abroad. The couple returned shortly thereafter to their home in Sydney, where young White grew up against the landscape of a country that would become the background for all but one of his eleven novels. Cited by the Swedish Academy "for an epic and psychological art which has introduced a new continent into literature," he was awarded the Nobel Prize in literature in 1973—a distinction that defied those Australian critics who had once condemned his work as that of an intellectual elitist, alien to the mind and manners of his countrymen.

Ironically, White's identity as an Australian writer was forged directly out of a sense of cultural alienation that separated his work from a more overtly indigenous literature peopled by bushmen, aborigines, mates, and squatters. The ambiguities of White's cultural heritage imposed a certain expatriotism. Born into the Australian gentry, he was a member of an aristocratic minority strongly rooted in an imperialistic British tradition. White's English birthright and Australian childhood established an early pattern of divided national alliance, and he was rejected equally by his Australian compatriots for his English manners and by his British peers for his colonial status.

At age thirte, White returned to England to attend public school at Cheltenham College. After graduating from Cheltenham, he went back to Australia to become a jackaroo—a sort of gentleman apprentice—on a sheep farm. Estranged from his countrymen by his English accent and education, White also felt a growing alienation from his parents. His determination to become a writer met with their strong disapproval, and his search for personal identity was further complicated by a growing awareness of his homosexuality.

White once more returned to England to enroll at Cambridge University, entering King's College to read modern languages. After completing the B.A. degree in 1935, he decided to take up lodgings in London and now began to write in earnest. He had already published two slim volumes of verse, *Thirteen Poems* in 1930 and *The Ploughman and Other Poems* in 1935, neither of which had stirred much enthusiastic critical response. From 1933 to 1940 he experimented with a number of literary forms, writing plays, short stories, and reviews. He also set to work on his first novel.

In London during the prewar years, White discovered an unorthodox artistic elite—painters, writers, musicians—who rejected a traditional rigid morality and encouraged him to develop an independent sense of himself and his art. The political situation in Germany and Spain seemed distant, and

White took little interest in the increasing tensions abroad. When Britain entered the war in 1939, he heard the news while traveling in the United States, finalizing the sale of his first novel, *Happy Valley*, to Viking Press. He returned to London only to discover what he described as a "cynical, uneventful, dispiriting phase of life" in the wartime city. His optimism about his writing career tempered by the historical threat of world war, White was now at work on his second novel, *The Living and the Dead*, a "wretched book" that he later admitted hating to write.

Seeking temporary refuge from the oppressive London environment, White fled to the United States, where he became involved in a short-lived relationship with a New York physician. When he returned to England a year later, he was quickly drafted into the Royal Air Force as an intelligence officer, beginning a four-year stint in the Middle East. While on leave in Alexandria during an assignment to Egypt, White met Manoly Lascaris, a "small Greek of immense moral strength," who was to become his lifelong lover and companion following the war. In his later autobiographical "self-portrait" entitled *Flaws in the Glass* (1981), White would credit Lascaris with giving "direction and meaning to what up till now had been a pointless and often desperate existence."

Meanwhile, White's first two novels had attracted mixed critical reviews. *Happy Valley* was published in England in 1939 and in the United States in 1940; *The Living*

and the Dead appeared in 1941. Located within a space of Australian landscape stretching "more or less from Moorang to Kambala," *Happy Valley* interweaves the provincial lives of its small-minded residents—an introspective physician, a villainous hired hand, a self-indulgent schoolteacher, a spinster piano teacher, an oversensitive adolescent—through a somewhat contrived series of plot maneuvers ranging from adultery to murder. Although the novel met with a generally enthusiastic public response and was awarded the Australian Literary Society Gold Medal in 1941, White calls *Happy Valley* his "best forgotten novel." Certainly it lacks the unified vision, compelling psychological depth, and creative stylistic innovation of his later work. Indeed, the book was never reprinted and is now studied largely within the context of White's mature prose fiction.

The Living and the Dead offers a sharp contrast to *Happy Valley*. It is decidedly more complex in conception and style, shifting beyond circumscribed Australian boundaries to "the confused sea that was anybody's London." White's second novel is the product of the oppressive prewar years he spent in London. The apparent failure of British cultural life that the young author experienced during this period is evident in his protagonist, Elyot Standish, a literary critic and London intellectual who finds himself paralyzed by what he perceives as the ultimate futility of human possibility. Most critics agreed that *The Living and the Dead* offered a bitter statement, yet recognized the potential talent of the author beginning to assume a mature artistic style and philosophy.

It would be seven years until White's next novel was published. After the war, Lascaris offered to relocate to Australia with him, and White returned "home" to the Australian landscape he loved. He set up household in Castle Hill outside Sydney, waiting for Lascaris to join him, sensitively aware that his British sensibility, his profession as a writer, and his relationship with another man would all mark him as an outsider in his native land. During this period of mixed hope and anxiety, White was working on *The Aunt's Story*, admittedly his favorite novel.

Published in 1948, *The Aunt's Story* traces the psychological disintegration of Theodora Goodman, the spinster aunt of the tale, exploring the contradictory relationship between sanity and the reality of human experience. The novel was received coolly by Australian critics, who were reluctant to admit White to the closed ranks of the country's literary greats—nationalist authors like Joseph Furphy, Kylie Tenant, Eleanor Dark, and Henry Lawson, who wrote about Australia's true "out back." While Theodora is ostensibly an Australian protagonist, the story's geographical focus shifts to Europe and concludes somewhere in the American Midwest. In addition, the novel was attacked for its obscure intellectualism and fractured syntax, a mode of psychological and metaphoric exploration that White was to develop fully in his later works.

White's keen disappointment over the negative critical response to *The Aunt's Tale* was exacerbated by his ill health, and it was another seven years before his next novel appeared. He set to work on *The Tree of Man* against remittent asthmatic attacks, often sitting up late at night to write when he could not lie down because of his respiratory disease. White's fourth novel was to be his version of the Australian epic. It is, most simply, the story of an Australian pioneer named Stan Parker and his wife and family, of one man's battle against the wilderness of a continent and against the effacement of history.

But White's themes are more humanistic than nationalistic in *The Tree of Man*. Despite the apparent simplicity of his subject and approach—the novel opens with Stan's young efforts to clear a space in the untamed landscape and ends with his death as an old man—White's attempt in this novel was "to discover the extraordinary behind the ordinary, the mystery and the poetry which alone could make bearable the lives of such people." The quotidian reality of daily life, of history itself, becomes the vehicle for exploring an inner human reality illuminated by spiritual insight.

First published in the United States in 1955, *The Tree of Man* won significant public acclaim and was awarded the Australian Literary Society Gold Medal two years later. But White was suspicious of such easy acceptance, doubting the depth of understanding of his popular reading audience. He was already at work on his next novel, once more pursuing his artistic themes in the guise of Australian history. Like *The Tree of Man*, *Voss* (1957) is White's own version of historical reality. Rooted in fact, the novel is a fictional reinterpretation of the adventures of Ludwig Leichhardt, a German explorer who set off on a failed mission to reach the Australian interior in the 1840s. But again, White's work reaches beyond the scope of simple historical fiction to sound the depths of the human soul. Material reality is subsumed by a more urgent apperception of some greater truth, dramatized in the mysterious spiritual empathy between Voss and Laura Trevelyan that negates the spatial and temporal constructs of historical action.

Voss was immediately recognized as a remarkable if difficult work of art, receiving the Miles Franklin Award in 1958 and the W. H. Smith & Son literary award in 1959. Not surprisingly, the book confused many readers, who tended to judge it by the conventions of more traditional historical romances. In *Voss*, however, White was forging his own genre in "a struggle to create completely fresh forms out of the rocks and sticks of words."

In *Riders in the Chariot* (1961) and *The Solid Mandala* (1966), White continued to develop the contradictions he perceived between spiritual apprehension and logical experience, between visionary insight and ordinary reality, between the infinite truths of human existence and the boundaries of time and space. These two novels were separated by White's relocation with Lascaris to an affluent part of Syd-

ney known as Centennial Park. Although White was apprehensive about the move after almost twenty productive years at "Dogwoods," their small suburban farm in Castle Hill, the continuity of vision in these two novels is evidence of a successful artistic rerooting.

In *Riders in the Chariot*, White uses the chariot as a symbol for a mode of interior understanding beyond the processes of cognitive reasoning and sense perception. His "riders" are a motley group—an aging spinster, a common working woman, a Jewish intellectual, an aborigine painter—who share a special grace derived from no common principle of conventional morality. These four seers share a transcendental recognition that is sharply at odds with the dull, uninspired, and often mean circumstances of their existence. The novel is enigmatic and inconclusive, suggesting rather than moralizing, and remains one of White's most difficult and controversial works.

The Solid Mandala is less problematic because it is more narrowly focused. White's central metaphor is the mandala, a geometric square-within-a-circle, symbolic of a universal creative principle variously identified as God, infinity, or truth. The novel explores the relationship between twin brothers, Waldo and Arthur Brown, and their individual psychic-spiritual understanding of reality. Again, White denies any correlation between spiritual sensitivity and logical perception, endowing the half-witted Arthur with superior visionary insight. Interpretations of *The Solid Mandala* have been various. White himself explains the characters of Arthur and Waldo as "my two halves," suggesting the good-evil, spiritual-rational duality within each individual.

From the spiritually illuminated, White turned to the morally flawed in his next novels, *The Vivisector* (1970) and *The Eye of the Storm* (1973). Unlike his visionary riders or the dim-witted but morally sensitive Arthur, Hurtle Duffield and Elizabeth Hunter, the respective protagonists of these works, demonstrate the mean and egotistic perversities of the human spirit. Nevertheless, there is a strange hint of grace available even in their limited capacities. The paralyzed artist Hurtle, "stroked by God," begins his final great painting in a frenzied creative outburst before collapsing in death. The selfish and petty old widow Mrs. Hunter, awaiting death in an invalid state of physical and spiritual decay, relives a mysterious religious moment experienced years before during the passing calm at the heart of a tropical storm. If they ultimately fail to redeem themselves, White seems to say, there is still the hint of spiritual possibility in these flawed human souls.

When White was announced for the Nobel Prize in 1973, many reacted with surprise. White's work was contrary to the spirit of the prize, claimed some critics, noting the original provision of Nobel's will that the award be made for the most distinguished literary work of an idealistic tendency. That White's work could be labeled "idealistic" was debatable. *The Vivisector*, published just three years prior, was

openly pornographic and questionably blasphemous; and in *The Eye of the Storm*, published the same year as the award, White broaches such topics as incest, adultery, hypocrisy, alienation, decay, and death through a caustic wit more irreverent than redemptive. Despite these objections, most readers recognize in White's work a therapeutic effort to identify the spiritual potential of human experience.

White's post-Nobel output includes two major novels and a long autobiographical work entitled *Flaws in the Glass: A Self-Portrait* (1981). *A Fringe of Leaves* (1976), like *Voss*, is White's own brand of historical fiction. The novel is based on the legend of one Eliza Fraser, who was shipwrecked off Australia's Great Barrier Reef in 1836 and escaped to live with a tribe of aborigines. White uses this bare historical sketch to create a probing psychological study of the conflict between civilized aesthetic and primitive will in the character of Ellen Roxburgh. In *The Twyborn Affair* (1979), White examines the theme of self-identity through the confused physiological and psychological states of a male-female protagonist variously named Eudoxia-Eddie-Eadith. The novel is difficult and complex, marked by a bitterly ironic humor and sense of cosmic indifference uncharacteristic of White.

Though most commonly recognized for his novels, White has also experimented with other literary forms, most notably the drama. In the early 1960s a series of his plays was produced in Adelaide with moderate success and later collected under the published title *Four Plays* (1965). A fifth play, *Big Toys*, was produced in Sydney in 1977. Generally dismissed as experimental, White's dramas remain controversial. His two collections of short stories, *The Burnt Ones* (1964) and *The Cockatoos* (1975), were generally well received, but the shorter genre curtails the ponderous deliberation of White at his best—in his novels.

Variously labeled a prophet, a mystic, a blasphemer, Patrick White offers a rich and complex vision of the human state. If there is a common thesis to be found in his work, it might best be illustrated by the epigraph from *The Living and the Dead*, perhaps his bleakest novel. From the eighteenth-century French philosopher Helvétius, White cites "les principes simples, au développement desquels sont attachés l'ordre et le bonheur du monde moral" —"through our absurd and fumbling errors in life, we may somehow chance to uncover those simple principles which underlie the order and good fortune of a moral world."

DOREEN L. BUCHMAN

Selected Bibliography

PRIMARY SOURCES

White, Patrick. *The Aunt's Story*. New York: Viking Press, 1948.

———. *The Cockatoos*. New York: Viking Press, 1974.

———. *The Eye of the Storm*. New York: Viking Press, 1973.

———. *Flaws in the Glass: A Self-Portrait*. New York: Viking Press, 1981.

———. *Happy Valley*. New York: Viking Press, 1940.

———. *The Living and the Dead*. New York: Viking Press, 1941.

———. *Riders in the Chariot*. New York: Viking Press, 1961.

———. *The Solid Mandala*. New York: Viking Press, 1966.

———. *The Tree of Man*. New York: Viking Press, 1955.

———. *The Twyborn Affair*. New York: Viking Press, 1980.

———. *The Vivisector*. New York: Viking Press, 1970.

———. *Voss*. New York: Viking Press, 1957.

SECONDARY SOURCES

Beatson, Peter. *The Eye in the Mandala. Patrick White: A Vision of Man and God*. London: Paul Elek, 1976.

Colmer, John. *Contemporary Writers: Patrick White*. London: Methuen, 1984.

Kiernan, Brian. *Patrick White*. New York: St. Martin's Press, 1980.

Walsh, William. *Patrick White's Fiction*. London: George Allen & Unwin, 1977.

Weigel, John. *Patrick White*. Boston: Twayne, 1983.

WILLIAM BUTLER YEATS 1923

A few months after he heard that he had been awarded the 1923 Nobel Prize in literature Yeats (1865–1939) wrote, "Of course I know quite well that this honour is not given to me as an individual but as a representative of a literary movement and of a nation, and I am glad to have it so." Since self-effacement and exaggerated humility were not among Yeats's character flaws, it is likely that his claim is, at least in part, correct. The prize came just over a year after the establishment of the Irish Free State government, in which Yeats had been appointed to a six-year term as senator, and only months after the end of the Irish Civil War. The award was presented as much to the "sixty-year-old smiling public man" (as Yeats referred to himself a few years later in "Among School Children") as it was to Ireland's best-known poet. Whatever the political motivations of the Nobel Committee, the award certainly did not mark the zenith of Yeats's literary achievement. Renown, financial security, lecture circuits, and university sinecures often lead recipients away from the very talents and accomplishments recognized by the Nobel Prize, but Yeats's finest work came in the fifteen years following the award.

In fact, his constant development of new poetic techniques, the uneasy interaction between his public image and his private concerns, and the conflict between his Anglo-Irish "ascendancy" roots and his interest in and identification with Irish peasant lore and the Celtic past are all hallmarks of his long career as poet, playwright, theater manager, essayist, and political activist. From the publication of a few lyric poems in 1885 when he was twenty years old to the completion of the play *Death of Cuchulain* in 1939 just before he died, Yeats built a literary reputation second to none in scope, critical acclaim, and influence on other writers.

After a brief attempt to follow his father's example and become a painter, Yeats turned to writing verse and verse drama while supporting himself with compilations of folklore, with editorial projects such as his and Edwin Ellis's *Works of William Blake*, and with short stories and essays on Irish literature and folklore that he churned out for English periodicals. Though he was born in Dublin and spent his summers with grandparents in Sligo, much of his early life was spent in London. As a result, he was as involved with English "symbolists," "aesthetes," and "decadents" as he was with the writers of the "Irish revival" or "Celtic Renaissance." His first book of poetry, *The Wanderings of Oisin and Other Poems* (1889), won praise from such established writers as William Morris and Oscar Wilde, while his membership in the Rhymers' Club brought him in contact with Arthur Symons and so with French literature and critical theory. These varied influences, together with his ill-fated infatuation with the Irish nationalist and actress Maud Gonne, led to plays such as *The Countess Kathleen* (1892), *The Land of Heart's Desire* (1894), *The Shadowy Waters* (begun 1894), *Diarmuid and Grania* (1901, in collaboration with George Moore), and *Cathleen ni Houlihan* (1902); collections of essays and short stories, including *John Sherman* (1891), *The Celtic Twilight* (1893), and *The Secret Rose* (1897); his first collected *Poems* (1895), and the exquisite culmination of his early work, *The Wind Among the Reeds* (1899).

This early work established Yeats as an heir to Pre-Raphaelite ornamentation, Pateresque "bejeweled" language, Baudelaire-like sadness, and nineteenth-century romantic "Celticism." Late in life Yeats looked back on his career in the poem "Coole Park and Ballylee, 1931," concluding that "we were the last romantics—chose for theme/ Traditional sanctity and loveliness." Along with his beautiful though dreamy, somewhat vague, symbol-laden language, Yeats was experimenting with a variety of metrical forms, from the deceivingly simple ballad stanzas of "The Cap and Bells" and "The Host of the Air" to what he called the long, "wavering, meditative, organic" hexameters of "He Bids His Beloved Be at Peace" or "The Lover Tells of the Rose in His Heart." The rich ambiguities of his poetic style echoed the ambiguity of his themes. Although his Irish nationalism was nostalgic and dreamy rather than active and clear-sighted, his *Cathleen ni Houlihan* inspired many of the young men who would later give their lives in the 1916

Easter Uprising. In the last year of his life Yeats commented on the practical power of emotion-filled art, asking himself and his readers, "Did that play of mine send out/ Certain men the English shot?"

During the first decade of the new century Yeats's life and work became sharper, more focused, less ornate, more intellectual—in short, more "modern." This was, in part, the result of his involvement, along with Lady Gregory and John Synge, in the Abbey Theatre and what Yeats called "theatre business, management of men." Yeats plunged into the day-to-day management of a theater and a new theatrical movement, he wrote essays outlining his dramatic theory, he defended Synge and others against the philistines in Ireland, and he developed his own reputation as dramatist with *The Pot of Broth* (1904), *The King's Threshold* (1904), *On Baile's Strand* (1904), *Deirdre* (1907), *The Unicorn from the Stars* (1908), *The Green Helmet* (1910), and a revision of *The Shadowy Waters* (1911)—all plays based on Irish folklore and mythology. Later, his association with Ezra Pound (who acted as Yeats's literary secretary in 1913) and his discovery, partly through Pound's translations, of the *Noh* plays of Japan, led to further theatrical experimentation, most notably the plays *At the Hawk's Well* (1917), *The Only Jealousy of Emer* (1919), *The Dreaming of the Bones* (1919), *Calvary* (1920), and *The Player Queen* (1922). Musical instruments, symbolic dances, masks, the absence of elaborate sets all reflect Yeats's belief in the ritual roots of drama, the primacy of language over action, and his abhorrence of "realism" and "naturalism" on stage.

By 1914 Ezra Pound claimed that he was assailed with questions such as "Will Mr. Yeats do anything more?" "Is Yeats in the [imagist] movement?" "How *can* the chap go on writing this sort of thing?" Pound's answer is a review of Yeats's 1914 collection of poems entitled *Responsibilities* in which he calls Yeats "the best poet in England" and demonstrates that Yeats has forged a new style and made himself into a thoroughly modern poet. These poems emerge from the Celtic twilight to examine Ireland and himself in the cold, hard light of the twentieth century, contrasting the idealism and martyrdoms of Ireland's past with "the old Paudeen[s]," the money-hungry and hypocritical middle class. The tone of the poems in *Responsibilities* can be exemplified by the sardonic first lines of "September 1913":

What need you, being come to sense,
But fumble in a greasy till
And add the halfpence to the pence
And prayer to shivering prayer, until
You have dried the marrow from the
    bone?

The uncompromising vision, the natural speech rhythms, the enjambed lines, and the long unanswerable question are all common to the poetry in this and later volumes. In his work, Yeats demonstrated why he was able to remain a major voice in poetry from the turn of the century until the eve of World War II—his style constantly changed and evolved.

In 1917, at the age of fifty-two, Yeats made a change in lifestyle that was to be reflected in his work; after pursuing Maud Gonne (and then her daughter Iseult) for over twenty years, he married George Hyde-Lees. Shortly before his marriage, he lamented the vanishing of his early visions and inspiration symbolized by "the dark leopards of the moon"; he concluded his "Lines Written in Dejection" with "And now that I have come to fifty years/ I must endure the timid sun." This and other poems in *The Wild Swans at Coole* (1919) are intensely personal, reflective, and retrospective. In his brilliant elegy for Major Robert Gregory, his friend and patron's son who was killed fighting for the British in World War I, he used the occasion of settling in to home and marriage to call to mind dead companions of his youth and to come to terms with "that discourtesy of death." Yeats perfected a conversational style counterpointing traditional meters and natural speech rhythms that allowed him to castigate pedantic "scholars" in an apt if unflattering synecdoche, "Bald heads forgetful of their sins"; to strive toward poems "maybe as cold/ And passionate as the dawn"; and to create complex philosophical dialogues between Hic and Ille, Michael Robartes and Aherne, and a Hunchback and a Saint—all manifestations of Yeats's own inner conflicts.

The volumes *Michael Robartes and the Dancer* (1921) and *The Tower* (1928) take these ideas and techniques further while demonstrating Yeats's political reactions to the Easter Uprising, the chaos of World War I and the Bolshevik Revolution, and the Irish Civil War. Although Yeats was ambivalent in his assessment of the Easter martyrs who were "bewildered" by an "excess of love," he concluded "Easter 1916" with a reference to the martyrs that became another rallying call for Irish nationalists; these men,

Now and in time to be,
Wherever green is worn,
Are changed, changed utterly:
A terrible beauty is born.

In "A Prayer for My Daughter," Yeats looked beyond a world in a chaos of war to a state of mind in which "all hatred driven hence,/ The soul recovers radical innocence/ And learns at last that it is self-delighting,/ Self-appeasing, self-affrighting. . . ."

In the years after he won the Nobel Prize, Yeats published his most accomplished poetry in *The Tower* (1928), *The Winding Stair and Other Poems* (1933), *New Poems* (1938), and a collection editors called *Last Poems and Two Plays* (1939). The plays of the late 1920s and 1930s—including *The Cat and the Moon* (1926), *The Resurrection* (1931), *The Words Upon the Window-Pane* (1934), *A Full Moon in March* (1935), *The King of the Great Clock Tower* (1935), *The Herne's Egg* (1938), *Purgatory* (1939), and *The Death of Cuchulain* (1939)—established him as a major force in modern drama. In addition, Yeats continued to give public lectures, do radio shows for the BBC, and write critical and philosophical prose, most notably *A Vision* (1925, 1937)—his study of history, personality, and the occult.

The last twelve years of his life, though plagued by serious illnesses, were among his most productive and were dominated by a philosophy that he describes in a letter to his lifelong friend Olivia Shakespear, "How strange is the subconscious gaiety that leaps up before danger or difficulty." In the late poem "Lapis Lazuli" he conveys this thought poetically when he examines the reactions of actors and audience to Shakespeare's great tragic figures; beneath Hamlet's rambling and Lear's raging is "gaiety transfiguring all that dread." This concentration on "tragic joy" and the process of history and time—symbolized for Yeats by great turning "gyres" or spirals—is indicative of the personal and artistic courage that was, perhaps, Yeats's dominant character trait. This included a deeply religious and philosophical world view that was positive without the bathos or pathos of some established world views. Yeats created the character "Crazy Jane" to express his conviction that "'Fair and foul are near of kin,/ And fair needs foul. . . .'" and to shock pusillanimous moralists with Crazy Jane's view of love:

'A woman can be proud and stiff
When on love intent;
But Love has pitched his mansion in
The place of excrement;
For nothing can be sole or whole
That has not been rent.'

For Yeats "truth" could only be expressed as a dialectic process, as the convergence of opposites: "Between extremities/ Man runs his course."

Yeats died in France on January 28, 1939, and was buried in Roquebrune. In September 1948 his body was returned to Ireland and buried with full honors in Drumcliff churchyard in County Sligo in accordance with Yeats's own poetic testament: "Under bare Ben Bulben's head/ In Drumcliff churchyard Yeats is laid." The final poems of Yeats's life are among his most courageous and his most technically perfected. There is evidence that in his final weeks he drew up a list stating the order in which his last poems should be arranged (Finneran, 676). According to this list "Under Ben Bulben," which ends with his famous enigmatic epitaph:

Cast a cold eye
On life, on death.
Horseman, pass by!

would begin the volume rather than end it. In this way his final poetic testament seems to speak from beyond the grave, reinforcing the idea that life, history, and time are part of a process inexorably kept in motion by the interaction of primary and antithetical forces, and life and death are antipodes worth only a passing glance. It was as though Yeats anticipated what W. H. Auden would write as elegy: "The death of the poet was kept from his poems." Yeats continues to be a major influence on poets and playwrights in Ireland, England, and throughout the world.

STEVEN D. PUTZEL

Selected Bibliography

PRIMARY SOURCES
Yeats, William Butler. *The Autobiography of William Butler Yeats.* New York: Macmillan, 1965.

———. *The Collected Plays of W. B. Yeats.* New York: Macmillan, 1952.

———. *Essays and Introductions.* New York: Macmillan, 1961.

———. *Explorations.* New York: Macmillan, 1962.

———, ed. *Fairy and Folk Tales of Ireland.* Gerrards Cross, Buckinghamshire: Colin Smythe, 1976.

———. *Mythologies.* New York: Macmillan, 1959.

———. *The Poems of W. B. Yeats.* Edited by Richard Finneran. New York: Macmillan, 1983.

———. *A Vision.* New York: Macmillan, 1965.

SECONDARY SOURCES
Ellmann, Richard. *Yeats: The Man and the Masks.* New York: Oxford University Press, 1948; rev. ed. 1979.

Finneran, Richard, ed. *Yeats: An Annual of Critical and Textual Studies.* Ithaca, N.Y.: Cornell University Press, an annual.

Henn, Thomas R. *The Lonely Tower: Studies in the Poetry of W. B. Yeats.* London: Methuen, 1950.

Orr, Leonard, ed. *Yeats and Postmodernism.* Syracuse, N.Y.: Syracuse University Press, 1990.

Parkinson, Thomas F. *W. B. Yeats, Self-Critic: A Study of His Early Verse, and the Later Poetry.* Berkeley: University of California Press, 1971.

Putzel, Steven D. *Reconstructing Yeats: "The Secret Rose" and "The Wind Among the Reeds."* Dublin: Gill & Macmillan; Totowa, N.J.: Barnes & Noble, 1986.

Torchiana, Donald T. *W. B. Yeats and Georgian Ireland.* Evanston, Ill.: Northwestern University Press, 1966.

INDEX

Fleres, Ugo, 331
Fletcher, Valerie, 110
Fokin, Mikhail, 318
Folejewski, Zbigniew, 282
Foscolo, Ugo, 307
France, Anatole, 127–132
Frankenheuser, Cilla, 196
Franklin, Estelle Oldham, 121
Freud, Sigmund, 31, 36, 197, 238, 260, 271, 427
Friar, Kimon, 111, 112, 113
Friele, Christian, 44
Fröding, Gustaf, 271
Furphy, Joseph, 453

Gaitán, Jorge, 137
Galsworthy, Ada, 133, 134
Galsworthy, Arthur, 133
Galsworthy, John, xiv, 132–135
Galsworthy, Lilian, 133
Galsworthy, Mabel, 133
Gandhi, Mahatma, 443
Gandhi, Mohandas Karamehand, 352
Garborg, Arne, 45
García Lorca, Federico, 195, 309
García Márquez, Gabriel, 135–140
Garibaldi, Giuseppe, 86
Garland, Hamlin, 242
Garrard, Florence, 215
Gauguin, Paul, 219
Gaulle, Charles de, 280
Ge, Nikolai, 317
Geibel, Emanuel, 183
Gelsted, Otto, 188
George, Henry, 381
George, Lloyd, 94, 95
Ghéon, Henri, 142
Giacometti, Paolo, 114
Gibbon, Edward, 95
Gide, André, 76, 141–147, 197, 265, 279, 325, 376
Gioanola, Elio, 343
Gjellerup, Karl Adolph Sr., 147
Gjellerup, Karl Adolph, 147–150, 335

Gladkov, Aleksandr, 322
Gliere, Reinhold, 318
Godoy Alcayaga, Lucila, see Gabriela Mistral
Goebbels, Joseph, 145
Goethe, Johann Wolfgang von, 39, 40, 90, 145, 164, 178, 181, 193, 260, 321
Golding, William, 151–155
Goldoni, Carlo, 330
Goldschmidt, Meir, 336
Gonne, Maud, 458, 459
Gorky, Maxim (Aleksei Maksimovich Peshkov), xiii, 73, 99, 353
Gorodetsky, Sergei, 319
Gotthelf, Jeremias, 427
Gounod, Charles, 290
Goya, Francisco, 11
Gracchus, C., 300
Graf, Arturo, 330
Gramitto, Caterina Ricci, 330
Grass, Günter, xiv, xv, 363
Greene, Graham, 279
Grenier, Jean, 75
Grillparzer, Franz, 160, 163
Gromoslavskaia, Maria, 386
Grotius, Hugo, 271
Grudinina, Natalia, 60
Grundtvig, Nicolai, 40, 335, 336
Guérein de Sauville, Marie-Valérie, 128
Guerrini, Olindo (Lorenzo Stecchetti), 99
Guillén, Jorge, 7, 195
Gumiler, Nikolai, 319
Guðjonsson, Halldór, see Halldór Laxness

Ha'am, Ahad, 2
Haeckel, Ernst, 161
Ḥaggī, Yaḥyā, 252
Haigh-Wood, Vivienne, 107
al-Hakīm, Tawfīg, 252, 253
Hálek, Vítěszlav, 378
Hall, Tord, 273